THE GLOBAL REGIME FOR THE ENFORCEMENT OF INTELLECTUAL PROPERTY RIGHTS

In *The Global Regime for the Enforcement of Intellectual Property Rights*, Xavier Seuba offers a comprehensive description of the international norms and bodies dealing with the enforcement of intellectual property rights. The book analyses multilateral, plurilateral and bilateral treaties, and their national implementation, along with civil, border and criminal enforcement. The book also explores the interface between the enforcement of intellectual property rights and the norms regulating international trade, competition and human rights, as well as the conceptual and systemic aspects of enforcement, while illustrating the importance of these rights with examples in litigation. The book should be read by anyone interested in how intellectual property rights are being enforced around the world and how these efforts relate to other legal regimes.

Xavier Seuba, Ph.D., is Senior Lecturer at the Center for International Intellectual Property Studies (CEIPI) of the University of Strasbourg. At CEIPI he is Academic Coordinator and Judicial Training Manager and co-directs the CEIPI-BETA Project in the Law and Economics of Intellectual Property. He teaches courses in various European and American universities in international intellectual property law, international health law and international economic law. His research is focused on intellectual property enforcement, intellectual property and health and the economics of intellectual property. Seuba has advised national governments and has also been a consultant for several international organizations.

The Global Regime for the Enforcement of Intellectual Property Rights

XAVIER SEUBA
Center for International Intellectual Property Studies, University of Strasbourg

CAMBRIDGE UNIVERSITY PRESS

CAMBRIDGE
UNIVERSITY PRESS

University Printing House, Cambridge CB2 8BS, United Kingdom

One Liberty Plaza, 20th Floor, New York, NY 10006, USA

477 Williamstown Road, Port Melbourne, VIC 3207, Australia

314-321, 3rd Floor, Plot 3, Splendor Forum, Jasola District Centre, New Delhi - 110025, India

79 Anson Road, #06-04/06, Singapore 079906

Cambridge University Press is part of the University of Cambridge.

It furthers the University's mission by disseminating knowledge in the pursuit of education, learning and research at the highest international levels of excellence.

www.cambridge.org
Information on this title: www.cambridge.org/9781108400893
DOI: 10.1017/9781108231510

First published 2017
First paperback edition 2019

A catalogue record for this publication is available from the British Library

Library of Congress Cataloging in Publication data
NAMES: Seuba, Xavier, 1977– author.
TITLE: The global regime for the enforcement of intellectual property rights / Xavier Seuba, Senior Lecturer, Center for International Intellectual Property Studies University of Strasbourg.
DESCRIPTION: Cambridge, United Kingdom ; New York, NY, USA : Cambridge University Press, 2017. | Includes bibliographical references and index.
IDENTIFIERS: LCCN 2017012156 | ISBN 9781108415163 (hardback)
SUBJECTS: LCSH: Intellectual property infringement. | Agreement on Trade-Related Aspects of Intellectual Property Rights (1994 April 15) | BISAC: LAW / Intellectual Property / General.
CLASSIFICATION: LCC K1401 .S48 2017 | DDC 346.04/8–dc23
LC record available at https://lccn.loc.gov/2017012156

ISBN 978-1-108-41516-3 Hardback
ISBN 978-1-108-40089-3 Paperback

To Cecilia and Martí

Contents

Detailed Contents

Acknowledgements

This book has greatly benefited from exchanges with many people. In some cases, the conversations maintained have been decisive when drafting chapters or developing ideas. This has been the case of exchanges with Frederick Abbott, Carlos Correa, Christophe Geiger, Mariano Genovesi, Henning Grosse Ruse-Khan, Elena Izyumenko, Roger Kampft, José Massaguer, Juan Camilo Pérez, Antoni Puig-Rubí, Santiago Ripol, Pedro Roffe, Miguel Vidal-Quadras, Horst Vissel, Raquel Xalabarder and Peter Yu. Thomas Colon and Anja Halle have reviewed the book for linguistic consistency. Rebecca Jackaman and Jeevitha Baskaran have taken care of the final editing of the book.

Elena Dan has carefully peer-reviewed the entire book. Her comments have greatly improved the quality of the text and footnotes and have also influenced the substantive content of several chapters. This is, in particular, the case of the two chapters on criminal enforcement and Chapter 8, which she co-authors. While she deserves big credit for her contribution, all possible errors are mine.

This book has been possible thanks to the research environment of the Center for International Intellectual Property Studies (CEIPI) and the Internet Interdisciplinary Institute (IN3), which hosted me while conducting the research.

Abbreviations

AC	– Law Reports: Appeal Cases (UK)
ACTA	– Anti-Counterfeiting Trade Agreement
AIDS	– acquired immunodeficiency syndrome
AIM	– European Brands Association
AIPPI	– International Association for the Protection of Intellectual Property
AR	– Alberta Reports (Canada)
ASEAN	– Association of Southeast Asian Nations
AUSFTA	– Australia-United States Free Trade Agreement
BCSC	– Supreme Court of British Columbia
BGH	– Bundesgerichtshof [Federal Court of Justice of Germany]
BGHZ	– Amtliche Sammlung des Bundesgerichtshof in Zivilsachen [Official Reporter for Decisions of the German Federal Court of Justice in Civil Matters]
CAFTA	– Central America Free Trade Agreement
Cal.	– California Reports (US)
CanLII	– Canadian Legal Information Institute
CARICOM	– Caribbean Community and Common Market
CARIFORUM	– Forum of the Caribbean Group of African, Caribbean and Pacific States
CBP	– Customs and Border Protection (US)
CCIA	– Computer and Communications Industry Association
CD Cal.	– United States District Court, Central District of California
Ch.D	– Law Reports Chancery Division (UK)
CJEU	– Court of Justice of the European Union
CP	– Law Reports, Common Pleas (UK)
CPR	– Canadian Patent Reporter
Cr App Rep	– Criminal Appeal Reports
CU	– Customs Union

D.Del.	– United States District Court, District of Delaware
D.Minn.	– United States District Court, District of Minnesota
D.Mass.	– United States District Court, District of Massachusetts
D.N.J.	– United States District Court, District of New Jersey
DG	– Directorate General
Dist. Ct./USDC	– United States District Court
DMCA	– US Digital Millennium Copyright Act
DMd	– United States District Court, District of Maryland
DR	– Dominican Republic
DSB	– Dispute Settlement Body
DSS	– Dispute Settlement System
DSU	– Dispute Settlement Understanding
E.D.Mich.	– United States District Court, Eastern District of Michigan
E.D.La.	– United States District Court, Eastern District of Louisiana
EC	– European Community
ECHR	– European Convention on Human Rights
ECJ	– European Court of Justice
ECommHR	– European Commission of Human Rights
ECOSOC	– United Nations Economic and Social Council
ECR	– European Court Reports
ECtHR	– European Court of Human Rights
ED Tex.	– United States District Court, Eastern District of Texas
EEA	– European Economic Area
EFTA	– European Free Trade Association
EIA	– Economic Integration Agreement
Eng. Rep.	– English Reports
EPA	– Economic Partnership Agreement
EPO	– European Patent Office
ER	– England Reports
ESCR Committee	– United Nations Committee on Economic, Social and Cultural Rights
ETS	– European Treaty Series
EU	– European Union
EU Charter	– Charter of Fundamental Rights of the European Union
EUIPO	– European Union Intellectual Property Office
EWCA	– England and Wales Court of Appeal
EWCA Civ.	– England and Wales Court of Appeal (Civil Division)
EWHC	– England and Wales High Court
F.	– Federal Reporter (US)
F. Cas.	– Federal Cases (US)
F. Supp.	– Federal Supplement (US)
F.2d	– Federal Reporter, Second Series (US)

F.3d	– Federal Reporter, Third Series (US)
FBI	– Federal Bureau of Investigation
FCA	– Federal Court of Appeal (Canada)
FCCA	– Federal Circuit Court of Australia
FCTD	– Federal Court Trial Division (Canada)
Fed. Appx.	– Federal Appendix (US)
Fed. Cir.	– Federal Circuit (US)
FRG	– Federal Republic of Germany
FSR	– Fleet Street Reports (UK)
FTA	– Free Trade Agreement
GA	– United Nations General Assembly
GAO	– United States Government Accountability Office
GAOR	– United Nations General Assembly Official Records
GATS	– General Agreement on Trade in Services
GATT	– General Agreement on Tariffs and Trade
GDP	– gross domestic product
GfK	– Growth from Knowledge
HADOPI	– Haute Autorité pour la Diffusion des Oeuvres et la protection des Droits sur Internet (France)
HCJ	– High Court of Justice (Canada)
HIV	– human immunodeficiency virus
HL	– House of Lords (UK)
HR	– House of Representatives (US)
HRC	– United Nations Human Rights Committee
IACtHR	– Inter-American Court of Human Rights
ICCPR	– International Covenant on Civil and Political Rights
ICESCR	– International Covenant of Economic, Social and Cultural Rights
ICJ	– International Court of Justice
ICT	– information and communication technologies
ICTSD	– International Centre for Trade and Sustainable Development
IFPI	– International Federation of the Phonographic Industry
IIC	– International Review of Intellectual Property and Competition Law
ILC	– International Law Commission
ILM	– International Legal Materials
InfoSoc	– Directive 2001/29/EC of the European Parliament and of the Council of 22 May 2001 on the harmonisation of certain aspects of copyright and related rights in the information society

INTERPOL	– International Criminal Police Organization
IP	– intellectual property
IPD	– Intellectual Property Decisions (UK)
IPRED2	– Second European Union Intellectual Property Rights Enforcement Directive
IPRs	– intellectual property rights
IR	– Irish Reports
ISP	– Internet service provider
JIPITEC	– Journal of Intellectual Property, Information Technology and E-Commerce Law
KEI	– Knowledge Ecology International
LDC	– least developed countries
LJN	– Landelijk JurisprudentieNummer (the Netherlands)
MD Florida	– United States District Court, Middle District of Florida
MERCOSUR	– Southern Common Market
N.D.Ill.	– United States District Court, Northern District of Illinois
N.M.	– United States District Court, District of New Mexico
NAFTA	– North American Free Trade Agreement
NDCal.	– United States District Court, Northern District of California
NDOhio	– United States District Court, Northern District of Ohio
NDTex.	– United States District Court, Northern District of Texas
NDGa	– United States District Court, Northern District of Georgia
NGOs	– non-governmental organizations
NJW	– Neue Juristische Wochenschrift (Germany)
NPEs	– non-practicing entities
OAS	– Organization of American States
OECD	– Organisation for Economic Co-operation and Development
OHIM	– Office of Harmonization for the Internal Market (Trade Marks and Designs)
OJ/OJEU	– Official Journal of the European Union
OR	– Ontario Reports (Canada)
PIBD	– Propriete Industrielle Bulletin Documentaire (France)
PIIPA	– public interest intellectual property advisors
PTAs	– Preferential Trade Agreements
R&D	– research and development
RAE	– Royal Spanish Academy
RPC	– Reports of Patent, Design and Trade Mark Cases (UK)
RSC	– Revised Statutes of Canada
S. Ct.	– Supreme Court Reporter (US)

S.W.	– South Western Reporter (US)
SACU	– Southern African Customs Union
SADC	– Southern African Development Community
SC	– Statutes of Canada
SCC	– Supreme Court of Canada
SCR	– Supreme Court Reports (Canada)
SD Iowa	– United States District Court, Southern District of Iowa
SD Tex.	– United States District Court, Southern District of Texas
SDNY	– United States District Court, Southern District of New York
SQ	– Statutes of Quebec
STC	– Sentence of the Supreme Court (Spain)
TPMs	– technological protection measures
TPP	– Trans-Pacific Partnership
TRIPS	– Agreement on Trade-Related Aspects of Intellectual Property Rights
UDHR	– Universal Declaration of Human Rights
UK	– United Kingdom of Great Britain and Northern Ireland
UK Ct. App.	– United Kingdom Court of Appeal
UKHL	– United Kingdom House of Lords
UKSC	– United Kingdom Supreme Court
UN	– United Nations
UNCTAD	– United Nations Conference on Trade and Development
UNGA	– United Nations General Assembly
UNSC	– United Nations Security Council
UNTS	– United Nations Treaty Series
UPC	– European Unified Patent Court
UPR	– Universal Periodic Review
US	– United States of America
USC	– United States Code
USCA	– United States Code Annotated
USLW	– United States Law Week
USPQ	– United States Patents Quarterly
USPQ2d	– United States Patents Quarterly Second Series
USPTO	– United States Patent and Trademark Office
USTR	– United States Trade Representative
VCLT	– Vienna Convention on the Law of Treaties
W.D. Tenn.	– United States District Court, Western District of Tennessee
WCO	– World Customs Organization
WCT	– WIPO Copyright Treaty
WHO	– World Health Organization

WIPO	– World Intellectual Property Organization
WL	– Westlaw (US)
WLR	– Weekly Law Reports (UK)
WPPT	– WIPO Performances and Phonograms Treaty
WTO	– World Trade Organization

Introduction

I

Norms on enforcement have a capital importance in any legal system. From a practical point of view, they determine the effectiveness of the system, thus transforming rights and obligations of substantive content into tangible entitlements. From a systemic point of view, they determine whether a legal system does in fact exist as such. Norms on intellectual property enforcement, hence, are a constituent component of the intellectual property regime and are crucial both in practical and systemic terms, since they shape the relations between right holders and other relevant stakeholders of the intellectual property system.

In the past two decades national developments in the area of intellectual property enforcement have been paralleled by unprecedented international normative and institutional action in this same domain. *The Global Regime for the Enforcement of Intellectual Property Rights* identifies and analyses the norms of international origin dealing with the enforcement of intellectual property rights. It does so by building upon the portrayal and study of the theoretical, systemic and economic aspects of intellectual property enforcement.

The objective is twofold. On the one hand, *The Global Regime for the Enforcement of Intellectual Property Rights* aims to introduce a resource book that addresses most of the questions relating the international aspects of intellectual property enforcement. On the other hand, it seeks to advance current knowledge and research in this area of intellectual property law by providing systematization, legal analysis and *lege ferenda* proposals in order to better understand and improve the enforcement-related aspects of international and national intellectual property regimes.

In order to achieve these objectives, the book identifies and critically reviews the present international normative *acquis* for the enforcement of intellectual property rights. Multilateral, plurilateral and bilateral treaties regulating intellectual property enforcement are analysed in the wider context of the norms of public international law, in particular with regard to fundamental international trade principles and international human rights norms. The differentiation between primary and secondary norms, the principle of systemic integration and the understanding of enforcement as a weighting and balancing process for the implementation of norms are key aspects that cut across this work.

The Global Regime for the Enforcement of Intellectual Property Rights contains fourteen chapters organized in five parts. The first of these is devoted to the foundations of intellectual property enforcement and includes chapters on the concept of enforcement, the interface between enforcement and fundamental rights and the economics of enforcement. Part II discusses the international normative and institutional aspects of enforcement and addresses the international normative architecture for the enforcement of intellectual property rights, the international institutional aspects of intellectual property enforcement and the transplantation of the law as a normative technique frequently used in this domain. Part III addresses civil enforcement. It includes three chapters targeting key remedies, namely measures for the preservation of evidence, interim injunctions and damages. Part IV touches upon border enforcement, its international regulation and the interface between border enforcement, free trade and human rights. Finally, Part V is devoted to criminal enforcement of intellectual property rights and describes its international regulation and the relationship with fundamental rights. Next, a brief introduction of these chapters is made.

II

Part I of *The Global Regime for the Enforcement of Intellectual Property Rights* contains three chapters falling under the title 'Foundations of Intellectual Property Enforcement'. Part I defines the object of interest of the book by providing a study of the concept of enforcement, which is followed by the examination of the interaction of norms on enforcement with human rights norms and the analysis of the economics of intellectual property enforcement.

Chapter 1, 'Intellectual Property Enforcement, from Concept to Practice', emphasizes that while enforcement is a term much used in daily legal practice and policy discussions, very little theorization exists on its meaning and scope in the intellectual property context. This chapter examines the concept of enforcement under several legal theories and provides the conceptual framework that shapes the rest of the book. The concept of enforcement is closely related to the concept of law, which gives sense and determines the relevance of enforcement norms, in this case, intellectual property enforcement norms. H.L.A. Hart's legal positivism provides the tools necessary to accurately define and classify norms on intellectual property enforcement. From that standpoint, Chapter 1 builds upon the relevance and practical implications of the differentiation between primary and secondary norms while acknowledging the thin and often easily blurred line between the two. It also discusses the instrumental nature of intellectual property enforcement *vis-à-vis* the power to exclude and/or to remuneration that characterizes intellectual property rights and analyses whether a number of norms allegedly on enforcement can be ascribed to that group.

Chapter 2, 'Intellectual Property Enforcement and Human Rights', analyses the intense relationship between intellectual property enforcement and the protection and promotion of human rights. Historically far less explored than the interaction between substantive intellectual property norms and human rights norms, the interface between enforcement and human rights is powerful, both in daily judicial practice and in national and international policy discussions currently taking place. Chapter 2 covers the range of relations between both legal regimes, categorizing these as mutually supportive, conflictive or ambiguous. It is held that international human rights law must have a decisive impact on both the drafting and implementation of intellectual property enforcement norms. This chapter also identifies several paradigmatic cases of interaction and describes the available normative tools and hermeneutic approaches to address this interaction. Chapter 2 introduces relationships between human rights and intellectual property rights that are studied in greater depth throughout the book and pays particular attention to the right to a fair trial, of vital importance given the close connection between enforcement and the administration of justice.

Chapter 3, 'The Economics of Intellectual Property Enforcement', addresses one of the contemporary focuses of interest among researchers and policy-makers. Analyses of the scale and impact of intellectual property infringement are now regularly invoked to justify the need of new enforcement norms and institutions. Chapter 3 identifies these studies, their findings and their methodologies and argues that a large number of them contain important methodological deficiencies. The chapter holds that economic estimates of intellectual property enforcement do not generally reflect the *net* impact of intellectual property protection. They fail to do so because studies generally neglect aspects such as the investment necessary to set up and run a proper system for the enforcement of intellectual property rights, the legally condemnable but economically relevant benefits arising from intellectual property infringement and the potentially anti-competitive and extraterritorial effects of some enforcement remedies and practices. Moreover, conventional estimates assume that a homogeneous and infallible enforcement system is in place, while in reality enforcement is better described as a variable and complex process with generally variable outcomes. Chapter 3 also proposes a number of measures to improve economic estimates of intellectual property enforcement so as to better inform policy-makers and judges.

Part II of *The Global Regime for the Enforcement of Intellectual Property Rights* is titled 'The International Architecture for the Enforcement of Intellectual Property Rights'. This part contains three chapters studying the normative and institutional international dimension of intellectual property enforcement as well as a normative technique frequently employed to develop new norms on intellectual property enforcement: legal transplantation.

Chapter 4, 'International Normative Architecture for the Enforcement of Intellectual Property Rights', emphasizes that national governments have traditionally been unwilling to surrender sovereignty over the implementation of intellectual property rights. However, since the Uruguay Round negotiations in the late 1980s, intellectual property enforcement has been incorporated as a priority issue in the international intellectual property normative agenda. This chapter identifies and describes the content of all international treaties dealing with the enforcement of intellectual property rights. It is based on the analysis of hundreds of international treaties, classified into legal instruments of multilateral, plurilateral and bilateral nature. Once identified, the objectives and content of intellectual property enforcement provisions set forth therein are described in order to better frame the specific remedies and enforcement-related mechanisms analysed in subsequent chapters of the book.

Chapter 5, 'International Bodies for the Enforcement of Intellectual Property Rights', identifies and analyses international bodies set up to oversee the implementation of international intellectual property obligations. The objective of these bodies is achieved either by the activation of dispute settlement mechanisms or the application of political pressure through monitoring and reporting systems. In fact, both diplomatic and jurisdictional means of dispute settlement coexist in international intellectual property law. The former include consultations, mediation, good offices and conciliation, generally managed by committees of a political nature in charge of the treaty or its intellectual property chapter. In contrast, the jurisdictional mechanisms include judicial or arbitral settlement by international courts and quasi-judicial bodies as well as *ad hoc* temporary bodies. Chapter 5 identifies the relevant institutions, their record of action and the unsettled question of jurisdictional overlaps in international intellectual property dispute settlement.

Chapter 6, 'Transplantation of the Law as a Technique to Foster New Enforcement Regulations', builds upon the productivity of transplantation of the law as a technique to legislate in a broad range of legal fields, including intellectual property. Legal transplantation in the area of enforcement is presently accomplished through a range of channels. These include the emulation of other nations' legal responses to similar situations or topics, the negotiation and implementation of international treaties, the negotiation of a nation's access to regional or multilateral organizations, the pressure sometimes directly exerted on some countries to adopt specific legal responses, technical cooperation and international dispute settlement. Chapter 6 analyses these procedures and focuses in particular on the experiences of the United States and the European Union to illustrate how a number of remedies set up for the enforcement of intellectual property rights have moved from national statutes to other nations' legal orders. While transplantation of intellectual property law is frequently related to power asymmetries, Chapter 6 also argues that transplantation does not take place just in the context of asymmetric interests.

Part III focuses on civil enforcement of intellectual property rights and contains three chapters addressing several remedies and the award of damages in case of intellectual property infringement.

Chapter 7 is devoted to measures for the preservation of evidence. These measures allow the seizing and safeguarding of evidence even before proceedings leading to a decision on the merits of the case have begun. While they foster the efficiency of enforcement procedures, measures for the preservation of evidence are often in tension with human rights. In particular, the rights to privacy, property and a fair trial may be impacted by these provisional measures. In essence, measures for the preservation of evidence permit competent authorities to allow the entrance and search of the defendant's business and domicile, thus impacting on the property and privacy of the alleged infringer. The international legal framework on measures for the preservation of evidence is underdeveloped. Norms set forth in bilateral and plurilateral treaties adopted after the TRIPS Agreement are generally vague and fundamentally concerned about right holders' interests. The responses proposed in Chapter 7 essentially rely on comparative intellectual property law and the implementation of the requirements deriving from due process and fair trial principles.

Chapter 8 analyses interim injunctions. International regulation of interim injunctions tends to allow a considerable margin of manoeuvre. This is recognition of the notable differences that exist across national legal orders with respect to provisional measures, which in turn respond to a set of factors, including States' different approaches to the right balance between protection of intellectual property, the public interest and fundamental rights. In practice, national courts still maintain extensive discretion with regard to the actual award of a preliminary injunction as well as the conditions applicable to each injunction awarded. The likelihood of success on the merits of the case, the harm avoided or caused if the injunction is granted, the balance of convenience and, in some national legal orders, the public interest are among factors regularly assessed when awarding an injunction. Chapter 8 analyses these factors, how they are regulated in international intellectual property law and the interaction between the public interest and fundamental rights when granting or rejecting interim injunctions.

The last chapter of Part III, Chapter 9, introduces the award of damages. In their quest to improve the enforcement of intellectual property rights, States have concluded multilateral, plurilateral and bilateral treaties that order compensating the right holder in case of intellectual property infringement and, in some cases, punishing the infringer and discouraging him and others from committing further infringements. However, the boundaries between compensation, punishment and deterrence are frequently vague. In this respect, the international regulation of damages illustrates some of the main difficulties arising from the process of global harmonization of legal standards concerning intellectual property enforcement. On the one hand, the promotion of conflicting standards at the international level shows the existence of limits to global harmonization. On the other hand, the potential clash between some forms of damages and fundamental rights becomes apparent, in particular the right to a fair trial and an overarching principle of proportionality in the human rights field.

Part IV focuses on border measures for the enforcement of intellectual property and their relationship with free trade principles and human rights norms. It also includes three chapters.

Chapter 10, 'The Global Regime on Border Measures', deals with the international regulation of border controls of goods protected by intellectual property rights. Since the TRIPS Agreement introduced the first comprehensive multilateral regulation on border measures relating goods protected by intellectual property rights, numerous plurilateral and bilateral treaties have expanded border measures. Chapter 10 states that border measures are the enforcement-related remedy most frequently regulated in post-TRIPS treaties. Originally focused on the control on importation of counterfeit and pirated goods, international obligations related to border controls have expanded to cover all customs situations and intellectual property categories. New regulations have expanded right holders' rights in the context of border enforcement while paying little attention to the rights of other concerned parties. This expansion has had an impact on fundamental principles of the intellectual property regime as well as the international trade regime. It may also impact on fair trial standards, as this chapter sustains and Chapter 12 analyses in greater depth.

Chapter 11 studies the close relationship between border measures and free trade. The possibility of controlling products under any suspensive procedure, the increase in the number of intellectual property categories subject to border control and the application of the law of the country of customs procedures – even when there is no direct link between the goods and the country in question – may give place to a regime that is difficult to reconcile with basic intellectual property and free trade principles, including the principles of territoriality and freedom of transit. This chapter further develops the interface between border measures against goods allegedly infringing intellectual property rights and free trade norms and the way this tension has been addressed in different legal orders, in particular in the European Union. While the chapter generally rejects the control of transit, it proposes a number of reforms in order to enable the control of trademark counterfeited goods.

Chapter 12, 'Border Measures and Human Rights', introduces the positive, conflictive and ambiguous relations between border enforcement and human rights that can be identified through analysing customs norms and practices worldwide. Taking into consideration the multifaceted interactions described in Chapter 12 and the fact that customs procedures may sometimes have contradictory effects when observed from the human rights perspective, this chapter not only presents the general framework but also addresses three different cases of interaction. The first of these relates to the impact of the implementation of border measures on access to vital products, particularly those that apply to products in transit. The second concerns arguments made in favour of border measures as an instrument to ensure consumer safety and whether these measures are acceptable, or even necessary, to implement a number of human rights. The third case of interaction touches upon ambiguous relations and pays particular attention to border measures regulation of poor normative quality.

Part V focuses on criminal enforcement of intellectual property rights, its international regulation and the relationship between criminal enforcement and human rights.

National and regional differences on criminal enforcement have determined the development of a global regime on criminal enforcement of intellectual property rights consisting of norms limited both in number and scope. Despite the recent promotion of new international norms on criminal enforcement, this area of law is the least harmonized when compared to civil and border enforcement. This is changing due to the adoption of new trade agreements that contain obligations on criminal enforcement. Chapter 13, 'The Global Regime on Criminal Enforcement', identifies the norms on criminal enforcement adopted in those treaties and analyses both the reasons that favour and those that militate against the use of criminal sanctions to respond to intellectual property infringement. This chapter holds that there is no correlation between strengthened use of criminal enforcement and higher ratios of efficiency in intellectual property enforcement, that criminal sanctions should apply only in cases of infringements endangering chief legal interests, that individual infringers must be distinguished from large-scale organized crime networks and that criminal sanctions must be the last resort given their severe effects on individual freedoms and social interests.

Chapter 14 analyses the interface between criminal enforcement and human rights and the pressure on a number of fundamental rights that the expansion of criminal enforcement norms by means of international treaties has introduced. This chapter focuses particularly on the impact that the expansion of criminal measures has on basic principles of justice and the right to a fair trial. Emphasis is placed upon the principle of legality and one of its four main pillars, namely the principle of legal certainty. The analysis of key terms contained in the definitions giving way to new criminal offences reveals that the principle of legal certainty is not satisfied in a number of recent treaties. Importantly, this chapter also holds that the current pressure put on human rights norms relates to an ongoing debate on the goals, functions and scope of criminal law to respond to specific intellectual property infringements. This debate is taking place at both the internal and international levels.

III

The Global Regime for the Enforcement of Intellectual Property Rights proposes a dynamic concept of enforcement, i.e. enforcement understood as a weighting and balancing process for the implementation of norms. From this standpoint, enforcement does not amount to a preset state of things or a situation where a homogeneous implementation of the same norms exists. To the contrary, enforcement entails balancing different and frequently competing interests. To enforce also means taking into consideration the public interest, fundamental rights, competition and free trade principles. Differentiation between primary and secondary norms, their interaction and independence, is also a key factor in such a weighting and balancing process.

Other factors must be taken into account when approaching enforcement from an international perspective. New international treaties include vague and incomplete provisions relating to intellectual property enforcement. Likewise, by means of legal transplantation selected national intellectual property statutes are partially exported. Unfortunately, they rarely take into account local circumstances and the overall balance normally existing in the original norm. These trends militate against a dynamic and multifaceted concept of enforcement. Instead, they reflect a poor understanding of the legal system and may ultimately run against the objectives pursued in those very same treaties and transplants. In a way, they reduce the diversity of elements of relevance in the weighting and balancing process necessary for the enforcement of intellectual property rights.

Contrary to current legislative practices, the judiciary has in general a much richer vision of the compounded elements of the legal system. Relevant contemporary jurisprudence favours differentiation between primary and secondary norms and the consideration of the public interest, fundamental rights, free trade and competition principles when adjudicating intellectual property cases, in particular cases relating to enforcement. In this sense, the judiciary also favours a dynamic concept of enforcement and guides intellectual property reform. This is naturally not always the case, and the judiciary cannot always withstand deeper trends and stronger pressures, including those that have been affixed in national and international law. In this last regard, *The Global Regime for the Enforcement of Intellectual Property Rights* holds that a number of international and national norms touching upon intellectual property enforcement need to be re-assessed and amended so as to introduce missing elements deriving from fundamental principles of justice. When conducting this exercise, comparative intellectual property law and rules and principles deriving from other areas of law, in particular fundamental rights law, become particularly useful.

PART I

Foundations of Intellectual Property Enforcement

1

Intellectual Property Enforcement, from Concept to Practice

I ENFORCEMENT AND THE LEGAL SYSTEM

1 *The Meaning of Enforcement*

Norms on enforcement have a capital importance in any legal system. From a practical point of view, they determine the effectiveness of the system, thus transforming rights and obligations of substantive content into tangible entitlements. From a systemic point of view and following H.L.A. Hart's approach to the concept of law, norms on enforcement determine whether a legal system, as such, does in fact exist.[1]

While enforcement is a term much used in daily legal practice and policy discussions, very little theorization exists on its meaning and scope in the intellectual property context. In light of the variable uses of the term by academia, States, international organizations and private stakeholders, it is timely to dig into its meaning and content.

The definition of enforcement and the delimitation of its content have vast implications. First, the definition of enforcement is closely related to the concept of law, which will give sense and determine the relevance of norms on enforcement. Second, the delimitation of enforcement implies drawing a thin and often easily blurred line between primary and secondary norms, the first dealing with substantive entitlements and the latter generally addressing adjudication. Third, the definition and delimitation of enforcement may put into question current labels and groupings of norms. In this sense, some norms that are commonly considered norms on enforcement have rather a substantive – or at best mixed – content. This may have important legislative and systemic implications. Fourth, the diversity of enforcement norms invites the establishment of some distinctions among them depending on their nature, addressees and the role of the State and public authorities in their implementation.

A central element of intellectual property rights is the faculty of preventing others from undertaking activities that fall within the object of protection. The majority of

[1] *See* Section 3.

intellectual property enforcement remedies are tributary to this right to exclude and have been built around this primary entitlement. This feature can be observed in the civil, criminal and border enforcement areas. Regarding civil enforcement, take for instance the case of injunctions, which permit impeding unauthorized uses of goods that involve the infringement of an intellectual property right. In the area of criminal enforcement, criminal sanctions apply when the magnitude of the unauthorized use surpasses a relevant threshold or the effects of the unauthorized use are particularly damaging. Likewise, border measures are intended to impede the unauthorized exploitation of a foreign product in the local market or national products in foreign markets.

The *parasitic* or instrumental nature of intellectual property enforcement *vis-à-vis* the power to exclude becomes clear in light of the definition of enforcement. To 'enforce' means 'to compel or ensure compliance with something, to give effect or force to a law or command'.[2] It therefore evokes an action, 'to make effective',[3] i.e. the activity 'by which a legally constituted power is applied to make the law's dictates actual'.[4] Law's dictates go however beyond intellectual property law, which means that the finalistic function of enforcement does not take place in isolation but in the context of the broader legal order.

On the basis of this definition, we next analyse in three different sections three different approaches to the concept of enforcement. First, a positivist analysis establishes a parallelism between law and *enforced* law. Under this view, without effective enforcement there is no law. Second, the so-called 'enforcement chain' considers that enforcement norms are rules of conduct and thus places particular attention on the addressees of those rules. Third, a systemic approach underlines the importance of generally efficacious enforcement and is particularly interested in the place and role of enforcement norms on the entire legal system. This is indeed the most comprehensive and useful perspective and the one that matches with current judicial and policy practices regarding enforcement.

2 *Intellectual Property Law as* Enforced *Intellectual Property*

The enactment and enforcement of norms with the threat of sanctions are reserved to the legitimate sovereign, and this is precisely what is usually called law.[5] Law shapes human behaviour for reasons and with tools distinct from those employed by morality. Where there is law, the human conduct is made in a way non-optional or mandatory.[6] For this reason, the enforcement of sanctions whenever legal rules are disobeyed is plainly distinct from the social disapproval and guilt that stem from

[2] *See* Garner (1999), p. 549.

[3] *See The Law Dictionary*, Featuring Black's Law Dictionary Free Online Legal Dictionary (2nd ed.), available at: http://thelawdictionary.org/enforce/ (last accessed April 2015).

[4] *See* Kleinfeld (2011), p. 293.

[5] *See* however next section for qualification to this proposition.

[6] *See* Hart (1997), p. 82.

morally reprehensible acts.[7] The nature and enforceability of rules thus distinguish law from morality and politics, areas where the fulfilment of commitments responds to incentives of a different nature. This is one of the reasons why modern States treat moral and legal rejection separately, even if they may stem from the same actions or facts.

The enforcement of any law has capital importance in practical terms, since the value of a non-enforced statute is little less than marginal. In the case of intellectual property this has been expressed in many different ways, sometimes with nice metaphors – 'without effective enforcement, IPRs are nothing but empty shells'[8] – and on other occasions in a more descriptive fashion, reminding for instance that 'the value of intellectual property rights depends in practice on whether the holder can take effective measures to prevent others from infringing them'.[9] Authors generally equate the value of an intellectual property right to its effective enforcement and note that 'without effective remedies for the enforcement of these rights, the rights are worthless'[10] or, similarly, that 'the best substantive protection is only as good as the means for its enforcement in practice'.[11]

The importance of enforcement, however, goes beyond daily practice. Legal positivism underlines the constitutive importance of enforcement. According to positivists, the possibility to enforce a law is precisely what makes law, law. Put differently, enforcement is part of law's very nature. John Austin's description of law captures very well not only the teleological but also the constitutive importance of norms on enforcement. According to Austin, laws properly so-called are commands issued by a sovereign backed by the power of affecting others with evil or pain.[12] That is, with the power to impose and enforce sanctions.[13] Under this view, sanctions and consequences for infringement are an 'identity-making feature of law'.[14]

The inextricable link that Hans Kelsen established between law and coercion is closely related to the constitutive nature of enforcement. According to Kelsen 'the first characteristic, then, common to all social orders designated by the word "law" is that they are orders of human behaviour. A second characteristic is that they are coercive orders'.[15] Enforcement, following Kelsen, is particularly related to the efficacy of the legal order and to the validity-conferring nature attributed to efficacy. This trait was suitably captured by Dieter Stauder, who affirmed that '[e]nforcement before the courts is therefore a major test of effectiveness for the rights conferred by the intellectual property system'.[16] For Kelsen, however, efficacy is more than a test since it relates to the validity of law. Congruently, 'a norm is only valid if and only if,

7 *See* Shavell (2002), p. 227. 8 *See* Hilty (2012), p. 11. 9 *See* Stauder (2005a), p. 291.

10 *See* Blair and Cotter (2005), p. 2.

11 *See* Dreier (1996), p. 255. *See*, along the same lines, WIPO (2004), p. 207; Doane (1994), p. 482.

12 *See* Austin (1832), pp. vii, 5–6. *See* also Hathaway and Shapiro (2011), p. 265.

13 *See* Austin (1832), p. 8. 14 *See* Kleinfeld (2011), p. 296. 15 *See* Kelsen (1967), p. 33.

16 *See* Stauder (2005a), p. 291. Along these lines, Joel Trachtman has held that '[l]egislation without adjudication at least raises greater concerns regarding the application and effectiveness of the legislation'. *See* Trachtman (1999), p. 339.

it belongs to a system which is on the whole efficacious'.[17] This is an extreme position which H.L.A. Hart softened by rather requiring a context of *general* efficacy.[18]

Although many scholars persuasively deny the constitutive relevance of enforcement and coercion,[19] and this is still a major area of discussion among legal philosophers,[20] the weight presently conferred to intellectual property enforcement is well understood in light of the positivist approach. In this line, the doctrine emphasizes that 'rights without sanctions are no rights',[21] and States redouble efforts for the codification of powerful intellectual property enforcement mechanisms, while international adjudication bodies such as Dispute Settlement Body of the World Trade Organization underline the constitutive relevance of enforcement of intellectual property law.[22] A note of caution, however, needs to be introduced, since the specific content of 'sanctions' and the practical effects of enforcement will be determined on a case-by-case basis, taking into account varied norms and legal interests.

Certainly, the approach that reduces law to 'orders backed by sanctions' cannot capture the complexities of the present legal system and modern States' law. Austin's theory falls short of that objective in particular. The legal system contains other classes of norms, for instance norms conferring the power to create other norms or prescribing how to interpret existing obligations, none of them considered law within Austin's model. In fact, sources of law such as custom, as well as the continuity of legislative authority that characterizes any modern legal system, would also be hardly explicable from that standpoint.[23] The very notion of rule and, more importantly, the functioning of a system integrated by different types of rules have been better described by H.L.A. Hart. Before moving on to Hart, however, another possible approach to enforcement is briefly introduced.

3 *The Enforcement Chain*

A different perspective to the nature and function of norms on enforcement is that based upon the so-called 'enforcement chain'. The enforcement chain has been described as a 'connected sequence of legal norms whose first link is a conduct

17 *See* Hart (1997), pp. 293–294.

18 Hart noted that 'though the efficacy of the system is the normal context for making statements of validity, none the less, in special circumstances, such statements may be meaningful even if the system is no longer efficacious'. *See* Hart (1997), p. 294.

19 *See* Cowan (1971), pp. 683–694; Raz (1975), pp. 158–160; Lowenfeld (1994), p. 488; Lamond (2001), pp. 35–51; Shapiro (2011), pp. 169–170.

20 *See* Kleinfeld (2011), pp. 306–307.

21 *See* Keplinger (2007), p. 648. *See*, along these lines, Hilty (2012); Stauder (2005a); Blair and Cotter (2005); Dreier (1996).

22 For instance, 'it is difficult to conceive that copyright would continue to exist, undisturbed, after the competent authorities had denied copyright protection to a work'. *See* WTO Panel Report, *China – measures affecting the protection and enforcement of intellectual property rights*, WT/DS362/R, 26 January 2009, para. 7.66 (hereinafter WTO Panel, *China –Intellectual Property Rights*).

23 *See* Hart (1997), pp. 44–49, 80.

rule . . . and subsequent links are rules that are designed to enforce previous links'.[24] In this context, conduct rules are integrated by rules laying down prohibitions, permissions and obligations, and norms on enforcement are described as a subset of conduct rules. Norms named 'primary' and 'secondary' enforcement rules – not to be confused with the primary and secondary rules described by H.L.A. Hart – are moreover identified within the category of conduct rules, their function being 'to ensure that that conduct rules are followed'.[25]

In order to guarantee the respect of conduct rules, primary enforcement norms impose on the violators of the norms the duty to perform some costly act or deny them a beneficial right. This is for instance the case of the payment of damages in case of infringement. Secondary enforcement rules, in turn, come into play if primary enforcement rules are not respected. In this case, the norms allow or oblige third parties to impose some consequences on infringers. An example is the taking of property in case of lack of payment of civil debts. A basic difference between primary and secondary enforcement norms is found in the fact that the former are firstly applied by the infringer himself while the latter are implemented by third parties at a later stage.

The 'enforcement chain' theory does, however, have some flaws. First, pursuant to this theory, rules laying down substantive rights and rules enacted to implement those very same rights belong to the same broad category, namely 'conduct rules'. Although subsequent distinctions are made, this initial grouping seems confusing, particularly when examining specific rights and remedies. For instance, according to this approach, the right to exclude others from using patented subject matter falls within the same category as the injunction that permits the enforcement of such a right. Second, it is not clear to what category measures directly adopted in response to an infringement should be ascribed in the situation when the measures are implemented not by the infringer himself, but by a third party. Take for instance the forfeiture and destruction of pirated goods: would forfeiture and destruction be primary or secondary enforcement rules? Along this line, the distinction between primary and secondary enforcement norms made by the 'enforcement chain' theory is vague, since they are frequently interdependent.[26] Finally, the role of procedural and institutional rules is uncertain in the 'enforcement chain' theory. If enforcement rules are considered to be conduct norms, rules shaping institutions in charge of enforcing intellectual property cannot be considered enforcement norms. Similarly, even if procedural rules can be considered norms laying down prohibitions, permissions and obligations, they can only be considered 'conduct rules' in a loose sense.

H.L.A. Hart's concept of law permits understanding enforcement norms in a wider and more productive context than the approach presenting them as a subset of rules of

[24] *See* Hathaway and Shapiro (2011), pp. 259, 271. [25] *Ibid.*, p. 271.

[26] The examples given by Hathaway and Shapiro (2011), p. 271, pose some difficulties. If an example of primary enforcement rule is to pay a fine and an example of a secondary rule is to be detained, it is difficult to see how a fine can be paid if an authority has not imposed it previously and how a prison sentence can be enforced if it is not imposing it on the infringer.

conduct. Hart's concept of law also permits understanding the crucial role of these norms in systemic terms, without reducing the legal system merely to coercion.

4 The Place of Enforcement in Intellectual Property Law as a System of Rules

In *The Concept of Law* H.L.A. Hart put the emphasis on the articulation of primary and secondary rules in order to ascertain the existence of law. It is in the combination of primary and secondary rules, and not in the combination of orders and sanctions, that the constitutive characteristic of a legal system lies or, more vividly expressed, where 'the key to the science of jurisprudence'[27] is to be found.

In this system, primary rules require undertaking, or abstaining from, certain acts, while secondary rules establish how primary rules are created, modified, terminated and adjudicated.[28] The centre of gravity therefore moves from Austin's orders and sanctions to H.L.A. Hart's combination of rules of a different nature and with different functions. This is a more comprehensive approach and one that permits studying the nature and content of intellectual property enforcement provisions in greater depth.

If law was made up of only primary rules of obligation it would be uncertain, static and inefficient.[29] To respond to these problems, legal systems have developed three sets of secondary norms: rules of recognition, rules of change and rules of adjudication. Rules of recognition respond to the problem of *uncertainty* and specify the characteristics that rules must meet to belong to the legal system. Rules of change correct the *static* nature of a regime of primary norms by prescribing how these norms are created or amended. Importantly for the purposes of this book, norms of adjudication remedy *inefficiency*, empower the making of 'authoritative determinations of the question of whether, on a particular occasion, a primary rule has been broken',[30] and identify both the individuals who are to adjudicate and the procedure to be followed in that adjudication.[31]

Secondary norms make up a vast group sharing a fundamental characteristic, that of referring to primary rules. A distinguishing feature of enforcement norms is that they are instrumental to the fulfilment of the rights of the right holder, his competitors and users. Hence, while primary rules deal with substantive rights and obligations, secondary rules relate to the primary rules themselves and clarify how these norms are ascertained, created, eliminated, changed or adjudicated.[32] It is precisely in this tributary context where norms on intellectual property enforcement find their place.

Rules of adjudication focus on the area of judicial enforcement, since H.L.A. Hart described them as relating to the concepts of judge (or court), jurisdiction and judgement.[33] They include, for instance, norms specifying the remedies in case of

27 *See* Hart (1997), p. 81. 28 *Ibid.*, p. 97. 29 *See* Hart (1997), pp. 91–93. 30 *Ibid.*, p. 96.
31 *Ibid.*, p. 97. 32 *Ibid.*, p. 94.
33 *See* Hart (1997), p. 97. Thomas Dreier also seems to restrict enforcement to 'legal consequences of infringement of the rights granted and the fundamental procedural principles of assertion of rights in court'. *See* Dreier (1996), p. 249.

violation as well as rules on the execution of court decisions. This basic content must be enlarged, and rules of adjudication may require a more ample definition. In this regard, decisions taken by administrative authorities to enforce primary norms can be considered within the context of rules of adjudication as well as civil, criminal and administrative procedural rules to adjudicate primary rules.[34] Both the legal consequences of infringement and the procedural principles of assertion of rights in court or administrative bodies must be considered enforcement norms.[35]

While they are interwoven, a central content of intellectual property rights, the right to exclude, must be differentiated from rights, institutions and procedures relating to enforcement. Intellectual property enforcement provisions establish the mechanisms and the legal framework that compel observance with the rights conferred by each intellectual property type. There is hence a close link between enforcement provisions and norms enshrining substantive rights and obligations. They are, however, norms of different nature and belong to different groups. This separation is fundamental because it allows taking into consideration rights and interests of relevance in specific disputes but different and going beyond right holders' rights.

The Supreme Court of Justice of the United States differentiated in *eBay, Inc., v. MercExchange* 'the creation of a right' from 'the provision of remedies for violations of that right'.[36] This apparently trivial observation was however the basis to reverse the practice of the Court of Appeals for the Federal Circuit of granting an injunction almost automatically once infringement and validity had been adjudged. More importantly, as a matter of principle, the differentiation between a right and a remedy recognizes that a powerful remedy such as an injunction does not necessarily follow a right to exclude[37] since other norms and principles may come into play, there may be other interests at stake, and intellectual property rights may go beyond the power to exclude.[38]

The separation between 'the creation of a right' and 'the provision of remedies for violations of that right' has important consequences. First, it permits bringing into consideration in the daily practice of intellectual property adjudication fundamental values and legal interests found in other branches of the legal system. It also enhances the role of core principles of the legal order, such as the principle of proportionality, which become of particular relevance when passing sentences that actually match primary and secondary rights. Additionally, it invites considering intellectual property rights from a different point of view. In this sense, while the right to exclude is a central tenet of intellectual property protection, the right to remuneration is also characteristic of intellectual property law.

In this last respect, as further developed in Chapter 8, the possibility of awarding damages instead of granting a permanent injunction finds correlation, in the substantive field, with classic intellectual property mechanisms, such as non-voluntary licenses,

34 In fact, H.L.A. Hart himself mentioned as example of secondary rules 'procedures for setting doubts, either by reference to a text or to an authority'. *See* Hart (1997), p. 92.

35 *See* Dreier (1996), p. 249.

36 *eBay, Inc., v. MercExchange, LLC*, 126 S.Ct. 1837 (2006), at 1840.

37 Sarnoff (2009), p. 103.

38 *See* Chapter 8, Sections IV.2.2 and IV.4.2.

which also transform the right to exclude into a right to remuneration. In addition to the classic and well-known compulsory licenses for public interest and competition purposes, modernity has led to the development of new classes of non-voluntary licenses, intended for instance to promote innovation in the domain of biotechnological research tools.[39] In a different domain, resale royalty rights and the original *droit de suite* also share the characteristic of entitling creators to remuneration, but not to exclusion.[40] Still, in the context of integrated circuit layout design protection there is also the possibility to continue to trade in stock in hand if a reasonable royalty is paid to the right hodler.

The Agreement on Trade-Related Aspects of Intellectual Property Rights also acknowledges the different nature of substantive norms and enforcement-related norms. Article 41 of the TRIPS Agreement states that enforcement procedures shall 'permit effective action against any act of infringement of intellectual property rights'; thus it is with reference to the conferred rights that enforcement provisions make sense,[41] particularly whenever an infringement is committed.[42] Likewise, legal texts exclusively addressing the enforcement of intellectual property rights declare that they 'should not affect substantive law on intellectual property'.[43] They recognize thus a separation between enforcement and substantive rights, a distinction that has been also emphasized in the context of negotiations of enforcement-related treaties.[44]

II THE OBJECT OF INTELLECTUAL PROPERTY ENFORCEMENT

1 *Laws and Commands*

The definition of enforcement is the point of departure to draw up boundaries and identify the material content of the legal framework for the enforcement of

[39] Article 40 b of the Swiss Patents Act, on research tools, establishes that any person who intends to use a patented biotechnological invention as an instrument or means for research is entitled to a non-exclusive license.

[40] *See* Ricketson (2015).

[41] For instance, the legal framework for enforcement enshrined in Party III of the TRIPS Agreement functions with reference to the granted rights, which are set in Articles 11 and 14 for copyright, Article 16 for trademarks, Article 22 for geographical indications, Article 26 for industrial designs, Article 28 for patents, Article 36 for layout-designs of integrated circuits and Article 39 for the protection of undisclosed information.

[42] The concept of infringement is therefore central, and this takes place whenever acts under the exclusive control of the title holder, not subject to admissible exceptions, are performed by third parties without the consent of the title holder. *See* UNCTAD-ICTSD (2005), p. 575. In infringement proceedings, 'the plaintiff is the owner (or licensee) of a right which the defendant has allegedly breached'. *See* Stauder (2005a), p. 295.

[43] The EU Directive on Enforcement states that it is tributary to substantive protection since 'it should not affect substantive law on intellectual property'. *See* Recital 15 of the Directive 2004/48/EC of the European Parliament and of the Council of 29 April 2004 on the enforcement of intellectual property rights, OJEU L 157 of 30 April 2004.

[44] For instance, 'ACTA delegates would like to make clear that ACTA is not about substantive standards. It is not to expand existing rights'. *See* Chair of the Swiss Delegation in name of ACTA delegates, Luzern, July 2010, available at: http://christianengstrom.wordpress.com/2010/07/01/qa-session-with-acta-negotiators (last accessed April 2015).

intellectual property rights. As mentioned above, 'enforce' means 'to compel or ensure compliance with something, to give effect or force to a law or command', hence the activity of making sure that laws and commands are properly followed. Therefore, the object of law enforcement is a *law* or a *command*. In the context of intellectual property enforcement, these naturally refer to intellectual property-related laws and commands.

To enforce a law implies making sure that legal rules are respected. Law enforcement must be hence differentiated from the implementation of policies and standards. Certainly, policies and standards may relate to intellectual property enforcement and may even prescribe the adoption of laws on intellectual property enforcement. They belong, however, to a larger group of mechanisms and tools that fall within the area of 'enforcement facilitation'.[45] Policy initiatives that enhance the effectiveness and facilitate the enforcement of intellectual property rights must be differentiated from law enforcement. Policies and standards are generally *implemented* or *developed* rather than enforced; thus referring to 'enforcement' of policies only makes sense if the law enshrines an obligation to implement them.

The definition of enforcement alludes not only to laws but also to commands and to the effect or force given to them. In the legal context 'commands' are found in different documents, such as writs, mandates or sentences. These commands will be generally instrumental to fulfil the law and need to be enforced through distinct channels and eventually be backed by force. Therefore, the mechanisms intended to execute an interlocutory order or a sentence in the area of intellectual property also fall within the reach of norms on enforcement.

2 *Enforcement Activities*

'Enforce' and 'enforcement' are broad-ranging terms. They commonly imply activities taking place at least in three different stages. First of all, the alleged infringement must be identified and reported, and a rapid reaction may be necessary. This stage encompasses the provisions that permit identifying the infringement and the norms that establish the mechanisms to take action when such an infringement occurs. Second, a process of adjudication must be undertaken. This process may eventually lead to sanctioning, and the resulting sanctions must be executed. Accordingly, some norms will establish the consequences of the infringement while others will lay down the channels for ensuring the implementation of the sentence.[46] Between the stages of identification and adjudication, or even before, other activities may take place. This is the case of rules of a preventive nature, which permit taking action before an alleged infringement is reported.

45 *See* Yu (2011c), p. 1088.

46 For Shavell this would be the third stage, the imposition of sanctions. *See* Shavell (2002), pp. 228, 230.

Law enforcement requires the existence of institutions and bodies to oversee and implement the aforementioned activities. These are enforcement-related bodies, such as courts, police and customs authorities. Courts probably require specific consideration in this context. The function of the judge is primarily adjudication,[47] but there is a relevant difference between judges and other enforcement-related authorities. In this regard, courts determine the facts and interpret the dictates of the law but do not actually enforce the law.

The enforcement-related activities and the enforcement-related institutions change in the international context. The implementation of international norms ultimately depends on national institutions. There is no such thing as an international police or international customs authorities surveying intellectual property rights. On the contrary, in the international context, intellectual property enforcement-related institutions are restricted to the dispute settlement bodies established in international treaties.[48]

3 *Areas of Enforcement*

The civil, criminal and administrative branches of law are the legal branches enacting national intellectual property enforcement norms and mechanisms to enforce intellectual property rights. International treaties establish obligations for States to regulate these areas in a particular manner and, in some cases, to attain specific outcomes.

Intellectual property rights are private rights of a proprietary nature. Pursuant to this nature, the procedures and mechanisms for intellectual property enforcement are mainly found in civil law and in the civil enforcement provisions set forth in international treaties. Civil enforcement procedures and remedies typically lay down the tools at the disposal of the right holder to enforce his or her rights. Hence, as noted by in the *China – Intellectual Property Rights* Panel report, initiation of procedures is generally the responsibility of private right holders.[49] Typical remedies regulated in international agreements include measures for the preservation of evidence, production of evidence, right of information, precautionary measures, damages, interim and final injunctions, and provisions on the destruction or disposal of the infringing goods. Civil enforcement, however, goes beyond the mentioned remedies.[50]

47 *See* Yankwich (1957), p. 376. 48 *See* Section III.5 and Chapter 5.

49 The WTO Panel noted that a common feature of the Sections 2, 3 and 4 of Part III of the TRIPS Agreement (civil, administrative and border enforcement) is that 'the initiation of procedures under these sections is generally the responsibility of private right holders'. By contrast, 'acquisition procedures for substantive rights and civil enforcement procedures generally have to be initiated by the right holder and are not done ex-officio by the authorities'. *See* WTO Panel, *China – Intellectual Property Rights*, para. 7.247.

50 According to Heath and Cotter, 'enforcement procedures in civil matters would have to encompass: availability of pre-trial measures; contents of the initial claim; service of such claim and other documents submitted to the court; rules of jurisdiction; rules for obtaining and interpreting evidence; role of the judge and the legal representatives in an action; rules on who should have standing to sue; owers of legal representatives and rules on who would be capable of being a legal representative (patent attorneys?); rules for interim measures; rules on how a trial should be conducted; rules on the

Intellectual property infringement may be committed wilfully, on a considerable scale and with the intention to commercially exploit the infringing product. The infringement may also be related to the commercial exploitation of deceptive products or products that endanger consumer health or security. In all these cases, and particularly in the case of trademark counterfeiting and copyright piracy, criminal law has been considered an adequate instrument to respond to the infringement. As Chapters 13 and 14 of this book detail, international treaties increasingly enact criminal enforcement provisions to respond to certain intellectual property infringements.

Administrative enforcement of intellectual property rights is not so common in comparative intellectual property law. Most of the countries that have developed administrative procedures to enforce intellectual property rights are found in Asia, this being notably the case of China. One specific area, however, stands apart. Indeed, in some specific contexts the State is particularly well-suited to impede or react against intellectual property infringement. This is the case of border and customs controls, where border authorities may be asked to impede the importation, exportation or transit of products infringing intellectual property rights. The intellectual property categories that will be controlled by public authorities and the border situations that may be supervised are regulated differently across States and in international treaties.[51]

The last decade has seen the development of a new area of intellectual property law enforcement. The so-called 'digital enforcement' concerns the protection of intellectual property rights in the digital domain. Although in reality the reaction to infringements in the digital environment usually materializes through measures of civil, criminal or/and administrative nature,[52] some measures have been specifically crafted for and are only applicable in the digital domain. This is particularly the case with respect to technological protection measures, such as rights-management information and anti-circumvention measures, as well as with respect to some of the reactions that can be undertaken against infringement or alleged infringement – such as notice-and-takedown. Enforcement in the digital domain faces different technological and legal challenges when compared to enforcement in the 'analogue' world and requires a great dose of reshaping and redefining. To start with, it would be more accurate using the expression 'enforcement in the digital domain' instead of 'digital enforcement'.

4 *Terminology*

The TRIPS Agreement, in its official English, Spanish and French versions, uses the expressions 'enforcement', 'observancia' and 'moyens de fair respecter les droits de

interpretation of IP rights; relationship between infringement and nullity; rules on what remedies would be available; rules on appeals.' Heath and Cotter (2015), p. 8.

51 *See*, in particular, Chapters 10, 11 and 12 of this book.

52 For instance, Article 27 ACTA requires 'that the civil and criminal chapters shall be applied in their entirety to infringements occurring online'.

propriété intellectuelle' respectively to allude to the provisions found in Part III of the Agreement. However, the dictionary meaning of these terms is slightly different in the respective languages, which proves that in the area of procedural law it is particularly unrewarding to attempt the translation of similar terms.[53]

In effect, while 'enforcement' is the action that permits observance, the Spanish term 'observancia' evokes either the result of the action to enforce[54] or the quality of observing the law.[55] Hence, while the English term makes reference to the action, the Spanish term evokes the final outcome. If the translation is done the other way around, the more approximate translation of 'observancia' into English is probably not 'enforcement' but 'fulfilment'. Interestingly, some treaties concluded between Spanish-speaking countries do not use the term 'observancia' but 'aplicación',[56] a word more akin to that of 'enforcement'. In fact, even in English 'enforcement' and 'application' are used as synonymous in some international treaties.[57] In the French version of the TRIPS Agreement the translation of 'enforcement' is not a term but a definition: 'moyens de fair respecter les droits de propriété intellectuelle',[58] which can be shortened to 'mise en œuvre'. In the latter case, the linguistic expression truthfully describes the dynamic content of enforcement norms.

5 *Rights and Duties*

The analysis undertaken so far could seem to imply that enforcement only refers to the implementation of the rights of the right holders. However, right holders' rights do not exist in isolation. First, rights conferred by each intellectual property category are accompanied by limitations, which in some instances may be read as rights of potential infringers or the public in general. Second, procedural and institutional intellectual property enforcement norms expressly enact rights for alleged infringers. In this regard, norms on enforcement commonly allude to the balance between the parties and in that context mention the right to be heard, the need to ensure proportionality in the context of enforcement litigation and the requirement to set up fair procedures and processes.[59]

53 *See* Stauder and Llewelyn (2004), p. 49.

54 According to the Royal Spanish Academy of the Language, 'observancia' is the exact and punctual fulfilment of what has been ordered to be executed, such as a law, statue or rule. It remits, therefore, to the final situation and not to the action or activity of enforcement. *See* RAE (2001).

55 The suffix '-ancia' in Spanish creates nouns denoting either some result or quality.

56 *See* Articles 14–27 Costa Rica-Mexico FTA and EIA (1995); Article 17–26 Mexico-Nicaragua FTA and EIA (1998).

57 Article 23 WIPO Performances and Phonograms Treaty, on 'Enforcement of Rights', states that 'Contracting Parties undertake to adopt, in accordance with their legal systems, the measures necessary to ensure the *application* of this Treaty' (emphasis added).

58 Which could be translated to 'means to compel respect to intellectual property'.

59 Some authors seem to go even a bit further and establish a parallelism between some norms on enforcement and norms on anti-competition practices. In this sense, it has for instance been held that 'some plaintiffs will try to use their intellectual property rights to restrict legitimate trade, and

National legal orders generally reflect the content described and try to ensure a balance between the rights of title holders and competitors. However, most of the new international treaties dealing with enforcement primarily strengthen the position of right holders. They rarely enshrine norms for the protection of the alleged infringer or the interests of consumers. In the majority of new treaties, few or no procedural guarantees favouring competitors are laid down, while new norms on enforcement may even extend substantive intellectual property rights.[60] This prevailing trend in international intellectual property law should not make one lose sight of the fact that most of the time there is policy and normative space in the national context to develop enforcement provisions that contribute to an overall balance between right holders and competitors.

III CONTROVERSIAL CASES OF ENFORCEMENT

The delimitation of the international legal framework for the enforcement of intellectual property is particularly important in light of the growing international attention paid to intellectual property enforcement. Some States negotiating new international standards on enforcement have affirmed that not all provisions presented as 'enforcement norms' can be considered as such.[61] If this was true, the consequences exceed the terminological aspect and relate to the ultimate justification of the norms, since it is generally easier to justify and achieve consensus to enforce an already existing right than to create a new substantive entitlement.

The presentation and analysis of the controversial cases of enforcement cannot ignore the fact that the boundary between substantive and enforcement norms is sometimes blurred. Indeed, a number of cases seem to prove that at times 'matters of enforcement and procedure cannot be sharply contrasted with matters of substance'.[62] Take, for instance, liability standards. Certainly, 'if a particular mental state is required (or not) for an act to be deemed infringing, then the scope of the IPR owners' rights is narrower (or broader) than if the rule were otherwise'.[63] In a related fashion, the cost of enforcing intellectual property rights impacts and changes the private value of those rights.[64] For instance, with respect to TRIPS it has been noted that 'domestic enforcement requirements may affect the nature and scope of the substantive rights incorporated into TRIPS'[65] and that 'to the extent that TRIPS requires injunctive relief or damage awards calculated to deter further unauthorized

enforcement rules have to guard against those abuses'. *See* Bronckers, Verkade and McNelis (2000), p. 14.

60 *See* Section III.1.

61 With respect to ACTA, the Indian delegate to the WTO Council for TRIPS held that substantive and not merely enforcement-related norms were promoting. *See* WTO Council for Trade-Related Aspects of Intellectual Property Rights (2010), para. 332.

62 *See* Blair and Cotter (2005), p. 5. 63 *Ibid.* 64 *See* Lanjouw and Lerner (1997).

65 *See* Netanel (1996–1997), pp. 461–462.

use, it may effectively provide for a more robust set of substantive copyright owner rights than is actually required under Berne'.[66]

1 *Norms Creating New Substantive Rights to Exclude*

In several treaties and under the enforcement label, new provisions enable title holders to exclude third parties from acts that are not excluded by the corresponding intellectual property type. This means that substantive rights granted to title holders are extended by expanding the right holder's power to exclude, an expansion not achieved through the amendment of the corresponding intellectual property category but through the amendment of the specific enforcement provisions.

An example of this type of expansion can be found in the area of border enforcement of patented products. Some international treaties and regional legal orders have included a commitment to allow the detention – either *ex parte* or *ex officio* – of goods that are in transit, regardless of whether they are protected in the jurisdictions of exportation and/or importation.[67] Granting the power to block the transit of products protected by patents in the jurisdiction of transit, where the product will not be exploited, expands the substantive rights of the patent holder. In effect, patentee rights commonly include the possibility to impede the use, offer for sale, sale, importation or production of the product, or the product obtained by a patented process.[68] While these provisions can be found in the enforcement section or chapters of the corresponding treaties, they should not actually be considered enforcement provisions.

Something similar happened with the Anti-Counterfeiting Trade Agreement. When leaked drafts of the Agreement started to circulate, it was noted that some provisions went far beyond enforcement and entered into the domain of substantive rights.[69] In response to the criticism, ACTA drafters included several references stating that the Agreement only relates to intellectual property enforcement. They clarified, for instance, that the Agreement related to enforcement but did not affect the acquisition, availability, scope and maintenance of intellectual property rights and also that the provisions of the Agreement did not create any obligation on a party to apply measures where a right in intellectual property was not protected under its laws and regulations.[70]

2 *Norms Creating a New Right to Have the Intellectual Property Right Enforced by Third Parties*

New enforcement obligations included in international treaties oblige States to impose third-party liability, particularly but not only in the digital enforcement domain. Accordingly, if the infringement is not impeded by the party in a position to

[66] *Ibid.* [67] *See* Chapter 10, Section IV.2. [68] *See* Chapter 11, Section II.2.

[69] For instance, according to Geist, ACTA 'represents a shift in intellectual property law that extends beyond mere enforcement'. Geist (2012), pp. 35–36.

[70] *See* Articles 3.1 and 3.2 of ACTA.

do so once it has been informed about the infringement, the right holder must be compensated by that party. Although the specific regulation varies from treaty to treaty, a good example is found in provisions relating to the hosting of infringing materials by intermediary service providers. Some European trade agreements establish that, where the service provided consists of the storage of information provided by a recipient of the service, the service provider will be liable if he is aware of the illicit nature of the activity or information or does not act expeditiously to remove or disable access to the information upon obtaining such knowledge.[71]

The obligation put on the third party to compensate for the infringement and to impede it can be assessed in two different ways. On the one hand, it can be held that it creates a new right that compels third parties to ensure the respect of a private right.[72] In this sense, it confers the right holder a new legal entitlement: requiring a third private party to take on the surveillance of the title holder's right. On the other hand, it could also be held that this is merely a privatization of enforcement: given the singular position held by some private parties, such as Internet service providers, it is more effective to transfer the responsibility to them. Certainly, while the circle of those responsible for the enforcement of intellectual property is extended, the substantive entitlement has not been modified. In principle there would be no reason to exclude it from the definition of enforcement offered above, which laid down a link between the substantive rights granted by each intellectual property category and the mechanisms and remedies deployed for its fulfilment.

In reality, extending the responsibility to enforce upon third parties reflects a deeper trend, i.e. the expansion of the protection of intellectual property in such a manner that it alters the characteristics of the right. Thus, while it is generally affirmed that intellectual property rights are private rights and therefore the costs of their enforcement must be borne by the right holder, who should 'act as his own policeman',[73] the normative reality reflects a greater involvement of the State – hence taxpayers – and other private parties in the enforcement of private rights.[74]

Recital 4 of the Preamble of the TRIPS Agreement recognizes that intellectual property rights are private rights. In *China – Intellectual Property Rights*, the WTO Panel noted that it is a common feature of the TRIPS Agreement's acquisition procedures for substantive rights and civil enforcement procedures to consider the launch of procedures as the responsibility of private right holders.[75] According to the panel, several provisions in those sections identify the right holder as the initiator of procedures. Moreover, 'a condition that authority shall only be available

[71] *See* for instance Article 253.1 EU-Colombia and Peru FTA and EIA (2013).

[72] *See*, in this sense, Weatherall (2010); American Association of Law Libraries *et al.* (2010).

[73] As WIPO underlines, the right-owner 'must keep an eye on the industrial and commercial markets in which he sells his products, or provides his services, or in which his processes might be used. He must keep abreast of his competitor's activities'. *See* WIPO (2004), p. 207. *See*, in a similar sense, Abbott, Cottier and Gurry (2007), p. 608; Correa (2007), p. 10. *See* also in this book Chapter 3, Section II.2.2.

[74] *Ibid.*

[75] *See* WTO Panel, *China – Intellectual Property Rights*, para. 7.247 (emphasis in original).

upon application or request seems to be assumed in much of Sections 2, 3 and 4 of Part III'[76] of the TRIPS Agreement. Importantly, the panel confirmed that 'this is consistent with the nature of intellectual property rights as private rights'.[77] In light of this jurisprudence, new obligations that extend the responsibility to enforce upon third parties strengthen the right to exclude in such a powerful way that the substantive right itself is modified.

3 *Expansion of the Legal Standing*

International treaties dealing with intellectual property enforcement often indicate who may bring legal action in case of infringement. The TRIPS Agreement alludes to 'right holders' and contains a footnote specifying that for the purpose of enforcement part of the Agreement, the term 'right holder' includes federations and associations having legal standing to assert such rights.[78] Thus, it is pursuant to national law that legal standing of federations and associations is determined. Moreover, the TRIPS Agreement permits its members to decide on whether licensees should have legal standing.[79]

New agreements, however, go beyond TRIPS and recognize legal standing to a broader group of parties. These include the holders of intellectual property rights, persons authorized to use those rights, collective rights management bodies and professional defense bodies. Certainly, in many cases this is conditioned to the provisions of the applicable law; thus domestic law will be still decisive.[80] In any case, the question that ultimately needs to be posed is whether new international agreements that recognize legal standing to licensees are provisions on intellectual property enforcement.

From a purely proprietary point of view it could be thought that licensees' power to litigate increases the economic value of the right holders' right. Right holders will be able to trade a more powerful right, that permits licensees to litigate, which allows sustaining that the right holder's right has become more valuable. Nevertheless, treaties enabling this possibility foresee that it will be implemented 'in so far as permitted by and in accordance with its applicable law'.[81]

[76] 'This is reflected in the first sentence of Article 42 and the first sentence of Article 51, the reference to an "applicant" in Article 50.3 and 50.5, the reference to "request[s]" in Articles 46 and 48.1, and the option (not obligation) to make *ex officio* action available under Article 58'. *See* WTO Panel, *China – Intellectual Property Rights*, para. 7.247 (emphasis in original).

[77] *Ibid.* [78] *See* Footnote 11 to Article 41 TRIPS Agreement.

[79] However, it has been held that a distinction needs to be made 'between licensee as such, and licensees that have received a power of attorney from the right-holder to initiate or participate in proceedings. It is more difficult to read the TRIPS Agreement as permitting a Member to disregard such power of attorney'. *See* Bronckers, Verkade and McNelis (2000), p. 16.

[80] *See* Article 152 EU-CARIFORUM States FTA and EIA (2008). On other occasions, reference is made to right 'holders having the legal standing and authority to assert such rights'. *See* footnotes 17–21 to Article 17.11.15 US-Australia FTA and EIA (2005).

[81] *See* Article 236 EU-Colombia and Peru FTA and EIA (2013).

The reference to the applicable law is relevant because standing in patent law responds to different rationales and is differently regulated from, for instance, standing in trademark and copyright law. Whether a more flexible law on standing to sue for intellectual property infringement is in the interest of the right holder is not as evident as suggested. The Supreme Court of the United States has traditionally held that patent rights are indivisible and that only the holder of the entire patent has standing to sue.[82] While this norm has exceptions[83] and some variations in comparative patent law,[84] the principle of patent unity, the precedence given to the patent owner and the convenience of avoiding multiple suits and successive awards of damages prevail.[85]

4 *Norms Pertaining to Other Areas*

It has been held that provisions on acquisition and maintenance are aimed at ensuring the exercise of registered rights.[86] Pursuant to this view, provisions on acquisition and maintenance do not concern enforcement in the narrow sense of the word but 'as regards the issue of effectiveness, the aim of these provisions as well is to guarantee the practical, undisturbed exercise of the registered rights described in the substantive provisions'.[87] In our view, this description of norms on acquisition and maintenance may create some confusion, since it gathers together provisions that have different objectives and fulfil different functions.

Norms on acquisition and maintenance are a pre-requisite for the existence and legal validity of most of intellectual property rights, not a means to enforce the rights. In fact, in the majority of cases rights would not exist or would not be enforceable without, precisely, their registration and maintenance. Once the rights have been granted, and if they are duly maintained, their infringement or threat of infringement can activate enforcement norms. Even in the case of rights not conditioned to registration, such as copyright, the creation of the right and its power to exclude needs to be distinguished from its enforcement.

[82] *See Waterman v. Mackenzie*, 138 U.S. 252 (1891).

[83] Licensees can join with the patentee as a plaintiff when the court deems this procedure necessary to protect licensees' interest. Courts have also limited the initiation of procedures to the patentee but have allowed the licensee to join to recover his actual damages. Moreover, licensees can also sue when the patentee himself violates the rights granted under the license.

[84] In France the patent owner and the exclusive licensee – provided that the contract does not establish otherwise – are entitled to ask for interim injunctions. The licensee of a compulsory license or a licensee of the right may ask for precautionary measures if the owner of the patent does not exercise the action. *See* Article L615-2 and 3 Intellectual Property Code.

[85] *See Gayler v. Wilder*, 51 US 477, 494–5 (1850). In the case of copyright, the US Copyright Act of 1976, Title 17 USC §§ 101 *et seq.*, abolished the indivisibility principle, and since then the assignee of exclusive rights and the exclusive licensee may bring action for infringement. *See Eden Toys, Inc. v. Florelee Undergarment Co.*, 697 F.2d27, 36 (2d cir.1982).

[86] *See* Dreier (1996), p. 249. [87] *Ibid.*

5 *Obligations Enshrined in International Instruments*

Enforcement provisions enacted in international treaties may pertain to two distinct realms. On the one hand, treaties frequently contain norms dealing with the enforcement of intellectual property in the national context and refer to domestic civil, criminal and border enforcement. On the other hand, treaties also enshrine norms concerning the enforcement of the treaty itself, which include dispute settlement provisions as well as other mechanisms to supervise the fulfilment of the treaty, thus including the fulfilment of the enforcement-related norm.

Keeping with the *hartian* divide between primary and secondary norms, civil, criminal and border enforcement provisions are ascribed to the group of secondary norms in national legal systems. By contrast, norms that relate to the enforcement of a treaty are also secondary norms, but in this case secondary norms of public international law. Provisions on treaty enforcement and articles on the enforcement of intellectual property rights found in international treaties differ therefore in terms of the relations they are meant to shape,[88] the legal consequences of their infringement[89] and the nature of the targeted disputes.[90]

ACTA is a good example of a treaty laying down both types of provisions. Its Chapter II enshrines intellectual property enforcement provisions intended to apply to private parties. It regulates civil, administrative and criminal enforcement as well as enforcement in the digital environment. By contrast, ACTA Chapter IV is devoted to international cooperation in the area of enforcement and regulates law enforcement cooperation with respect to criminal enforcement and border measures, information sharing, capacity building and technical assistance.[91] ACTA Chapter V includes institutional arrangements and sets up the ACTA Committee.[92] Thus, while Chapters IV and V are ultimately intended to promote the fulfilment of commitments in the intellectual property area, they are designed to influence only the behaviour of Member States.

In addition to elucidating the divide and differentiating the two groups of enforcement norms, the example of ACTA illustrates the importance of further clarification of the content of the treaty norms on intellectual property enforcement. Although the classification is rudimentary, it is possible to differentiate horizontal, vertical and interpersonal provisions relating to intellectual property enforcement found in international treaties. Horizontal provisions are meant to rule the relations

88 On the one hand, relations between private parties, on the other, inter-state relations.

89 The infringement of the normative content of civil, criminal and administrative intellectual property provisions will give place to civil or criminal responsibility of the infringer, while the infringement of the obligation to fulfil the treaty obligations in good faith will give rise to international responsibility of the State.

90 On the one hand the interest is found in intellectual property disputes, on the other, in the other public international law.

91 *See*, respectively, Article 33, Article 34 and Article 35 of ACTA.

92 The ACTA Committee has been tasked to 'review the implementation and operation of this Agreement'. *See* Article 36 ACTA.

between contracting Member States and may be directly[93] or indirectly[94] related to enforcement. In vertical provisions States agree to regulate their relations with legal or natural persons in a specific manner.[95] Finally, in interpersonal provisions States undertake to shape the relationship between private parties in a particular fashion.[96] This classification is not intended to alter the State-centred nature of the norms[97] but to reflect the content of the compromises undertaken by States.

Even if international treaties generally prescribe how States must regulate the enforcement of intellectual property internally and foresee the mechanisms to ensure that they fulfil their international commitments, both vertical and interpersonal provisions on intellectual property enforcement may become relevant in a suit of law. In effect, depending on the specific wording of the provision and the national approach to the direct applicability of international law, an intellectual property enforcement provision of vertical or interpersonal nature may be directly invoked in national courts. That is, international norms on intellectual property enforcement can

93 Take for instance Article 16.11.3 US-Colombia FTA and EIA (2012), establishing that '[e]ach Party shall publicize information on its efforts to provide effective enforcement of intellectual property rights in its civil, administrative, and criminal systems, including any statistical information that the Party may collect for such purposes'. The same compromise can be found in Article 18.10.2 Republic of Korea-US FTA and EIA (2012); Article 17.11.3 US-Australia FTA and EIA (2005); Article 14.10.2 US-Bahrain FTA and EIA (2006); Article 15.10.2 US-Morocco FTA and EIA (2006); Article 16.11.3 US-Peru FTA and EIA (2009); Article 15.11.3 US-Panama FTA and EIA (2012); Article 16.9.3 US-Singapore FTA and EIA (2004).

94 Article 36(1) Berne Convention provides that '[a]ny country party to this Convention undertakes to adopt, in accordance with its constitution, the measures necessary to ensure the application of this Convention'. This type of provision is commonly found in international treaties pertaining to a wide range of areas. In the case of intellectual property-related treaties, *see* Article 25 Paris Convention; Article 26 Rome Convention; Article 9.4 WIPO Phonograms Convention. In our view this provision specifies the *pacta sunt servanda* principle, codified in Article 27 Vienna Convention on the Law of Treaties.

95 For instance, Article 42 TRIPS Agreement states that 'Members shall make available to right holders civil judicial procedures concerning the enforcement of any intellectual property right covered by this Agreement . . . '

96 For instance, Article 159 EU-CARIFORUM States FTA and EIA (2008) establishes that 'in appropriate cases and at the request of the person liable to be subject to the measures provided for in Part III of the TRIPS Agreement and in this Chapter, the competent judicial authorities may order pecuniary compensation to be paid to the injured party instead of applying the measures provided for in Part III of the TRIPS Agreement or in this Chapter if that person acted unintentionally and without negligence, if execution of the measures in question would cause him disproportionate harm and if pecuniary compensation to the injured party appears reasonably satisfactory'. While most of the conventional norms dealing with enforcement regulate the relations between private parties, in the majority of occasions they are of vertical nature. The customary way to frame intellectual property enforcement obligations is to start declaring that 'Members shall provide', 'Parties shall ensure', 'judicial authorities shall have the authority' and similar expressions. This introduction is generally followed by the regulation of the specific remedy.

97 With the very relevant particularities deriving from the emergence of international organizations and specific branches of international law, particularly international human rights law, humanitarian law and investment law, we still give credit, in general, to Lassa Oppenheim when affirming that 'since the Law of Nations is a law between States only and exclusively, States only and exclusively are subjects of the Law of Nations'. *See* Oppenheim (1905), p. 341.

effectively determine the relations between right holders, alleged infringers and users in daily litigation. For instance, even if TRIPS 'is not a model law, and for the most part, its text is ill suited to be converted directly into domestic legislation',[98] some of its enforcement provisions have been the object of national litigation. This has been the case in the Netherlands with regard to Article 45 of the TRIPS Agreement on damages[99] and in Poland[100] and Argentina in relation to Article 50 of the TRIPS Agreement on provisional measures.[101] On the contrary, the Court of Justice of the European Union has rejected the direct application of very same Article 50.[102]

While the direct invocation of international norms and whether international treaties create rights for individuals is a matter of local law,[103] and in some areas such as the European Union it is conditioned by regional integration rules, it should be kept in mind that norms on enforcement *of the treaty* are not directly applicable, since they allude to inter-State mechanisms.

In this context, reference must also be made to provisions on cooperation and capacity-building, frequently found in the enforcement part of international intellectual property treaties.[104] These provisions do not generally deal with the enforcement of intellectual property rights *per se* but address the enforcement of

98 Taubman (2011), pp. 12, 45.

99 *See* Supreme Court, 19 December 2003, LJN AF9714, para. 5.2.3 (quoted from Sloss (2009), p. 368).

100 *Ibid.*, p. 395.

101 For a collection of an important number of cases where Article 50 of the TRIPS Agreement was directly invoked in Argentina, *see* Genovesi and Kors (2005), pp. 153–181.

102 CJEU, Case C-300/98 and C-392/98 *Parfums Christian Dior SA v Tuk Consultancy*, 2000.

103 The German Basic Law (Grundgesetz) for instance provides in Article 25 that '[t]he general rules of public international law shall be an integral part of federal law. They shall take precedence over the laws and *shall directly create rights and duties* for the inhabitants of the federal territory' (emphasis added). A somewhat scholarly paradox is that provisions on intellectual property enforcement found in an international treaty are, from the point of view of public international law, primary norms, since they establish rights and obligations in the area of enforcement. By contrast, in the context of an international treaty secondary norms are those devoted to the enforcement of the treaty. However, when the norms on enforcement recognized in a treaty are directly applied in the local legal order, they operate as secondary norms, since their function will be to enforce intellectual property rights and obligations.

104 *See* Article 256.1 EU-Colombia and Peru FTA and EIA (2013) and equivalent provisions found in the treaties between: Australia-Chile FTA and EIA (2009); Brunei Darussalam-Japan FTA and EIA (2008); Chile-China FTA and EIA (2006/2010); Chile-Japan FTA and EIA (2007); Chile-Mexico FTA and EIA (1999); China-Costa Rica FTA and EIA (2011); China-New Zealand FTA and EIA (2008); Costa Rica-Mexico FTA and EIA (1995); CAFTA-DR-US FTA and EIA (2006); EFTA-Mexico FTA and EIA (2001); EFTA-Montenegro FTA (2012); EU-Cameroon FTA (2014); EU-CARIFORUM States FTA and EIA (2008); EU-Chile FTA and EIA (2003); EU-Colombia and Peru FTA and EIA (2013); EU-Republic of Korea FTA and EIA (2011); EU-South Africa FTA (2000); ASEAN-India FTA and EIA (2010/2015); Japan-Indonesia FTA and EIA (2008); Japan-Malaysia FTA and EIA (2006); Japan-Mexico FTA and EIA (2005); Japan-Peru FTA and EIA (2012); Japan-Singapore FTA and EIA (2002); Japan-Switzerland FTA and EIA (2009); Japan-Thailand FTA and EIA (2007); Japan-Viet Nam FTA and EIA (2009); New Zealand-Malaysia FTA and EIA (2010); Nicaragua-Chinese Taipei FTA and EIPA (2008); NAFTA FTA and EIA (1994); Panama-Peru FTA and EIA (2012); Panama-Chinese Taipei FTA and EIA (2004); Peru-Republic of Korea FTA and EIA (2011); Singapore-Australia FTA and EIA (2003); Thailand-Australia FTA and EIA (2005); Thailand-New Zealand FTA and EIA (2005); Turkey-Chile FTA (2011).

international obligations that have intellectual property as their main object. They refer to inter-State actions, commonly implying cooperation in areas such as the judiciary, customs[105] or the promotion of public awareness.[106]

Provisions on cooperation for the enforcement of intellectual property invite a consideration of the abundance of soft law in the area of enforcement. Soft law can be approached in two different ways.

Traditionally, soft law refers to 'international instruments other than a treaty containing principles, norms, standards, or other statements of expected behaviour',[107] hence, non-binding law.[108] This type of soft law instruments abound in the area of intellectual property enforcement. Take, for instance, the statements issued in the context of the G8 conferences,[109] the compromises agreed in bilateral conferences of a fundamentally political nature,[110] or the 'codes of conduct', 'model provisions' and similar texts adopted by international organizations such as the World Customs Organization.[111] While the non-binding nature could in principle diminish their relevance, in reality these initiatives impact enforcement from the top down and the bottom up. At the macro level, the G8 has been a powerful engine to coordinate and foster normative and policy international initiatives proposing stringent standards for intellectual property enforcement.[112] At the administrative level, the WCO has promoted interpretations of the TRIPS Agreement that go beyond this agreement and that have been implemented by local customs authorities.[113]

Soft law may also have a material or substantive meaning rather than a formal one. In this second sense, soft law alludes to the content of treaty provisions containing promotional and oratory language[114] with respect to intellectual property

105 References to customs cooperation concerning intellectual property are not only found in intellectual property chapters.

106 The areas of cooperation may be very ample. Take for instance Article 119 of the Japan-Philippines FTA and EIA (2008) that mentions (a) exchange of information and experts; (b) strengthening the intellectual property protection system; (c) promotion of mutual understanding of intellectual property protection system of each party; (d) promotion of public; (e) organizing international symposiums, workshops and fairs; and (f) technical assistance to be agreed upon between the parties in the development of information and communications technology-related projects for efficient administration of intellectual property protection system.

107 *See* Shelton (2006), p. 180.

108 *See* Footer (2010), p. 2.

109 *See* in particular the G8 *Gleneagles Statement on Reducing IPR Piracy and Counterfeiting Through More Effective Enforcement*, July 2005; the G8 *St. Petersburg Statement on Combating Intellectual Property Rights Piracy and Counterfeiting*; July 2006; the G8 *Heiligendamm Summit Declaration, Growth and Responsibility in the World Economy* June 2007; and the G8 *Hokkaido Summit Declaration, World Growth*, July 2008.

110 For instance, the EU-US Vienna Summit Declaration identified intellectual property enforcement as one of the central areas of transatlantic cooperation and endorsed the new Action Strategy on the Enforcement of Intellectual Property Rights against piracy and counterfeiting. *See EU-US Summit – Vienna*, 21 June 2006, Council of the European Union, 10783/06, 21 June 2006, Brussels, available at: www.consilium.europa.eu/uedocs/cms_data/docs/pressdata/en/er/90176.pdf (last accessed April 2015), p. 7.

111 *See* World Customs Organization (2003).

112 *See* Blakeney (2012) pp. 43–44.

113 *See* an example in Chapter 10, Section II.5.1.

114 *See* Weil (1983), p. 414.

enforcement. In these treaty articles parties undertake 'obligations' preceded by expressions such as 'seek to', 'make efforts to', 'promote', 'examine with understanding' or 'take due steps with a view to'.[115] These commitments and their implementation are sometimes reinforced at a later stage, either unilaterally[116] or by means of subsequent bilateral agreements.[117]

Chapter 5 of this book introduces the international bodies set up to monitor the enforcement of intellectual property undertakings. These bodies and the process of international adjudication do not give effect to intellectual property obligations. Unlike municipal law, the execution of the decisions of international dispute settlement bodies is the responsibility of the infringing party.[118] Although it is relatively common to allude to the existence of international institutions with 'enforcement power' to ensure that countries comply with their international intellectual property obligations,[119] in reality there is no international body with direct power to execute decisions[120] or enforce intellectual property law. To the contrary, the infringing State will enforce the command originating from that body,[121] generally amending national laws or correcting infringing practices.[122]

115 For instance, pursuant to Article 17 of the Annex on intellectual property rights of the EFTA-Montenegro FTA (2012), parties 'agree to enhance their cooperation in the field of intellectual property rights'. A similar level of lassitude can be found in Article 256.1 EU-Colombia and Peru FTA and EIA (2013), 'The Parties agree to cooperate with a view to supporting implementation of the commitments and obligations undertaken under this Title. . . . (b) exchange of experiences between the EU Party and each signatory Andean Country on enforcement of intellectual property rights'.

116 The European *Strategy for the Enforcement of Intellectual Property Rights* announced that articles on cooperation for intellectual property enforcement should be carefully monitored and effectively implemented, notably with respect to the more 'problematic' countries. *See* European Commission (2005b), p. 6.

117 For instance, according to the EU Commission, the Customs Co-operation Agreement between the EU and China (2004) provides a legal framework for in-depth co-operation to stop illegal traffic. *See* Commission of the European Communities (2005a), p. 14.

118 Even in the WTO, which arguably has the most effective international dispute settlement system, enforcement depends on the parties themselves. This has led some authors to portray WTO as a 'self-enforcing contract'. *See* Matsushita, Schoenbaum and Mavroidis (2006), p. 143.

119 *See* Lee (2011), p. 405. 120 *See* Damrosch (1997), pp. 19–24.

121 In the WTO context rulings can be solely enforced by means of economic and political pressure on WTO Members. While the goal of the process is 'to secure either settlement or prompt compliance with recommendations or rulings of the DSB', as provided in Article 21.1 of the Dispute Settlement Understanding (DSU), States will be ultimately the ones enforcing the reports of panels or the Appellate Body. A different view, however, suggests that because the authorization of trade sanctions is equivalent to the level of nullification or impairment suffered by the complainant, trade sanctions can be seen as positive tool to re-balancing the level of commitments between the two countries, which would be a positive remedy or process in its own right, instead of a means to induce compliance. *See* Grosse Ruse-Khan (2008b), pp. 325–326.

122 *See* McNelis (2003), pp. 651–652, 656–657. Also, Harold H. Koh has noted that 'like most laws, international rules are rarely enforced, but usually obeyed'. *See* Koh (1997), p. 2603. *See*, generally, Franck (1988). For some, this feature reflects 'the ultimate limitation of today's international society'. *See* Taniguchi (2009), p. 7.

IV CONCLUSIONS

Norms on intellectual property enforcement are norms of adjudication adopted with the intention to remedy the *inefficiency* of the law. These norms determine the general efficacy that is required by any legal system. They belong to the group of secondary norms that, together with primary norms, make up the legal system. It is in the combination of primary and secondary norms, and not in the combination of orders and sanctions, where the constitutive characteristic of a legal system lies.

Intellectual property enforcement norms are tributary to rules laying down substantive rights and obligations, both in sequential and functional terms. There is an inherent link between enforcement provisions and norms that enshrine the rights and obligations of intellectual property right holders. However, this relationship must not be overemphasized. Although enforcement norms serve substantive rules, it is occasionally difficult to draw a sharp distinction between them, since enforcement norms may alter so significantly the value of the primary right that the latter may seem to have been transformed. Importantly, norms on enforcement have to be read in the context of the entire legal system, since intellectual property enforcement describes a process where diverse norms are taken into consideration rather than a predefined state of things.

Norms on enforcement allow making authoritative determinations on whether, on a particular occasion, a primary rule has been infringed and permit the identification of both the individuals who are to adjudicate and the procedure that must be followed for that adjudication. Nevertheless, norms on enforcement include not only those relating to civil or criminal courts, jurisdiction or judgement but also norms that shape decisions taken by administrative authorities such as border authorities as well as procedural rules in all areas of intellectual property enforcement.

Laws and *commands* are the object of law enforcement; hence legal enforcement must be differentiated from the implementation of *policies* and *standards*. Typical enforcement activities include the identification of the infringement, precautionary reaction to infringement, the imposition of sanctions and the execution of sanctions. Carrying out these activities requires setting up enforcement-related bodies and authorities not only in the judicial but also in the administrative and security-related domains. The civil, criminal and administrative branches of the law are the legal branches that commonly enact intellectual property enforcement norms and mechanisms. Additionally, the enforcement of intellectual property rights in the digital environment has implied the development of activities of a different nature, involving new technological means and actors.

Norms on enforcement relate to the execution of both the rights of right holders and alleged infringers. Nevertheless, new international norms on enforcement fundamentally strengthen right holders' position and rarely enshrine norms for the protection of the alleged infringer. In the majority of occasions, however, States maintain the power to develop in their national legal orders the guarantees absent in international treaties but necessary to preserve a balance between the conflicting parties.

It is disputable whether all provisions presented as enforcement norms can be considered as such, particularly in the international context. Even if the dividing line between substantive and enforcement norms is sometimes blurred, it is necessary to clarify the nature of some norms generally presented as enforcement norms. First, norms creating new rights to exclude cannot be considered norms on enforcement: on the contrary, they create new substantive entitlements. Second, norms creating a new right to have the intellectual property right enforced by third parties alter the generally private nature of intellectual property rights in such a manner that it modifies the substantive right as well. Third, recognizing the power of States to entitle right holders to sue is not an expansion of substantive rights but recognition of the differences existing across States and intellectual property categories in this regard. Fourth, provisions on acquisition and maintenance have traditionally been dissociated from enforcement rules, and this should continue to be the case. Fifth, international treaties enshrine provisions related to the enforcement of the treaty itself as well as provisions on intellectual property rights enforcement. The latter will be directly applicable depending on their drafting and the national approach to the direct application of public international law.

Intellectual property enforcement is frequently the object of international soft law norms. Soft law may be found not only in texts such as resolutions, statements or declarations but also in international treaties. Conventional rules enacting vague and weak commitments (material soft law) in the area of intellectual property enforcement are also frequently found in international treaties.

2

Intellectual Property Enforcement and Human Rights

I THE EMERGING RELATIONSHIP BETWEEN ENFORCEMENT AND HUMAN RIGHTS

1 A *Traditionally Neglected Area*

The relationship between human rights and intellectual property came to the forefront in the late 1990s. The sudden attention to these two bodies of law 'that were once strangers'[1] was largely due to the implosion of the HIV/AIDS crisis and the lack of access to pharmaceutical products. In effect, the latter was linked to the enhancement of intellectual property standards as a result of the entry into force of the Agreement on Trade-Related Aspects of Intellectual Property Rights. The TRIPS Agreement became a distal determinant of health in the eyes of the public health community, and increased attention was put on its impact on access to products as well as on the impact of intellectual property in general on a range of public goods.

The effect of intellectual property on numerous socially relevant areas, such as environment and culture, and the incidence of intellectual property on a range of civil liberties, such as freedom of expression and privacy, also became the object of attention of activists, scholars and institutions in the early 2000s. Since then, the strengthening of intellectual property standards, in particular due to the mushrooming of bilateral and plurilateral agreements containing detailed intellectual property obligations,[2] has only increased the level of interest in the interface between human rights and intellectual property.

[1] Helfer (2003), p. 47.

[2] On the substantive side, UN Special Rapporteurs, UN treaty bodies, the Human Rights Council and the former UN Commission on Human Rights and UN Sub-Commission on Human Rights have expressed their preoccupation with respect to the potential impact of intellectual property bilateral commitments on the protection of human rights. In the area of intellectual property and health, for instance, *see* the Report of the UN Special Rapporteur on the Right to Health, which contains a section on 'TRIPS-plus standards in the area of patent law in free trade agreements', UN Human Rights Council (2009), pp. 23–28. *See* also specific comments on the relationship between bilateral trade

Analysis in this area has generally focused on the interaction between intellectual property and social and economic rights,[3] particularly on rights such as the right to health,[4] the right to food[5] and the right to access to knowledge.[6] The relationship between norms on human rights and intellectual property enforcement has been far less explored by international bodies and scholars active in the area of intellectual property and human rights. Certainly, this started to change following the negotiation of plurilateral agreements enshrining relevant enforcement provisions[7] and, in particular, with the advent of new mechanisms and norms relating to enforcement in the digital domain.

The little attention paid to the interface between human rights and intellectual property enforcement at the international level contrasts with the practice in national and regional contexts, where courts, legislators and academia have more frequently addressed this relationship. Proportionality of damages awards, the protection of privacy when implementing measures for the preservation of evidence or the right of information and the protection of defendant's rights when granting an injunction have been, in particular, traditional areas of concern of courts adjudicating intellectual property cases. On the contrary, a number of reasons permit understanding why the relationship between human rights and intellectual property enforcement has been a relatively neglected area in international debates.

First, intellectual property enforcement belongs to a new generation of topics in international intellectual property law-making. Although international cooperation in this area of enforcement has been going on for a long time,[8] only in recent years has enforcement become a central concern of international regulation. As studied

compromises and human rights in the context of the examination of national periodic reports by the UN Committee on Economic, Social and Cultural Rights (2010a; 2010b, p. 3). The former Human Rights Commission and Sub-Commission of Human Rights also adopted numerous resolutions on access to medicines. *See* UN Human Rights Council (2013), p. 3.

3 Probably the first UN document discussing the impact of intellectual property on a variety of human rights – mainly economic and social – was adopted by the former Sub-Commission on the Promotion and Protection of Human Rights in 2000; *see* UN Sub-Commission on Human Rights (2000). *See* also UN Sub-Commission on Human Rights (2001).

4 Among the first documents, *see* World Health Organization (2001); UN ECOSOC Sub-Commission on the Promotion and Protection of Human Rights (2001). *See* a list of bibliographic references on intellectual property and the right to health in Correa, Velasquez and Seuba (2012).

5 *See* Cullet (2004); Helfer (2004); Jonsén and Söllner (2007); McManis (2009); Trade – Human Rights – Equitable Economy (3D) (2009); van Overwalle (2009).

6 *See* Suthersanen (2005); Brown, Guadamuz and Hatcher (2010); Busaniche (2012).

7 Negotiations to conclude the Anti-Counterfeiting Trade Agreement triggered scholarly attention in this area. *See* Geiger (2010); Geiger (2012b); D'Erme *et al.* (2013); Korff and Brown (2011).

8 Bilateral activities started to multiply in the 1990s, while the traditional activities conducted by the World Intellectual Property Organization at the national level were grouped under the label of 'enforcement' also in the late 1990s and early 2000s. Enforcement – and cooperation in this area – became a separate item in the early 2000s, and the WIPO Advisory Committee on Enforcement was set up. Since then and until 2016, this committee has held eleven sessions, always giving account of technical cooperation activities developed in this field. *See* www.wipo.int/meetings/en/topic.jsp?group_id=142 (last accessed September 2016).

in Chapter 4, while the TRIPS Agreement sets forth a complete catalogue of enforcement-related procedures, more recent treaties have gone beyond them in a selective and frequently unbalanced fashion. The present focus on the development of norms on intellectual property enforcement at the international level makes it foreseeable that increased attention will be paid to its human rights aspects.

Second, the relationship between norms on intellectual property enforcement and human rights raises concerns in areas generally distinct from access to vital goods. Scholarly literature, specialized non-governmental organizations and think tanks have however traditionally devoted most of their attention to access-related concerns. Even if access to goods may also become a matter of relevance when codifying and implementing intellectual property enforcement rules, these rules usually impact upon civil rights and issues of procedural nature. In that context, while fair trial may be the most contentious aspect at the international level, privacy issues are probably the ones attracting most of the attention of ordinary citizens.

Third, intellectual property enforcement has been generally regarded as impacting companies but rarely of direct relevance to human beings. However, the increasing pervasiveness of intellectual property in daily life and the emergence of the digital domain brought enforcement of intellectual property rights close to common citizens. In fact, in some instances the consequences of infringement have even become a subject of social debate, in particular because of the perceived lack of proportionality with the actual damage inflicted. Disproportionate awards of damages and criminalization of intellectual property infringement stand out in that context.

Fourth, as exemplified by norms on civil remedies and border measures, tensions between human rights and intellectual property enforcement become apparent when actually enforcing intellectual property rights. While these rules may have become international, enforcement *per se* is still reserved to national bodies. Litigation takes place in national courts, and there are numerous cultural, linguistic and legal barriers that make it difficult to extract lessons of global relevance. While these lessons exist, international bodies and literature have in general refrained from approaching topics that were largely perceived to be of national concern.

2 *A Compound Relationship*

Relations between norms on intellectual property and those on human rights can be mutually supportive, conflictive and, very frequently, ambiguous. While many chapters of this book explore in detail these different possibilities, the present chapter broadly introduces examples taken from the area of intellectual property enforcement to illustrate each possibility. For instance, while the enforcement of intellectual property rights is instrumental to the fulfilment of rights such as the right to property or the right to a remedy, poor drafting of enforcement norms may result in either ambiguous or conflictive relations with a variety of other human rights, ranging from the right to a fair trial to the right to health.

As it happens with substantive intellectual property obligations, human rights law provides an external and values-based criterion to assess intellectual property enforcement-related obligations. Human rights law permits assessing the design and the acceptability of the normative framework resulting from international compromises and local developments relating to intellectual property enforcement. In this regard, intellectual property law is a technical area, mostly devoid of axiological orientation. By contrast, human rights law has been developed to protect fundamental legal interests inextricably related to values. Hence, international human rights law offers guidance when drafting laws and identifying limits to the protection of intellectual property. It becomes, in fact, a tool to identify fundamental interests and needs of citizens, thus essential to implement the instrumental function of intellectual property rights.[9]

Norms of general public international law regulate the relations between international regimes. More precisely, they set the normative context and lay down the rules that permit addressing specific situations. Neither intellectual property nor human rights are islands in the sea of public international law, but part of it. Therefore, norms of international law on treaty interpretation and treaty conflicts are a useful resource when analysing the relationship between both regimes. In this regard, it is worth noting that the level of detail in which some international treaties prescribe how to enforce intellectual property rights at the national level is quite unique in terms of international law. Thus, the potential for conflict and the sources of tension are also notable. In that context, human rights standards, of both national and international origin, become a particularly valuable resource, since they permit responding to those conflicts and tensions.

3 *Human Rights Related to Intellectual Property Enforcement*

The relationship between intellectual property enforcement and human rights is intense, and almost all generations of human rights are related to intellectual property enforcement.[10] While most of the attention is being currently placed on

9 Rights created through the enactment of intellectual property laws are instrumental rights that 'should serve the interests and needs that citizens identify through the language of human rights as being fundamental'. *See* Drahos (1999), p. 32.

10 At present, human rights are generally classified in three 'generations'. The first generation of human rights are 'negative' rights, in the sense that states must abstain from interfering with individual freedoms, which are primarily included in the International Covenant on Civil and Political Rights. The second generation of human rights are 'positive' rights, meaning that states must take 'positive' action to implement them, and they broadly correspond to the human rights provided under the International Covenant on Economic, Social and Cultural Rights. The third generation of rights, also called 'rights of solidarity', specifies rights such as the right to economic and social development, the right to peace or the right to a healthy environment. *See*, for an in-depth analysis on this classification of human rights, Tomuschat (2014), pp. 136–154; Vasak (1977), p. 29. Criticism exists nevertheless of this classification. *See* in this sense Wellman (2000), p. 641; UN Human Rights Council (2007), para. 41.

the potential impact of intellectual property enforcement norms on a range of civil rights and liberties, these rules equally impact on the second and third generations of human rights.

In relation to the effect of intellectual property enforcement on civil rights, there is a close relationship between enforcement and the rights to access to a court and to a fair trial. Many norms on intellectual property enforcement identify the judicial body that will settle the controversy and the measures that judges may order to respond to the infringement.[11] On the other hand, enforcement transforms entitlements into reality. Hence, the right to exclude that many intellectual property rights confer comes into effect due to enforcement procedures. As a consequence, specific enforcement-related measures, such as injunctions[12] and measures for the preservation of evidence,[13] or entire areas of enforcement, such as enforcement in the digital domain,[14] may impact upon human rights such as freedom of expression[15] or the right to privacy and protection of personal data.[16]

The attention to the impact of enforcement norms on civil rights has been recently complemented by a growing interest in the relationship between the enforcement of intellectual property rights and social and economic rights. Certainly, some consequences derive from the impact that new types of enforcement-related obligations have on businesses and economic stakeholders. This is for instance the case in respect to the freedom to conduct a business,[17] in the sense that obligations concerning the enforcement of intellectual property rights in the digital environment may have various consequences for different stakeholders, notably on the Internet service providers. However, the reason for the recent interest in the impact of enforcement on economic and social rights may also be found in the

[11] *See* Section IV. [12] *See* Kalbfus and Wehlau (2012). [13] *See* Sherlock (1989), pp. 476–477.

[14] New PTAs chapters on the digital environment have created new sources of intrusion on the right to privacy and the right to freedom of expression. The general argument is that said chapters enact a detailed system favouring the right holder, while its limits have to be inferred from provisions drafted in very general terms. *See* for instance Matulionyte (2011).

[15] *See* Lemley and Volokh (1998); Psychogiopoulou (2012); Akester (2006); Angelopoulos (2008); Carter (2009); Firth (2008); Geiger (2007); Strowel and Tulken (2005).

[16] *See* Smith (2013); Yu (2010b). The right to privacy may be at stake in numerous situations. The area that has attracted most of the attention in recent years is digital enforcement, in particular the provision of information relating to Internet users accused of intellectual property infringement. Whether a third party should provide information impacting on the privacy of another private party allegedly infringing an intellectual property right is particularly sensitive from the point of not only the right to privacy but also other fundamental rights, such as the right to freedom to conduct a business. In *Promusicae* the CJEU held that it does not follow from the right of information concerning infringers and infringing networks an obligation to communicate personal data in the context of civil proceedings. *See* ECJ, Case C-275/06, *Productores de Música de España (Promusicae) v. Telefónica de España SAU* [2008], Judgment of the Court (Grand Chamber) of 29 January 2008, ECR I-00271, paras. 58 and 70.

[17] The right to freedom to conduct a business is provided by Article 16 of the Charter of Fundamental Rights of the European Union, OJEU C 326 of 26 October 2012, p. 391 (hereinafter EU Charter of Fundamental Rights).

increasingly demanding and detailed international regulation of intellectual property enforcement, which has revealed unforeseen economic effects on welfare.[18]

First, new norms on intellectual property enforcement may impact on trade, competition and access to the second-generation rights, such as culture and health. The case of the rules on intellectual property enforcement at the border, and the restrictions they caused to the transit of patented medicines, is telling to illustrate the potential impact of new enforcement norms on the second-generation rights such as the right to health.[19] In a similar vein, rules on injunctions may impact on access to a number of vital goods, impede access to information and hinder competition.[20] However, as Chapter 12 on border measures notes, some enforcement-related measures may also be instrumental to protect consumer safety and therefore be instrumental for the protection of rights such as the right to health or the right to food.

Another relevant phenomenon in terms of welfare and impact on fundamental rights is the 'chilling effect' caused by certain enforcement obligations or enforcement practices. Unbalanced norms on enforcement not only conflict with fair trial and due process standards[21] but may also deter legal activities[22] and impinge upon other fundamental rights, such as freedom of expression. The eventual consequences of an adverse ruling or just the costs of litigation may be too severe to risk undertaking what probably are legal activities. Something similar can be said with respect to the fear caused by certain monitoring practices or the retention of sensitive data, which may impact on the right of freedom of expression.[23] Ambiguous and unbalanced enforcement regimes feed this fear and cause the mentioned 'chilling effect'. In its turn, this may impair competition, hence reducing the supply of goods and increasing their price, with the concomitant effect on cultural and social rights such as health, food and culture.[24]

This area closely relates to the empirical analysis on the economic value of intellectual property enforcement. So far, the majority of analyses focus on the positive economic outputs that enforcement of intellectual property rights produces.[25] In fact, the value of the entire intellectual property system has been considered synonymous to the value of norms on intellectual property enforcement. The underlying understanding has been that, without enforcement, the system has

18 *See*, in particular, Chapter 3, Section IV.

19 The area of intellectual property enforcement and border measures was the first where the consequences became clear, with impact on the transit of generic medicines derived from the EU Border Enforcement Regulation. *See* Chapters 10–12.

20 *See* Chapter 8.

21 *See*, in regard to statutory damages, Samuelson and Wheatland (2009), pp. 495–496.

22 *See* Netcoalition-CCIA (eds.) (2010).

23 *See* CJEU, Joined cases C-293/12 and C-594/12, *Digital Rights Ireland Ltd (C-293/12) v Minister for Communications, Marine and Natural Resources and Others and Kärntner Landesregierung (C-594/12) and Others* [2014], Judgment of the Court (Grand Chamber) of 8 April 2014, Reports of Cases, para. 28.

24 *See* in detail Chapter 3, Section IV.3.1.

25 *See* Chapter 3, Section II.

no value; hence the value of the system can be attributed to intellectual property enforcement. This is a sound equation but insufficient to capture the complexities of the economics of enforcement. Essentially, it fails to reflect any independent value of the norms on enforcement themselves and impedes capturing other relevant economic outcomes of norms on enforcement.[26]

In addition to their impact on human rights pertaining to distinct categories, norms on intellectual property enforcement fulfil an 'intermediary' role. That is, they permit to materialize either the positive or the conflictive relations between intellectual property and human rights. This is clear in relation to fundamental rights closely related to intellectual property, such as the right to property[27] and the right to enjoy the moral and material benefits resulting from scientific, literary or artistic production.[28] In regard to the latter, the United Nations Committee on Economic, Social and Cultural Rights has underlined its relationship with enforcement procedures, stating that effective protection of the moral and material interests of authors 'would be hardly conceivable without the possibility of availing oneself of administrative, judicial or other appropriate remedies'.[29] Enforcement procedures, however, not only materialize positive relations but may also become the mechanism to violate human rights as such. For instance, an injunction may be the instrument to materialize the intrusion on the right to freedom of expression justified on copyright protection. This apparently naïve observation helps to explain why specific human rights violations that have their origin in intellectual property regulation are materialized by norms on intellectual property enforcement. In fact, confusion may sometimes exist on whether the norm on enforcement or the intellectual property right *per se* causes tensions with human rights entitlements.

4 *Intellectual Property Enforcement and Rights Related to the Administration of Justice*

Norms on enforcement have an instrumental function not only for the fulfilment of rights closely related to intellectual property, as mentioned in the previous section, but also concerning rights and principles of a cross-cutting nature, with ample scope and critical impact on the protection of other fundamental rights. This is particularly

[26] *See* in detail Chapter 3, Section IV.4.

[27] Not all legal systems consider property a human right, and not all systems considering property a human right accept human rights protection in favour of non-human entities, such as companies. In the European context, this dimension has received important attention. On the one hand, Additional Protocol no. 1 to the European Convention on Human Rights establishes the right to property as a fundamental right, and this has been considered to include intellectual property, even of legal entities. On the other hand, the European Charter of Fundamental Rights provides for protection of intellectual property in Article 17.2, a provision that is open to discussion/interpretation.

[28] *See* UN Committee on Economic, Social and Cultural Rights (2006).

[29] Consequently, the committee has considered the 'failure to enforce relevant laws or to provide administrative, judicial or other appropriate remedies' a violation of the right of creators and inventors to the material and moral benefits resulting from their work. *Ibid.*, para. 51.

the case of rights and principles related to the administration of justice, such as the right to remedy, the right to a fair trial and the principle of legality. In these cases, intellectual property enforcement is the vehicle to fulfil these rights, which moreover are frequently mechanisms that enable the protection of other fundamental rights. The relationship is reciprocal, and norms on enforcement must also be adjusted to the requirements resulting from rights related to the administration of justice.

Rights and principles related to the administration of justice are therefore especially connected with norms on enforcement. On the one hand, rules on intellectual property enforcement come into play when a substantive intellectual property right is infringed or is about to be infringed. It is precisely when there is a threat of intellectual property infringement or an actual infringement occurs that the fundamental right to an effective remedy becomes of relevance. On the other hand, numerous norms on enforcement set up procedural standards and frame the rights of the parties to the procedure. These remedies and procedural rights are those very precise standards that implement the broader right to a fair trial or that can be also clustered under the more general title of fundamental procedural guarantees.[30]

For instance, inherent components of the right to a fair trial mentioned in the TRIPS Agreement include the right to a reasoned sentence in writing, the right to a procedure and sentence within reasonable time limit, the right to affordable procedures, the right to be heard, the right to a review, the right to a timely and detailed written notice, the right to representation by independent legal counsel and the right to procedures without burdensome requirements concerning mandatory personal appearances. That is, when regulating intellectual property enforcement, the TRIPS Agreement lays down a very complete charter of due process standards.[31] While posterior treaties may have remained silent with respect to many of the mentioned guarantees, there is nothing in these agreements preventing parties from implementing them. In fact, constitutional obligations, international human rights treaties, the TRIPS Agreement and, very probably, local intellectual property statutes oblige states to implement inherent components of the right to a fair trial in the context of enforcement procedures.[32]

30 These 'fundamental procedural guarantees' would include (a) judicial competence, judicial independence, judicial impartiality, procedural equality, due notice or the right to be heard, publicity, reasoned decisions; (b) prompt and accelerated justice; (c) professional independence of counsel, right to assistance of counsel, attorney client privilege; (d) privilege against self-incrimination. *See* Andrews (2012), p. 22.

31 *See* Chapter 4, Section II.2.2.

32 Pursuing Article 3 of the EU Enforcement Directive, for instance, all Member States of the European Union have the obligation to adopt domestic enforcement measures of intellectual property rights that are 'fair' and 'proportionate', which invoke elements of due process. *See* Directive 2004/48/EC of the European Parliament and of the Council of 29 April 2004 on the enforcement of intellectual property rights (OJEU L 157 of 30 April 2004), OJEU L195 of 2 June 2004 (hereinafter EU Enforcement Directive)/Corrigendum to Directive 2004/48/EC of the European Parliament and of

II MUTUALLY SUPPORTIVE RELATIONS BETWEEN INTELLECTUAL PROPERTY ENFORCEMENT AND HUMAN RIGHTS

This section addresses the interaction between the right to a remedy and intellectual property enforcement, one of the examples of the potential mutually supportive relations between enforcement of intellectual property rights and human rights. International human rights treaties provide a good starting point to introduce this relationship in greater depth.

Take for instance Article 14.1 of the International Covenant on Civil and Political Rights,[33] which encompasses the right of access to a court in cases of determination of rights and obligations in a suit at law and lays out fundamental conditions of due process. This article sets forth two important obligations. First, it establishes that everyone is 'entitled to a fair and public hearing by a competent, independent and impartial tribunal established by law'. Second, it also states that '[a]ll persons shall be equal before the courts and tribunals'. The Human Rights Committee, the body in charge of monitoring the ICCPR, has addressed the content of the right of access to justice in a similar way[34] to the European Court of Human Rights[35] and has clarified that it relates not only to judicial cases but also to administrative proceedings.[36]

Intellectual property enforcement articles included in international treaties lay out the remedies that permit reacting against a violation of an intellectual property right or preventing its occurrence. Intellectual property enforcement provisions also enact the guarantees and options available to the alleged infringer for responding to an accusation of infringement, which also imply the judicial process. Therefore, enforcement provisions are aimed at the implementation of the right to a remedy in the specific context of intellectual property litigation, both for right holders and alleged infringers. Hence, in international human rights law, the basis of the right to

the Council of 29 April 2004 on the enforcement of intellectual property rights (OJEU L 157 of 30 April 2004), OJEU L195 of 2 June 2004 (hereinafter EU Enforcement Directive).

33 It is Article 14.1 and not Article 2.3 of the ICCPR that obliges Member States to lay out remedies to enforce legal entitlements set forth in the Convention – the basis of the human right to access to a court. In fact, Article 2.3 is not drafted in terms of a subjective right but as an obligation of Member States to ensure that individuals have accessible and effective remedies to vindicate the rights recognized in the Covenant. Hence, Article 2.3 is not the correct basis of the right to have non-human rights (or human rights not foreseen in the Convention) claims adjudicated in court. The reason for this is the link made between the text of Article 2.3 and the 'rights or freedoms' recognized in the Covenant. As the Human Rights Committee recalls, Article 2.3 requires that 'in addition to effective protection of *Covenant rights* States Parties must ensure that individuals also have accessible and effective remedies to vindicate *those rights*' (emphasis added). The same correlation extends to reparation. As stated by the committee, Article 2.3 'requires that States Parties make reparation to individuals whose Covenant rights have been violated'. *See* UN Human Rights Committee (2004), paras. 15 and 16. The basis for the more general right to a remedy is found elsewhere, more precisely in Article 14 of the ICCPR.

34 *See*, more generally for a comparative approach on this aspect, Scheinin (2007).

35 *See* European Union Agency for Fundamental Rights and Council of Europe (2016), pp. 15 *et seq.*

36 *See* UN Human Rights Committee (2007).

have claims arising from intellectual property entitlements, and also the basis to respond to those claims, may be found in Article 14 of the ICCPR.

Many international agreements regulating intellectual property enshrine an article that obliges parties to ensure that 'measures, procedures and remedies' are available so as 'to permit effective action against any act of infringement of intellectual property rights'.[37] The relationship between this type of provisions and the right to access to a court has been underlined in the jurisprudence of the World Trade Organization. In *United States – Section 211 Omnibus Appropriations Act*[38] WTO dispute, the European Communities invoked Article 42 of the TRIPS Agreement, on 'fair and equitable procedures', and argued that US legislation made a trademark 'devoid of any practical value' by restricting access to the courts.[39]

Another provision commonly found in intellectual property treaties concerns legal standing. Intimately related to the right to access to a court, the article on 'entitled applicants' found in treaties determines who is entitled to the right to a remedy in the context of intellectual property proceedings. In the most ample versions, entitled applicants include intellectual property right holders, other persons authorized to use those rights (in particular, licensees), intellectual property collective rights management bodies and federations or associations having the legal standing and authority to assert those rights.[40]

Human rights bodies have addressed the conditions that should be met by remedies aimed at guaranteeing the respect of fundamental rights related to intellectual property norms. In the case of the right to enjoy the moral and material rights arising from intellectual assets, the conditions that judicial remedies should fulfil are coincidental with those set forth in intellectual property treaties and intellectual property chapters of preferential trade agreements. The Committee on Economic, Social and Cultural Rights, which is the body in charge of monitoring the International Covenant on Economic, Social and Cultural Rights, has stated that 'such remedies should not be unreasonably complicated or costly, or entail unreasonable time limits or unwarranted delays'.[41] This is exactly the same wording that

37 *See* Article 10.41.2 EU-Republic of Korea FTA and EIA (2011). Another example can be Article 16.9.5 US-Singapore FTA and EIA (2004), which establishes that '[e]ach Party shall provide for civil remedies against the actions described in paragraphs 7 and 8 of Article 16.4', the latter being articles describing infringements in cases related to anti-circumvention measures and rights management information.

38 *See* WTO Panel Report, *United States – Section 211 Omnibus Appropriations Act of* 1998, WT/DS176/R, 6 August 2001.

39 *Ibid*., paras. 4.6, 4.7, 4.11. While the WTO Panel found US law to be inconsistent with Article 42 of the TRIPS Agreement because the provision deprived the claimant from having a chance to substantiate its claim in court, the Appellate Body reversed the WTO Panel's finding and stated that Members are not obliged by virtue of Article 42 to permit adjudication of each substantive claim regarding trade mark rights a party might assert, if that party is fairly determined *ab initio* not to be the holder of an interest in the subject mark. *See* WTO Appellate Body Report, *United States – Section 211 Omnibus Appropriations Act of* 1998, WT/DS176/AB/R, 2 January 2002.

40 *See* Article 10.42 EU-Republic of Korea FTA and EIA (2011).

41 *See* UN Committee on Economic, Social and Cultural Rights (2006), para. 52.

can be found in the TRIPS Agreement and in the intellectual property provisions enacted in many trade agreements.[42] Such a coincidence evidences that the remedies that the Committee on Economic, Social and Cultural Rights had in mind were, precisely, the remedies set forth in provisions regulating intellectual property enforcement, naturally under the condition that they fulfil the requirements identified by the Committee.

Importantly, 'the right to an effective remedy need not be interpreted as always requiring a judicial remedy. Administrative remedies will, in many cases, be adequate ... Any such administrative remedies should be accessible, affordable, timely and effective'.[43] This precision is important since measures and actions for the enforcement of intellectual property rights may be of administrative nature. This is the case in particular in some countries and also in some areas, such as border enforcement, where customs authorities can assume the entire process that may eventually result in the destruction of an infringing product.[44]

The reference to judicial and administrative remedies as necessary to implement the right to an effective remedy may be of relevance when assessing the increasingly frequent private enforcement of intellectual property rights. In this regard, it must be noted that while human rights law may require the existence of judicial and administrative mechanisms for the enforcement of intellectual property rights, the same reasoning does not apply with respect to private enforcement. Hence, practices such as mandating third parties to impede the infringement of an intellectual property right do not have a human rights standing. This does not mean that they are in conflict with human rights norms, but just that they are unrelated to the right to a remedy as enshrined in international human rights conventions.[45]

The considerations made relating to some mechanisms found in the digital environment apply as well to other intellectual property enforcement areas. For instance, some initiatives in the field of criminal enforcement have invoked the protection of human rights as its ultimate basis. In the European Union this has been for example the case of the failed directive on criminal enforcement, the IPRED2, which linked its very adoption to the need to satisfy Article 17(2) of the EU Charter on Fundamental Rights. In a reference of ambiguous wording and many possible readings, Article 17(2) states that '[i]ntellectual property shall be protected'.[46]

42 *See* Article 151.2 EU-CARIFORUM States FTA and EIA (2008).

43 *See* UN Committee on Economic, Social and Cultural Rights (1998), para. 9.

44 *See* Chapter 1, Section II.3.

45 While these practices do not have a basis on human rights entitlements, their implementation may indeed raise human rights concerns. Implementation of private enforcement systems in the field of intellectual property rights might raise some question in relation to, for instance, ensuring a fair and independent review of the alleged infringement or in relation to the independence and impartiality of the bodies that monitor private enforcement instruments. For a more general assessment on private enforcement mechanisms and human rights, *see* Bridy (2012)

46 The argument was that 'the direct objective of this initiative is to implement Article 17(2) of the EU Charter of Fundamental Rights which states that "Intellectual property shall be protected"; it does this by approximation of legislation while respecting the different legal traditions and systems of the

However, and contrary to what could be inferred from the directive, states are only bound to adopt criminal measures in reaction to the most serious violations of human rights.[47] This indicates that 'European lawmaker's suggestion that the proposed expansion of criminal sanction for intellectual property infringement under IPRED2 "implements" article 17(2) of the EU Charter is a rhetorical flourish rather than the statement of legal obligation'.[48]

III AMBIGUOUS RELATIONS

1 *Vagueness and Imbalance*

The relationship between human rights and intellectual property rules is frequently more complex than merely supportive or conflictive. In fact, ambiguous relations are rather common, and the ultimate assessment on whether there is a conflict depends on the intricacies of interpretation and implementation, the latter, by definition, being highly contextual and national-specific. This is particularly evident when international human rights norms are put into relation with international norms on intellectual property enforcement.

Two prominent characteristics of new intellectual property enforcement undertakings adopted in bilateral and plurilateral compromises illustrate such complex relations. The vague drafting of some articles and the imbalance that characterizes those and other articles may give rise to tense relationships between intellectual property and human rights if enforcement provisions are not correctly interpreted and implemented.

Important bilateral and plurilateral treaties include intellectual property enforcement articles of uncertain meaning. Diverging interests between contracting parties and conflictive views as to the relevance and function of some enforcement-related norms as well as national political considerations ultimately explain that phenomenon. In search of an agreement, parties insert vague compromises and open terms in the text. That language is part of a 'constructive ambiguity',[49] which is aimed at facilitating the conclusion of the treaty and convincing domestic stakeholders that no major concessions have been made while there are different views on the meaning and scope of the provisions adopted. In other occasions, general reservations made to specific obligations make it difficult to understand the real scope of that obligation. For instance, some treaties enshrine 'national conformity clauses' declaring that the adopted compromises are subjected to national law or national interpretation. Therefore, even if national law contradicts what has been actually agreed

Member States as well as other fundamental rights and principles recognised by the Charter'. *See* Commission of the European Communities (2005b), p. 2.

47 Human rights jurisprudence in this regard relates to the cases of rape, physical punishment to children, violent homicide and slavery. *See*, for the corresponding sentences, Griffiths (2012), p. 198.

48 *See* Griffiths (2012), p. 198.

49 *See* Watal (1999).

to in the treaty, 'national conformity clauses' would still allow parties to fulfil the treaty.[50]

Ambiguity must be distinguished from another important feature, particularly of trade agreements, which is the creation of unbalanced regimes where typically the interests of the right holders take the central – and sometimes even the exclusive – role.[51] Unbalanced intellectual property provisions raise a range of questions from the human rights point of view. In some cases, problems relate to the overall impact of an unbalanced system on very diverse social interests, such as food, health or, in a distinct arena, competition. On other occasions, enforcement provisions with unbalanced content may also affect civil and political rights, such as the rights to a fair trial, privacy or freedom of expression. Moreover, the same provision may have a double impact, both on social and civil rights.

The absence of procedural guarantees in favour of the alleged infringer is particularly troubling from the point of view of due process and fair trial. In the agreements negotiated by the European Union, the provisions on precautionary measures, permanent injunctions, right of information, evidence and measures for the preservation of evidence frequently do not mention very basic rights of alleged infringers.[52] For instance, in the case of provisional measures, unmentioned are the right to be informed without delay, the right to a review of the measures, the right to be heard, or the right to have the measures revoked in case proceedings are not instituted within a reasonable period. Contradictorily as it may seem, all these are guarantees that the European legislation on injunctions effectively provides.[53]

2 *The Relevance of the Right to a Fair Trial in the Implementation of Norms on Intellectual Property Enforcement*

Once the right to access to a court has been guaranteed, attention focuses on the characteristics of the proceedings that the said right gives access to. International human rights norms on due process and fair trial set the framework to assess procedural rules.[54] This makes the right to a fair trial of the utmost interest when analysing norms on intellectual property enforcement, since these norms specifically regulate the powers and processes available to right holders and alleged infringers in case an intellectual property right has been infringed or it is about to be infringed.

50 *See* Chapter 4. 51 *See* Chapter 6, Section V.5. 52 *See* Chapter 6, Section III.1.

53 *See* Article 9 of the Enforcement Directive.

54 The European Court of Human Rights stated that Article 6 of the European Convention on Human Rights, on the right to fair trial, 'extends only to "contestations" (disputes) over (civil) "rights and obligations" which can be said, at least on arguable grounds, to be recognised under domestic law; it does not in itself guarantee any particular content for (civil) "rights and obligations" in the substantive law of the Contracting States'. *See* ECtHR, *James and others v. United Kingdom*, no. 8793/79, 21 February 1986, Series A no. 94, para. 81.

A first question to elucidate is whether the right to a fair trial applies to intellectual property proceedings. The main international covenants regulating the right to a fair trial allude to the determination of rights and obligation 'in a suit of law',[55] the determination of 'civil rights and obligations'[56] or the determination of 'rights and obligations of a civil, labor, fiscal, or any other nature'.[57]

According to the Human Rights Committee, the determination of rights and obligations 'in a suit of law' encompasses '(a) judicial procedures aimed at determining rights and obligations pertaining to the areas of contract, property and torts in the area of private law, as well as (b) equivalent notions in the area of administrative law ... and it may (c) cover other procedures which ... must be assessed on a case by case basis'.[58] The right to a fair trial as enshrined in the European Convention on Human Rights is also applicable to disputes involving private parties, such as actions in contract or tort law,[59] and has been effectively applied to intellectual property litigation. In this regard, the European Court of Human Rights has expressly stated that copyright 'proceedings concern the determination of the applicants' 'civil rights and obligations' within the meaning of Article 6 § 1'.[60] Hence, intellectual property law is covered by the reference to the determination of rights and obligations pertaining to the fields of contract, property and torts in the area of private law.

The right to a fair trial has an ample content, intensively analysed and developed by courts and human rights bodies. The Human Rights Committee has emphasized the importance for the respect of the right to a fair trial, of the principles of equality of arms, adversary proceedings, preclusion of *ex officio reformatio in pejus* and expeditious procedures.[61] In the European context, the right to a fair trial also has been linked to the principles of equality of arms,[62] effective access to a court[63] and the effective participation in the process.[64] Many, if not all, of these requirements are relevant in the context of intellectual property litigation. For instance, in respect to 'expeditious procedures' human rights bodies have expressly mentioned that proceedings related to

55 *See* Article 14.1 ICCPR. 56 *See* Article 6.1 ECHR.

57 *See* Article 8.1 of the American Convention on Human Rights.

58 *See* UN Human Rights Committee (2007), para. 16. 59 *See* Vitkauskas and Dikov (2012), p. 14.

60 In *Nemec v. Slovakia* the European Court of Human Rights noted 'that the proceedings in issue concern a copyright. It is satisfied, and this was not contested by the parties, that the proceedings concern the determination of the applicants' 'civil rights and obligations' within the meaning of Article 6 § 1'. *See* ECtHR, *Nemec v. Slovakia*, no. 48672/99, 15 November 2001, unreported, para. 29.

61 It has been established that 'the concept of a fair hearing in the context of article 14 (1) of the Covenant should be interpreted as requiring a number of conditions, such as equality of arms, respect for the principle of adversary proceedings, preclusion of *ex officio reformatio in pejus*, and expeditious procedure'. *See* Human Rights Committee, *Yves Morael v. France*, Communication no. 207/1986, 28 July 1989, UN Doc Supp. no. 40 (A/44/40), 1989, 210, para. 9.3 (emphasis in original).

62 *See* ECtHR, *Borgers v. Belgium*, no.12005/86, 30 October 1991, Series A no. 214-B; ECtHR, *Dombo Beheer BV v. the Netherlands*, no. 14448/88, 27 October 1993, Series A no. 274, para. 33.

63 *See* ECtHR, *Golder v. United Kingdom*, no. 4451/70, 21 February 1975, Series A no. 18.

64 *See* ECtHR, *V v. United Kingdom*, no. 24888/94, 16 December 1999, Reports of Judgments and Decisions 1999-IX.

particular intellectual property rights should not be 'unreasonably complicated or costly, or entail unreasonable time limits or unwarranted delays'.[65]

It is not within the reach of this chapter to thoroughly depict the right to a fair trial and infer all its potential implications in the context of intellectual property rights enforcement. Other chapters of this book target several components of the right to a fair trial, as applied in specific situations and with respect to diverse enforcement procedures. By contrast, one of the requirements of the right to a fair trial – i.e. equality of arms – is selected and analysed in light of one of the mentioned characteristics of new norms on intellectual property enforcement found in some trade agreements, which is its unbalanced content.

3 *The Principle of Equality of Arms and Intellectual Property Enforcement*

New international compromises on intellectual property enforcement frequently prioritise the rights and interests of right holders. This may respond to the perception that right holders are not being sufficiently protected and that the currently existing mechanisms are unsatisfactory to fulfil substantive rights recognized elsewhere. However, a more complete account for the little attention paid to the rights of alleged infringers and other relevant stakeholders includes as well factors such as the unequal representation of concerned stakeholders in international negotiations. This, added to shortcomings in terms of transparency of the negotiating processes, has facilitated the adoption of texts largely criticized because of their overall lack of balance.

Several chapters of this book study in greater depth this phenomenon and provide specific examples of such unbalance and its relationship with the protection of human rights. From the point of view of human rights, the right to a fair trial and its associated principle of equality of arms are of chief importance when analysing such unbalance.

Take for instance the human rights jurisprudence of the European system. In a case specifically concerning measures for the enforcement of an intellectual property right, the European Court of Human Rights addressed the existence of appropriate safeguards for the defendant. Unsurprisingly, the court held that 'it is essential that this measure should be accompanied by adequate and effective safeguards against arbitrary interference and abuse'.[66] On its part, in the context of that very same case, when the European Commission of Human Rights previously upheld the measures and accepted the interference with the right to privacy, it alluded to the 'quality of the law' and also to the compatibility 'with the rule of law' of the denounced measures.[67] In a similar vein, it can be held that an unbalanced

[65] *See* UN Committee on Economic, Social and Cultural Rights (2006), para. 52.

[66] *See* ECtHR, *Chappel v. United Kingdom*, no. 10461/83, 30 March 1989, Series A no. 152-A, para. 57 (hereinafter ECtHR, *Chappel v. United Kingdom*).

[67] 'The phrase 'in accordance with the law' does not merely refer back to domestic law but also relates to the quality of the law, requiring it to be compatible with the rule of law; it thus implies that there must be a measure of protection in domestic law against arbitrary interferences by public authorities with

regime on intellectual property enforcement does not fulfil the quality requirement mentioned by the European Commission of Human Rights, nor does it provide safeguards against arbitrary interference and abuse.

The principle of equality of arms is particularly relevant in that context. This principle is a basic component of the right to a fair trial[68] and has been enshrined in all the major international human rights treaties and declarations.[69] Essentially, it implies 'that the same procedural rights are to be provided to all the parties unless distinctions are based on law and can be justified on objective and reasonable grounds, not entailing actual disadvantage or other unfairness to the defendant'.[70] Hence, each party in a particular controversy must have reasonable possibility to present his cause, in conditions that will not put him in disadvantage against the other contending part.[71]

In contrast, important guarantees are frequently absent in new international compromises on intellectual property enforcement. If these international norms were transposed without any further changes or additions into the national legislation or no other principle of general law or norms found elsewhere in the legal order were applied, the imbalance between the right holder and the alleged infringer would generate a conflict with the principle of equality of arms. That legislative framework or lack of hermeneutic re-balancing would indeed facilitate that 'arbitrary interference and abuse' occurred frequently.[72]

IV CONFLICTIVE RELATIONS

1 *Conflicts of Regimes*

Both human rights treaties and intellectual property treaties are living instruments. International organizations, states and treaty-bodies interpret, modify and litigate the norms enshrined therein. The internal dynamics of both the human rights regime and the trade and intellectual property regime lead to regular adoption of norms and

the rights safeguarded by, inter alia, paragraph 1 of Article 8 (art. 8–1) ... '. *See* ECtHR, *Olsson v. Sweden (no. 1)*, no. 10465/83, 24 March 1988, Series A no. 130, para. 61.b.

68 *See* ECtHR, *Feldbrugge v. the Netherlands*, no. 8562/79, 29 May 1986, Series A no. 99, para. 44; ECtHR, *Delcourt v. Belgium*, no. 2689/65, 17 January 1970, Series A no. 11, para. 28.

69 Starting with Article 10 UDHR, which also guarantees that '[e]veryone is entitled in full equality to a fair and public hearing ... in the determination of his rights and obligations and of any criminal charge against him'.

70 *See* UN Human Rights Committee (2007), para. 13.

71 *See* ECtHR, *Werner v. Austria*, no. 21835/93, 24 November 1997, Reports 1997-VII, para. 63; ECtHR, *Coëme and Others v. Belgium*, nos. 32492/96, 32547/96, 32548/96, 33209/96 and 33210/96, 22 June 2000, Reports of Judgments and Decisions 2000-VII, para. 102; ECtHR, *G.B. v. France*, no. 44069/98, 2 October 2001, Reports of Judgments and Decisions 2001-X, para. 58; ECtHR, *Ankerl v. Switzerland*, application no. 17748/91, 23 October 1996, Reports 1996-V, para. 38. *See* also Husovec and Peguera (2015), p. 25.

72 Condemned by the European Court of Human Rights. *See* ECtHR, *Chappel v. United Kingdom*.

'authoritative' interpretations of already existing norms. Moreover, both regimes have built-in mechanisms that determine who is going to judge disputes and under what premises the decision will be taken.[73] Hence, even if analysis of normative conflicts quite predictably focuses on norms, the relationship between international regimes is more complex and has to do with an increasingly intricate web of relations at different levels.[74]

From the systemic point of view conflicts of policies are more significant than jurisdictional and normative conflicts. It is not rare that States take contradictory stances in distinct forums – a contradictory positioning that gives rise to inconsistent trends in international organizations. The Secretary General of the United Nations affirmed the existence of these incoherencies when appointed, in November 2015, the High Level Panel on Access to Medicines with a mandate 'to review and assess proposals and recommend solutions for remedying the policy incoherence between the justifiable rights of inventors, international human rights law, trade rules and public health in the context of health technologies'.[75]

In the context of enforcement, the same phenomenon has been underlined when analysing the Anti-Counterfeiting Trade Agreement *vis-à-vis* other international developments in the sphere of intellectual property.[76] On the substantive side, the unbalanced content of some enforcement provisions would be inconsistent with Recommendation 45 of the World Intellectual Property Organization Development Agenda, which instructs 'to approach intellectual property enforcement in the context of broader societal interests, and especially development-oriented concerns'.[77] On the membership side, plurilateral and bilateral compromises used to enhance enforcement would be *per se* at odds with the promotion of 'multilateral, multi-stakeholder, democratic, and transparent' policy dialogue announced in other forums.[78]

Examples of policy incoherence related to intellectual property provisions in trade agreements are numerous and concern both developed and developing countries. In the case of developed countries, some aspects and substantive content of a number of PTAs are contradictory with both the letter and spirit of the Doha Declaration on the TRIPS Agreement and Public Health.[79] Similarly, some developing countries have also held positions of intricate articulation. For instance, developing countries adopting treaties with TRIPS *plus* and *extra* provisions have

[73] Their respective power to attract the controversy and deliver a response to the controversy makes the final answer predictable. This has to be read as advice against de-contextualized analysis of conflicts of norms.

[74] This phenomenon was widely discussed at the end of the 1990s with the emergence of the WTO trade regime and the concomitant power and attractiveness of its Dispute Settlement System. Areas such as environment, food security and health suddenly became 'trade issues'. *See* Jackson (1996); Trachtman (1998). In Chapter 5 we argue that dispute settlement bodies of trade agreements may be asked to decide on human rights aspects of intellectual property ligation.

[75] *See* UNSG High-Level Panel on Access to Medicines (2015), p. 3.

[76] *See* Yu (2009a); Yu (2011b). [77] *See* WIPO (2007a), p. 157. [78] *See* Yu (2011b), p. 1076.

[79] *See* Abbott (2004a).

also been very active in proposing alternative models to the patent-based innovation system, a combination of positions of difficult articulation.[80]

Public international law provides some answers and tools in cases where norms are in conflict or need to be interpreted. However, public international law cannot solve discrepancies reflecting international or national contradictory policy goals. Public international law is simply not the right instrument to address incongruous policies of international organizations and states. It is in the phases of treaty negotiation and adoption when countries should strike an appropriate balance between the protection and enforcement of intellectual property rights and the commitments made in international or regional human rights instruments. Doing otherwise and allowing treaty bodies to make what would naturally be states' decisions will probably result in further controversy.

2 *Conflicts of Norms*

In the past fifteen years, a growing volume of academic literature has focused on the conflictive relations between intellectual property and human rights. The TRIPS Agreement and plurilateral and bilateral agreements with TRIPS *plus* and *extra* provisions have caused concern given their impact on fundamental rights. The relationship between certain intellectual property rights categories, mainly patents and copyright, with a number of human rights has led to affirm the existence of 'actual or potential conflicts' between the two.[81] Nevertheless, eventual conflicts arising from intellectual property enforcement norms have rarely been studied.

The lack of clarity of enforcement statues may create conflicts with both civil and social rights. For instance, in the case of social rights the ambiguity of border enforcement rules made the Kenyan Supreme Court holding that 'it would be in violation of the state's obligations to the petitioners with respect to their right to life and health to have included in legislation ambiguous provisions subject to the interpretation of intellectual property holders and customs officials when such provisions relate to access to medicines essential for the petitioners' survival'.[82] For the court, 'there can be no room for ambiguity where the right to health and life of the petitioners and the many other Kenyans who are affected by HIV/AIDS are at stake'.[83]

80 A telling example is that of Colombia, which has concluded PTAs enacting demanding intellectual property compromises while also promoting a multilateral treaty on alternative R&D mechanisms in the context of the World Health Organization, perceived as a criticism to the systema that those PTAs intended to strengthen. On the activism of Colombia, *see* Mursak Hermann (2012); Knowledge Ecology International (2012); 'El "oso" de Colombia en Ginebra', 23 May 2013, available at: http://m.semana.com //nacion/articulo/el-oso-colombia-ginebra/344189–3 (last accessed September 2016).

81 *See* UN Sub-Commission on the Promotion and Protection of Human Rights (2000), p. 1.

82 *See* High Court of Kenya, *Patricia Asero Ochieng, Maurine Atieno and Joseph Munyi v. The Republic*, Petition no. 409 OF 2009, 20 April 2012, para. 94. *See* Chapter 14, Section IV.

83 *Ibid.*

Regarding civil rights, some norms on enforcement, particularly in the area of criminal enforcement, may not fulfil the minimum requirements that any criminal law statute should meet. This claim was raised in relation to ACTA and can also be made regarding a number trade agreements. In ACTA, the lack of clarity of the definition of 'commercial scale' activities triggering criminal responsibility was understood to violate fair trial guarantees. According to Article 23, 'acts carried out on a commercial scale include at least those carried out as commercial activities for direct or indirect economic or commercial advantage'. [84] As Chapter 14 analyses, this provision contains a 'definition highly problematic with regard to the principle of legal certainty and legality of criminal offenses'.[85] The principle of legality prescribes the need for clarity, concision and predictability. *Lex scripta, lex certa, lex previa* and *lex stricta* are the four pillars of this principle.[86] Likewise, the principle of legality 'expresses the fundamental premise that those subject to the law must know what the law is so as to be able to plan their actions accordingly'.[87]

Several US trade agreements lay down criminal measures in response to circumvention activities of effective technological measures. These measures will 'be applied when any person, other than a nonprofit library, archive, educational institution, or public noncommercial broadcasting entity, is found to have engaged willfully and for purposes of commercial advantage or private financial gain in any of the foregoing activities'.[88] The reference to 'private financial gain' as a benchmark to apply criminal measures is also found in the context of the provisions on rights management information.[89]

Similarly, several trade agreements of the United States oblige providing for criminal sanctions in cases of wilful piracy or counterfeiting on a commercial scale. In the case of copyright, 'commercial scale' includes 'significant willful infringements for purposes of commercial advantage or private financial gain' as well as 'willful infringements that have no direct or indirect motivation of financial gain, provided that there is more than a *de minimis* financial harm'.[90] Other treaties where it is established that 'significant wilful copyright or related rights infringements that have no direct or indirect motivation of financial gain'[91] also make room for criminal sanctions and do not mention the '*de minimis*' requirement. Hence, in one case the mere existence of 'significant willful copyright infringement' is requisite enough; in the other case 'more than a *de minimis* financial harm' is required.

[84] *See* the same construction for instance in Article 15.11.26(a) CAFTA-DR-US FTA and EIA (2006).
[85] *See* Geiger (2015c), p. 105. *See* Chapter 14. [86] *See* Chapter 14.
[87] *See* Tridimas (1999), p. 163.
[88] *See* Article 18.4.7(a) 2 (ii) Republic of Korea-US FTA and EIA (2012); Article 15.5.7(a) 2 (ii) CAFTA-DR-US FTA and EIA (2006); Article 17.4.7 US-Australia FTA and EIA (2005).
[89] *See* Article 18.4.8(a) Republic of Korea-US FTA and EIA (2012).
[90] *See* Article 15.11.26(a) CAFTA-DR-US FTA and EIA (2006).
[91] See Article 18.10.26 Republic of Korea-US FTA and EIA (2012).

The interpretation of these provisions is unclear. The meanings of 'private financial gain', 'significant', 'wilful infringements', '*de minimis* financial harm' and 'indirect motivation of financial gain' raise, in all cases, doubts would seem incompatible with the principle of legal certainty.[92]

In light of the doubts existing in respect to the meaning of some contemporaneous provisions on criminal enforcement enshrined in international treaties, the 'duty on legislators to ensure that it is clear what conduct will give rise to sanctions and to the deprivation of liberty' is hardly met.[93] The requirement of clarity and intelligibility of the law, crucial in criminal law, is not entirely satisfied in contemporaneous agreements regulating enforcement. The UN Human Rights Committee has affirmed that the 'broad definition' of a crime may negatively impact fundamental rights, including rights of non-derogable nature.[94] According to the Committee, the vagueness of the definitions directly contradicts the principle of legality,[95] this being particularly the case of 'ambiguous wording of the provisions and the use of several evidentiary presumptions to the detriment of the defendant'.[96]

3 *How to Address Ambiguous and Conflictive Relations*

Since the early 2000s, the need to have a holistic view of public international law as a coherent legal order and not as a conglomerate of isolated branches touching upon a range of substantive issues has been underlined.[97] The proliferation of international norms in diverse substantive areas and the diverse power of the respective dispute settlement systems have attracted a renewed interest in general public international law, which includes the norms of treaty conflict and treaty interpretation. As we will see, both the principle of systemic integration and the norms of treaty conflict have been invoked in the pursuit of answers to the increasingly complex questions arising from the interaction of norms of international law, including trade and human rights norms.

In order to address ambiguous and conflictive relations it is useful to briefly recall the distinction made in Chapter 1 between primary and secondary norms. On the one hand, primary norms are rules of substantive content, namely norms that enact rights and obligations. On the other hand, secondary norms are 'norms on norms' and address issues such as the interaction between primary norms, the methods and

92 *See* Chapter 14. 93 *See* Irish Law Reform Commission (1997), p. 99.

94 *See* HRC, Estonia, ICCPR, A/58/40, vol. I, 2003, 41, para. 79.8.

95 For instance, 'extremist activity' has been considered too vague to satisfy the principle of legality. *See* HRC, Russian Federation, ICCPR, A/59/40, vol. I, 2003, 20, para. 64.20; *see* similarly, HRC, Morocco, ICCPR, A/60/40, vol. I, 2004, 35, para. 84.20.

96 *See* HRC, Israel, ICCPR, A/58/40, vol. I, 2003, 64, para. 85.14.

97 *See* International Law Commission (2006b); Abi-Saab (1999); Dupuy (1999); Leathley (2007); Marceau (2001).

techniques applied in the creation and extinction of norms, the interpretation of norms and the solution to eventual conflicts.[98]

On the substantive side – i.e. primary norms – the proliferation of detailed and demanding intellectual property obligations implies that the sources of tension with human rights norms are more and more numerous. Presently, almost all intellectual property rights categories are the object of international regulation, which implies that very diverse areas of public interest – such as food, health or knowledge – relate with intellectual property rights. Moreover, the detailed regulation of intellectual property enforcement in trade agreements means that other legal interests, in particular those protected by civil rights, will also have to be accommodated as to address the possible tension and conflict with intellectual property rights.

3.1 The Relevance of Norms on Treaty Interpretation

General international law contains an important set of secondary rules to address the relations between international treaties.[99] The starting point is the presumption against conflict between norms of public international law and the instruction to implement these norms in good faith.[100] Accordingly, ambiguous relations existing between intellectual property norms and those on human rights should in principle be solved through interpretation, allowing for the implementation of both.

The hermeneutic techniques to conduct such an operation are found in the Vienna Convention on the Law of Treaties, particularly in Article 31. This article enacts a single operation of textual, teleological and contextual interpretation. That is, the various means mentioned in Article 31 are all to be employed and are all of equal value.[101] The principle of systemic integration forms part of this operation.[102] This principle is enshrined in Article 31.3(c)[103] of the Vienna Convention on the Law of Treaties and instructs to take into account other obligations of international law binding on the parties when interpreting a specific rule. That is, when interpreting the meaning of an intellectual property norm contained in a treaty, other rules, for instance those enshrined in a human rights convention, can be taken into consideration.[104]

98 For the concepts of primary and secondary norms, *see* Chapter 1, Sections I.3 and I.4. For their contextualization in public international law, *see* Casanovas y La Rosa (2001).

99 Particularly Articles 30, 31 and 32 VCLT. These norms constitute an authentic 'tool-box' in the words of the International Law Commission (2006b), p. 250.

100 Under the 'principle of harmonization', '[i]t is a generally accepted principle that when several norms bear on a single issue they should, to the extent possible, be interpreted so as to give rise to a single set of compatible obligations'. *See* International Law Commission (2006a), p. 1. Among the doctrine, *see* also Jennings and Watts (1992), p. 1275; Pauwelyn (2003), pp. 240–244.

101 *See* Villiger (2011), pp. 113–114. 102 *See* McLachlan (2005), pp. 279–320.

103 Article 31.3(c) VCLT states '[t]here shall be taken into account, together with the context: . . . (c) any relevant rules of international law applicable in the relations between the parties'.

104 For the specific implementation of this principle in the context of the WTO dispute settlement system in the area of intellectual property, *see* Seuba (2010b), pp. 204–208; Hestermeyer (2007).

The principle of systemic integration[105] has acquired central importance in the exploration of the interplay of different international legal regimes, and both comprehensive[106] as well as in-depth studies relating to specific intellectual property areas[107] have underlined the potential relevance of this principle to achieve greater unity and coherence of the international legal order. Fundamentally, the principle of systemic integration establishes that, in interpreting international rules, norms binding on the parties and distinct to the interpreted rule need to be taken into account.[108]

Ideally, unbalanced provisions giving rise to ambiguous relations should be redrafted internationally and their meaning duly clarified. This is, however, not foreseeable. By contrast, reforms undertaken in the context of national implementation are perfectly feasible. In this regard, interpretation pursuant to international human rights standards can be decisive to re-shape and interpret intellectual property legislation, usually in combination with teachings extracted from comparative intellectual property law.

As the case of measures for the preservation of evidence illustrates in Chapter 7, the regime enshrined in several international texts is not satisfactory from the human rights point of view, either because it creates uncertainty or because parties' interests are not protected equitably. Something similar happens with respect to interim injunctions, as detailed in Chapter 8. However, the very same provisions that give rise to vague and incomplete regimes also allow margin for action. Given that it is possible to react and redress the identified problems, the basis of reaction and the content of new norms can be found in the right to a fair trial as regulated in both international human rights law and its specific implementation in comparative law.

Two important operations would improve the situation. First, when implementing an international agreement, the missing guarantees set forth by the right to a fair trial should be incorporated in national legislation. Guidance on the balance achieved by other states may be a useful source of inspiration to adopt new legislation, but it is not the only possibility, and countries may want to be more creative. Second, in case the treaty is implemented without passing national legislation, the recourse to the principle of systemic integration would allow the local interpreter – the judge – to bring into consideration fair trial and due process international national standards when passing sentences.

In both instances, an overarching principle may be of crucial relevance. The call for proportionality is common in the human rights field and has been applied not only as an independent principle in the area of intellectual property[109] but also when dealing with the interface between intellectual property enforcement and human rights.[110] Proportionality has in fact a much broader scope and function, namely that

[105] *See* McLachlan (2005), pp. 279–320. [106] *See* Pauwelyn (2003); Zapatero (2003).

[107] *See* Seuba (2008); Hestermeyer (2007). [108] *See* Article 31.3(c) VCLT.

[109] *See* ECJ, Case C-275/06, *Productores de Música de España (Promusicae) v. Telefónica de España SAU* [2008], Judgment of the Court (Grand Chamber) of 29 January 2008, ECR I-00271.

[110] *See* Seuba (2015b), pp. 71–72.

of a balancing mechanism rooted in general principles of public international law.[111] Although the specific meaning and scope of the principle of proportionality may vary in different legal regimes and legal theories, it provides in all cases the tools to balance conflicting rights[112] and is a 'key legal concept to assist the trading-off of competing values'.[113] That is, it requires taking into account the nature of the conflicting interests at stake and the degree to which those interests need to be protected in the circumstances of the case.[114]

The principle of proportionality goes beyond litigation in specific disputes or the assessment of whether intrusive measures are justified in a particular case. In fact, its function is not only judicial but also legislative, since it permits assessing norms themselves. In this particular regard, the Court of Justice of the European Union has stated that 'it is necessary to ascertain whether the penalty laid down by the provision in question to achieve the aim in view corresponds with the importance of that aim and whether the disadvantages caused are not disproportionate to the aims pursued'.[115]

The principle of proportionality is not just a legal principle shared by domestic legal orders but has also been adopted in the sphere of public international law. On the one hand, dispute settlement bodies regularly apply it as a fundamental general legal principle informing adjudication. In that same sense, some intellectual property treaties explicitly acknowledge the role of proportionality, both in general regarding enforcement procedures[116] and with respect to specific remedies.[117] On the other hand, the principle of proportionality has experienced an autonomous development in several material regimes of public international law.[118] While its development is not comparable to the relevance acquired in other areas of international law, the principle of proportionality lies behind the checks and balances found in international intellectual property treaties, and it is a tool to foster the competing objectives pursued in

[111] *See* Geiger (2016), p. 661. [112] *Ibid.* [113] Adenas and Zlepting (2006), p. 2.

[114] *See* ECtHR, *Neij and Sunde Kolmisoppi v. Sweden*, no. 40397/12, 19 February 2013.

[115] *See* ECJ, Case C-356/97, *Molkereigenossenschaft Wiedergeltingen eG v. Hauptzollamt Lindau* [2000], Judgment of the Court (Sixth Chamber) of 6 July 2000 ECR I-05461, para. 36. *See* also ECJ, Case C-8/89, *Vincenzo Zardi v. Consorzio agrario provinciale di Ferrara* [1990], Judgment of the Court (Fifth Chamber) of 26 June 1990, ECR I-02515, para. 10; and ECJ, Joined Cases C-133/93, C-300/93 and C-362/93 *Antonio Crispoltoni v. Fattoria Autonoma Tabacchi and Giuseppe Natale and Antonio Pontillo v. Donatab Srl* [1994], Judgment of the Court (Fifth Chamber) of 5 October 1994, ECR I-04863, para. 41.

[116] *See* in particular Article 6.3 of ACTA, which states that 'in implementing the provisions of this Chapter, each Party shall take into account the need for proportionality between the seriousness of the infringement, the interests of third parties, and the applicable measures, remedies and penalties'; or the more broader formulation in provisions found in some bilateral trade agreements, such as Article 234.2 of the EU-Colombia and Peru FTA and EIA (2013).

[117] This is the case of the TRIPS Agreement, which explicitly alludes to proportionality when regulating the right to information and the article relating to the destruction of infringing copies (*see* Articles 37 and 36 respectively).

[118] Proportionality has, indeed, greatly developed in material regimes such as the human rights regime, humanitarian law regime, international sea law regime and international trade regime, among others. *See* Cannizzaro (2000).

those treaties.[119] In light of its status both in domestic and international law, whether intellectual property treaties explicitly allude to this principle or not, whether they do it in general or with respect to concrete legal provisions and whether they do it with more or less intensity should not influence its actual implementation on the part of judges and competent authorities.[120]

3.2 Norms on Conflict of Treaties

The principle of systemic integration has some limits. In particular, this principle is of no relevance whenever treaty articles are clear, regardless of whether provisions eventually conflict with human rights norms. On the other hand, the principle of systemic integration only permits taking into consideration norms binding on all the parties of the dispute.[121] In this sense, a human rights treaty could not be invoked for interpreting non-human rights norms if states involved in the controversy were not parties to both conventions.

There will be cases where human rights and intellectual property rights cannot be reconciled and the relationship between the norms concerned can only be approached in terms of treaty conflict. Although the very notion of conflict is disputed, and more or less flexible approaches to the identification of conflicts can be adopted,[122] once its existence is asserted some public international law rules apply.

Article 30 of the VCLT sets forth the basic rules on the application of successive treaties dealing with the same subject matter. It envisages the possibility that treaties themselves incorporate conflict clauses – either of subordination or primacy[123] – and codifies the chronological criteria (*lex posterior derogat priori*) in regard to treaty provisions that are incompatible with posterior obligations whenever the parties to the conflicting treaties coincide. However, when parties to treaties in conflict do not coincide, the situation becomes more difficult. In this case, the *lex posterior* rule is applied between parties that coincide in both treaties (Article 30.4(a)), but for the rest of the states the treaty where they do coincide will be applied, irrespective of its

119 The need to balance conflicting values and goals is clear in Articles 7 and 8 of the TRIPS Agreement.

120 The specific relevance of proportionality is discussed in this book when introducing aspects such as the relationship between criminal enforcement and freedom of expression or the award of damages. *See* Chapter 14, Section III.1, and Chapter 9, Section V.2.

121 As stated in Article 31.3(c) VCLT.

122 As the International Law Commission has summarized, '[a] strict notion would presume that conflict exists if it is possible for a party to two treaties to comply with one rule only by thereby failing to comply with another rule. This is the basic situation of incompatibility. An obligation may be fulfilled only by thereby failing to fulfil another obligation. However, there are other, looser understandings of conflict as well. A treaty may sometimes frustrate the goals of another treaty without there being any strict incompatibility between their provisions. Two treaties or sets of rules may possess different background justifications or emerge from different legislative policies or aim at divergent ends'. *See* International Law Commission (2006b), p. 19.

123 This is what Article 30.2 VCLT foresees, '[w]hen a treaty specifies that it is subject to, or that it is not to be considered as incompatible with, an earlier or later treaty, the provisions of that other treaty prevail'.

temporal precedence (Article 30.4(b)). This framework is completed with the customary *lex specialis* rule, which prescribes the precedence of the more detailed norm. Moreover, it must be noted that *ius cogens* norms will always prevail over any other contradictory norm.

Conflicts involving *ius cogens* norms are theoretically the easiest to solve, since these are the sole public international law norms with hierarchical status. Conflicts with these norms are considered *inherent* conflicts and have the most drastic outcomes, namely the nullity of both the contradicting norm and the treaty enshrining it.[124] Nevertheless, only a few and very basic human rights have the *ius cogens* status – i.e. freedom from torture, prohibition of slavery, prohibition of racial discrimination.[125] It has been proposed that specific components of certain human rights – that compound the 'core content' of each right – have *ius cogens* status.[126] It has also been held that certain levels of intellectual property protection may impinge upon the core content of some human rights,[127] thus conflicting with *ius cogens* norms.

Although intellectual property protection may impact the core content of a number of human rights norms,[128] public international law does not permit (yet) drawing a parallel between human rights' core content and *ius cogens*. The existence of a peremptory norm of general international law requires its acceptance and recognition 'by the international community of states as a whole',[129] a consensus that simply does not exist in this respect.

Once ruling out the relevance of *ius cogens* norms, Article 30 of the VCLT enters into play. This article limits its application to successive treaties dealing with the *same subject matter*, hence, whether an intellectual property norm and a human rights norm can be deemed to refer to the same subject matter, is decisive. A formalistic application of this rule[130] would imply that most interactions between norms pertaining to different international legal regimens would be out of the reach of Article 30. By contrast, a more accepted thesis, and the one supported by the International Law Commission, holds that 'the test of whether two treaties deal with the "same subject matter" is resolved through the assessment

124 *See* Pauwelyn (2003), pp. 276–277, 281.

125 *See* International Law Commission (2001a), p. 85. *See* also ICJ, *Questions of Interpretation and Application of the 1971 Montreal Convention Arising from the Aerial Incident at Lockerbie (Libyan Arab Jamahiriya v. United States of America)*, Order of 14 April 1992, ICJ Reports 1992, 114, p. 126.

126 *See* Orakhelashvili (2007), p. 183.

127 *See* UN Committee on Economic, Social and Cultural Rights (2001), para. 12; UN Committee on Economic, Social and Cultural Rights (2006), para. 35.

128 *See* Seuba (2008), p. 402.

129 *See* Article 53 VCLT.

130 For instance, the United States held that 'the WTO is not a successive treaty relating to the same subject matter as the NAFTA. The NAFTA is a free trade agreement establishing preferential treatment among the NAFTA parties. The WTO is a multilateral trade agreement providing for multilateral trading rules'. *See North American Free Trade Agreement, Arbitral Panel Established Pursuant to Article 2008 in the Matter of Tariffs Applied by Canada to Certain US-Origin Agricultural Products*, CDA-95-2008-01, 2 December 1996, para. 87.

of whether the fulfilment of the obligation under one treaty affects the fulfilment of the obligation of another'.[131] Therefore, whenever it is possible to demonstrate that the fulfilment of an obligation under an intellectual property treaty affects the fulfilment of the obligation contained in a human rights treaty, that condition would be satisfied.

The states party to the treaties in conflict and the ratification date of these treaties determine the applicable rule. Article 30 of the VCLT is, in principle, clear: if both states coincide in the relevant treaties, the latter prevails, but should states not coincide, only the treaty in which they do concur will be applied. In practical terms, both situations would seem – in principle and in most cases – to imply that intellectual property treaties would prevail over a provision contained in a human rights treaty. One of the reasons is quite prosaic: most human treaties were adopted in the 1970s or 1980s, while intellectual property provisions are set forth in more recent treaties. The other is more practical: relevant proponents of trade agreements enshrining provisions allegedly in conflict with human rights entitlements (particularly the United States) have not ratified some of the human rights treaties concerned.

It can be held, however, that the aforementioned rules are of no application to human rights. It is widely accepted that human rights treaties have special features that exempt them from a number of general international law rules. The objective nature of these norms, the special regime on treaty reservations, the debate surrounding its *ius cogens* status and the qualification of human rights as *erga omnes* obligations all refer to the singular relationship that exists between international human rights law and public international law.[132]

Among the abovementioned characteristics, the fact that human rights treaties set forth obligations of an objective nature stands out. That is to say, treaties of this nature exclude reciprocity and oblige parties to comply with treaty obligations regardless of other members' infringements. Human rights treaty provisions are designed to protect fundamental rights, not state's interests,[133] a radical departure from the majority of international treaties. For example, the demand for *effective protection* characteristic of human rights treaties would result in the *lex posterior* and *lex specialis* rules being of reduced application when dealing with human rights.[134] A human rights convention 'is an absolute or "integral treaty"', which differs from those laying down sinalagmatic and interdependent obligations since '[t]he obligations it imposes are independent of any expectation of reciprocity or performance on the part of other parties of their obligations'.[135]

131 *See* International Law Commission (2006b), p. 130.

132 *See* Seuba (2008), p. 412; Seuba (2010b), p. 212.

133 *See* ECtHR, *Ireland v. The United Kingdom*, no. 5310/71, 18 January 1978, Series A no. 25. In a similar vein, *see* IACtHR, *The Effect of Reservations*, Advisory Opinion OC-2/82, 24 September 1982, Series A no. 2; IACtHR, *Restrictions to the Death Penalty*, Advisory Opinion OC-3/83, 8 September 1983, Series A no. 3, 76, 77, para. 50.

134 *See* Roucounas (1987-VI), p. 197.

135 *See* International Law Commission (2006b), p. 161.

It was mentioned that Article 30 of the VCLT would probably result in giving precedence to intellectual property rules, either because these are posterior or because these are the only applicable rules to both parties. This outcome would not exempt parties, however, from the obligation to continue the application of the human rights treaty in regard to the other Member States not involved in the conflict. This is what is prescribed in Article 30.4(b) of the VCLT. However, it is obvious that it is impossible to fulfil both obligations altogether.

The very nature of human rights treaties and obligations – absolute, integral, objective – implies that a state cannot infringe a human rights treaty with respect to another party to the covenant and nevertheless continue its application with respect to the other parties. Due to the fact that human rights obligations imply respecting, protecting and fulfilling the human rights of those persons under the jurisdiction of the treaty Member, it is just not possible to respect said duty partially. Because of the integral nature of human rights treaties and the *erga omnes* consideration of the obligations set forth therein, the nature of the breach would be of such a character as to radically change the position of all the other states to which the obligation is owed.

The International Law Commission has affirmed that integral obligations, and more precisely human rights obligations, enjoy some precedence to merely transactional instruments. This is the reason why Article 30 of the VLCT finds its limit precisely when integral obligations come into play.[136] Human rights treaties cannot be operated through the same techniques as 'ordinary' treaties creating bilateral relationships. As far as the consequence of the violation of *erga omnes* and integral obligations are concerned, they are particularly serious: it will not be possible to invoke the violating obligations and other states will be compelled to not recognize the resulting situation.[137] Hence, this would result in the non-application of intellectual property obligations whenever they conflict with human rights norms.

This is indeed a drastic outcome, which may lead one to argue that norms of public international law on treaty conflict do not realistically address the complexity of contemporary interactions between legal regimes. So, albeit technically correct, this outcome would respond to this inadequacy. However, it is also possible to sustain that the international community does recognize precedence to human rights norms and the abovementioned results are really the desired ones. The *pro homine* and evolutionary principles inherent to the international human rights

136 According to the cCommission, '[a]lthough such clauses [conflict clauses] are undoubtedly useful, there is a limit to what they can achieve. They cannot, for instance, affect the rights of third parties or interfere with the operation of *jus cogens* or other hierarchical principles (such as those having to do with integral or interdependent obligations)'. *See* International Law Commission (2006b), p. 137 (emphasis in original).

137 *See* for instance ICJ, *Legal Consequences of the Construction of a Wall in the Occupied Palestinian Territory*, Advisory Opinion of 9 July 2004, ICJ Reports 2004, para. 159.

regime, and the identification of human dignity as a basic legal interest protected by international legal system, give credit to the latter view.

V CONCLUSIONS

The relationship between human rights and norms on intellectual property enforcement had been far less explored than the relationship between substantive intellectual property obligations and human rights regulations. This has however changed in recent years. Among other factors, the rapid adoption of detailed international obligations concerning intellectual property enforcement and the efforts to monitor intellectual property enforcement in the online environment have put the interface between intellectual property enforcement and human rights centre-stage.

This may not be so surprising to legal scholars and other experts working with domestic statutes. Indeed, judicial adjudication at the national level has usually dealt with the balancing of competing interests in the context of enforcement-related litigation. This has also been the case of legislators when passing statutes enacting enforcement obligations. At the international level, however, international human rights law has only recently become a benchmark to assess new enforcement-related obligations. Gradually, the mutually supportive, conflicting and ambiguous relations between intellectual property enforcement and human rights have been identified and analysed and have also become a pivotal element of campaigns against new enforcement-related treaties.

In effect, by invoking human rights concerns, enforcement initiatives have been derailed, to the extent that the given impression may have been that human rights law is generally against intellectual property enforcement, or at least against the new initiatives concerning the enforcement of intellectual property rights. There is not, however, such a general conflict between enforcement and human rights. Instead, what exists in abundance is poor drafting of international treaties as well as partial readings of those very same treaties. Human rights law has been sufficiently developed both at the local and international level to respond to the problems caused by poor and unbalanced drafting. At the same time, a clear distinction should be made between statements using human rights language, generally found in the political discourse, and situations of proper tension between legal norms belonging to the human rights regime and the intellectual property regime. The latter are more precise, objective and easier to remedy.

3

The Economics of Intellectual Property Enforcement

I INTRODUCTION

The economics of the intellectual property system has become a central focus of interest among researchers and policy-makers. The number of economists who in the 1970s and 1980s became interested in patent law[1] has grown exponentially to the extent that economic studies now flourish in almost all areas of intellectual property law. Likewise, intellectual property enforcement has become a priority at the international level, prompting the adoption of ambitious policies and demanding obligations. Invariably, economic analyses on the scale and impact of intellectual property infringement have been invoked to justify the need of new enforcement norms and institutions.

Economic analyses have frequently touched upon the *scale* and *impact* of intellectual property infringement, i.e. they have studied the magnitude in terms of quantity and the socioeconomic relevance of infringement. However, these studies have numerous methodological shortcomings. Estimates frequently fail to recognize relevant economic variables as well as the positive – even if illegal – effects of infringement, the potential anti-competitive effects of some enforcement norms and their impact on welfare. Some of these problems can be solved if a broader view is taken of the social relevance of intellectual property and the reasons behind infringement.

In a related but distinct set of matters, the importance of enforcement stands in stark contrast with the lack of scholarly attention and little knowledge about the economic significance of civil, border and criminal enforcement remedies and sanctions considered independently. An explanation for this vacuum can be found

[1] In 1986 Professor George Priest from Yale University still stated that 'economists can tell lawyers very little about how to enforce or interpret the law of intellectual property'. *See* Priest (1986), p. 21. By that time, however, the pioneering work of Arrow (1962) had already fructified and economists studied specific topics such as patent damages and patent litigation. Particularly influential in the area were the works of Calabresi and Melamed (1972).

in the confusion between the value of enforcement and the value of the intellectual property system itself. However, there are different possible levels of enforcement; thus it must be possible to estimate the economic impact of enforcement norms *per se*.

As mentioned in Chapter 1, legal positivism understands that the 'enforcement' and the 'efficacy' of the system are constitutive traits of the law. Indicating a similar relevance but for different reasons, a *hartian* approach to the law does not conceive the existence of a legal system without norms on enforcement. When assessed in the context of the intellectual property system, the crucial role that enforcement norms play in the theories of Austin, Kelsen and Hart may make it difficult to distinguish between the economic impact of the *enforced* intellectual property system and the economic impact of intellectual property enforcement mechanisms themselves. Nevertheless, even if secondary norms may ultimately determine the value of substantive rights, an independent estimation of the value of secondary norms is possible.

II SCALE AND IMPACT OF INTELLECTUAL PROPERTY INFRINGEMENT

Estimations of the scale and impact of intellectual property infringement are helpful in understanding the relevance of intellectual property enforcement. The *scale* of infringement alludes to the magnitude of infringement in terms of quantity, while the *impact* of infringement echoes its socioeconomic relevance. A large number of studies have tried to estimate the number of infringing products, the value of those products and the socioeconomic effects of infringement.

Concerning the scale of intellectual property infringement, estimates frequently reflect the quantities of intellectual property-infringing goods and the situations or specific spots where such goods are found. This is, for instance, the case of studies indicating the number of goods seized at the border and studies showing the products that are most frequently infringed.[2] Other estimates illustrate the quantity of counterfeit goods in particularly sensitive domains, such as military equipment[3] or pharmaceutical products.[4] Frequently, studies take a step further and assign a monetary value to the infringing goods, reflecting, *inter alia*, the value of international trade of counterfeit goods or the value of infringing goods in different product markets.[5] In other cases, the estimates determine the loss of profits to the right

[2] *See* the numbers on border seizures and detentions in the United States in US Customs and Border Protection Office of International Trade (2012), p. 6.

[3] In 2012, a year-long investigation of the US military found 1.800 cases of counterfeit parts in military equipment. *See* Committee on Armed Services United States Senate (2012), p. 1.

[4] In the Operation 'Pangea IV', involving eighty-one countries, INTERPOL seized 2.4 million counterfeit pills valued at US$6.3 million in only one week. *See* INTERPOL (2011).

[5] The OECD, for instance, stated that international trade in counterfeit and pirated products could have been up to US$200 billion in 2005 (updated to US$250 billion in 2007). This figure would have been higher if Internet infringement and domestic production and consumption had been considered. *See* OECD (2008), p. 13; OECD (2009), p. 1.

holders in specific industries and countries.[6] These estimates can be considered to reflect either the scale or the impact of infringement.[7]

The impact of intellectual property is usually illustrated by evoking the social benefits arising from intellectual property protection for consumers, right holders, governments and the economy as a whole.[8] In this sense, consumer protection is enhanced thanks to the link existing between (primarily) trademark protection and health and security concerns. For right holders, the respect of their rights impacts their brand value and firm reputation, as well as the volume and price of their sales. The effectiveness of the system will also influence right holders' incentive to innovate and the quantity they need to invest to ensure the enforcement of their rights. In the case of governments, intellectual property protection is positively transformed in tax revenues and permits avoiding the introduction of dangerous products (fakes) to supply chains with national security or safety implications. At the macro level, the economy as a whole benefits from intellectual property protection given the effects of the latter on investment, trade, wealth creation, innovation, employment, knowledge dissemination and foreign direct investment. Naturally, the benefits depend on the interaction of many other factors and vary across intellectual property categories, products and right holders.

Estimates of the impact of intellectual property infringement have resulted in impressive figures. Studies on the socioeconomic effects at the macro level put the emphasis on the impact of infringement on economic growth,[9] foreign direct investment[10] and employment.[11] An additional area of research relates to the impact

6 In 2000 the Centre for Economics and Business Research estimated annual lost revenues in the European Union at €7.581 million in clothing and footwear, €3.731 million in toys and sports equipment, €3.017 million in perfumes and cosmetics and €1.554 million in pharmaceuticals. In terms of profits, the estimates indicated that these industries annually lost €1.266 million in clothing and footwear, €627 million in toys and sports equipment, €555 million in perfumes and cosmetics and €292 million in pharmaceuticals. *See* Centre for Economics and Business Research (2000), pp. 2–3. Another private report, commissioned by the Australian Toy Association, the Business Software Association and the Interactive Entertainment Association, valued lost sales at AUD$131.7 million in the toy industry in Australia. *See* Allen Consulting Group (2003), p. v. Concerning the effect on right holders' revenues, the International Federation of the Phonographic Industry (IFPI) noted that '[t]he overall impact of digital piracy has been to contribute substantially to the dramatic erosion in industry revenues in recent years. Despite the surge by more than 1000 per cent in the digital music market from 2004 to 2010 to an estimated value of US$4.6 billion, global recorded music revenues declined by 31 per cent over the same period'. *See* IFPI (2011), p. 14.

7 *See* Hoorens *et al.* (2012), p. 20.

8 Put the other way around, the impact of infringement is usually presented as a concatenation of deleterious socioeconomic effects. *See* for instance Directorate General Taxation and Customs Union (TAXUD) (2014).

9 The Centre for Economics and Business Research affirmed, for instance, that counterfeiting reduced European GDP by €8042 million (at 1995 prices) per annum. *See* Centre for Economics and Business Research (2000), p. 14.

10 The OECD notes that counterfeiting may result in 'small, negative effects on levels of foreign direct investment flows' and 'possible effect on structure of foreign direct investment'. *See* OECD (2008), pp. 134, 140, 166, 308.

11 According to the International Chamber of Commerce, creative industries 'represent a major European economic force, corresponding to 6.9 per cent of European GDP, and 6.5 per cent of the

of intellectual property infringement on public finance. In this case, estimates pertain to customs revenues,[12] tax revenues[13] and the costs of crime prevention and eradication.[14] A third area has to do with the effects infringement on right holders and, particularly, their lost revenue.[15] Finally, the impact of infringement on consumer interests has generally focused on the relationship between infringement and health and safety. As noted, this relation is particularly intense in products infringing trademark rights.[16]

Finally, when alluding to the socioeconomic impact of infringement, a link is frequently drawn between intellectual property infringement and some of the worst kinds of criminal activity. In some cases, intellectual property infringement has been linked to drug trafficking and other forms of organized crime[17] and in some other instances even to terrorism.[18]

European workforce. This translates into €860 billion in revenues and 14 million jobs'. *See* TERA Consultants (2010), p. 6. For the US Patent and Trademark Office, IP-intensive industries were directly responsible for 40 million jobs, or 27.7 per cent of all jobs. These IP-intensive industries also indirectly supported an additional 12.9 million supply-chain jobs throughout the economy. Economics and Statistics Administration and United States Patent and Trademark Office (2012), pp. vi–vii. For the EPO and the OHIM, IPR-intensive industries contribute 26 per cent of employment and 39 per cent of GDP in the European Union. *See* EPO-OHIM (2013), pp. 3, 6. Similarly, *see* Europe Economics (2008); Pham (2010).

12 *See* OECD (2008), p. 35.

13 Consumers and producers of some infringing goods will not pay the taxes generally applied to licit activities. This is particularly the case of infringements taking place in the informal or grey economy, particularly counterfeiting and piracy. Moreover, tax revenues may also decrease as a result of the impact that illicit activities have on intellectual property owners or producers of legitimate goods. *See* US Government Accountability Office (GAO) (2010), p. 12. According to a GfK study commissioned by the Spanish Right Holders Coalition, in 2012 illegal access to audiovisual content meant that Spanish tax authorities failed to receive €249.6 million and 24.766 jobs were lost. *See* Jimenez, Martin and Palao (2013). *See* as well Fink (2009a), p. 13; Frontier Economics (2011); Thompson (2004).

14 *See* Frontier Economics (2011).

15 *See* International Trademark Association (1998); Rob and Waldfogel (2006); Motion Picture Association of America (2006).

16 This is particularly the case when infringement concerns pharmaceuticals, food, consumer electrical components, toys or household goods. *See* GAO (2010), p. 5. *See* also Wall and Large (2010), p. 1094; Commission of the European Communities (2006), p. 2; Satchwell (2004); Forzley (2003).

17 The preamble of the failed EU Intellectual Property Rights Enforcement Directive (IPRED2) noted that infringements of intellectual property 'are a constantly growing phenomenon which nowadays has an international dimension, since they are a serious threat to national economies and governments. ... In addition to the economic and social consequences, counterfeiting and piracy also pose problems for consumer protection, particularly when health and safety are at stake. Increasing use of the Internet enables pirated products to be distributed instantly around the globe. Finally, this phenomenon appears to be increasingly linked to organized crime'. *See* Commission of the European Communities (2006), p. 2. *See* also Roudaut (2012), p. 84.

18 Among other sources linking intellectual property infringement and terrorism *see* Treverton *et al.* (2009); International Anti-Counterfeiting Coalition (2005); Global Options (2003).

III DIVERSITY AND DIVERGENCE OF DATA

The reliability of the studies measuring the scale and impact of intellectual property infringement is controversial. Some of the difficulties are inherent to the object of the research. For instance, like other illicit activities, many infringements are furtively performed and therefore remain unreported, particularly when they amount to criminal activity. This naturally makes data on them inherently difficult to obtain[19] and requires the use of proxy indicators or incomplete and limited data to estimate the scale of the infringement.[20] Other difficulties relate to the studies themselves and concern the sometimes contentious methodologies implemented and the conflicts of interest of the authors and funders of the studies.

1 *Sources of Information*

Until recently, public institutions were not involved in the estimation of the global extent and relevance of infringement, and data collection on illicit activities was mostly carried out by private actors.[21] This has implied that estimates concerning the scale of infringement, the value of intellectual property or the impact of intellectual property infringement have been elaborated by private stakeholders who often have a direct interest in the object of analysis.

In fact, even figures quoted by public sources to describe the magnitude of the problem or to justify the action of public authorities have been frequently produced by private stakeholders.[22] On some occasions, estimates of private origin evoked by public authorities have proved to be unsustainable, and when authorities were asked to endorse the very figures they were quoting, they were unable to do so.[23] Unsurprisingly, this has provoked a broader trend of scepticism with regard to the estimates' consistency and reliability.[24]

On other occasions, the source of the information may have direct interest in demonstrating a specific result.[25] Sometimes this is expressly stated, and studies openly announce that they intend to convince those not aware of the gravity of infringement

19 *See* GAO (2010), p. 15; Fink (2009a), p. 1. 20 *See* OECD and EUIPO (2016), p. 16.

21 *See* Yu (2010a), p. 7; GAO (2010), pp. 16–17; Roffe and Seuba (2015), p. 1 *et seq.*

22 *See* GAO (2010), p. 16.

23 A 2002 FBI press release contained an estimate affirming that US businesses lose US$200–250 billion to counterfeiting on an annual basis. Another 2002 press release, from the US CBP, estimated that US businesses and industries lose US$200 billion a year in revenue and 750,000 jobs due to counterfeits of merchandise. Various sources attributed to the Federal Trade Commission estimate that the US automotive parts industry lost US$3 billion in sales due to counterfeit goods. None of these estimates could be confirmed by their sources when they were asked. *See* GAO (2010), pp. 18–19.

24 *See The Economist* (2005); Tekeste and Muñoz (2008), p. 20; Matthews (2008), p. 6; Xuan (2009), p. 25; Chow (2011), p. 785; Dubuisson (2012), p. 22.

25 For instance, the study by Stijn Hoorens used 'confidential data made available to us by a multinational technology firm producing consumer goods targeted by counterfeiters'. *See* Hoorens *et al.* (2012), p. xi.

or the value of intellectual property.[26] The tendency to overstate figures has reduced their credibility and, paradoxically, may have downplayed the extent and relevance of infringement. The use of alarming terms such as 'robbery' or 'theft' or the indiscriminate reference to 'piracy' to allude to the infringement of any intellectual property,[27] even in public reports[28] and normative texts,[29] is a manifestation of that tendency.[30]

In 2008, the Organization for Economic Co-operation and Development report on *The Economic Impact of Counterfeiting and Piracy* started to change this pattern. Notwithstanding its disputed methodology and data,[31] the OECD report was the first of a number of reports adopted by public institutions trying to ascertain the socio-economic impact of intellectual property. The European Patent Office and the European Union Intellectual Property Office,[32] the United States Government Accountability Office,[33] the United States Patent and Trademark Office[34] and the World Intellectual Property Organization[35] have elaborated or published reports trying to solve previous methodologically shaky aspects. While some of these reports also resort to controversial methodologies, the fact that public institutions produce their own estimates is a positive step.

2 *Methodological Aspects*

2.1 Diversity and Comparability

The use of one or another methodology may respond to the necessity to adapt to the object of research. Nevertheless, when estimates on the same object use different methodologies and arrive at different conclusions, it is natural to wonder which of the methodologies is correct. Take, for instance, some of the methodologies to assess

26 For instance, the EPO-OHIM joint study was developed 'in view of the question marks which, in public debate, have sometimes been raised over IP's role in supporting innovation and creativity'. *See* EPO-OHIM (2013), p. 2.

27 *See* Casey (2012), pp. 1–2; Gursey (1995); Alliance against IP Theft (2005).

28 In the recent OECD and EUIPO report it is clarified that the 'study uses the term "counterfeit" to describe tangible goods that infringe trademarks, design rights or patents'. See OECD and EUIPO (2016), p. 16.

29 Take, for instance, in the United States, the cases of the *No Electronic Theft Act* 1996 or the *Preventing Real Online Threats to Economic Creativity and Theft of Intellectual Property Act* of 2011, S.968, 112h Cong.

30 Words such as 'theft', 'thief', 'stealing', 'burglar's tools' and 'robbery' are increasingly employed to describe the unauthorized use of intellectual property. *See* Loughlan (2007), p. 401.

31 *See*, more generally in this sense, Fink (2009b), p. 15: 'Close inspection of the methodology applied to arrive at this figure reveals that it is more an 'educated guess' than a true estimate.'

32 Formerly known as European Union Office of Harmonization for the Internal Market. *See* EPO-OHIM (2013). The Office of Harmonization for the Internal Market (Trade Marks and Designs) is now called the European Union Intellectual Property Office (EUIPO), following the entry into force on 23 March 2016 of the Regulation (EU) No. 2015/2424, OJEU L 341 of 24 December 2015, p. 21.

33 *See* GAO (2010).

34 *See* Economics and Statistics Administration and United States Patent and Trademark Office (2012).

35 *See* WIPO (2013); WIPO (2007c).

right holders' losses. Some studies have combined information on the number of infringements, the substitution rate[36] and the price at which products would probably have been sold.[37] A different methodology to assess right holders' losses uses company forecasts combined with information on country-level measures related to counterfeiting. The latter model presumes that unexplained unfulfilled demand is in part due to intellectual property infringement.[38]

Other studies reflect different information concerning intellectual property infringement. In some cases, consumer surveys have been carried out with the intention of determining the prevalence of counterfeiting.[39] In other cases, data has been triangulated with the objective of ascertaining the global trade of counterfeiting and piracy across sectors. For instance, the 2008 OECD study mentioned previously extrapolated seizure data provided by customs authorities, compared that data to international trade data and used these data in an econometric model.[40]

These examples show that estimates are not readily comparable.[41] In order to facilitate comparability,[42] a joint study produced by EPO and EUIPO in 2013 proposed a similar approach to that used in the USPTO 2012 study.[43] The goal was to quantify the overall contribution made by intellectual property-intensive industries to the economy in terms of output, employment, wages and trade. In order to achieve this goal, the study identified the number of intellectual property rights per employee for each industry, and those above average were considered to be intellectual property-intensive. The EPO and EUIPO study, however, is open to criticism for a number of assumptions it makes.[44] Similarly, statements made in the study inferring a causal relationship between the granting of intellectual property rights and the data collected have also been prone to criticism.[45]

In reality, producing a reliable evaluation of the general effects of intellectual property infringement on the economy as a whole is still out of reach.[46] The specific characteristics of products, markets and intellectual property categories impede the development of a single methodology to collect and analyse data, applicable across industries. The collection of data, the substitution rate, the value of goods and the extent of deceit by consumers are critical aspects that change across industries and products. Different types of intellectual property infringements produce different

36 *See* Section 2.3.

37 *See* Centre for Economics and Business Research (2000); Allen Consulting Group (2003).

38 *See* Hoorens *et al.* (2012), p. 41. 39 *See* Gallup Organization (2007).

40 The OECD itself seems to doubt the projected data: 'the overall degree to which products are being counterfeited and pirated is unknown and there do not appear to be any methodologies that could be employed to develop an acceptable overall estimate'. *See* OECD (2008), p. 71.

41 As it has been noted 'methods for extrapolating to other markets or countries lack clarity'. *See* Hoorens *et al.* (2012), p. ix.

42 'If cross-national comparisons are to be undertaken, it is imperative that comparable methods be employed so that the studies measure the same items in the same way'. *See* WIPO (2012), p. 44.

43 *See* Economics and Statistics Administration and United States Patent and Trademark (2012).

44 *See* Section 3.2.3. 45 *See* Kur and Harhoff (2014), p. 617.

46 *See* in this sense GAO (2010), p. 27; Band and Gerafi (2014).

welfare effects depending on underlying market failures and characteristics.[47] For these reasons, it has been suggested that efforts need to focus on the development of a model that works for specific products[48] or very restricted markets.[49]

2.2 Limitations Regarding the Scale of Infringement

Several methods have been used to estimate the scale of intellectual property infringement. The lack of information as to the real extent of intellectual property infringements has made it necessary to use indirect measures that approximate or represent real phenomena. These proxy indicators commonly stem from the activity of custom authorities (i.e. seizures) and surveys conducted among consumers or producers of intellectual property-protected goods. Other methods are sampling exercises such as 'mystery shopping' and economic and econometric models.[50]

Problems related to methodology and data reliability in current estimations of the magnitude of infringement are severe and put estimates into question.[51] As regards frequently quoted data on border enforcement, it is uncertain whether detentions at the border should be counted as reflecting the extent and types of infringement, the quantity of the goods detained or the effort made by customs authorities.[52] In fact, enforcement data reflect an unknown fraction of the total amount of infringing products and a subset of cases in which infringers are caught.[53] The quantity of infringing products that in reality make their way into the market is just not known, and therefore seizures at the border cannot be indicative of the actual imports of counterfeit goods. Moreover, border seizures do not reflect infringements occurring in the digital environment or infringements within national borders.

Surveys of supply and demand of infringing products[54] compile data on the consumption or sales patterns of counterfeit or pirated goods, showing consumer behaviour in terms of preferences. Although surveys have advantages, they also present a number of shortcomings. Among the latter, mention is commonly made of the costs of the studies, the difficulty of detecting bias and the uncertain extrapolation of the results to broader settings or countries.[55]

Economic models are also used to predict the scale of infringement. These models do not estimate but forecast the level of infringement using information obtained from either enforcement actions or surveys of supply and demand. Taking this information as a basis, studies 'build mathematical models following the logic of

47 *See* Fink (2009b), pp. 3, 15; WIPO (2012), p. 44; Hoorens *et al.* (2012), p. 26.
48 *See* Hoorens *et al.* (2012), p. ix. 49 *See* GAO (2010), p. 1.
50 *See* Hoorens *et al.* (2012), pp. 18–19. 51 *Ibid.*, pp. vii, ix, 27. 52 *See* GAO (2010), p. 16.
53 *See* Hoorens *et al.* (2012), p. 31.
54 For instance, by means of 'mystery shopping' (i.e. consumers are recruited to go out and buy products from various vendors) or direct questionnaires to consumers.
55 *See* Directorate General Internal Market and Services (2013), p. 5; GAO (2010), pp. 20–21, 27. Surveys also have been considered unreliable; *see* Hargreaves (2011), p. 73.

economics, but incorporating elements of uncertainty, to predict what is unknown about the specific market under scrutiny'.[56] The main difficulty facing economic models is that they rely on information that may not be exact and that the consistency of the logic that underpins them also determines their ultimate value.[57]

2.3 Limitations of the Studies on the Impact of Infringement

In estimating the impact of infringement, a common practice consists of relating the scale of infringement with consumers' desire to substitute legitimate goods for counterfeits. The so-called 'substitution rate' is therefore a crucial part of the equation. Despite this importance, the rate at which the consumer is willing to switch from purchasing a fake good to paying for the genuine article is controversial. It varies from sector to sector, across intellectual property categories[58] and even with respect to the same product depending on the price.[59] These reasons explain the general rejection of one-to-one substitution[60] and the search of more sophisticated approaches to capture consumers' attitudes.

Some reports have effectively tried to capture markets for intellectual property-infringing products more accurately. They have made a distinction between a primary market, where infringing products infiltrate the market of the genuine good and the substitution rate is 1 (i.e. the infringing product is a perfect substitute if the consumer is deceived),[61] and a secondary market, where consumers chiefly focus on price and disregard quality and authenticity, thus creating an opportunity for producers of fakes and counterfeits.[62] In the primary market, the fake good is almost identical in quality to the genuine one, and the unaware consumer purchases the counterfeit product at full retail price.[63] While estimates that assume a one-to-one substitution rate should in principle relate to the primary market, in practice many estimates of secondary markets also assume one-to-one substitution.

56 *See* Hoorens *et al.* (2012), p. 32. 57 *Ibid.*, p. 33.

58 For example, respondents from the cinema sector have reported 20 per cent, those from the digital music sector have reported between 10 and 50 per cent, seed producers from 0 to 70 per cent depending on the species, and book publishers have reported almost a one-to-one ratio. According to some respondents the substitution rate of IPR infringement is zero, and online infringement of copyrighted works in the field of digital media is even considered by some to increase the awareness of consumers about the author and the author's works. *See* Directorate General Internal Market and Services (2013), p. 5.

59 *See* Hui and Png (2003), p. 2; GAO (2010), pp. 17–18; Yu (2010a), p. 8.

60 *See* Fink (2009a), p. 13; Hui and Png (2003), p. 2; Yu (2010a), p. 8. *See* as well Hoorens *et al.* (2012), p. 34; GAO (2010), pp. 17–18.

61 If consumers themselves cannot distinguish fakes from originals, the presence of counterfeit goods undermines the signalling function of trademarks. Consumers will invariably be worse off. Purchasers of counterfeit products will, at best, derive a value from the product that is lower than the price they paid for it and, at worst, be exposed to physical harm if counterfeit products create health or safety risks. *See* Fink (2009a), p. 6.

62 *See* Hoorens *et al.* (2012), p. ix; *See* Fink (2009a), p. 12. 63 *See* GAO (2010), p. 17.

Assumptions regarding the size of infringement need to be combined with those concerning the value of infringing goods in order to estimate the full impact of infringement. For instance, the number of seizures at the border can be combined with the estimated domestic value of seized goods.[64] With regard to establishing an overall monetary value of intellectual property infringement, once the number of infringing goods has been estimated, several measures can be used to calculate value, including production costs, the domestic value, landed cost plus profit or the manufacturer's suggested retail price.[65] Estimates of final value also sometimes combine the aggregate value of infringing goods and other economic impacts, such as unpaid taxes or jobs allegedly lost.[66]

Another methodology to estimating the impact of infringement is based on the use of economic multipliers. The theory of multipliers shows how capital changes in one industry affect production and employment in related industries.[67] In principle, this makes it possible to estimate the impact of an industrial investment in terms of employment, manufacturing or construction. Interestingly, this methodology corroborates the assumption that the effect of infringement goes beyond the industry immediately concerned. However, the applicability of this methodology to intellectual property infringement is somewhat limited since it was developed to look at a one-time change in output and employment[68] and does not allow taking into account consumer savings or expenditures deriving from the use of infringing goods.

In addition to the constraints highlighted above, other factors may render existing estimates questionable. Some of them relate to incorrect use of legal terminology,[69] others to very debatable assumptions. Take, for instance, one of the more important studies conducted in recent times, the study jointly undertaken by the EPO and EUIPO. In order to reflect the contribution of intellectual property-intensive industries to employment and gross domestic product, the two institutions ascertained the relevance of several intellectual property categories for different areas of economic activity. The authors then decided the level above which industries are considered intellectual property-intensive. Finally, they linked the volume of employment in each sector to the estimates.

64 For instance, it has been reported that in 2011, the US Customs and Border Protection seized 24.792 counterfeit or pirated goods, which represented more than US$1.1 billion in lost sales. *See* US Customs and Border Protection Office of International Trade (2012), p. 6.

65 *See* GAO (2010), pp. 6, 17.

66 For instance, according to a report commissioned by Business Action to Stop Counterfeiting and Piracy, the impact of counterfeiting and piracy is estimated at US$650 billion annually. This estimate includes costs to the trademark owners in lost profits as well as costs to national economies. In this last regard, the report states that G20 governments annually lose US$125 billion in tax revenue. *See* Frontier Economics (2011), p. 6.

67 *See* GAO (2010), p. 23. 68 *Ibid.*

69 In some instances, new terms are coined to define intellectual property infringement without rigor. In other instances, counterfeiting is used to imply not only trademark counterfeiting but also piracy or any type of intellectual property infringement.

The EPO and EUIPO study contains several controversial aspects, such as the choice of covered rights, the fact that the report avoids the years of economic crisis, the definition of intellectual property-intensive industry and the weight given to different intellectual property rights.[70] While these aspects are debatable, others actually distort objective conclusions. In the case of patents the study considers a proxy for innovation patents that have been filed, instead of those effectively granted.[71] However, counting filed patents does not reflect an objective level of innovation. For one, numerous patent applications are rejected. In addition, when patents are granted, defendants in lawsuits usually file a counter-claim for revocation of the patent, an argument relating to the validity of patents that happens to be successful in roughly half of the cases.[72] In fact, as the US Supreme Court has noted, patent litigation frequently arises because of 'the notorious difference between standards applied by the Patent Office and by courts'.[73] So, contrary to what could be inferred from the EPO-EUIPO study, there is a long way between patent filing and a valid patent, not to mention a valid patent that has resulted in an innovation that has been ultimately marketed.

As the EPO-EUIPO study has shown, the selection of the relevant industries for assessing such an impact is difficult. Peter Yu has noted that 'with the ubiquity of intellectual property-related goods and services, intellectual property protection and enforcement affects virtually all industries'.[74] Paradoxically, both the industries that rely heavily on the protection of intellectual property and those that promote competition are in a way related and contribute to national economies and welfare. Hence, taking into account the economic contribution of pharmaceutical innovators or copyright-based companies, but not the contribution of generic producers or 'fair-use industries',[75] only partially reflects reality.

IV OTHER SOCIOECONOMIC EFFECTS OF INTELLECTUAL PROPERTY ENFORCEMENT

Estimates focusing on socially desirable benefits of intellectual property protection are of paramount importance, but they generally omit significant aspects. Among them, mention must be made of the potential positive effects arising from intellectual

70 *See* Nurton (2013).

71 A similar argument can be made in relation to trademarks, where the European study counts the registered trademarks when the majority of trademarks are not exploited.

72 A study conducted by John Allison and Mark Lemley found that, from 1989 to 1996, 46 per cent of patents were invalidated in final written decisions on validity. *See* Allison and Lemley (1998).

73 *See Graham v. John Deere Co.* 383 U.S. 1, 18 (1966). Similarly, in the context of the Pharmaceutical Sector Inquiry, the final report of DG Competition quoted a European judge stating 'one cannot ever expect the grant of a patent by a Patent Office to be also a certificate of validity. It never has been and never will be. In truth the Patent Office is a kind of coarse filter – rejecting clearly bad cases but having to allow those which may be good.' See European Commission (2009b), p. 110.

74 *See* Yu (2010a), p. 7.

75 *See* for instance Rogers and Szamosszegi (2010).

property infringement as well as the costs associated with the protection of intellectual property and the eventual negative impact on welfare arising from certain intellectual property enforcement measures. Moreover, it is necessary to evaluate the impact of enforcement institutions *per se*, i.e. to distinguish between primary and secondary norms, and study the impact of the latter.

1 Positive Effects Arising from Intellectual Property Infringement

Legal analyses cannot conceive taking into consideration the benefits of law infringement. After all, the rule of law prescribes that 'if laws do not serve the public interest, they ought to be changed rather than disregarded'.[76] However, economic analysis may suggest otherwise. That is, from a purely economic angle, the net economic impact of intellectual property will result from subtracting the positive from the negative impact of infringement.[77] This is indeed an approach of interest from the policy perspective. However, current estimates rarely compute the potential gains deriving from intellectual property infringements, which, we hold, should be taken into account to estimate 'how much of the losses the intellectual property industries claimed to have suffered would be cancelled out'.[78]

First, reference must be made to consumer surplus. Consumers may purchase infringing products purposely, since these may be cheaper than genuine goods. In this manner, consumers reduce expenditure, generating savings that may ultimately benefit consumption in other areas.[79] Consumers who knowingly purchase fake products are likely to be better off from counterfeiting activity, since 'their choice reflects a rational trade-off between price, status value, and quality'.[80]

Second, lower prices of goods infringing intellectual property may enable access to products that otherwise would have not been bought, for instance (fake) luxury goods.[81] In a related fashion, cheaper counterfeit goods may exert pressure to lower prices for legitimate goods and therefore also benefit consumers.[82]

Third, price set aside, intellectual property-infringing goods may also be the only source for accessing products not available in the market, sometimes of similar, or even equal, quality to the original.[83] An example is that of movies not yet released in cinemas and that may not be released at all in a given country. Something similar, but with more serious consequences, may happen with regard to patented pharmaceuticals, which may not be available at all or be available only in insufficient quantities in poor and commercially weak markets.

Fourth, economists also allude to network externalities or demand-side economies of scale to explain some benefits arising from infringement. The valuation of

[76] *See* Fink (2009b), p. 3. [77] *See* GAO (2010), p. 27. [78] *See* Yu (2010a), p. 8.
[79] *See* GAO (2010), p. 1. [80] *See* Fink (2009b), p. 8. [81] *See* GAO (2010), p. 14.
[82] *See* Correa (2012), p. 64.
[83] Peter Yu introduces the example of the 'ghost shifts', where infringing goods are made to the same specifications by the same factories using the same personnel and raw materials. *See* Yu (2010a), p. 12.

products may increase with the number of consumers who own the same product. Take for instance a computer program: the more users it has, the more it enhances interaction and the more value it has to consumers.[84] This may have positive welfare effects not only for the consumer of both the original and the infringing product but also for the right holder himself, since 'illegal copying activity in the presence of network externalities can allow the software producer to segment the market and to price-discriminate, reaping higher profits compared to a scenario where there is no illegal copying'.[85]

Fifth, economic activity may also improve as a consequence of infringement. Beneficiaries may be directly related to the infringement but may also be unrelated third parties or even the right holder. The positive output of intellectual property-intensive industries in terms of creation and quality of employment is frequently highlighted. However, 'employment effects are unclear, because employment may decline in certain industries or rise in other industries as workers are hired to produce counterfeits'.[86] Similarly, industrial activity and manufacturing capacities may also benefit from infringement,[87] particularly in developing and emerging countries. As mentioned, third parties may also indirectly benefit from infringement. For example, Internet infrastructure manufacturers are possible beneficiaries of digital piracy because of the bandwidth demands related to the transfer of pirated digital content.[88] Finally, even right holders may reap benefits from infringements. In this regard, companies experiencing losses in one line of business may increase revenues in related or complementary businesses due to increased brand awareness.[89] Moreover, in the context of copyright, infringing copies may stimulate the acquisition of originals by parties related in different ways to the infringer.[90] In fact, it has even been held that some companies have allowed a period of flexibility regarding infringement with the intention to become popular in the local market. Once this objective has been achieve, demands for effective enforcement have increased.[91]

It should also be kept in mind that there is a contradictory relationship between infringement and creativity. Even if economic revenues deriving from copyright

84 'If the value of a software program is directly enhanced by the opportunities to reduce learning and customization costs, as well as for data exchange and skill transfer, then piracy, because it increases the size of the total installed base, may raise the value of the program to all users.' *See* Conner and Rumelt (1991), p. 126. *See* also Takeyama (1994), pp. 155–166.

85 *See* Fink (2009b), p. 11. *See* Takeyama (1994), p. 156; Hui and Png (2003), p. 11.

86 *See* GAO (2010), p. 29. This is the reason why 'stronger trademark enforcement may well lead to substantial short-run employment losses in the concerned countries'. *See* Fink (2009a), p. 6. More precisely, 'in many developing countries, the distribution of counterfeit and pirated goods often offers an important source of employment for low-skilled workers'. *See* Fink (2009a), p. 9.

87 *See* Correa (2012), p. 64.

88 *See* GAO (2010), p. 15.

89 Pirated music and film may act as a marketing tool for producers. For instance, they may incentivize increased revenues due to the sales of merchandise that are based on movie characters whose popularity is enhanced by sales of pirated movies. *See* GAO (2010), p. 15; Hoorens *et al.* (2012), p. vii.

90 *See* Hui and Png (2003), p. 1. These authors also hold that piracy helps the legitimate producer by enabling more effective price discrimination, p. 19.

91 *See* Piller (2006).

protection are vital for the majority of artists, online copyright infringement can help artists at the early stage of their careers to achieve some popularity.[92] This relative fame can result in concerts and sale of merchandising. In a related context, it has been underlined that infringement may increase sales of legitimate goods based on consumer 'sampling' of pirated goods. Consumers may use pirated goods to 'sample' music, movies, software or electronic games before purchasing legitimate copies.[93]

In reference to the benefits arising from infringement it has been held that 'these arguments are, naturally, not valid if a State wants to maintain its international reputation and participate in the international exchange of culture, information and entertainment'.[94] Even if correct, this answer is partial and the full response is more complex. Educated consumers, companies, decision-makers and the public in general need to know the exact benefits arising from intellectual property protection. If the overall balance is positive, the full understanding of positive and negative effects should improve innovation policies, maximizing the former and minimizing the latter. Indeed, when assessing the usually neglected effects of infringement attention should also be paid to the static cost-dynamic cost trade-offs. While, pursuant to a number of the abovementioned arguments, underenforcement may improve social welfare, it can also lead to social welfare reductions as a consequence of reduced returns to innovative actions (and expectations thereof). Even if difficult to model and theorize, the sacrifice of static efficiency in exchange of dynamic efficiency is, after all, a pillar of the intellectual property system.

2 *Costs*

2.1 What Costs?

Intellectual property enforcement requires significant public investment.[95] Although this applies to all types of countries, it has been particularly noted that in the case of developing countries the transition to stronger protection involves short-run costs that are not trivial.[96] Certainly, right holders and alleged infringers will bear a substantial part of the costs, but the State will still need to invest in a meaningful manner. Hiring personnel, setting up institutional infrastructures, restructuring existing agencies and acquiring the necessary means for implementing enforcement activities are just the first steps. Afterwards, the state will have to assume the running costs of the system, which will probably surpass those of setting it up.

92 *See* DG Internal Market and Services (2013), p. 5.

93 *See* GAO (2010), p. 15.

94 *See* WIPO (2004), p. 217.

95 While this has been a relatively neglected topic at the international level, the provision of resources for enhanced protection forms part of the normal process for the adoption and implementation of national laws. *See* for instance the *Prioritizing Resources and Organization for Intellectual Property Act* of 2008, P.L. 110–403, adopted to strengthen and improve the protection of intellectual property and which included the creation of the Office of the United States Intellectual Property Enforcement Representative.

96 *See* World Bank (2001), p. 136.

Scholars have only started to analyse these costs,[97] which are generally unnoticed when estimating the economic impact of intellectual property and adopting new obligations.

In order to assess the investment required, it is necessary to identify the activities falling within the enforcement domain and the investment items related to them. Among such activities are identification of the infringement, storage of allegedly infringing goods, adjudication of controversies, disposal and destruction of infringing goods and imprisonment of those responsible for criminal infringement.

The identification of the infringement of an intellectual property right may require significant resources and expertise, particularly when it implies searches into the premises of the infringer or conducting raids to identify and seize infringing materials sold, for instance, in the streets. Particularly in the case of criminal enforcement it has been noted that costs 'have to do with the expenses of identifying violators and of adjudication, which can be substantial, especially when public enforcement agents are involved'.[98]

Destruction and disposal are also expensive activities. Recycling, open-air burning, shredding, crushing and burying in landfill sites are typical disposal activities.[99] When infringers are identified, they will generally bear part of the costs arising from these activities. However, this will not always be the case, and both right holders and the state will assume part of the costs. In the case of the state, it will frequently pay the running costs of the specialized infrastructure, machinery and skilled personnel.

In a different context and level of complexity, temporary storage of allegedly infringing goods also represents a significant investment. Take for instance the case of products detained at the border. Seized goods have to be secured in warehouses while other enforcement actions or even judicial proceedings take place, which may mean prolonged storage. Naturally, as seizures increase, customs agencies' storage and destruction costs grow and become increasingly burdensome.[100]

In the context of criminal enforcement, there are two main types of sanctions: monetary and imprisonment. Monetary sanctions imply a transfer of command over resources; this is why they are socially free.[101] Conversely, the administration of monetary sanctions and imprisonment requires substantial investment. In the case of imprisonment, funds are needed to set up and run the penitentiary system.[102]

Even if part of the running costs will be borne by the losing party, the public investment necessary for an efficient system of intellectual property enforcement will still be significant. This raises several questions, including what should be the optimal level of public investment in IP enforcement, should the investment

97 *See* Trainer and Allums (2008), pp. 705–706; Trainer (2008), pp. 57, 69–72; Yu (2010a), p. 3; Fink (2009b).

98 *See* Shavell (2002), p. 240.

99 *See* Soentgen (2012).

100 US Custom and Border Protection reported that it spent about $41.9 million to destroy seized property between fiscal years 2007 and 2009. *See* GAO (2010), p. 13.

101 Shavell (2002), p. 240.

102 On the resource implications of criminal enforcement, *see* Grosse Ruse-Khan (2012); Pinyosinwat (2007).

change depending on the level of development of the country concerned, and what does this investment tell about intellectual property rights as 'private' rights?

2.2 Optimum Levels of Investment and Private Rights

While an intellectual property legal practitioner would probably hold that the optimal level of investment in enforcement is just the amount necessary to guarantee right holders' rights, from the economic perspective the answer is rather more pragmatic. In this sense, it has been noted that 'it is optimal for governments to devote a level of public spending on law enforcement, such that the marginal benefit of fighting IPRs violations equals the marginal cost of enforcement activity'.[103] Hence, there are optimum levels of investment in enforcement: the benefit arising from law enforcement must be at least equivalent to its cost. This means, in effect, that there are rational levels of intellectual property infringement or, put in economic terms, investments not worth making.

Existing estimates on the budgetary investment needed for enforcement are partial or indirect, and the amount required globally is just unknown. To remedy this gap, it is possible to study the investment made by countries or donors when implementing enforcement provisions in preferential trade agreements,[104] the economic allotments of technical assistance programs[105] or reforms in countries that strengthen their intellectual property enforcement regime.[106] While this task is feasible with respect to specific norms and intellectual property enforcement areas, such as graduated-response systems in specific countries,[107] it becomes far more complex when the same norms and mechanisms fulfil enforcement functions in respect to other areas of the law.

Developing countries will have fewer incentives to invest in intellectual property enforcement. These countries typically face other pressing priorities for public spending, and the costs of enforcement constitute opportunity costs, since they may be used for other purposes. Hence, given the resource constraints in developing countries, 'an increased use of resources in the enforcement area inevitably will lead to the withdrawal of resources from other competing, and at times more important, public needs',[108] such as health, security, food security or education.

103 *See* Fink (2009a), p. 15.

104 *See* Seuba, Rovira and Bloemen (2010), p. 10. Estimations of these costs are rare. *See* for instance Finger and Schuler (1999).

105 *See* Commission on Intellectual Property Rights (2002), pp. 149–151; May (2007), pp. 61–66; Correa (2009), p. 35.

106 *See* Fink (2009b), p. 21.

107 In the case of France, '[t]he governmental contribution has been tens of millions of euros so far'. *See* Giblin (2014), p. 155. Also, the budget for 2013 was €8 million, while in previous years the budget amounted to €12.5 million. *See Le Monde* (2012). For a discussion on the costs of the so-called graduated response systems, *see* Rayna and Barbier (2010), p. 294.

108 *See* Abbott and Correa (2007), p. 31. Along these lines, *see* Tekeste and Muñoz (2008), p. 4; Correa (2009), p. 43; Correa (2012), p. 74; Yu (2010a), p. 1; Urbas (2005), p. 321; Fink (2011), p. 396.

TABLE 1 *Investment Items Required for Enforcement Activities*

Enforcement Activity	Area of Enforcement	Investment Items
Identification of the infringement	Civil, border, criminal	• Personnel: judges, clerks, border authorities, police • Infrastructure: judicial, police and customs facilities • Technical means: needed for conducting a civil search or criminal raid
Storage of allegedly infringing goods	Border, criminal	• Personnel: border authorities, police, workers in warehouses • Infrastructure: warehouses, free zones • Technical means: machinery, trucks
Adjudication	Civil, border, criminal	• Personnel: judges, police, prosecutors • Infrastructure: courts and judicial facilities • Technical means: forensic means
Destruction and disposal (recycling, open-air burning, shredding, crushing, burying in landfill sites)	Civil, border, criminal	• Personnel: judges, police, prosecutors, technicians in the field of disposal and recycling • Infrastructure: open air facilities, factories, warehouses, incineration plants • Technical means: specialized machinery, means of transport, air pollution filtering mechanisms
Imprisonment	Criminal	• Personnel: judges, police, prosecutors, prison wardens • Infrastructure: courts, prisons, means of transport • Technical means: security devices

During the Uruguay Round developing countries 'did not see any benefit in incurring in the costs of establishing mechanisms for the administrative or judicial protection of intellectual property rights of foreign companies',[109] although it was clear that they would have to devote resources to establishing the domestic machinery needed to enforce intellectual property rights.[110] However, they succeeded in inserting into the TRIPS Agreement Article 41.5, which states that WTO Members are not required to devote more resources to intellectual property enforcement than to other areas of law enforcement. This article is frequently invoked as recognition that resource constraints will play a role when allocating investment in enforcement.[111]

109 *See* Stewart (1993), p. 468.

110 *See* Ross and Wasserman (1993); Reinbothe and Howard (1991), pp. 157–164.

111 *See* Chapter 4, Section II.2.2.

Some trade agreements recognize the costs specifically deriving from the implementation of intellectual property enforcement provisions. In some cases, in recognition of the effort required, countries are allowed a number of years to undertake the necessary reforms and investment.[112] In other cases, the recognition of the costs is not accompanied by an exemption or moratorium. On the contrary, it is expressly stated that decisions on the distribution of enforcement resources shall not excuse the parties from complying with those commitments.[113]

New international commitments on intellectual property enforcement are characterized by high levels of exigency and detail and by the inclusion of provisions requiring 'increased pressure to use the state machinery to reduce the cost of private enforcement'.[114] New agreements oblige states to invest more in terms of infrastructure. At the same time, the expansion of measures applicable *ex officio* shifts to the state the cost of such measures as well as potential liability when measures are wrongly adopted.[115] In response, it has been argued that 'such pressures should be resisted, and right owners assume the initiative and costs of enforcing their private rights'.[116]

The TRIPS Agreement recognizes that intellectual property rights are private rights.[117] Consequently, it is understood that right holders and not governments should take the lead and generally assume the costs of enforcing their rights.[118] The panel set up in the WTO *China – Intellectual Property Rights* case noted that a common feature of the enforcement provisions of the TRIPS Agreement is that the launch of procedures is normally the responsibility of private right holders.[119]

112 For instance, the treaty between the USA and Chile states that '[i]n those cases in which the full implementation of the obligations contained in this Chapter requires a Party to amend its domestic legislation or additional financial resources those amendments and financial resources shall be in force or available as soon as practicable, and in no event later than: . . . four years from the date of entry into force of this Agreement, with respect to the obligations in Article 17.11 on enforcement (including border measures).' *See* Article 17.12.2(b) of the US-Chile FTA and EIA (2004).

113 For instance, Article 15.10.3 of the US-Oman FTA and EIA (2009) states that '[t]he Parties understand that a decision that a Party makes on the distribution of enforcement resources shall not excuse that Party from complying with this Chapter.' *See* also US-Chile FTA and EIA (2004) Articles 17.11.1 and 17.11.2 (take however into account transitory periods allowed in Article 17.12.2(b)).

114 *See* Matthews (2008), pp. 2, 25. In fact, this has also been noted at the internal level. According to Christophe Geiger, HADOPI 'amounts to an indirect funding by the state of a record industry that is facing difficulties, and hence to support sector-based interests'. *See* Geiger (2014a), p. 712.

115 Carlos Correa's remarks alluded to criminal enforcement but are also applicable to border enforcement. *See* Correa (2012), p. 74.

116 *See* Commission on Intellectual Property Rights (2002), p. 147.

117 The nature of intellectual property rights as private rights clarified in Recital 4 of the Preamble of the TRIPS Agreement was particularly underlined by some national delegations during the Uruguay Round. *See* UNCTAD-ICTSD (2005), p. 11, footnote 21.

118 *See* Matthews (2008), p. 26; Abbott, Cottier and Gurry (2007), p. 608; WIPO (2008), p. 207.

119 For the panel, '[a]cquisition procedures for substantive rights and civil enforcement procedures generally have to be initiated by the right holder and are not *ex officio*'. *See* WTO Panel Report, *China – measures affecting the protection and enforcement of intellectual property rights*, WT/DS362/R, 26 January 2009, para. 7.247 (emphasis in original) (hereinafter WTO Panel, *China – Intellectual Property Rights*).

According to the panel, 'a condition that authority shall only be available upon application or request seems to be assumed in much of Sections 2, 3 and 4 of Part III',[120] a feature consistent 'with the nature of intellectual property rights as private rights'.[121]

The grounds for rejecting public investment because of the private nature of intellectual property rights could be, however, limited. States already invest in police, the judiciary and, among other areas of enforcement, border enforcement. Devoting public resources to the enforcement of private rights has sound grounds, since 'helping individual intellectual property owners enforce their rights using public resources is justified because, in aggregate, it serves the public good'.[122] This, however, does not say much about the precise monetary implications of that investment and the specific activities that should be funded with public resources. Indeed, many consider law enforcement a public[123] or collective consumption[124] good, in the sense that once it is produced for some consumers, it can be consumed by additional consumers without additional costs.[125] In a more lax sense, it has been noted the 'enforcement of legal norms is a public good because it generates widespread benefits, including safety from violence and anarchy and affirmative support of the pursuit of individual happiness'.[126] Generally, the state will supply the necessary resources to guarantee the provision of public goods, including law enforcement.

It must be underlined, however, that the public good nature of law enforcement does not improve or validate the substantive content of norms. Instrumentalism sees property as an institutional mechanism that has to serve moral values,[127] and at least in the international context, these values are generally identified with the legal interests protected by international human rights law.[128] While certainly broad, this caveat introduces a note of caution and reveals the importance of looking mostly at the effects of substantive (or primary) norms and not at procedural (or secondary) rules. Both legitimate and legal reasons to decline enforcement may exist in particular cases in light of the primary norms' impact on the values that the legal system aims to protect. These should be differentiated from those legitimate but legally controversial reasons to decline enforcement, such as resource constraints.

[120] This would be proved by 'the first sentence of Article 42 and the first sentence of Article 51, the reference to an 'applicant' in Article 50.3 and 50.5, the reference to 'request[s]' in Article 46 and 48.1, and the option (not obligation) to make *ex officio* action available under Article 58'. *See* WTO Panel, *China – Intellectual Property Rights*, para. 7.247 (emphasis in original).

[121] *Ibid.* [122] *See* Gervais (2012), p. 270.

[123] Yang (2006), p. 1149; Tullock (1971), p. 913; Dasgupta (2011), p. 49; Sandler (2013), p. 17. However, see a critique to inaccuracy of this term to describe government output, including legislation and law enforcement, in Holcombe (1997), p. 11.

[124] *See* Samuelson (1954), pp. 387–389.

[125] Reference is being made here to the general concept of enforcement (compliance); thus the different activities that make up this concept – such as dispute resolution – can be better described as intermediate goods, since they are 'an input into compliance with socially desired standards of behavior'. *See* Landes and Posner (1979), p. 236.

[126] Yang (2006), p. 1150. [127] Drahos (2001), p. 214. [128] *See* Chapter 2.

While this does not specify the enforcement-related activities that should be funded with public resources, it facilitates reaching a common understanding with respect certain discussions. There is for instance growing consensus among scholars rejecting the replacement of civil enforcement by criminal enforcement. In response to the increasing criminalization of intellectual property infringement, it has been noted that such a replacement amounts to subsidizing right holders and 'transferring wealth from the taxpayers, in the form of *ex officio* police investigations and prosecution, to the cultural industries',[129] among others.

As noted above, there is an optimum level of investment in enforcement. This level, however, does not necessarily coincide with the investment needed to fulfil international intellectual property commitments. Arguably, in strictly economic terms, only public investment made by countries with intellectual property-intensive industries is sound. However, more and more states adopt commitments that require greater public investment. This can be explained by taking into account three different factors: first, the bargaining process that characterizes the adoption of new intellectual property obligations, where interests different from innovation and competition take centre-stage;[130] second, the lack of knowledge of both the scale of infringement and its socioeconomic impact;[131] and third, the economic relevance of specific enforcement institutions is just unknown. In response to the existence of legal commitments on enforcement that require economically inefficient levels of investment, reforming the system and privatizing these costs are appealing options.[132]

3 *Negative Impact*

Norms on enforcement are not neutral. Strengthening right holders' position to the detriment of their competitors' procedural rights may deter legal competition and restrict access to legal products. Moreover, new norms on enforcement may expand their impact to third countries and jurisdictions. These examples relate to the broader, much more complex debate concerning the content of legally accurate norms in terms of social welfare maximizing. Transparency (norms must contain well-defined words, with universally accepted meanings), accessibility (norms must be easily applicable to concrete situations and intended audience) and congruity (the substantive words included in the norm must result in the intended behaviour)[133] are the elements that have been identified as compounding regulatory precision. Ideally, policy-makers are 'profit-maximizing entrepreneurs who

129 *See* Mylly (2012), p. 244. Along similar lines, *see* Correa (2009), p. 42; Xuan (2009), pp. 28–31; Grosse Ruse-Khan (2009), pp. 51–52.

130 *See* Chapter 6, Section V.1.

131 As one author noted, '[i]f intellectual property enforcement provisions in agreements are to be introduced, this must be done on the basis of adequate evidence on the level of counterfeiting and piracy and its effects. At present there is insufficient reliable evidence to confirm whether or not additional enforcement provisions are necessary.' *See* Matthews (2008), p. 30.

132 *See* Fink (2009a), p. 21. 133 Diver (1983) p. 66.

manufacture standards' by selecting that mix of accessibility, congruity and transparency that maximizes net income.[134] The effects and examples introduced next illustrate, however, that the precision of normative trends in intellectual property enforcement may be far from optimal.

3.1 Chilling Effect

Some intellectual property enforcement norms may provoke overdeterrence and discourage legal activities in fear of the consequences of eventual lawsuits and the costs of litigation. Unjustified threats of infringement actions, abuse of interim injunctions, unreasonable claims for damages and the obligation to assume lawyer's fees independently of the judicial decision are potential sources of this 'chilling effect'.

Injunctions are a case in point. Preliminary injunctions in patent cases may be used to impose financial stress on competitors. Certainly, if a plaintiff can temporarily shut down a defendant's operations while an issue is resolved, the defendant will experience a sharp reduction in cash flows.[135] Facilitating the grant of interim injunctions may also raise legal expenditure, a highly dissuasive increase in countries where each party bears the cost of litigation. In this case, competitors may be forced out of business even before the infringement investigation is completed.[136]

Excessively high damages also are a factor deterring competition. Take for instance the United States, where statutory damages have allegedly caused 'technology companies to withhold new products and services from the market'.[137] More generally, scholars have reflected upon the specific amount of damages awarded. In this context, Blair and Cotter asked in 2005 'what sort of monetary relief should courts provide in order to preserve the incentive structure upon which the system is premised while at the same time avoiding the overdeterrence of lawful conduct?',[138] thus clearly implying that the discretion is not without effects on the system.

The 'chilling effect' of criminal sanctions is particularly worth examining.[139] Take, for instance, the case of pharmaceutical patents. In light of the complexities of drug development and commercialization, both competitors and innovators take risks in their daily activity, including the possibility of infringing a patent. The criminalization of patent infringement may have deleterious effects on innovation and competition, since the eventual infringer – the scientist, the entrepreneur – would be highly unlikely to proceed if he knew that he could face criminal prosecution.[140]

As the last example indicates, the consequences of the 'chilling effect' are not limited to competitors in the market. Several socioeconomic interests may be

[134] *Ibid.*, p. 102. [135] *See* Lanjouw and Lerner (1996), p. 4. [136] *See* Casey (2012), p. 3.
[137] *See* Netcoalition-CCIA (eds.) (2010). [138] *See* Blair and Cotter (2005), p. 3.
[139] *See* Grosse Ruse-Khan (2012), p. 174.
[140] *See* European Generic and Biosimilar Medicines Association (2006), p. 3.

affected. For instance, commerce may suffer since 'the threat of having to defend oneself against an intellectual property suit could have a discouraging effect on trade'.[141] Fundamental rights may also be endangered. In the context of copyright, it has been noted that 'a true strict liability system' could have a 'chilling effect upon the publication of new works', a problematic outcome both from the economic point of view and for the guarantee of freedom of speech.[142] Similarly, the blurring of definitions of the term 'counterfeit' may impact on the availability of generic drugs and, consequently, on access to health.[143]

3.2 Restricting Access to Legal Products

The restriction of access to legal products may also be a direct and anticipated consequence of new norms on intellectual property enforcement. Some enforcement statutes have enhanced right holders' position in such a manner that new substantive rights have been granted. A case in point is that of the faculty to detain patented products in transit by invoking right holders' rights in the country of transit.

The so-called 'local-manufacturing fiction' permitted the control of foreign markets from the Netherlands, since it enabled the obstruction of trade and limited access to products that were perfectly legal both in origin and destination.[144] This proposal was indeed rejected in the context of the ACTA negotiations, but it has made its way in some trade agreements.[145] Moreover, some normative proposals in the European Union intend to modify the European Court of Justice jurisprudence regarding the control of counterfeit goods in transit. The amendment to the trademark regulation entitles right holders to prevent third parties from bringing goods from third countries bearing without authorization a trademark that is essentially identical to the trademark registered in respect of those goods into the customs territory of the Union, regardless of whether they are released for free circulation.[146]

The socioeconomic relevance of seizures and detentions of products in transit invoking local patent rights was raised in 2009, when seizures of pharmaceutical products in transit occurred as a result of the implementation of the EU Border Enforcement Regulation.[147] The 'manufacturing fiction' permitted Dutch courts to

[141] *See* Bronckers, Verkade and McNelis (2000), p. 11.

[142] *See* Blair and Cotter (2005), p. 107.

[143] *See* Spenneman (2015). *See* Chapter 12 and the references therein for the definition of counterfeit.

[144] See Chapter 11, Section II.2, for the 'local manufacturing fiction' and Chapter 1, Section III.1, on controversial cases of enforcement.

[145] See Chapter 10, Sections III and IV.

[146] *See* the proposed Article 9(5), of the Proposal for a Regulation of the European Parliament and of the Council amending Council Regulation (EC) No 207/2009. *See* Chapter 11, Section II.3.

[147] *See* Council Regulation (EC) No. 1383/2003 of 22 July 2003 concerning custom action against goods suspected of infringing certain intellectual property rights and the measures to be taken against goods found to have infringed such rights, OJEU L 196 of 2 August 2003, repealed by Regulation (EU)

detain in-transit products even if there was no risk of diversion into the Dutch market.[148] In that context it was held that given the nature of the seized goods and their relevance to the protection of health, seizures would have an impact on the right to health in third countries.[149] The reform of the European regulation and directive concerning trademarks has given rise to similar debates and concerns.[150] To our knowledge, there are no socioeconomic estimates on the impact that border enforcement measures have in third markets. Similarly, while voices have been raised in relation to the socioeconomic effects of new controls on trademark protected goods in transit, arguing that this would increase transaction costs and prevent traders from using the most efficient transit routes[151], no economic impact assessment on this particular measure has been conducted, nor have the consequences on access to legal goods been assessed.

4 *Economic Impact of Intellectual Property Enforcement Remedies*

4.1 The Value of the System, Substantive Norms and Secondary Norms

Studies on the economic value of intellectual property rights generally focus on the positive economic output resulting from the enforcement of intellectual property. In those studies, enforcement is generally understood as a given or neutral activity, scant attention is paid to the fact that the economic impact of each enforcement mechanism or remedy differs, i.e. the very same remedy can be implemented in different manners, and 'enforcement' is the result of a complex mechanism and variable processes.

The study of the economic impact of intellectual property enforcement *per se* has not attracted the attention it deserves, and the impact of enforcement remedies is in general terms poorly understood.[152] It has been noted that 'even within the burgeoning literature on the law and economics of intellectual property rights, there is still relatively little discussion on the appropriate remedies for infringement'.[153] Even this statement overlooks the fact that remedies[154] are only part of a complex mechanism integrating criminal enforcement and border enforcement as well as numerous processes and institutions that result in the enforcement of intellectual property.

No. 608/2013 of the European Parliament and of the Council of 12 June 2013 concerning customs enforcement of intellectual property rights, OJEU L 181 of 29 June 2013.

148 *See* Chapter 11, Section II.2.

149 *See* Seuba (2009), p. 19; Grosse Ruse-Khan and Jaeger (2009); Seuba (2010a); Kumar (2010); Micara (2012). *See* in detail Chapter 12.

150 *See* Chapter 12, Section III.1.

151 'Civil Society letter regarding proposed rules for EU trademark legislation', Brussels December 1, 2014, available at: www.msfaccess.org/content/civil-society-letter-regarding-proposed-rules-eu-trademark-legislation (accessed December 2014).

152 *See*, in this same sense, Savin (2006), p. F160.

153 *See* Blair and Cotter (2005), p. 2.

154 In this context, following the approach adopted by Scotchmer, 'remedies' include both injunctions plus damages. *See* Scotchmer (2004), p. 206

Intellectual property enforcement norms are secondary rules, frequently secondary rules of adjudication.[155] While in *hartian* terms it is in principle easy to differentiate between primary norms enshrining substantive rights and obligations and secondary norms enacting the procedures to, among other activities, adjudicate disputes, sometimes it is almost impossible to distinguish the contours of the two sets of norms. Take, for instance, the example of damages. While awarding very substantial damages strengthens the value of a patent or a copyright, a system that awards minimal or no damages or that imposes insurmountable difficulties in proving damages weakens those rights. This exemplifies the difficulty in delineating the contours of primary and secondary norms and some of the difficulties that will face those trying to give independent value to intellectual property enforcement remedies and mechanisms.

4.2 Specific Areas of Research

The economic analysis of remedies has delivered interesting results in the areas of liability standards, standing, injunctions and, in particular, damages. Litigation *per se* and other intellectual property enforcement institutions, such as technological protection measures, have also attracted research.

One of the first enforcement-related areas to rouse the interest of economists was patent litigation.[156] Data and evidence on litigation have been studied to reach conclusions such as (i) the more valuable patents are, the more frequently litigated;[157] (ii) small firms avoid research and development if this may attract litigation on the part of larger firms[158] or, as Scotchmer says, 'where litigation is prevalent';[159] (iii) the costs of litigation affect the willingness to enforce patents;[160] (iv) there is a relationship between portfolios' size and litigation;[161] (v) the cost of enforcing patents changes the value of patent rights;[162] (vi) patent litigation impacts on innovation;[163] (vii) the use of preliminary injunctions can discourage research and development of small companies;[164] (viii) some courts are more likely to favour patents and patent holders than others;[165] and (ix) the propensity to litigate patents varies with the expected benefits of litigation.[166] More broadly, litigation modifies

155 *See* Chapter 1, Section I.4.

156 *See* Meurer (1989), pp. 77–91; Duchêne and Serfes (2012), p. 399.

157 *See* Lanjouw and Schankerman (2001), p. 4.

158 As stated 'Firms with high litigation costs appear less likely to patent in the same subclass as rivals. These firms seem particularly reluctant to patent after awards to firms that have low litigation costs.' *See* Lerner (1995).

159 *See* Scotchmer (2004), p. 203.

160 *See* Lanjouw and Lerner (1997).

161 *See* Lanjouw and Schankerman (2001), p. 4, 'having a larger portfolio of patents reduces the probability of filing a suit on any individual patent, conditional on its observed characteristics'. The same authors reached similar results in respect to the size of the company: the smaller the company, the more probable litigation; *see* Lanjouw and Schankerman (2004), pp. 45–74. *See* also Scotchmer (2004), p. 203.

162 *See* Lanjouw and Lerner (1997).

163 *Ibid.*

164 *See* Lanjouw and Lerner (1996).

165 *See* Scotchmer (2004), p. 205; Harmon (1998).

166 *See* Lanjouw and Lerner (1997).

the profitability of intellectual property rights in a manner that differs across types of firms and technologies.[167]

A remedy that has attracted the interest of law and economics scholars is preliminary injunctive relief. Among the aspects that have been explored, mention can be made of the use of interim injunctions as a predatory instrument against financially weak competitors.[168] Economic analysis has also proved that injunctive relief generally favours large litigants and is likely to increase expenditures on legal fees in the process of dispute resolution.[169]

In regard to damages, both the nature of the award and the specific calculation of monetary damages have been studied intensively.[170] In the model developed by Cotter and Blair,[171] the prevailing right holder in a patent, trade secret, copyright or trademark infringement action should be able 'to recover the greater of her lost profits attributable to the infringement or the defendant's profits so attributable. In some cases the award should be further modified for optimal deterrent effect',[172] i.e. to avoid over- or underdeterrence.[173] Analysed in the context of the United States law, the authors indicate that trade secret law satisfactorily conforms to this model and that copyright, trademark and patent law are also satisfactory in general terms. However, there are a number of departures from the model. In this context, Cotter and Blair underline that the impossibility to claim restitution of profits in patent law is problematic,[174] and statutory damages in copyright law is prone to criticism but ultimately justifiable,[175] whereas the limitation of restitution in the context of trademark law to cases of wilful infringement is correct.[176]

Scotchmer's analysis of patent damages leads to different conclusions. While Cotter and Blair criticize the absence of restitutionary damages in United States patent law,

[167] *See* Scotchmer (2004), p. 204. [168] *See* Lanjouw and Lerner (1996).

[169] *Ibid.*, p. 3. Scotchmer invokes a number of these findings in Scotchmer (2004), pp. 202–204.

[170] The economics of the calculation of monetary damages have been analysed by many of authors, such as Blair and Cotter (2005), pp. 208–262; Schlicher (2000), p. 503; Addanki (1998); Conley (1987); Schlicher (2003); Werden *et al.* (1999), p. 305.

[171] *See* Blair and Cotter (1998), pp. 1585–1694. [172] *See* Blair and Cotter (2005), p. 68.

[173] It is particularly clear that the goals of the specific remedy will condition the assessment of its economic efficiency. Whether the emphasis is put on deterrence, restitution or prevention from unjustified benefits will condition the ulterior assessment of the economic rationale.

[174] The impossibility to claim restitution is in effect at odds with the recommendation put forward, in the sense that the prevailing party should be entitled to the greater of her own lost profit or the defendant's profit. For the authors, the difficulty of properly calculating the proportion of profit attributable to the infringing conduct is not sufficient to impede claiming restitution. *See* Blair and Cotter (2005), p. 73; Blair and Cotter (1998), p. 1647.

[175] The possibility to claim a quantity unrelated to the actual loss or to the infringer's profits does not conform to the model. However, in this case the departure is a reasonable response to the 'pervasiveness of small-scale infringements'. *See* Blair and Cotter (2005), p. 71; Blair and Cotter (1998), p. 1651.

[176] The restriction of restitution to the cases of wilful trademark counterfeiting is justified, since exactly assigning the benefits in case of 'nonwilful' trademark infringement is very difficult and the possibility to award damages exceeding restitution may exceed deterrence. *See* Blair and Cotter (2005), p. 72; Blair and Cotter (1998), p. 1672.

Scotchmer held that awarding lost profits may be better suited to the interests of product patent owners and that both lost profits and unjust enrichment fulfil compensatory and deterrent goals. In the model developed by Scotchmer, lost profits of the right holder are superior to the unjust enrichment of the infringer. The benefit of the monopolist right holder is superior to his own benefit after the infringement *plus* the unjust enrichment of the infringer. This is due to the fact that both the price of the product and the market share decrease in an infringement situation. Thus, 'due to price erosion, the lost-profit rule yields larger damages for the right-holder than the unjust enrichment rule does'.[177] Given that lost profits are higher than unjust enrichment, deterrence is accomplished if awarded damages amount to lost profits. However, unjust enrichment would also have a deterrent effect, since there is no incentive to infringe. Although an audacious infringer under the rule of unjust enrichment risks losing nothing, and paying punitive damages is mostly limited to the United States, Scotchmer arguments give a powerful basis to the lost profits rule.[178]

Concerning mental states of the alleged infringer, economists have studied the implications of the diverse liability standards, and have tried to ascertain whether, when, and in what circumstances a strict liability regime, proof of intent or negligence should be required. Their analysis has concluded that statutory limitations to the strict liability regime[179] are roughly justified. Conversely, it has also been held that actual or constructive notice of patent infringement,[180] negligence or intent in trade secret infringement,[181] and copying copyrighted material[182] construe economic rationales to impose strict liability.[183] Similarly, the rationales of recognizing

177 *See* Scotchmer (2004), p. 208. The difficulty, recognized by Scotchmer, is that price erosion should be calculated with respect to an unknown equilibrium that should have occurred but did not occur. This is solved by referring to a benchmark level of profit that could be achieved in various ways, with or without licensing.

178 Estimating lost profit becomes even more difficult when licensors and licensees are not competitors in the market. Scotchmer utilizes the example of licensing of research tools. In this case, the price of the license fee that would have been paid in case infringement did not occur is also unknown. Under the damages doctrine, damages may be the price of the license: the maximum that the licensee would be willing to pay is the damage that he would have to pay. At the same time, this is also the minimum that the licensor will expect; otherwise a court would concede it to her. Nothing tells us, however, which should be the specific price. In the example provided by Scotchmer, if the licensor establishes a specific price for the license and, for whatever reason the demand increases, he/she may be willing to increase the price. However, in that new situation those willing to acquire the technology may be inclined to infringe, since the price for the license has been already established and paying damages equivalent to that price will be more convenient than paying the new price. *See* Scotchmer (2004), p. 212.

179 Which it is defined as liability without fault. *See* Restatement (Second) of Torts (1959 § 504-24A).

180 This is treated differently from other cases where the state of mind of the infringement is relevant for a number of procedural and material aspects. For instance, wilful infringement may determine the imposition of aggravated damages, and intent also becomes relevant in cases of infringement under the doctrine of equivalents. *See* Blair and Cotter (2005), pp. 99–100.

181 *See* Blair and Cotter (2005), pp. 105–106.

182 For copyrights, independent creation is a defense. *See* Blair and Cotter (2005), pp. 103–104.

183 *Ibid.*, p. 98.

independent discovery as a defense in cases of trade secret and copyright infringement but not in cases of patent and trademarks are generally found acceptable.[184] The particular situation in trademark law – where compensatory damages are due in case of actual confusion regardless of the intent, whereas wilful infringement allows imposing restitution[185] – is also found acceptable. Proposals for improvement are put forward in several respects, particularly in the case of patent law and constructive notice.[186]

Standing has also been the object of economic analysis in the US context, more precisely whether only the right holder or also licensees and other assignees should be entitled to enforce the right.[187] The rules of patent law, copyright and trademark law diverge significantly. Sometimes only the owner or the assignee is entitled to sue, while on other occasions the licensee may assert claims for infringement if the owner also joins, and in some cases the licensee has the right to file a suit on its own. The great diversity of situations may give the impression of arbitrariness. Nevertheless, economic analysis has concluded that the rationales for such a differentiation are acceptable, although traditional rules 'are at best only approximations for the optimal set of rules to be applied in different settings'.[188]

Finally, in a different context, technological protection measures have also been the object of economic study. A first reflection is that all technical protection measures involve wasted costs, since they represent an unnecessary investment in an ideal world where users respect intellectual property.[189] Second, truly effective technological protection measures will negatively impact on welfare when welfare is enhanced by fair use, since technological protection measures will be equally effective to impede licit and illicit uses of the protected material. Similarly, truly effective technological protection measures may extend protection further than the period of exclusivity granted by the intellectual property right and may also avoid the disclosure requirement in the case of patents. In both situations, they will nullify the intellectual property protection trade-off. Scotchmer also studied the potential interaction between technological protection measures and price and found that they could have a moderating influence. However, given that they may perpetuate protection and that the system of protection is costly, one potential conclusion is that circumvention may enhance social welfare.[190]

4.3 Research Agenda

The research conducted on the independent economic significance of intellectual property enforcement institutions is meagre. Most of the attention has been traditionally directed to rules of substantive law, while important civil, border and criminal enforcement norms have largely been ignored. For this reason, a complex and rich research agenda almost remains unexplored.

184 *Ibid.*, p. 107. 185 *Ibid.*, p. 105. 186 *Ibid.*, p. 98. 187 *Ibid.*, p. 160. 188 *Ibid.*, p. 161.
189 *Ibid.*, p. 216. 190 *Ibid.*, p. 218.

Except in the case of damages and, to a lesser extent, injunctions and standing, the rest of civil enforcement remedies have not been studied by law and economics scholars. Unresearched remedies play a crucial role in any intellectual property system. Think for instance about the cases of the right of information, provisions on evidence, measures for the preservation of evidence or corrective measures, all of them virtually unresearched. But even in cases of injunctions and standing, it is clear that more research is needed. Take, for instance, the promising field of study on the relevance of legal fees in the context of non-practicing entities.[191]

If civil enforcement is largely an unresearched area, border enforcement has not been studied at all by law and economics scholars. While pursuant the TRIPS Agreement States must solely impede the importation of counterfeit and pirated products, new international norms make Sates responsible for the control of a large number of border situations and almost all intellectual property categories. However, from the economic point of view, it is just not known what difference it makes to right holders, competitors and the entire system controlling the transit, exportation and re-exportation of products. The same applies with respect to intellectual property categories different from trademarks and copyright. Similarly, aspects as important as the economic impact of the presumption of infringement in the context of border measures, and therefore the automatic destruction of goods, have not been studied at all.

Criminal enforcement has so far attracted minimal attention.[192] Indeed, it was already affirmed in the late 1990s that the rent-seeking model commonly applied in the non-criminal context was also applicable to the criminalization of copyright infringement.[193] Conscious of the relevance of using the tools of law and economics,[194] later studies have held that the assessment of benefits and costs indicates that 'the deterrent benefit of criminalizing infringement may be limited, while the costs to copyright policy and long-term effectiveness of the criminal law may be large'.[195]

Researchers should also take into consideration the need for further refinement and differentiation between intellectual property categories. While the problems detailed in this piece are applicable to many intellectual property categories, the specific calculation of the economics of enforcement will require attention to the particularities of enforcement norms of each intellectual property category.

191 *See* Messen and Meurer (2012); Schwartz and Kesan (2014).

192 *See* Wechsler (2012), p. 123.

193 *See* Saperstein (1997), pp. 1472–1473.

194 Daniel Gervais has noted that 'with the emergence of data and a better understanding of the impact of intellectual property, using in particular the tools of law and economics . . . one not need to assume that measures of strict enforcement using criminal law necessarily serve the public interest in every case'. *See* Gervais (2012), p. 271.

195 *See* Szott Moohr (2005), p. 805.

V CONCLUSIONS

Estimates of the scale and impact of intellectual property infringement have proliferated in the past two decades. In the majority of cases, studies have been commissioned by concerned parties and have implemented controversial methodologies, frequently containing objectionable assumptions. Fortunately, public institutions show a growing interest in the economic aspects of intellectual property. While this is positive news, the complexities and the multifaceted socioeconomic impacts of intellectual property have received only limited attention.

Economic estimates of the impact of intellectual property do not generally reflect the *net* impact of intellectual property. Studies neglect capital aspects such as the investment necessary to set up and run a proper system for the enforcement of intellectual property rights, the eventual benefits arising from intellectual property infringement and the anti-competitive and extraterritorial effects of new enforcement institutions. Moreover, estimates assume that a homogeneous and infallible enforcement system is in place, while in reality enforcement is better described as a variable and complex process, as was described in Chapter 1.

The elaboration of reliable estimates reflecting the general impact of intellectual property infringement on the economy, taking into account all aspects mentioned above, is just not possible at the present moment. Current estimates of the socioeconomic effects of intellectual property protection at the macro level are particularly questionable and, at maximum, can only be considered 'educated guesses'. In contrast, narrowing the object of research and studying specific products, markets or institutions may result in more credible estimates.

Activities that commonly fall within the realm of enforcement and investment items related to those activities need to be identified in order to calculate the investment needed to enforce intellectual property law. In this chapter we identify these items and activities and propose some indirect sources to conduct the calculation. The result should be assessed against the fact that levels of investment in enforcement that are optimal from the economic point of view do not necessarily coincide with the level of enforcement required to fulfil intellectual property law. A number of factors explain the mentioned gap, such as the adoption of international treaties where states assume obligations with the sole intention to reap benefits in fields other than intellectual property, internal pressures to adopt higher standards of protection and the lack of reliable information on the socioeconomic impact of new enforcement commitments. New sources of funding, probably right holders, should bear the costs of the economically inefficient investment in enforcement.

Enforcement norms should preserve the function devised for substantive norms and the objectives of the intellectual property system. If enforcement overdeters competition, the trade-off that underpins some intellectual property norms – to spur innovation and creativity by temporarily restricting competition – is nullified. On the other hand, the strengthening of the right holder's position may result in unexpected situations, where alleged enforcement rights become substantive rights or trespass national borders and confer to the right holder the power to control foreign markets. In this context, it must be recalled that the drafting of legally accurate rights in terms of social welfare maximizing is not by any means straightforward. While judging the quality of the rules should be accompanied by positive proposals relating to the actual degree of formal precision of administrative rules, determining the latter is a contextual and frequently inconclusive exercise.

Finally, it is necessary to draw a distinction between the value of the intellectual property system and the value of enforcement institutions. Civil, criminal and border enforcement norms diverge greatly across nations, and the legally available options result in critical differences in terms of economic impact. However, up until now, with the exception of damages, the institutions that make up the intellectual property enforcement arsenal have been largely ignored by law and economics scholars.

PART II

The International Architecture for the Enforcement of Intellectual Property Rights

4

International Normative Architecture for the Enforcement of Intellectual Property Rights

I INTERNATIONALIZATION OF ENFORCEMENT AND CLASSIFICATION OF TREATIES

1 *Scope of This Chapter*

Obligations dealing with domestic enforcement of intellectual property rights have become a common feature of international agreements. Their international codification has changed the historical neglect of this important area of regulation and has done so with a level of detail not found in other areas of international law. As a result, a loosely organized regime has emerged, where both repetitive and conflictive norms coexist. In order to give the full picture of the international normative architecture for the enforcement of intellectual property rights, this chapter identifies and classifies international treaties touching upon intellectual property enforcement and introduces the objectives and main obligations established therein. The purpose is to describe the content of the treaties and the general obligations set forth therein while reserving the analysis of specific enforcement remedies and institutions for later chapters.

The identification of treaties depending on whether they are multilateral or bilateral is a first and useful step in building a picture of the current international normative architecture for the enforcement of intellectual property rights.[1] Multilateral treaties[2] can be further differentiated into regional and plurilateral agreements. For descriptive purposes, the classification of treaties depending on their membership can be complemented with references to other relevant aspects, such as the regulated subject matter, the openness of the treaty to the participation of

[1] Criteria for classifying international treaties include (i) the number of participants, (ii) the degree of openness to other Member States not having participated in the negotiations, (iii) the subject matter of the treaty, (iv) their function *vis-à-vis* the creation of obligations, (v) the nature of the Members of the treaty, (vi) their duration, and (vii) the formalities of their conclusion.

[2] Those concluded between three or more States. *See* Aust (2007), p. 10.

third States, the sophistication of the articles of the treaty and the addressees of the obligations undertaken.

This chapter takes into account additional criteria and characteristics when describing the relevant treaties, such as the moment of adoption and the substantive content of the treaty. With respect to the moment of adoption, the chronological criterion is used to ascribe intellectual property treaties to different groups, creating 'generations of treaties', which may also correspond to varying levels of sophistication.[3] On the other hand, from the substantive point of view, enforcement-related treaties may be differentiated depending on whether they only regulate intellectual property[4] or address other subjects as well, particularly trade in goods.[5] The nature of the norms enshrined in the treaty (civil, criminal or administrative) is an additional criterion for classification, although treaties regulating enforcement generally do not restrict their reach to just one type of enforcement. Finally, intellectual property enforcement provisions may also be differentiated according to whether they operate at the national level or are of an international impact.[6]

2 *Evolution of the International Codification of Enforcement*

National governments have been traditionally unwilling to surrender sovereignty over the implementation of intellectual property rights.[7] This reluctance was evident in the old intellectual property conventions, which contain very few regulations on enforcement of rights.[8] The Paris and Berne Conventions, for instance, contain 'few minimum standards on enforcement beyond national treatment and certain optional provisions'[9] and do not provide 'governments with the necessary guidance concerning appropriate and modern' enforcement standards.[10]

In the late 1970s and early 1980s, industrialized nations manifested their discontent with respect to the lack of effective enforcement within some countries and the concomitant problems their industries faced.[11] These countries sustained that

[3] More recent treaties are, in general, the most sophisticated, while older treaties enshrine more rudimentary intellectual property commitments. *See* Fink (2011), pp. 398–399.

[4] The case of the treaties of the World Intellectual Property Organization is the clearest one (for instance, the WIPO Internet treaties). However, it is also possible to find bilateral treaties only dealing with intellectual property. *See* Section III.

[5] Bilateral agreements addressing intellectual property enforcement have, in the majority of cases, a trade-related component. However, it is worth mentioning the existence of treaties regulating intellectual property enforcement in the area of science and technology and other treaties on the protection of foreign investment. *See* Section IV.

[6] Reinbothe differentiates purely internal enforcement rules from 'trade-related enforcement measures'. The latter include rules on border enforcement as well as 'international enforcement disciplines'. *See* Reinbothe (2010), p. 5.

[7] *See* Abbott (2009), pp. 6–7.

[8] *See* Dreier (1996), p. 249.

[9] *See* WTO Panel Report, *China – measures affecting the protection and enforcement of intellectual property rights*, WT/DS362/R, 26 January 2009, para. 7.241 (hereinafter WTO Panel, *China – Intellectual Property Rights*).

[10] *See* WIPO (2004), p. 214.

[11] *See* Bronckers, Verkade and McNelis (2000), p. 10.

inadequate enforcement was a trade barrier, since their exports were being substituted by locally manufactured infringing products.[12] Counterfeiting was a central topic of discussion during the 1973–1979 GATT Tokyo Round,[13] although the practical effects in terms of normative changes were meagre.[14] In any case, since that moment the 'lack of an international discipline on sanctions and remedies for tackling counterfeiting and piracy'[15] has been on the international normative agenda.

Domestic enforcement of intellectual property rights was at the heart of the Uruguay Round negotiations.[16] The divide between developed and developing nations was also clear in this domain. Right from the beginning, developed nations had a clear agenda in mind. In the early stages of the Round, the European Union and Japan underlined the problems existing with respect to national remedies and procedures[17] as well as with insufficient inter-State collaboration.[18] The United States was even more specific and identified concrete subjects that needed to be tackled. Among these were border enforcement, police enforcement, access to judicial and administrative bodies, procedural and evidentiary provisions, injunctions and damages.[19] From a very different perspective, developing countries held that the only area that needed attention was border enforcement.[20]

Part III of the Agreement on Trade-Related Aspects of Intellectual Property Rights, which is specifically devoted to enforcement, did not attempt to achieve full harmonization. Instead, it established general standards[21] to be implemented according to the method chosen by each World Trade Organization Member State[22] and often left judges ample discretion to ponder different legal interests involved in adjudication.[23] At the time that the TRIPS Agreement was adopted, national differences were very relevant, which made it unfeasible to adopt a uniform set of rules or the universal recognition and execution of national rulings.[24] Instead, the goal was to agree on the first international and comprehensive set of norms on enforcement,[25]

12 *Ibid.*

13 Scholars noted that 'as early as 1978, the USA and the European Community had taken the initiative in proposing an agreement on counterfeiting in the Tokyo Round'. *See* Reinbothe and Howard (1991), p. 157.

14 *See* Blakeney (2004b), p. 10.

15 *See* Reinbothe (2010), p. 7; Reinbothe and Howard (1991), p. 157.

16 *See* Dreier (1996), p. 249; Stewart (1993), pp. 463, 466.

17 *See* GATT (1987a), paras. 2–5.

18 *Ibid*, para. 7.

19 *See* GATT (1987b), paras. 2–3. *See* as well Watal (2010), p. 605.

20 *See* GATT (1988a).

21 These standards were something more than 'a bullet point list of required elements for an IPR enforcement system'. *Contrario sensu, see* Trainer (2008), p. 56.

22 *See* UNCTAD-ICTSD (2005), p. 255.

23 *See* following the comments made with regards to the wording of the TRIPS Agreement on 'judges shall have the authority'.

24 *See* Dreier (1996), p. 254.

25 'One of the major reasons for the conclusion of the TRIPS Agreement was the desire to set out a minimum set of procedures and remedies that judicial, border and other competent authorities must have available to them'. *See* WTO Panel, *China –Intellectual Property Rights*, para. 7.241; Watal (2010), p. 604; Correa (2007), p. 409; Grosse Ruse-Khan (2012), p. 171; Pauwelyn (2010), p. 391.

generally modelled on the national laws existing in developed countries,[26] which is precisely what can be found in Part III of the TRIPS Agreement. This was considered 'one of the most spectacular merits of the WTO TRIPS Agreement',[27] a 'major achievement'[28] and 'perhaps the most significant milestone in TRIPS'.[29]

The multilateral legal regime on intellectual property enforcement set up in the TRIPS Agreement corresponded 'to large extent to the desires of industrialized countries',[30] which tried to remedy the perceived inadequacies of enforcement remedies and procedures of the Paris and Berne Conventions.[31] Its practical consequences were considered to be 'enormous',[32] particularly because of the enhancement of the position of right holders[33] and the creation of an efficient international dispute settlement mechanism tied to trade sanctions.[34]

Notwithstanding these achievements, approximately a decade after the TRIPS Agreement entered into force, intellectual property enforcement returned to the forefront of international norm-making. Countries that had promoted the adoption of the TRIPS Agreement underlined the need to enhance the international normative *acquis* on intellectual property enforcement. In order to achieve that objective, the adoption of numerous bilateral agreements and ambitious plurilateral treaties was promoted.[35]

The reason for promoting new enforcement norms in trade agreement post-TRIPS can be found in the relative disenchantment with respect to enforcement norms found in the TRIPS Agreement. In effect, even if the enforcement regime in the TRIPS Agreement was initially considered revolutionary, with the passage of time its norms were criticized for being crafted as too broad of legal standards.[36] In fact, while the majority of early commentators praised the enforcement rules of the TRIPS Agreement, some claimed that the ambiguity of these rules would 'make it harder for mediators or dispute-settlement panels to pin down clear-cut violations',[37] something that would 'greatly disappoint rightholders in the developed countries'.[38] Even if the reality is far more complex – and only the combination of a set of historical, economic, tactical, disciplinary and technological challenges can

26 *See* Chapter 6, Section II.1. 27 *See* Reinbothe (2010), p. 5.
28 *See* Gervais (2008), p. 440; Trainer (2008), p. 47. 29 *See* Cordray (1994), p. 135.
30 *See* Dreier (1996), p. 257. 31 *See* Netanel (1996–1997), p. 454; Cordray (1994), pp. 135–136.
32 *See* Reinbothe and Howard (1991), p. 163. 33 *See* Straus (2000), p. 807.
34 See Chapter 5, Section II.2.1.
35 Namely, the Anti-Counterfeiting Trade Agreement and the Trans-Pacific Partnership Agreement. As of October 2016, nor the ACTA or the TPP had been adopted.
36 *See* criticism made by the Assistant USTR for Services in 1999 of the space left in TRIPS enforcement provisions to national authorities and judges in 'USTR official predicts difficulty in forcing compliance with TRIPS", *Inside US Trade*, 16 July 1999, citing Mr Papovich, (quoted from Watal (2010), p. 607). Also, reflecting on the PTAs goal of eliminating ambiguities of the enforcement provisions in the TRIPS Agreement and raising the enforcement standards set forth therein, *see* Trainer (2008), p. 61.
37 *See* Reichman and Lange (1998), p. 35. It has also been affirmed that the enforcement norms of the TRIPS Agreement were 'new and primitive'. *See* Yu (2011b), p. 1048.
38 *See* Reichman and Lange (1998), pp. 38–39; Trainer (2008), p. 47.

explain the difficulties of the TRIPS Agreement to provide effective enforcement[39] – new treaties, particularly trade agreements, were adopted to remedy the alleged shortcomings, transform what in the TRIPS Agreement were permissions into obligations and convert ambiguous provisions in the TRIPS Agreement into detailed articles.

The possibility to conclude agreements of bilateral or plurilateral nature in the area of intellectual property has been recognized since the time of the Paris and Berne Conventions.[40] In this context, it is worth clarifying that while there are cases of treaties of bilateral nature exclusively dealing with intellectual property,[41] these are relatively rare. In the majority of cases, intellectual property provisions are enshrined in treaties of broader economic or commercial scope. By and large, the most important strategy for intellectual property codification has been the conclusion of Preferential Trade Agreements, which include bilateral and plurilateral trade agreements as well as customs unions, economic integration agreements and partial scope agreements.[42]

Trade agreements have become a major source of international intellectual property regulation, including enforcement regulation. This is not, however, a new phenomenon. PTAs were already a factor of normative change in the context of the negotiations of the TRIPS Agreement.[43] The influence of provisions set forth in the North American Free Trade Agreement – including its articles on enforcement – in subsequent PTAs has probably not been recognized enough.[44] In 2013, there were 141 PTAs addressing intellectual property norms in a significant manner,[45] a number that continues to grow since then.[46] Some of these treaties enshrine very complete intellectual property enforcement statutes, while others

39 *See* Yu (2011a), pp. 325–326.

40 Article 19 of the Paris Convention states that Members 'reserve the right to make separately between themselves special agreements for the protection of industrial property, in so far these agreements do not contravene the provisions of this Convention'. Similarly for the Berne Convention *see* Article 20.

41 *See* Agreement regarding Intellectual Property Rights, Annex, § 1(G), US-China; Agreement between the United States of America and the Kingdom of Cambodia on Trade Relations and Intellectual Property Rights Protection (1996); Agreement between the United States of America and the Republic of Latvia on Trade Relations and Intellectual Property Rights Protection (1995); Agreement on Intellectual Property between the Government of the United States of America and the Government of the Republic of Hungary (1994); Agreement concerning the Protection and Enforcement of Intellectual Property Rights between the Government of the United States of America and the Government of Jamaica (1994); Agreement Between the United States of America and the Government of Ecuador Concerning the Protection and Enforcement of Intellectual Property Rights (1993); Agreement between the Government of the Federal Republic of Germany and the Government of the State of Israel on Cooperation in the Area of Intellectual Property (1989).

42 *See* Article XXIV paragraphs 8(a) and 8(b) of GATT 1994; Article V of GATS, and para. 4(a) of the Enabling Clause.

43 *See* Stewart (1993), p. 495.

44 *See* however Stewart (1993), p. 563; *see* Chapter 6.

45 *See* Seuba (2013b).

46 In 2014, for instance, the European Union concluded trade agreements with Ukraine, Georgia, Moldova, Singapore and Canada that include significant intellectual property provisions.

contain a reduced number of provisions dealing with specific mechanisms, notably border measures.

Turning to plurilaterals, the Anti-Counterfeiting Trade Agreement tried to introduce a major systemic shift. While the TRIPS Agreement was a compromise subject to specific boundaries, ACTA was akin to a framework agreement, which opened new avenues for the intellectual property enforcement agenda. There is a general perception that ACTA constituted just a springboard for new initiatives to expand enforcement standards. The Agreement's in-built mechanisms would have permitted moving in that direction.[47] Similarly, ambiguous provisions within ACTA would permit, if other conditions were met, a number of maximalist implementations.[48] This is why it has been noted that the main problem in ACTA was 'the vague and uncertain nature of some provisions and the lack of clear limits'.[49] Even if the implementation of the treaty failed, ACTA is shaping new bilateral and plurilateral initiatives and has been used as a standard to assess other countries' performance in the context of unilateral evaluations, in particular by the United States and the European Union.

Similar considerations can be made with respect to the Trans-Pacific Partnership Agreement. Another failed plurilateral initiative, the TPP will not be adopted in its original form. This plurilateral agreement would have strengthened the obligations set forth in many bilateral treaties and would have added a new layer of repetitive obligations. For members of the TPP with no bilateral treaties with the United States, or for those whose treaties were old, the TPP would have implied entering into a world of high intellectual property (enforcement) standards supervised by a new forum for the settlement of disputes.

II MULTILATERAL TREATIES

1 *The Berne and Paris Conventions*

1.1 The Little Attention Paid to Enforcement

Intellectual property enforcement was generally ignored in the Paris Convention for the Protection of Industrial Property and in the Berne Convention for the Protection of Literary and Artistic Works. The affirmation that 'the obligation of States to provide adequate means for enforcement of rights is clearly present' in the Berne Convention[50] is an excessively generous reading of the Convention. In reality, both the Paris and Berne Conventions contain very little guidance as to the specific means for intellectual property enforcement,[51] in particular with respect to 'appropriate and modern standards for the enforcement of rights'.[52] The provisions

[47] *See* Chapter 5. [48] *See* Geist (2015), pp. 345–356; Matulionyte (2015), pp. 115–142.

[49] *See* Geiger (2015a), p. 323. [50] *See* WIPO (2004), p. 214. [51] *See* Gervais (2012), p. 269.

[52] *See* WIPO (2004), p. 214.

enshrined in these treaties are very limited in number and scope, afford States a great margin of discretion and have had a limited impact.[53]

The Paris and the Berne Conventions recognize a large autonomy of the Parties to decide on the implementation of most of enforcement provisions. The Paris Convention states that it is for the Parties to decide on judicial and administrative procedures as well as on the jurisdiction of the courts.[54] On its turn, the Berne Convention establishes that 'the means of redress ... shall be governed exclusively by the laws of the country where protection is claimed'.[55] In a similar vein, the Berne Convention emphasizes domestic autonomy concerning enforcement and establishes that seizure of infringing copies of a work 'shall take place in accordance with the legislation of each country'.[56]

1.2 Isolated References to Enforcement

The Paris and Berne Conventions contain no references to general goals or principles relating to enforcement. References to remedies exist, but they are occasional and target specific remedies. This is the case of injunctions for specific rights and situations, the seizure of imported goods, some procedural rights and references to norms on legal standing.

Enforcement provisions in the Paris Convention can be briefly summarized. A first case in point is the seizure on importation,[57] the prohibition of importation or the seizure inside the country[58] of goods unlawfully bearing a trademark or trade name.[59] However, Members may replace these measures by actions and remedies available to nationals under national law.[60] That is, non-discrimination suffices. Exactly the same approach applies to direct or indirect use of a false indication.[61] In both cases, as well as in the case of anti-competitive practices, Parties are bound to provide appropriate legal remedies to nationals of the other countries of the Union for the 'effective' protection against those acts.[62] Finally, the Paris Convention obliges Parties to offer procedural national treatment before courts and administrative authorities to associations and organizations of business, manufacturers and retailers.[63]

The award of an injunction in favour of the owner of a renowned trademark seems implicit in the Paris Convention. In this regard, Members undertake 'to refuse or to cancel the registration and to prohibit the use' of trademarks creating confusion with regard to well-known trademarks.[64] Additionally, the proprietor of a trademark is

53 *See* Yu (2012), p. 287. 54 *See* Article 2.3 Paris Convention.
55 *See* Articles 5.2 and *6bis*.3 Berne Convention. 56 *See* Article 16.3 Berne Convention.
57 *See* Article 9.1 Paris Convention. 58 *See* Article 9.5 Paris Convention.
59 This is a provision that can be traced back to the Madrid Arrangement for the Repression of False and Deceptive Indications of Source on Goods of 14 April 1891 (1967).
60 *See* Article 9.6 Paris Convention. 61 *See* Article 10.1 Paris Convention.
62 *See* Article 10ter.1 Paris Convention. 63 *See* Article 10*ter*.2 Paris Convention.
64 *See* Article *6bis*.1 Paris Convention.

entitled to oppose or demand the cancellation of a registration applied for his agent or representative without the right holder's authorization.[65] However, there is no explicit reference to injunctions, and certainly the same outcome can be achieved by other means.

Enforcement-related provisions in the Berne Convention are similarly succinct. The Convention allows for the seizure of infringing copies of protected music works upon their importation,[66] defines standing[67] and establishes that 'infringing copies of a work shall be liable to seizure in any country of the Union where the work enjoys legal protection',[68] even when copies come from a country where the work is not or no longer protected.[69] It also prescribes that the means of redress are governed by the law of the country where protection is claimed.[70] The rest of the enforcement-related measures were left to national discretion, until the TRIPS Agreement was adopted.

2 *The TRIPS Agreement*

2.1 The Content of Part III of the TRIPS Agreement

Part III of the TRIPS Agreement is devoted to intellectual property enforcement within national jurisdictions.[71] Five sections make up this part and address general obligations, civil and administrative enforcement, provisional measures, border measures and criminal enforcement. The twenty articles contained in Part III create a relatively sophisticated reference for WTO Members states, whilst leaving considerable margin of manoeuvre for adjustment and national implementation. In terms of content, the provisions of the TRIPS Agreement on enforcement can be divided into three groups depending on their expected outcome.

First, some articles state how enforcement must be put into practice and use an imperative terminology. An example is Article 41.1 of the TRIPS Agreement, which establishes that the Members of the WTO 'shall ensure that enforcement procedures as specified in this Part are available'. While 'shall' provisions abound in Part III of the TRIPS Agreement and touch upon both the rights of the right holder and the alleged infringer,[72] subsequent treaties regulating enforcement of intellectual property rights include an even higher number of imperative provisions.

In other cases, the TRIPS Agreement instructs Members to empower their courts to do something or to adopt certain decisions, but it does not prescribe a specific result. In fact, this is the most common type of provision in the Agreement and is

[65] *See* Article *6septies*.2 Paris Convention. [66] *See* Article 13.3 Berne Convention.
[67] *See* Article 15 Berne Convention. [68] *See* Article 16.1 Berne Convention.
[69] *See* Article 16.2 Berne Convention. [70] *See* Article *6bis*.3 Berne Convention.
[71] From the systemic point of view, it has been rightly held that Part IV of the TRIPS Agreement, on acquisition and maintenance of intellectual property, should have preceded Part III of the treaty. *See* Dreier (1996), p. 249.
[72] *See* respectively Articles 41.1–4, 42.1, 46, 49, 50.4, 50.6, 50.8, 51, 52, 54, 55, 58, 59, 61 TRIPS Agreement.

generally introduced under a construction stating that 'judicial authorities shall have the authority to . . . '.[73] When passing sentences, judges take into consideration the entire legal order, including obligations belonging to areas of law distinct from intellectual property. It is in this context that such an authority to adopt, or not, certain decisions must be understood.

Finally, the TRIPS Agreement also proposes some further possibilities of enforcement but leaves their implementation to the discretion of the Parties. When this is the case, usual expressions are 'Members may provide that the judicial authorities shall have the authority to . . . ', or 'Members may authorize the judicial authorities to . . . '.[74]

Section 2 of Part III of the TRIPS Agreement addresses civil and administrative enforcement and opens with a general article relating to the fairness of procedures and due process principles. This section regulates crucial measures and remedies, namely the production and preservation of evidence, the award of injunctions and damages, the destruction of goods and the provision of information on the infringer and infringing goods. It also allows implementing administrative procedures, which shall conform to the same principles as laid down for civil procedures. It seems obvious, however, that there is a clear preference for civil measures.[75]

Section 3 of Part III also relates to civil enforcement since it regulates, in a single article, precautionary measures.[76] It must be noted that other international agreements regulating provisional measures, particularly trade agreements, include precautionary measures in the civil enforcement section and do not create an independent section as the TRIPS Agreement does. In fact, the TRIPS Agreement is also somewhat original in the sense that the articles set forth in Sections 2 and 3 do not appear in the sequence of civil procedure. In daily litigation practice, precautionary measures are granted before a decision on the merits has been adopted, thus before the award of a permanent injunction and the adoption of a decision on damages. In the TRIPS Agreement, this order is altered.

Section 4, on border measures, consists of ten articles describing the border situations subject to controls and the intellectual property rights categories that must or may be controlled.[77] Importantly, Section 4 also alludes to the applicable law to decide on the infringing status of imported products as well as to the administrative procedures that need to be implemented in the context of border measures. As Chapters 10, 11 and 12 of this book explore, this regime has given place to crucial changes in domestic legal orders and bears a close relation with trade-related objectives as well as human rights protection.

Finally, Section 5, on criminal measures, contains just a single article, which prescribes that wilful trademark counterfeiting or copyright piracy on a commercial

[73] *See* Articles 43.1, 44.1, 45.1, 46, 47, 48.1, 50.1, 50.2, 50.3, 50.7, 53.1, 56, 59 TRIPS Agreement.

[74] *See* also Articles 44.2, 45.2, 47, 48.1, 51, 50.5, 57 and 60 TRIPS Agreement.

[75] *See* Heath and Cotter (2015), p. 10.

[76] *See* Chapter 9, Section III.1.

[77] *See* Chapter 10, Section II.1.

scale shall be the object of criminal sanctions.[78] Again, this book explores in depth how this obligation, as well as the obligations set forth in ulterior treaties expanding the reach of criminal enforcement, closely interacts with public order, fundamental rights and national sovereignty.

2.2 General Obligations Concerning Enforcement

The first section of Part III of the TRIPS Agreement, on general obligations, incorporates crucial articles shaping the implementation of all enforcement-related provisions in the Agreement. Article 41, on general obligations, is particularly important since it clarifies the goals and sets out the principles for the interpretation and implementation of the entire Part III. Several sub-sections of Article 41 have been transplanted to numerous plurilateral and bilateral agreements.[79]

2.2.1 THE DEMAND FOR EFFECTIVENESS. The 'primary obligation'[80] of WTO Members in the area of enforcement is to set up effective methods for the enforcement of intellectual property rights. This is the commitment undertaken by WTO Members in Article 41.1 of the TRIPS Agreement, which requires the availability of enforcement procedures and remedies so as to permit the prevention of and effective action against infringement.

Whether this is an obligation of result or an obligation of means has been the subject of debate. While some claim that WTO Members must ensure the effectiveness of remedies and underline that both effectiveness and deterrence are prescriptive outcomes,[81] others hold that the TRIPS Agreement requires implementing mechanisms and remedies for the enforcement of intellectual property as mandated by the treaty.[82] In this line of reasoning, it has been held that the enforcement provisions of the TRIPS Agreement are 'institution-oriented, not outcome-oriented'.[83]

When the WTO Panel in the *China – Intellectual Property Rights* case addressed a claim relating to effectiveness, it sustained that effectiveness at least implies the existence of the measures and remedies enshrined in the TRIPS Agreement. The WTO Panel underlined that Part III of the Agreement 'includes a multilaterally-agreed minimum set of enforcement procedures that Members must make available to right holders against any infringement of intellectual property rights'.[84] It further considered that '[w]here a Member chooses to make available other procedures' for the enforcement of intellectual property rights or other policies, 'that policy choice does not diminish the Member's obligation under Article

[78] *See* Chapter 13.

[79] This is interesting because the transplanted sub-section have their origin in the North American Free Trade Agreement. In this sense, compare Article 41 of the TRIPS Agreement with Article 1714 of the NAFTA FTA and EIA (1994). *See* Chapter 6.

[80] *See* Abbott (2004b), p. 427. [81] *See* Smith (1996), pp. 46–45. [82] *See* Correa (2007), p. 412.

[83] *See* Brewster (2011), p. 31. [84] *See* WTO Panel, *China – Intellectual Property Rights*, para. 7.180.

41.1 of the TRIPS Agreement to ensure that enforcement procedures as specified in Part III are available'.[85]

Overall, the words of the WTO Panel reinforce the view holding that enforcement provisions of the TRIPS Agreement enshrine commitments of a different nature and content and that most of the time the emphasis is on the tools rather than on specific results. In some cases the provisions of the Agreement lay down clear and immediately enforceable mandates, while in other cases the text is open and the possibilities for implementation are many. It is important to keep in mind that the TRIPS Agreement was not conceived as a tool to ensure full harmonization and homogeneous implementation of enforcement obligations. On the contrary, it is an instrument that lays down minimum standards and commits parties to an overall satisfactory level of intellectual property enforcement.[86] That is, the obligations in the TRIPS Agreement 'have been formulated rather as requirements that certain results be possible, rather than mandating the outcome of actions'.[87]

2.2.2 THE TRIPS AGREEMENT AND RESOURCE-RELATED CONCERNS. Article 41.1 of the TRIPS Agreement must be read in light of the private nature of intellectual property rights[88] and in conjunction with Article 41.5, which states that nothing in the Agreement 'creates any obligation with respect to the distribution of resources as between enforcement of intellectual property rights and enforcement of law in general'.[89] The latter resulted from a proposal put forward by India[90] and is commonly regarded as a concession made to developing countries,[91] which wanted to contextualize the new obligations in the broader framework of general law enforcement[92] and preempt demands for resources to set up specialized courts or strengthen intellectual property enforcement.[93]

This provision is frequently invoked in policy-related forums, under the general understanding that it 'should temper IPR owners' expectations'.[94] Developing countries invoke Article 41.5, since they see in it a justification of the priority given to laws and policies addressing more urgent needs.[95] In this sense, the WTO Panel report in *China – Intellectual Property Rights* case has been interpreted as giving meaningful impact to this article as a justification for non-compliance. Whereas the WTO Panel made clear that it does not establish a general permission to infringe, it stated that

85 *Ibid.* 86 *See* Bronckers, Verkade and McNelis (2000), p. 14. 87 *Ibid.*, p. 15.

88 *See* Chapter 1, Section II.3 and Section III.2. 89 *See* as well Article 2.2 ACTA.

90 *See* GATT (1989), p. 3, para. 4(e). *See* also Dreier (1996), p. 261.

91 *See* Stewart (1993), p. 541; UNCTAD-ICTSD (2005), p. 585; Correa (2007), p. 417.

92 *See* Watal (2010), p. 337. 93 *See* Yu (2011a), p. 326. 94 *See* Trainer (2008), p. 51.

95 For instance, the Chinese delegate to the TRIPS Council stated in 2010 that 'the TRIPS Agreement was clear about resource allocation, and gave due consideration to the limited resources of developing country governments to enforce IPR laws relative to other laws which might call for more urgent priority. Article 41.5 was cognisant of the capacity constraints of Members and therefore created no obligation with the respect to distribution of resources as between the enforcement of IPRs and the enforcement of law in general.' *See* WTO Council for Trade-Related Aspects of Intellectual Property Rights (2010), para. 266.

'Article 41.5 is an important provision in the overall balance of rights and obligations in Part III of the TRIPS Agreement'.[96]

In our view, however, Article 41.5 does not provide a safe haven to countries with resource constraints. In fact, the WTO Panel report *China – Intellectual Property Rights* noted that the Article refers to the deployment of resources for enforcement of intellectual property rights, but does not impact on or detract from the standard set for enforcement in any particular provision.[97] The WTO Panel seems to disentangle resource considerations and fulfilment of the norms. This is particularly important in light of the manifold economic implications of enforcement norms, including the considerable expense required for their implementation.[98] Fulfilling this obligation while simultaneously making use of the right to not modify the distribution of resources seems difficult to reconcile.[99]

2.2.3 FAIR TRIAL STANDARDS. Enforcement provisions in the TRIPS Agreement set up 'minimum standards of due process'[100] that crystallize general principles of law,[101] such as general principles on judicial procedure widely accepted in domestic legal orders. Inherent components of the right to a fair trial mentioned in Articles 41 and 42 include the right to a reasoned sentence in writing, the right to a procedure and sentence within reasonable time limit, the right to affordable procedures, the right to be heard, the right to a review, the right to a timely and detailed written notice, the right to representation by independent legal counsel and the right to procedures without burdensome requirements concerning mandatory personal appearances. That is, a very complete charter touching upon due process standards.

Article 41.2 of the Agreement establishes that remedies and procedures must be 'fair and equitable' and prescribes that 'they shall not be unnecessarily costly, or entail unreasonable time limits or unwarranted delays'. This is, in fact, a provision already found in the 1994 North American Free Trade Agreement.[102] It lays down fundamental due process principles that may have decisive effects on adjusting enforcement procedures to the requirements resulting from the right to a fair trial.[103] In particular, it sets forth the principles of equity and fairness in enforcement procedures, which apply to all parties in a dispute.[104]

Something similar occurs with respect to Article 41.3 of the TRIPS Agreement, which specifies further the right to a fair trial in the context of intellectual property enforcement and introduces the right to be heard. This construction, also easily traceable in the North American Free Trade Agreement,[105] establishes that decisions on the merits of a case shall preferably be in writing and reasoned, made

96 *See* WTO Panel, *China – Intellectual Property Rights*, para. 7.594. 97 *See* Watal (2010), p. 610.
98 *See* Chapter 3, Section IV.2. 99 *See* Seuba (2013a), pp. 417–418.
100 *See* Reichman and Lange (1998), p. 34. 101 *See* Blakeney (2004b), p. 7.
102 *See* Article 1714.2 NAFTA FTA and EIA (1994). 103 *See* Chapter 2, Section III.2.
104 *See* UCTAD-ICTSD (2005), p. 582; Straus (2000), p. 811; Heath (2005), p. 12.
105 *See* Article 1714.3 NAFTA FTA and EIA (1994).

available to the Parties without undue delay and based only on evidence in respect of which Parties were offered the opportunity to be heard.

The TRIPS Agreement also enshrines the right to a review. Pursuant to Article 41.4, 'Parties to a proceeding shall have an opportunity for review by a judicial authority' of both final administrative decisions and initial judicial decisions on the merits of a case, the latter at least as regards 'the legal aspects of initial judicial decisions on the merits of a case. However, there shall be no obligation to provide an opportunity for review of acquittals in criminal cases.'

In respect to civil enforcement, guarantees that integrate the right to fair trial are complemented with the text of Article 42. This is a particularly important article for alleged infringers, since it recognizes the right to a timely and detailed written notice, to representation by independent legal counsel and to procedures without 'burdensome requirements concerning mandatory personal appearances'. It also orders that all parties must be 'entitled to substantiate their claims and to present all relevant evidence'. Likewise, it orders the protection of confidential information. The language used in Article 42 makes non-derogable the standards set forth therein.[106]

2.2.4 OBJECTIVES AND PRINCIPLES OF THE TRIPS AGREEMENT. The general provisions and basic principles of the TRIPS Agreement impact on Part III of the Agreement. The potential of Articles 7 and 8 of the Agreement is vast and it has been explored in great depth by doctrine[107] as well as by some WTO case law.[108] Moreover, these articles are repeatedly quoted in policy statements in multilateral fora,[109] mostly by developing countries[110] and in some intellectual property chapters of PTAs.[111]

Although some caution must be expressed concerning their practical impact, the principles and objectives enshrined in Articles 7 and 8 are relevant for enforcement-related obligations. This is particularly the case for references made in Article 7 to the link between intellectual property enforcement and the promotion of technological innovation, the transfer and dissemination of technology, the mutual advantage of producers and users, social and economic welfare, and the balance of rights and obligations. As it has been noted, this text 'essentially captured centuries of past legislative evolution at the national level'.[112] The reference made to taking equally into account the legitimate interests of intellectual property owners and those of their competitors should be especially meaningful in the area of enforcement.[113]

106 *See* Section 2.2.5. 107 *See* Grosse Ruse-Khan (2008a); Yu (2009b);.

108 *See* WTO Dispute Settlement Panel, *Canada – Patent Protection of Pharmaceutical Products*, WT/DS114/R, 17 March 2000, para. 7.26, stating that the goals and limitations stated in Articles 7 and 8.1 must be borne in mind when interpreting Article 30 of the TRIPS Agreement on exceptions.

109 *See* Recommendation 45 WIPO (2007a).

110 *See* Request for Consultations by India, *European Union and a Member State – Seizure of Generic Drugs in Transit*, WT/DS408/1, 19 May 2010, p. 3.

111 *See* Article 139.2 EU-CARIFORUM States FTA and EIA (2008); Article 195 EU-Colombia and Peru FTA and EIA (2013).

112 Taubman (2011), p. 11. 113 *See* Straus (2000), p. 808.

In this last regard, the account to the principle of equality of arms and, therefore, to the guarantees of the right to a fair trial seems clear.[114]

2.2.5 IS THE TRIPS AGREEMENT THE LIMIT TO FURTHER STRENGTHENING ENFORCEMENT? The TRIPS Agreement has been commonly considered an agreement that lays down minimum standards of protection and enforcement.[115] Its *de minimis* nature is confirmed by Article 1.1, which states that 'Members may, but shall not be obliged to, implement in their law more extensive protection'. Treaties and national provisions strengthening the protection of intellectual property have been justified pursuant to this article. In the specific area of enforcement, Part III of the TRIPS Agreement is recognized as the basis and reference point for international treaties that followed.[116]

Almost a decade ago, however, it started to be widely recognized that the TRIPS Agreement not only lays down minimum standards of protection but, in some cases, also specifies maximum levels of protection, also in the area of enforcement.[117] This is evident in the last phrase of Article 1.1, which establishes that increased protection is possible 'provided that such protection does not contravene the provisions of this Agreement'. This has been the point of departure for the view that sees the TRIPS Agreement as an agreement prescribing the 'ceiling' of protection and not only the floor.[118] Pursuant to this view, whenever a provision of the TRIPS Agreement is drafted in mandatory terms, it should be read as limiting further regulation that would strengthen the level of protection set forth. Nevertheless, provisions in bilateral and plurilateral agreements oblige to either think otherwise or to conclude that this prohibition is circumvented. The abundance of open terms, permissive provisions and ambiguous wording in the TRIPS Agreement facilitates the emergence of new norms that avoid clear conflicts with mandatory provisions in the treaty. Whereas the avoidance of direct normative conflicts is thus frequent, conflicts do exist in certain cases, both in substantive and enforcement-related domains.[119]

2.2.6 INTELLECTUAL PROPERTY PROTECTION AND FREE TRADE. The Preamble of the TRIPS Agreement compels WTO Members to 'ensure that measures and procedures to enforce intellectual property rights do not themselves become barriers to legitimate trade'. This reference is reiterated in the context of enforcement norms and

[114] *See* Chapter 2, Section III.2. [115] *See* Reichman (1995), p. 345.

[116] *See* Reinbothe (2010), p. 5. [117] *See* Pires de Carvalho (2002), p. 32.

[118] Former WTO Director General Pascal Lamy noted that while the TRIPS Agreement does not preclude its Members from introducing additional measures to protect intellectual property, such protection cannot contravene the Agreement. *See* letter from Pascal Lamy, Director General of the World Trade Organization to EU Parliament Members, 4 May 2010, available at: http://keionline.org/sites/default/files/WTO-Lamy_Answer-to-MEP-letter.pdf (last accessed October 2016). For a doctrinal elaboration of the TRIPS Agreement as a treaty establishing ceilings, *see* Yu (2006), p. 402; Dinwoodie (2006b), p. 214; Kur and Grosse Ruse-Khan (2008); Grosse Ruse-Khan (2011), pp. 653–657.

[119] *See* Chapter 9, Section IV.3, for a specific case of normative conflict and Chapter 11 for a broader case of conflictive relations between free trade and intellectual property protection.

procedures, since Article 41.1 of the Agreement announces that enforcement procedures 'shall be applied in such a manner as to avoid the creation of barriers to legitimate trade and to provide for safeguards against their abuse'. As it has been underlined, several provisions of the TRIPS Agreement 'contain binding language which sets out general principles upholding procedural guarantees for the defendant or preventing the creation of trade barriers, as well as specific obligations limiting enforcement measures'.[120] These references have proven to be instrumental in the context of controversies relating to the strengthening of some intellectual property standards or the expansive interpretation of already existing standards. One of the clearest cases is that of border measures relating to intellectual property protected goods, namely the restriction of the transit of patented products invoking the manufacturing fiction.[121] Enforcement procedures can also be used abusively, for instance to 'interfere with time-sensitive sales'[122] and therefore contradict both free trade principles and the prohibition of abusive use of enforcement mechanisms.

3 *The WIPO Internet Treaties*

The World Intellectual Property Organization's 1996 Copyright Treaty and Performances and Phonograms Treaty are commonly known as the 'WIPO Internet treaties'. The TRIPS Agreement was outdated in this particular domain as soon as it entered into force, since it did not address enforcement on the Internet. The WIPO Internet treaties had been negotiated in parallel to the conclusion of the TRIPS Agreement,[123] were adopted just one year after the TRIPS Agreement and entered into force in 2002. Since then, PTAs[124] and regional treaties[125] have actively promoted the adoption of WIPO Internet treaties and have expanded on the obligations set forth therein, in particular regarding digital enforcement.

The WIPO Internet treaties require States to 'ensure that enforcement procedures are available under their law so as to permit effective action against any act of infringement of rights covered by this Treaty, including expeditious remedies to prevent infringements and remedies which constitute a deterrent to further infringements'.[126] These treaties codified the first attempts to respond to online infringement of intellectual property rights, in particular copyright, which were made by means of technological protection measures against unauthorized access and copying as well as electronic rights management information.[127] The technological protection measures and electronic

120 *See* Kur and Grosse Ruse-Khan (2011), p. 381.

121 *See* Chapter 11.

122 Therefore also contrary to Article 41.1 of the TRIPS Agreement. *See* Heath and Cotter (2015), p 11.

123 *See* Reinbothe and von Lewinski (2002).

124 *See* for instance EU-Chile FTA and EIA (2003/2005); EU-CARIFORUM States FTA and EIA (2008).

125 *See* Article 10, Convention on Cybercrime (2001).

126 *See* Article 14.2 WCT and Article 23.2 WPPT.

127 According to WIPO 'the answer to the machine is in the machine'. This 'answer' to the problems raised by the 'machine' – by the computer and the related elements of information and telecommunication technologies – 'consists in technological protection measures (such as encryption of the

rights management information are usually jointly referred to as digital rights management;[128] however, they 'raise different legal issues', and the WIPO Internet treaties regulate them separately.[129] In any case, the WIPO Internet treaties only order States to adopt legal protection and effective legal remedies on technological measures[130] and electronic rights management information,[131] but they do not mandate detailed legal remedies or enforcement mechanisms relating to domestic implementation.

3.1 Technological Protection Measures

Article 11 of the WCT and Article 18 of the WPPT require States to provide 'adequate legal protection' and 'effective legal remedies' for technological measures. It has been generally implied that an 'adequate' level of protection refers to a balanced set of rules, in the sense that the protection should take into account both right holders' rights and the public interests at stake, since such a balance impacts on the scope and mechanisms of protection and the exceptions and limitations available.[132] In relation to the means to guarantee 'effective legal remedies' against circumvention of technological protection measures, States can implement civil and criminal measures as well as provisional and border measures.[133]

Article 11 of the WCT applies in respect to literary and artistic works, and Article 18 WPPT in relation to phonograms (sound recordings) and performances (related rights). As noted by Mihaly Ficsor, these obligations 'only apply to works, performances and phonograms protected under the two Internet Treaties', but naturally not 'to works, performances and phonograms which have fallen into the public domain'.[134]

There is controversy as to whether the protection provided by the WIPO Internet treaties covers acts of circumvention only or if it also covers the so-called 'preparatory acts'.[135] While at a first glance the text seems to refer just to the protection against acts of circumvention,[136] many interpret the relevant norms in the sense that 'the obligation to provide for "adequate protection" under Article 11 WCT would seem to require that rightholders enjoy protection also against *preparatory acts* on top of protection against the acts of circumvention themselves'.[137]

protected material) and electronic rights management information (such as digital identifiers) to be included in the "machine."' *See* WIPO (2003), pp. 215–216.

128 *See* Ficsor (2010), pp. 257–258. 129 *Ibid.* 130 *See* Article 11 WCT and Article 18 WPPT.

131 *See* Article 12 WCT and Article 19 WPPT.

132 *See* Reinbothe and von Lewinski (2015), pp. 143–145. *See* also Ficsor (2010), p. 287 *et seq.*

133 *See* WIPO (2003), p. 218. *See* also Hinze (2016), p. 792. 134 *See* Ficsor (2010), p. 293.

135 Meaning 'manufacturing and distribution of devices which permit or facilitate circumvention'. *See* Reinbothe and von Lewinski (2015), p. 144.

136 *See* also Hinze (2016), p. 785.

137 *See* Reinbothe and von Lewinski (2015), p. 144. *See* also WIPO (2003), pp. 217–218; Ficsor (2010), pp. 259 *et seq.*; Ricketson and Ginsburg (2006), p. 977. Nevertheless, for a comment that 'there does not appear to be any *legal* necessity for interpreting Article 11 to require this conclusion', *see* Hinze (2016), p. 786 (emphasis in the original).

While the WCT and WPPT provisions include 'copy-control' technological protection measures, whether 'access-control' technological protection measures are likewise shielded is open to question.[138] An argument against such inclusion is that the word 'access' does not appear in the WCT, WPPT or Berne Convention. Therefore, there would be no legal basis to 'creating a new and potentially very broad exclusive right, with full economic status'.[139] Others, however, consider that the WIPO Internet treaties require protection of access-control technological measures because this type of legal coverage adequately protects reproduction rights of the authors as provided by the Berne Convention, and it further establishes reproduction and communication rights as under the WCT.[140]

One significant element in relation to the technological protection measures of the WIPO Internet treaties is the commonly known as the 'digital lock'.[141] It has been noted that the 'dire scene presupposes that works will no longer be available in non-protected formats, which may not soon be likely, but for works that are 'digital original', it is at least conceivable'.[142] The experience of national implementation and interpretation of technological protection measures provided by the WIPO Internet treaties,[143] as well as the growing number of countries urged to adopt them in the context of trade agreements, make the implications of 'digital locks' a real scenario.

3.2 Rights Management Information

Article 12 of the WCT and Article 19 of the WPPT provide obligations of States in relation to rights management information, starting with the obligation to provide for 'adequate and effective legal remedies',[144] including civil and administrative remedies, provisional measures, and criminal penalties. Parties must adopt adequate rules to ban the acts sanctioned under these provisions and also effective legal remedies if a violation of such ban occurs.[145] In this context 'adequate' has been interpreted to involve a balanced approach between the 'strength and consequences of the remedy, on the one hand, and the importance and consequences of the act

138 Access-control refers to 'those TPMs which protect works and objects of related rights against unauthorized access', while copy-control refers to TPMs protecting works and objects of related rights against unauthorized copying. *See* Ficsor (2010), p. 265. Examples consist in copy-controls on CDs, region coding on DVDs, and access-controls on electronic books. *See* Geist (2010a), p. 205.

139 *See* Hinze (2016), p. 789.

140 *See* Hinze (2016), pp. 789–790; Ricketson and Ginsburg (2006), pp. 975, 978; Reinbothe and von Lewinski (2015), pp. 143, 145; Ficsor (2010), pp. 264 *et seq.*

141 Term employed to describe the downside effect of implementing technological protection measures. For example, one author simply defines 'digital locks' as 'technological measures that can be used to restrict access to, and use of copyright works'. *See* Hinze (2016), p. 780.

142 *See* Ricketson and Ginsburg (2006), p. 981. *See* also Hinze (2016), more generally. For a different opinion on the risk of 'digital locks', *see* Ficsor (2010), pp. 295 *et seq.*

143 *See* Hinze (2016).

144 *See* Article 12.1 of the WCT and Article 19.1 of the WPPT.

145 *See* WIPO (2003), p. 220.

sanctioned'[146] by the WIPO Internet treaties, on the other hand. With respect to the demand of effectiveness of legal remedies, similarly nuanced comments can be made as with respect to the TRIPS Agreement.[147]

The acts prohibited by Article 12.1 of the WCT and Article 19.1 of the WPPT are 'to remove or alter any electronic rights management information without authority' and 'to distribute import for distribution, broadcast or communicate [or make available] to the public, without authority, works or copies of works [performances, copies of fixed performances or phonograms] knowing that electronic rights management information has been removed or altered without authority'.[148] The definition of rights management information provided in Articles 12.2 and 19.2 includes reference to linking the prohibition of the acts involved to copyright infringement, which is different from Article 11 of the WCT and Article 18 of the WPPT, where the question if a nexus between technological protection measures and copyright infringement is required has given place to different implementation in national systems.[149]

WIPO Internet treaties articles on rights management information carry an 'agreed statement', which is meant to clarify the scope of the provisions and to confirm that formalities are prohibited under the respective provisions. In relation to the scope of provisions, it is stated that 'any right covered by this Treaty' incorporates both 'exclusive rights and rights of remuneration'.[150] The second sentence of the agreed statement explains that the implementation of Article 12 of the WCT and Article 19 WPPT must not violate the principle formulated under the Berne Convention that 'the enjoyment and the exercise of ... rights shall not be subject to any formality'.

III PLURILATERAL AGREEMENTS

1 *The Anti-Counterfeiting Trade Agreement*

1.1 Content of the Anti-Counterfeiting Trade Agreement

The Anti-Counterfeiting Trade Agreement[151] is a plurilateral treaty on international and national enforcement of intellectual property rights negotiated between a closed group of nations and signed in 2011.[152] The ratification of the Agreement was

146 *See* Reinbothe and von Lewinski (2015), p. 181.

147 *See* Section II.2.2.1. *See* also Reinbothe and von Lewinski (2015), p. 181.

148 These acts must be performed with knowledge, 'that is, mere inadvertent acts are not covered', or with reasonable ground to know. *See* WIPO (2003), p. 221.

149 *See* Hinze (2016), pp. 790–791.

150 *See* footnote 10 to Article 12.2 WCT and footnote 16 to Article 19.2 WPPT.

151 The content of Sections 1, 2 and 3 of Part III of this chapter is based on Seuba (2015a) and Seuba (2015b).

152 On 1 October 2011, in Tokyo, eight representatives of the negotiating countries signed ACTA, namely Australia, Canada, Japan, Republic of Korea, Morocco, New Zealand, Republic of Singapore and the

however rejected by the European Parliament in 2012, a rebuff that in practical terms meant the end of ACTA as standalone international treaty. Nevertheless, ACTA erected the most complete international regime on intellectual property enforcement developed so far, and the provisions set forth therein heavily influence intellectual property enforcement standards adopted in other plurilateral and bilateral agreements.

ACTA is not concerned with trade or trademarks, as the name suggests. Instead, it is the only international treaty ever adopted with an exclusive focus on intellectual property enforcement, and more particularly on the enforcement of all intellectual property rights that are the subject of Sections 1 through 7 of the TRIPS Agreement. The wording of ACTA becomes particularly relevant given its unique scope and influence on other international agreements.

The proposed 'new international standard for intellectual property enforcement'[153] includes a preamble and six chapters, the first two of which are subdivided into sections. The Preamble and Chapter I announce the objectives and some basic understandings. The initial provisions address the relationships between ACTA and other international agreements, the possibility and conditions to increase the levels of protection, the applicability of the objectives and principles of the TRIPS Agreement and the protection of information held by public authorities.[154] The section on definitions, consisting of a single article, is particularly important because in many respects it defines the scope of the Agreement.

Chapter II of ACTA forms the core of the treaty. It regulates the legal framework for enforcement of intellectual property rights and includes sections on general obligations, civil enforcement, border measures, criminal enforcement and enforcement in the digital environment. The section on general obligations has been heavily modelled upon the corresponding articles of the TRIPS Agreement, except for the fact that a number of guarantees in favour of the alleged infringer have vanished in ACTA.

The second section of Chapter II enshrines specific civil enforcement remedies, together with the general obligation to make available civil judicial procedures.[155] Members are to make available injunctions to compel alleged infringers to desist from the infringement and to prevent infringing goods from entering into the channels of commerce, a power extended to acts performed by third parties. In line with the TRIPS Agreement, ACTA limits the power of injunctions in case of governmental use or use by third parties authorized by a government. In these cases, Parties may limit the remedies to the payment of monetary compensation.

United States. The European Union and 22 of its Member States (Austria, Belgium, Bulgaria, the Czech Republic, Denmark, Finland, France, Greece, Hungary, Ireland, Italy, Latvia, Lithuania, Luxembourg, Malta, Poland, Portugal, Romania, Slovenia, Spain, Sweden and the United Kingdom) signed the treaty on 26 January 2012, and the United Mexican States signed on 12 July 2012.

[153] *See* Kaminski (2011), p. 387. [154] *See* Articles 1–4 ACTA.

[155] Parties may exclude patents and protection of undisclosed information from the scope of this section.

ACTA establishes that judicial authorities will have the authority to order infringers to pay damages to right holders. In awarding damages, judicial authorities shall have the authority to consider any legitimate measure of value submitted by the right holder, which is indeed a controversial criterion.[156] The article on damages also requires the availability of pre-established damages, presumptions and additional damages at least for infringement of copyright and related rights and for cases of trademark counterfeiting. In a related context, ACTA confirms the right to order the destruction of the goods without compensation as well as the destruction or disposal outside channels of commerce of materials and implements used to manufacture or create the infringing goods.[157]

Article 11 deals with the obligation of the infringer or the alleged infringer to provide information, while Article 12 establishes that judicial authorities must have the authority to order provisional measures against an alleged infringer or a third party within its jurisdiction to prevent goods from entering the stream of commerce and to preserve evidence.

Section 3 regulates border measures and allows Parties to exclude patents and undisclosed information.[158] A general prohibition of 'unjust' discrimination between intellectual property rights is laid down, which conversely means that Parties are not barred from some types of 'justified' discrimination. The most important provision in this section is probably Article 16, which requires States to control import and export shipments either *ex parte* or *ex officio*, and permits (but does not oblige) them to maintain procedures regarding goods in transit.[159] The section on border measures also regulates the provision of information and the possibility to require a security or assurance, both to prevent abuse and to protect the defendant and the authorities.

Section 4 deals with criminal measures and, like the TRIPS Agreement, it requires that criminal procedures and penalties be made available at least in cases of wilful trademark counterfeiting and copyright piracy.[160] The most important feature is the redefinition of the 'commercial scale' requirement for the applicability of criminal measures, to include at least acts carried out as commercial activities 'for direct or indirect economic or commercial advantage'.[161] ACTA also expands criminalization when it obliges Parties to sanction the wilful importation and domestic use of labels or packaging to which a mark has been applied without authorization and which is intended to be used in the course of trade on goods or services for which the trademark is registered.

Section 5 deals specifically with enforcement of intellectual property rights in the digital environment. Article 27.1 obliges Parties to make available civil and criminal enforcement procedures against acts of infringement taking place in the digital context. It is, therefore, a major change with respect to the TRIPS Agreement and

156 *See* Chapter 9, Section III.2.1. 157 *Ibid.* 158 *See* Chapter 10, Section III.1.2.

159 *See* Chapter 10, Section III.1.1. 160 *See* Chapter 13, Section II.

161 This is indeed an important and controversial change. *See* Chapter 13, Section III.1.

also with respect to PTAs. Section 5 also sets forth the obligation to provide adequate legal protection and effective remedies against the use of anti-circumvention devices of technological measures used to protect works. It also alludes to electronic rights management information, requiring protection against copyright or related rights infringement by removing or altering rights management information or the public dissemination of works from which rights management information has been removed or altered.

Chapters III, IV and V of ACTA include articles devoted to relations between States. They concern the enforcement of intellectual property rights but are not designed to rule relationships between private parties. To the contrary, they establish how States can collaborate to foster the enforcement of intellectual property rights and how the Agreement will be monitored as well as how ACTA itself will be governed.

1.2 ACTA in Relation to the TRIPS Agreement

From a normative point of view, ACTA has two notable characteristics. First, in relation to civil, criminal and border enforcement it incorporates the obligations set forth in the TRIPS Agreement but remains silent on the many instances where the TRIPS Agreement regulates the rights of alleged infringers.[162] Second, the ACTA strengthens the standards of protection for right holders and creates new rights in areas not specifically regulated in the TRIPS Agreement, such as the digital environment.

Several provisions of ACTA go beyond the TRIPS Agreement. In the area of civil enforcement, this is also the case of injunctions, which pursuant to ACTA would apply to both imports and exports instead of imports only,[163] as well as the case of calculation of damages.[164] There are also fundamental differences in key definitions[165] and in the perspective adopted with regard to several situations. For instance, ACTA advances the moment of action when it refers to 'alleged infringer' instead of 'infringer' and 'suspect goods' instead of 'infringing goods'.[166] Similarly, several mandatory provisions in ACTA are merely optional in the TRIPS Agreement.

For many, the most disturbing provisions in ACTA are those relating to criminal measures, mainly because of their difficult compatibility with due process standards

162 There are many examples in this sense. For instance, the rules on the search and seizure of alleged infringing goods or the silence with respect to the right of the alleged infringer to be heard and to be given notice enshrined in the TRIPS Agreement.

163 Compare Article 8 ACTA and Article 44.1 TRIPS Agreement.

164 Compare Article 9 ACTA and Article 24.1 TRIPS Agreement. *See* Chapter 9.

165 This is a noticeable for instance in respect to the definitions contained in Chapter I of ACTA relating to 'counterfeit trademark goods' and 'pirated copyright goods'.

166 Compare Article 11 ACTA and Article 47 TRIPS Agreement as well as Article 25 ACTA and Article 49 TRIPS Agreement.

and the principle of legality.[167] In addition to criminal enforcement, border enforcement is also an area of tension. The sections on border measures in the TRIPS Agreement and ACTA diverge in important respects. For instance, ACTA's section on border measures does not solely mention counterfeit and pirated goods as its mandatory target but applies as well to goods infringing any intellectual property rights except patents and data protection. Moreover, it introduces an ambiguous definition of 'commercial scale', particularly controversial in light of the WTO jurisprudence.[168]

1.3 General Obligations of ACTA

Chapter I of ACTA addresses fundamental issues and shapes the scope and the interpretation of the entire treaty. Despite their importance, the implications of the six articles that make up Chapter I are not entirely clear. Some of the provisions merely transplant twin provisions of the TRIPS Agreement and, together with them, some doubts and questions. Not all the links originally made by the norms transplanted from the TRIPS Agreement have been incorporated into ACTA, something that further contributes to speculation, particularly with regard to the most ambiguous provisions.

Article 1 of ACTA contains an important conflict clause of subordination[169] stating that nothing in ACTA 'shall derogate from any obligation of a Party with respect to any other Party under existing agreements, including the TRIPS Agreement'. This conflict clause raises significant doubts, such as which agreements ACTA does not derogate from and what happens with provisions that only enshrine rights but not obligations as well as potential conflicts between agreements concluded between ACTA and non-ACTA Members. The answer to these questions illustrates the potentially broad reach of this article. First, all international agreements, and not only those on intellectual property, may be affected by this subordination clause. Second, the mandate to respect previous 'obligations' and the silence with respect to previous 'rights' concern inter-State relations, not private ones. Moreover, it has to be read under the main obligation found in many treaties and a basic principle of international law, *pacta sunt servanda*, which refers both to rights and obligations. Finally, the limitation of the conflict clause to relations between ACTA Members acts as an 'incentive to become a Member of the ACTA club. In effect, if an explicit treaty guarantee of no supersession is sought, becoming a Member of ACTA would be the only way of guaranteeing it."[170]

167 *See* Chapter 2 and Chapter 13, Section III.1. 168 *See* Chapter 10.

169 This clause falls within the third category of conflict clauses that the International Law Commission distinguished in 2006, namely 'clauses in the subsequent treaty providing that it 'shall not affect' the earlier treaty'. *See* International Law Commission (2006b), pp. 135–138. This is a category that may be understood as an evolution to those clauses identified in 1952 by Aufricht: clauses contained in the later treaty declaring that 'it is not at variance with the letter or spirit of an earlier treaty'. *See* Aufricht (1952), p. 657.

170 *See* Seuba (2015a), p. 49.

Article 2 of ACTA announces important principles with regard to the obligations undertaken, the implementation of the provisions of the Agreement and the resource implications deriving from enforcement commitments. It also transplants the objectives and principles of the TRIPS Agreement to ACTA.

First phrase of Article 2.1 – '[e]ach Party shall give effect to the provisions of this Agreement' – codifies the *pacta sunt servanda* principle. As is the case in the TRIPS Agreement, there is no specific indication of how ACTA obligations must be fulfilled. Parties are free to determine the appropriate method for implementing the provisions of the treaty, and while both the direct invocation of the Agreement and its domestic reception would be acceptable, the provisions of ACTA generally favour national implementation. In any case, the freedom to determine the appropriate method of implementation does not allow the adoption of a lower standard, as WTO case law shows,[171] nor does it exclude the implementation from being scrutinized.[172] This possibility may become controversial in ACTA, since it lacks a dispute settlement system guaranteeing neutrality and balance. As pointed out by the WTO Panel report in *China – Intellectual Property Rights*, deference to domestic implementation is particularly important in the area of enforcement, where national differences tend to be notable.[173]

Article 2.1 of ACTA sets up an obligation also present in the TRIPS Agreement and other intellectual property treaties:[174] Parties may implement more extensive protection provided that it does not contravene the Agreement. This reminds Parties that ACTA contains minimum standards of protection while allowing them to enact more extensive protection provided it does not contradict the minimum standards established in the treaty.

Article 2.2 of ACTA states that 'nothing in this Agreement creates any obligation with respect to the distribution of resources as between enforcement of intellectual property rights and enforcement of law in general'. The provision parallels Article 41.5 of the TRIPS Agreement. Therefore, the considerations made above with respect to the implications of Article 41.5 of the TRIPS Agreement may apply to ACTA as well.[175] Deference to national choices with regard to resource allocation can also be found in the chapter dealing with international cooperation.[176]

Article 2.3 of ACTA declares that the 'objectives and principles set forth in Part I of the TRIPS Agreement, in particular Articles 7 and 8, shall apply, *mutatis mutandis*, to this Agreement'. This provision could play a key role in the interpretation of ACTA, or it may be merely hortatory, something that depends to a great extent on

171 *See* WTO Panel, *China – Intellectual Property Rights*, para. 7.513. Even stronger, it 'does not permit differences in domestic legal systems and practices to justify any derogation from the basic obligation to give effect to the provisions on enforcement'. *Ibid.*

172 *See* UNCTAD-ICTSD (2005), p. 28.

173 *See* WTO Panel, *China – Intellectual Property Rights*, para. 7.513.

174 *See* Article 1.1 TRIPS Agreement; Article 19 Paris Convention; Article 22 Rome Convention; Article 5.1 Berne Convention.

175 *See* Section II.2.2.2.

176 *See* Article 33.3 ACTA.

the views held by the participants on the effective impact of Articles 7 and 8 of the TRIPS Agreement. Before analysing this question, it should be noted that a number of other principles set forth in Part I of the TRIPS Agreement would be applicable in the context of ACTA as well, namely those relating to national treatment, the most favoured nation treatment and exhaustion of rights.[177]

While the principles and objectives embodied in the TRIPS Agreement have been transplanted into ACTA, the immediate objective of ACTA drafters was to enhance the legal regime for the enforcement of intellectual property rights. However, where ACTA states only in the Preamble that it is aimed at strengthening intellectual property enforcement,[178] all declarations of the drafting States converged on noting that the Agreement's goal was to guarantee proper enforcement of intellectual property rights.[179] Only at a very advanced stage of the negotiations was it deemed necessary to introduce some balancing provisions. In fact, the reference to Articles 7 and 8 of the TRIPS Agreement was included at the last moment, just before the final text was concluded.[180]

One of the corollaries of the general rule of interpretation codified by the Vienna Convention on the Law of Treaties is that interpretation must give meaning and effect to all the terms of a treaty.[181] Accordingly, the goals and principles of the TRIPS Agreement referenced in ACTA form part of the Agreement and must be interpreted in a meaningful way. Articles 7 and 8 of the TRIPS Agreement may in fact be more important in the context of ACTA than in that of the TRIPS Agreement. The reason is simple: in comparison to ACTA, the TRIPS Agreement is a balanced treaty. Numerous provisions of ACTA are drafted in either permissive or ambiguous terms or do not mention other rights and interests at stake. This is the reason why Articles 7 and 8 of the TRIPS Agreement could play a quasi-legislative function in the context of ACTA or in posterior treaties merely copying ACTA provisions.

A relevant area of concern *vis-à-vis* enforcement regulation is the protection of privacy. ACTA establishes that Parties are not required to release information in contradiction with their law or in cases where it would 'be contrary to the public

177 *See* Blakeney (2012), p. 107.

178 Although there are different views as to the practical value of preambles, for many they merely have an interpretative function.

179 *See* a compilation of declarations of Member States in that regard in Seuba (2015a), p. 54.

180 In July 2010, Canada, Australia, New Zealand and Singapore proposed to incorporate the entire text of Articles 7 and 8 of the TRIPS Agreement. In contrast, the United States and Mexico objected mentioning these articles, while the European Union proposed the inclusion of 'some principles' enshrined in these articles in the Preamble of ACTA. In October 2010, the proposal by Canada, Australia, New Zealand and Singapore was substituted by a reference to Articles 7 and 8 of the TRIPS Agreement in Article 2.3 of ACTA.

181 As the WTO Appellate Body has recalled, the interpreter cannot adopt a reading that would result in reducing whole clauses or paragraphs of a treaty to redundancy or inutility. *See* Appellate Body Report, *United States – Standards for Reformulated and Conventional Gasoline*, WT/DS2/AB/R, 20 May 1996, p. 23; Appellate Body Report, *Japan – Taxes on Alcoholic Beverages*, WT/DS8/AB/R, WT/DS10/AB/R, WT/DS11/AB/R, 1 November 1996, p. 11; Appellate Body Report, *United States – Section 211 Omnibus Appropriations Act of* 1998, WT/DS176/AB/R, 2 January 2002, para. 161.

interest', impede law enforcement or 'prejudice the legitimate commercial interests of particular enterprises'. It also establishes an obligation for the Party receiving the information, which constrains the use or disclosure of the information to the purpose for which the information was provided. This is a cross-cutting provision that applies to the entire Agreement and deals with rights and obligations of States but does not apply in the context of private relations.[182] This is the reason why the provisions of ACTA totally or partially addressing private relations contain autonomous references to the precedence of local laws 'governing privilege, the protection of confidentiality of information sources, or the processing of personal data'[183] or their implementation in a manner that 'preserves fundamental principles such as freedom of expression, fair process, and privacy'.[184]

Article 5 enshrines general definitions of terms that later appear throughout the Agreement.[185] This article is critical to understanding the meaning of some provisions and the reach of ACTA.[186] Some of the definitions notably expand the scope of enforcement when compared to the TRIPS Agreement, and as such Article 5 was considered one of the most significant points of departure from existing intellectual property law.[187] The departure is particularly noticeable in the case of the definitions of 'counterfeit trademark goods' and 'pirated copyright goods':[188] while in the TRIPS Agreement the infringing nature is assessed in accordance with the law of the country of importation, in ACTA the relevant law is that of the country where the procedures are invoked.[189]

Article 5(h) does not provide a definition of 'intellectual property' but maintains the reach given to this term by the TRIPS Agreement, which specifies that 'intellectual property' refers to the 'categories of intellectual property that are the subject of Sections 1 through 7 of the Part II'. Although the scope of ACTA and the TRIPS Agreement is apparently the same, the conclusion is rather different. First, 'categories' of intellectual property rights in the TRIPS Agreement should not be confused with the headings of Sections 1 through 7. Instead, they refer to the categories that are the *subject* of those sections, which leads to a different outcome and includes, for instance, *sui generis* plant variety protection. Second, the reference

182 Hence, Article 4 is not a provision that could, for instance, be invoked by an Internet service provider to protect the privacy of Internet users by not providing the data to another private entity, such as a right holders organization.

183 *See* Article 11 ACTA. 184 *See* Article 27 ACTA.

185 However, not all definitions in ACTA are enshrined in Article 5. An important case in point is the definition of 'commercial scale', found in Article 23 and solely affecting Section 4, on criminal enforcement.

186 Since setting up definitions in the initial chapter affects the scope of the entire treaty. For instance, moving the definition of counterfeiting from the section on border measures – where it was in the drafts of ACTA – to the section on initial provisions impacts the reach of the definition, which is not limited to a specific field but applies to the entire Agreement. *See* Kaminski (2011), p. 422.

187 *Ibid.*, p. 387.

188 Included in Articles 5(d) and 5(k) ACTA. *See*, in this same sense, Mercurio (2012), p. 369.

189 *See* Chapter 10, Section III.3.

to the categories of the TRIPS Agreement as the object of application of enforcement norms of ACTA expands the reach of enforcement provisions of the TRIPS Agreement, which are often restricted to specific categories.[190] However, more surprisingly, in some regards ACTA also reduces the scope of protection and does not include some intellectual property rights covered by the TRIPS Agreement and some free trade agreements.[191] Regarding the categories covered in the TRIPS Agreement but eventually not in ACTA, this would be the case of 'utility models' and 'trade names', which are not the *subject of* Sections 1 through 7 of Part II of the TRIPS Agreement but are included in the TRIPS Agreement by its Article 2.1.[192]

2 *The Trans-Pacific Partnership Agreement*

The P4 trading group, set up in 2005 by Chile, Brunei Darussalam, Singapore and New Zealand, was at the origins of the TPP. In 2009 the United States joined the P4 negotiations, followed later on by a larger group of nations with the view of becoming a major trading block.[193] Once negotiations concluded, the TPP became the most sophisticated trade agreement enshrining intellectual property standards, including enforcement standards. However, signed in February 2016, the prospects for successful entry into force in its original form disappeared when President Trump withdrew from the TPP in January 2017.[194] However, as it happens with ACTA, the TPP is basis for future bilateral agreements and the new benchmark for intellectual property negotiations.

Section I of Chapter 18 of the TPP is devoted to the enforcement of intellectual property rights. It includes general principles and detailed articles touching upon civil, criminal and border enforcement measures. It also enshrines important references to enforcement of intellectual property rights in the digital domain. It largely builds upon previous agreements, in particular ACTA and the PTA between the United States and the Republic of Korea. In this regard, even if the TPP sometimes goes beyond these treaties, in some other instances it is more balanced and includes checks and balances that are frequently absent in PTAs. This is particularly the case

190 For instance, while in ACTA patents and trade secrets are excluded from the section on border measures and the rest of categories are included, the TRIPS Agreement only obliges to adopt border measures with respect to piracy and counterfeiting.

191 Utility models are covered for instance in the entire section on enforcement of the EU-CARIFORUM States FTA and EIA (2008) in Article 148, and a provision on criminal enforcement refers also to utility models in Article 121 of the Japan-Indonesia FTA and EIA (2008).

192 *See* also Chapter 10, Section II.1.2.

193 These countries are Australia, Brunei Darussalam, Canada, Chile, Japan, Malaysia, Mexico, New Zealand, Peru, Singapore, the United States and Vietnam.

194 Even if candidates to the US presidential elections of 2016 expressed their dissatisfaction with the TPP, in the majority of cases their concerns were unrelated to the intellectual property chapter and rather focused on aspects they consider to be missing.

of the general provisions, which enshrine a number of guarantees and basic principles missing in PTAs.

Take for instance the case of the references to fair trial and enforcement procedures. In much the same way as ACTA did, and in many respects also reiterating the TRIPS Agreement, the TPP establishes that enforcement procedures shall be fair and equitable, not 'unnecessarily complicated or costly, or entail unreasonable time-limits or unwarranted delays'.[195] This is an improvement over many PTAs, which are silent in this regard. Interestingly, given the scope of the TPP, it also extends fair trial principles to the digital environment.

The article touching upon distribution of resources and intellectual property enforcement confirms what was already agreed upon in ACTA and the TRIPS Agreement and improves a number of PTAs.[196] Essentially, it confirms the latitude that States have when deciding how to allocate resources for the enforcement of intellectual property rights and restates that States are not obliged to create specialized bodies for the enforcement of intellectual property rights.[197] These affirmations may represent an interesting and probably unexpected development, since they seem to contradict PTAs concluded by TPP Members, where it is stated that decisions relating to the allocation of resources do not justify lack of enforcement.[198]

General provisions of the enforcement section of the TPP restate as well some of the 'ceilings' and guarantees set forth in the TRIPS Agreement, in particular that enforcement procedures must 'be applied in such a manner as to avoid the creation of barriers to legitimate trade' and that 'safeguards against their abuse' must be provided.[199] While previous references made to the relevance of the ceilings established in the TRIPS Agreement are also applicable with respect to TPP,[200] the specific significance of the obligation not to create barriers to legitimate trade is analysed in the chapters touching upon border measures.

The influence of ACTA over the TPP is apparent. The provision relating to proportionality is a case in point.[201] In both treaties the reference to proportionality is almost identical and orders States to 'take into account the need for proportionality between the seriousness of the infringement', 'the interests of third parties' and the applicable measures, remedies and penalties.[202] This is an improvement with respect to the TRIPS Agreement, since the proportionality principle in TPP applies

195 *See* Article 18.71.3 TPP. *See* also above previous references to Article 6.2 ACTA and Article 41.2 TRIPS Agreement.

196 Article 18.71.4 of the TPP says that Section I does not oblige 'to put in place a judicial system for the enforcement of intellectual property rights distinct from that for the enforcement of law in general' and does not create obligation 'with respect to the distribution of resources as between the enforcement of intellectual property rights and the enforcement of law in general'. The references already made with respect to Article 41.5 of the TRIPS Agreement and Article 2.2 of ACTA are fully applicable in this respect.

197 *See* Section IV.2.

198 This is the case of Peru, Chile and Singapore. *See* Section IV.2.

199 *See* Article 18.71.1 TPP.

200 *See* Section II.2.2.2.

201 *See* Article 18.71.5 TPP.

202 *See* Seuba (2015b), pp. 71–72.

to all enforcement-related areas, whereas in TRIPS explicit reference to proportionality is just made in the context of civil enforcement.[203]

However, a troubling feature of the TPP and other agreements adopted after the TRIPS Agreement is the lack of reference to the rights and guarantees that protect all parties, not just right holders. As Chapter 6 of this book further develops, there are several, not particularly complex, mechanisms to correct this neglect. However, it is a feature that confirms the description of the TPP and similar agreements as treaties essentially conceived to favour right holders' rights, with little interest in the functioning of the intellectual property system as a whole. In fact, lack of balance can be detected even in articles that in principle would seem an improvement with respect to previous treaties.

Take for instance the case of the article of the TRIPS Agreement that elaborates on several fair trial guarantees that must be applicable in the context of civil procedures.[204] The TPP contains a very general article relating to fair trial. However, it remains silent with respect to the guarantees specifically applicable in the context of civil procedures. Something similar happens with respect to the article ordering to empower judicial authorities to award compensation and payment of legal expenses to the party that has been wrongly enjoined as a result of abuse of enforcement procedures.[205] This is a novelty and a positive feature when compared to ACTA and PTAs. However, when compared to national legal orders the analysis is not so positive. Indeed, national legal orders do not restrict the compensation to damages and expenses but foresee as well sanctions in case of abuse. Likewise, in national legal orders it is not necessary that an abuse exists to compensate the party wrongly enjoined.[206]

IV BILATERAL AGREEMENTS

1 *Relevance of Enforcement Norms in Preferential Trade Agreements*

Since the mid-1990s the number of PTAs has constantly grown, particularly after the TRIPS Agreement was adopted. PTAs have been considered an ideal tool to foster increased protection of intellectual property while negotiations in other fora make no progress. While the normative and policy implications of intellectual property provisions in PTAs have attracted significant academic attention, their specific impact on intellectual property enforcement has been rarely studied.

203 Thus, 'all authorities related to intellectual property enforcement, and not only the judiciary, are requested to assess the alleged infringement and its consequences, and discretionally decide whether or not to proceed in light of the foreseeable impact on balance'. *See* Seuba (2015b), p. 71.

204 These are Article 42 of the TRIPS Agreement and Article 18.74.1 of the TPP. *See* Section 2.2.3.

205 *See* Article 18.74.15 TPP.

206 *See* Weatherall (2015), p. 27.

PTAs have been a leading source of new normative commitments in the area of intellectual property enforcement. Beginning with the United States, and soon thereafter with the European Union, the main trading powers have made intellectual property enforcement a prominent component of the PTAs negotiated in the past ten years. The Trade Promotion Authority Act of the United States establishes that the purpose of the United States in the area of enforcement is 'providing strong enforcement of intellectual property rights, including through accessible, expeditious, and effective civil, administrative, and criminal enforcement mechanisms'.[207] The other text of relevance is the European Union's Strategy for the Enforcement of Intellectual Property Rights in Third Countries of 2004,[208] which mapped out the future actions of the European Union with regard to international enforcement. Among other activities, it announced the promotion of the adoption of new legal undertakings on enforcement. In accordance with that goal, the European Union has inserted powerful intellectual property enforcement provisions in ambitious PTAs.[209]

Of course, not all PTAs that regulate intellectual property address enforcement,[210] and not all agreements that regulate enforcement do it with the same intensity. A differentiation can be made between treaties that make a general reference to intellectual property enforcement[211] and those that regulate this area

[207] *See* Trade Act of 1974, 19 USC § 3802, 4.A(v).

[208] *See* European Commission (2005). The European Commission adopted a revised Strategy for the Enforcement of Intellectual Property Rights in Third Countries in 2014. *See* European Commission (2014).

[209] *See* European Commission (2010a), p. 4.

[210] This is the case of the agreements concluded between ASEAN-China FTA and EIA (2005/2007); ASEAN-Australia-New Zealand FTA and EIA (2010); ASEAN-Republic of Korea FTA and EIA (2010/2009); Canada-Chile FTA and EIA (1997); Canada-Costa Rica FTA (2002); Canada-Peru FTA and EIA (2009); Caribbean Community and Common Market CU and EIA (1973/2002); Chile-Costa Rica (Chile-Central America) FTA and EIA (2002); Chile-El Salvador (Chile-Central America) FTA and EIA (2002); Chile-Guatemala (Chile-Central America) FTA and EIA (2010); Chile-Honduras (Chile-Central America) FTA and EIA (2008); Chile-Nicaragua (Chile-Central America) FTA and EIA (2012); Panama-Chile FTA and EIA (2008); China-Hong Kong FTA and EIA (2003); Egypt-Turkey FTA (2007); EU-Egypt FTA (2004); EU-Palestinian Authority FTA (1997); Faroe Islands-Norway FTA (1993); Gulf Cooperation Council CU (2003); India-Singapore FTA and EIA (2005); Israel-Mexico FTA (2000); Pakistan-Malaysia FTA and EIA (2008); Panama-Honduras (Panama-Central America) FTA and EIA (2009); Peru-Chile FTA and EIA (2009); Southern African Development Community FTA (2000); Southern Common Market (MERCOSUR) CU and EIA (1991/2005); Turkey-Jordan FTA (2011); Turkey-Palestinian Authority FTA (2005); Turkey-Syria FTA (2007); Turkey-Tunisia FTA (2005); Ukraine-Former Yugoslav Republic of Macedonia FTA (2001); Ukraine-Moldova FTA (2005); US-Israel FTA (1985).

[211] *See* EU-Mexico FTA and EIA (2000); EU-Montenegro FTA and EIA (2008/2010); EU-Morocco FTA (2000); EU-Serbia FTA and EIA (2010/2013); EU-Tunisia FTA (1998); EU-Turkey CU (1996); European Economic Area EIA (1994); European Free Trade Association FTA and EIA (1960/2002); Hong Kong, China-New Zealand FTA and EIA (2011); India-Japan FTA and EIA (2011); Republic of Korea-Chile FTA and EIA (2004); Republic of Korea-India FTA and EIA (2010); Republic of Korea-Singapore FTA and EIA (2006); Panama-Costa Rica (Panama-Central America) FTA and EIA (2008); Panama-El Salvador (Panama-Central America) FTA and EIA (2003); Turkey-Albania FTA (2008); Turkey-Bosnia and Herzegovina FTA (2003); Turkey-Croatia FTA (2003); Turkey-Former Yugoslav Republic of

in detail.[212] Although our attention has focused on the latter, next, some differentiation is made among treaties that contain general references to intellectual property enforcement.

First, not all levels of generality are equal. Some treaties only mention enforcement in a general fashion, and it is difficult to extract concrete consequences.[213] On other occasions, treaties require the protection of intellectual property rights in accordance with the 'highest international standards, including effective means of enforcing such rights',[214] an obligation so vague that it resembles a political undertaking rather than a legal commitment. There are, however, other treaties that contain general references with more practical implications. This is the case of treaties that oblige Parties to fulfil enforcement obligations as foreseen in the TRIPS Agreement[215] or treaties that oblige Parties to respect the level of protection existing in other jurisdictions than of their own.[216] In the first case, this frequently adds nothing to the already existing obligations of the Parties, since all of them are Members to the WTO.[217] However, it may have relevance if dispute settlement mechanisms set forth in the respective treaties are triggered.

Macedonia FTA (2000); Turkey-Georgia FTA (2008); Turkey-Israel FTA (1997); Turkey-Montenegro FTA (2010); Turkey-Morocco FTA (2006); Turkey-Serbia FTA (2010).

212 *See* Andean Community CU (1988); Australia-Chile FTA and EIA (2009); Chile-China FTA and EIA (2006/2010); Chile-Japan FTA and EIA (2007); Chile-Mexico FTA and EIA (1999); China-Costa Rica FTA and EIA (2011); Colombia-Mexico FTA and EIA (1995); Costa Rica-Mexico FTA and EIA (1995); CAFTA-DR-US FTA and EIA (2006); EC Treaty CU and EIA (1958); EFTA-Albania FTA (2010); EFTA-Colombia FTA and EIA (2011); EFTA-Hong Kong, China FTA and EIA (2012); EFTA-Mexico FTA and EIA (2001); EFTA-Montenegro FTA (2012); EFTA-Peru FTA (2011); EFTA-Serbia FTA (2010); EFTA-Ukraine FTA and EIA (2012); EU-CARIFORUM States FTA and EIA (2008); EU-Colombia and Peru FTA and EIA (2013); EU-Republic of Korea FTA and EIA (2011); Japan-Indonesia FTA and EIA (2008); Japan-Malaysia FTA and EIA (2006); Japan-Peru FTA and EIA (2012); Japan-Philippines FTA and EIA (2008); Japan-Switzerland FTA and EIA (2009); Japan-Thailand FTA and EIA (2007); Japan-Viet Nam FTA and EIA (2009); Republic of Korea-US FTA and EIA (2012); Mexico-El Salvador FTA and EIA (2001); Mexico-Guatemala FTA and EIA (2001); Mexico-Honduras FTA and EIA (2001); Mexico-Nicaragua FTA and EIA (1998); Nicaragua-Chinese Taipei FTA and EIA (2008); NAFTA FTA and EIA (1994); Pakistan-China FTA and EIA (2007/2009); Panama-Peru FTA and EIA (2012); Panama-Chinese Taipei FTA and EIA (2004); Peru-China FTA and EIA (2010); Peru-Republic of Korea FTA and EIA (2011); Singapore-Australia FTA and EIA (2003); Thailand-Australia FTA and EIA (2005); US-Australia FTA and EIA (2005); US-Bahrain FTA and EIA (2006); US-Chile FTA and EIA (2004); US-Colombia FTA and EIA (2012); US-Jordan FTA and EIA (2001); US-Morocco FTA and EIA (2006); US-Panama FTA and EIA (2012); US-Oman FTA and EIA (2009); US-Peru FTA and EIA (2009); US-Singapore FTA and EIA (2004).

213 Apart from those derived from declarations of good intentions.

214 For instance Article 168 EU-Chile FTA and EIA (2003/2005).

215 This is frequently the case of agreements concluded by EFTA. *See* for instance Article 5 of Annex XII EFTA-Turkey FTA (1992).

216 This is the case of the treaties of the European Union with candidate members.

217 Exceptions would be in the case of those treaties benefiting from periods of transition.

Treaties can also be identified depending on the area or areas of intellectual property enforcement that they regulate, namely civil,[218] criminal,[219] border[220] and digital[221] enforcement.

218 *See* Andean Community CU (1988); Australia-Chile FTA and EIA (2009); Chile-Japan FTA and EIA (2007); Chile-Mexico FTA and EIA (1999); Colombia-Mexico FTA and EIA (1995); Costa Rica-Mexico FTA and EIA (1995); CAFTA-DR-US FTA and EIA (2006); EC Treaty CU and EIA (1958); EFTA-Colombia FTA and EIA (2011); EFTA-Mexico FTA and EIA (2001); EFTA-Montenegro FTA (2012); EFTA-Peru FTA (2011); EU-CARIFORUM States FTA and EIA (2008); EU-Colombia and Peru FTA and EIA (2013); EU-Republic of Korea FTA and EIA (2011);; Japan-Indonesia FTA and EIA 2008); Japan-Malaysia FTA and EIA (2006); Japan-Peru FTA and EIA (2012); Japan-Philippines FTA and EIA (2008); Japan-Switzerland FTA and EIA (2009); Japan-Thailand FTA and EIA (2007); Japan-Viet Nam FTA and EIA (2009); Republic of Korea-US FTA and EIA (2012); Mexico-El Salvador FTA and EIA (2001); Mexico-Guatemala FTA and EIA (2001); Mexico-Honduras FTA and EIA (2001); Mexico-Nicaragua FTA and EIA (1998); NAFTA FTA and EIA (1994); US-Australia FTA and EIA (2005); US-Bahrain FTA and EIA (2006); US-Chile FTA and EIA (2004); US-Colombia FTA and EIA (2012); US-Jordan FTA and EIA (2001); US-Morocco FTA and EIA (2006); US-Panama FTA and EIA (2012); US-Oman FTA and EIA (2009); US-Peru FTA and EIA (2009); US-Singapore FTA and EIA (2004).

219 *See* Andean Community CU (1988); Australia-Chile FTA and EIA (2009); Chile-Japan FTA and EIA (2007); Chile-Mexico FTA and EIA (1999); Colombia-Mexico FTA and EIA (1995); Costa Rica-Mexico FTA and EIA (1995); CAFTA-DR-US FTA and EIA (2006); EC Treaty CU and EIA (1958); EFTA-Mexico FTA and EIA (2001); EFTA-Montenegro FTA (2012); EU-CARIFORUM States FTA and EIA (2008); EU-Colombia and Peru FTA and EIA (2013); EU-Republic of Korea FTA and EIA (2011); Japan-Indonesia FTA and EIA (2008); Japan-Malaysia FTA and EIA (2006); Japan-Peru FTA and EIA (2012); Japan-Philippines FTA and EIA (2008); Japan-Switzerland FTA and EIA (2009); Japan-Thailand FTA and EIA (2007); Japan-Viet Nam FTA and EIA (2009); Republic of Korea-US FTA and EIA (2012); Mexico-El Salvador FTA and EIA (2001); Mexico-Guatemala FTA and EIA (2001); Mexico-Honduras FTA and EIA (2001); Mexico-Nicaragua FTA and EIA (1998); NAFTA FTA and EIA (1994); US-Australia FTA and EIA (2005); US-Bahrain FTA and EIA (2006); US-Chile FTA and EIA (2004); US-Colombia FTA and EIA (2012); US-Jordan FTA and EIA (2001); US-Morocco FTA and EIA (2006); US-Panama FTA and EIA (2012); US-Oman FTA and EIA (2009); US-Peru FTA and EIA (2009); US-Singapore FTA and EIA (2004).

220 *See* EFTA-Albania FTA (2010); Andean Community CU (1988); Australia-Chile FTA and EIA (2009); Chile-Japan FTA and EIA (2007); Chile-Mexico FTA and EIA (1999); China-Costa Rica FTA and EIA (2011); Colombia-Mexico FTA and EIA (1995); Costa Rica-Mexico FTA and EIA (1995); CAFTA-DR-US FTA and EIA (2006); EC Treaty CU and EIA (1958); EFTA-Colombia FTA and EIA (2011); EFTA-Hong Kong, China FTA and EIA (2012); EFTA-Mexico FTA and EIA (2001); EFTA-Montenegro FTA (2012); EFTA-Peru FTA (2011); EFTA-Serbia FTA (2010); EFTA-Ukraine FTA and EIA (2012); EU-CARIFORUM States FTA and EIA (2008); EU-Colombia and Peru FTA and EIA (2013); EU-Republic of Korea FTA and EIA (2011); Japan-Indonesia FTA and EIA (2008); Japan-Malaysia FTA and EIA (2006); Japan-Peru FTA and EIA (2012); Japan-Philippines FTA and EIA (2008); Japan-Switzerland FTA and EIA (2009); Japan-Thailand FTA and EIA (2007); Japan-Viet Nam FTA and EIA (2009); Republic of Korea-US FTA and EIA (2012); Mexico-El Salvador FTA and EIA (2001); Mexico-Guatemala FTA and EIA (2001); Mexico-Honduras FTA and EIA (2001); Mexico-Nicaragua FTA and EIA (1998); NAFTA FTA and EIA (1994); Pakistan-China FTA and EIA (2007/2009); Panama-Peru FTA and EIA (2012); Panama-Chinese Taipei FTA and EIA (2004); Peru-Republic of Korea FTA and EIA (2011); Peru-China FTA and EIA (2010); Singapore-Australia FTA and EIA (2003); Thailand-Australia FTA and EIA (2005); US-Australia FTA and EIA (2005); US-Bahrain FTA and EIA (2006); US-Chile FTA and EIA (2004); US-Colombia FTA and EIA (2012); US-Jordan FTA and EIA (2001); US-Morocco FTA and EIA (2006); US-Panama FTA and EIA (2012); US-Oman FTA and EIA (2009); US-Peru FTA and EIA (2009); US-Singapore FTA and EIA (2004).

221 *See* Australia-Chile FTA and EIA (2009); CAFTA-DR-US FTA and EIA (2006); EC Treaty CU and EIA (1958); EU-Colombia and Peru FTA and EIA (2013); EU-Republic of Korea FTA and EIA (2011);

One of the major post-TRIPS Agreement changes is the regulation of intellectual property enforcement in the digital domain. Since the adoption of the WIPO Internet Treaties in 1996, many PTAs have included an obligation to ratify digital enforcement-related treaties. In other cases, treaties directly regulate the digital enforcement measures to be adopted and address in particular anti-circumvention of effective technological measures and electronic rights management information.[222]

As regards border enforcement, numerous treaties contain measures that potentially affect goods protected by intellectual property rights. These are however measures of general nature, such as the inspection of goods entering into the country. However, many other treaties regulate the specific relationship between intellectual property rights and border measures, and these are the treaties that attract our interest.[223] Fundamentally, these treaties expand both the categories of intellectual property rights and the border situations object of control.

2 *General Provisions Concerning Intellectual Property Enforcement*

The diversity existing across PTAs regulating intellectual property enforcement makes it impossible to generalize with respect to the contents of the general provisions specifically targeting these enforcement measures. Probably the only valid generalization is that, in the majority of cases, there is no section on general provisions for intellectual property enforcement. The PTAs promoted by the United States and the European Union are, however, an exception as they often enshrine some general principles and understandings on how enforcement should be implemented, and coincide in aspects such as mandating *ex officio* action in the context of border and criminal enforcement or requiring final decisions on the merits of a case be made in writing.

Agreements concluded by the United States commonly mention the possibility to provide more extensive enforcement of intellectual property rights under its law than required by the treaty, providing that 'the more extensive protection does not contravene' the PTA itself.[224] This is reminiscent of the construction of Article 1.1 of the TRIPS Agreement, generally presented as the provision limiting the ever-increasing protection of intellectual property rights.

Japan-Peru FTA and EIA (2012); Japan-Switzerland FTA and EIA (2009); Republic of Korea-US FTA and EIA (2012); Mexico-Nicaragua FTA and EIA (1998); NAFTA FTA and EIA (1994); US-Australia FTA and EIA (2005); US-Bahrain FTA and EIA (2006); US-Chile FTA and EIA (2004); US-Colombia FTA and EIA (2012); US-Morocco FTA and EIA (2006); US-Panama FTA and EIA (2012); US-Oman FTA and EIA (2009); US-Peru FTA and EIA (2009); US-Singapore FTA and EIA (2004).

222 *See* footnote above on the treaties directly regulating digital enforcement, excepting the EC Treaty CU and EIA (1958), Mexico-Nicaragua FTA and EIA (1998) and NAFTA FTA and EIA (1994).

223 *See* Chapter 13.

224 *See* Article 18.1.5 Republic of Korea-US FTA and EIA (2012); Article 17.1 US-Australia FTA and EIA (2005); Article 14.1.4 US-Bahrain FTA and EIA (2006); Article 15.1.4 US-Morocco FTA and EIA (2006); Article 16.1.7 US-Peru FTA and EIA (2009); Article 16.1.7 US-Colombia FTA and EIA (2012).

Due process and fair trial standards are also commonly mentioned in treaties promoted by the United States in the context of intellectual property enforcement. In some cases, the incorporation of due process principles is made in general terms, alluding, for instance, to the assumption that procedures and remedies for enforcement of intellectual property rights 'are established in accordance with the principles of due process that each Party recognizes and the foundations of its own legal system'.[225] On other occasions, however, only specific aspects related to due process are mentioned. This is the case of the right to have judicial decisions and administrative rulings related to the enforcement of intellectual property rights in writing, published or 'available to the public, in its national language in such a manner as to enable governments and right holders to become acquainted with them'.[226] As mentioned before, ACTA and TPP have generally improved references to fair trial principles in international agreements relating to intellectual property rights.

Another aspect expressly regulated in the United States' PTAs is the presumption of authorship that, according to the treaties, applies in the context of civil, administrative and criminal proceedings involving copyright or related rights. Accordingly, 'in the absence of proof to the contrary, the person whose name is indicated as the author, producer, performer, or publisher of the work, performance, or phonogram in the usual manner is the designated right holder ... Each Party shall also provide for a presumption that, in the absence of proof to the contrary, the copyright or related right subsists in such subject matter.'[227] The first part of this presumption was already found in the Berne Convention and, by reference, in the TRIPS Agreement.[228] This is not the case of the second part of the presumption (subsistence of right). Moreover, this presumption has been extended by the TPP to the much more challenging areas of trademarks and patents.[229]

The United States' PTAs articles on enforcement mix obligations intended to shape State action with many other articles relating to right holders' rights and obligations.[230] In Chapter 1 reference was made to the difference between

225 *See* Article 16.11.1 US-Peru FTA and EIA (2009); Article 16.11.1 US-Colombia FTA and EIA (2012); Article 15.11.1 US-Panama FTA and EIA (2012); Article 17.11.1 US-Chile FTA and EIA (2004).

226 *See* Article 18.10.1 Republic of Korea-US FTA and EIA (2012); Article 17.11.2 US-Australia FTA and EIA (2005); Article 14.10.1 US-Bahrain FTA and EIA (2006); Article 15.11.1 US-Morocco FTA and EIA (2006); Article 16.11.2 US-Peru FTA and EIA (2009); Article 16.11.2 US-Colombia FTA and EIA (2012); Article 15.11.3 US-Panama FTA and EIA (2012); Articles 16.9.1 and 16.9.2 US-Singapore FTA and EIA (2004); Article 17.1.12 US-Chile FTA and EIA (2004).

227 *See* Article 18.10.3 Republic of Korea-US FTA and EIA (2012); Article 17.11.4 US-Australia FTA and EIA (2005); Article 14.10.4 US-Bahrain FTA and EIA (2006); Article 15.11.4 US-Morocco FTA and EIA (2006); Article 16.11.5 US-Peru FTA and EIA (2009); Article 16.11.5 US-Colombia FTA and EIA (2012); Article 15.11.5 US-Panama FTA and EIA (2012); Article 16.9.6 US-Singapore FTA and EIA (2004).

228 *See* Articles 15.1 and 15.2 Berne Convention; Article 9.1 TRIPS Agreement.

229 *See* Articles 18.72.2 and 18.72.3 TPP.

230 For instance, among the former, reference must be made to the obligation to publicize 'efforts to provide effective enforcement of intellectual property rights in its civil, administrative, and criminal systems, including any statistical information that the Party may collect for such purposes'. *See* Article 18.10.2 Republic of Korea-US FTA and EIA (2012); Article 17.11.3 US-Australia FTA and EIA

intellectual property enforcement provisions intended to apply to private parties and other provisions touching upon issues such as international cooperation, exchange of information or transparency of enforcement practices, which are addressed to States and not to right holders or alleged infringers.[231]

One of the central elements of Article 41 of the TRIPS Agreement is the affirmation in paragraph 5 that nothing in the Agreement 'creates any obligation with respect to the distribution of resources as between enforcement of intellectual property rights and enforcement of law in general'. While some PTAs transplant this provision,[232] the actual implications of Article 41.5 are contentious.[233] Some PTAs have tried to make sure that references of this type do not impact on the actual respect of substantive rights. Hence, in some PTAs it is stated that 'Parties understand that a decision that a Party makes on the distribution of enforcement resources shall not excuse that Party from complying with the provisions of this Chapter'.[234]

In the case of the European Union, only treaties concluded after the adoption of the 2005 Strategy for the enforcement of intellectual property rights include a detailed regulation on intellectual property, including intellectual property enforcement. Whenever an article on general obligations concerning enforcement is incorporated, it is modelled upon Article 3 of the EU Enforcement Directive.[235]

The requirements enshrined in Article 3 frequently refer to the interests of the right holder, this being for instance the case of the condition that enforcement procedures must be 'dissuasive'. Other conditions set forth in Article 3 are of interest for not only right holders but also competitors and users of intellectual property-protected goods. This is the case of the 'affordable' nature of such procedures. Most importantly, Article 3 contains some balancing requirements that must guide the implementation of enforcement provisions. Notably, the corresponding procedures, remedies and sanctions must be fair, equitable and proportionate. This call for fairness, equity and proportionality is a useful reference when the specific consequences of enforcement procedures and remedies seem out of balance or, simply,

(2005); Article 14.10.2 US-Bahrain FTA and EIA (2006); Article 15.11.2 US-Morocco FTA and EIA (2006); Article 16.11.3 US-Peru FTA and EIA (2009); Article 16.11.3 US-Colombia FTA and EIA (2012); Article 15.11.4 US-Panama FTA and EIA (2012); Article 16.9.3 US-Singapore FTA and EIA (2004).

231 *See* Chapter 1, Section III.4.

232 *See* Article 234.4 EU-Colombia and Peru FTA and EIA (2013).

233 *See* Section II.2.2.

234 *See* Article 14.10.3 US-Bahrain FTA and EIA (2006); Article 15.11.3 US-Morocco FTA and EIA (2006); Article 16.11.4 US-Peru FTA and EIA (2009); Article 16.11.4 US-Colombia FTA and EIA (2012); Article 15.11.2 US-Panama FTA and EIA (2012); Article 16.9.4 US-Singapore FTA and EIA (2004); Article 17.11.2 US-Chile FTA and EIA (2004).

235 *See* Directive 2004/48/EC of the European Parliament and of the Council of 29 April 2004 on the enforcement of intellectual property rights (OJEU L 157 of 30 April 2004), OJEU L 195 of 2 June 2004 (hereinafter EU Enforcement Directive)/Corrigendum to Directive 2004/48/EC of the European Parliament and of the Council of 29 April 2004 on the enforcement of intellectual property rights (OJEU L 157 of 30 April 2004), OJEU L 195 of 2 June 2004 (hereinafter EU Enforcement Directive). *See* Chapter 6.

not appropriate in a given situation.[236] Importantly, Article 3 of the EU Enforcement Directive, both in its original and its transplanted versions, establishes that enforcement cannot create barriers to legitimate trade and safeguards against abuse of enforcement procedures shall be provided. Whereas in its original version this reference relates only to civil enforcement, in the 'last-generation' European PTAs it is drafted in a way that its effects expand to both civil and border enforcement measures.

[236] *See* Chapter 2.

5

International Bodies for the Enforcement of Intellectual Property Rights

I INTRODUCTION

1 *Scope*

Numerous international bodies oversee the implementation of international intellectual property commitments undertaken by States. To the extent that these bodies compel or ensure compliance with those obligations, they are considered international institutions for the enforcement of intellectual property rights.[1] As detailed below, the focus is put on state obligations for the enforcement of intellectual property rights and not on the enforcement of intellectual property rights in the context of private disputes. The objective of the bodies identified in this chapter is achieved by the administration of dispute settlement mechanisms or the application of political pressure. In this regard, even if dispute resolution is 'the place where legislation becomes binding and effective',[2] international bodies may also enhance enforcement through systems based on soft law processes and mechanisms such as monitoring and reporting.

The bodies selected in this chapter are those related to the treaties identified in Chapter 4, which depicted the international normative framework for the enforcement of intellectual property rights. In Section I, international dispute settlement mechanisms and relevant bodies are introduced. Section II identifies dispute settlement bodies set up in the treaties and describes their institutional aspects and the dispute settlement methods administered. Section III identifies treaty-monitoring bodies with diplomatic functions in the area of treaty enforcement and describes the councils and intellectual property committees established in treaties. Finally, Section IV addresses interaction between intellectual property enforcement-related bodies.

[1] Enforcement implies to compel or ensure compliance with something, or to give effect or force to a law or command. *See* Chapter 1, Sections I and II.

[2] *See* Trachtman (1999), p. 339.

The scope of this chapter could be broader if all international treaties that deal with intellectual property, even indirectly, were taken into account. In that case, bodies created in the context of bilateral investment treaties, environmental treaties or human rights treaties would also be addressed. In effect, bodies and procedures set up in these treaties can be also considered part of the overall international intellectual property enforcement regime. In the case of investment treaties, the inclusion of intellectual property among the categories of protected investment entitles *ad hoc* panels to rule on investor-state disputes touching upon intellectual property. Environmental and human rights bodies have also settled intellectual property-related disputes in cases where close links exist between the respective regimes.[3] In this regard, several chapters of this book analyse the interaction between enforcement norms and norms pertaining to different international regimes. In addition, the principles related to jurisdictional overlaps depicted in Section IV of this chapter apply as well to the interrelation between bodies pertaining to different material regimes.

To date, the most successful body for the settlement of international intellectual property disputes has been the World Trade Organization Dispute Settlement Body. Its dispute settlement procedures are among the most developed in international law and influence dispute settlement practices in other areas.[4] Moreover, the possibility of linking trade sanctions and the infringement of international commitments in the area of intellectual property has proven to be a generally efficient way to enhance intellectual property enforcement. These features must be contextualized in a situation where there is no adjudicatory body specializing in inter-State intellectual property disputes. Prior to the conclusion of the WTO Agreement, the World Intellectual Property Organization promoted a treaty for the settlement of intellectual property disputes.[5] That initiative ultimately failed as it was found unnecessary in light of the creation of the WTO.[6] In effect, the absorption of the major intellectual property conventions into the Agreement on Trade-Related Aspects of Intellectual Property Rights[7] implied that the WTO Dispute Settlement Body would also be competent to adjudicate disputes concerning the major intellectual property conventions.[8] However, as this chapter analyses, similar dispute settlement bodies created in the context of bilateral trade agreements have not had a workload comparable to that of the WTO Dispute Settlement Body.[9]

3 The European Court of Human Rights has an impressive record of cases relating to the interface between intellectual property and human rights. *See* Geiger and Izyumenko (2017a); Geiger and Izyumenko (2017b).

4 *See* Petersmann (2006), p. 274.

5 *See* WIPO (1997).

6 *See* Petersmann (1997), p. 467; Dinwoodie, Hennessey and Perlmutter (2001), p. 781; Abbott (2004b), p. 435; Petersmann (2006), p. 332.

7 *See* Article 2.2 TRIPS Agreement.

8 The Paris Convention for the Protection of Industrial Property; the Berne Convention for the Protection of Literary and Artistic Works; the Rome Convention for International Convention for the Protection of Performers, Producers of Phonograms and Broadcasting Organizations; and the Washington Treaty on Intellectual Property in Respect of Integrated Circuits.

9 *See* Section III.3.

2 *International Dispute Settlement Mechanisms and Relevant Bodies*

Diplomatic and jurisdictional means of dispute settlement coexist in international law. The former typically include diplomatic negotiations, good offices, mediation and conciliation, while the latter comprise international inter-State arbitration and judicial settlement.[10] Jurisdictional means of dispute settlement are characterized by the participation of a third Party invested with the power to adjudicate the dispute, a decision that will be based on law and binding on the Parties. International law, however, does not prescribe a preference of one method over others. By virtue of the principle of free choice regarding the means of dispute settlement,[11] States may establish their preference, for instance in an international treaty or in a specific agreement.

Negotiation is the most popular means of international dispute settlement,[12] mainly for reasons of convenience, flexibility and reduced political and economic costs.[13] Numerous intellectual property treaties prescribe either direct consultations between Parties[14] or consultations in the context of the committee in charge of administering the agreement.[15] Having recourse to diplomatic means of dispute settlement, particularly negotiation, can be compulsory in international law,[16] including in international intellectual property law.[17] As in many other areas of international law, in the case of intellectual property treaties consultations may often be the only available mechanism for solving the dispute, since jurisdictional systems for dispute settlement have been expressly excluded.[18] On other occasions, treaties specify that Parties can resort to other dispute settlement mechanisms only after holding consultations.[19]

10 *See* Section I of the UN General Assembly (1982), para. 5; Article 33 UN Charter.

11 This is a principle of customary international law, codified as well in Article 2.3 of the UN Charter.

12 *See* Anderson (1998), pp. 111–121; Merrills (2005); Merrills (2006), p. 535; Sobrino Heredia (2009), p. 926.

13 *See* Petersmann (2006), p. 300.

14 *See* Article 15.5 EFTA-Turkey FTA (1992); Article 26.6 EFTA-SACU FTA (2008); Article 24.4 Egypt-Turkey FTA (2007); or Article 20.2 Turkey-Bosnia and Herzegovina FTA (2003).

15 *See* Article 15.3 EFTA-Palestinian Authority FTA (1999); Article 12.2(a) EU-Mexico FTA and EIA (2000); Article 69.3 EFTA-Mexico FTA and EIA (2001).

16 *See* ICJ, *North Sea Continental Shelf Cases*, Judgment of 20 February 1969, ICJ Reports 1969, p. 48, para. 85; Article 283.1 United Nations Convention on the Law of the Sea.

17 Concerning disputes that arise from WTO Agreements, including the TRIPS Agreement, and according to Article 4.3 of the WTO Understanding on Rules and Procedures Governing the Settlement of Disputes '[i]f a request for consultations is made pursuant to a covered agreement, the Member to which the request is made shall . . . enter into consultations in good faith'.

18 *See* Article 8 of the Memorandum of Understanding between the Governments of the Member States of the Association of Southeast Asian Nations and the Government of the People's Republic of China on Cooperation in the Field of Intellectual Property (2009).

19 *See* Article 46.1 Vienna Trademark Registration Treaty; Article 166.1 China-New Zealand FTA and EIA (2008); Article 16.1 Vienna Agreement Establishing an International Classification of the Figurative Elements of Marks; Article 235 Central American Agreement for the Protection of Industrial Property; Article 173 Convention on the Grant of European Patents.

Good offices and mediation are also political methods of dispute settlement. In these cases, Parties to the dispute accept the intervention of a third Party, who may either have an active role in proposing solutions (mediation) or simply act as a channel of communication (good offices).[20] While there is no record of their use in the context of international intellectual property disputes, some intellectual property treaties,[21] or treaties for the settlement of intellectual property disputes,[22] list mediation and good offices among the means available to the disputing Parties.

Conciliation is another diplomatic means of dispute settlement. In this case, a body – usually nominated by the Parties to the dispute – is entrusted with proposing a solution after examining all the relevant facts and law. The solution, however, is not mandatory.[23] Although it is similar to arbitration, the search for a solution 'acceptable' to the Parties makes it different – i.e. more political – from arbitration, which results in a compulsory arbitral award. However, conciliation is infrequent in the intellectual property domain. Indeed, there are very few references to conciliation in intellectual property-related international treaties and no citations of its actual use.[24]

Jurisdictional dispute settlement mechanisms lay down rules-based procedures and result in legally binding decisions adopted by independent arbitrators or judges. International dispute settlement bodies may have general competence to adjudicate disputes relating to a wide range of matters, or their competence may be narrow and limited to intellectual property cases. The first group comprises the majority of international courts and bodies, while the second group includes *ad hoc* temporary bodies and regional courts. As regards the first group of institutions, mention must be made of the International Court of Justice as well as of the adjudicatory bodies that have been created to rule on the controversies arising from specific treaties or in the context of a particular regime, the prime example being that of the WTO Dispute Settlement Body. As to the second group of institutions, some intellectual property treaties have chosen to create *ad hoc* bodies of a temporary nature for the adjudication of disputes resulting from a treaty.[25] In the regional context, the possible creation of the Unified Patent Court is an almost unique example of an

[20] *See* Bindschedler (1992), p. 721; Bercovitch and Rubin (1992); Merrills (2006), p. 537; Sobrino Heredia (2009), pp. 927–928.

[21] *See* Article 14.2 of the Washington Treaty on Intellectual Property in Respect of Integrated Circuits.

[22] *See* Article 5 of the WTO Understanding on Rules and Procedures Governing the Settlement of Disputes.

[23] *See* for instance Cot (1972), p. 9.

[24] This is for instance the case of Article 14 of the Washington Treaty on Intellectual Property in Respect of Integrated Circuits, which describes the conciliation process in detail: proceedings before the conciliation panel will result in a written report containing the facts and recommendations. After its reception, the Assembly shall 'make recommendations to the parties to the dispute, based upon its interpretation of [the] Treaty and the report of the panel'. *See* also Article 5 of the WTO Understanding on Rules and Procedures Governing the Settlement of Disputes.

[25] *See* Article 4.3 of the Washington Treaty on Intellectual Property in Respect of Integrated Circuits.

international, specialized and permanent jurisdiction for the settlement of patent disputes.[26]

Enforcement is also enhanced through systems of a distinct nature, based on the supervision of States' compliance with international obligations, conceived to function as a forum for discussion. In effect, while 'teeth'[27] – namely, dispute settlement bodies with power to impose sanctions or overturn trade advantages – are important to law enforcement, intellectual property treaties may also create dispute prevention and management bodies. Even if these mechanisms are closely tied to dispute settlement processes, their role is different. A good example is the WTO where, on the one hand, diplomatic means of dispute settlement coexist with judicial means of dispute settlement and where, on the other hand, a political body – the TRIPS Council – is tasked with several functions relating to the supervision of the treaty and the prevention and management of disputes. As will be seen, this is also the case of bilateral and plurilateral agreements in the area of intellectual property.

II INTERNATIONAL DISPUTE SETTLEMENT BODIES

International dispute settlement bodies with competence to rule on controversies arising from intellectual property treaties are particularly relevant for the enforcement of international obligations on intellectual property. On the one hand, the existence of a powerful dispute settlement body may deter the infringement of international obligations, which may be instrumental in the proper functioning of the national intellectual property system. On the other hand, in cases of infringement of an international undertaking, the dispute settlement body will order either the cessation of the infringement and reparation for its consequences[28] or the specific consequence mandated in the treaty itself. Hence, dispute settlement bodies both deter the infringement and facilitate reaction when infringement occurs.

1 *The International Court of Justice*

The jurisdiction of the International Court of Justice may be asserted on different grounds. First, States may conclude a special agreement, called 'compromise', declaring their determination to have a particular dispute settled by the Court. Second, treaties may enshrine a binding clause by virtue of which Parties

26 The Andean Court of Justice would eventually qualify in that context, although the fact that the Andean Court is a body of a regional integration organization, and addresses disputes concerning other topics, differentiates it from the Unified Patent Court.

27 *See* Muntañá Mora (1993).

28 According to Article 30 of the International Law Commission (2001a), '[t]he State responsible for the internationally wrongful act is under an obligation: (a) to cease that act, if it is continuing'. According to Article 31, '[t]he responsible State is under an obligation to make full reparation for the injury caused by the internationally wrongful act'. Treaties may foresee *lex specialis* rules *vis-à-vis* these provisions.

accept the competence of the Court. This is the so-called 'compromissory' clause. Third, States may use the optional clause enshrined in the Statute of the International Court of Justice. By virtue of this clause, they recognize the compulsory jurisdiction of the Court without special agreement in relation to other States that accept the same obligation.[29] Finally, States may have concluded a judicial settlement treaty recognizing the general or specific jurisdiction of the Court.[30]

Numerous intellectual property treaties include compromissory clauses that refer controversies to the International Court of Justice. Although the trend is to not include this type of clause anymore, older multilateral treaties made provision for the submission of disputes to the International Court of Justice. In addition to the Paris and Berne Conventions, six international intellectual property treaties empower parties to bring before the International Court of Justice any dispute concerning the interpretation or application of the corresponding convention.[31] This is, however, an opt-out clause since the same article also affirms that States may declare that they do not consider themselves bound by the compromissory clause[32] or choose any other means of dispute settlement.[33]

Despite the abundance of treaty provisions enabling the referral of inter-State intellectual property disputes to the International Court of Justice, this option has proved to be unsuccessful. In fact, not a single intellectual property dispute has been brought to the International Court of Justice. While the Court has addressed numerous controversies relating to very sensitive and complex disputes, the intellectual property community does not seem to consider it an attractive option. The Court's machinery has been described as 'toothless'[34] and its dispute settlement mechanisms 'worthless'.[35] More radically, current references to the Court tend to portray it as a 'moribund'[36] mechanism that belongs to the past,[37] and States choose the WTO Disputes Settlement System even when they could refer the dispute to the International Court of Justice.[38]

29 *See* Article 36 of the Statute of the International Court of Justice.

30 *See* Article XXXI of the *American Treaty on Pacific Settlement 'Pact of Bogota'*, 30 April 1948.

31 *See* Article 28 Paris Convention; Article 33 Berne Convention; Article 30 Rome Convention; Article 59 Patent Cooperation Treaty; Article 46 Vienna Trademark Registration Treaty; Article 16 Vienna Agreement Establishing an International Classification of the Figurative Elements of Marks; Article XV Universal Copyright Convention; Article 173 Convention on the Grant of European Patents.

32 Article 28 Paris Convention; Article 33 Berne Convention; Articles 59 and 64 Patent Cooperation Treaty.

33 *See* Article 30 Rome Convention.

34 *See* Dinwoodie (2006a), p. 597.

35 *See* Nimmer (1995), pp. 1385, 1393. *See* as well Lee (2011), p. 406; Cordray (1994), pp. 131–133; Su (2000), pp. 183–184.

36 *See* Pauwelyn (2010), p. 391.

37 Tellingly, when addressing dispute settlement in the field of intellectual property, scholars allude to the International Court of Justice when referring to 'how disputes were handled before TRIPS'. *See* Dinwoodie, Hennessey and Perlmutter (2001), p. 781.

38 This is, however, not particularly noticeable. In fact, international trade or trade-related disputes have hardly ever been decided by the ICJ or by its predecessor. *See* Abbott (2004b), p. 421; Petersmann (2006), p. 301; Murphy (1991), p. 442.

There are a number of reasons that explain the reluctance of Parties to use the dispute settlement system of the International Court of Justice. Some have underlined the lack of intellectual property expertise of the judges sitting in the Court[39] as well as the perception that patent disputes are too trivial to be brought before the Court.[40] Others believe that the Court does not provide a 'well-functioning authoritative interpretation mechanism'.[41] Mention must also be made of the general perception regarding the Court's time-consuming process to adopt decisions[42] and the inexistence of 'effective means to effect compliance with a decision rendered by the Court'.[43] In this line of reasoning, particularly in light of the old intellectual property conventions' relations with the International Court of Justice, it has been held that 'the Achilles' heel of all the Great Conventions is that they uniformly lack enforcement tools'.[44]

2 *The World Trade Organization Dispute Settlement Body*

2.1 A Turning Point in International Dispute Settlement

The Uruguay Round marked a turning point in international dispute settlement. First and foremost, it successfully set up an effective international dispute settlement system[45] that combines diplomatic and jurisdictional mechanisms. Second, and very important in our context, the WTO Dispute Settlement System was made applicable to disputes related to the TRIPS Agreement.[46]

The original GATT system for dispute settlement was 'relatively informal'[47] and heavily influenced by diplomatic considerations.[48] Crucially, under the old system every decision had to be made by consensus, which meant that the defendant had an effective right to veto every step of the process, including trade retaliation.[49] Unsurprisingly, the veto power resulted in the losing Party's blocking the rulings,

39 This opinion, however, should be put into question in light of the experience of some judges of the Court. Take for instance the case of the current, as of 2016, Vice President of the Court, Abdulqawi Ahmed Yusuf, with an important record of publications on intellectual property and experience in intellectual property-related international organizations. The same applies with respect to Judge Dalveer Bhandari.

40 *See* Emmert (1990), pp. 1317, 1344–1347.

41 *See* Cottier and Foltea (2012), p. 161.

42 *See* Reinbothe and Howard (1991), p. 157.

43 *See* Okediji (2002), p. 594.

44 *See* Netanel (1996–1997), pp. 441–442.

45 *See* Lowenfeld (1994), p. 479; Dreyfuss and Lowenfeld (1997), p. 276; Hudec (1998), p. 101; Merrills (2006), p. 211; Castel-Fodor (2013), p. 207.

46 The relevance of the applicability of dispute settlement disciplines to the TRIPS Agreement has been underlined in Pauwelyn (2010), p. 391; Brewster (2009), pp. 1133–1134; Siegel (2002), p. 583; Okediji (2002), p. 634.

47 *See* Hudec (1999), p. 2.

48 *See* Hudec (1970), pp. 615–616. Although Hudec also noted that 'after 1980, the GATT dispute settlement procedure transformed itself into an institution based primarily on the authority of legal obligation'. *See* Hudec (1999), p. 4.

49 As it has been noted, 'from the appointment of a panel to the adoption of the panel's legal ruling and the authorization of trade sanctions'. *See* Hudec (1999), p. 9. Along similar lines, *see* Lorcher (2003), p. 204.

which made the system inefficient,[50] in particular with regard to the most sensitive cases.[51]

The application of dispute settlement disciplines to the intellectual property context was the object of intense discussions during the Uruguay Round. Delegates to the negotiations expressed conflicting views on the relationship between the TRIPS Agreement and cross-retaliation and, more broadly, on the specificities of intellectual property when settling disputes in the WTO context.[52] In a remarkable achievement,[53] the final text confirmed the application of the WTO Dispute Settlement Understanding to the TRIPS Agreement.[54]

2.2 The Dispute Settlement Body, Panels and Appellate Body

Three institutions were devised in the Uruguay Round for the settlement of disputes: the Dispute Settlement Body, panels and the Appellate Body. The WTO General Council, consisting of representatives of all WTO Members, acts under different capacities, including as the DSB.[55] Pursuant to the general mandate of administering 'rules and procedures and (. . .) the consultation and dispute settlement provisions of the covered agreements',[56] the DSB has four basic functions: the establishment of panels, the adoption of panel and Appellate Body reports, the supervision of their implementation and the authorization of retaliatory measures.[57] While the panels and the Appellate Body are responsible for deciding on the legal aspects of the controversy, the formal and final adoption of the report is the responsibility of the DSB. Notwithstanding its political composition, in practice and by virtue of the negative consensus rule, the reports drafted by the panels and the Appellate Body are adopted automatically.

The WTO panels are temporary bodies composed of three well-qualified individuals selected from a roster of experts nominated by the WTO Member

50 *See* Bello (1995), pp. 772–774.

51 Whereas the number of implemented cases was in effect high, sensitive cases were effectively blocked by the losing party. *See* the example of the GATT Panel Report, *European Economic Community-Production Aids Granted on Canned Peaches, Canned Pears, Canned Fruit Cocktail and Dried Grapes*, L/5778, 20 February 1985, discussed in Hudec (1993), p.155.

52 In this sense, it has been argued that a violation of the TRIPS Agreement would entitle to retaliate in other sectors, or vice versa. *See* Gervais (2003), p. 340.

53 For the WTO itself, but also for the international intellectual property system. *See* Gutowski (1999), p. 754; Okediji (2000), pp. 149–150; Okediji (2002), p. 594; Davey (2005), p. 32.

54 The Preamble of the TRIPS Agreement recognizes 'the importance of reducing tensions by reaching strengthened commitments to resolve disputes on trade-related intellectual property issues through multilateral procedures', and Article 64.1 TRIPS Agreement confirms the application of the WTO Dispute Settlement Understanding to the TRIPS Agreement disputes.

55 Pursuant to Article IV.3 of the Agreement establishing the World Trade Organization, the General Council 'shall convene as appropriate to discharge the responsibilities of the Dispute Settlement Body', while pursuant to Article IV.4, the General Council may meet as well as Trade Policy Review Body. The General Council assumes, moreover, the executive functions and the adoption of important decisions that later on will have to be endorsed by the Ministerial Conference.

56 *See* Article 2.1 Dispute Settlement Understanding.

57 *Ibid.*

States.[58] In the intellectual property context, they could include renowned legal experts, employees of national intellectual property offices or international intellectual property-related organizations, provided that they participate in their individual capacity.[59] Panellists are appointed by the disputing parties or, in case of lack of consensus, by the WTO Director-General.[60] In contrast, the Appellate Body is a permanent body in charge of reviewing panel rulings.[61] It comprises seven 'persons of recognized authority, with demonstrated expertise in law, international trade and the subject matter of the covered agreements',[62] three of whom shall serve on any one case.[63] While cases are attributed to divisions of three judges, all seven members 'shall stay abreast of dispute settlement activities and other relevant activities of the WTO'.[64]

These bodies are at the centre of a system that closely resembles a court[65] and have the competence to settle disputes relating to the 'covered agreements'[66] in accordance to the norms set up in the Dispute Settlement Understanding,[67] which also determines the consequences of infringement. Once adopted by the DSB, panel and Appellate Body decisions are final and mandatory, and retaliation may follow in case rulings are not fulfilled.

The objectives of the Dispute Settlement Understanding are to 'secure a positive solution' to disputes, to provide 'security and predictability to the multilateral trading system' and 'to preserve the rights and obligations of Members'.[68] The DSU enacts the legal procedure to settle disputes and ensure that parties have 'recourse to, and abide by, the rules and procedures' of the WTO whenever they 'seek the redress of a violation of obligations' and enforce the obligations appended to the WTO Agreement.[69] Pursuant to the Dispute Settlement Understanding, dispute settlement is compulsory and panel and Appellate Body reports 'shall be adopted by the DSB' unless it decides '*by consensus* not to adopt the Appellate Body

58 *See* Article 8.5 Dispute Settlement Understanding. Exceptionally, panels are composed of five members.

59 More broadly, these individuals may have served as State representatives or in the Secretariat, taught or published on international trade law or policy, or served as a senior trade policy official of a Member. *See* Article 8.1 Dispute Settlement Understanding. *See* Hudec (1999), pp. 34–39.

60 *See* Articles 8.6 and 8.7 Dispute Settlement Understanding.

61 *See* Article 17.1 Dispute Settlement Understanding. Its permanent nature emerged when the Uruguay Round negotiations were advanced. *See* Hudec (1999), p. 27.

62 According to Article 17.3 Dispute Settlement Understanding, members of the Appellate Body 'shall be unaffiliated with any government. The Appellate Body membership shall be broadly representative of membership in the WTO.'

63 *See* Article 17.1 Dispute Settlement Understanding. For a discussion on the criteria to be met by the Members and politics behind their appointment, *see* Elsig and Pollack (2012).

64 *See* Article17.3 Dispute Settlement Understanding.

65 For some, the court represents the most important international tribunal. *See* in this sense Matsushita, Schoenbaum and Mavroidis (2006), p. 104; Georgiev and Van der Borght (2006), p. 11.

66 The 'covered agreements' are the Agreements listed in Appendix 1 to the Dispute Settlement Understanding, which include all the multilateral WTO Agreements.

67 *See* Article 1 Dispute Settlement Understanding.

68 *See* Articles 3.7 and 3.2 Dispute Settlement Understanding.

69 *See* Article 23 Dispute Settlement Understanding; Hudec (1998), p. 101.

report within 30 days following its circulation to the Members'.[70] The DSU also prescribes steps to incentivize the enforcement of Appellate Body and panel decisions, which may include retaliatory measures.[71]

2.3 Dispute Settlement Mechanisms Available to Parties

The Dispute Settlement Understanding recognizes a broad standing[72] and, in order to settle disputes, authorizes Members to have recourse to consultations,[73] good offices,[74] conciliation,[75] mediation[76] and arbitration[77] as well as the panel process.

By far most of the controversies are solved through bilateral or multilateral negotiations.[78] As is the case with many other international agreements,[79] recourse to 'consultations' is required before invoking the panel process. However, recourse to good offices, conciliation and mediation is voluntary and unusual[80] and so far irrelevant in the area of intellectual property. From the institutional point of view, it will be up to the WTO Director-General to initiate these procedures upon request from the parties.[81]

Arbitration in the WTO may relate to the implementation of panel reports or may function as well as an independent dispute settlement mechanism. In the first case, arbitration may be instrumental to the determination of the period of time to implement rulings[82] and may also address specificities concerning the sanctions or principles for the implementation of the rulings.[83] This type of arbitration will be conducted

70 *See* Articles 16.4 and 17.14 Dispute Settlement Understanding (emphasis added). *See* also Hudec (1993), pp. 235–236; Pauwelyn (2005), pp. 26–27; Romano (2007), p. 791.

71 *See* Section 2.3.

72 'Neither Article 3.3 nor 3.7 of the DSU nor any other provision of the DSU contain any explicit requirement that a Member must have a "legal interest" as a prerequisite for requesting a panel.' *See* WTO Appellate Body Report, *European Communities – Regime for the importation, sale and distribution of bananas*, WT/DS27/AB/R, 9 September 1997, para. 132.

73 *See* Article 4 Dispute Settlement Understanding. In the more general language, consultations amount to negotiations.

74 *See* Articles 5 and 24 Dispute Settlement Understanding. 75 *Ibid.* 76 *Ibid.*

77 *See* Articles 21.3 and 25 Dispute Settlement Understanding.

78 It has been suggested that dispute settlement before a panel or the Appellate Body is merely the continuation of diplomatic means of dispute settlement. *See* Taniguchi (2009), p. 15; Davey (2000), p. 291.

79 *See* Section 3 on dispute settlement in PTAs.

80 In 2001 the Director-General notified WTO Members of his readiness to implement Article 5 and assist them in good offices, mediation and conciliation. *See* WTO (2001). In 2002 was received the first request for mediation by the Philippines, Thailand, and the European Communities. *See* WTO General Council (2002a).

81 *See* Article 5.6 Dispute Settlement Understanding.

82 This would be the case if the parties do not successfully agree within forty-five days. *See* Article 21.3(c) Dispute Settlement Understanding.

83 *See* Article 22.6 Dispute Settlement Understanding. In this context, though, it must be underlined that the function of the WTO arbitration is not to suggest the means for specific implementation of the ruling. *See* WTO, *Australia – Measures Affecting Importation of Salmon, Arbitration under Article 21.3(c) of the Understanding on Rules and Procedures governing the settlement of disputes*, WT/DS18/9, 23 February 1999, para. 35.

by a sole arbitrator, appointed by the Director-General, if the parties cannot agree within ten days after referring the matter to arbitration.[84] Arbitration may also be an independent means of dispute settlement to solve clearly defined differences.[85] In this case, parties are free to decide how to appoint the arbitrator or arbitrators.

Only States have access to the DSB, and only State laws or conducts are addressed in the rulings.[86] Given the inherently political context, launching a dispute in the WTO context is accompanied by a careful evaluation of all circumstances. This keeps the number of cases low compared to the situation that would exist if intellectual property owners had direct access to the system.[87] Moreover, the fact that laws and State conducts are the main object of the WTO disputes also helps explain why systemic rather than immediately commercial issues are generally the object of the DSB rulings.[88]

After the consultation period expires, parties can request the establishment of a panel.[89] WTO dispute settlement proceedings are adversarial, thus permitting parties to present their claims and counter-claims. In the panel process, parties can present written submissions[90] followed by oral hearings. The panel will then prepare an interim report describing the facts and the applicable law as well as its conclusions. Once the parties have given their feedback on the interim report, the panel will finalize its report.[91]

The system designed in the Uruguay Round treats panel and Appellate Body rulings as judicial decisions. As such, and probably to counterbalance the loss of their power to veto the adoption of panel reports,[92] parties are given the opportunity to appeal 'both to correct errors that might be made by an *ad hoc* panel and to give participants dissatisfied with the outcome a second chance to be heard'.[93] The Appellate Body conducts this task in a speedy process[94] that culminates in a ruling on the 'issues of law covered in the

84 *See* footnote 12 to Article 21.3(c) Dispute Settlement Understanding.

85 Article 25 Dispute Settlement Understanding allows WTO Members to agree to settle their differences by arbitration and leaves ample margin to agree upon a procedure. The award of the arbitral body does not need to be adopted by the Dispute Settlement Understanding as panel reports but can be enforced in the same manner.

86 Some claim it is necessary to open the Dispute Settlement Body to private parties as well. *See* Zekos (2007), pp. 441–451.

87 Several internal mechanisms (the Technical Barriers Regulation in Europe or the Section 301 of the US Trade Act) permit, however, private parties to influence a State's decision on the initiation of cases, as exemplified in the WTO Appellate Body Report, *United States – Section 211 Omnibus Appropriations Act 1998*, WT/DS176/AB/R, 2 January 2002 (hereinafter WTO Appellate Body, *US-Havana Club*).

88 *See* Abbott (2004b), pp. 428–429; Pauwelyn (2010), p.421.

89 According to Articles 4.7 and 4.8 Dispute Settlement Understanding, a consultation period of sixty days, a period that may be shortened to twenty days in case of urgency.

90 *See* Article 12.6 Dispute Settlement Understanding.

91 *See* Article 15 Dispute Settlement Understanding.

92 *See* Lorcher (2003), p. 207.

93 *See* Dreyfuss and Lowenfeld (1997), p. 316.

94 In sixty days from the date of appeal, exceptionally in ninety days. *See* Article 17.5 Dispute Settlement Understanding.

panel report and legal interpretations developed by the panel'.[95] The Appellate Body may 'uphold, modify or reverse the legal findings and conclusions of the panel'.[96]

Even if WTO panels and Appellate Body reports are only binding upon the parties to the controversy and do not give place to jurisprudence conditioning future cases,[97] they are however highly influential. First, it is common practice among WTO panels to quote Appellate Body reports as well as reports issued by other panels. Moreover, panel reports can also influence the development of intellectual property treaties, 'which are often negotiated or implemented in the shadow of these reports'.[98] Moreover, the reports may also feed the debate and add arguments in the context of the processes taking place in the TRIPS Council and other intellectual property-related organs and organizations.[99]

2.4 Enforcement of Dispute Settlement Body Decisions

The implementation process or enforcement procedure starts once the Appellate Body has delivered its decision, provided that further clarification or specifications are not needed. It is in this context that the losing party will inform the DSB of its intentions with regard to implementing the recommendations and rulings of the DSB.[100] Given that the objective of the rulings of WTO panels and the Appellate Body is to restore the situation that existed before the infringement,[101] the first objective of the adopted report will be the withdrawal of incompatible measures.

If the infringing party does not implement the recommendations within a reasonable period of time, parties can agree on trade compensation.[102] This remedy will entail additional trade concessions in favour of the winning party,[103] which will be applied temporarily until the situation is restored. If no compensation is agreed upon, the complainant(s) may request the DSB to authorize the suspension of concessions or other obligations under the covered agreements.[104] Trade retaliation must be equivalent to the level of the nullification or impairment of benefits

95 *See* Article 17.6 Dispute Settlement Understanding. *See* also Article 17.5 Dispute Settlement Understanding.

96 *See* Article 17.13 Dispute Settlement Understanding.

97 *See* Matsushita, Schoenbaum and Mavroidis (2006), p. 112.

98 *See* Yu (2011f), p. 743.

99 *Ibid.*

100 *See* Article 21.3 Dispute Settlement Understanding. The reasonable period of time may be proposed by the infringing party (and approved by the Dispute Settlement Understanding), agreed by the parties or decided by arbitration if parties do not agree.

101 *See* Article 3.7 Dispute Settlement Understanding.

102 *See* Articles 3.7 and 22.2 Dispute Settlement Understanding.

103 *See* Articles 22.1 and 22.2 Dispute Settlement Understanding. An example, in the intellectual property context, is the compromise of the United States in the dispute concerning Section 110(5) of US Copyright Act to pay a lump sum to compensate for the nullification or impairment of the benefits the European Community was entitled to under the TRIPS Agreement. *See* WTO, Notification of a Mutually Satisfactory Temporary Arrangement, *United States-Section 110(5) of the US Copyright Act*, WT/DS160/23, 26 June 2003, para. 2.

104 *See* Articles 22.1 and 22.2 Dispute Settlement Understanding.

inflicted[105] and will last until the inconsistent measure is removed.[106] Among the possible options, retaliation in the same economic sector where the violation occurred is preferred,[107] while cross-agreement retaliation is particularly problematic in the intellectual property field.

In fact, the rationale for retaliation is strange when observed from the intellectual property perspective, in principle contrary to the drastic measures that retaliation implies.[108] However, from the point of view of the national interest the conclusions are different, particularly if the view taken is that of developing countries.[109] In this case, 'intellectual property retaliation is far more advantageous to developing states, compared to retaliation in goods, when targeting developed states'.[110] This is due to several reasons: first, because it 'improves net welfare for the developing state'[111] given that it does not require to bear an economic loss to sanction the violating state, as do most suspensions of trade in goods or services; second, the threat of sanctions is credible since it is fundamentally self-interested;[112] and third, retaliation effects in intellectual property are felt by 'very influential interest groups in the respondent state'[113] and may be more effective than retaliation in other sectors.

The possibility to agree on compensation or, instead, to retaliate has created a debate concerning whether DSB reports are actually binding or whether they can be substituted by compensation or trade retaliation.[114] While legally speaking parties are obliged to fulfil the rulings – and the DSU clearly establishes that 'neither compensation nor the suspension of concessions or other obligations is preferred to full implementation of a recommendation'[115] – in practical terms parties may choose to maintain the incompatible measure, practice or regulation and pay a price for it.

2.5 The Dispute Settlement Body's Record in the Intellectual Property Area

This section provides a general account of the DSB's activity in the intellectual property domain. It does not aim to provide an in-depth analysis of the intellectual

105 *See* Article 22.4 Dispute Settlement Understanding.

106 *See* Article 22.8 Dispute Settlement Understanding.

107 *See* Article 22.3(e) Dispute Settlement Understanding.

108 Retaliation would imply the suspension of rights of foreign right holders, a measure that would probably be considered unacceptable even by domestic right holders. Moreover, retaliation in the intellectual property context could be controversial when assessed against other international treaties and legal regimes, such as investment law or human rights law, or even other intellectual property treaties. *See* WTO Decision by the Arbitrators, *European Communities – Regime for the Importation, Sale and Distribution of Bananas – Recourse to Arbitration by the European Communities under Article 22.6 of the DSU*, WT/DS27/ARB/ECU, 24 March 2000, paras. 157–158; Pauwelyn (2010), p. 426.

109 The purpose of accepting cross-agreement retaliation came from the government of the United States, concerned about the enforcement of the TRIPS Agreement: 'by linking intellectual property and the trade in goods (the trade in which developing countries are most politically sensitive), the developed states would have a more effective weapon against violations of the TRIPS Agreement'. *See* Brewster (2011), pp. 39–40.

110 *See* Brewster (2011), p. 7. 111 *Ibid.* 112 *Ibid.* 113 *Ibid.*

114 In favour of the binding nature of the rulings, *see* Jackson (1998a), pp. 169–170.

115 *See* Article 22.1 Dispute Settlement Understanding.

property-related jurisprudence of the DSB, a task undertaken in other chapters of this book with respect to some enforcement-related areas. As has been noted, the applicability of the WTO Dispute Settlement System to the TRIPS Agreement disputes was a major achievement and a central element of the international intellectual regime that emerged from the TRIPS Agreement. Right after the adoption of the TRIPS Agreement observers predicted that the number of controversies would grow exponentially[116] and that the DSB would be flooded with intellectual property disputes,[117] mainly affecting developing countries.[118]

The reality has been very different. Disputes concerning intellectual property have been few compared to the larger category of trade disputes. Although the frequency of disputes involving the TRIPS Agreement placed the agreement in the eleventh position among the twenty-one WTO treaties, the difference in the number of cases between the TRIPS Agreement and the top five agreements in terms of controversies is enormous. For instance, the GATT has been cited in consultation requests in 385 cases, while the TRIPS Agreement has been cited in just 34 cases.[119] In fact, the number of disputes seems to have declined[120] or at least stabilized at a relatively low level.[121]

Even more important, controversies relating to the TRIPS Agreement are frequently settled through consultations and thus do not make their way into the panel process.[122] Hence, if the focus is put on controversies that reach the panel and Appellate Body stages, the difference between trade disputes and intellectual property disputes is even greater. It has, in fact, been argued that 'the positive and often complex and costly steps that TRIPS requires countries to take may explain why complainants have focused on consultations and cooperative strategies rather than confrontation and litigation'.[123] Indeed, when the objective is the development of norms or institutions rather than, for instance, lowering tariffs, States that have a particular interest in intellectual property may prefer giving technical or financial support or exercising political or diplomatic pressure rather than resorting to direct confrontation.[124]

[116] *See* Watal (2001), p. 363; Reichman (2003), p. 125. Similarly, but referring to disputes in general, *see* Petersmann (2006), p. 288.

[117] *See* Pires de Carvalho (2005), pp. 416–417.

[118] *See* Dreyfuss and Lowenfeld (1997), p. 282; Otten (1998), p. 528; Mota (2000), p. 533.

[119] The number of cases citing each agreement in the request for consultations by June 2014 was: GATT 1994, 385 cases; Subsidies and Countervailing Measures, 102 cases; Anti-dumping, 102 cases; Agriculture, 74 cases; Agreement Establishing the WTO, 53 cases; Technical Barriers to Trade, 49 cases; Safeguards, 44 cases; Sanitary and Phytosanitary Measures, 41 cases; Import Licensing, 41 cases; Trade-Related Investment Measures, 39 cases; Intellectual Property, 34 cases; Protocol of Accession, 26 cases; Services, 23 cases; Textiles and Clothing, 16 cases; Customs Valuation, 16 cases; DSU, 15 cases; Rules of Origin, 7 cases; Preshipment Inspection, 2 cases; Government Procurement, 4 cases; GATT 1947, 1 case; Civil Aircraft, 0 cases. *See* www.wto.org/english/tratop_e/dispu_e/dispu_agreements_index_e.htm?id=A29 (last accessed October 2016).

[120] *See* Fukunaga (2008), p. 888.

[121] *See* Pauwelyn (2010), p. 393; Lee (2011), p. 405.

[122] *See* Fukunaga (2008), pp. 882, 888; Lee (2011), pp. 405, 408, 409; Okediji (2002), p. 633.

[123] *See* Pauwelyn (2010), p. 422.

[124] *Ibid.*

The prediction that developing countries would be most frequently denounced in the context of the TRIPS Agreement has not been fulfilled either. In fact, most intellectual property complaints have targeted developed countries, which have, in some cases, been denounced by developing countries.[125] While developed countries consider the DSB a central body for the promotion of intellectual property enforcement, the possibility of achieving the same objectives through other means – together with the socio-political consequences of launching an intellectual property-related case against a developing country – may have forestalled a more intensive use of the dispute settlement system.[126]

The relevance of the TRIPS Agreement and its Dispute Settlement System has been primarily systemic. The majority of controversies have not addressed substantive intellectual property matters.[127] Instead, disputes have dealt with aspects such as transitory periods and the relationship between the TRIPS and other WTO domains as well as trade discrimination issues.[128] This may respond to the fact that the TRIPS Agreement was chiefly 'designed to address systemic intellectual property enforcement issues, and not to serve as a court of appeals on individual cases or controversies'.[129] That is, disputes have not arisen in relation to specific situations that particular companies may face but 'to force the specific country to align its legislation with TRIPS and, in some cases even more so, to send a signal to, and set a precedent for, all WTO members'.[130]

The articles of the TRIPS Agreement on enforcement have been rarely addressed by the WTO adjudicatory organs. In *Havana Club*, a dispute between the United States and the European Union concerning the ban on the protection and recognition of trademarks and trade names in connection with Cuban business relations, the Appellate Body found that the procedural obligations of Article 42 of the TRIPS Agreement do not prevent legislating whether 'courts must examine each and every requirement of substantive law at issue before making a ruling'.[131] That is, the WTO Parties are not obliged to permit adjudication of substantive claims regarding trademarks if it has been previously determined that the claimant is not the holder of an interest in the subject mark.[132] *China – Intellectual Property Rights*[133] is the most comprehensive WTO Panel report to have examined TRIPS norms on enforcement, and as such it is studied in several chapters of this book. Part III of the TRIPS Agreement remains, however, largely

[125] *See* Fukunaga (2008), pp. 879, 887; Lee (2011), pp. 405, 411.

[126] In this regard, it has been suggested that the debates on the relationship between public health and intellectual property may explain the low number of the TRIPS Agreement disputes filed against developing countries. *See* Pauwelyn (2010), p. 427.

[127] The exception being the cases WTO Panel Report, *Canada-Patent Protection of Pharmaceutical Products*, WT/DS114/R, 17 March 2000; WTO Panel Report, *United States-Section 110(5) of US Copyright Act*, WT/DS160/R, 15 June 2000; WTO Panel Report, *China – measures affecting the protection and enforcement of intellectual property rights*, WT/DS362/R, 26 January 2009 (hereinafter WTO Panel, *China – Intellectual Property Rights*).

[128] *See* Abbott and Cottier (2003), pp. 396–397.

[129] *Ibid.*, p. 443.

[130] *See* Abbott and Cottier (2003), p. 399.

[131] *See* WTO Appellate Body, *US-Havana Club*, para. 226 (emphasis omitted).

[132] *See* Petersmann (2006), p. 311.

[133] *See* WTO Panel, *China – Intellectual Property Rights*.

non-interpreted, something that is particularly relevant in light of its open and vague content. By contrast, mutually agreed solutions affecting Argentina, Greece, Sweden, Denmark, Denmark and the European Union have targeted enforcement related issues, including criminal enforcement, injunctions and border measures.

3 *Dispute Settlement Bodies in Preferential Trade Agreements*

Preferential Trade Agreements largely replicate the WTO model and create an array of diplomatic and jurisdictional dispute settlement procedures. This is particularly the case of the most advanced PTAs, on which this chapter's analysis is based.[134] From the institutional point of view, the major difference between the dispute settlement systems of the WTO and PTAs is the stability and permanence of the former. PTAs do not create a permanent jurisdictional body in charge of settling disputes. The scheme generally followed in PTAs consists of setting up *ad hoc* bodies, generally inter-State arbitral panels. PTAs do, however, create permanent governing bodies and bodies specifically in charge of monitoring the intellectual property section.[135] These political bodies oversee the enforcement of the treaty and may play a role in dispute settlement proceedings, particularly with respect to political mechanisms for the settlement of disputes.

Non-jurisdictional or diplomatic mechanisms are the first option for settling disputes arising from PTAs. All agreements mention consultations as the initial dispute settlement mechanism. Indeed, in some cases recourse to consultations is mandatory,[136]

[134] The analysis of this section is based on the study of the intellectual property and dispute settlement provisions of 54 PTAs, namely those concluded by the United States, the European Free Trade Association, the European Union (its five last generation agreements), Mexico, Australia and Japan: ASEAN-Australia-New Zealand FTA and EIA (2010); Australia-Chile FTA and EIA (2009); Chile-Japan FTA and EIA (2007); Chile-Mexico FTA and EIA (1999); Colombia-Mexico FTA and EIA (1995); CAFTA-DR-US FTA and EIA (2006); EFTA-Albania FTA (2010); EFTA-Chile FTA and EIA (2004); EFTA-Colombia FTA and EIA (2011); EFTA-Croatia FTA (2002); EFTA-Egypt FTA (2007); EFTA-Former Yugoslav Republic of Macedonia FTA (2002); EFTA-Hong Kong, China FTA and EIA (2012); EFTA-Israel FTA (1993); EFTA-Jordan FTA (2002); EFTA-Republic of Korea FTA and EIA (2006); EFTA-Lebanon FTA (2007); EFTA-Mexico FTA and EIA (2001); EFTA-Montenegro FTA (2012); EFTA-Morocco FTA (1999); EFTA-Peru FTA (2011); EFTA-Serbia FTA (2010); EFTA-Singapore FTA and EIA (2003); EFTA-Turkey FTA (1992); EFTA-Ukraine FTA and EIA (2012); EU-CARIFORUM States FTA and EIA (2008); EU-Colombia and Peru FTA and EIA (2013); EU-Republic of Korea FTA and EIA (2011); India-Japan FTA and EIA (2011); Japan-Indonesia FTA and EIA (2008); Japan-Malaysia FTA and EIA (2006); Japan-Mexico FTA and EIA (2005); Japan-Peru FTA and EIA (2012); Japan-Philippines FTA and EIA (2008); Japan-Singapore FTA and EIA (2002); Japan-Switzerland FTA and EIA (2009); Japan-Thailand FTA and EIA (2007); Japan-Viet Nam FTA and EIA (2009); Republic of Korea-US FTA and EIA (2012); Mexico-El Salvador FTA and EIA (2001); Mexico-Guatemala FTA and EIA (2001); Mexico-Honduras FTA and EIA (2001); Thailand-Australia FTA and EIA (2005); US-Australia FTA and EIA (2005); US-Bahrain FTA and EIA (2006); US-Chile FTA and EIA (2004); US-Colombia FTA and EIA (2012); US-Jordan FTA and EIA (2001); US-Morocco FTA and EIA (2006); US-Panama FTA and EIA (2012); US-Oman FTA and EIA (2009); US-Peru FTA and EIA (2009); US-Singapore FTA and EIA (2004).

[135] *See* Section III.

[136] *See* Article 1802 Thailand-Australia FTA and EIA (2005); Article 204 EU-CARIFORUM States FTA and EIA (2008); Article 14.3 EU-Republic of Korea FTA and EIA (2011); Article 301 EU-Colombia

while good offices, mediation and conciliation are voluntary.[137] Consultations may take place bilaterally in the context of the general committee governing the treaty[138] or in thematic sub-committees such as intellectual property committees.[139]

The so-called 'right to a panel', which recognizes the possibility of requesting the establishment of an *ad hoc* dispute settlement body to adjudicate a specific controversy, is a central component of the WTO Dispute Settlement System.[140] PTAs also recognize the right to request the establishment of an arbitral tribunal[141] – generally

and Peru FTA and EIA (2013). It is not entirely clear, but it could also be the case of Article 21.3(3) of Chapter 21 Australia-Chile FTA and EIA (2009).

137 *See* Articles 6 and 7 of Chapter 17 ASEAN-Australia-New Zealand FTA and EIA (2010); Article 63 ASEAN-Japan FTA (2008); Article 21 of Chapter 21 Australia-Chile FTA and EIA (2009); Article 1803 Thailand-Australia FTA and EIA (2005); Article 89 EFTA-Chile FTA and EIA (2004); Article 12.2 EFTA-Central America FTA and EIA (2014); Article 12.4 EFTA-Colombia FTA and EIA (2011); Article 10.2 EFTA-Hong Kong, China FTA and EIA (2012); Article 9.2 EFTA-Republic of Korea FTA and EIA (2006); Article 12.4 EFTA-Peru FTA (2011); Article 9.2 EFTA-Ukraine FTA and EIA (2012); Article 205 EU-CARIFORUM States FTA and EIA (2008); Article 323 EU-Colombia and Peru FTA and EIA (2013); Article 135 India-Japan FTA and EIA (2011); Article 141 Japan-Indonesia FTA and EIA (2008); Article 206 Japan-Peru FTA and EIA (2012); Article 141 Japan-Singapore FTA and EIA (2002); Article 140 Japan-Switzerland FTA and EIA (2009); Article 161 Japan-Thailand FTA and EIA (2007); Article 118 Japan-Viet Nam FTA and EIA (2009); Article 151 Japan-Philippines FTA and EIA (2008); Article 147 Japan-Malaysia FTA and EIA (2006); Article 21.4 of Chapter 21 Australia-Chile FTA and EIA (2009); Article 20.5 CAFTA-DR-US FTA and EIA (2006); Article 21.5 US-Peru FTA and EIA (2009); Article 21.5 US-Colombia FTA and EIA (2012); Article 20.5 US-Panama FTA and EIA (2012); Article 22.5 US-Chile FTA and EIA (2004); Article 18.05 Chile-Mexico FTA and EIA (1999); Article 19.06 Mexico-El Salvador FTA and EIA (2001); Article 19.06 Mexico-Guatemala FTA and EIA (2001); Article 19.06 Mexico-Honduras FTA and EIA (2001); Article 19.06 Colombia-Mexico FTA and EIA (1995).

138 This is the case of the agreements concluded by the United States and Mexico.

139 *See* Article 301 EU-Colombia and Peru FTA and EIA (2013).

140 *See* Jackson (1998b), p. 72.

141 *See* Articles 6.5 and 8.1 of Chapter 17 ASEAN-Australia-New Zealand FTA and EIA (2010); Article 1804 Thailand-Australia FTA and EIA (2005); Article 20.6 CAFTA-DR-US FTA and EIA (2006); Article 21.7 US-Australia FTA and EIA (2005); Article 19.7 US-Bahrain FTA and EIA (2006); Article 20.7 US-Oman FTA and EIA (2009); Article 21.6 US-Peru FTA and EIA (2009); Article 21.6 US-Colombia FTA and EIA (2012); Article 17.1(c) US-Jordan FTA and EIA (2001); Article 22.9 Republic of Korea-US FTA and EIA (2012); Article 20.6 US-Panama FTA and EIA (2012); Article 22.6 US-Chile FTA and EIA (2004); Article 19.1(d) US-Israel FTA (1985) (alluding to conciliation instead of arbitration); Article 20.7 US-Morocco FTA and EIA (2006); Article 20.4.4 US-Singapore FTA and EIA (2004); Article 18.06 Chile-Mexico FTA and EIA (1999); Article 33 EFTA-Albania FTA (2010); Article 91 EFTA-Chile FTA and EIA (2004); Article 12.4 EFTA-Central America FTA and EIA (2014); Article 12.6 EFTA-Colombia FTA and EIA (2011); Article 41 EFTA-Egypt FTA (2007); Article 10.4 EFTA-Hong Kong, China FTA and EIA (2012); Article 25 *bis* EFTA-Israel FTA (1993); Article 31 EFTA-Jordan FTA (2002); Article 9.4 EFTA-Republic of Korea FTA and EIA (2006); Article 34 EFTA-Lebanon FTA (2007); Article 43 EFTA-Montenegro FTA (2012); Article 24 EFTA-Morocco FTA (1999); Article 12.6 EFTA-Peru FTA (2011); Article 34 EFTA-Serbia FTA (2010); Article 38 EFTA-Tunisia FTA (2005); Article 9.4 EFTA-Ukraine FTA and EIA (2012); Article 136 India-Japan FTA and EIA (2011); Article 142 Japan-Indonesia FTA and EIA (2008); Article 209 Japan-Peru FTA and EIA (2012); Article 143 Japan-Singapore FTA and EIA (2002); Article 141 Japan-Switzerland FTA and EIA (2009); Article 162 Japan-Thailand FTA and EIA (2007); Article 119 Japan-Viet Nam FTA and EIA (2009); Article 153 Japan-Philippines FTA and EIA (2008); Article 148 Japan-Malaysia FTA and EIA (2006); Article 178 Chile-Japan FTA and EIA (2007); Article 19.07 Mexico-El Salvador FTA and EIA (2001); Article 19.07 Mexico-Guatemala FTA and EIA (2001); Article 19.07 Mexico-Honduras FTA and EIA (2001); Article 19.07 Colombia-Mexico FTA and EIA (1995).

composed of three members[142] – in case consultations do not deliver a positive outcome or one of the parties does not engage in the consultations.

While the criteria and procedure for designating panel members vary across treaties, their ultimate goal is to achieve a balanced composition. Negotiations between the parties to select the members of the panel are important,[143] and a frequent option is to nominate one arbitrator for each party, sometimes selected among the members of an agreed-upon roster of experts. In this case, the appointed arbitrators will designate a third arbitrator, who will chair the tribunal.[144] This nomination may be also done by drawing lots, particularly if parties cannot agree or do not appoint an arbitrator.[145] Another option implies involving an independent authority in the decision, such as the WTO Director-General,[146] the Secretary-General of the Permanent Court of Arbitration[147] or the President of the International Court of Justice.[148]

Some agreements prescribe the elements that panel reports must address. Among them, mention is frequently made of the need to adopt an initial and a final report[149] and the requirement that the panel summarizes the issues of fact and addresses legal controversies.[150] In all cases the decisions of the panel will be final and binding on the parties.

142 Exceptionally, some Mexican agreements establish that the arbitral panel will be integrated by five members. *See* for instance Article 18.09 Chile-Mexico FTA and EIA (1999).

143 *See* for instance Article 11.3 of Chapter 17 ASEAN-Australia-New Zealand FTA and EIA (2010); Article 64 ASEAN-Japan FTA (2008).

144 *See* Article 11.6 of Chapter 17 ASEAN-Australia-New Zealand FTA and EIA (2010); Article 21.7 of Chapter 21 Australia-Chile FTA and EIA (2009); Article 1805.1 Thailand-Australia FTA and EIA (2005); Article 143.4 Japan-Singapore FTA and EIA (2002).

145 *See* Article 136 India-Japan FTA and EIA (2011); Article 142 Japan-Indonesia FTA and EIA (2008); Article 210 Japan-Peru FTA and EIA (2012); Article 162 Japan-Thailand FTA and EIA (2007); Article 180 Chile-Japan FTA and EIA (2007); Article 19.09 Mexico-El Salvador FTA and EIA (2001); Article 19.07 Mexico-Guatemala FTA and EIA (2001); Article 19.07 Mexico-Honduras FTA and EIA (2001); Article 20.9 CAFTA-DR-US FTA and EIA (2006); Article 21.7 US-Australia FTA and EIA (2005); Article 19.7 US-Bahrain FTA and EIA (2006); Article 20.7 US-Oman FTA and EIA (2009); Article 21.9 US-Peru FTA and EIA (2009); Article 21.9 US-Colombia FTA and EIA (2012); Article 22.9 Republic of Korea-US FTA and EIA (2012); Article 20.9 US-Panama FTA and EIA (2012). This is however not mentioned in Article 17.1(c) US-Jordan FTA and EIA (2001); Article 22.9 US-Chile FTA and EIA (2004); Article 20.7 US-Morocco FTA and EIA (2006); Article 20.4.4 US-Singapore FTA and EIA (2004). Some treaties only mention negotiations, and in case negotiations fail, they mention selection by lot. *See* Article 207 EU-CARIFORUM States FTA and EIA (2008); Article 14.5 EU-Republic of Korea FTA and EIA (2011); Article 303 EU-Colombia and Peru FTA and EIA (2013).

146 *See* Article 65.3 ASEAN-Japan FTA (2008); Article 92.5 EFTA-Chile FTA and EIA (2004); Article 9.5.4 EFTA-Republic of Korea FTA and EIA (2006); Article 12.8.4 EFTA-Peru FTA (2011); Article 119.5 Japan-Viet Nam FTA and EIA (2009).

147 *See* Article 33.6 EFTA-Albania FTA (2010); Article 12.9 EFTA-Colombia FTA and EIA (2011).

148 *See* Article 10.5.5 EFTA-Hong Kong, China FTA and EIA (2012); EFTA-Lebanon FTA (2007).

149 At the same time, in the US-Jordan FTA and EIA (2001), only one report is foreseen. *See* Article 17(d).

150 *See* Articles 20.13 and 20.14 CAFTA-DR-US FTA and EIA (2006); Articles 21.9 and 21.10 US-Australia FTA and EIA (2005); Article 19.9 US-Bahrain FTA and EIA (2006); Article 20.9 US-Oman FTA and EIA (2009); Articles 21.13 and 21.14 US-Peru FTA and EIA (2009); Articles 21.13 and 21.14

The consequences of the PTAs' arbitral decisions follow the pattern of reparation, compensation and trade retaliation found in the WTO system. In the first instance, the Party complained against shall eliminate the non-conformity, nullification or impairment as determined in the report. If the decision is not implemented and Parties are unable to reach agreement on a solution, the two sides shall enter into negotiations with a view to finding mutually acceptable compensation. Finally, if the Parties are unable to agree on compensation or have agreed on compensation and this is not satisfied, the complaining State may suspend the application of benefits of equivalent effect.[151]

One particularly interesting feature of some agreements is the enactment of a system for referring matters from national judicial or administrative proceedings. Similar to a prejudicial question but merely consultative, pursuant to this system interpretation or implementation issues arising in domestic judicial or

US-Colombia FTA and EIA (2012); Articles 22.11 and 22.12 Republic of Korea-US FTA and EIA (2012); Articles 20.12 and 20.13 US-Panama FTA and EIA (2012); Articles 22.12 and 22.13 US-Chile FTA and EIA (2004); Articles 20.9 US-Morocco FTA and EIA (2006); Articles 20.4.5 US-Singapore FTA and EIA (2004); Articles 18.13–18.14 Chile-Mexico FTA and EIA (1999); Articles 208 and 209 EU-CARIFORUM States FTA and EIA (2008); Articles 14.6 and 14.7 EU-Republic of Korea FTA and EIA (2011); Article 137 India-Japan FTA and EIA (2011); Article 143 Japan-Indonesia FTA and EIA (2008); Article 212 Japan-Peru FTA and EIA (2012); Article 144 Japan-Singapore FTA and EIA (2002); Article 142 Japan-Switzerland FTA and EIA (2009); Article 163 Japan-Thailand FTA and EIA (2007); Article 120 Japan-Viet Nam FTA and EIA (2009); Article 154 Japan-Philippines FTA and EIA (2008); Article 149 Japan-Malaysia FTA and EIA (2006); Article 181 Chile-Japan FTA and EIA (2007); Articles 19.13 and 19.14 Mexico-El Salvador FTA and EIA (2001); Articles 19.13 and 19.14 Mexico-Guatemala FTA and EIA (2001); Articles 19.13 and 19.14 Mexico-Honduras FTA and EIA (2001); Articles 19.14 and 19.15 Colombia-Mexico FTA and EIA (1995).

151 *See* Article 17 of Chapter 17 ASEAN-Australia-New Zealand FTA and EIA (2010); Article 71 ASEAN-Japan FTA (2008); Articles 21.11 and 21.12 of Chapter 21 Australia-Chile FTA and EIA (2009); Article 1811 Thailand-Australia FTA and EIA (2005); Articles 20.15 and 20.16 CAFTA-DR-US FTA and EIA (2006); Articles 21.10 and 21.11 US-Australia FTA and EIA (2005); Articles 19.10 and 19.11 US-Bahrain FTA and EIA (2006); Articles 20.10 and 20.11 US-Oman FTA and EIA (2009); Articles 21.15 and 21.16 US-Peru FTA and EIA (2009); Articles 21.15 and 21.16 US-Colombia FTA and EIA (2012); Articles 22.12 and 22.13 Republic of Korea-US FTA and EIA (2012); Articles 20.14 and 20.14 US-Panama FTA and EIA (2012); Articles 22.14 and 22.15 US-Chile FTA and EIA (2004); Articles 20.10 and 20.11 US-Morocco FTA and EIA (2006); Articles 20.5 and 20.6 US-Singapore FTA and EIA (2004); Articles 18.15 and 18.16 Chile-Mexico FTA and EIA (1999); Article 34 EFTA-Albania FTA (2010); Article 96 EFTA-Chile FTA and EIA (2004); Article 46 EFTA-Bosnia and Herzegovina FTA (2015); Articles 12.8 and 12.9 EFTA-Central America FTA and EIA (2014); Articles 10.9 and 10.10 EFTA-Hong Kong, China FTA and EIA (2012); Article 9.10 EFTA-Republic of Korea FTA and EIA (2006); Article 44 EFTA-Montenegro FTA (2012); Articles 12.16 and 12.17 EFTA-Peru FTA (2011); Article 35 EFTA-Serbia FTA (2010); Articles 9.8 and 9.9 EFTA-Ukraine FTA and EIA (2012); Article 213 EU-CARIFORUM States FTA and EIA (2008); Article 14.11 EU-Republic of Korea FTA and EIA (2011); Article 310 EU-Colombia and Peru FTA and EIA (2013); Article 140 India-Japan FTA and EIA (2011); Article 146 Japan-Indonesia FTA and EIA (2008); Articles 218 and 219 Japan-Peru FTA and EIA (2012); Article 147 Japan-Singapore FTA and EIA (2002); Article 145 Japan-Switzerland FTA and EIA (2009); Article 166 Japan-Thailand FTA and EIA (2007); Article 123 Japan-Viet Nam FTA and EIA (2009); Article 157 Japan-Philippines FTA and EIA (2008); Articles 152 Japan-Malaysia FTA and EIA (2006); Article 185 Chile-Japan FTA and EIA (2007); Articles 19.15 and 19.16 Mexico-El Salvador FTA and EIA (2001); Articles 19.15 and 19.16 Mexico-Guatemala FTA and EIA (2001); Articles 19.15 and 19.16 Mexico-Honduras FTA and EIA (2001); Articles 19.16 and 19.17 Colombia-Mexico FTA and EIA (1995).

administrative proceedings may be posed to the joint committee and the other parties will be notified. The joint political body administering the treaty shall endeavour to agree on an appropriate response as expeditiously as possible, which shall be submitted to the local court or administrative body.[152]

In most treaties, intellectual property falls within the scope of the dispute settlement chapter, because it is either expressly mentioned or, at least, not specifically excluded. There are some exceptions, however. The first of these relates to treaties that expressly preclude intellectual property from dispute resolution.[153] A second exception concerns the exclusion or inclusion of only some intellectual property-related aspects. In this regard, the jurisdiction of the dispute settlement body may be limited to a number of topics, such as most favoured nation treatment within the area of intellectual property[154] or 'difficulties which affect trade' and relate to intellectual property.[155]

Some PTAs have tried to resolve the controversy regarding non-violation complaints, which have been the subject of heated discussions for the past twenty years in the WTO. In line with the positions defended in the global debate, PTAs' solutions vary widely. On the one hand, some treaties extend the competence of the dispute settlement body to cases where no infringement exists but a party claims that a benefit expected from the PTA has been nullified or impaired. This is the case of agreements concluded not only by the United States[156] but also by other States,[157] including developing countries.[158] On the other hand, in a limited number of cases,

[152] *See* Article 20.20 CAFTA-DR-US FTA and EIA (2006); Article 21.19 US-Peru FTA and EIA (2009); Article 21.19 US-Colombia FTA and EIA (2012); Article 20.18 US-Panama FTA and EIA (2012); Article 22.19 US-Chile FTA and EIA (2004); Article 18.17 Chile-Mexico FTA and EIA (1999); Article 19.17 Mexico-El Salvador FTA and EIA (2001); Article 19.18 Mexico-Guatemala FTA and EIA (2001); Article 19.18 Mexico-Honduras FTA and EIA (2001); Article 19.18.1(b) Colombia-Mexico FTA and EIA (1995).

[153] *See* Article 12.6 Republic of Korea-India FTA and EIA (2010); Article 100 Brunei Darussalam-Japan FTA and EIA (2008); Article 115 Chile-China FTA and EIA (2006/2010).

[154] According to Article 2(c) of Protocol 6 of the EU-Bosnia and Herzegovina FTA and EIA (2008/2015), dispute settlement mechanisms of the dispute settlement chapter apply to Article 73.2, which is the Article on the most favoured nation treatment in the area of intellectual property.

[155] *See* Article 44.2 EU-Algeria FTA (2005); Article 73.5 EU-Bosnia and Herzegovina FTA and EIA (2008/2015); Article 46.2 EU-South Africa FTA (2000).

[156] *See* Article 20.2(c) CAFTA-DR-US FTA and EIA (2006); Article 21.2(c) US-Australia FTA and EIA (2005); Article 19.2.(c) US-Bahrain FTA and EIA (2006); Article 22.2(c) US-Chile FTA and EIA (2004); Article 21.2(c) US-Colombia FTA and EIA (2012); Article 20.2(c) US-Morocco FTA and EIA (2006); Article 20.2(c) US-Panama FTA and EIA (2012); Article 20.2(c) US-Oman FTA and EIA (2009); Article 21.2(c) US-Peru FTA and EIA (2009).

[157] *See* Article 21.1.1 Australia-Chile FTA and EIA (2009); Annex 22.02(c) Nicaragua-Chinese Taipei FTA and EIA (2008).

[158] That is, agreements solely between developing countries. *See* Annex 18.02.1(d) Chile-Mexico FTA and EIA (1999); Article 19.02.1 Colombia-Mexico FTA and EIA (1995).

non-violation complaints have been expressly excluded from the dispute settlement bodies' competence.[159]

One of the noteworthy aspects of the relationship between PTAs, dispute settlement and intellectual property relates to an intriguing feature of many of these agreements, namely the repetition of the content of the treaties. Indeed, many treaties repeat the content of the Parties' domestic legislation and/or the content of PTAs they have concluded with third States. This apparently innocuous redundancy[160] has important effects. Given the link established between the material area covered by the treaty and the dispute settlement mechanism, Parties may have an interest in repeating substantive law. By re-enacting a provision already provided for in another treaty or already enshrined in the national legal order, the jurisdiction of the dispute settlement body of the new treaty can be triggered.[161] Similarly, the obligation to ratify multilateral WIPO conventions – even if these have already been ratified by the Parties – opens the door to submitting controversies arising from those conventions in the context of the bilateral dispute settlement regime.

Even if the main trading powers announce that dispute settlement mechanisms enshrined in PTAs 'will be triggered in cases of non-compliance with the required high(est) standards of IP protection',[162] the reality is that not a single intellectual property-related controversy has thus far been adjudicated in the context of a PTA.[163] Although the lack of transparency could imply that controversies have been adjudicated but not communicated, this does not seem to be the case. However, the lack of actual controversies does not diminish the relevance of the dispute settlement system of PTAs since its mere existence may have a powerful deterrent effect. Moreover, the system remains available regardless of its actual use. In this regard, if dispute settlement systems in PTAs start to be triggered and disputes are settled bilaterally, some countries may be worse off chiefly because they lose the power that broader coalitions and joint litigation may give in the context of the WTO.[164]

159 *See* Article 2(b) of Chapter 17 Australia-New Zealand FTA and EIA (1983/1989); Article 141 China-Costa Rica FTA and EIA (2011).

160 The fact that the implementation of international treaties generally requires the adoption of internal rules, added to the national treatment principle, is enough to extend the benefits deriving from intellectual property provisions contained therein to the nationals of any other country.

161 *See* Burrell and Weatherall (2008), p. 265; Seuba (2014a), p. 299.

162 *See* European Commission (2005a), p. 9.

163 The United States Trade Representative has created a special webpage on dispute settlement proceedings in the context of PTAs. By June 2014 the webpage only displayed a single dispute, in the context of the CAFTA-DR-US FTA and EIA (2006), between Guatemala and the United States, concerning labour standards. That information is now found on the webpage of the United States Department of Labor. *See Guatemala Submission under* CAFTA-DR, available at: www.dol.gov/ilab/trade/agreements/guatemalasub.htm (last accessed October 2016).

164 *See* Drahos (2007), p. 191.

III TREATY MONITORING BODIES

1 The TRIPS Council

The Agreement establishing the WTO created numerous committees and councils,[165] including the Council for Trade-Related Aspects of Intellectual Property Rights, commonly known as the TRIPS Council.[166] Open to the participation of all WTO Member States and to some organizations having observer status,[167] the TRIPS Council is the body charged with supervising and managing the operation of the Agreement.[168] This function is closely related to other tasks, such as serving as a forum for discussions, facilitating technical guidance and receiving notifications as established in the TRIPS Agreement. Since its creation, the Council has held between three and six formal meetings annually.[169]

Several articles of the TRIPS Agreement identify the TRIPS Council as the body responsible for receiving notifications relating to a range of matters.[170] This is notably the case of Article 63.2, which commands Member States to notify national laws, regulations, sentences and administrative rulings of general application relating to the Agreement.[171] This information, which has been further detailed in a number of documents,[172] will assist the Council in its review of the operation of

165 *See*, respectively, Articles IV.7 and IV.4 of the Agreement Establishing the World Trade Organization.

166 *See* Article IV.5 of the Agreement Establishing the World Trade Organization.

167 Intergovernmental organizations may have either regular or *ad hoc* observer status. The Food and Agriculture Organization, the International Monetary Fund, the International Union for the Protection of New Varieties of Plants, the Organisation for Economic Co-operation and Development, the United Nations, the United Nations Conference on Trade and Development, the World Bank, the World Customs Organization and the World Intellectual Property Organization enjoy regular observer status. The World Health Organization has *ad hoc* observer status, while other organizations have *ad hoc* observer status on a meeting-by-meeting basis: the African Regional Intellectual Property Organization, the African Intellectual Property Organization, the Cooperation Council of the Arab States of the Gulf and the European Free Trade Association. The Joint United Nations Programme on HIV/AIDS has observer status during the Council's discussions on the TRIPS Agreement and public health.

168 *See* Article 68 TRIPS Agreement.

169 *See* IP/C/8, 6 November 1996, six formal meetings; IP/C/12, 28 November 1997, six formal meetings; IP/C/15, 4 December 1998, five formal meetings; IP/C/19, 22 October 1999, four formal meetings; IP/C/22, 6 December 2000, four formal meetings; IP/C/23, 5 October 2001, three formal meetings; IP/C/27, 6 December 2002, five formal meetings; IP/C/30, 1 December 2003, four formal meetings; IP/C/32, 8 December 2004, four formal meetings; IP/C/44, 4 December 2006, three formal meetings IP/C/48, 7 December 2007, three formal meetings; IP/C/51, 4 December 2008, three formal meetings; IP/C/52, 5 November 2009, three formal meetings; IP/C/56, 10 November 2010, three formal meetings; IP/C/59, 7 November 2011, three formal meetings; IP/C/62, 26 November 2012, three formal meetings; IP/C/67, 23 October 2013, three formal meetings.

170 Notifications are received pursuant to Articles 1.3, 3.1, 4(d), 63.2, 69, 70.8 and 70.9 TRIPS Agreement.

171 That is, relating to the availability, scope, acquisition, enforcement and prevention of intellectual property abuse.

172 *See* WTO Council for Trade-Related Aspects of Intellectual Property Rights (1995a); WTO Council for Trade-Related Aspects of Intellectual Property Rights (1995b); Council for Trade-Related Aspects

the TRIPS Agreement in what has been considered a 'systemic approach' to monitor compliance.[173] This notification requirement has been well respected.[174]

The notification obligation is closely related to the review process as well as the so-called 'regulatory teaching'[175] and monitoring[176] functions of the TRIPS Council. The information provided by Members is the starting point of the process, with written questions and replies submitted to a review meeting, where further follow-up questions and replies are discussed. The legislation under review is distributed in advance to Member States, which study it and prepare questions. At subsequent meetings of the Council, Members are given an opportunity to follow up on topics that surfaced but were not sufficiently addressed in the review session.[177]

The review mechanism has a strong link to the enforcement provisions of the TRIPS Agreement, since it enhances compliance with the Agreement and contributes to preventing formal dispute settlement proceedings.[178] Among the benefits associated with the mechanism, mention is commonly made of the enhancement of the quality of the legislation and the clarification of the meaning of national norms.[179] The review mechanism helps raise awareness and understanding of obligations in the TRIPS Agreement, identify flaws in the notified norms, clarify eventual misunderstandings and, ultimately, reduce discrepancies in the interpretation of the norms.[180] While interpreting the Agreement or determining whether a Member complies with its obligations is not the function of the Council, it has been suggested that its deliberations should be taken into account in the context of dispute settlement proceedings.[181]

In addition to its notification and review functions, the Council also acts as a forum for discussion. The debates of the Council relate to topics that the TRIPS Agreement expressly instructs it to supervise as well as issues that attract international attention because of either the technical difficulties implied or their controversial nature. Among repeatedly raised topics are the implementation of Article 70 of the TRIPS Agreement (particularly Articles 70.2, 70.8 and 70.9, relating to the protection of existing subject matter[182]); the protection of geographical indications and the

of Intellectual Property Rights (1995c); WTO Council for Trade-Related Aspects of Intellectual Property Rights (1997).

173 *See* Article 63.2 TRIPS Agreement and Otten (1998), p. 524.

174 By 2013, 130 Members had notified all or part of their implementing legislation of the TRIPS Agreement. *See* WTO (2013), para. 2.1.

175 The concept of 'regulatory teaching' could be seen as reversed to the role played by the WTO as a 'regulatory learning'. *See* Lang and Scott (2009), p. 575.

176 *See* Article 68 TRIPS Agreement.

177 The review mechanism implemented by the TRIPS Council is supposedly more effective than the review taking place in other WTO councils and committees, due to the limited scope of the TRIPS Agreement by comparison to other WTO agreements. *See* Fukunaga (2008), p. 898.

178 *See* Otten (1998), p. 525. 179 *Ibid.*, p. 526.

180 *See* Vandoren (1999), p. 29; Fukunaga (2008), pp. 870, 894; Watal (2001), pp. 50–57, 84.

181 *See* Abbott (2004b), pp. 431–432.

182 *See* Annual Reports IP/C/8, 6 November 1996; IP/C/12, 28 November 1997; IP/C/15, 4 December 1998; IP/C/19, 22 October 1999; IP/C/22, 6 December 2000; IP/C/23, 5 October 2001.

establishment of a multilateral system of notification and registration of geographical indications for wines;[183] the implementation of Article 27.3(b) and the relationship between the TRIPS Agreement, the Convention on Biological Diversity and the protection of traditional knowledge;[184] the implementation of the commitment in Article 66.2 to provide incentives for promoting technology transfer to least-developed countries;[185] and the treatment of non-violation complaints in the context of the TRIPS Agreement.[186]

In parallel, Members have used the Council as a forum to discuss sensitive issues and new and emerging topics. Probably the first topic of global concern raised in the context of the TRIPS Agreement was the relationship between intellectual property and public health. While the Council has been the forum of intense discussions on this issue, it has also addressed specific topics, such as the implementation of compulsory licenses in countries that lack the capacity to manufacture pharmaceuticals and the detention of medicines in transit.[187] The Council also developed a proposal on non-voluntary licenses, which was

183 The protection of geographical indications has been on the agenda of the TRIPS Council on a regular, almost permanent, basis. *See* Annual Reports IP/C/8, 6 November 1996; IP/C/12, 28 November 1997; IP/C/15, 4 December 1998; IP/C/19, 22 October 1999; IP/C/22, 6 December 2000; IP/C/23, 5 October 2001; IP/C/27, 6 December 2002; IP/C/32, 8 December 2004; IP/C/44, 4 December 2006; IP/C/48, 7 December 2007; IP/C/52, 5 November 2009; IP/C/56, 10 November 2010; IP/C/59, 7 November 2011; IP/C/62, 26 November 2012; IP/C/67, 23 October 2013.

184 Article 27.3(b) and its diverse ramifications have been discusses in the TRIPS Council each and every year. *See* Annual Reports IP/C/8, 6 November 1996; IP/C/12, 28 November 1997; IP/C/15, 4 December 1998; IP/C/19, 22 October 1999; IP/C/22, 6 December 2000; IP/C/23, 5 October 2001; IP/C/27, 6 December 2002; IP/C/30, 1 December 2003; IP/C/32, 8 December 2004; IP/C/44, 4 December 2006; IP/C/48, 7 December 2007; IP/C/51, 4 December 2008; IP/C/52, 5 November 2009; IP/C/56, 10 November 2010; IP/C/59, 7 November 2011; IP/C/62, 26 November 2012; IP/C/67, 23 October 2013.

185 *See* Annual Reports IP/C/15, 4 December 1998; IP/C/19, 22 October 1999; IP/C/22, 6 December 2000; IP/C/27, 6 December 2002; IP/C/30, 1 December 2003; IP/C/32, 8 December 2004; IP/C/44, 4 December 2006; IP/C/48, 7 December 2007; IP/C/51, 4 December 2008; IP/C/52, 5 November 2009; IP/C/62, 26 November 2012; IP/C/67, 23 October 2013.

186 The TRIPS Agreement provided the TRIPS Council the role to discuss and propose the adequate framework within the WTO Dispute Settlement Understanding for non-violation complaints relating to the TRIPS Agreement. While Article 64.2 TRIPS Agreement provides a five-year moratorium for non-violation complaints, Article 64.3 instructs the TRIPS Council to examine the scope and modalities for that type of complaints and submit its recommendations to the Ministerial Conference. *See* Annual Reports IP/C/15, 4 December 1998; IP/C/19, 22 October 1999; IP/C/22, 6 December 2000; IP/C/27, 6 December 2002; IP/C/30, 1 December 2003; IP/C/32, 8 December 2004; IP/C/44, 4 December 2006; IP/C/48, 7 December 2007; IP/C/51, 4 December 2008; IP/C/52, 5 November 2009; IP/C/56, 10 November 2010; IP/C/62, 26 November 2012; IP/C/67, 23 October 2013.

187 *See* Annual Reports IP/C/23, 5 October 2001; IP/C/27, 6 December 2002; IP/C/30, 1 December 2003; IP/C/32, 8 December 2004; IP/C/44, 4 December 2006; IP/C/48, 7 December 2007; IP/C/51, 4 December 2008; IP/C/52, 5 November 2009; IP/C/56, 10 November 2010; IP/C/59, 7 November 2011; IP/C/62, 26 November 2012; IP/C/67, 23 October 2013.

adopted by the General Council on 30 August 2003.[188] In addition, it prepared an amendment to Article 31(f) of the TRIPS Agreement,[189] whose ratification period has been repeatedly extended in order to reach the required number of ratifications. Another substantive topic raised in the TRIPS Council is electronic commerce, which was on the Council's agenda in the late 1990s and early 2000.[190] A number of emerging issues have recently been brought up for discussion in the Council, including three relatively new topics in 2013: intellectual property and innovation; intellectual property and sports; and intellectual property, climate change and development.[191] More recent topics have included innovation and the public interest.

Discussions taking place in the Council reflect global debates. While developing countries were not very active participants in the deliberations in the past, their attitude has changed in recent years.[192] The present use of the Council as a platform for contestation is unprecedented,[193] largely triggered by the legal and policy advances with respect to enforcement. While enforcement was introduced as an issue of discussion in the context of the TRIPS Council by developed countries in 2005,[194] initiatives in the enforcement domain have prompted strong reactions from developing countries.[195] The concerns generally expressed relate to the impact of new and stringent enforcement standards beyond the balance achieved in the TRIPS Agreement,[196] the impact of new enforcement obligations on other legal interests[197] and the effect of new enforcement commitments on the allocation of public resources.[198] Moreover, developing and emerging countries have claimed that enforcement issues should be addressed in the context of dispute settlement and not in the TRIPS Council.[199] This demonstrates the radically different views that exist between some developed

[188] During the meeting of 28 August was considered the item 'Paragraph 6 of the Doha Declaration on the TRIPS Agreement and Public Health', *see* IP/C/M/38–42. For the decision *see* WTO General Council (2002a).

[189] *See* WTO General Council (2005).

[190] *See* IP/C/15, 4 December 1998; IP/C/19, 22 October 1999; IP/C/22, 6 December 2000; IP/C/23, 5 October 2001; IP/C/27, 6 December 2002; IP/C/30, 1 December 2003.

[191] *See* IP/C/67, 23 October 2013. [192] *See* Yu (2011a), p. 329. [193] *See* Abdel Latif (2015), p. 357.

[194] In 2005 the European Union proposed to include enforcement of intellectual property rights in the agenda of the Council as a specific and permanent item. *See* IP/C/M/47, 3 June 2005, para. 261. While Japan and Switzerland welcomed the initiative, the reaction of emerging and developing nations was, in general, to ask for more time to receive orders from their respective capitals. *See* IP/C/M/47, 3 June 2005, paras. 262–271. In successive years, developed countries filed communications on the issue of enforcement. *See* IP/C/W/448, IP/C/W/468, IP/C/W/471, IP/C/W/485, IP/C/W/488, IP/C/W/492, IP/C/W/501.

[195] *See* comments of the representative of China at the TRIPS Council, and particularly her summary of intellectual property enforcement trends, in WTO Council for Trade-Related Aspects of Intellectual Property Rights (2010), para. 250.

[196] *See* comments in this regard of the representative of China at the TRIPS Council in WTO Council for Trade-Related Aspects of Intellectual Property Rights (2010), paras. 264–265.

[197] *Ibid.*, para. 254. [198] *Ibid.*, paras. 256–259, 266. [199] *See* New (2005); Gerhardsen (2006).

and emerging economies with regard to the level of attention that enforcement deserves at the multilateral level.[200]

While assessing violations of the TRIPS Agreement is not the role of the Council, it performs several tasks of relevance in the context of dispute settlement. Indeed, the low number of formal TRIPS-related complaints and the high settlement rate of these complaints have been attributed to the success of the Council.[201] Not only is the Council regularly informed of developments taking place in the WTO Dispute Settlement System,[202] but the TRIPS Agreement also authorizes it to intervene in the area of dispute prevention and assist Members in the context of dispute settlement as well as the selection of panel members. With regard to dispute prevention, the meetings of the Council are useful in the mitigation and settlement of disputes. The review process plays an important role in this regard.[203] During the review process, inconsistencies in Members' laws are identified and discussed, thus allowing their amendment before they become the subject of formal disputes. Moreover, the review process permits gathering information useful for preparing or resolving disputes before they reach the adversarial phase.[204] Additionally, the Council may play a role in the selection of the members of the panels that will adjudicate a dispute.[205] In this regard, although it is the Secretariat's task to appoint the panellists, WTO Members may oppose that nomination. In that event, the Director-General will appoint the panel in consultation with the Chair of the DSB and the Chair of the TRIPS Council.

2 *The ACTA Committee*

The Anti-Counterfeiting Trade Agreement set up an interesting body, the ACTA Committee, which partially innovated and partially transplanted into the plurilateral domain the model followed in PTAs. Even if the provisions on the ACTA Committee are apparently 'mundane and highly administrative',[206] they would have helped 'institutionalize ACTA as a freestanding, self-evolving forum'[207] if the agreement had entered into force.

200 A European Union Commission staff working paper noted that 'attempts by the European Union and other supporters of an effective IPR system to constructively address enforcement problems in multilateral fora (World Trade Organisation, World Intellectual Property Organisation, World Customs Organisation) have been opposed by countries like Brazil and India, often supported by China, Argentina and others. This has prevented some of these institutions from addressing pressing IPR enforcement issues that could suitably be resolved multilaterally.' *See* European Commission (2009a), p. 4.

201 *See* Lang and Scott (2009), pp. 575–614.

202 *See* IP/C/19, 22 October 1999; IP/C/22, 6 December 2000; IP/C/23, 5 October 2001; IP/C/27, 6 December 2002; IP/C/30, 1 December 2003.

203 *See* Fukunaga (2008), pp. 870, 894; Watal (2001), pp. 50–57, 84.

204 *See* Fukunaga (2008), p. 894.

205 *See* Article 8.1 Dispute Settlement Understanding.

206 *See* Yu (2015), p. 142.

207 *Ibid.*

The ACTA Committee was conceived as the political body governing ACTA, an autonomous institution where all Member States would be represented and decisions would be taken by consensus. The interest of the present Section is limited to the ACTA Committee's competence with regard to the enforcement of the treaty and intellectual property enforcement more generally. It is, however, worth a mention that the ACTA Committee's competences are far broader, and include the eventual normative development of the treaty and the acceptance of other Parties to the 'ACTA club'.[208]

Article 36 of ACTA differentiates between optional and mandatory functions. Both involve a mix of tasks that relate either to the implementation of the treaty or to the enhancement of intellectual property enforcement. Although ACTA clarifies that the Committee is not a dispute settlement body, and cannot supervise 'domestic or international enforcement or criminal investigations of specific intellectual property cases',[209] it is not entirely clear how this task can be differentiated from some of the functions effectively attributed to the Committee.

This confusion is due to the mandatory functions attributed to the ACTA Committee, some of which relate to the enforcement of the treaty. This is the case of the requirement to review the implementation and operation of the Agreement as well as the mandate to consider matters that may affect such implementation and operation.[210] Among the optional tasks, several relate to the implementation of the treaty and others to the enhancement of enforcement in general. The former concerns the possibility to establish *ad hoc* committees or working groups to assist the Committee in the implementation of its mandatory functions,[211] such as the implementation of the treaty, as well as the possibility to 'make recommendations regarding the implementation and operation of [ACTA], including by endorsing best practice guidelines'.[212] By contrast, the possibility of sharing 'information and best practices with third parties on reducing intellectual property rights infringements'[213] is a function clearly related to the enforcement of intellectual property in general.

Assuming that ACTA will never enter into force, it is uncertain what would have happened if the ACTA Committee had actually been created. In our view, the ACTA Committee itself (or an *ad hoc* sub-committee) would have effectively monitored the implementation of the treaty and therefore the implementation of its provisions on civil, border, digital and criminal enforcement. Hence, the ACTA Committee would have become the only international supervisory body specialized in intellectual property enforcement. This could have been a very influential and interesting role if it had taken place in the multilateral context, since a specialized institution would have clarified the expectations of the Parties concerning

208 *See* for instance Gervais (2012), p. 324; Yu (2013).

209 *See* Article 36.11 ACTA. In fact, ACTA only mentions consultations as a dispute settlement mechanism and restricts them to consultations between the parties. *See* Article 38 ACTA.

210 *See* Articles 36.2(a) and (e) ACTA.

211 *See* Article 36.3(a) ACTA.

212 *See* Article 36.3(c) ACTA.

213 *See* Article 36.3(d) ACTA.

international commitments on intellectual property enforcement, or at least the differences within the membership concerning the meaning of the Agreement. The constituency of ACTA, as well as the lack of participation of countries holding different views, drastically diminishes the interest of that function.

3 *Preferential Trade Agreements Committees*

The enforcement of intellectual property commitments enshrined in PTAs may be enhanced by means of two different types of committees. First, general committees set up in PTAs oversee the functioning and operation of the agreement. Second, PTAs may create specialized intellectual property committees. While the former can be found in almost all PTAs,[214] the latter have been included in a small but growing number of them.[215]

General committees are political bodies in the sense that they consist of representatives of the Parties, usually high-ranking officials.[216] While the names of these bodies differ across treaties (and include 'Joint Council', 'Trade Committee', 'Trade

[214] This affirmation is based on the same research described in Section 5.2.3 of this chapter, over more than 50 PTAs, most of them last-generation agreements.

[215] *See* Article 165 Chile-Japan FTA and EIA (2007); Article 123 Japan-Indonesia FTA and EIA (2008); Article 129 Japan-Malaysia FTA and EIA (2006); Article 187 Japan-Peru FTA and EIA (2012); Article 130 Japan-Philippines FTA and EIA (2008); Article 97 Japan-Singapore FTA and EIA (2002); Article 128 Japan-Switzerland FTA and EIA (2009); Article 143 Japan-Thailand FTA and EIA (2007); Article 97 Japan-Viet Nam FTA and EIA (2009); Article 17.9 Republic of Korea-Singapore FTA and EIA (2006); Article 17.05 Panama-Costa Rica FTA and EIA (2008); Article 17.05 Panama-El Salvador FTA and EIA (2003); Article 17.05 Panama-Honduras FTA and EIA (2009); Article 257 EU-Colombia and Peru FTA and EIA (2013).

[216] *See* Article 1.1 of Chapter 16 ASEAN-Australia-New Zealand FTA and EIA (2010); Article 11.3 ASEAN-Japan FTA (2008); Article 20.1.2 of Chapter 20 Australia-Chile FTA and EIA (2009); Article 1701 Thailand-Australia FTA and EIA (2005); Article 20.1.1 US-Peru FTA and EIA (2009); Article 20.1.1 US-Colombia FTA and EIA (2012); Article 19.1.1 US-Panama FTA and EIA (2012); Article 21.1.1(a) US-Australia FTA and EIA (2005); Article 18.2.1(a) US-Bahrain FTA and EIA (2006); Article 19.2.1(a) US-Oman FTA and EIA (2009); Article 22.2.1 Republic of Korea-US FTA and EIA (2012); Article 20.1.1(a) US-Singapore FTA and EIA (2004); Article 19.1.1 US-Panama FTA and EIA (2012); Article 31 EFTA-Albania FTA (2010); Article 85 EFTA-Chile FTA and EIA (2004); Article 43 EFTA-Bosnia and Herzegovina FTA (2015); Article 11.1 EFTA-Central America FTA and EIA (2014); Article 11.1 EFTA-Colombia FTA and EIA (2011); Article 37 EFTA-Egypt FTA (2007); Article 9.1 EFTA-Hong Kong, China FTA and EIA (2012); Article 26 EFTA-Israel FTA (1993); Article 29 EFTA-Jordan FTA (2002); Article 8.1 EFTA-Republic of Korea FTA and EIA (2006); Article 30 EFTA-Lebanon FTA (2007); Article 29 EFTA-Former Yugoslav Republic of Macedonia FTA (2002); Article 70 EFTA-Mexico FTA and EIA (2001); Article 41 EFTA-Montenegro FTA (2012); Article 11.1 EFTA-Peru FTA (2011); Article 34 EFTA-Tunisia FTA (2005); Article 8 EFTA-Ukraine FTA and EIA (2012); Article 19.1.1 CAFTA-DR-US FTA and EIA (2006); Article 227 EU-CARIFORUM States FTA and EIA (2008); Article 15.1 EU-Republic of Korea FTA and EIA (2011); Article 12 EU-Colombia and Peru FTA and EIA (2013); Article 14 India-Japan FTA and EIA (2011); Article 14 Japan-Indonesia FTA and EIA (2008); Article 148 Japan-Switzerland FTA and EIA (2009); Article 13 Japan-Thailand FTA and EIA (2007); Article 11 Japan-Viet Nam FTA and EIA (2009); Article 13 Japan-Philippines FTA and EIA (2008); Article 13 Japan-Malaysia FTA and EIA (2006); Article 14 Japan-Peru FTA and EIA (2012); Article 18.01 Mexico-El Salvador FTA and EIA (2001); Article 18.01 Mexico-Guatemala FTA and EIA (2001); Article 18.01 Mexico-Honduras FTA and EIA (2001).

Agreement Committee', 'Joint Commission', 'Free Trade Commission'), their role is similar and generally consists of the administration and overview of the implementation and operation of the PTA.

The competence of these general committees as far as intellectual property is concerned may be expressly recognized in the treaty[217] or, instead, stem from articles describing their general functions. In the second case, PTAs normally spell out the tasks of the committees, which include, *inter alia*, an overview of the implementation and operation of the agreement,[218] the creation and supervision of the work of the subsidiary bodies[219] and the adoption of decisions and recommendations of subsidiary bodies.[220]

[217] For instance, Annex V, on Intellectual Property, Article 2.3 EFTA-Egypt FTA (2007) and Article 15.3 EFTA-Palestinian Authority FTA (1999), establish in similar terms that that '[t]he Joint Committee shall hold consultations, upon request of any Party, relating to the administration and enforcement of intellectual property rights agreements'.

[218] *See* Article 1.2(a) of Chapter 16 ASEAN-Australia-New Zealand FTA and EIA (2010); Article 11.2(a) ASEAN-Japan FTA (2008); Article 20.1.3(a) of Chapter 20 Australia-Chile FTA and EIA (2009); Article 1701 Thailand-Australia FTA and EIA (2005); Article 19.1.2(a) CAFTA-DR-US FTA and EIA (2006); Article 21.1.2(b) US-Australia FTA and EIA (2005); Article 18.2.2(b) US-Bahrain FTA and EIA (2006); Article 19.2.2 US-Oman FTA and EIA (2009); Article 20.1.2(a) US-Peru FTA and EIA (2009); Article 20.1.2(a) US-Colombia FTA and EIA (2012); Article 15.1 US-Jordan FTA and EIA (2001); Article 22.2.2(a) Republic of Korea-US FTA and EIA (2012); Article 19.1.2(a) US-Panama FTA and EIA (2012); Article 17.2(a) US-Israel FTA (1985); Article 19.2.1 US-Morocco FTA and EIA (2006); Article 20.1.2 US-Singapore FTA and EIA (2004); Article 17.01.2(a) Chile-Mexico FTA and EIA (1999); Article 31 EFTA-Albania FTA (2010); Article 85 EFTA-Chile FTA and EIA (2004); Article 43 EFTA-Bosnia and Herzegovina FTA (2015); Article 11.1 EFTA-Central America FTA and EIA (2014); Article 11.1 EFTA-Colombia FTA and EIA (2011); Article 37 EFTA-Egypt FTA (2007); Article 9.1 EFTA-Hong Kong, China FTA and EIA (2012); Article 26 EFTA-Israel FTA (1993); Article 29 EFTA-Jordan FTA (2002); Article 8.1 EFTA-Republic of Korea FTA and EIA (2006); Article 30 EFTA-Lebanon FTA (2007); Article 29 EFTA-Former Yugoslav Republic of Macedonia FTA (2002); Article 70 EFTA-Mexico FTA and EIA (2001); Article 41 EFTA-Montenegro FTA (2012); Article 11.1 EFTA-Peru FTA (2011); Article 34 EFTA-Tunisia FTA (2005); Article 8 EFTA-Ukraine FTA and EIA (2012).

[219] *See* Article 1.2(c) of Chapter 16 ASEAN-Australia-New Zealand FTA and EIA (2010); Article 11.2(d) ASEAN-Japan FTA (2008); Article 20.1.3(c) of Chapter 20 Australia-Chile FTA and EIA (2009); Article 1702.1(d) Thailand-Australia FTA and EIA (2005); Article 19.1.2(d) CAFTA-DR-US FTA and EIA (2006); Article 21.1.1(b) US-Australia FTA and EIA (2005); Article 18.2.1(b) US-Bahrain FTA and EIA (2006); Article 19.2.1(b) US-Oman FTA and EIA (2009); Article 20.1.2(d) US-Peru FTA and EIA (2009); Article 20.1.2(d) US-Colombia FTA and EIA (2012); Article 15.3(b) US-Jordan FTA and EIA (2001); Article 22.2.2(b) Republic of Korea-US FTA and EIA (2012); Article 19.1.2(d) US-Panama FTA and EIA (2012); Article 17.3(b) US-Israel FTA (1985); Article 19.21(b)(c) US-Morocco FTA and EIA (2006); Article 20.1.1(b) US-Singapore FTA and EIA (2004); Article 17.01.2(d) Chile-Mexico FTA and EIA (1999); Article 31 EFTA-Albania FTA (2010); Article 85 EFTA-Chile FTA and EIA (2004); Article 83 EFTA-Bosnia and Herzegovina FTA (2015); Article 11.1 EFTA-Central America FTA and EIA (2014); Article 11.1 EFTA-Colombia FTA and EIA (2011); Article 37 EFTA-Egypt FTA (2007); Article 9.1 EFTA-Hong Kong, China FTA and EIA (2012); Article 26 EFTA-Israel FTA (1993); Article 29 EFTA-Jordan FTA (2002); Article 8.1 EFTA-Republic of Korea FTA and EIA (2006); Article 30 EFTA-Lebanon FTA (2007); Article 30 EFTA-Former Yugoslav Republic of Macedonia FTA (2002); Article 70 EFTA-Mexico FTA and EIA (2001); Article 41 EFTA-Montenegro FTA (2012); Article 11.1 EFTA-Peru FTA (2011); Article 34 EFTA-Tunisia FTA (2005); Article 8 EFTA-Ukraine FTA and EIA (2012); Article 230 EU-CARIFORUM States FTA and EIA (2008); Article 15.1 EU-Republic of Korea FTA and EIA (2011); Article 13 EU-Colombia and Peru FTA and EIA (2013).

[220] Including the decisions of intellectual property committees. *See* Article 1.2(d) of Chapter 16 ASEAN-Australia-New Zealand FTA and EIA (2010).

General committees may also play an important role in the avoidance and settlement of disputes related to the interpretation or application of the PTA,[221] including its intellectual property provisions. In cases of controversy, PTAs commonly empower general committees to create working/expert groups that may have recourse to good offices, conciliation or mediation as well as make recommendations that facilitate the resolution of the dispute.[222] Some treaties go beyond and give these bodies greater competences in the area of dispute settlement. For instance, they prescribe that general committees are empowered to receive requests for consultations and arbitration, appoint mediators and panellists, adopt rules of procedure for dispute settlement, decide whether the rulings will be made public and be regularly notified of the progress of the case.[223]

In addition to general committees, specialized bodies in charge of the administration and monitoring of the intellectual property component of a given PTA are also relevant in the context of enforcement. In effect, more and more PTAs create intellectual property 'committees', 'sub-committees' or 'joint committees'[224] that coexist with both general committees and other specialized committees. These are political bodies in the sense that they are composed of representatives of the Parties without excluding the possibility of inviting representatives of relevant entities other

[221] *See* Article 20.3(d) of Chapter 20 Australia-Chile FTA and EIA (2009); Article 19.1.2(c) CAFTA-DR-US FTA and EIA (2006); Article 21.1.2(c) US-Australia FTA and EIA (2005); Article 18.2.2(c) US-Bahrain FTA and EIA (2006); Article 19.2.2(c) US-Oman FTA and EIA (2009); Article 21.1.2(c) US-Peru FTA and EIA (2009); Article 21.1.2(c) US-Colombia FTA and EIA (2012); Article 15.2 (c) US-Jordan FTA and EIA (2001); Article 22.2(d) Republic of Korea-US FTA and EIA (2012); Article 19.1.2 (c) US-Panama FTA and EIA (2012); Article 17.2(b) US-Israel FTA (1985); Article 19.2(c) US-Morocco FTA and EIA (2006); Article 17.01.2(c) Chile-Mexico FTA and EIA (1999); Article 31 EFTA-Albania FTA (2010); Article 85 EFTA-Chile FTA and EIA (2004); Article 83 EFTA-Bosnia and Herzegovina FTA (2015); Article 11.1 EFTA-Central America FTA and EIA (2014); Article 11.1 EFTA-Colombia FTA and EIA (2011); Article 37 EFTA-Egypt FTA (2007); Article 9.1 EFTA-Hong Kong, China FTA and EIA (2012); Article 26 EFTA-Israel FTA (1993); Article 29 EFTA-Jordan FTA (2002); Article 8.1 EFTA-Republic of Korea FTA and EIA (2006); Article 30 EFTA-Lebanon FTA (2007); Article 30 EFTA-Former Yugoslav Republic of Macedonia FTA (2002); Article 70 EFTA-Mexico FTA and EIA (2001); Article 41 EFTA-Montenegro FTA (2012); Article 11.1 EFTA-Peru FTA (2011); Article 34 EFTA-Tunisia FTA (2005); Article 8 EFTA-Ukraine FTA and EIA (2012); Article 14 Japan-Peru FTA and EIA (2012); Article 148 Japan-Switzerland FTA and EIA (2009).

[222] *See* Article 21.4 of Chapter 21 Australia-Chile FTA and EIA (2009); Article 20.5 CAFTA-DR-US FTA and EIA (2006); Article 21.5 US-Peru FTA and EIA (2009); Article 21.5 US-Colombia FTA and EIA (2012); Article 20.5 US-Panama FTA and EIA (2012); Article 22.5 US-Chile FTA and EIA (2004); Article 18.05 Chile-Mexico FTA and EIA (1999); Article 19.06 Mexico-El Salvador FTA and EIA (2001); Article 19.06 Mexico-Guatemala FTA and EIA (2001); Article 19.06 Mexico-Honduras FTA and EIA (2001); Article 19.06 Colombia-Mexico FTA and EIA (1995).

[223] This is the case in the EU-CARIFORUM States FTA and EIA (2008).

[224] The names of these specialized bodies are also diverse. On occasions, these committees have a wider scope of interests, which implies that they do not necessarily bear 'intellectual property' in their title. This is for instance the case of committees on 'Business Environment', as in Article 99.1 Brunei Darussalam-Japan FTA and EIA (2008).

than governments.[225] In keeping with their inter-State nature, the committees' decisions will usually be adopted by consensus.

The functions of intellectual property committees are diverse. While not limited to the enforcement of the treaty, this is their chief task.[226] In this regard, mention must be made to the enforcement-related functions such as monitoring the implementation of intellectual property provisions[227] and promoting solutions to difficulties arising in the protection of intellectual property.[228] Other enforcement-related functions include discussions on 'any issues related to intellectual property with a view to enhancing' intellectual property protection and enforcement,[229] control of the implementation of specific intellectual property provisions,[230] the study and advancement on enforcement topics[231] and the oversight of the Parties' co-operation as regards intellectual property.[232]

Intellectual property committees have an ambiguous role as far as dispute settlement is concerned. Among the functions mentioned previously, several relate directly or indirectly to dispute settlement. This is the case of activities such as 'reviewing and monitoring the implementation and operation' of intellectual property provisions, or reviewing all issues related to intellectual property that arise from the treaty. However, agreements containing this type of provisions also include

[225] *See* Article 15 Japan-Indonesia FTA and EIA (2008); Article 97 Japan-Singapore FTA and EIA (2002); Article 128 Japan-Switzerland FTA and EIA (2009); Article 143 Japan-Thailand FTA and EIA (2007).

[226] That the objective of the these bodies is to promote the enforcement of intellectual property was made clear in the European Unions' Strategy for the Enforcement of Intellectual Property Rights, when the European Union committed to '[r]aise more systematically enforcement concerns at Summit meetings and in the Councils/Committees created in the framework of these bilateral agreements'. *See* European Commission (2005a), p. 5.

[227] *See* Article 12.1 of Chapter 13 ASEAN-Australia-New Zealand FTA and EIA (2010); Article 123(a) Japan-Indonesia FTA and EIA (2008); Article 187.2(a) Japan-Peru FTA and EIA (2012); Article 97.1 Japan-Singapore FTA and EIA (2002); Article 128.2(a) Japan-Switzerland FTA and EIA (2009); Article 143.2(a) Japan-Thailand FTA and EIA (2007); Article 130.2(a) Japan-Philippines FTA and EIA (2008); Article 129.1(a) Japan-Malaysia FTA and EIA (2006); Article 165.2(a) Chile-Japan FTA and EIA (2007).

[228] Including matters affecting the availability, acquisition, scope, maintenance, and enforcement of intellectual property rights as well as those matters affecting the use of intellectual property rights. *See* Decision No. 2/2000 of the EC-Mexico Joint Council of 23 March 2000, 2000/415/EC, OJEU L 157/10 of 30 June 2000. *See* also Article 17.06 Nicaragua-Chinese Taipei FTA and EIA (2008).

[229] *See* Article 123(b) Japan-Indonesia FTA and EIA (2008); Article 187.2(b) Japan-Peru FTA and EIA (2012); Article 97 Japan-Singapore FTA and EIA (2002); Article 128.2(b) Japan-Switzerland FTA and EIA (2009); Article 143.2(b) Japan-Thailand FTA and EIA (2007); Article 130 Japan-Philippines FTA and EIA (2008); Article 129 Japan-Malaysia FTA and EIA (2006); Article 165 Chile-Japan FTA and EIA (2007).

[230] According to Article 213.1 EU-Colombia and Peru FTA and EIA (2013), '[i]n the context of the Subcommittee on Intellectual Property, a Party may request from another Party information regarding the compliance of products bearing geographical indications protected pursuant to this Section with the respective product specifications and their modifications'.

[231] Article 130.2 Japan-Philippines FTA and EIA (2008) states that the intellectual property committee will address the issues of 'vi) liability of internet service providers; ... ix) adequate and effective enforcement; and x) fair and equitable enforcement procedures, including procedures for border measures'.

[232] *See* Article 17.9.1(a) Republic of Korea-Singapore FTA and EIA (2006).

chapters or articles specifically devoted to dispute settlement, which are applicable to the provisions on intellectual property.[233]

IV JURISDICTIONAL OVERLAPS

1 *The Proliferation of Enforcement-Related Bodies*

The proliferation of international dispute settlement and treaty oversight bodies with competence in the area of intellectual property enforcement is a notable feature of contemporaneous international intellectual property law. This trait is symptomatic of both the maturity and growing complexity of this international regime. States are not only ready to assume new substantive commitments, they are also willing to trust the resolution of eventual discrepancies to supranational bodies and accept international supervision of their obligations. Enhanced enforcement of international rules and therefore greater legal security are in principle foreseeable consequences of the creation of enforcement-related bodies.

The large number of bodies cited in previous sections suggests that the creation of enforcement-related entities has not followed a systematic approach. In reality, each bilateral, regional, plurilateral and multilateral treaty has created its own bodies while devoting little or no attention to the fact that similar institutions have already been established under other treaties dealing with the same subject matter. The lack of regulation of jurisdictional interaction and doubts concerning the relationship between international enforcement-related bodies characterize contemporaneous international intellectual property law. This explains why uncertainty, duplication and divergent responses are often associated with the proliferation of enforcement-related bodies.

The proliferation of political and legal dispute settlement bodies with overlapping jurisdictions has given rise to a range of problematic situations. The following scenarios can be envisaged: (i) a dispute between Members of a PTA may be brought before a trade panel established by that PTA or before an international tribunal having general jurisdiction (i.e. the International Court of Justice); (ii) a dispute between Members of a PTA may be brought before a trade panel established by virtue of the PTA or before the Dispute Settlement Body of the WTO; (iii) the same national regulation may be challenged before the dispute settlement panels of two or more PTAs, in each case by a different trading partner – in this case, the bodies involved in the dispute may arrive at contradictory conclusions; (iv) a controversy arising from the same national statute may be adjudicated by a PTA panel and, in parallel, settled by means of negotiation, good offices or mediation in the context of another PTA – again, the solutions to the controversy may be different in each

[233] *See* Article 138.2 Japan-Indonesia FTA and EIA (2008); Article 145.1 Japan-Malaysia FTA and EIA (2006); Article 204.1 Japan-Peru FTA and EIA (2012); Article 149.1 Japan-Philippines FTA and EIA (2008); Article 20.2 Republic of Korea-Singapore FTA and EIA (2006); Article 22.02 Nicaragua-Chinese Taipei FTA and EIA (2008).

context; (v) the same dispute may be adjudicated from different angles by a panel established by virtue of a trade-related body and by a dispute settlement body pertaining to another international regime, such as an investment or human rights dispute settlement body.

General rules of international law do not foresee a single response to the situations outlined above. In fact, in most cases either they do not provide a specific response to the proliferation and fragmentation of international enforcement fora or the available options are of a too general nature. It could be said that the only clear general rule is the absence of hierarchy among bodies created in international treaties. The lack of guidance on how to address relations between international bodies creates a number of problems, with forum-shopping and potentially inconsistent rulings being probably the most prominent examples.

Forum-shopping, or choosing the right tribunal to adjudicate a dispute as well as avoiding less advantageous dispute settlement fora, has become an important task for trade diplomats.[234] The reasons for choosing one dispute settlement forum rather than another vary widely and include the cost of litigation, the organizational context in which the dispute will be decided, the identity of the judges or arbitrators, eventual advantages in the applicable law, who can initiate a complaint and against whom, procedural advantages, the possibility of appeal, the remedies that can be obtained, who is bound by the eventual ruling and what happens in case of non-compliance.[235] On most occasions, some factors will weigh in favour of one dispute settlement body while other factors appear to favour another. In this regard, some factors point to developing and developed countries having different priorities.[236] In principle, the former are likely to choose a multilateral, cheap and development-sensitive forum, while the latter are likely to prefer a forum where more demanding intellectual property standards will be applied.[237]

2 *Possible Answers*

2.1 Options Found in Treaties

International law does not enshrine a general rule for addressing all jurisdictional overlaps. Some treaties specify the preferred option, but this is not always the case,

[234] *See* Petersmann (2006), p. 297.

[235] *See* Pauwelyn (2004b), p. 247; Petersmann (2006), pp. 280, 287.

[236] A number of reasons make the WTO forum preferable for developing countries. In this context, Pauwelyn alludes to the fact that the cost of litigation is borne largely by the WTO budget and the Advisory Centre on WTO Law; the neutral selection of panellists; the possibility to appeal; preferential treatment for least-developed countries; and the fact that the larger WTO membership may put political pressure on the parties to resolve the dispute. *See* Pauwelyn (2004b), pp. 302–303.

[237] If the choice has to be made between the WTO and PTAs adopted after the entry into force of the TRIPS Agreement, in the majority of occasions the defendant will probably prefer the WTO Dispute Settlement System while the plaintiff would be rather inclined for the PTA dispute settlement system, given that the latter generally enshrines a level of exigency higher than the TRIPS Agreement.

nor does it suffice to avoid many problems. This section provides an overview of the available options. First, it introduces the rules found in some treaties, which either determine the exclusive jurisdiction of a given dispute settlement body or establish a rule on the choice of forum. Second, it details the *lege ferenda* options that have been put forward.

Some treaties address the question of jurisdictional overlaps. The two main options consist of either establishing that the dispute settlement procedures of the treaty apply with exclusion of any other dispute settlement procedure or enacting a rule that allows parties to choose one forum and bars them from subsequently resorting to any other.

Treaties may specify that their dispute settlement systems have exclusive jurisdiction. This was the option chosen in the treaties creating regional integration areas, such as the European Community,[238] the Andean Community[239] and the Caribbean Community.[240] In the multilateral context, the WTO Dispute Settlement Understanding also provides for an exclusive dispute resolution clause.[241] However, while these clauses may avert some of the problems described previously, they cannot avoid many others. Think, for instance, about the interpretation of the same provision enshrined in two different treaties where one of the parties coincides. Even when both treaties include a clause on exclusive jurisdiction, it will not be possible to avoid the risk of reaching two incompatible rulings on the same subject and binding on the same Party.[242]

238 Members undertook 'not to submit a dispute concerning the interpretation or application of the Treaties to any method of settlement other than those provided for therein'. *See* Article 344 (ex Article 292 TEC) of the *Treaty on European Union and the Treaty on the Functioning of the European Union*. The European Community Court had therefore exclusive jurisdiction for the settlement of all disputes as between European Union Members falling under European Community treaties, including all trade disputes.

239 The Treaty Creating the Andean Court establishes that 'Member Countries shall not submit any dispute that may arise from the application of provisions comprising the legal system of the Andean Community to any court, arbitration system or proceeding whatsoever except for those stipulated in this Treaty'. *See* Article 42(1) of *Treaty Creating the Court of Justice of the Andean Community*, 28 May 1996.

240 Article XII.1 of the *Agreement Establishing the Caribbean Court of Justice*, 14 February 2001, provides that 'the Court shall have exclusive jurisdiction to hear and deliver judgment on: (a) disputes between Contracting Parties to this Agreement; (b) disputes between any Contracting Parties to this Agreement and the Community; (c) referrals from national courts or tribunals of Contracting Parties to this Agreement; (d) applications by nationals in accordance with Article XXIV, concerning the interpretation and application of the Treaty'.

241 Pursuant to Article 23 Dispute Settlement Understanding, '[w]hen Members seek the redress of a violation of obligations or other nullification or impairment of benefits under the covered agreements or an impediment to the attainment of any objective of the covered agreements, they shall have recourse to, and abide by, the rules and procedures of this Understanding'. *See* in this regard WTO Panel Report, *United States-Sections 301–310 of the Trade Act of 1974*, WT/DS152/R, 22 December 1999, para. 7.35 *et seq*.

242 Such exclusive jurisdiction clauses have not prevented simultaneous or successive trade disputes at the WTO and in regional fora to analyse the same governmental measures from different legal perspectives. *See* Petersmann (2006), p. 353.

Some treaties allow Parties to freely choose the dispute settlement forum and recognize 'the rights of Member States to seek recourse to other fora'[243] or spell out that the dispute settlement rules and procedures 'are without prejudice to the rights of the Parties to have recourse to dispute settlement procedures available under other agreements to which they are party'.[244] However, these provisions are not sufficient to avoid problems arising from divergent dispute settlements.

Many commercial agreements enshrining intellectual property provisions establish a rule on the choice of forum. This rule entitles the complaining Party to choose the adjudicatory body, in either the multilateral or bilateral context. Pursuant to this rule, once the forum has been chosen, making use of another adjudicatory body is forbidden.[245] That is, Parties are precluded from subsequently taking the same controversy to another dispute settlement body. This option is most frequently found when treaties allude to jurisdictional conflicts. However, this scenario is quite rare, and amending treaties to enact this type of clause is a relatively complex option.[246]

Some treaties also try to avoid conflicts and facilitate harmonious interpretations by granting some deference to existing jurisprudence. This is particularly the case of institutions enacted in the context of commercial agreements, which may contain references to the pre-eminence to be given to the jurisprudence of the WTO Dispute Settlement Body.[247]

The options concerning jurisdictional interaction described previously need to be distinguished from provisions on relations between norms. Some treaties recognize the pre-eminence of the TRIPS Agreement, or at least accord it some kind of precedence. This is the case of ACTA and many PTAs. The options are diverse: Parties to new treaties may reaffirm commitments made in the TRIPS Agreement,[248] undertake to 'comply with the substantive provisions set out in the TRIPS Agreement'[249] or, more broadly, confirm rights and obligations under WTO agreements and any other international treaties.[250] These references can be reinforced by expressly stating that the TRIPS Agreement prevails in any eventual conflict.[251]

[243] *See* Article 1.3 of the *ASEAN Protocol on Dispute Settlement Mechanism*, 20 November 1996. Similarly, the SADC Tribunal provides for 'exclusive jurisdiction over all disputes between the States and the Community' but recognizes that court's jurisdiction 'over disputes between States, and between natural or legal persons and States' is not exclusive. *See* Articles 17 and 15.1 of the *Protocol on Tribunal in the Southern African Development Community*, 7 August 2000.

[244] *See* Article 58.1 New Zealand-Singapore FTA and EIA (2001).

[245] *See* Article 2005.6 NAFTA FTA and EIA (1994); Article 77.3 EFTA-Mexico FTA and EIA (2001).

[246] Arguably, trade powers would have an interest in rejecting it. *See* Romano (2007), p. 842.

[247] *See* Article 14.16 EU-Republic of Korea FTA and EIA (2011).

[248] *See* Article 110 China-Costa Rica FTA and EIA (2011); Annex XIII, on Intellectual Property, Article 2.1 EFTA-Ukraine FTA and EIA (2012); Article 107.3(a) Japan-Switzerland FTA and EIA (2009).

[249] *See* Annex VI, on Intellectual Property, Article 2.2 EFTA-Montenegro FTA (2012); Article 229.1 EU-Central America FTA and EIA (2013).

[250] *See* Article 3 EFTA-Montenegro FTA (2012); Article 1.4 EFTA-Peru FTA (2011); Article 1.3 EFTA-Ukraine FTA and EIA (2012).

[251] An example of such provision is 'no provision of this Title will contradict or be detrimental to the provisions of such multilateral agreements', to be found, for example, in Article 196.2 EU-Colombia

The opposite – i.e. affirming the priority of the bilateral and posterior agreement *vis-à-vis* WTO obligations – is rather uncommon.[252]

2.2 *Lege ferenda* Proposals

The problems posed by jurisdictional overlaps are not limited to the intellectual property context. The proliferation of regional and bilateral trade agreements and, in the broader context, the expansion of public international law in terms of treaties and dispute settlement bodies have made of the interrelation between treaties and their institutions a central area of interest of contemporary public international law. Academia and international institutions have proposed many alternative options to address this interaction.

A number of proposals put the International Court of Justice at the centre of the potential solutions. One of these consists of transforming this court into a sort of international cassation body that has the competence to rule on eventual disagreements between specialized courts.[253] Another option consists of allowing the International Court of Justice to receive pre-judicial questions concerning treaty interpretation, similar to the questions posed to the European Court of Justice. These pre-judicial questions would be posed by specialized dispute settlement bodies and would relate to eventual conflictive interpretations of the same obligation.[254] Although these proposals could be really efficient, they are hardly achievable.

A more specific and far-reaching *lege ferenda* proposal consists of applying international rules relating to the relationship between substantive treaty norms to jurisdictional overlaps. These norms include both the rules contained in Article 30 of the Vienna Convention on the Law of Treaties and other customary rules.[255] In this line of reasoning, it has been proposed that where the subject matter, scope and substance of the dispute before the WTO and PTA dispute settlement bodies are the same, the issues of jurisdiction should be resolved by reference to the *lex posterior* and *lex specialis* rules. Where application of these rules favours the specific jurisdiction of one forum, the other forum should decline its jurisdiction to hear the dispute. This is a feasible option as long as the treaty provision in question binds all disputants and does not affect the rights of other Members.[256]

A different proposal to address jurisdictional tensions consists of adopting and adapting private international law rules, such as *forum non conveniens*, *res judicata*

and Peru FTA and EIA (2013); Article 12 Japan-Indonesia FTA and EIA (2008); Article 11 Japan-Malaysia FTA and EIA (2006).

252 *See* however Article 1.03 Chile-Mexico FTA and EIA (1999); Article 1.3 Costa Rica-Mexico FTA and EIA (1995).

253 *See* Abi-Saab (1999), p. 930.

254 *See* Dupuy (1999), pp. 791–807.

255 *See* Marceau (2001), p. 1110; Pauwelyn (2004b), p. 289; Lowe (1999), p. 195.

256 *See* Pauwelyn (2004a), p. 903.

and *lis alibi pendens*. The implementation of the doctrine of forum *non conveniens* would lead an international tribunal to decline jurisdiction on the grounds that some other forum is more suitable for the ends of justice.[257] The principle of *res judicata* imposes parties to a dispute to respect the final judgement of a competent court and requires three conditions: identity of parties, identity of object and identity of the legal cause of action.[258] A third relevant principle is that of *lis alibi pendens*. Pursuant to this principle, if a closely similar case is already pending before a competent tribunal, the other forum may decline to exercise its jurisdiction.[259]

Another proposal, of a more general nature and very ample reach, is that of fostering cooperation between enforcement-related bodies. This may take different forms, including 'international cooperation among judges so as to promote greater respect for international law throughout transnational judicial networks'.[260] Cooperation proposals may also be more specific and put, for instance, WIPO at the centre. In this regard, reference is frequently made to the central role of WIPO to articulate intellectual property norms.[261] The WTO panels have shown great deference to WIPO and WIPO conventions when adjudicating disputes.[262] Indeed, not only jurisdictional bodies but also the TRIPS Council may seek guidance from WIPO in the context of dispute settlement,[263] a coordination praised by some[264] and that, in the opinion of others, should be promoted further. [265]

Another *lege ferenda* option consists in centralizing all intellectual property disputes – including those unrelated to the TRIPS Agreement – in the WTO Dispute Settlement System. A feasible mechanism could be using the Dispute Settlement Understanding provisions on arbitration, since WTO law does not specify whether arbitration within the WTO requires procedural or substantive legal links with the WTO Dispute Settlement System.[266] Certainly, other *lege ferenda* proposals promote just the contrary and suggest that WTO panels and the

257 *See* Pauwelyn (2004b), p. 290. In practical terms, forum *non conveniens* would imply the application of a doctrine of national and private nature to a very different context, where disputes are of inter-State nature, a possibility that has been generally rejected. *See* Lowe (1999), p. 201; Kwak and Marceau (2002), p. 8.

258 *See* Lowe (1996), p. 40; Pauwelyn (2004b), pp. 292–293.

259 *See* Lowe (1999), p. 202.

260 *See* Petersmann (2006), p. 274.

261 In this sense, it has been noted that 'WIPO has a special claim to a role in articulating international intellectual property norms'. *See* Dreyfuss and Lowenfeld (1997), pp. 293–294.

262 A deference that explains that the 'umbilical cord between WIPO and the WTO remained and, if anything, was strengthened through WTO dispute settlement'. *See* Pauwelyn (2010), p. 416.

263 *See Agreement between the World Intellectual Property Organization and the World Trade Organization*, 22 December 1995.

264 *See* Cottier and Foltea (2012), p. 158.

265 *See* Dinwoodie and Dreyfuss (2009), p. 1196. In the context of dispute settlement, Cottier and Foltea argue in favour of 'substantive reliance of the WTO adjudicator on WIPO's normative developments, expertise and judicial norm interpretation'. *See* Cottier and Foltea (2012), pp. 158, 161.

266 The text of Article 25 suggests that these questions are left to the mutual agreement of the parties *See* Petersmann (2006), p. 321.

Appellate Body should use their 'inherent power of comity to decline to exercise jurisdiction so that the dispute can be resolved by an FTA tribunal where a dispute is inextricably connected with a dispute under an FTA'.[267] The implicit assumption is, however, debatable since it assumes that panels and the Appellate Body possess inherent judicial powers – including the power of comity – by virtue of being an international judicial tribunal.[268]

[267] *See* Henckels (2008). [268] *Ibid.*, pp. 593–595.

6

Transplantation of the Law as a Technique to Foster New Enforcement Regulations

I THE PHENOMENON

1 *Transplantation as a Legislative Technique*

Transplantation of the law has traditionally been a useful technique to legislate. The adoption into the national legal order of norms originating in a different state may be explained by different reasons, ranging from efficiency to coercion. In fact, all branches of law and a large number of states have experienced some levels of legal transplantation. In the case of intellectual property, not only have statutes pertaining to this area been moved from one country to another,[1] but some of the clearest examples of the present dynamism of legal transplantation can be observed in this domain.[2]

There are opposing views regarding the benefits and the very possibility of transposing the law of one country to another. In the 1970s, Alain Watson coined his theory on legal transplantation and made two central points: first, transplantation is a common phenomenon that allows the improvement of national legal orders,[3] and second, according to Watson norms move easily and are accepted without difficulty in other legal systems.[4] In contrast, other authors have emphasized the difficulties, if not the impossibility, of legal transplants. Legal comparativists such as Pierre Legrand and Otto Kahn-Freund[5] have underlined the lack of relation

[1] For instance, '[t]he history of intellectual property laws in China is a history of legal transplants. From the introduction of intellectual property laws during the late Qing dynasty and the Republican era to the recent laws and amendments adopted by the People's Republic, legal transplant was the primary means by which the modern Chinese intellectual property regime was established.' *See* Yu (2016), p. 20.

[2] *See* for example Dreyfuss (2004), p. 21; Yu (2004), p. 396; Yu (2007b), pp. 855–872. A strong criticism of that phenomenon can be found in Mattei (2003), pp. 403–407, whereas a more conciliatory approach may be found in Yu (2016), pp. 29–35.

[3] *See* Watson (1978), pp. 317–318. [4] *See* Watson (1993), p. 95.

[5] *See* for example Legrand (1997), p. 111; Kahn-Freund (1974), p. 1.

between the transplanted norm and the local context[6] as well as the somewhat reductionist view of Watson's theory, criticized for focusing solely on norms.[7] While these are indeed simplifications of an old and rich doctrinal debate,[8] they are fairly representative of the opposite poles of the discussion.

Transplantation of intellectual property norms happens through a range of channels, which include local emulation of foreign norms, conclusion of new international treaties, accession procedures to regional or multilateral organizations, direct pressure exerted on other countries, cooperation between intellectual property authorities and the use of international dispute settlement procedures. In the case of intellectual property enforcement, the adoption of new treaties has been the most efficient method for transplanting national statutes to foreign countries.

2 *Exporters and Importers of Norms*

Intellectual property transplantation is actively promoted by a small group of countries and regional integration areas. The United States, the European Union, the European Free Trade Association and, more recently, Japan promote the adoption and international expansion of increasingly demanding intellectual property norms found in their local legal orders. In the case of intellectual property enforcement, this group of norm-exporting countries is practically reduced to the United States and the European Union.

Developing nations, in particular the smaller or less-developed countries, frequently are importers of norms. In some instances, the less power these countries have, the more demanding the transplanted norms are. Take, for instance, norms found in the treaties concluded between Central American and Caribbean countries with the United States and the European Union. Both Central American and Caribbean countries accepted most of the North American and European intellectual property proposals. As a consequence, their local statutes are stricter than those

6 Gunther Teubner modifies the terminology: instead of alluding to legal transplants, reference should be made to 'legal irritants'. *See* Teubner (1998), p. 11.

7 This criticism may not be entirely correct, since Watson acknowledged that transplantation usually entails a change in the law due to numerous contextual factors (e.g. religion, economy). *See* Watson (1993), p. 93.

8 In 1748 Montesquieu affirmed that '[l]aw in general is human reason, inasmuch as it governs all the inhabitants of the earth: the political and civil laws of each nation ought to be only the particular cases in which human reason is applied. They should be adapted in such a manner to the people for whom they are framed that it should be a great chance if those of one nation suit another. They should be in relation to the nature and principle of each government; whether they form it, as may be said of politic laws; or whether they support it, as in the case of civil institutions. They should be in relation to the climate of each country, to the quality of its soil, to its situation and extent, to the principal occupation of the natives, whether husbandmen, huntsmen, or shepherds: they should have relation to the degree of liberty which the constitution will bear; to the religion of the inhabitants, to their inclinations, riches, numbers, commerce, manners, and customs. In fine, they have relations to each other, as also to their origin, to the intent of the legislator, and to the order of things on which they are established; in all of which different lights they ought to be considered.' *See* Montesquieu (2001), p. 23.

of more developed countries, such as Peru and Colombia. The latter have also concluded trade agreements with the two trading powerhouses, but their treaties contain softer standards.[9] In the area of intellectual property enforcement, border enforcement is a good example of this phenomenon.[10] In fact, the inversely proportional strictness of requirements in relation to the level of development of the trade partners and the correlation between power asymmetries and the negotiation of intellectual property chapters in trade agreements can be easily observed from the early beginning of the negotiations.[11]

Transplantation of intellectual property law is related to currently existing power asymmetries between countries exporting and importing norms.[12] There is a widespread perception that, to a large extent, intellectual property chapters represent the cost that developing countries pay to obtain benefits in other areas, particularly to gain access to developed country markets.[13] Accordingly, the content tends to be heavily influenced by the demands of developed countries.[14] Acknowledgement of this power asymmetry is useful to understanding a number of characteristics of present intellectual property law-making, including transplantation.[15]

A notable feature is the frequent lack of correlation between transplanted norms and the economic and social context of the country adopting them. Norms that in countries of legal exportation have kept pace with industrial and scientific development, frequently fine-tuned through administrative practice or judicial interpretation over time, are exported regardless of the level of the development of importers. This is clear with respect to substantive standards of protection. Take, for instance, the case of patent protection for pharmaceutical products. Numerous industrialized

9 In substantive intellectual property-related areas, the adoption of strictest standards on the part of the weakest states can be observed for instance with respect to the linkage between the patent status and the marketing authorization or the extension of the term of patent protection.

10 The number of intellectual property rights categories that must be controlled by Cariforum border authorities is larger than that resulting from the agreements between the European Union, Peru and Colombia. *See* Chapter 10.

11 The intensity of the debates during the drafting of international intellectual property law texts is a good example of how power asymmetry works. The changes introduced to the initial draft of an intellectual property chapter of an international agreement will most probably reflect the power of the trading partner.

12 The Commission on Intellectual Property Rights stated that '[d]eveloping countries – and in particular poor consumers of products which may be protected by IP rights – negotiate from a position of relative weakness. There is a fundamental asymmetry in relationships between developed and developing countries, based ultimately on their relative economic strength.' Commission on Intellectual Property Rights (2002), p. 7. On different types of asymmetry, *see* Seuba (2014a).

13 This aspect was recognized early also with respect to the TRIPS Agreement. *See*, in this sense, Otten (1997), p. 22.

14 The most detailed and demanding treaties are always participated in by a developed country and hardly ever by two developing countries alone, while treaties including provisions related to highly sensitive topics, such as digital enforcement or pharmaceutical test data protection, are never concluded by developing countries between themselves. *See* Seuba (2013b).

15 For a comprehensive study on legal transplantation and asymmetric interests in the area of intellectual property, *see* Morin and Gold (2014).

countries did not grant product patent protection for pharmaceuticals until the early 1990s.[16] This policy choice enabled them to develop competitive pharmaceutical industries that, with the passage of time, became innovative. Nevertheless, the Agreement on Trade-Related Aspects of Intellectual Property Rights obliged WTO Members to grant product patent protection without discrimination as to the field of technology. In practice, and even where transition periods were applicable, this implied that within a very short time frame the same level of protection would be available in developing and developed countries even if in many cases the latter had only recently started to grant such protection.

However, contrary to what could be inferred from the previous paragraphs, transplantation does not only take place in the context of asymmetric interests.[17] Examples of developed nations importing other developed nations' intellectual property norms abound in substantive regulation. For instance, the Bolar exception is a limitation to patent rights that has transited from the United States, Canada and the legislation of the European Union to finally reach the national statutes of European countries.[18] Some developed countries have, in fact, a notable record when it comes to transplantation. This is the case of the Republic of Korea with regards to issues such as the linkage between pharmaceutical marketing authorization and the patent status or the protection of pharmaceutical test data of biological and biotechnological medicinal products. While the former is modelled on the original version found in the US Hatch-Waxman Act,[19] the latter is based upon European Union proposals.[20] In the area of intellectual property enforcement, the Republic of Korea agreed to a proposal put forward by the European Union that in many aspects literally transplanted the European Directive on the enforcement of intellectual property rights and the European border measures regulation.[21]

Turning back to developing countries, an explanation for the importation of intellectual property norms originating from the United States and the European Union may be found in the value attributed to intellectual property in the overall context of the negotiated agreement. For developing countries, the overriding

16 *See* WIPO (1987).

17 'By asymmetric interests, we mean situations in which the originator country has a strong interest in exporting its rules while the prospective adopter perceives itself as having a strong interest in maintaining its dissimilar rules, at least with respect to the specific issue-area that the legal transplant covers'. *See* Morin and Gold (2014), p. 783.

18 *See* Vidal-Quadras (2013), pp. 295–330.

19 *See* Drug Price Competition and Patent Term Restoration Act of 1984, Pub. L. No. 98–417, 98 Stat. 1585, codified at 15 USC. §§ 68b-68c, 70b (1994); 21 USC §§ 301 note, 355, 360cc (1994); 28 USC § 2201 (1994); 35 USC §§ 156, 271, 282 (1994).

20 Footnote 67 to Article 10.36 of the EU-Republic of Korea FTA and EIA (2011) alludes to the definition of pharmaceutical product, in respect to which test data protection systems will apply, and sends the reader to the annex specifically devoted to pharmaceutical products. There, Article 6.1 of Annex 2-D considers pharmaceutical products both those of chemical synthesis, biologicals and biotechnologicals. This case is also to be found in footnote 72 to Article 231.1 EU-Colombia and Peru FTA and EIA (2013).

21 *See* Section III.

interest is gaining access to affluent markets. This is the reason why they negotiate a trade treaty with the European Union or the United States. From this contractualist perspective, intellectual property is a relatively marginal area, and certainly not a priority for developing countries. While in the case of developed countries negotiating with the United States and the European Union the importance of the regulation of intellectual property is duly recognized, this area is treated as currency for more immediate and tangible benefits in other sectors.[22]

II TRANSPLANTATION BY MEANS OF THE CONCLUSION OF INTERNATIONAL TREATIES

1 *Multilateral, Plurilateral and Bilateral Law-Transplanting Treaties*

Even if the adoption of a treaty generally is a paramount example of legal convergence, this may not be always the case. Some authors hold that coercion has been the driving force behind the adoption of many intellectual property-related treaties,[23] ultimately resulting in transplantation. However, in the majority of cases an essentially contractual or bargaining approach has been the driving force of transplantation. By virtue of this approach, norms originating in one country and reflecting the actual preferences of this country are adopted by others in exchange of compensation in other areas.

Multilateral, regional and bilateral 'law-transplanting international agreements' are the most successful tools to export norms from one legal order to another.[24] From the resulting international treaty, the transplanted norms are later imported into the national legal order of other Member State(s). In the area of intellectual property, the TRIPS Agreement is the first case in point.

Part III of the TRIPS Agreement, on enforcement, was modelled on existing laws in developed countries, both in general and with respect to specific enforcement areas.[25] The TRIPS Agreement codified the common denominator of the legislation of the countries of legal exportation and became a powerful mechanism for transplanting European and American intellectual property law in WTO Member States.[26] Reflecting on the enforcement rules of the TRIPS Agreement, authors have wondered how 'eighteenth-century European rules, updated in concert with other Western nations until 1989, can be successfully integrated into the social, cultural, economic, and legal fabric of dozens of developing nations'.[27]

The provisions on enforcement in the TRIPS Agreement have influenced not only national legislation but also plurilateral and bilateral treaties. This occurrence

22 *See* Geist (2003). 23 *See* Mattei (2003), pp. 403–407. 24 *See* Yu (2011b), p. 1038.

25 Part III Section 4 of the TRIPS Agreement was modelled on the national laws existing in developed countries at the time of the Uruguay Round negotiations. *See* Blakeney (2001); UNCTAD-ICTSD (2005), p. 609; Correa (2007), p. 439.

26 *See* Dreyfuss (2004), p. 21. 27 *See* Gervais (2009b), p. 2353.

is in some cases verbatim – i.e. the transplanting treaties reproduce the articles of the TRIPS Agreement exactly. A good example is Article 6 of the Anti-Counterfeiting Trade Agreement, which lays down general obligations with regard to enforcement and largely replicates Articles 41 and 46 of the TRIPS Agreement. On other occasions, transplantation becomes somewhat innovative, since it incorporates provisions of the TRIPS Agreement by reference. This is the case of Article 2.3 of ACTA, which brings Articles 7 and 8 of the TRIPS Agreement, on objectives and principles, into the context of ACTA.

Once the TRIPS Agreement had been adopted, intellectual property standards *demandeurs* continued influencing the content of international intellectual property law.[28] Their proposals for international (and third countries) legal reform were also largely modelled on the legislation of the United States and the European Union. In the plurilateral domain, ACTA and the Trans-Pacific Partnership Agreement transplanted the content of relevant local statutes, copying and taking one step forward previously agreed bilateral agreements. The exportation of relevant aspects of the Digital Millennium Copyright Act, the United States system for the award of damages, and the European Union regime on border enforcement are particularly telling. The source of many articles of plurilateral and bilateral agreements touching upon these topics can be traced back to the law of the United States and of the European Union, although fragments of the TRIPS Agreement are also part of the final patchwork.

In the case of the Preferential Trade Agreements, the influence of United States intellectual property law started in the early nineties, with the North American Free Trade Agreement. In turn, NAFTA heavily influenced subsequent multilateral and bilateral negotiations. The NAFTA provisions were in many cases the inspiration for the corresponding articles of the TRIPS Agreement,[29] including those on intellectual property enforcement.[30] Interestingly, NAFTA reinforced its influence by means of PTAs that replicated provisions of the treaty, including some that could not be found in the TRIPS Agreement. Contrary to conventional thinking, this was not only done through the promotion of PTAs by the United States, but also through agreements promoted by Mexico with other developing countries.[31]

2 *The Special Relevance of Bilateral Agreements*

The relevance of legal transplantation for the promotion of normative harmonization is particularly evident in the bilateral context. Trade agreements are possibly the clearest example of transplantation instruments, since they frequently incorporate entire passages of the legislation of one of the trading partners. This is, in fact, an explicit objective of some trading partners.

28 *See* Chapter 4, Section I.2. 29 *See* Stewart (1993), p. 563.

30 *See* for instance our analysis of the general obligations enshrined in the TRIPS Agreement, in Chapter 4, Section I.2.

31 This situation has led to identify Mexico as a 'pollinator'. *See* X. Seuba (2013a), p. 245.

In 2002, the United States adopted its Trade Promotion Authority Act,[32] declaring that one of its negotiating objectives was 'ensuring that the provisions of any multilateral or bilateral trade agreement governing intellectual property rights that is entered into by the United States reflect a standard of protection similar to that found in United States law'.[33] Further, the Trade Promotion Authority Act states that the objective of the United States in the area of enforcement when concluding trade agreements is 'providing strong enforcement of intellectual property rights, including through accessible, expeditious and effective civil, administrative, and criminal enforcement mechanisms'.[34]

The European Union also reiterates that one of its objectives in the domain of intellectual property is the transplantation of European law in other countries.[35] In the area of enforcement, the text of reference is the European Union's Strategy for the Enforcement of Intellectual Property Rights in Third Countries.[36] The scope of this document is more ample than that of the United States' Trade Promotion Authority Act. The Strategy for the Enforcement of Intellectual Property Rights mapped the future actions of the European Union in the enforcement domain.[37] In that text, the European Commission anticipated numerous activities intended to guarantee enforcement in third countries, among others the promotion of the adoption of new legal undertakings on enforcement, which had to be modelled on the European Union legislation.[38] In keeping with that goal, the European Union has inserted powerful intellectual property enforcement chapters in 'ambitious'[39] economic treaties subscribed with both developed and developing countries. It has also declared that dispute settlement mechanisms contained in these treaties 'will be triggered in cases of non-compliance with the required high(est) standards of IP protection'.[40]

The general justification provided by these two texts has been made operational through the transplantation of specific normative texts. We will now examine the United States Digital Millennium Copyright Act and the European Union Enforcement Directive and the way that the intellectual property framework contained in these statutes has been transplanted into international treaties.

32 *See* Trade Act of 1974, 19 USC § 3802. 33 *Ibid.*, Article 4.A(i)(II). 34 *Ibid.*, Article 4.A(v).

35 For instance it has been noted that '[t]he Commission has also been discussing the E-Commerce Directive in a bilateral context . . . by requiring the full transposition of the E-Commerce Directive in Association Agreements concluded in the context of the European Neighbourhood Policy'. *See* European Commission (2012), p. 108.

36 *See* European Commission (2005a).

37 In the Strategy for the Enforcement of Intellectual Property Rights in Third Countries, the European Union committed to '[r]evisit the approach to the IPR chapter of bilateral agreements, including the clarification and strengthening of the enforcement clauses'. *See* European Commission (2005a), p. 5.

38 The European Commission stated for instance that 'instruments such as the new EU Directive harmonising the enforcement of IPR within the Community, as well as the new customs' Regulation on counterfeit and pirated goods may constitute an important source of inspiration and a useful benchmark'. *See* European Commission (2005b), p. 5.

39 *See* European Commission (2010a), p. 4. 40 *See* European Commission (2005b), p. 9.

III TWO EXPORTED INTELLECTUAL PROPERTY ENFORCEMENT STATUTES

1 *The European Directive on the Enforcement of Intellectual Property Rights*

The intellectual property template used by the European Union when negotiating international intellectual property texts is based on a collection of European statutes. Among the ones used to craft the European proposals are the civil enforcement directive,[41] the border enforcement regulation,[42] the supplementary protection certificates regulation,[43] the temporary test data articles enshrined in the broader pharmaceutical directive[44] and the European norms on geographical indications.[45]

In the area of civil enforcement, the European Directive on the enforcement of intellectual property rights is the basis of international legal commitments adopted by the European Union.[46] The EU Enforcement Directive sets the framework for harmonizing the means available to right holders to fight against infringement and enforce their intellectual property rights. The European legal framework for civil enforcement goes beyond the measures enshrined in the TRIPS Agreement and promotes the adoption of the practices and legislation of those Member States that

[41] *See* Directive 2004/48/EC of the European Parliament and of the Council of 29 April 2004 on the enforcement of intellectual property rights (OJEU L 157/45 of 30 April 2004), OJEU L 195/16 of 2 June 2004 (hereinafter EU Enforcement Directive).

[42] *See* Council Regulation (EC) No. 1383/2003 of 22 July 2003, concerning customs action against goods suspected of infringing certain intellectual property rights and the measures to be taken against goods found to have infringed such rights, OJEU L 196/7 of 2 August 2003, repealed by Regulation (EU) No. 608/2013 of the European Parliament and of the Council of 12 June 2013 concerning customs enforcement of intellectual property rights, OJEU L 181/15 of 29 June 2013.

[43] EU proposals just copy and paste the European Union Supplementary Protection Certificate Regulation, last version found in Regulation (EC) No. 469/2009 of the European Parliament and of the Council of 6 May 2009 concerning the supplementary protection certificate for medicinal products, OJEU L 152/1 of 16 June 2009.

[44] *See* Directive 2004/27/EC of the European Parliament and of the Council of 31 March 2004 amending Directive 2001/83/EC on the Community code relating to medicinal products for human use, OJEU L 136/34 of 30 April 2004.

[45] The relevant regulatory framework of the European Union for protection of geographical indications is composed of the Council Regulation (EC) No. 510/2006 of 20 March 2006 on the protection of geographical indications and designations of origin for agricultural products and foodstuffs, OJ L 93/12 of 31 March 2006; Commission Regulation (EC) No. 1898/2006 of 14 December 2006 laying down detailed rules on implementation of Council Regulation (EC) No. 510/2006 on the protection of geographical indications and designations of origin for agricultural products and foodstuffs, OJ L 369/1 of 23 December 2006; Council Regulation (EC) No. 1234/2007 of 22 October 2007 establishing a common organization of agricultural markets and on specific provisions for certain agricultural products (Single CMO Regulation), OJ L 299/1 of 16 November 2007, as last amended by Commission Regulation (EU) No. 513/2010 of 15 June 2010, OJ L 150/40 of 16 June 2010; Commission Regulation (EC) No. 753/2002 of 29 April 2002 laying down certain rules for applying Council Regulation (EC) No. 1493/1999 as regards the description, designation, presentation and protection of certain wine sector products, OJ L 118/1 of 4 May 2002; Regulation (EC) No. 110/2008 of the European Parliament and of the Council of 15 January 2008 on the definition, description, presentation, labelling and the protection of geographical indications of spirits drinks and repealing Council Regulation (EEC) No. 1576/89, OJ L 39/16 of 13 February 2008.

[46] *See*, as well, Govaere (2011), pp. 413–414.

have proven to be the most effective for the protection of intellectual property rights.

A comparison between the EU Enforcement Directive and a number of last-generation European trade agreements[47] shows a close correlation with regard to the order, the naming and most of the content of the articles that deal with civil enforcement.[48] The rights granted to title holders in last-generation European PTAs are almost identical to those found in the EU Enforcement Directive. In fact, the main differences are found in provisions that deal with the limits of right holders' entitlements and the rights of alleged infringers and consumers. These provisions are virtually non-existent or enshrine a catalogue of limits and entitlements far more limited than those found in the EU Enforcement Directive. The absence of balancing provisions in the European trade agreements compared to the Directive should be a matter of concern, since the Directive itself has been criticized for its inclination to favour right holders.[49] Paradoxically, when comparing the EU Enforcement Directive to the articles on enforcement enshrined in several European PTAs, the Directive becomes a relatively balanced text.

1.1 Provisions Regarding Evidence

Rules for obtaining evidence are essential in a world of intangible assets.[50] Rules on evidence help determine fundamental issues for the right holder, such as the moment when the infringement started and the quantity of infringing goods that have been marketed. Essential as they may be, they also entail a number of risks. Pursuant to these provisions the infringer is requested to provide information that lies in his control. This information is likely to involve sensitive data, regardless of its contribution to assess the existence of an infringement. The provision of this information may impinge upon the right to privacy or the right to not self-incriminate, which needs to be appropriately balanced against the interest in requiring the evidence.[51]

Article 6 of the EU Enforcement Directive obliges Member States to empower judicial authorities to order the opposing party to present evidence that lies in her control. It clarifies that this possibility must follow an *ex parte* petition and is subject to several guarantees. The information that may be ordered to be produced includes relevant banking, financial or commercial documents when the case has to do with an infringement committed on a commercial scale. This possibility is established in

47 This includes one association agreement (EU-Central America FTA and EIA (2013)), one multi-party trade agreement (EU-Colombia and Peru FTA and EIA (2013)), one bilateral free trade agreement (EU-Republic of Korea FTA and EIA (2011)) and one economic and partnership agreement (EU-CARIFORUM States FTA and EIA (2008)).

48 *See* Seuba (2013a). 49 *See* Cornish, Drexl, Hilty and Kur (2003), p. 447.

50 *See* Heath (2005), p. 15. 51 *See* Chapter 7.

all last-generation European PTAs.[52] Differences between the EU Enforcement Directive and the European trade agreements, however, are found in the guarantees foreseen to benefit the opposing party.

The EU Enforcement Directive requires the applicant to specify and identify the requested evidence allegedly under the control of the opposing party. This prevents unspecific searches and ensures the normal functioning of the economic activity of the alleged infringer, whose privacy and business will not be unjustifiably intruded in search of unknown evidence. Similarly, the Enforcement Directive orders the applicant to present 'reasonably available' evidence to substantiate his claims and makes the communication of banking, commercial or financial information conditional upon the protection of confidential information.

When these limits and guarantees are contrasted with those found in the trade agreements concluded by the European Union, they are largely absent. In effect, neither the specification of the evidence nor the presentation of evidence by the applicant are required in the large majority of agreements. If the articles on evidence found in the PTAs with these countries were directly applicable, they could be abused by right holders, who would easily 'fish' for evidence.

Another provision dealing with evidence relates to measures for the preservation of evidence. Safeguarding of evidence on the alleged infringement (even when proceedings have not yet been initiated) is an important measure to foster the efficiency of remedies and procedures. International regulation of the provision on preservation of evidence is studied in greater depth in Chapter 7. Nevertheless, it is timely to introduce some key aspects of this remedy in the context of legal transplantation.

Article 7 of the Enforcement Directive regulates measures for obtaining evidence by mixing features originating from the French 'saisie-contrefaçon' and the British 'Anton Piller orders'. Some of these features have been transferred into the articles of trade agreements negotiated by the European Union and finally to the national regulation of the European trading partners. Hence, the transplanted norms have transited from national (the United Kingdom and France) to regional (European Union) legal orders, from regional to international statutes (PTAs) and, from there, back to national legal orders (European Union trading partners).

According to the EU Enforcement Directive, judicial authorities must be able to order provisional measures to preserve relevant evidence in respect to the alleged infringement. This may entail detailed description or the physical seizure of the infringing goods and, in appropriate cases, of the materials and implements used, as well as related documents. These *ex parte* measures are subject to the presentation of reasonably available evidence, must be prompt and effective, may be taken without

[52] *See* Article 237 EU-Colombia and Peru FTA and EIA (2013); Article 262 EU-Central America FTA and EIA (2013); Article 10.43 EU-Republic of Korea FTA and EIA (2011); Article 153 EU-CARIFORUM States FTA and EIA (2008).

the other party having been heard and may be adopted even before the commencement of judicial proceedings.[53]

The general legal regime described previously coincides closely with the regulation established in the European trade agreements.[54] The differences, however, are found in the guarantees contained in the European legislation. These are intended to avoid interference with fundamental rights and the activity of the alleged infringer. In effect, notice, possibility of review and of revocation, provision of adequate security or assurance and awarding of compensation in different circumstances are the guarantees instituted in the EU Enforcement Directive to mitigate harmful effects of the measures.[55] These are absent in the European PTAs.

1.2 Right of Information

The right of information is an important provision in the fight against counterfeiting and piracy, since it allows investigating the origin and distribution networks of the infringing goods or services. However, if no strict limits are laid down, the right of information may also become controversial when observed from the perspective of protection of personal data.[56]

The origin of Article 8 of the Enforcement Directive can be traced back to the German Anti-Piracy Law of 1990,[57] which enshrined the 'Auskunftsanspruch' (right of information) and permitted requesting information on the identity of infringers and their suppliers and customers. Pursuant to the Enforcement Directive, Member States shall ensure that judicial authorities may order that information on the origin and distribution networks of the infringing goods or services is facilitated to the right holder. This is a departure from the TRIPS Agreement, where the right of information is an optional remedy and States may decide to include it or not in their intellectual property statutes.

According to the Enforcement Directive and the texts of European trade agreements, judges may order to make available information on the origin and distribution networks of infringing goods or services. The *ex parte* request for information

53 *See* Article 7.1 EU Enforcement Directive.

54 *See* Article 238 EU-Colombia and Peru FTA and EIA (2013); Article 10.44 EU-Republic of Korea FTA and EIA (2011); Article 154 EU-CARIFORUM States FTA and EIA (2008); and Article 263 EU-Central America FTA and EIA (2013).

55 *See* Articles 7.1–7.4 EU Enforcement Directive.

56 In *Promusicae* case, the European Court of Justice stated that the right of information requires that 'the competent judicial authorities may order that information on the origin and distribution networks of the goods or services which infringe an intellectual property right be provided. However, it does not follow from those provisions, which must be read in conjunction with those of paragraph 3(e) of that article, that they require the Member States to lay down, in order to ensure effective protection of copyright, an obligation to communicate personal data in the context of civil proceedings.' *See* ECJ, Case C-275/06, *Productores de Música de España (Promusicae) v. Telefónica de España SAU* [2008], Judgment of the Court (Grand Chamber) of 29 January 2008, ECR I-00271, para. 58.

57 *See* Law of 7 March 1990, Bundesgesetzblatt I, 422 *et seq*.

must be justified and proportionate, and it can be made to the infringer and to the person found in possession of infringing goods, using infringing services or providing services used in infringing activities.[58] Except in the case of the infringer itself, in the rest of situations the activity must be performed on a commercial scale.

Article 8 of the EU Enforcement Directive establishes several guarantees aimed at fostering a balanced implementation of the right of information.[59] These guarantees have been transferred to most European PTAs enshrining this provision[60] but not to the treaty concluded with Central America.[61] In this case, there is no reference to the precedence of rules related to civil and criminal proceedings on this kind of information or to rules that govern the responsibility for the misuse of information. Moreover, the agreement with Central America does not mention aspects closely related to fundamental rights. For instance, there is no mention of either the right to not admit personal culpability by not providing information or the precedence of rules that protect the confidentiality of information and the processing of personal data.

1.3 Provisional and Precautionary Measures

The Enforcement Directive sets up three main options regarding provisional and precautionary measures: issuing of interlocutory injunctions,[62] the seizure or delivery of allegedly infringing goods[63] and the seizure of both movable and immovable property belonging to the alleged infringer.[64] Each option has its own specific requirements and guarantees, but other requirements and the potential consequences if these measures are abused are common in all cases.[65]

The first provisional and precautionary measure mentioned in the Enforcement Directive concerns the issuance of interim injunctions. This possibility is meant to prevent an imminent infringement from taking place or to stop the continuation of the alleged infringement. In these cases, interlocutory injunctions may be issued both against the alleged infringers and intermediaries and with respect to all intellectual property rights categories.[66]

58 *See* Article 8.1 EU Enforcement Directive.

59 *See* Article 8.3 (b) through (e) of the EU Enforcement Directive: i) Prevalence of statutory provisions that 'govern the use in civil or criminal proceedings of the information communicated' pursuant to the right of information; ii) prevalence of provisions that afford 'an opportunity for refusing to provide information' which would force to admit oneself participation – or that of his/her close relatives – 'in an infringement of an intellectual property right'; iii) prevalence of statutory provisions that 'govern the protection of confidentiality of information sources or the processing of personal data'.

60 *See* Article 10.45.2, (b) through (e) EU-Republic of Korea FTA and EIA (2011); Article 155.3 (b) through (e) EU-CARIFORUM States FTA and EIA (2008); Article 239.3, (b) through (e) EU-Colombia and Peru FTA and EIA (2013).

61 *See* EU-Central America FTA and EIA (2013).

62 *See* Article 9.1(a) EU Enforcement Directive.

63 *See* Article 9.1(b) EU Enforcement Directive.

64 *See* Article 9.2 EU Enforcement Directive.

65 *See*, in particular, Chapters 7 and 8.

66 Copyright interlocutory injunctions have their own *lex specialis* and are covered by Directive 2001/29/EC of the European Parliament and of the Council of 22 May 2001 on the harmonization of certain

As detailed in Chapter 8, European Union trade agreements fundamentally copy and paste the content of the EU Enforcement Directive relating to interim injunctions, although almost only inasmuch as it relates to the protection of right holder rights. The many references found in the EU Enforcement Directive aimed at ensuring that provisional measures are not abused have not been included in the treaties concluded by the European Union, which remain largely silent in that respect. The requirement to show a good case – i.e. that the claimant is the right holder and that the corresponding right is being infringed upon or that such infringement is imminent – and the references aimed at ensuring that provisional measures are not abused – meaning the obligation to revoke the measure, the lodging of an adequate security or equivalent assurance and the compensation if the measures are revoked or lapse – have been put aside in the texts promoted by the European Union.[67] It seems, hence, that a fundamental unbalanced legal regime may be set up unless European trading partners supplement the wording of their agreements in the implementation process.

1.4 Measures Resulting from a Decision on the Merits of the Case

In the Enforcement Directive, measures resulting from a decision on the merits of the case are regulated in three provisions dealing with corrective measures, injunctions and alternative measures. The European trade agreements have transplanted this regime, with some slight but important differences with regard to corrective measures and injunctions.

1.4.1 CORRECTIVE MEASURES. The EU Enforcement Directive[68] and the European trade agreements[69] foresee three distinct actions concerning goods found to be infringing intellectual property rights and in some cases also with regard to materials used to produce those goods: recalling infringing goods from the channels of commerce, definitive removal from the channels of commerce and destruction. As a balancing criterion when considering the request for corrective measures, the EU Enforcement Directive and two trade agreements[70] allude to the need for proportionality as well as to the need to take into account the interests of third parties. All of these are important and useful references for delivering balanced decisions on corrective measures.

aspects of copyright and related rights in the information society, OJ L 167/10 of 22 June 2001 (hereinafter Information Society Directive). *See* Chapter 8.

67 *See* Chapter 8, Section II.3.2. 68 *See* Article 10 EU Enforcement Directive.

69 *See* Article 241 EU-Colombia and Peru FTA and EIA (2013); Article 266 EU-Central America FTA and EIA (2013); Article 10.47 EU-Republic of Korea FTA and EIA (2011); Article 157 EU-CARIFORUM States FTA and EIA (2008). Corrective measures apply to all intellectual property rights, except in the case of the EU-Central America FTA and EIA (2013), which limits corrective measures to pirated and counterfeited goods. *See* Article 266.1 EU-Central America FTA and EIA (2013).

70 The EU-Central America FTA and EIA (2013) and the EU-Republic of Korea FTA and EIA (2011).

1.4.2 INJUNCTIONS. Once a judicial decision confirms the existence of an infringement, an injunction prohibiting the continuation of the infringing activity usually will follow.[71] Injunctions stop the infringement and forbid its reoccurrence in the future. They are one of the most valued civil remedies as in principle they permit the restoration of market exclusivity for the right holder. Because of their correlation with the market exclusivity, they are closely related to damages.

The majority of European last-generation PTAs[72] repeat the pattern of the Enforcement Directive as regards injunctions:[73] in case of infringement, judicial authorities may issue an injunction against the infringer to prohibit the continuation of the infringement. In all cases, this possibility is subject to national legislation and will be implemented 'where appropriate'.

Injunctions may also be issued against intermediaries whose services are used to infringe an intellectual property. The Enforcement Directive opens this possibility in cases of infringements of 'an intellectual property right' and recalls Article 8.3 of the Information Society Directive.[74] In principle, this means that all categories of intellectual property rights would be covered, as is the case of the treaty with Cariforum and the text with Peru and Colombia. The agreement with the Republic of Korea, however, limits actions against intermediaries to copyright and related rights, geographical indications and trademark infringements.[75]

An important difference is found in the treaty with Colombia and Peru, which legislates 'by reference' and incorporates Article 44.2 of the TRIPS Agreement on regulation of remedies with respect to use by governments or third parties authorized by a government.[76] Transplantation has followed an interesting path in this case, since Article 44.2 of the TRIPS Agreement has its origins in US law.[77] It was transferred to the TRIPS Agreement from the United States and later included in plurilateral and bilateral agreements. The latter do not necessarily include the United States among their Members. Article 44.2 of the TRIPS Agreement makes it possible to limit the remedies available to payment of adequate remuneration in the circumstances of each case, taking into account the economic value of the authorization, or to issue a declaratory judgement and grant adequate compensation. Thus, infringing activities may continue if adequate remuneration and compensation are satisfied. There may be different circumstances in which it will be

[71] *See* Chapter 8, Section IV.2.

[72] *See* Article 242 EU-Colombia and Peru FTA and EIA (2013); Article 10.48 EU-Republic of Korea FTA and EIA (2011); Article 158 EU-CARIFORUM States FTA and EIA (2008). The EU-Central America FTA and EIA (2013) is silent on the matter of injunctions.

[73] *See* Article 11 EU Enforcement Directive.

[74] The content is coincidental. According to Article 8.3 of the Information Society Directive, 'Member States shall ensure that rightholders are in a position to apply for an injunction against intermediaries whose services are used by a third party to infringe a copyright or related right'.

[75] *See* Article 10.48.2 EU-Republic of Korea FTA and EIA (2011).

[76] *See* Article 242 EU-Colombia and Peru FTA and EIA (2013).

[77] More precisely, in Title 28 USC §1498, Patent and Copyright Cases.

socially preferable or more equitable to allow the continuation of the infringing activity, as detailed in greater depth in Chapter 8.[78]

1.5 Damages

The regulation of damages is one of the most disputed areas of civil enforcement. The continental law tradition and the conception prevailing in common law countries differ in important aspects, particularly on whether damages fulfil compensatory or punitive functions. The European trade agreements have 'copy-pasted' the wording of the article on damages contained in the Enforcement Directive.[79]

The European regulation of damages draws a distinction between the infringer who knowingly infringed or had reasonable grounds to know and the infringer who did not know or had no reasonable grounds to know. With regard to the 'conscious' infringer there are two alternatives. In the first case, when judicial authorities set damages, they must take into account lost profits of the right holder or unfair profits obtained by the infringer and elements other than economic factors, such as moral damage. The second alternative permits setting damages as a lump sum on the basis of elements such as the amount of royalties and fees due if an authorization had been requested. By contrast, in the case of the infringer that did not know, judicial authorities may order the recovery of profits or the payment of damages, which may be pre-established.

Chapter 9 analyses the regulation of damages in European agreements. In particular, it describes both the partial transplantation that, again, characterizes the regulation of this remedy in those agreements and, more importantly, the conflict existing with the mirror provision set forth in US trade agreements. It is argued that conflicting regulation in this domain may be indicative of some of the limits of international harmonization in the area of intellectual property enforcement.

2 *The United States Digital Millennium Copyright Act*

Among the intellectual property statutes exported by the United States through the conclusion of PTAs, the case of the Digital Millennium Copyright Act[80] is worth a mention.[81] While the DMCA implemented the 1996 WIPO Internet treaties, it has been a contentious statute. The DMCA included two new prohibitions in copyright law, one on circumvention of technological measures used by copyright owners to protect their works and one on tampering with copyright management information.

78 *See* Chapter 8, Section IV.2.

79 *See* Article 13 EU Enforcement Directive; Article 244 EU-Colombia and Peru FTA and EIA (2013); Article 267 EU-Central America FTA and EIA (2013); Article 10.50 EU-Republic of Korea FTA and EIA (2011); Article 160 EU-CARIFORUM States FTA and EIA (2008).

80 *See* Pub. L. No. 105–304, 112 Stat. 2860, 28 October 1998 (hereinafter Digital Millennium Copyright Act, of 1998).

81 *See* United States Copyright Office (1998).

These prohibitions were accompanied by civil remedies and criminal penalties in case of violation.[82] Importantly, the DMCA introduced four new limitations on the liability of online service providers for copyright infringement[83] and addressed as well a number of other significant copyright-related issues.

The DMCA has been subject to intense litigation,[84] ultimately resulting in reinterpretation.[85] Regardless of the criticism it has attracted[86] and the fact that alternative models have been proposed,[87] the original DMCA has been exported to numerous countries.

Many PTAs concluded by the United States regulate copyright enforcement in the digital domain in a detailed and prescriptive fashion. Articles on anti-circumvention measures[88] are an example of that.[89] In many PTAs, anti-circumvention provisions mirror Section 1201 of the DMCA.[90] The parallelism starts with the terminology used[91] and continues with punishable activities, types of liability and a model of tight and strictly defined exceptions.

As a result, legal reforms introduced by the trading partners of the United States have been heavily modelled on the DMCA. The majority of PTAs promoted by the United States do not just go beyond national statutes of trading partners, they also exceed multilateral commitments (the WIPO Internet treaties). Notably, they

82 This is found in Title I of the act, which received the name of the WIPO Internet treaties, namely 'WIPO Copyright and Performances and Phonograms Treaties Implementation Act of 1998'.

83 The limitations were based on four categories of conduct by a service provider, namely, transitory communications, as in § 512(a); system caching, as in § 512(b); storage of information on systems or networks at direction of users, as in § 512(c); and information location tools, as in § 512(d).

84 Pioneer cases were *Universal City Studios v. Reimerdes*, 111 F. Supp. 2d 346 (2d Cir. 2001) and *Universal City Studios v. Corley*, 243 F. 3d. 429 (2d Cir. 2001). In other cases, clarifications have been crucial. For example, DMCA was not clear on who has the burden to prove that the anti-circumvention technology is authorized. The case *Chamberlain Group, Inc. v. Skylink Technologies, Inc.*, 381 F3d 1178 (Fed. Cir. 2004) clarified that the burden is on the plaintiff alleging circumvention.

85 In 2005 the Digital Media Consumer Rights Act, HR 1201 was passed, having as its main purpose to restore some balance in copyright law.

86 *See* Samuelson (2003), p. 41; Burk and Cohen (2001), pp. 41–83.

87 For Ruth Okediji, 'the EU model of the WCT contains room for flexibility for member states to consider enacting limitations and exceptions that are consistent with those provided by national law'. *See* Okediji (2004), pp. 23–24.

88 Potential problems arising from these measures have been summarized by Pedro Roffe. They may 'impede lawful uses of works (making a copy of a music CD to listen to it in a notebook, making a backup copy of a computer program ... or copying small parts of a movie in a DVD for purposes of teaching or criticism. TPMs have also been used to bar the manufacture of competing products, to suppress speech, to limit the first sale doctrine and to fragment markets through the use of regional zone codes in DVDs. Moreover, the use of TPMs restricts access to works that have already fallen in the public domain' and create problems to 'developing countries access to information technology'. *See* Roffe (2004), pp. 33–34.

89 Take for instance the four conditions imposed in Title 17 USC § 512 of the Digital Millennium Copyright Act of 1998 for the limitation of the liability for service providers and Article 17.11.29 US-Australia FTA and EIA (2005).

90 The United States–based approach was applauded by the industry in the country. *See* Industry Functional Advisory Committee on Intellectual Property Rights for Trade Policy Matters (2004).

91 *See* Greenleaf *et al.* (2007), p. 3.

enshrine the obligation to introduce both criminal penalties and civil remedies for acts aimed at the circumvention of effective technological measures[92] and for the commercialization of circumvention services and devices.[93] Hence, tampering with embedded anti-piracy measures that restrict access to protected works and phonograms are subject to civil liability and may amount to a criminal offence. Anti-circumvention provisions also cover activities such as manufacturing, importing, distributing, selling or renting devices that permit the circumvention of technological protection measures. Additionally, in line with the model set forth in the DMCA, United States trade agreements contain a restricted set of exceptions to anti-circumvention provisions as well as instructions on how to manage those exceptions.[94]

The DMCA regime on anti-circumvention of technological protection measures differs from that already found in the legal orders of United States trading partners. The case of Australia is noteworthy. The PTA between Australia and the United States requires the Parties to enact civil and criminal liability for the act of circumventing technical protection measures and for trading in services and devices that permit circumvention. As soon as the agreement with the United States was adopted, the Australian Copyright Act narrowed the prohibition of the sale of circumvention devices.[95] This was a deliberate choice on the part of Australian legislators, who were of the view that the prohibition of circumvention intruded too significantly into the private sphere.[96]

Internal policy considerations could have motivated the inclusion by the United States Trade Representative of the DMCA text into the wording of the PTAs, with the expectation of consolidating the controversial provisions found within the DMCA. The aim would have been not only to export the DMCA but also to obstruct alternative legislative approaches, such as that of the European Union. The regime of the United States is based on the prohibition of acts of circumvention and a ban on commercial activities aimed at allowing circumvention. These prohibitions are accompanied by a limited set of exceptions, including cases that allow the sale and manufacture of circumvention devices. Leveraging clauses in the DMCA are stringent,[97] and there is no reference to 'fair use of access' as a potential argument

92 *See* Article 17.4.7(a)(i) US-Australia FTA and EIA (2005). *See* also Article 16.4.7(a)(i) US-Singapore FTA and EIA (2004).

93 It is provided that, 'manufactures, imports, distributes, offers to the public, provides, or otherwise traffics in devices, products, or components', in Article 17.4.7(a)(ii) US-Australia FTA and EIA (2005). *See* also Article 16.4.7(a)(ii) US-Singapore FTA and EIA (2004).

94 *See* Article 17.4.7(e)-(f) US-Australia FTA and EIA (2005).

95 *See* Copyright Act 1968, Act No. 63 of 1968 as amended, taking into account amendments up to Act No. 158 of 2006 (Superseded). *See* § 116AO(l)(b), providing that '[m]anufacturing etc. a circumvention device for a technological protection measure (1) An owner or exclusive licensee of the copyright in a work or other subject-matter may bring an action against a person if: (b) the person knows, or ought reasonably to know, that the device is a circumvention device for a technological protection measure', available at: www.comlaw.gov.au/Details/C2007C00045 (last accessed October 2016).

96 *See* Burrell and Weatherall (2008), p. 276.

97 As noted by Samuelson, 'the statutory exceptions are very drawn narrowly and fail to recognise many legitimate reasons for circumventing technical measures'. *See* Samuelson (2003), p. 42.

to widen the scope for legitimate grounds. The potentially unfair outcomes of the DMCA have been criticized since its inception.[98] By contrast, a different conception is promoted by the European Union through the 'fair use by design' approach underpinning the Information Society Directive.[99] Under this approach, copyright owners are encouraged 'to build space for users into their copyright protection strategy'[100] and 'if all else fails, can result in owners being compelled to make non-encrypted versions of works available to users'.[101] The net effect of the United States' PTAs is to effectively block the adoption of this alternative model.[102]

IV OTHER MEANS OF LEGAL TRANSPLANTATION

1 The Implementation Process

The implementation process may play a role as important as the negotiation of the agreement.[103] To start with, implementation merely limited to the transcription of the treaty text is problematic since the intellectual property chapter is often incomplete and unbalanced. On the other hand, implementation may sometimes entail a renegotiation of the agreement, which may limit options that are legitimate according to the treaty but deemed unacceptable by the counterpart. In fact, when implementing intellectual property chapters contained in trade agreements countries do not generally take advantage of all available options. While this may respond to a sovereign decision of the country, it may also arise from the features of the implementation process. This is usually observed with respect to the implementation of exceptions or flexible interpretations of the treaty commitments.[104]

In the case of agreements concluded by the United States, the United States Trade Representative oversees the implementation through both informal contacts and the exchange of diplomatic notes. The demands of the USTR are persuasive, and if the counterpart does not accept them, the treaty will probably not enter into force for the United States. The legal basis for the process of 'certification' of conformity with the United States' implementation of the agreement is found in the text of many agreements itself.[105]

98 *See* Therein (2001), p. 1023. For a comparative perspective, *see* De Werra (2001).

99 *See* Dusollier (2003).

100 *See* Burrell and Colleman (2005), p. 73.

101 *See* Burrell and Weatherall (2008), p. 289.

102 *Ibid.*

103 *See* Roffe and Genovesi (2009), p. 12.

104 *See* Burrell and Weatherall (2008), p. 274.

105 The agreements concluded by the United States usually contain a provision stating that '[a]t such time as the President determines that (*name of the country*) has taken measures necessary to comply with those provisions of the Agreement that are to take effect on the date on which the Agreement enters into force, the President is authorized to exchange notes with the Government of (*name of the country*) providing for the entry into force, on or after (*date*), of the Agreement with respect to the United States'. *See* for instance Section 101(b) US-Panama FTA and EIA (2012); Section 102(b) of the US-Peru FTA and EIA (2009).

This powerful tool is usually employed in a context of limited information to external stakeholders, since third parties rarely have access to the details of the implementation process. In fact, transparency may even be more limited in the implementation phase than during the negotiations of the treaty. Beyond some mid-range officials discussing technical aspects and a limited number of private stakeholders, the content of the negotiations in the implementation process is often unknown, thus facilitating the exertion of pressure and the formulation of new demands.

2 *Dispute Settlement*

The dispute settlement mechanism provided for inter-State differences in trade agreements is an additional channel to continue the exportation of the law. In the context of the TRIPS Agreement it has been rightly noted that rules resulting from adjudication in the WTO Dispute Settlement System 'might be accepted into the domestic laws of the parties (or at least, into the laws of the parties where the question has not been yet fully answered)'.[106] Its potential for legal transplantation has been also underlined when noting that it may be attractive for panels working on a difficult question to consult the laws of developed countries.[107]

The effects of the dispute settlement mechanisms set forth in bilateral trade agreements are more intriguing. As noted in Chapter 5, the usually *ad hoc*-appointed bodies may have the competence to rule on 'any dispute concerning the interpretation and application of this Agreement, in particular when one of the Parties considers that a measure taken by another Party is or could be inconsistent with its obligations under this Agreement'.[108]

Some bilateral agreements foresee special rules and, arguably, dispute settlement mechanisms for intellectual property disputes.[109] Moreover, in some cases the dispute settlement system is entrusted to solve disputes on matters not yet agreed upon in the multilateral context. This is, for example, the case of disputes concerning the nullification and impairment of benefits, even if the cause of such nullification and impairment does not contravene the agreement.[110] This naturally opens an uncertain scenario and may provoke a chilling effect with regard to what measures

[106] *See* Dreyfuss and Lowenfeld (1997), p. 292. [107] *Ibid.*, p. 295.

[108] *See* Article 299 EU-Colombia and Peru FTA and EIA (2013). *See* also Chapter 5, Section II.3.

[109] This is for instance the case of the decision concerning the registry or protection of a geographical indication under Article 250 EU-Central America FTA and EIA (2013).

[110] *See* Article 20.2(c) CAFTA-DR-US FTA and EIA (2006); Article 21.2(c) US-Australia FTA and EIA (2005); Article 19.2(c) US-Bahrain FTA and EIA (2006); Article 22.2(c) US-Chile FTA and EIA (2004); Article 21.2(c) US-Colombia FTA and EIA (2012); Article 20.2(c) US-Morocco FTA and EIA (2006); Article 20.2(c) US-Panama FTA and EIA (2012); Article 20.2(c) US-Oman FTA and EIA (2009); Article 21.2(c) US-Peru FTA and EIA (2009); Article 21.1.1 Australia-Chile FTA and EIA (2009); Article 22.02(c) Nicaragua-Chinese Taipei FTA and EIA (2008); Article 18–02 Chile-Mexico FTA and EIA (1999); Article 19.02.1 Colombia-Mexico FTA and EIA (1995).

can be adopted in the regulatory and intellectual property domains without fear of retaliation under the dispute settlement system of the treaty.

The dispute settlement system can be instrumental in exerting persistent pressure with regard to actions that can be undertaken by the other party. For instance, the European Union has stated that institutional mechanisms of agreements regulating intellectual property[111] 'can be used to monitor and discuss legislation and enforcement problems from a very early stage'.[112] From the perspective of countries importing intellectual property standards, this approach should be viewed with caution, since it can be a channel to go beyond the provisions of the treaty. Indeed, the dispute settlement mechanism can be instrumental in reintroducing old aspirations or insisting on the primacy of a particular interpretation among many other possibilities.

3 *Cooperation*

Cooperation is an additional channel for promoting the adoption of new legal standards on enforcement. Numerous intellectual property chapters contained in PTAs include articles on cooperation and exchange of good practices, including cooperation on the enforcement of intellectual property.[113] These articles provide the legal umbrella for an important number of activities currently taking place worldwide.

The activities undertaken, with or without an international umbrella agreement, are usually designed by countries that export their intellectual property standards,[114] which have an easily detectable influence on the content of the cooperation. In the case of the United States, both the Strategic Plan and the Annual Report of the

[111] Although these mechanisms are not dispute settlement bodies, they fulfil functions related to the monitoring of the agreement. They may also act as a forum to provide an amicable solution to a dispute concerning the meaning of the obligations of the parties pursuant to the agreement.

[112] *See* European Commission (2005a), p. 5.

[113] *See* Australia-Chile FTA and EIA (2009); Brunei Darussalam-Japan FTA and EIA (2008); Chile-China FTA and EIA (2006/2010); Chile-Japan FTA and EIA (2007); Chile-Mexico FTA and EIA (1999); China-Costa Rica FTA and EIA (2011); China-New Zealand FTA and EIA (2008); Costa Rica-Mexico FTA and EIA (1995); CAFTA-DR-US FTA and EIA (2006); East African Community CU and EIA (2000/2010); EC Treaty CU and EIA (1958); EFTA-Mexico FTA and EIA (2001); EFTA-Montenegro FTA (2012); EU-Cameroon FTA (2014); EU-CARIFORUM States FTA and EIA (2008); EU-Chile FTA and EIA (2003/2005); EU-Colombia and Peru FTA and EIA (2013); EU-Republic of Korea FTA and EIA (2011); EU-South Africa FTA (2000); European Economic Area EIA (1994); European Free Trade Association FTA and EIA (1960/2002); ASEAN-India FTA and EIA (2010/2015); Japan-Indonesia FTA and EIA (2008); Japan-Malaysia FTA and EIA (2006); Japan-Mexico FTA and EIA (2005); Japan-Peru FTA and EIA (2012); Japan-Singapore FTA and EIA (2002); Japan-Switzerland FTA and EIA (2009); Japan-Thailand FTA and EIA (2007); Japan-Viet Nam FTA and EIA (2009); New Zealand-Malaysia FTA and EIA (2010); Nicaragua-Chinese Taipei FTA and EIA (2008); NAFTA FTA and EIA (1994); Panama-Peru FTA and EIA (2012); Panama-Chinese Taipei FTA and EIA (2004); Peru-Republic of Korea FTA and EIA (2011); Singapore-Australia FTA and EIA (2003); Thailand-Australia FTA and EIA (2005); Thailand-New Zealand FTA and EIA (2005); Trans-Pacific Strategic Economic Partnership FTA and EIA (2006); Turkey-Chile FTA (2011).

[114] *See* Dreyfuss (2004), p. 21; Blakeney and Mengistie (2011), p. 75.

Intellectual Property Enforcement Coordinator are awash with examples of enforcement-related cooperation activities. They include workshops-and-trainings as well as direct involvement in local intellectual property enforcement[115] and the amendment of enforcement-related statutes.[116] Similarly, the European Union's cooperation on legislative aspects, including 'regulatory approximation with the EU *acquis* and enforcement practices',[117] is a relevant aspect of its enforcement-related cooperation.

4 *Monitoring outside the Dispute Settlement System*

Both the European Union and the United States have set up their own mechanisms for unilaterally monitoring the intellectual property policies and practices of other countries. Processes such as United States Section 301 of the Omnibus Trade and Competitiveness Act[118] or the mechanism set up in European Regulation No. 3286/94[119] are important channels for putting pressure on trading partners' legislation and administrative practices. In fact, as USTR points out, compliance with the TRIPS Agreement is not an obstacle to exerting pressure on trading partners.[120]

In the case of the European Union, the 2004 Strategy for the Enforcement of Intellectual Property Rights put in place a mechanism to periodically monitor the enforcement of intellectual property rights in third countries, a blacklisting activity that relies on the collaboration of public and private entities.[121] In a related fashion, both the 2004 and 2014 strategies for the enforcement of intellectual property rights target the complaints mechanism under the Trade Barriers Regulation as proper means to improve enforcement of intellectual property rights. More recently, the

115 *See* for instance the detentions of the persons 'allegedly responsible for massive worldwide online piracy through Megaupload.com', in Intellectual Property Enforcement Coordinator (2013), p. 25.

116 For instance, '[i]n October 2011, Ukraine adopted a new law making the manufacture or distribution of counterfeit medicines a crime. This legislation resulted from a legislative recommendation put forward at a May 2011 workshop on counterfeit medicines put on by U.S. Embassy Kyiv and the U.S. Commercial Law Development Program'. *See* Intellectual Property Enforcement Coordinator (2012), p. 27.

117 *See* European Commission (2013), p. 19.

118 *See* Omnibus Trade and Competitiveness Act of 1988, Pub. L. No. 100–418, 102 Stat. 1107, 23 August 1988.

119 *See* Council Regulation (EC) No. 3286/94 of 22 December 1994 laying down Community procedures in the field of the common commercial policy in order to ensure the exercise of the Community's rights under international trade rules, in particular those established under the auspices of the World Trade Organization, OJ L 349/71 of 31 December 1994.

120 For the United States Trade Representative, non-reasonable acts or policies include those impeding the effective protection of intellectual property 'notwithstanding the fact that the foreign country may be in compliance with the specific obligations of the Agreement on Trade-Related Aspects of Intellectual Property Rights referred to in section 3511(d)(15) of this title'. *See* Title 19 USC § 2411, (d)(3)(B)(i)(II), (2006).

121 Among others, Commission delegations, embassies of Member States, right holders and associations and chambers of commerce.

2014 strategy foresees the deployment of retaliatory measures, in particular the possibility of restricting 'participation or funding in specific EU-funded programmes in sufficiently serious and clearly targeted cases'.[122]

Concerns specifically mentioning civil enforcement are frequent in the United States Section 301 reports. They may target specific enforcement-related remedies and mechanisms, such as damages,[123] or, by contrast, introduce a range of civil enforcement concerns. In the US Section 301 Report of 2014, for instance, the United States cited 'important weaknesses in China's civil enforcement system that relate to mechanisms for gathering evidence; procedures for obtaining preliminary injunctions; and the relative weight afforded certain kinds of evidence, as reflected in the overreliance on original documentary evidence over oral testimony'.[124] It also highlighted Indonesia's 'inefficiencies in its judicial and prosecutorial systems which include a lack of transparency and deterrent-level sentences'.[125] Belarus was castigated for its lack of 'civil remedies or criminal penalties for online piracy',[126] and Turkmenistan came under fire over its lack of 'effective administrative, civil or criminal procedures or penalties'.[127]

5 *Compromise to Adopt or Fulfil Specific Norms in the Future*

Another channel for maintaining normative influence on trading partners involves inserting into international treaties the obligation to adopt or amend specific norms in the future. The examples are numerous.

In the intellectual property enforcement context, under the association agreement between Cariforum and the European Union the 'Cariforum States agree to collaborate to expand' the scope of border measures so that goods infringing all intellectual property rights are covered.[128] Another example is found in the agreements concluded by the European Union with states willing to access the EU. In these treaties a clause announcing the compromise to fulfil European standards of intellectual property protection in a short period of time is included. That is, reference is made not to a list of obligations but to the European Union law on intellectual property and a short period of time to conform to it.[129]

122 European Commission (2014) p. 17.

123 It has been noted that 'the U.S. Trade Representative, predominantly at the urging of the International Intellectual Property Association, can single out countries with trade practices that affect domestic intellectual property interests. Criticisms are directed at countries (1) without statutory damages, (2) that employ various efforts to curtail the severity of statutory damages, and (3) that provide some the same limitations as present in the United States.' *See* Samuelson, Hill and Wheatland (2013).

124 *See* United States Trade Representative (2014), p. 31. 125 *Ibid.*, p. 45. 126 *Ibid.*, p. 47.

127 *Ibid.*, p. 57. 128 *See* Footnote 2(c) to Article 163 EU-CARIFORUM States FTA and EIA (2008).

129 A provision of this type is found in EU-Albania FTA and EIA (2006/2009); EU-Former Yugoslav Republic of Macedonia FTA and EIA (2001/2004); EU-Croatia FTA and EIA (2002/2005); EU-Bosnia and Herzegovina FTA (2008); EU-Montenegro FTA and EIA (2008/2010); EU-Serbia FTA and EIA (2010/2013); and EU-Turkey CU (1996).

V CHARACTERISTICS OF TRANSPLANTATION

1 *Contractualization via International Negotiation*

Numerous norms are transplanted from one country to another via commercial agreements. These treaties commonly tackle a large number of topics, including tariffs, services, investment and intellectual property. The aspiration of the Parties is to reach an overall balance or equilibrium of advantages and concessions in the agreement, thus not expecting all their demands to be recognized in the treaty. This implies that countries will reach positive results in some areas while making concessions in others. This *quid pro quo* rationale is carried out through the technique of the 'package deal', which implies the acceptance of the entire agreement, meaning that in some areas concessions are made while in others benefits are obtained.

Parties to trade agreements see intellectual property negotiations as a bargaining process, haggling with their counterparts rather than focusing on a positive contribution to the construction of a coherent intellectual property legal regime. The 'package deal' implies accepting compromises that are not optimal for an entire legal branch, such as intellectual property, in exchange of trade concessions. In fact, the adoption of new intellectual property commitments is frequently part of a larger trade-off responding to interests unrelated to local needs in terms of innovation and competition.[130]

This is quite different from accepting a trade-off in the tariffs context. Gaining benefits in certain economic sectors while neglecting key policy areas may be logical in the short term but not in the long run. In the course of the negotiations, parties may exaggerate or feign interest in compromises that are not really a priority for them, with the objective of reaching more moderate goals. Treaty proposals may also include demands currently debated domestically or demands that may not even be acceptable under the local legislation of the proponent. In reaction to these negotiating techniques, a formal response proposing the extension of the principle of good faith to treaty negotiations has been put forward.[131]

2 *Competitive Transplantation*

Transplantation may take place in a competitive fashion, in the sense that the first country capable of transferring its own regulation will generally block the adoption of proposals with different content originating from other commercial powers. In the case of transplantation through trade agreements, this introduces an extra incentive to be the first to negotiate and to do so as quickly as possible. For instance, the

130 *See* Principle 1 of the Max Planck Principles in Bilateral and Regional Trade Agreements, Max Planck Institute for Innovation and Competition (2013).

131 This principle is, however, customarily constrained to the implementation phase of the treaties. *See* Seuba (2013c).

European Union has been successful in having its civil enforcement *acquis* transplanted into the Cariforum agreement and key features of its border enforcement regime transplanted into the treaty with the Republic of Korea. Similarly, the United States has managed to export standards and remedies that are regulated differently in the European Union. This is for instance the case of the award of punitive damages, the registration of scent marks,[132] the patentability requirement of utility,[133] and the *linkage* between marketing authorization and patent status. In some cases, the changes may be minor, and therefore it may not really matter whether the European Union or the United States negotiates first, but in other areas the differences can be relevant. Although a State is free to adopt either the American or the European model, it cannot subscribe to both.

3 *Conflicting Transplantation*

Competitive transplantation does not necessarily end with only one of the foreign statutes being transplanted. Instead, countries may have accepted the incorporation of two different norms into their national law. Moreover, the obligations undertaken may not necessarily be coincidental or shared by the exporters of the norms. In fact, the imported norms may even be conflicting.

An example of conflicting importation relates to the model of protection for geographical indications, based either on the protection of trademarks – as promoted by the United States – or on a particular system of protection as advocated by the European Union. Both have tried to export their systems into the national law of their trading partners, frequently targeting the very same countries. As a consequence, the texts of those countries' trade agreements with either major commercial power reflect the fact that only by infringing one agreement will it be possible to fulfil the other.[134]

Chapter 9 deals with the award of damages. The regulation of punitive damages in PTAs gives rise to a confusing legal scenario that involves two distinct situations. One of these relates to the inharmonious regulation of the institution globally, and the other concerns the specific situation of countries that adopt treaties where punitive damages are regulated in a very different manner. Countries exporting domestic standards that have not been globally harmonized – due to the existence of

[132] This is the objective of Article 17.2.2 US-Australia FTA and EIA (2005): 'neither party may require, as a condition of registration, that [trade] marks be visually perceptible, nor may a Party deny registration of a mark solely on the ground that the sign of which it is composed is a sound or a scent'. This seems to have been specially conceived to obstruct the adoption of the European model, which makes it almost impossible to register an olfactory trademark. *See* Burrell and Weatherall (2008), p. 284.

[133] *See* Genovesi (2013), p. 331.

[134] Compare Articles 15.2.3 and 15.3.7 CAFTA-DR-US FTA and EIA (2006) with Article 144.F EU-CARIFORUM States FTA and EIA (2008).

fundamental discrepancies with regard to the nature and functions of such norms – contribute to the creation of incoherent and conflictive national statutes.

In a related context, the exportation of the United States regime on damages requires the awarding of damages not only to compensate for the infringement but also to provide a deterrent and eventually explicitly punish the infringer. The fact that the United States statutory damage regime has been widely criticized has not impeded the United States from insisting 'upon exporting this extraordinary remedy to other nations through bilateral and plurilateral treaties, as well as other mechanisms'.[135]

4 *Defensive and Offensive Transplantation*

Depending on the point of view of the country that exports its norms, transplantation may play an offensive or a defensive function. On the one hand, concluding a treaty that transcribes part of the national legislation is a manner of exporting that legislation and making it more difficult to modify the local statute. This can be called 'offensive transplantation', a clear case being for instance that of the DMCA. On other occasions, States pursue not the transplantation of local law but the drafting of an international agreement that permits sustaining the international legality of national norms. This is our understanding of 'defensive transplantation'.

Defensive transplantation may be more subtle, but its effects can be equally crucial. In the context of ACTA, for instance, the European Union failed in its attempt to transplant its entire regime on enforcement at the border.[136] However, the European Union achieved the objective of negotiating a regime that did not directly conflict with the controversial European border enforcement system, particularly with regard to the control of products in transit. From this angle, and absent a decision in the World Trade Organization concerning the legality of the European system, ACTA permits the European Union to sustain that its regime does not contradict international law.

5 *Unbalanced Transplantation*

Another important feature of transplantation is the frequently unbalanced content of the exported norms. This is an aspect commonly underlined when commenting on the content of the intellectual property chapters of PTAs.[137] In effect, countries exporting intellectual property standards have developed comprehensive and complex national legal regimes to promote innovation, reward authors, foster competition and ensure intellectual property enforcement. However, it has become frequent

[135] *See* Samuelson, Hill and Wheatland (2013), p. 531. [136] *See* Chapter 5.

[137] *See* Section III. For all the academic references alluding to the imbalance between provisions favouring right holders and provisions favouring alleged infringers, *see* Max Planck Institute for Innovation and Competition (2013), para. 7.

practice to attempt to transpose in treaties sections found in national laws that best reflect the interests of some industrial sectors to the detriment of other stakeholders.

In some cases, the challenges do not result from lack of balance or vagueness of the exported norms. Some imported norms may bring in-built problems that can become more acute in their new context. For instance, the transplantation of some provisions of the TRIPS Agreement into ACTA has implied importing old uncertainties and unsettled questions into the new agreement, particularly with regard to the initial provisions, definitions and general principles. Their real meaning, scope and implications are still open to speculation twenty years after the TRIPS Agreement was concluded. These uncertainties are exacerbated in ACTA, since not all the links made in the TRIPS Agreement to related norms within that Agreement have been incorporated into ACTA.

The partial transplantation of intellectual property norms has resulted in the adoption of norms protecting the rights of right holders while neglecting the interests of competitors and users of protected works or inventions. The perplexing effect of this practice is that countries importing norms have, in some areas, developed a regime that is stricter than the original source. If implemented as enshrined in the corresponding treaty, the regime is likely to be anti-competitive and dysfunctional and may even generate problems from the point of view of the protection of fundamental rights.

VI POSSIBLE RESPONSES

Problems resulting from lack of balance and vagueness of the exported norms mostly refer to issues related to access to public goods, the protection of fundamental rights and the coherence of the system. Responding to the lack of procedural and substantive safeguards in the context of intellectual property enforcement requires first a proper identification of the unbalanced provisions. Once that identification has been made it will be possible to consider appropriate responses. In principle, nothing in the agreements that contain new and transplanted enforcement standards bars parties from legislating in a sense not expressly forbidden in those agreements. If the needs are known and the normative answer is not prohibited, members may just implement it.

There are several ways to address the problems posed by transplantation, and transplantation lacking balance in particular. One way is to take into account other provisions in the same agreement or in other agreements, which may help resolve ambiguity or prescribe obligations that incorporate some balance. Some of the characteristics of treaties laying down enforcement provisions may be also instrumental. For instance, the abundance of vague definitions, the frequent referral to other laws and the adoption of national conformity clauses and let-out clauses as well as the invocation of general principles of due process and fair trial standards are avenues for reintroducing the lost equilibrium.

Sometimes the answer may be found in provisions of the same agreement. For instance, Article 1 of ACTA permits understanding that fundamental rights take precedence over conflicting obligations when their impact negatively affects fundamental rights.[138] More broadly, the principles set forth in the initial provisions of ACTA and the general obligations concerning enforcement could also have been useful to introduce some balance. Article 6, for instance, mandates respect for fundamental due process principles. Invoking fairness and equity, it lays out an overarching proportionality principle. This could have been useful in the daily interpretation of the agreement as well as in the interpretation of national legislation implementing the treaty. In case of doubt or when the apparent interpretation is contrary to the principles established in the initial provisions and in Article 6, these provisions would have come into play. Moreover, and probably more importantly, they also have a legislative function since, as stated with regard to Article 6 of ACTA, the Agreement 'allows Parties to maintain and apply additional procedural safeguards'.[139]

When attention is focused on the impact of unbalanced norms on the entire system and its coherence, a more comprehensive approach is needed. Complementing the norms with additional legislation and interpreting commitments adopted pursuant to basic principles and fundamental rights are ways to tackle important imbalances. These operations may be facilitated in the same treaties, which sometimes oblige parties to take into account other international conventions. This is particularly the case of references to the TRIPS Agreement, which permit the incorporation of more balanced principles, including parties' commitments under Part III of the TRIPS Agreement.[140] A different path is the implementation of the principle of systemic interpretation, taking into account the rest of international law obligations binding on the parties. As noted, this will permit invoking obligations that originate in the area of human rights, particularly with regard to due process and fair trial standards.[141]

There are other sources of inspiration for reconstructing the system by introducing the missing balance. European and North American law as well as national and international jurisprudence are among them. In fact, more exportation may mean more balanced exportation. If the 'exporting' legal order is well understood, it will be possible to devise different implementation options. This also applies to the sources of that legal order. For instance, the Enforcement Directive originates from different European legal traditions, and its language often allows several implementing options. Hence, it would be useful to identify the origin of the provisions adopted by States that have concluded PTAs. This knowledge can be useful when adopting secondary legislation, passing sentences or litigating. Sometimes the preferred option may be to repeat the response given in the original legal order. On other occasions, however, that knowledge may help to avoid a repetition of errors that

138 *See* Chapter 4, Section III. 139 *See* Kamperman Sanders (2015), p. 86.

140 *See*, however, some predictable limits to that operation in Chapter 10, Section IV.3.3.

141 *See* Chapter 2, Section IV.3.1.

others may have committed or just to appreciate the differences justifying a different response. In this last regard, nuanced interpretations and carefully drafted implementing legislation may improve the legal texts of origin.[142]

With the intention of reaching an agreement, States negotiating an international treaty frequently leave open the specific implications of controversial terms or obligations. The abundance of ambiguous terms and flexible commitments can be also used to adjust intellectual property legislation to national choices.[143] Similarly, permissive language is frequent in international treaties. With regard to enforcement, European PTAs leave injunctions to the discretion of judicial authorities: it is stated that 'judicial authorities *may* order' or that 'judicial authorities *may* issue'.[144] These enabling references may be understood as meaning that a permanent injunction does not necessarily or automatically follow a decision finding an infringement. The US Supreme Court backed this view in the *eBay, Inc. v MercExchange* decision, stating that 'the decision whether to grant or deny injunctive relief rests within the equitable discretion of the district courts, and that such discretion must be exercised consistent with traditional principles of equity'.[145]

'National conformity clauses' and let-out clauses can also be useful in addressing problems arising from lack of balance and partial transplantation. 'National conformity clauses' refer to provisions that remit to national law the specific implementation, if any, of the obligations set forth in the treaty. In this sense, it is not strange to find references such as 'if the domestic legislation permits' or 'in accordance to domestic law' in articles enshrining controversial institutions.[146] With regard to let-out clauses found in international treaties, it is not uncommon to find references to

[142] For instance, when interpreting a local statute that essentially copied an European one, a South African judge stated: 'The Act remains a South African statute, which must be interpreted and applied in the light of our law and circumstances. Local policy considerations may differ from those applicable in Europe. The application of rules remains, even in Europe, a matter for local courts and they differ occasionally amongst themselves.' *See Beecham Group Plc v. Triomed (Pty) Ltd* [2002] ZASCA 109, para. 7.

[143] For instance, in the European agreements EU-CARIFORUM States FTA and EIA (2008) and EU-Central America FTA and EIA (2013), it is stated that the provision of evidence lying in the control of the opposing party will only be requested 'where appropriate' (Article 262 EU-Central America FTA and EIA (2013) and Article 153 EU-CARIFORUM States FTA and EIA (2008)). 'Appropriate' remits to 'suitable' or 'proper'. These terms open an important window either for policy definition through additional legal specification or for judicial autonomy to take a decision concerning the obligation to show the requested documentation.

[144] *See* Article 240 EU-Colombia and Peru FTA and EIA (2013) (emphasis added).

[145] *See eBay, Inc. v MercExchange*, LLC., 547 US 388, 391 (2006).

[146] For instance, as in the EU-Colombia and Peru FTA and EIA (2013) regarding the physical seizure of the infringing goods. Similarly, with regards to the attribution of legal costs to the unsuccessful party, *see* Article 245 EU-Colombia and Peru FTA and EIA (2013); Article 268 EU-Central America FTA and EIA (2013). *See* as well the case of interlocutory injunctions, as provided in Article 240.1 EU-Colombia and Peru FTA and EIA (2013), '[i]n accordance with their domestic legislation, each Party shall provide that its judicial authorities may, upon request of the applicant, issue an interlocutory injunction against any party'.

the fact that action on the part of applicants will be carried out 'in so far as permitted by and in accordance with the provisions of its applicable law'.[147] This can be construed either as a let-out clause or as a provision granting an important margin to legislate.

Finally, the importance that the principle of proportionality may play in the specific implementation of enforcement procedures must be underlined. As stated in almost all enforcement-related sections of international treaties, proportionality must guide enforcement procedures. The call for proportionality is also common in the human rights field, and it requires an assessment of the potential impact of some enforcement provisions on related rights.[148] In this regard, it is worth mentioning that 'the concept of "proportionality" stands as a proscription against unreasonable criminal prosecutions and an assertion that, in civil matters, intellectual property rights may not exceed the bounds of equity under any circumstance'.[149]

Transplantation may have however some external limits. That is, the exportation of national norms may at some stage result in a stalemate that does not permit further legislative advances. The example of ACTA is telling. ACTA is plagued with vague provisions that in some instances exceed the international framework for intellectual property enforcement. The insistence of the European Union and the United States on the exportation of their own legislation was probably one of the causes of ACTA's failure, since it frequently resulted in ambiguous language, essentially aimed at avoiding conflicts with either European or US law. As Bryan Mercurio has noted, the key to achieving an efficient enforcement regime is the negotiation of a *real* international treaty, meaning an agreement that contains clear enforcement norms reached through an authentic compromise and, hence, harmonization in law-making.[150] In other words, transplantation may be useless when harmonization has attained high levels or when none of the parties is in a position to derogate from its own statutes.

147 *See* Article 236 EU-Colombia and Peru FTA and EIA (2013). 148 *See* Chapter 4, Section III.2.
149 *See* DeLaurell (2012), p. 185. 150 *See* Mercurio (2015).

PART III

Civil Enforcement

7

Measures for the Preservation of Evidence

I INTRODUCTORY ASPECTS

1 *International Norms and Conflicting Interests*

The infringer of an intellectual property right may not collaborate with the justice in order to clarify his responsibility. In fact, the infringer may withhold evidence relating to the violation or even hide or destroy related information or materials.[1] In order to foster the efficiency of enforcement procedures, international treaties and national statutes have enacted provisional measures that permit seizing and safeguarding evidence even before proceedings leading to a decision on the merits of the case have begun. Together with speedy injunctive relief, measures for the preservation of evidence are critical tools to foster the efficacy of infringement procedures.[2]

Measures for the preservation of evidence are regulated in multilateral, plurilateral and bilateral treaties as well as in domestic laws. In the multilateral context, in the Agreement on Trade-Related Aspects of Intellectual Property Rights, the article devoted to provisional measures alludes to actions aimed at producing and safeguarding evidence of the infringement. The same occurs at the plurilateral level, in the Anti-Counterfeiting Trade Agreement and the Trans-Pacific Partnership Agreement. In the TRIPS, ACTA and TPP, the relevant article is drafted in general terms and maintains a level of generality that permits applying the principles laid down therein both to specific national provisions regulating measures for the preservation of evidence as well as to other interlocutory orders.

Several Preferential Trade Agreements include articles that specifically regulate the measures for the preservation of evidence. This is particularly the case of the treaties promoted by the European Union, where the article on measures for the preservation of evidence is modelled on parallel European institutions, such as the French

[1] *See* Blakeney (2005), p. 30. [2] *See* Stauder (2005), p. 1.

saisie-contrafaçon and the English Anton Piller order. The PTAs promoted by the United States include some references to preservation of evidence, with respect to copyright and trademark infringement as well as in the digital domain. Moreover, the general conditions set forth for the implementation of precautionary measures are also of application to measures for the preservation of evidence.

Measures for the preservation of evidence are frequently in tension with fundamental rights. This is an almost unavoidable feature because the preservation measures are intended to address, among others, a situation where the possessor of incriminatory documents or materials may not want to release them. In order to respond to this situation, interlocutory orders aimed at preserving evidence may for instance allow entrance into the premises of the alleged infringer before proceedings are initiated. Thus, due to their invasive nature, the implementation of measures for preservation of evidence must be balanced against fundamental rights that protect privacy, property and due process.

When regulating measures for the preservation of evidence, states have tried to guarantee the balance between the parties and impede unjustified intrusions upon fundamental rights. Among the guarantees in benefit of the alleged infringer there is the requirement to prove a strong *prima facie* case of infringement and a strong likelihood of destruction of evidence. States particularly sensitive to the risks associated with this type of interlocutory measures have enacted or implemented strict requirements for their award and implementation. Not surprisingly, these states have also developed the most sophisticated and powerful regimes on measures for the preservation of evidence. In contrast, many international treaties do not reflect most of the desirable guarantees and limitations. In this chapter, it is argued that full understanding of the implications of the relevant agreements and their analysis *vis-à-vis* fundamental rights standards may shed light on the eventual amendment and re-drafting of international norms on measures for the preservation of evidence.

2 *Other Enforcement-Related Measures concerning Information*

Measures for the preservation of evidence are among a larger group of remedies concerning information. These remedies include measures intended to produce evidence by the opposing party as well as the possibility to order the infringer to inform the right holder of a number of aspects touching upon the infringement. While this chapter focuses on measures of preservation of evidence, international norms touching upon the production of evidence and the right of information are briefly introduced in this section.[3] On the one hand, the three of them form part of the larger group of investigative measures. On the other hand, the challenges posed by the regulation and implementation of measures for the preservation of

[3] *See* also Chapter 6, Section III.

evidence, in particular in relation to fundamental rights and the normative features of their international regulation, are also identifiable with respect to the other investigative measures.

To be successful in the context of intellectual property litigation it may be necessary to provide information concerning aspects that only the alleged infringer knows, such as the number of products sold or the benefits made from that sale. Judicial authorities have the power to order the production of evidence lying in the control of the opposing party. In order to do so, the party requesting the evidence must fulfil two conditions. First, she must present reasonably available evidence sufficient to support its claims, and second, she must specify the evidence relevant to substantiation of its claims that lies in the control of the opposing party.[4] The protection of confidential information is usually set as the limit for exercising such a power.[5] As it happens with respect to measures for the preservation of evidence, a sound legal regime integrated by checks and balances is essential to avoid conflicts with privacy, property and the right to a fair trial.

Judicial authorities may also be entitled to order the infringer to inform the right holder of the identity of third persons involved in the production and distribution of the infringing goods or services and their channels of distribution.[6] Bilateral and plurilateral agreements have transformed what in the TRIPS Agreement is a faculty into an obligation. The scope of this right has also been thoroughly amended since TRIPS was adopted. Pursuant to PTAs and plurilaterals, information will concern not only third persons and the channels of distribution but also the person found in possession of the infringing goods, using the infringing services, providing services used in infringing activities or indicated by any of the previous ones as involved in the production, manufacture or distribution.[7] As it happens with the measures for the preservation of evidence, the right of information can be abused if no strict limits are laid down, something particularly worrying given its close relationship to privacy and the protection of personal data.[8]

[4] Article 43.1 of the TRIPS Agreement. [5] *See* Chapter 6, Section III.1.1.

[6] Article 47 of the TRIPS Agreement. [7] *See* Chapter 6, Section III.1.2.

[8] In *Promusicae*, the European Court of Justice stated that 'Article 8(1) of Directive 2004/48 admittedly requires Member States to ensure that, in the context of proceedings concerning an infringement of an intellectual property right and in response to a justified and proportionate request of the claimant, the competent judicial authorities may order that information on the origin and distribution networks of the goods or services which infringe an intellectual property right be provided. However, it does not follow from those provisions, which must be read in conjunction with those of paragraph 3(e) of that article, that they require the Member States to lay down, in order to ensure effective protection of copyright, an obligation to communicate personal data in the context of civil proceedings.' The ECJ concluded that 'Directives 2000/31, 2001/29, 2004/48 and 2002/58 do not require the Member States to lay down, in a situation such as that in the main proceedings, an obligation to communicate personal data in order to ensure effective protection of copyright in the context of civil proceedings'. *Productores de Música de España (Promusicae) v. Telefónica de España SAU*, Case C-275/06, 28 January 2008.

II INTERNATIONAL LEGAL FRAMEWORK ON MEASURES FOR THE PRESERVATION OF EVIDENCE

1 *The Regime Set Forth in the TRIPS Agreement*

Article 50 of the TRIPS Agreement was the first international norm ever adopted relating to measures for the preservation of evidence.[9] The scope of Article 50 of the TRIPS Agreement is broad and regulates all types of precautionary measures,[10] including measures for the preservation of evidence. It is in this ample context that Article 50 sets up the relevant multilateral legal framework to adopt more specific national rules.

Article 50.1(b) of the TRIPS Agreement obliges WTO Members to empower judges to order prompt and effective provisional measures to preserve evidence regarding a possible infringement. This section is closely related to Article 50.2 of the TRIPS Agreement, which mandates empowering judicial authorities to adopt provisional measures *inaudita altera parte*, in particular where delays are likely to cause irreparable harm to the right holder or where there is a demonstrable risk of evidence being destroyed. This is, thus, an explicit derogation from the adversarial principle. The latter provision captures the essence of the corresponding institutions in the national context: measures will be adopted *inaudita parte*, on a provisional basis, with the intention to avoid irreparable harm or the destruction of evidence. The specific measures that can be adopted are left at the discretion of Member States.

Other sections of Article 50 of the TRIPS Agreement enshrine a number of general guarantees that should help at keeping the award of provisional measures, including measures for the preservation of evidence, in conformity with due process and fair trial standards. In this sense, Article 50.3 permits judicial authorities to require the applicant to provide any reasonably available evidence to show that he is the right holder and that his right is being infringed or that the infringement is imminent and to order the applicant to provide a security sufficient to protect the defendant and to prevent abuse.

Also relevant in the context of measures for the preservation of evidence is Article 50.5 of the TRIPS Agreement, which establishes that the applicant may be required to supply other information necessary for the identification of the goods concerned in order to assist the authority enforcing the provisional measure. Also in the TRIPS Agreement and in a number of national laws that regulate in detail measures for the preservation of evidence[11] is found the obligation to empower judges to order compensation for the defendant 'where the provisional measures are revoked or

[9] On the general meaning and implications of Article 50 of the TRIPS Agreement, *see* UNCTAD-ICTSD (2005), pp. 601–608. Regarding its relevance for measures for the preservation of evidence, *see* Blakeney (2004), p. 15; Blakeney (2005), pp. 30–31.

[10] *See* Chapter 8.

[11] *See* following references to Article 7 of the EU Enforcement Directive, the French *saisie-contrefaçon* and the common law Anton Piller orders.

where they lapse due to any act or omission by the applicant, or where it is found subsequently that there has been no infringement or threat of infringement'.[12]

Article 50.4 of the TRIPS Agreement establishes that whenever measures are adopted *inaudita altera parte*, the parties affected shall be given notice without delay after the execution of the measures at the latest. This article may have limited importance in light of the characteristics of some of the measures for the preservation of evidence developed at the national level. This is the case of Anton Piller orders and *saisie-contrafaçon*, remedies that permit entrance into the premises of the alleged infringer. In the case of Anton Piller orders, an authorization from the infringer must be obtained. This will not happen without significant pressure,[13] but the authorization must indeed exist, thus the reference of Article 50.4 to inform the alleged infringer without delay is not relevant. In the case of *saisie-contrafaçon*, the alleged infringer is informed when the *saisie* is conducted. This means that the alleged infringer is informed right in the moment of the execution of the measure.

Article 50.4 of the TRIPS Agreement also provides for 'a review, including a right to be heard' upon the request of the defendant 'with a view to deciding, within a reasonable period of notification of the measures' whether they should be 'modified, revoked or confirmed'. The fulfilment of this general requirement, conceived to reintroduce the adversarial principle, can become particularly challenging in the case of the measures for the preservation of evidence.[14]

2 *Plurilateral Agreements*

Article 12 of the Anti-Counterfeiting Trade Agreement regulates the adoption of 'prompt and effective provisional measures' and specifically mentions measures adopted to preserve relevant evidence in regard to the alleged infringement.[15] These measures may be adopted *inaudita altera parte*, in particular where any delay is likely to cause irreparable harm to the right holder or where there is a demonstrable risk of evidence being destroyed. In proceedings conducted *inaudita altera parte*, judicial authorities shall have the authority to act expeditiously on requests for provisional measures and to adopt a decision without undue delay.[16] This drafting emulates that of Article 50 of the TRIPS Agreement and establishes the general framework for the adoption of measures for the preservation of evidence, which is accompanied by a number of guarantees. By contrast, the Trans-Pacific Partnership Agreement lays down a shorter and succinct provision, in particular when compared to TRIPS but also in comparison to ACTA.

In effect, Article 12 of ACTA also sets up the guarantees that apply to all types of provisional measures, including measures for the preservation of evidence. Coincidentally with the TRIPS Agreement, ACTA orders Parties to empower

[12] *See* Article 50.7 TRIPS Agreement. [13] *See* Section III.3. [14] *Ibid.*
[15] *See* Article 12.1(b) ACTA. [16] *See* Article 12.2 ACTA.

judicial authorities to require reasonably available evidence to prove the infringement or the imminence of the infringement and to order the provision of a security or equivalent assurance sufficient to protect the defendant and to prevent abuse.[17] In a novelty with respect to the TRIPS Agreement and tilting the balance in favour of right holders, ACTA establishes that 'such security or equivalent assurance shall not unreasonably deter recourse to procedures for such provisional measures'.[18] ACTA also establishes that the applicant may be compelled to provide compensation for any injury caused by the provisional measures if it is subsequently found that there has been no infringement of an intellectual property right.[19]

Although the mentioned guarantees are relevant, they are not mentioned in the TPP, and moreover, they do not include all the guarantees enshrined in the TRIPS Agreement. In this sense, it is noticeable that ACTA does not mention guarantees such as the right to be heard and the right to be informed promptly after the execution of the measure, a feature that it shares with other plurilaterals and bilaterals.

Article 12.3 of ACTA specifically addresses the adoption of measures for the preservation of evidence and essentially coincides with Article 18.75.3 of the Trans-Pacific Partnership Agreement. In a novelty with respect to the TRIPS Agreement but almost coincidentally with the content of the United States PTAs, Article 12.3 of ACTA states that '[a]t least in cases of copyright or related rights infringement and trademark counterfeiting, each Party shall provide that ... its judicial authorities have the authority to order the seizure or other taking into custody of suspect goods, and of materials and implements relevant to the act of infringement, and, at least for trademark counterfeiting, documentary evidence, either originals or copies thereof, relevant to the infringement'.

Article 12.3 of ACTA has to be read as a *lex specialis* within provisional measures, obliging to permit the seizures at least in the case of copyright and trademark infringement. The sole difference with respect to the provision found in the TPP is that this is explicitly limited to copyright or related rights infringement and trademark counterfeiting, while in ACTA measures relating to other types of intellectual property rights are possible. This is important because, as it happens with the TRIPS Agreement, nowhere else are stated which are the 'prompt and effective provisional measures' that judges may adopt. Hence, Article 12.3 of ACTA is the first plurilateral norm regulating measures for the preservation of evidence specifically and explicitly involving the seizure of relevant material.

3 *Preferential Trade Agreements*

3.1 European Union Preferential Trade Agreements

As it happens with the regulation of other enforcement-related measures, the European legislation on measures for the preservation of evidence gives important

[17] *See* Article 12.4 ACTA. [18] *Ibid.* [19] *See* Article 12.5 ACTA.

clues about the content of the most recent European PTAs.[20] A brief presentation of the European harmonized rules on this matter allows a better understanding of the meaning of the equivalent measures in PTAs and also of the relevance of the missing parts of the European legislation on the matter.

According to Article 7 of the EU Enforcement Directive,[21] judicial authorities must be able to order provisional measures 'to preserve relevant evidence in respect of the alleged infringement'. This is further defined with the identification of two potential actions that may be adopted in this context: 'the detailed description, with or without the taking of samples, and the physical seizure of the infringing goods and, in appropriate cases, of the materials and implements used . . . and the documents relating thereto'.[22]

These *ex parte* measures are subject to the presentation of reasonable available evidence to support that the right has been or is about to be infringed. Measures for the preservation of evidence must be prompt and effective and may be taken without the other party having been heard – although the defendant must be informed promptly – and before the commencement of proceedings leading to a decision on the merits of the case. The defendant has the right to ask for a review of the measure, a reintroduction of the adversarial principle allowing the judge to reconsider whether the measure must be revoked, maintained, or modified. The Enforcement Directive also requires the initiation within a reasonable period of time of proceedings on the merits of the case and the possibility to award compensation if an infringement is not found or proceedings are not duly initiated. As guarantee of this compensation, the measures to preserve evidence 'may be subject to the lodging by the applicant of adequate security or an equivalent assurance'.[23]

The European regime described greatly coincides with the one in the TRIPS Agreement[24] and with the regulation foreseen in the European trade agreements,[25] in particular with respect to the rights of the right holder. It is interesting, though, to make a double comparison of the agreements. On the one hand, it is useful to compare them since this allows identifying relevant differences across the agreements and understanding their implications. Second, it is also suitable to compare

[20] *See* Chapter 6, Section III.1.

[21] *See* Directive 2004/48/EC of the European Parliament and of the Council of 29 April 2004 on the enforcement of intellectual property rights, OJEU L157 of 30 April 2004 (hereinafter EU Enforcement Directive).

[22] *See* Article 7.1 EU Enforcement Directive.

[23] *See*, for all them, Article 7.1 to 7.4 EU Enforcement Directive.

[24] Article 7.1 of the EU Enforcement Directive first subparagraph is almost identical to Articles 50.2 and 50.3 of the TRIPS Agreement. Article 7.1 of the EU Enforcement Directive second sub-paragraph parallels Article 50.4 of the TRIPS Agreement. Article 7.2 of the EU Enforcement Directive relates to Article 50.3 of the TRIPS Agreement, while Article 7.3 of the EU Enforcement Directive is related to Article 50.6 of the TRIPS Agreement. And Article 7.4 of the EU Enforcement Directive is almost equal to Article 50.7 of the TRIPS Agreement.

[25] *See* Article 10.44 EU-Republic of Korea FTA and EIA (2011); Article 154 EU-CARIFORUM States FTA and EIA (2008); Article 263 EU-Central America FTA and EIA (2013); Article 238 of EU-Colombia and Peru FTA and EIA (2013).

the articles set forth in the European PTAs with the corresponding article in the EU Enforcement Directive, since this permits observing what has been transplanted into the PTAs and what has been omitted.

Although the structure and content of recent European PTAs greatly concur, these agreements contain slight variations that may have significant consequences. The case of the treaty between the European Union, Colombia and Peru offers some relevant examples. First, this treaty contains a 'national conformity clause' regarding the physical seizure of the infringing goods and materials and implements related with the infringement.[26] Pursuant to this clause, the acceptability of such a physical seizure is made conditional upon its compatibility with national legislation. Second, in addition to the mentioned conditionality, the relevant provision states that measures must be not only prompt and effective but also proportionate, an important requirement not foreseen in the other texts. The call for fairness and balance gives to national legislators and judges a broader margin to implement measures for the preservation of evidence in a balanced manner.

Another comparison to be made is that between the EU Enforcement Directive and the correlative provisions in PTAs. Drawing from the experience acquired with Anton Piller orders and *saisie-contrafaçon*, the EU Enforcement Directive enshrines several guarantees to avoid abuse of enforcement procedures and undesired outcomes of the implementation of measures for the preservation of evidence. The guarantees set forth in Article 7 of the EU Enforcement Directive include the right to be informed promptly of the measure and to ask for a review, the possibility to revoke the measure if proceedings are not initiated in a reasonable period of time and the possibility to ask for a security before executing the measures and for compensation in case the measures were unduly granted.

However, none of these safeguards has been introduced in the trade agreements promoted by the European Union.[27] This absence may be particularly problematic because not only deviations from the original intent of the provision on measures for preservation of evidence may occur but also procedural abuses may take place. For instance, if title holders know that no compensation in favour of the defendant will be awarded when no infringement is found, they may be tempted to use measures for the preservation of evidence as a tool to harass competitors. Seizures of legitimate goods or disclosure and examination of trade secrets may be unintended consequences from the absence of the relevant guarantees.[28]

3.2 United States Preferential Trade Agreements

The PTAs concluded by the United States do not include an article exclusively devoted to the measures for the preservation of evidence. Contrary to the European

[26] *See* Article 238 EU-Colombia and Peru FTA and EIA (2013) and the reference made therein 'if the national legislation so permits'.
[27] *See* Chapter 6, Section III.1.1. [28] *See* Section III.

agreements, there is no such a thing like a specific provision on the preservation of evidence applicable with respect to all categories of intellectual property rights. The United States treaties are not totally silent, though. Three instances can be found where measures for the preservation of evidence are regulated, either with respect to some categories of intellectual property rights or in some specific contexts.

First, an article commonly found in United States agreements establishes that in civil judicial proceedings concerning copyright infringement and trademark counterfeiting, judicial authorities shall have the authority to order the seizure of suspected infringing goods, any related materials and implements and, at least for trademark counterfeiting, documentary evidence relevant to the infringement.[29] This power may fulfil other functions apart from preserving evidence, such as preventing the entrance of allegedly infringing products into the market or impeding its production. Tellingly, the agreement between Chile and the United States affirms for instance that these measures will be adopted 'where necessary to prevent further infringement'.[30] However, the reference to the preservation of documentary evidence and the possibility of seizing products, materials and implements are indeed characteristic of measures for the preservation of evidence.

Second, the United States agreements widen the scope of measures for the preservation of evidence. In these agreements reference is made to the seizure of devices and products suspected of being involved in the prohibited activity with respect to the circumvention of technological protection measures and removal or alteration of rights management information.[31] That is, precautionary measures for the preservation of evidence are explicitly made applicable in the digital domain.

Third, the United States PTAs contain an article enshrining the conditions for the implementation of precautionary measures in general, conditions that are of application to measures for the preservation of evidence. Pursuant to this article, the award of provisional measures must satisfy two pre-requisites: the plaintiff must provide any reasonably available evidence in order to prove that his right is being infringed or that such infringement is imminent, and the plaintiff must provide a reasonable security or equivalent assurance set at a level sufficient to protect the defendant and to prevent abuse.[32]

[29] *See* Article 18.10.8 Republic of Korea-US FTA and EIA (2012); Article 17.11.9 US-Australia FTA and EIA (2005); Article 14.10.9 US-Bahrain FTA and EIA (2006); Article 17.11.11 US-Chile FTA and EIA (2004); Article 16.11.10 US-Colombia FTA and EIA (2012) and US-Peru FTA and EIA (2009); Article 15.11.9 US-Morocco FTA and EIA (2006); Article 15.11.10 US-Panama FTA and EIA (2012); Article 16.9.11 US-Singapore FTA and EIA (2004).

[30] *See* Article 17.11.11 US-Chile FTA and EIA (2004).

[31] *See* Article 14.10.14(a) US-Bahrain FTA and EIA (2006); Article 17.11.13(a)(i) US-Australia FTA and EIA (2005); Article 15.10.14(a) US-Oman FTA and EIA (2009); Article 16.11.15(a) US-Peru FTA and EIA (2009); Article 16.11.15(a) US-Colombia FTA and EIA (2012); Article 15.11.14(a) US-Morocco FTA and EIA (2006); Article 15.11.14(a) US-Panama FTA and EIA (2012); Article 16.9.5(a) US-Singapore FTA and EIA (2004).

[32] *See* Article 14.10.18 US-Bahrain FTA and EIA (2006); Article 17.11.17 US-Australia FTA and EIA (2005); Article 15.10.18 US-Oman FTA and EIA (2009); Article 16.11.19 US-Peru FTA and EIA (2009); Article 16.11.19 US-Colombia FTA and EIA (2012); Article 15.11.18 US-Morocco FTA and EIA (2006);

In the domestic legislation of the United States, impounding orders found in the Copyright Act[33] and the civil actions arising out of use of counterfeit marks as established in the Trademark Act[34] fulfil a similar function. In the case of copyright, impounding orders allow the court to seize 'copies or phonorecords claimed to have been made or used in violation of the exclusive right of the copyright owner'; 'plates, molds, matrices, masters, tapes, film negatives, or other articles by means of which such copies of phonorecords may be reproduced'; and 'records documenting the manufacture, sale, or receipt of things involved in any such violation',[35] subject to the protection of confidential information.[36] In a similar fashion, the Trademark Act establishes that in the case of a civil action arising out of use of counterfeit marks,[37] the court may, upon *ex parte* application, grant an order 'providing for the seizure of goods and counterfeit marks involved in such violation and the means of making such marks, and records documenting the manufacture, sale, or receipt of things involved in such violation'.[38]

III HOW TO REDRESS VAGUENESS AND LACK OF BALANCE

The international legal framework on measures for the preservation of evidence is underdeveloped. The comparison against parallel remedies existing at the national level reveals the absence of important pieces of this remedy. Treaties adopted after the TRIPS Agreement are generally vague, and the regulation enshrined is fundamentally concerned about the rights of the right holders. In this regard, ACTA and TPP remain silent with respect to a number of basic guarantees present in the TRIPS Agreement, European agreements transplant the EU Enforcement Directive text only as far as rights of title holders are concerned, and the United States agreements are relatively vague and also concerned about the rights of the right holders. Said lack of balance and vagueness may create tensions when analysed from the point of view of fundamental rights. However, these tensions may be attenuated with a contextualized reading of the texts and the implementation of fundamental principles of public international law.

A first step to ensure a balanced implementation requires conducting a more complete reading of the relevant texts. This reading implies contextualizing the treaty provisions in a more ample framework, where references to other treaties and basic principles have been inserted. A second and also necessary operation requires interpreting and implementing the concerned articles under the principle of

Article 15.11.18 US-Panama FTA and EIA (2012); Article 16.9.15(a) US-Singapore FTA and EIA (2004); Article 17.11.16(a) US-Chile FTA and EIA (2004).

33 *See* Title 17 USC, § 503(a). 34 *See* Title 15 USC, § 1116(d)(1)(A).

35 *See* Title 17 USC, § 503(a)(1) (A) through (C). 36 *See* Title 17 USC, § 503(a)(2).

37 Under § 1114(1)(a) of the same Title, or § 220506 of Title 36 with respect to a violation that consists of using a counterfeit mark in connection with the sale, offering for sale or distribution of goods or services.

38 *See* Title 15 USC, § 1116(d)(1)(A).

systemic integration. This principle prescribes taking into consideration, when interpreting an international norm, other norms of public international law binding on the parties.[39] In this case, human rights norms will re-define the parameters of implementation of measures for the preservation of evidence. A third operation focuses on national implementation. In this particular regard, international human rights norms may also be useful, but the experience of other countries can be particularly inspiring, as will be seen in the case of Anton Piller orders.

1 A *Contextualized Reading*

While the isolated reading of articles found in bilateral and plurilateral agreements leads to the conclusion that vagueness and imbalance are problematic features of the agreements, a broader reading of the texts results in a rather more positive conclusion. In an important number of cases, enforcement-related treaties contain general provisions declaring the prevalence of previous agreements and/or articles enshrining general principles related to due process and fair trial standards. These provisions are useful to clarify the reading of the article on measures for the preservation of evidence as well as other articles of ambiguous or poor content.

ACTA specifically declares that it complements the TRIPS Agreement and that nothing in the treaty shall derogate from any obligation existing in the TRIPS Agreement or in other agreements. Moreover, Article 6 of ACTA includes several principles and guarantees that are useful in remedying potential problems posed by the silences regarding rights protecting alleged infringers. References to the TRIPS Agreement can also be found in other problematic treaties, where it is specifically stated that 'Parties affirm their rights and obligations with respect to each other under the TRIPS Agreement',[40] or, more generally, reaffirm the rights and obligations under the Agreement establishing the World Trade Organization – and therefore its annexes.[41]

The reaffirmation of the rights and obligations under the TRIPS Agreement is a useful compromise when interpreting intellectual property-related treaties. It may be ambiguous to 'reaffirm' an agreement but not clarify whether it prevails over new treaties in case of conflict. In this regard, it would seem that when new treaties reaffirm or 'state again strongly'[42] the TRIPS Agreement, recognize its prevalence. However, this may not be the case if posterior norms are clear and specific. In any case, and concerning measures for the preservation of evidence, no conflicts

[39] *See* Chapter 2, Section IV.3.

[40] *See* Article 17.1.3 US-Australia FTA and EIA (2005); Article16.1.4 US-Peru FTA and EIA (2009); Article 16.1.6 US-Colombia FTA and EIA (2012); Article 15.1.5 US-Panama FTA and EIA (2012); Preamble US-Chile FTA and EIA (2004).

[41] *See* Preamble US-Singapore FTA and EIA (2004).

[42] *See* Oxford Dictionary meaning of 'reaffirm'.

between the TRIPS Agreement and posterior agreements exist, and the key is found in treaty interpretation rather than addressing normative conflicts. Thus, while guarantees foreseen in the TRIPS Agreement are obviated in PTAs and plurilaterals, the 'reaffirmation' of the TRIPS Agreement reinforces a broader and more balanced reading of plurilaterals and bilaterals.

In addition to the guarantees set forth in Article 50 of the TRIPS Agreement, applicable to measures for the preservation of evidence, the TRIPS Agreement is also of relevance because of the objectives and principles announced in Articles 7 and 8 and because of the principle of 'fair and equitable procedures' enshrined in Article 42. The systemic relevance of Articles 7 and 8 of the TRIPS Agreement to clarify the provisions of the treaty has already been underpinned.[43] The references to technological innovation, transfer of technology, the interests of producers and users, social and economic welfare and balance of rights and obligations imply that the TRIPS Agreement must be read in a broader socioeconomic context, where the interests of both right holders and alleged infringers are taken into account.

In the context of civil enforcement, Article 42 of the TRIPS Agreement and its prescription of fair and equitable procedures are also crucial.[44] As stated in Chapters 2 and 4, Article 42 of TRIPS includes a complete charter touching upon fair trial standards. Mention is made therein to the right to written, timely and detailed notice; the right to be represented by independent legal counsel; the right to procedures that do not impose overly burdensome requirements concerning mandatory personal appearances; the right to be entitled to substantiate claims and to present all relevant evidence; and the right to provide a means to identify and protect confidential information.[45]

2 *Systemic Integration*

Norms found in international treaties are part of a broader legal framework that needs to be taken into account when determining their concrete meaning.[46] Article 31 of the Vienna Convention on the Law of the Treaties enacts a single operation of textual, teleological and contextual interpretation. The principle of systemic integration enshrined in Article 31.3(c)[47] forms part of this operation.[48] Pursuant to this principle, when interpreting a specific norm contained in an international treaty, other obligations of international law binding on the parties need to be taken into account. These naturally include norms pertaining to the international human rights regime.

43 *See* Chapter 4, Section II.2.2.4. 44 *See* Straus (2000), p. 808.

45 *See* Chapter 2, Section I.3, and Chapter 4, Section II.2.2.3. 46 *See* Chapter 2, Section IV.3.

47 Article 31.3(c) reads, 'There shall be taken into account, together with the context: . . . (c) any relevant rules of international law applicable in the relations between the parties.'

48 *See* McLachlan (2005).

2.1 Fundamental Rights Impacted by Measures for the Preservation of Evidence

Measures for the preservation of evidence may cause a range of problems from the point of view of fundamental rights. The protection of the right to privacy, the right to property and the right to a fair trial may be impinged upon by the invasiveness of some interlocutory orders, the entrance into the defendant's premises, the seizure of documents and objects and the partial derogation of the adversarial principle. A carefully balanced regulation is necessary to mitigate the impact on the legal interests protected by these fundamental rights.

The entrance and search into the defendant's business and domicile allowed by some measures for the preservation of evidence may impact on the right to privacy. Certainly, in some cases the implementation of measures for the preservation of evidence requires the consent of the alleged infringer; thus it would seem that the impact on the right to privacy is minimal or non-existent. The permission given by the alleged infringer in the context of measures for the preservation of evidence like Anton Piller orders distinguishes them from criminal search warrants.[49] In reality, however, consent is relative, since in the case of Anton Piller orders failure to permit the search may be sanctioned by contempt of court, which has severe consequences in terms of criminal punishment. This implies that 'such a subtlety will be of little comfort to a defendant who is confronted with an order in those terms',[50] since permission is extracted under severe pressure. Thus, there must be other grounds distinct to the permission granted by the defendant to justify the impact on the right to privacy.

The search into the premises, records and secrets of the alleged infringer may also impact on the right to property. Measures for the preservation of evidence may allow the right holder to have access to crucial information on the defendant's business. This is particularly relevant in light of the fact that the defendant and the plaintiff are probably competitors. The access gained to documentation containing trade secrets, frequently legitimate and unrelated to the infringement, is difficult when not impossible to undo.[51] Moreover, measures for the preservation of evidence have

[49] In the original case, the judge strived to differentiate Anton Piller orders from search warrants: 'Let me say at once that no court in this land has any power to issue a search warrant to enter a man's house so as to see if there are papers or documents there which are of an incriminating nature, whether libels or infringements of copyright or anything else of the kind. ... But the order sought in this case is not a search warrant. It does not authorise the plaintiffs' solicitors or anyone else to enter the defendants' premises against their will. It does not authorise the breaking down of any doors, nor the slipping in by a back door, nor getting in by an open door or window. It only authorizes entry and inspection by the permission of the defendants.' *See Anton Piller KG v. Manufacturing Processes Limited, Bernard Preston Wallace and Alfred Henry Stephen Baker*, [1975] EWCA Civ. 12, p. 60 (hereinafter *Anton Piller KG v. Manufacturing Processes Ltd. and Others*).

[50] *See* Rock (1984–1985), p. 193.

[51] As it has been stated, '[s]ince Anton Piller orders give compulsory rights of inspection, once those inspections have taken place the information procured from it is in the hands of the other side and the situation is irreversible'. *See Thermax Limited v. Schott Industrial Glass Limited*, [1981] FSR 289 (Ch.

been used sometimes as 'fishing expeditions' or oppressive procedural measures designed to put small business competitors out of business.[52] These practices may 'have the effect of destroying the defendant's business without any opportunity to apply to the court for it to be set aside, before it was executed'.[53] In fact, in some cases the order may give 'the plaintiff the opportunity to appropriate trade secrets, exactly what, in many cases, the plaintiff is accusing the defendant of doing'.[54]

Local versions of measures for the preservation of evidence also have a difficult relationship with the right to not self-incriminate. The privilege against self-incrimination permits one not to facilitate evidence or answering questions that may eventually result in the incrimination of the concerned person. However, Anton Piller orders require the defendant to disclose sensitive information to judicial authorities and to the plaintiff. Although it is disputed whether the privilege against self-incrimination can be extended to civil proceedings,[55] controversial situations may arise even if that extension is not uphold. Take for instance cases depicted in Section 2.2, the cases where a civil infringement may also have criminal implications, since the same information may prove both a civil infringement and a criminal offence or, still, the situation depicted in Chapter 9, where the award of damages also has a punitive nature.

2.2 Responses Given to the Tensions Existing between Measures for the Preservation of Evidence and Fundamental Rights

Measures for the preservation of evidence have been analysed by human rights courts and national and regional tribunals in numerous instances. Most of the jurisprudence has focused on the impact of these measures on the right to privacy, the right to a fair trial and incidentally on the right to property.

The right to privacy is a right of non-absolute nature; thus intrusions on privacy are permitted for legitimate purposes. The European Court of Human Rights has explored the grounds that permit interfering with the right to privacy. Article 8.2 of the European Convention on Human Rights tolerates intrusions on the right to privacy if these interferences are necessary for the protection of 'the rights of others', a precision of great importance in the context of measures for the preservation of evidence. When this justification concurs – for instance to avoid the violation of intellectual property rights – the permitted 'interference' must fulfil a number of conditions. The European Convention on Human Rights requires examining

D), p. 294 (hereinafter *Thermax Limited v. Schott Industrial Glass Ltd.*), as quoted in *Netsmart Inc. v. Poelzer*, 2002 ABQB 800 (CanLII), 2002 ABQB 800, 324 AR 260, para. 31.

52 *See* Godin (1996), p. 111.

53 *See Columbia Pictures Industries Inc. v. Robinson and Others*, [1987] 1 Ch. 38 (hereinafter *Columbia Pictures v. Robinson*).

54 *See* Godin (1996), p. 121.

55 *See* Zuckerman (2007), p. 395.

whether the challenged measures are established by the law[56] and are necessary in a democratic society.[57] This has led the European Court of Human Rights to examine the implementation of Anton Piller orders and ruling that, even if in the particular case examined problems were found with regard to the implementation of the order, Anton Piller orders *per se* are compatible with the protection that the Convention awards to privacy.[58]

The European Court of Human Rights has tied the acceptability of measures for the preservation of evidence not only to the right to privacy but also to the right to a fair trial. In this sense, it has for instance stated that the evidence presented to the court should be valid and admissible and that the way in which the evidence is taken should ensure fairness.[59] Moreover, courts and national statutes have subjected the legitimacy of any deprivation of property to the respect of due process standards. In this regard, although deprivation of property has been associated with a fair hearing, the characteristics of some measures for the preservation of evidence imply a tense relationship with fair hearing standards. Indeed, the Court of Justice of the European Union has underlined the tension between rules on the taking of evidence and the right to a fair hearing.[60] Citizens may be deprived of their property and their businesses closed down 'by orders made ex parte, on applications of which they know nothing and at which they cannot be heard, by orders which they are forced, on pain of committal to obey, even if wrongly made'.[61] In fact, the defendant may be left in a very precarious circumstance, since measures for the preservation of evidence may impact on the fundamental principle of *audi alteram partem*, and although the defendant may oppose the execution of the order, the merits of the order will not be discussed.

Early case law in the United Kingdom recognized the potential impact on self-incrimination arising from measures for the preservation of evidence. As a result, the implementation of the measures requested was initially rejected.[62] Later on, the

56 This requires interferences to have some basis in domestic law but also that the law meets some quality requirements. *See* ECtHR, *Chappel v. United Kingdom*, no. 10461/83, 30 March 1989, Series A no. 152-A, para. 57 (hereinafter ECtHR, *Chappell v. United Kingdom*).

57 Which implies considering whether they are proportionate to the legitimate aim pursued.

58 *See* ECtHR, *Chappell v. United Kingdom*, para. 57.

59 *See* ECtHR, *Barbera, Messegne and Jabardo v. Spain*, application no. 10590/83, 6 December 1988, Series A no. 146, para. 68.

60 *See* CJEU, Case C-276/01, *Joachim Steffensen* [2003], Judgment of the Court (Fifth Chamber) of 10 April 2003, ECR 2003 I-03735, para. 80.

61 The full quote read as '[i]t is a fundamental principle of civil jurisprudence in this country that citizens are not to be deprived of their property by judicial or quasi-judicial order without a fair hearing ... What is to be said of the Anton Piller procedure which, on a regular and institutionalised basis, is depriving citizens of their property and closing down their businesses by orders made ex parte, on applications of which they know nothing and at which they cannot be heard, by orders which they are forced, on pain of committal to obey, even if wrongly made?'. *See Columbia Pictures v. Robinson*, pp. 73–74.

62 *See Rank Film Distributors Ltd and Others v. Video Information Centre and Others*, [1982] AC 380 (Ch.D) (hereinafter *Rank Film Distributors Ltd. v. Video Information Centre*).

English Parliament abrogated the privilege against self-incrimination in areas where intellectual property infringement is involved.[63] In accordance with the present legislation, the defendant must respond to the questions posed and comply with any order made to disclose information. Nevertheless, he also receives statutory protection and the information collected as a result of the Anton Piller orders is not admissible in criminal proceedings. This reflects the, for some, 'most desirable situation', which is to permit Anton Piller orders to be made and 'at the same time protect the served party from subsequent criminal ramifications which could result from the disclosures'.[64]

The relationship between measures for the preservation of evidence and trade secrets has also been addressed in court. While national tribunals have recognized the existing tension and have exempted the alleged infringer from disclosing information 'in cases where the respondent invokes business secrets in a field that would become apparent upon presentation for inspection, and if the subject matter and the circumstances make it likely that such business secrets exist',[65] they have also 'realised that invoking business secrets by the defendant may be frivolous in itself if invariably used to frustrate the applicant's right of inspection.'[66] This tension is acknowledged in legal texts, which subject the adoption of measures to preserve relevant evidence to the protection of confidential information.[67]

2.3 Problems Raised by the Codification of Measures for the Preservation of Evidence in Bilateral Agreements

Tensions between fundamental rights and measures for the preservation of evidence are almost unavoidable and may be exacerbated as a result of the adoption of imbalanced international norms. The comparative analysis of the relevant PTAs provisions on measures for the preservation of evidence permits identifying the guarantees that are missed in the agreements and that would protect the alleged infringers. The treaties promoted by the European Union do

[63] Section 72 of the United Kingdom's Senior Courts Act of 1981 establishes that '(1) In any proceedings to which this subsection applies a person shall not be excused, by reason that to do so would tend to expose that person, or his or her spouse or civil partner to proceedings for a related offence or for the recovery of a related penalty – (a) from answering any questions put to that person in the first-mentioned proceedings; or (b) from complying with any order made in those proceedings. (2) Subsection (1) applies to the following civil proceedings in the High Court, namely – (a) proceedings for infringement of rights pertaining to any intellectual property or for passing off; (b) proceedings brought to obtain disclosure of information relating to any infringement of such rights or to any passing off; and (c) proceedings brought to prevent any apprehended infringement of such rights or any apprehended passing off'.

[64] *See* McInnes (1987–1988), p. 344.

[65] Düsseldorf High Court, 17 August 1981, Gewerblicher Rechtsschutz und Urheberrecht (GRUR) 1983, 741 – 'Interest in Secrecy and Right of Inspection I' (quoted from Heath and Cotter, 2015, p. 19).

[66] Heath and Cotter, 2015, p. 19.

[67] *See* Article 7.1 EU Enforcement Directive.

not mention the obligation to notify immediately after the execution of the measure, the right (to be heard and) to ask for a review of the measure, the right to have the measures revoked if proceedings on the merits of the case are not established in a reasonable period of time, the possibility to ask for an adequate security or equivalent assurance and the right to be awarded compensation in case measures are revoked or lapse.[68]

If the unbalanced and vague PTAs provisions on measures for the preservation of evidence are implemented as drafted in the treaties, intellectual property holders will know that no compensation in favour of the defendant will be awarded even if no infringement is found and that the alleged infringer will have fewer chances to make his argument and defend his rights in court. The actions that the right holder or the authorities may undertake by virtue of this regulation may imply the violation of fundamentals rights related to privacy, due process and property. That is, the unbalanced procedural regime, which does not satisfy key elements of the right to a fair trial, may lead to the violation of substantive rights.

In *Chappell v. United Kingdom*, the European Court on Human Rights addressed an alleged violation of the right to privacy arising from the implementation of an Anton Piller order.[69] The Court rejected the existence of a violation of the right to privacy but made several considerations of interest when analysing new provisions in PTAs on measures for the preservation of evidence.

The Court focused its analysis on whether the interference with the right to privacy had been 'in accordance with the law' and 'necessary in a democratic society'. The possibility to grant an Anton Piller order was obviously part of the English law, which meant that the standards of foreseeability and accessibility had been duly fulfilled. The observations of the Court were however interesting with respect to the necessity of the order, i.e. the necessity of the interference with the right. It was in this context that the Court addressed the existence of appropriate safeguards, holding that 'it is essential that this measure should be accompanied by adequate and effective safeguards against arbitrary interference and abuse'.[70] Previously, the European Commission of Human Rights upheld the measures and accepted the interference with the right to privacy. The Commission alluded to the 'quality of the law' and to the compatibility 'with the rule of law' of the denounced measures.[71]

These considerations on the legal framework for the implementation of measures for the preservation of evidence bring into the debate on PTAs some of the standards

[68] *See* Section II.3.1. [69] *See* ECtHR, *Chappel v. United Kingdom*.

[70] *See* ECtHR, *Chappel v. United Kingdom*, para. 57.

[71] 'The phrase "in accordance with the law" does not merely refer back to domestic law but also relates to the quality of the law, requiring it to be compatible with the rule of law; it thus implies that there must be a measure of protection in domestic law against arbitrary interferences by public authorities with the rights safeguarded by, inter alia, paragraph 1 of Article 8 (art. 8-1)'. *See* ECtHR, *Chappel v. United Kingdom*, para. 57. *See* also ECtHR, *Olsson v. Sweden (No. 1)*, no. 10465/83, 24 March 1988, Series A no. 130, para. 61(b).

embraced by the right to fair trial. Effectively, in its analysis of the Anton Piller orders the European Court underlined the need of 'safeguards against arbitrary interference and abuse', the need to satisfy minimum quality requirements and the compatibility of the measures with the rule of law. The PTAs regime described does not seem to fulfil the quality requirement, nor does it provide safeguards against arbitrary interference and abuse.

Among other aspects concerned, the principle of equality of arms is particularly relevant. This principle is a basic component of due process and implies 'that the same procedural rights are to be provided to all the parties unless distinctions are based on law and can be justified on objective and reasonable grounds, not entailing actual disadvantage or other unfairness to the defendant'.[72] In contrast, a number of important guarantees are absent in bilateral and plurilateral agreements. In case their norms were transposed without changes into the national legislation, the imbalance between the rights of the right holder and the guarantees for the alleged infringer would be obvious. That legislative framework would indeed facilitate the frequent 'arbitrary interference and abuse' against which the European Court of Human Rights cautions.

3 *Comparative Law as a Resource to Local Normative Development: The Case of Anton Piller Orders*

3.1 Introduction

The current international framework on measures for the preservation of evidence insufficiently ponders all the interests at stake. For the majority of countries, international obligations relating to measures for the preservation of evidence are not particularly significant or demanding. For other countries, in particular those that have recently concluded bilateral and plurilateral agreements, the situation differs; thus they must implement new and generally imbalanced or vague obligations. These countries – it is foreseeable that the number will increase in the near future – may benefit from the experience of other countries so that that they can implement their international commitments in an equitable and fair manner.

In the European Union, the EU Enforcement Directive regulation of the measures for the preservation of evidence mixes features originating from the French *saisie-contrafaçon* and the British Anton Piller orders. Although inquisitive in nature, *saisie-contrafaçon* and Anton Piller orders have been carved out so that the alleged infringer is not found defenseless. As mentioned, the European Court of Human Rights has specifically examined Anton Piller orders and has found that its legal regime is compatible with the prescriptions of the European Convention on

[72] *See* UN Human Rights Committee (2007), para. 13.

Human Rights. The analysis of the Court underpins the features and guarantees needed to avoid abuse and satisfy human rights standards.

Several common law legal orders[73] presently recognize a particular and sophisticated form of private 'civil search warrant',[74] namely *ex parte* interlocutory orders with significant local adaptations.[75] In these countries, Anton Piller orders have become a rather frequent and useful mechanism to preserve vital evidence concerning the infringement. Originally developed in the United Kingdom, the name derives from the second case that dealt with the granting of the order and the guarantees relating to its award and process of execution, the *Anton Piller KG v. Manufacturing Processes Ltd. and Others* case.[76]

Awarded without notice to the defendant,[77] Anton Piller orders request that the alleged infringer authorize entrance into his professional or even private premises. The objective of the entry is to search for evidence,[78] either to preserve it for trial or to obtain evidence that may be withheld during discovery. Additionally, they also permit the securing of materials related to the intellectual property infringement.[79] Furthermore, the defendant may be obliged to provide information about other aspects related to the case, such as sources of supply and the destination of the allegedly infringing products. Although they were originally conceived as an extraordinary remedy,[80] their use has become frequent and 'particularly crucial in copyright, patent, and trade mark cases, where modern technology easily facilitates the systematic pirating'.[81]

Anton Piller orders do not oblige to permit access to private premises. However, they caution the alleged infringer of the fact that, in case permission to entry is not granted, he will be charged with contempt of court.[82] In this case, the substantive aspects of the controversy are of little importance. This extremely coactive 'request'

73 This is the case at least of United Kingdom, Australia, New Zealand, Canada, Hong Kong, South Africa, Nigeria, India and Ireland.

74 The aptness of the term is frequently denied; *see* Rock (1984–1985), p. 191. For allusions to Anton Piller orders as '*ex parte* interlocutory orders akin to a private search warrant', *see* Judge and Al-Sharieh (2012), p 713.

75 *See* Berryman (2009–2010), p. 509.

76 The first reported case on Anton Piller orders was *EMI v. Pandit*, [1975] 1 All ER 418 (Ch.D) (hereinafter *EMI v. Pandit*). Nevertheless, the famous case that has given name to the institution, *Anton Piller KG v. Manufacturing Processes Ltd and Others*, was ruled one year later.

77 It has been affirmed that 'the very essence of the Anton Piller Order is surprise'. *See* Rock (1984–1985), p. 197.

78 Such as blueprints, plans, business records, any documents or articles.

79 However, 'raison d'être of the Anton Piller order has been the preservation of evidence rather than the confiscation of infringing property'. *See* Berryman (2007), p. 129.

80 It 'can only be justified in the most exceptional circumstances'. *See Anton Piller KG v. Manufacturing Processes Ltd. and Others*, p. 58.

81 *See* Gao (2000), p. 61.

82 Further, in the *Anton Piller KG v. Manufacturing Processes Ltd. and Others* case the process was described in a manner sufficiently clear as to 'make evident that the measure cannot be adopted without permission to enter. No constable or bailiff can knock at the door and demand entry so as to inspect papers or documents. The householder can shut the door in his face and say "Get out". That

has been duly termed the 'nuclear weapon of the law'[83] and even an 'instrument of oppression'.[84]

3.2 Safeguards

The invasive nature of Anton Piller orders implies that their award must be carefully monitored. However, with the passage of time these orders have become increasingly requested and commonly implemented. As a result of their popularity, abuses have been committed in both the granting and the execution of the orders. Courts have reacted to excesses identifying numerous safeguards on three distinct levels: legal thresholds to have the order granted (substantive principles or pre-requisites), procedural protections in framing the orders also apply (framing of the order) and practical safeguards must be observed when carrying out the order (service requirements).[85]

3.2.1 SUBSTANTIVE PRINCIPLES GOVERNING THE AWARD OF ANTON PILLER ORDERS. The plaintiff must fulfil three essential conditions to have an Anton Piller order authorized: first, he must present a strong *prima facie* case; second, he has to prove the gravity of the damage inflicted or that is going to be inflicted and, finally, he must show evidence regarding the defendant's possession and possible destruction of incriminating documents. These conditions were established in the original Anton Piller case[86] and have become basic principles in all common law countries where the order has been transplanted. Their adoption and development on the part of the judiciary indicate the will to safeguard defendants' fundamental rights against the coercion and intrusion that Anton Piller orders imply.

The first condition obliges the applicant to present a good case. Courts and national statutes require the satisfaction of a high standard of proof before authorizing an Anton Piller order. Applicants have to show an 'extremely strong prima facie case',[87] 'strong *prima facie* case'[88] or 'clear or compelling evidence'.[89] This standard is considerably higher than that required to grant regular interlocutory injunctions. Although the latter may vary across jurisdictions, in the United Kingdom the granting of ordinary interlocutory injunctions requires proving that the request is not

was established in the leading case of Entick v Carrington. None of us would wish to whittle down that principle in the slightest.' *See Anton Piller KG v. Manufacturing Processes Ltd. and Others*, p. 60.

83 *See Bank Mellat v. Nikpour*, [1985] FSR 87 (CA).

84 Justice Brightman stated, 'it seems to me that an Order on the lines sought might become an instrument of oppression, particularly in a case where a plaintiff of big standing and deep pocket is ranged against small man who is alleged on the evidence of one side only to have infringed the plaintiff's rights'. *See Anton Piller KG v. Manufacturing Processes Ltd. and Others*, p. 60.

85 *See* Godin (1996), p. 107.

86 *See Anton Piller KG v. Manufacturing Processes Ltd. and Others*, p. 62. 87 *Ibid.*

88 In the United Kingdom, *see Thermax Limited v. Schott Industrial Glass Ltd.*, p. 298, and *Columbia Pictures v. Robinson*, p. 70. In Canada, *see Bardeau Ltd. v. Crown Food Services Equipment Ltd.*, [1982] 38 OR (2d) 411 (HCJ), p. 413; *Nintendo of America Inc. v. Cornex Video Games Inc.*, [1982] 69 CPR (2d) 122, pp. 130–131 (FCA).

89 *See Rank Film Distributors Ltd. v. Video Information Centre*, p. 439.

'frivolous nor vexatious'.[90] This is a threshold lower than proving a 'strong *prima facie* case'.[91]

In *Anton Piller KG v. Manufacturing Processes Ltd. and Others* case, the Court also required that the potential or actual damage 'must be very serious for the plaintiff'.[92] The Court must be convinced by the arguments presented by the plaintiff that, unless the order is given, the damage will be severe. This standard brings up two concerns. The first relates to a difficulty inherent not only to Anton Piller orders but also to other measures for the preservation of evidence, since only the plaintiff will be in the position to provide information regarding the infringement and the seriousness of the damage. The second concern relates to the vagueness of the requirement, since it may be difficult to agree on which damage must be deemed 'very serious'.[93]

The third requirement alludes to the need to show clear evidence of the fact that defendants have in their possession incriminating documents or materials as well as the likelihood of the destruction of such material.[94] It refers, thus, to two separate elements, one related to the incriminating documents, the other concerning the possible destruction of the relevant proofs.

The obligation to show clear evidence of the fact that the alleged infringer is in possession of incriminating materials is closely related to the requisite of being honest, in the sense of fully disclosing all the information relevant to the case. Courts have demanded applicants to hand out all the information that may aid the judge deciding on the measure.[95] Given the dependency existing with respect to the information provided by the plaintiff, courts have considered that this requirement must be strictly applied. As a result, not fulfilling this requirement[96] will result in discarding the order, even if it seemed to be justified from the substantive point of view.[97]

3.2.2 GUARANTEES ACCOMPANYING THE ORDER. A number of guarantees protect the defendant in the framing of an Anton Piller order. Some of them have been identified by courts and are now part of the relevant jurisprudential principles that

90 *See American Cyanamid Co. v. Ethicon Ltd.*, [1975] AC 396 (HL).

91 In this same sense, *see* Godin (1996), p. 117.

92 *See Anton Piller KG v. Manufacturing Processes Ltd. and Others*, p. 61. In fact, this condition was announced in the very first case, *EMI v. Pandit*, where it was stated that the measure 'must be shown that irreparable harm will accrue, or there is a high probability that irreparable harm may accrue to the plaintiffs, unless the particular form of relief now sought is granted to them'.

93 *See* Godin (1996), p. 119.

94 In this sense, Anton Piller orders are different from *saisie-contrefaçon*, since the latter can be conducted without providing evidence of infringement.

95 In *Thermax Limited v. Schott Industrial Glass Ltd.*, the Court affirmed that 'the rule of full disclosure to the court is almost more important in *Anton Piller* cases than in other ex parte applications. Since *Anton Piller* orders give compulsory rights of inspection, once those inspections have taken place the information procured from it is in the hands of the other side and the situation is irreversible.' *See Thermax Limited v. Schott Industrial Glass Ltd.*, p. 298.

96 Either intentionally or innocently. For instance, in *Thermax Limited v. Schott Industrial Glass Ltd.*, the Anton Piller order was discharged because the plaintiff failed to disclose material facts, although unintentionally.

97 *See Columbia Pictures v. Robinson*, p. 77.

guide the execution of Anton Piller orders. Other guarantees have been directly codified in national statutes and have been transplanted afterwards into regional and international texts.

A general safeguard is to require the plaintiff to pay damages eventually resulting from the execution of the order, a requisite already stated in the *Anton Piller KG v. Manufacturing Processes Ltd. and Others* case[98] and other early[99] and relevant[100] jurisprudence. This requirement is also enshrined in the TRIPS Agreement, where it is linked to cases where it is subsequently found that there has been no infringement or threat of infringement.[101] In this same context, some legal orders enshrine the possibility to ask the plaintiff for a security or post a bond before executing the measures.

The items copied or seized may be of vital importance for the suspected infringer. They probably relate to his business and may be crucial for the continuation of his economic activity. This is the reason why courts require elaborating an exhaustive record of the materials seized in the execution of the order,[102] which shall be returned to the defendant as soon as practicable.[103] Also in relation to the seized goods, it has also been ordered that the disputed materials not returned to the defendant may be given for its custody to a neutral officer of the court or, in case this is not possible, to the defendant's solicitor.[104]

Courts have also underscored the importance of carefully framing the order, in the sense of delimiting, to the extent possible, the physical areas to be searched, the types of goods that may be inspected and the nature of the documentation and information that may be examined when entering into the premises of the defendant.[105]

3.3.3 EXECUTION OF THE ORDER. In addition to satisfying some pre-requisites to obtain the order and to comply with a number of guarantees, the execution of the order itself has benefited from jurisprudence related to the practical aspects of the service of the order.

In the *Anton Piller KG v. Manufacturing Processes Ltd. and Others* case, it was already established that in the execution of the order the plaintiff must be accompanied by a solicitor, who will act for the plaintiff but also as an officer of the court.[106] This implies that the solicitor will have to properly explain the order to the defendant,[107] present the materials associated to the order and ensure that the order is not abused.[108]

98 *See Anton Piller KG v. Manufacturing Processes Ltd. and Others*, p. 61.
99 *See Vapormatic Co. Ltd. v. Sparex Ltd. and Another*, [1976] 11 WLR 939 (Ch.D).
100 The Supreme Court of Canada, in its jurisprudence, alluded to the undertaking in damages, 'in the event that the order turns out to be unwarranted or wrongfully executed'. *See Celanese Canada Inc. v. Murray Demolition Corp.*, [2006] 2 SCR 189, para. 40.1(ii) (hereinafter *Celanese Canada Inc. v. Murray Demolition Corp.*).
101 *See* Article 50.7 TRIPS Agreement.
102 *See Columbia Pictures v. Robinson*, p. 76.
103 *See* Godin (1996), p. 122.
104 *See Columbia Pictures v. Robinson*, p. 77.
105 *See Columbia Pictures v. Robinson*, p. 86; Godin (1996), p. 123.
106 *See* Godin (1996), p. 125.
107 *See* Rock (1984–1985), p. 200.
108 *See Anton Piller KG v. Manufacturing Processes Ltd. and Others*, p. 61.

The involvement and characteristics of the solicitor accompanying the execution of the order have been a matter of controversy. His role and activity may be strictly delimited,[109] and he must not exceed the terms of the order.[110] Although originally that role was performed by the solicitor of the plaintiff himself, later on it has been required that an experienced solicitor not linked to the plaintiff manage the execution of the order,[111] which has given way to the so-called 'independent supervising solicitor'.[112]

Case law has also regulated the possibility to receive legal advice before the order is carried out. The defendant must have the opportunity to see and examine the application and any supporting materials. This will permit looking for legal aid and eventually ask for the exclusion of materials revealing trade secrets.[113] It will also allow the defendant to oppose entry, fully informed though of the fact that contempt proceedings with the threat of imprisonment will probably follow.[114] The requirement to allow the defendant to consult and look for legal aid is also linked to the condition imposed to carry out the order in reasonable business hours[115] 'when counsel for the party about to be search is more likely to be available'.[116]

IV CONCLUSIONS

Measures for the preservation of evidence are a relevant tool in the context of infringement procedures; thus they permit having access to relevant evidentiary pieces. However, their invasive nature may impact on several fundamental rights. In particular, the rights to privacy, to property and to a fair trial may be affected by this subtype of provisional measures. For this reason, national legal orders normally

109 *See* Rock (1984–1985), p. 201, quoting *RTZ Services Ltd. v. Stewart*, unreported, 'It is important that the order go no further than is necessary to protect the plaintiffs' interest until the matter can be further dealt with by the court. I have provided for representatives of the Clarkson Company Limited to be the only persons with access to the material. The plaintiffs' representatives will attend for the sole purpose of identifying what it considers to be relevant material and a representative of Fasken & Calvin as officers of the court [will attend] to ensure compliance with the order.'

110 *See* Berryman (2009–2010), p. 522.

111 This was first the case in the United Kingdom, where in *Universal Thermosensors Ltd. v. Hibben and Others*, [1992] FSR 361 (Ch.D) (hereinafter *Universal Thermosensors v. Hibben and Others*) reference was made to serve and carried out the order in the presence of an independent solicitor. The Supreme Court of Canada endorsed the requirement to appoint 'a vigilant court-appointed supervising solicitor who is independent of the parties'; *see Celanese Canada Inc. v. Murray Demolition Corp.*, para. 1. This requirement has however been questioned by some. *See* Berryman (2007).

112 In Canada, this was required in *Celanese Canada Inc. v. Murray Demolition Corp.*, while in the United Kingdom this requirement has been statutorily established. The origin has been allegedly found in the South African Supreme Court, that execution of the order should require evidence and property seized to be placed into the hands of an impartial court officer or sheriff. *See* Berryman (2009–2010), p. 520.

113 *See* Godin (1996), p. 126.

114 *See Anton Piller KG v. Manufacturing Processes Ltd. and Others*, pp. 61–62.

115 *See Universal Thermosensors Ltd. v. Hibben and Others*, p. 386.

116 *See Celanese Canada Inc. v. Murray Demolition Corp.*

demand the fulfilment of strict criteria in order to execute measures for the preservation of evidence.

While some treaties regulate measures for the preservation of evidence in detail, in other occasions they just provide the general framework for the adoption of precautionary measures, thus also conditioning measures for the preservation of evidence. A number of bilateral and plurilateral treaties enshrine a regime on measures for the preservation of evidence of unbalanced content. In other occasions treaties remain vague, and their specific implications are uncertain. These are situations that need to be corrected to preserve fundamental rights and ensure the balance between the rights of the right holder and the alleged infringer.

This chapter holds that international human rights standards and comparative law are useful tools to complement the legislation of countries that subscribe to treaties of unbalanced and vague content. International standards on fair trial and the regulation of Anton Piller orders in the United Kingdom may be a good source of inspiration. Indeed, British courts have historically ruled on the tensions between fundamental rights and measures for the preservation of evidence, and their jurisprudence may be useful to other countries with less experience and new international obligations to fulfil.

A second tool to redress the *lacunae* and problems affecting provisions on preservation of evidence set forth in bilateral and plurilateral agreements is found in the TRIPS Agreement. Neither plurilateral nor bilateral treaties rule out the applicability of TRIPS. Hence, guarantees established therein are fully applicable, in addition to the more detailed articles enshrined in bilateral and plurilateral agreements. The resulting regime, hence, is one that favours right holders but requires at least the implementation of the guarantees embodied in the TRIPS Agreement.

Finally, international human rights law is also helpful at redressing the insufficiencies of the international intellectual property law. The standards resulting from the right to a fair trial, the right to property and the right to privacy improve legislation and jurisprudence on civil enforcement, in particular measures for the preservation of evidence. These standards oblige legislation and judges to introduce the missing guarantees, and their implementation is a reminder of the fact that intellectual property norms cannot be invoked in isolation but as part of a broader and richer legal system, either at the national or at the international level.

8

Interim Injunctions

I INTRODUCTION

The award of an interim injunction has far-reaching consequences. It may prevent an imminent infringement from taking place, or it may temporarily impede the continuation of an allegedly infringing activity. Wrongly granted, it may stop legal activities of all sorts. From a corporate point of view, interim injunctions impact on goodwill, market share and eventually the very survival of the company. From the point of view of individuals, interim injunctions may protect right holder's entitlements but also impede the exercise of relevant activities, for instance activities relating to fundamental freedoms such as freedom of expression or freedom to conduct business.

Injunctions are not just important because they restore or maintain the *status quo* and provide relief before the end of lengthy judicial proceedings. They also play an important role from the procedural point of view. Thanks to the interim process to decide on whether the injunction deserves to be granted, parties acquire good knowledge about the opponent's case. Moreover, and partially because of that important informative role, precautionary injunctions may easily be transformed into final decisions, since cases where interim procedures conclude the litigation abound.[1] In fact, interim injunctions are also a key preventive tool in cases where the award of damages would not suffice to repair the injury caused once proceedings come to an end.[2]

While interim injunctions may be 'the sharpest sword amongst the IP owner's weapons',[3] their relevance goes beyond the economic aspects and their actual impact in the litigation. In this regard, and given that injunctions materialize right

[*] This chapter is authored by Xavier Seuba and Elena Dan.

[1] In the context of trademark litigation, Bastian and Knaak have noted that interim injunction may conclude 80 per cent of the cases in the United Kingdom, 65 per cent in the Netherlands, around 50 per cent in Belgium and 50 per cent in Germany. *See* Bastian and Knaak (1995), pp. 149–174.

[2] *See* European Commission (2010a), p. 14.

[3] Heath and Cotter (2015), p. 19.

holders' faculty of preventing others from undertaking diverse activities, they are closely related to a range of fundamental rights and may also have an important impact on the public interest.

Interim injunctions are instituted in international, regional and national legal texts. In the case of international treaties, interim injunctions are frequently regulated in articles dealing with provisional measures, often drafted in broad terms. Given the differences existing across national legal orders with respect to the regulation and execution of interim injunctions, international norms tend to be flexible and allow considerable margin of manoeuvre to States and judicial authorities.

Temporary injunctions have a number of distinctive features. First, even though national norms generally set the conditions under which such measures are granted, in practice courts have extensive discretion as to whether to order an injunction as well as regarding the conditions of the injunction. Such discretion is, in fact, a feature of precautionary measures in general, not only in the intellectual property domain. Frequently considered a remedy of equity, injunctions typically require a careful analysis of the balance of interests, eventually including the public interest, as well as the strength of the conflicting parties' arguments.

Second, the need to balance the continuation of activities which in principle are legal and to protect the right holder from the consequences of infringing acts makes it difficult to define the precise scope and conditions of preliminary measures. National courts have adopted different views as to the appropriateness and conditions for the award of preliminary injunctions. In fact, differences across national legal orders, and even between courts in the same legal order, may be important. While a flexible approach enables responding to a range of relevant interests, concerns as to the legal security and eventual forum-shopping may be justified.[4]

Third, preliminary injunctions are available to all forms of intellectual property rights, but their regulation and the interests at stake widely differ. For instance, injunctions may pose complex challenges from the point of view of the protection of fundamental rights. These problems, however, are specific to each intellectual property category. The right to freedom of expression, for instance, is of major relevance when awarding injunctions in copyright-related cases. By contrast, when injunctions are ordered in patent-related cases, challenges may arise in relation to access to life-saving products. The importance of the intellectual property category at stake also becomes apparent when comparing the urgency that the award of an interim injunction has for the right holder. In this sense, while in cases involving trademarks the award of an interim injunction may be decisive to avoid irreparable reputational loss, other intellectual property categories may experience less pressure since damages may be relatively easier to quantify.

[4] At least at the national level: a well-known example of forum-shopping is the District Court for the Eastern District of Texas, widely recognized as a friendly jurisdiction for NPEs, where injunctions are easily granted. *See* Leichkis (2007).

Issuing preliminary injunctions is in direct connection with a range of human rights. The right to freedom of expression, the right to health and the right to a fair trial are examples of the interface between interim injunctions and human rights. The right to health and the right to a fair trial are particularly studied in this chapter. Another area that is presently attracting a great deal of litigation concerns the interface between injunctions and freedom of expression,[5] particularly in the digital environment.

II PRELIMINARY INJUNCTIONS IN INTERNATIONAL LAW

1 *The Global Standard on Preliminary Injunctions*

Article 50 of the TRIPS Agreement provides for several types of provisional measures,[6] including measures to react against infringements or threats of infringement by restraining a party from engaging in particular acts. Pursuant to Article 50.1 (a), Members shall authorize courts to order prompt and effective provisional measures to prevent an infringement of any intellectual property right from occurring. In combination with Article 50.3, which alludes to actual infringements, the TRIPS Agreement covers not only the reaction to alleged infringements that have already started but also the action with respect to those that are imminent but have not yet occurred.[7]

The TRIPS Agreement also establishes the conditions under which judicial authorities grant preliminary injunctions. First, in line with national provisions that require showing a good case and that both *fumus boni iurius* and *periculum in mora* exist,[8] judicial authorities may demand that the applicant submit any reasonably available evidence in order to provide a sufficient degree of certainty that he is the right holder and that his right is being infringed or that such infringement is imminent.[9] Second, in order to protect the defendant and to prevent abuse, the applicant may also be requested to provide a security or equivalent assurance.[10] Third, the applicant may also be ordered to provide 'other information necessary' for the identification of goods concerned by the authority that will execute the measure.[11]

In parallel to these requirements, there are also a number of safeguards for the defendant. The TRIPS Agreement recognizes the right of the defendant to ask for

5 The impact of preliminary injunctions on freedom of expression commonly arises in connection to cases related to copyright. This has been considered by national laws, such as in the United Kingdom, where Section 12.3 of the Human Rights Act of 1998 has introduced an important qualification to the threshold of preliminary injunction as set out by courts. *See* for a comment Bently and Sherman (2008), p. 1104; Bainbridge (2012), p. 929. For a more general analysis on the issue, *see* Lemley and Volokh (1998).

6 Article 50 of TRIPS includes both interim measures to preserve relevant evidence and measures to prevent an infringement from occurring or stop its continuation. This is different from the EU Enforcement Directive, which treats separately measures for preserving evidence (Article 7) and precautionary measures to prevent or stop infringements (Article 9).

7 *See* Vander (2009), p. 742. 8 *See* Section III.2.1. 9 *See* Article 50.3 TRIPS Agreement.

10 *Ibid.* 11 *See* Article 50.5 TRIPS Agreement.

the revocation of the measure in case an action on the merits of the case is not launched within a reasonable period of time.[12] More precisely, where an *inter partes* interim injunction has been adopted, the judicial authority will determine the period of time available to initiate the main proceedings. In any case, this 'reasonable period' will not exceed twenty working days or thirty-one calendar days.[13] Another specific safeguard for the defendant is the right to claim compensation for any injury caused if the interim measure is later revoked or lapses due to acts or omissions of the applicant or it is found that there was no infringement.[14] Hence, compensation will follow if an injunction wrongly granted causes injury, regardless of the existence of any mistake on the part of the right holder.

Article 50.2 of the TRIPS Agreement specifies that preliminary injunctions must be available *inaudita altera parte* 'where appropriate'. This includes at least situations where delay may result either in irreparable harm or in the destruction of evidence. Freezing orders, for instance, preventing the dissipation of assets of the alleged infringer before the final decision of the court, can address situations where delay may result in irreparable harm. As far as the guarantees for the defendant are concerned, where a decision has been made *inaudita altera parte*, the alleged infringer must be notified without delay after the execution of the measure, and a review, including a right to be heard, of this decision shall be available to the defendant. The purpose of such a review is to decide within a reasonable period of time whether the measure has to be modified, revoked or confirmed.[15]

Some claim that the regulation of interim injunctions in TRIPS reflects the ambitions of developed countries.[16] Certainly, by the time it was adopted, such a regulation was without precedent in international intellectual property law. Article 50 lays down the minimum requirements for the preliminary protection of intellectual property rights. However, the scope and comprehensive content of this article make it a norm with unique character on the global arena.[17] While Article 50 has a unique character, seen in historical perspective and in light of his content, it is also fair to describe Article 50 as a norm setting forth a quite flexible regime to determine 'whether, when and how to award injunctive relief for infringements of intellectual property rights'.[18] Countries retain, hence, a great margin to fine-tune their own provisions on injunctions. For instance, the *periculum in mora* requirement set forth in TRIPS may be implemented differently in national jurisdictions, both by statute and in judicial decisions. In Spain, for instance, patent holders not practicing their patents are not entitled to interim injunctions, since it is

12 *See* Article 50.6 TRIPS Agreement.
13 For a national implementation of this requirement, *see* Article L615-3 combined with Article R615-1 of the French Intellectual Property Code.
14 *See* Article 50.7 TRIPS Agreement.
15 *See* Article 50.4 TRIPS Agreement.
16 *See* Dreier (1996), p. 255.
17 *See* UNCTAD-ICTSD (2005), p. 601; Heath (2005), p. 9.
18 *See* Sarnoff (2009), p. 107.

understood that whenever the invention is not practiced, there is no *periculum in mora* since the alleged injury can be repaired awarding damages.[19]

While the flexibility of Article 50 in benefit of legislators and judges has been applauded,[20] its alleged lack of precision, in particular as to the conditions for granting injunctions, has also been criticized.[21] Critics claim that judges have excessive freedom in considering the evidence and adopting decisions[22] and argue that Article 50 is 'vague' and does not guide national judges in complex infringement procedures.[23] This criticism is, however, unjustified. As a matter of course an injunction is a discretionary remedy, since the circumstances of the case always play a central role in the final judicial decision.[24] Flexibility is a good strategy since national legal orders may add relevant criteria or conditions, legitimately subject to different interpretations.[25] In fact, the TRIPS Agreement enshrines the principles and norms recognized in the most important legal orders while respecting their specificities. The respect of major national differences enables coexistence and the adoption of international standards. National differences and judicial discretion exist in fact for good reasons, as demonstrated by the fact that even in a fairly harmonized area, such as in the European Union, differences persist.

Another line of criticism focuses on the requirement of 'irreparable harm', set forth in Article 50.2 of the TRIPS Agreement, and contends that the judicial application of this requirement 'frequently results in the denial of preliminary injunctions even in developed countries, which further weakens the thrust of these provisions'.[26] As abovementioned, pursuant to Article 50.2, judicial authorities must have authority to adopt provisional measures without the defendant being heard in particular where 'any delay is likely to cause irreparable harm to the right holder'. The critical factor causing the 'irreparable harm' is the 'delay';[27] however, this has to be balanced against the right of the defendant to be heard, as established in Article 50.4[28] and, naturally, against the consequences that the award of the preliminary injunction will have on the defendant. This is in fact common practice in national

19 *See* Article 133 of the Spanish Patent Law, and Audiencia Provincial, de Barcelona (Sección 15ª) Auto de 23 octubre 2003, JUR\2004\16152; Audiencia Provincial de Madrid (Sección 19ª) Auto num. 152/2004 de 12 mayo JUR\2004\246491.

20 *See* UNCTAD/ICTSD (2005), p. 601.

21 *See* Straus (2000); Dreier (1996).

22 *See* Reichman (1997), footnote 29, p. 341.

23 For a conclusion that the guidelines advanced in developed countries such as France or Germany should be followed internationally (e.g. by developing countries or countries of transition), *see* Straus (2000), p. 823.

24 As noted in *Coflexip v Stolt*, 'Where a patentee has conclusively established the validity of his patent and that it had been infringed, as a general rule an injunction will be granted. However that will not happen as a matter of course as an injunction is a discretionary remedy. It is for that reason there have been cases where injunctions have been refused, for example, where the defendant satisfied the court that further infringement was not likely.' *Coflexip SA v Stolt Comex Seaway MS LTD* [2000] EWCA Civ 242.

25 This is for instance the case of the analysis of the public interest in the United States.

26 *See* Reichman (1997), footnote 29, p. 341.

27 *See* UNCTAD/ICTSD (2005), p. 604.

28 *See* in more detail Section IV.1.

legal orders. National judicial authorities are very careful and grant preliminary injunctions *inaudita altera parte* only in case of urgency, when there is a real likelihood of substantial injury being caused to the right holder and the claim is supported by hard evidence.[29] As it has been stated, '[t]he mere possibility of producing harm to the right holder would not be sufficient to ignore the defendant's basic right to be heard before an injunction or other relief is granted'.[30]

Finally, it has been stressed that the vagueness of Article 50 impacts on its self-executing nature.[31] Jurisprudence shows, however, contradictory views in this respect. Whereas Argentinean courts have considered Article 50 self-executing,[32] the Court of Justice of the European Union has held the contrary[33] inasmuch as the procedural requirements of Article 50 'are not such as to create rights upon which individuals may rely directly before the national courts'.[34] Ultimately, the diversity of views as to whether Article 50 is directly applicable has to do with the stand of national legal orders towards international law and the views regarding the nature of WTO obligations. In this last respect, even in countries following a monist approach, it may be understood that the articles of the TRIPS Agreement belong to a wider legal system where compensation (hence, cross-retaliation) occupies a central place and, for this reason, it is up to the State, and not to national courts, deciding on the precise effect of the TRIPS Agreement within the national legal order.

2 *Plurilateral Agreements*

2.1 The Anti-Counterfeiting Trade Agreement

Article 12 of ACTA regulates different types of provisional measures. This Article is modelled upon Article 50 of the TRIPS Agreement, thus the structure and the aspects addressed are highly coincidental. In essence, both provisions set forth that

[29] *See* Malbon, Lawson and Davison (2014), p. 678. *See* Section III.2.4.

[30] *See* UNCTAD/ICTSD (2005), p. 605. *See* also Straus (2000), p. 813. *See* Section IV.1.

[31] For details on both interpretations, *see* UNCTAD/ICTSD (2005), p. 601.

[32] *See* UNCTAD/ICTSD (2005), footnote 100, p. 601.

[33] *See* Gielen (2002).

[34] *See* ECJ, C-89/99, *Schieving-Nijstad and Others* [2001], Judgment of the Court of 13 September 2001, ECR I-05851, para. 53 (hereinafter ECJ, C-89/99, *Schieving-Nijstad and Others*). The CJEU limited the effect of Article 50 of the TRIPS Agreement to that of guiding the interpretation of national courts when applying national rules on preliminary injunctions. In the words of the Court, 'where the judicial authorities are called upon to apply national rules with a view to ordering provisional measures for the protection of intellectual property rights falling within a field to which TRIPs applies and in respect of which the Community has already legislated, they are required to do so as far as possible in the light of the wording and purpose' of Article 50 of the TRIPS Agreement. *See* ECJ, C-89/99, *Schieving-Nijstad and Others*, para. 55. Also, the Court has interpreted Article 50 in its case law, to guide Member States and to avoid rise of various interpretation of these provisions. *See* ECJ, Case C-53/96, *Hermès International v FHT Marketing Choice BV* [1998], Judgment of the Court of 16 June 1998, ECR 1998 I-03603, para. 32. See also As. Christian Dior c. Tuk Consultancy BV, C-53/96, 14 December 2000.

judicial authorities shall have the authority to order prompt and effective provisional measures.[35] Likewise, both articles explicitly identify the prevention of infringement and the preservation of evidence as the objectives of provisional measures.[36] However, some differences are relevant and in the majority of occasions follow the pattern already noticed in other contexts. Thus, while ACTA broadens the scope of provisional measures in some respects, it omits relevant guarantees protecting the alleged infringer.

In comparison to the TRIPS Agreement, ACTA permits both restricting and expanding the scope of provisional measures. It permits restricting the scope of provisional measures since, by virtue of the footnote found in the very same title of the civil enforcement section, patents and protection of undisclosed information can be excluded from the scope of the articles on provisional measures.[37] As it has been noted, 'this then reduces the coverage of ACTA below the level of the TRIPS Agreement'.[38] However, in a different respect, ACTA also expands the scope of provisional measures since it explicitly establishes that they may be ordered against third parties.[39] Whereas the TRIPS Agreement does not preclude this possibility, it does not mention it and, as noted elsewhere in this chapter, the power to grant injunctions against third parties is crucial in some environments, such as the Internet.[40]

While the basic regulation in TRIPS and ACTA is coincidental, differences are important with respect to measures adopted *inaudita altera parte*. As in the TRIPS Agreement, ACTA allows *inaudita altera parte* measures where appropriate, in particular where any delay is likely to cause irreparable harm or where there is a demonstrable risk of evidence being destroyed.[41] Nevertheless, ACTA does not mention the obligation to notify the alleged infringed after the execution of the measure nor the right to a review of the *inaudita altera parte* measure, including the right to be heard, as set forth in the TRIPS Agreement.[42]

As to what can be requested of the applicant in order to process his demand for provisional measures, the TRIPS Agreement asks for evidence that the applicant is the right holder, that the right is being infringed or is about to be infringed and, eventually, a security or equivalent assurance. ACTA however qualifies these requirements, since it omits the reference to the proof that the applicant is the right holder and explicitly establishes that the requested security or assurance shall not deter recourse to provisional measures.[43]

Finally, a note relating to compensation and revocation. ACTA does not explicitly provide that provisional measures may be revoked or otherwise cease to have effect if proceedings leading to a decision on the merits of the case are not initiated within

35 *See* Article 50.1 TRIPS Agreement; Article 12.1 ACTA.

36 *See* Article 50.1(a) and (b) TRIPS Agreement; Article 12.1(a) and (b) ACTA.

37 *See* footnote 2, p. E-5 ACTA. 38 *See* Blakeney (2012), p. 138. 39 *See* Article 12.1(a) ACTA.

40 *See* Section II.3.2 and Section III.2. 41 *See* Article 50.2 TRIPS Agreement; Article 12.2 ACTA.

42 *See* Article 50.4 TRIPS Agreement. 43 *See* Article 12.4 ACTA.

a reasonable period of time. However, ACTA implicitly recognizes this possibility, since it regulates the consequences of revocation. In this regard, it establishes that compensation follows for the injury caused when measures are revoked or where they lapse due to any act or omission by the applicant or where it is subsequently found that there has been no infringement or threat of infringement.[44]

As noted when comparing TRIPS and ACTA,[45] guarantees foreseen in the TRIPS Agreement have been left out in ACTA. Even if the lack of specific provision of safeguards for provisional injunctions has been rightly criticized,[46] and it has been claimed that Article 12 lacks remedies rooted in the right to be heard,[47] it is possible to restore the missing balance. While Sections III and IV of this chapter provide some external normative tools to conduct such an exercise, the solution may also be found in the text of the ACTA agreement itself. In this regard, Article 6 of ACTA provides for general safeguards and establishes that procedures for enforcing intellectual property must be applied 'in such a manner as to . . . provide for safeguards against their abuse'[48] and 'shall be fair and equitable'.[49] Therefore, ACTA commands the respect of fundamental principles of due process, through invoking fairness and equity,[50] and this order is fully applicable to Article 12. Additionally, Article 1 of ACTA states that '[n]othing in the treaty shall derogate from any obligation of a Party with respect to any other Party under existing agreements, including the TRIPS Agreement'. Likewise, the Preamble of ACTA states that it complements TRIPS.[51] Therefore, Article 12 of ACTA can be read in conjunction with Article 50 of the TRIPS Agreement and in light of the procedural safeguards set forth therein. Naturally, to the extent that those procedural safeguards are mandatory, they are not modified by ACTA.[52]

2.2 The Trans-Pacific Partnership Agreement

The TPP Article on provisional measures is rather succinct.[53] It includes a reference to *inaudita altera parte* measures, it addresses some conditions to be fulfilled when providing the evidence and security that judicial authorities may require, and it includes as well a specific sub-section devoted to measures for the preservation of evidence.[54] Even if the article on provisional measures in the TPP is based upon the treaties subscribed by the United States, in some respects it improves previous treaties.

This is the case of the section relating to *inaudita altera parte* injunctions. While it certainly strengthens the TRIPS Agreement, since it transforms the power of judicial

44 *See* Article 50.7 TRIPS Agreement; Article 12.5 ACTA. 45 *See* Chapter 4, Section III.1.2.
46 *See* Opinion of European Academics on Anti-Counterfeiting Trade Agreement (2011).
47 *See* also on this Metzger (2010). 48 *See* Article 6.1 ACTA. 49 *See* Article 6.2 ACTA.
50 *See* in more detail Chapter 4, Section III.1.3.
51 On the relation between ACTA and the TRIPS Agreement, *see* Seuba (2015a), p. 47.
52 *See* Kamperman Sanders (2015), p. 87. 53 *See* Article 18.75 TPP.
54 In this last respect, *see* Chapter 7, Section II.2.

authorities to adopt *inaudita altera parte* measures 'where appropriate' into an obligation to act 'expeditiously' on a request for relief,[55] it still improves the text of some PTAs. As analysed later, PTAs promoted by the United States include a very similar provision but without the final caveat introduced in the TPP, where it conditions *inaudita altera parte* injunctions to the Party's judicial rules.[56]

The TPP also entitles judicial authorities to require the applicant for a provisional measure to provide evidence to satisfy them that his right is being infringed or that the infringement is imminent. In the same article, it also allows judicial authorities to require the applicant to provide security or equivalent assurance set at a level sufficient to protect the defendant and to prevent abuse. This provision is common in the TRIPS Agreement, ACTA and PTAs. In contrast to TRIPS, but in line with PTAs and ACTA, the TPP establishes that 'such security or equivalent assurance shall not unreasonably deter recourse to those procedures'.[57]

3 *Interim Injunctions in Preferential Trade Agreements*

The large majority of the PTAs regulating intellectual property in a significant manner do not include specific references to interim injunctions.[58] The PTAs promoted by the United States and those – more recently – subscribed by the European Union represent an important exception in that regard. The regulation of provisional measures in European and United States PTAs is characterized by a feature common to other remedies: the inclusion of right holders' rights and the omission of the guarantees of the alleged infringers. Another feature commonly observed in the intellectual property enforcement domain is the frequent use of transplantation as a normative technique. Countries have not only imported provisions commonly found in the legislation of the United States and Europe but have also transplanted these provisions in agreements adopted later on with third countries.[59]

3.1 PTAs Concluded by the United States

When compared with the TRIPS Agreement, the main difference found in the PTAs concluded by the United States is the obligation of Parties to act

55 Whereas pursuant to Article 18.75.1 of the TPP 'authorities shall act . . . expeditiously', pursuant to Article 50.2 of the TRIPS Agreement judicial authorities simply 'shall have the authority to adopt provisional measures'.

56 As analysed later, the US-Australia FTA and EIA (2005), US-Peru FTA and EIA (2009), US-Colombia FTA and EIA (2012), US-Chile FTA and EIA (2004) partake this TPP feature.

57 Compare Article 18.75.2 of the TPP, against Article 50.3 of the TRIPS Agreement and Article 12.4 of ACTA. *See* Section II.3.1 for the references found in PTAs.

58 This is even the case of some treaties that set forth demanding obligations in other intellectual property-related fields, such as the EFTA agreements, but remain silent with respect to injunctions.

59 Notice for instance Article 17.37 Australia-Chile FTA and EIA (2009).

expeditiously on requests for provisional measures *inaudita altera parte*.[60] Hence, like in the TPP, the judicial faculty set forth in TRIPS becomes an obligation in PTAs, whereas the discretion allowed in TRIPS (i.e. 'where appropriate') is likewise significantly curtailed.

United States PTAs order, in effect, acting expeditiously *inaudita altera parte*, an adverb that is sometimes narrowly specified by establishing a number of days to execute the requests for relief.[61] The standards set forth in the TRIPS Agreement are, thus, drastically modified.[62] Moreover, in the majority of PTAs, this obligation is left unqualified since no limits or guarantees are foreseen. If this obligation is not further qualified by means of national legislation or interpretation, the adoption of provisional measures *inaudita altera parte* pursuant to United States PTAs would just depend on the request of the right holder. In this sense, interestingly, some treaties remedy that situation and include a reference expressing that *inaudita altera parte* measures will be adopted in accordance with the Party's judicial rules.[63]

As it also happens in other domains, some provisions of the PTAs of the United States just repeat parts of the TRIPS Agreement. This is, for instance, the case of the recognition that judicial authorities have the right to require the plaintiff requesting provisional measures to provide reasonable available evidence to convince them about the existence of an infringement or about the likelihood of an imminent infringement.[64] The repetition of already existing obligations may pursue several purposes,[65] and in this specific case must be seen in the broader context of agreements that also mandate the presumption of validity of patents,[66] an obligation sometimes specifically enacted in the context of provisional measures.[67]

60 *See* Article 18.10.17 Republic of Korea-US FTA and EIA (2012); Article 17.11.16 US-Australia FTA and EIA (2005).

61 In the case of the PTAs between the United States and Bahrain, the United States and Oman and the United States and Morocco, this is a period of ten days. *See* Article 14.10.17 US-Bahrain FTA and EIA (2006); Article 15.10.17 US-Oman FTA and EIA (2009); Article 15.11.17 US-Morocco FTA and EIA (2006).

62 For details in this regard *see* Section II.1.

63 Interestingly, the treaty between the United States and Australia includes a reference expressing that *inaudita altera parte* measures will be taken 'in accordance with the Party's judicial rules', and the treaties between the United States and Chile, the United States and Colombia and the United States and Peru allude to the procedural rules of the Party. *See* Article 17.11.16 US-Australia FTA and EIA (2005); Article 17.11.15 US-Chile FTA and EIA (2004); Article 16.11.18 US-Colombia FTA and EIA (2012); Article 16.11.18 US-Peru FTA and EIA (2009).

64 This is an obligation that restates Article 50.3 of the TRIPS Agreement. *See* Article 18.10.18 Republic of Korea-US FTA and EIA (2012); Article 17.11.17 US-Australia FTA and EIA (2005); Article 14.10.18 US-Bahrain FTA and EIA (2006); Article 17.11.16(a) US-Chile FTA and EIA (2004); Article 16.11.19 US-Colombia FTA and EIA (2012); Article 16.11.19 US-Peru FTA and EIA (2009); Article 15.10.18 US-Oman FTA and EIA (2009); Article 15.11.18 US-Panama FTA and EIA (2012); Article 15.11.18 US-Morocco FTA and EIA (2006).

65 For instance, attracting the dispute settlement system of the PTAs.

66 *See* Article 18.10.3 Republic of Korea-US FTA and EIA (2012).

67 *See* Article 17.11.18 US-Australia FTA and EIA (2005); Article 14.10.19 US-Bahrain FTA and EIA (2006); Article 15.10.19 US-Oman FTA and EIA (2009); Article 15.11.19 US-Panama FTA and EIA (2012); Article 15.11.19 US-Morocco FTA and EIA (2006).

The large majority of the PTAs of the United States do not mention many of the safeguards foreseen in the TRIPS Agreement.[68] Moreover, like in the case of ACTA and the TPP, the provision of a guarantee is qualified. In this respect, while the agreements concluded by the United States explicitly recognize that judicial authorities may require the provision of a reasonable security or equivalent assurance with the objective to protect the defendant and prevent abuse, they also establish that such security or assurance shall not deter recourse to provisional measures,[69] a limit absent in the TRIPS Agreement.

The agreements of the United States expressly mandate extending provisional measures, including injunctions, against the circumvention of effective technological measures that authors, performers and producers of phonograms use in connection with the exercise of their rights as well as to protect rights management information.[70] In some other occasions, they broadly demand the extension of civil measures – which would include provisional measures – against the circumvention of effective technological measures.[71]

3.2 PTAs Negotiated by the European Union

Last-generation PTAs concluded by the European Union regulate the award of interim injunctions in a rather homogeneous, brief and foreseeable manner. In fact, they fundamentally copy and paste the content of the EU Enforcement Directive,[72] although almost only inasmuch as it relates to the protection of right holder rights. Thus, European Union trading partners must ensure that judicial authorities have the power to grant an interlocutory injunction to prevent an imminent infringement from occurring or the continuation of an alleged infringement that is already taking place.[73] In some treaties, this power reaches third parties as well, since interlocutory

68 Namely, to be given notice in case of measures adopted *inaudita altera parte*, the right to a review, including a right to be heard, and the revocation of the measures if proceedings on the merits are not initiated within a reasonable period of time.

69 *See* Article 18.10.3 Republic of Korea-US FTA and EIA (2012); Article 17.11.17 US-Australia FTA and EIA (2005); Article 14.10.18 US-Bahrain FTA and EIA (2006); Article 17.11.16(a) US-Chile FTA and EIA (2004); Article 16.11.19 US-Colombia FTA and EIA (2012); Article 16.11.19 US-Peru FTA and EIA (2009); Article 15.10.18 US-Oman FTA and EIA (2009); Article 15.11.18 US-Panama FTA and EIA (2012); Article 15.11.18 US-Morocco FTA and EIA (2006).

70 *See* Article 18.10.13(a) Republic of Korea-US FTA and EIA (2012); Article 17.11.13(a) US-Australia FTA and EIA (2005); Article 14.10.14(a) US-Bahrain FTA and EIA (2006); Article 16.11.15(a) US-Colombia FTA and EIA (2012); Article 16.11.15(a) US-Peru FTA and EIA (2009); Article 15.10.14(a) US-Oman FTA and EIA (2009); Article 15.5.7(a) US-Panama FTA and EIA (2012); Articles 15.5.8(a) and 15.5.9(a) US-Morocco FTA and EIA (2006).

71 *See* Article 17.11.5 US-Chile FTA and EIA (2004).

72 *See* Directive 2004/48/EC of the European Parliament and the Council of 29 April 2004 on the Enforcement of Intellectual Property Rights, OJEU L 157of 30 April 2004 (hereinafter EU Enforcement Directive).

73 *See* Article 240 EU-Colombia and Peru FTA and EIA (2013); Article 265 EU-Central America FTA and EIA (2013); Article 156.1 EU-CARIFORUM States FTA and EIA (2008); Article 10.46 EU-Republic of Korea FTA and EIA (2011).

injunctions may also be issued against intermediaries whose services are being used to infringe an intellectual property right.[74] This is an important extension, since it enables precautionary measures for instance against a carrier, a commission agent or an Internet service provider.

Some European PTAs foresee that the injunction may be tied to a recurring penalty payment,[75] whereas it is seldom established that the plaintiff must provide reasonable available evidence to convince the court that an infringement is taking place.[76] As it happens with other missing guarantees, this requirement is, however, found in the EU Enforcement Directive and in national law of the Member States.[77]

It is again noticeable that the references found in the EU Enforcement Directive aimed at ensuring that provisional measures are not abused have not been included in the treaties concluded by the European Union. There is no reference, hence, to the obligation to revoke the measures if the applicant does not institute, within a reasonable period of time, proceedings leading to a decision on the merits of the case. In some cases, there is no reference either to the subjection of measures to the lodging of an adequate security or an equivalent assurance. Likewise, the EU Enforcement Directive provision on compensation that will follow if measures are revoked is absent in the PTAs concluded by the European Union.[78] In this last respect, according to the EU Enforcement Directive, compensation would follow even where the plaintiff did not act maliciously because, 'after all, the plaintiff entertains a calculated risk when requesting a provisional measure'.[79] But this will not be the case for the partners of the European Union, unless they supplement the wording of the respective agreements in the implementation process.

III INFORMED IMPLEMENTATION AND SELECTIVE TRANSPLANTATION

1 *Objective*

A central argument of this book is that human rights law and comparative intellectual property law are useful tools to remedy some of the most visible shortcomings of

74 *See* Article 156.1 EU-CARIFORUM States FTA and EIA (2008); Article 10.46 EU-Republic of Korea FTA and EIA (2011); Article 20.37 EU-Canada (2016). The treaty with Republic of Korea specifies that 'the scope of "intermediary" is determined in each Party's legislation, but shall include those who deliver or distribute infringing goods, and also where appropriate, include online service providers'. *See* footnote 69 to Article 10.46 EU-Republic of Korea FTA and EIA (2011).

75 *See* Article 240 EU-Colombia and Peru FTA and EIA (2013); Article 265.2 EU-Central America FTA and EIA (2013); Article 156.1 EU-CARIFORUM States FTA and EIA (2008); Article 10.46 EU-Republic of Korea FTA and EIA (2011).

76 *See* Article 265.2 EU-Central America FTA and EIA (2013). There are no references for instance in the agreements EU-Colombia and Peru FTA and EIA (2013) and EU-Republic of Korea FTA and EIA (2011).

77 *See* Section III.2.

78 *See*, respectively, Articles 9.5, 9.6 and 9.7 of the EU Enforcement Directive.

79 *See* Heath (2005), p. 27.

international law on intellectual property enforcement. Fair trial standards and lessons learnt from national experiences are effective tools to respond to the vagueness and unbalance that characterizes important intellectual property treaties. Quite often, the provisions that give place to ambiguous and incomplete regimes allow margin for action, both normative and judicial. States thus have the possibility to regain the missing balance, at least partially, by making use of that room of manoeuvre. As held in Chapter 2, legal reforms undertaken in the context of national implementation of international treaties are a good opportunity to conduct that exercise.

That argument entails, hence, that transplantation of intellectual property law is not considered a negative normative technique by its own nature. On the contrary, the experience in other states can become a valuable input. Emulation because of expected improvement of the quality of the law is a reasonable ground for selective transplantation. If the 'exporting' legal order is well understood and the right pieces of legislation are correctly selected, it is possible to devise positive options for implementation. This affirmation naturally implies that there is a situation to redress. In effect, both in plurilateral and bilateral treaties the normative regime for interim injunctions is essentially vague and lacking balance.

This section aims at widening the perspective on possible options when implementing interim injunctions in national legislation. In order to do that, the requirements set forth in the European Union and in the United States are depicted separately. In the European Union, the Enforcement Directive is used as the basis to introduce comparative national practices of the United Kingdom, Germany and France. Indeed, these three legal orders are not homogeneous, which demonstrates that it is certainly possible to abide to a demanding supranational text while maintaining local differences. In the case of the United States, the four-factor test is central.[80] This is in fact an even more interesting case because of the emphasis put on the public interest.[81]

2 *The Standard in the European Union*

The EU Enforcement Directive requires ensuring that judicial authorities may, at the request of the applicant, issue against the alleged infringer an injunction to prevent an imminent infringement of an intellectual property right, forbid on a provisional basis the continuation of alleged infringements or make such continuation subject to the lodging of guarantees.[82] This basic legal framework fundamentally transposes Article 50 of the TRIPS Agreement, but it also goes one step beyond in several important respects, particularly in regard to issuing injunctions against intermediaries. In effect, an interlocutory injunction may also be issued,

[80] *See* Section III.3. [81] *See* Section IV.2. [82] *See* Article 9.1(a) EU Enforcement Directive.

under the same conditions, against an intermediary whose services are being used by a third party to infringe on an intellectual property right.[83]

In order to have an interim measure granted, a number of requirements must be met. Courts will usually examine the validity of the right, the petitioner's likelihood of success on the merits of the case, the balance of convenience and the urgency of the measure.[84] Many years after the adoption of the EU Enforcement Directive, this field still proves to be divisive.[85] While a common approach exists, differences across national courts and legislations remain important. What follows is a comparative analysis on the conditions to fulfil to grant an interim injunction. The goal is to show available options to countries importing European Union law while making it clear that different approaches are acceptable and even recommendable. The option finally chosen will depend on a range of factors, including local legal traditions and national circumstances.

2.1 Validity of the Right and Likelihood of Infringement

The first important condition relates to the actual existence of the right holder's right and the likelihood of infringement. That is, the applicant must show that he has a good case, or, put differently, a ground for the grant of final relief,[86] *fumus boni iuris* or 'sufficient colour of right'.[87].This is indeed 'a basic issue of justice',[88] since 'no defendant shall be made subject to a measure that presumably would not stand up to a proper trial'.[89]

Notably in patent cases, the alleged infringer will typically claim the nullity of the patent and file a counter-claim for revocation. Either simultaneously or once the validity is upheld, he will also claim that no infringement has been committed. For

83 Recital 23 of the EU Enforcement Directive. As abovementioned, this implies the introduction of a flexible notion enabling precautionary measures for instance against a carrier, a commission agent, or an online intermediary. *See* the implementation of this provision in French intellectual property law in Article L615-3 of the Intellectual Property Code.

84 Legal orders may use different expressions, for instance, as in Spain, the requirement of *fumus boni iuris* plus *periculum in mora*. Essentially, however, legal orders coincide in conducting an assessment of the rights of the parties and the consequences that either awarding or rejecting the injunction would have.

85 *See also* Cotter (2013), pp. 240 *et seq*. Shortly after the entry into force of the EU Enforcement Directive, scholars made similar observations, invoking 'factors such as willingness of courts to grant preliminary injunctions in cases typically involving complex assessments, as in patent law'. *See* Kur (2004), p. 826.

86 *See Siskina v Distos Compania Naviera Sa* [1979] AC 210 [UK].

87 The High Court of Australia held that '[t]he corollary of the proposition stated by Sir Frederick Jordan is that a plaintiff seeking an interlocutory injunction must be able to show sufficient colour of right to the final relief, in aid of which interlocutory relief is sought'. See, *Australian Broadcasting Corp v Lenah Game Meats PTY LTD* [2001] HCA 63.

88 *See* Heath (2005), p. 28.

89 *Ibid.* Seen from the other side of the controversy, 'the plaintiff cannot have a legal interest in obtaining a measure that he is unlikely to obtain in proper procedures on the merit'. *See* Heath (2005), p. 28; Heath and Cotter (2015), p. 21.

this reason, the EU Enforcement Directive states that Member States must authorize courts to require the applicant to provide 'reasonably available evidence in order to satisfy themselves with a sufficient degree of certainty that the applicant is the rightholder and that the applicant's right is being infringed, or that such infringement is imminent'.[90] Certainly, countries, and not only judges, may have different views on the level of evidence required to grant an interim injunction.[91]

In Germany,[92] the actual or imminent infringement[93] must be satisfactorily substantiated[94] and the validity of the patent must be sufficiently certain both in *inaudita altera parte* cases and if challenged by the defendant. That is, the claim and the ground for the preliminary injunction are to be demonstrated to the satisfaction of the court.[95] In these respects, the plaintiff has to establish a strong *prima facie* case of infringement,[96] which implies that the infringement should be determined without difficulty.[97] A sufficient certainty that the patent is valid may typically be assumed if the patent has 'survived opposition or nullity proceedings at first instance'.[98] If there is a doubt as to the validity – for example, if the patent is being challenged in contradictory proceedings[99] – the preliminary injunction will be denied.[100]

In France plausible – '*vraisemblable*' – evidence is also requested to prove likelihood of infringement or that the infringement is imminent.[101] The alleged infringement or the likelihood of infringement must be 'credible', which means that it is insufficient to examine only the validity of the title,[102] and the 'credibility' of the

90 *See* Article 9.3 EU Enforcement Directive.

91 A negative view on this possibility can be seen in European Commission (2010), p. 14.

92 *See* Title 4, Section 940 German Code of Civil Procedure.

93 An author noted that '[p]reliminary measures can already be requested before an infringement has actually taken place, yet on condition that there is a real and immediate danger of such an infringement happening'. *See* Marshall (2005), p. 124.

94 However, full proof is not required, *see* Title 4, Sections 920 and 294 German Code of Civil Procedure.

95 *See* Title 4, Section 920.2 German Code of Civil Procedure.

96 *See* Straus (2000), p. 819. *See* also Perkins and Mills (1996), p. 596.

97 *See* Straus (2000), p. 819.

98 *See* Kühnen and Peterreins (2015), p. 569, para. 2037. *See* also Higher Regional Court Dusseldorf, no. 2 U 126/09 – Harnkatheterset, 29 April 2010; Higher Regional Court Karlsruhe, no. 6 U 52/15 – Ausrüstungssatz, 23 September 2015.

99 The probability of validity of a patent is one of the factors to be considered by national European courts in granting a preliminary injunction, including in Germany. For a comparative analysis, *see*, for example, Cotter (2013), pp. 242 *et seq*.

100 *See* Perkins and Mills (1996), p. 596.

101 Article L617-3 of the French Intellectual Property Code provides that '[s]aisie en référé ou sur requête, la juridiction ne peut ordonner les mesures demandées que si les éléments de preuve, raisonnablement accessibles au demandeur, rendent vraisemblable qu'il est porté atteinte à ses droits ou qu'une telle atteinte est imminente'. The old law required for a *caractère sérieux de l'action au fond*, while the new law seems lighter in this sense (the condition of *vraisemblance*).

102 However, some French courts have limited their evaluation to simply ascertaining the existence of the patent and the quality of the title holder. *See* Cour d'Appel Toulouse, RG no. 08/03793 (Section 1, Chambre 2), 2 December 2009.

infringement is also necessary.[103] That is, the focus is placed on the infringement. Indeed, this may imply an analysis similar to that carried out on the merits of the case.[104] As for the validity of the title, a mere patent application is not enough,[105] and the court may also dismiss an application for a preliminary injunction on the grounds of the obvious or serious invalidity of the patent[106] or if the alleged infringer challenges the validity of the patent with sound arguments.[107]

In the United Kingdom, the court generally operates in two stages: first, it decides whether there is a serious question to be tried, and afterwards it considers if 'it is fair'[108] that the preliminary injunction be granted.[109] In evaluating whether there is a serious issue worthy of trial, the evidence should reveal that the plaintiff has a real prospect of succeeding in his claim for a permanent injunction at full trial.[110] The claim must exist in substance and reality and not be merely frivolous or vexatious,[111] which 'inevitably involves establishing the existence of a right that founds the claim and the existence of an actual or threatened infringement of that right'.[112] It should then be considered where the balance of convenience lies, in either granting or rejecting the injunction.

2.2 Balance of Convenience

'Balance of convenience' is the concept defining the test conducted in common law countries to assess whether the injunction should be granted in light of the possible effects on the conflicting parties, i.e. to assess the 'degree of unquantifiable loss that one party will suffer as opposed to another'.[113] It entails a pragmatic and comprehensive assessment of a range of factors[114] so as to ascertain the likely impact of granting or withholding an injunction on each of the parties. In non-common law

[103] *See* Casalonga and Langlais (2010), p. 37. The jurisprudence is not, however, uniform. *See* for instance the different standard to examine the likelihood of infringement followed by some French courts in Tribunal de Grande Instance of Paris, *EI DuPont de Nemours v. Mylan*, no. 10/51453, 12 February 2010, confirmed by the Court of Appeal of Paris (Division 1, Chambre 3), 15 March 2011 (the court has granted the preliminary injunction), and in Tribunal de Grande Instance of Paris, *Novartis v. Actavis*, 28 January 2011, reversed by the Court of Appeal of Paris (Division 1, Chambre 4), 16 September 2011 (the court has denied the measure)

[104] This is similar to the requirement that the action on the merits appeared serious under the old law.

[105] *See* Casalonga and Langlais (2010), p. 36. [106] *Ibid.*, p. 37.

[107] *See* Cour d'Appel de Paris, *Novartis AG v. Mylan and Qualimed* (Pole 1, Chambre 2), 21 March 2012.

[108] *See* Bently and Sherman (2008), p. 1105.

[109] While the first stage represents a criterion in itself, the second requires looking at three factors: whether damages would be an adequate remedy, the balance of convenience and the merits of the case. *See* Bently and Sherman (2008), pp. 1103 *et seq*; Bainbridge (2012), pp. 927 *et seq*.

[110] *See* Bently and Sherman (2008), p. 1103. According to Thorley and Fysh (2015), it seems not a high hurdle and would merely require the case to be arguable. This would be confirmed in *Novartis AG v Dexcel-Pharma Ltd* [2008] *EWHC* 1266 (Pat).

[111] *See Mothercare Ltd v Robson Books Ltd* [1979] FSR 466. [112] *See* Brandreth (2005), p. 456.

[113] *See* Thorley and Fysh (2015). [114] *See* Cornish and Llewelyn (2005), p. 100.

countries similar exercises are conducted[115] and other principles are intended to achieve related objectives. This is the case of the comparative analysis of the interests involved in a given dispute as well as the overarching principle of proportionality.

In the United Kingdom, a criterion when considering the balance of convenience is whether damages would be an adequate remedy.[116] In order to determine the adequacy of damages, the court analyses whether damages awarded at full trial would be a satisfactory remedy for the plaintiff in the absence of an injunction and whether the defendant is able to pay damages.[117] If damages are not an adequate remedy, the court will additionally consider whether the defendant would be adequately compensated at trial for the loss suffered between the time of the interim injunction and full trial.[118]

Assessing the balance of convenience involves a variety of factors that depend on the circumstances of the case[119] and leave large discretion to the court.[120] For example, in the United Kingdom, public interest considerations have been taken into account in patent litigation relating to pharmaceutical products, in cases both denying[121] and granting the injunction.[122] Further, in evaluating the balance of convenience, the promptitude with which the plaintiff seeks the preliminary injunction may be relevant. In this regard, if the plaintiff delayed bringing the action, the court might assume that the effects of the infringement might not be serious.[123]

115 In France, the law does not require assessing the balance of convenience, but courts have taken into account the balance of interests of the parties, when both issuing or rejecting an injunction. For an example granting the injunction, *see* Tribunal de Grande Instance of Paris, *EI DuPont de Nemours v. Mylan*, no. 10/51453, 12 February 2010. In this case, the court held that '[t]he Judge in preliminary proceedings should, when confronted with a serious challenge, weigh opposing interests so as to ensure that a balance between the rights of the parties is maintained, that is, between the seriousness of an imminent damage and its potential compensation and the seriousness of the prohibition measure sought.' For an example rejecting the injunction, *see* Tribunal de Grande Instance of Paris, SA *Aventis Pharma*, SA *Sanofi-Aventis France* v. SAS *Teva Sante*, no. 10/56889, 19 August 2010 (hereinafter Tribunal de Grande Instance of Paris, no. 10/56889, 19 August 2010).

116 *See* Bently and Sherman (2008), footnote 43, p. 1106; Brandreth (2005), pp. 456, 458.

117 *See SKB v Generics* [2002] 25(1) IPD 25005.

118 *See* Bently and Sherman (2008), p. 1106.

119 *See* Bainbridge (2012), p. 927.

120 The discretion of the Court becomes central when assessing the balance of convenience. Take for instance this excerpt of a sentence by Justice Jacob: 'the only thing I think I can say with some certainty is that the order of damage to the claimant is likely to be a good deal greater than that to the defendant ... [because] claimant's damage is more unquantifiable than that of the defendants, but both are unquantifiable. There are degrees of unquantifiability, just as there are degrees of infinity'. *See SmithKline Beecham plc v Generics (UK) Ltd* [2001] All ER (D) 325.

121 In a case rejecting the injunction, it was held that 'the Court should in appropriate circumstances take into account the interests of persons who would be affected by the grant of the injunction. That may involve considering the interests of the public.' *See Chiron Corp vs Organon Teknika Ltd* (No. 10) [1995] FSR 325, 7.

122 A preliminary injunction might be denied if its granting endangers the public access to a life-saving drug. *See Roussel-Uclaf v GD Searle & Co Ltd* [1977] FSR 125 ('it is at very least doubtful if the court in its discretion even ought to grant and injunction').

123 *See* Bently and Sherman (2008), p. 1107.

2.3 Urgency

The so-called *periculum in mora*, or the necessity to adopt measures so that the final sentence does not become meaningless, is also a common requisite in comparative patent law. In Germany, the plaintiff must show an urgent need for an injunction, and filing a request for a preliminary injunction within one or two months of discovering the infringement is normally considered enough to demonstrate that there was urgency.[124] In this regard, however, it has been stated that '[i]t is not about the greatest speed, but about the petitioner prosecuting its action in a way that suggests the seriousness of its effort and that therefore objectively justifies granting it access to injunction proceedings'.[125] In cases where the injunction is aimed at impeding an infringement that has not yet commenced, the urgency requirement demands the plaintiff to show an imminent infringement.[126]

In order to ascertain the existence of *periculum in mora*, the behaviour and activities of both the right holder and the alleged infringer are of relevance. For instance, in the case of the right holder some countries require the effective exploitation of the patent in order to understand that there is *periculum in mora*.[127] As to the act of the alleged infringer, the condition that the infringement must be imminent in order to award a preliminary injunction leaves judges a margin of discretion because the meaning of 'imminent infringement' is nowhere defined. French courts, for instance, have decided that proving the existence of an imminent infringement requires something more than the grant of a marketing authorization for a pharmaceutical product,[128] the registration of a medicine on the list of refundable drugs[129] or the absence of reply to a warning letter.[130] Certainly, courts have also identified a number of situations that would indicate that an imminent infringement is likely. These situations include, for instance, a catalogue announcing the launching date of a product as well as company statements announcing the will to launch a product on the market.[131]

With respect to urgency, whereas in Germany and in the United Kingdom it is required that the issue is urgent,[132] the new wording of the French law does not

124 Local courts nevertheless, have dealt with the urgency requirement differently. *See* Marshall (2005), p. 124. For instance, in Hamburg Regional Court a preliminary injunction can be filed more than two months after discovery of the infringement, while in the Munich Regional Court it is necessary to file the request within one month. *See* Coury (2003), pp. 1135–1136; Managing Intellectual Property (1997), p. 39.

125 *See* Kühnen and Peterreins (2015), para. 2095, p. 577.

126 *See* Higher Regional Court Dusseldorf, *no.* 2 W 47/07 – *Olanzapin*, 29 May 2008; Cotter (2013), p. 244.

127 *See* references to Article 133 of the Spanish Patent Law in Section II.1.

128 *See* Tribunal de Grande Instance of Paris, 11 December 2002, Propriete Industrielle Bulletin Documentaire (PIBD) 2003, no. 767, III-338.

129 *See* Tribunal de Grande Instance of Paris, *SA Aventis Pharma, SA Sanofi-Aventis France v. SAS Teva Sante*, no. 10/56889, 19 August 2010.

130 *Ibid.* 131 *See* Tribunal de Grande Instance of Lyon, no. 2008/01373, 21 July 2008.

132 *See* Rule 25.2(2)(b) Civil Procedure Code.

request showing 'urgency' anymore.[133] Before the implementation of the EU Enforcement Directive, French law required filing the preliminary injunction promptly after the patentee became aware of the alleged infringing activities.[134] Urgency was satisfied if the plaintiff instituted the action for obtaining a preliminary injunction within six months.[135] In opposition to the previous law and the traditional jurisprudence of the French courts on the matter, this requirement has been removed from the Intellectual Property Code.[136]

2.4 Measures Adopted *inaudita altera parte*

The efficiency of the measure is also enhanced by establishing that the preliminary injunction can be granted without the defendant having been heard. This will happen 'where any delay would cause irreparable harm to the rightsholder', under the condition that the defendant is afforded an opportunity to be heard within a reasonable time after the execution of the measure.[137]

Courts are cautious when granting *inaudita altera parte* measures in the domain of patents. These are possible in Germany,[138] but in practice it is difficult to obtain an interim injunction without an oral hearing.[139] German courts are very careful in their interpretation of procedural pre-requisites, especially in cases concerning infringement of technical subject matters, such as in patents.[140] *Inaudita*

[133] *See* Article L615-3. Also, the lack of the condition of urgency in the letter of the new law suggests that an application for a preliminary injunction can be made anytime from the date at which the plaintiff became aware of the alleged infringement. Nevertheless, it can be noticed that courts have observed that more than twelve months far exceeds a 'prompt request' for a preliminary injunction, especially when comparing with the old law, where the former requirement of 'bref délai' was interpreted by courts as a period not exceeding six months. *See* Tribunal de Grande Instance of Paris, *Aventis Pharmaceuticals v. Teva Classics*, no. 09/56031, 12 January 2010, where the court stated that '[a] titre liminaire, le juge des référés note que sous l'empire de l'ancien texte la demande en référé de la société Aventis Pharmaceuticals aurait été déclarée irrecevable car l'exploitation du médicament générique par la société Teva Santé a été développée au vu et au su de la société demanderesse pendant *plus de douze mois avant la saisine du juge des référés ce qui implique que la notion de bref délai est largement dépassée*' (emphasis added).

[134] The previous wording of Article L615-3 read as 'only ... if the substantive proceedings appear well founded and *are instituted within a short time* of the day on which the patentee became aware of the facts on which the proceedings are based' (emphasis added). It could be noticed that the former conditions for preliminary injunctions in patent cases were more restrictive than the current law.

[135] *See* Cour de Cassation, no. 92–14361, 1 March 1994, Bulletin 1994 IV no. 83, p. 64. *See* also Petit (2005), p. 160.

[136] *See* Article L615-3 of the Intellectual Property Code. Tribunal de Grande Instance of Lyon, 3 June 2008, has stated that, 'l'application de cette disposition, qui nécessite seulement la constatation de l'existence des droits de propriété intellectuelle et d'une atteinte à ses droits, *n'est nullement conditionnée à l'existence d'une situation d'urgence*' (emphasis added).

[137] *See* Article 9.4 EU Enforcement Directive.

[138] *See* Section 937 German Code of Civil Procedure. For a comment, *see* Marshall (2005), p. 125.

[139] *See* Marshall (2005), p. 125.

[140] *See* Kühnen and Peterreins (2015), para. 2131, p. 586; Straus (2000), pp. 822–823; Dreier (1996), pp. 274–275.

altera parte injunctions seem to be granted in cases relating to exhibitions and trade fairs, when there are only a few days to enforce them. But even in these situations and even if differences across Higher Regional Courts remain, courts try to contact the attorney of the defendant.[141]

Under Article L615-3 of the French Intellectual Property Code, preliminary injunctions can be requested *inter partes* or *inaudita altera parte*.[142] An *inaudita altera parte* preliminary injunction will be ordered only in circumstances where any delay would cause irreparable harm to the right holder.[143] In regard to the number of successful actions in obtaining *inaudita altera parte* injunctions in France, even though it has been observed that the situation has slightly changed in the past years,[144] cases are still rare.[145] Like in France and Germany, *inaudita altera parte* preliminary injunctions are also available in the United Kingdom,[146] although circumstances must be exceptional[147] and injunctions are granted only the strictly necessary period of time.[148]

3 *The Four-Factor Test in the United States*

In the United States, injunctions are provided by statute and granted by courts in accordance with principles of equity.[149] The courts typically consider sequentially four factors:[150] (1) the plaintiff's likelihood of success on the merits; (2) whether the

141 In preliminary proceedings, no further appeal is possible to the Federal Court of Justice, which could harmonize the jurisprudence in the field. More broadly, the court has a large discretion in preliminary proceedings and has to balance the interests of the claimant against the interests of the defendant taking all factors into account. *See* Cotter (2013), pp. 243–244; Straus (2000), p. 819. *See* also Perkins and Mills (1996), p. 597.

142 Article L615-3 of the French Intellectual Property Code provides for proceedings 'en référé' or 'sur requete'.

143 Article L615-3 of the French Intellectual Property Code reads, '[l]a juridiction civile compétente peut également ordonner toutes mesures urgentes sur requête lorsque les circonstances exigent que ces mesures ne soient pas prises contradictoirement, *notamment lorsque tout retard serait de nature à causer un préjudice irréparable au demandeur*' (emphasis added). In *Novartis v. Sanofi-Aventis*, the French Supreme Court decided that *inaudita altera parte* preliminary injunctions should be available if the applicant can demonstrate the need for the defendant not being heard, if there is no doubt of the infringement and if an injunction is necessary because damages could not constitute adequate compensation. *See* Cour de Cassation, *Novartis AG v. Sanofi-Aventis*, no. 13–10189, 16 September 2014.

144 Under the former law, the procedure of preliminary injunctions has been rarely used. *See* Veron and Mandel (2005).

145 *See* in this sense Romet and Veron (2011); Casalonga and Langlais (2010).

146 *See* Bently and Sherman (2008), p. 1100.

147 *See* Thorley and Fysh (2015).

148 *See Warner-Lambert v Teva UK Ltd* [2011] EWHC 1691.

149 In the United States, Title 35 USC §283 provides for injunctions; '[t]he several courts having jurisdiction of cases under this title may grant injunctions in accordance with the principles of equity to prevent the violation of any right secured by patent, on such terms as the court deems reasonable'. For a detailed analysis of preliminary injunctions in historical perspective, *see* Meyer (1983).

150 *See Hybritech, Inc. v. Abbott Labs.*, 849 F.2d 1446 (Fed. Cir. 1988) (hereinafter *Hybritech, Inc. v. Abbott Labs.*). The Court explained that the preliminary injunction 'factors, taken individually, are not dispositive; rather, the district court must weigh and measure each factor against the other

plaintiff will suffer irreparable harm without interlocutory injunction, i.e. whether damages could compensate; (3) whether the balance of hardships favours the plaintiff; and (4) the impact of interlocutory injunction on the public interest.[151] The plaintiff must also pose a security in order to cover costs and damages that might occur on any party who is wrongfully enjoined,[152] and the rules of procedure also allow for *inaudita altera parte* preliminary injunctions.[153]

It has been generally held that the first two requirements, namely the likelihood of success and irreparable harm, are the most important,[154] even if in recent times the Supreme Court has also emphasized the relevance of the public interest criterion.[155]

Likelihood of success on the merits can be demonstrated by showing that the plaintiff will 'likely prove' infringement, and 'likely withstand' the defendant's challenge on patent validity.[156] Put the other way around, 'a reasonable likelihood of success requires a showing of validity and infringement'.[157] In order to overcome the plaintiff's showing of probable success on the merits, the defendant must demonstrate by 'clear and convincing evidence'[158] that either the patent is not infringed or the patent is invalid.[159] The Court of Appeals for the Federal Circuit developed a very strong presumption in favour of the grant of injunctions, a presumption rooted in the emphasis put on the existence of irreparable harm whenever sufficient proof that the patent was valid and infringed was provided.[160]

Putting the mentioned presumption aside for a moment, for a harm to be 'irreparable' it must be established to be 'neither remote nor speculative, but actual and imminent',[161] and damages must be insufficient to remedy it.[162] It is not,

factors and against the form and magnitude of the relief requested'. *See* for a comment, among others, Cotter (2013), p. 97.

151 *See*, among others, Manzo (2007); Laycock (2008); Griem and Brook (2008); Gergen *et al.* (2012); Wu (2014); Sherkow (2014).

152 *See* Boyce and Hollis (2007), pp. 386–387.

153 *See* Rule 65 of the US Federal Rules of Civil Procedure providing that: 'Temporary Restraining Order: (1) Issuing without notice: The court may issue a temporary retraining order without written or oral notice to the adverse party or its attorney only if: (A) specific facts in an affidavit or a verified complaint clearly show that immediate and irreparable injury, loss, or damage, will result to the movant before the adverse party can be heard in opposition; and (B) the movants attorney certifies in writing any efforts made to give notice and the reasons why it should not be required.'

154 *See Reebok International, Ltd. v. J. Baker, Inc.*, 32F.3d1552, 1556 (Fed. Cir. 1994).

155 As noted below, an evident difference between the European and US tests is the public interest standard that is examined in the United States, whereas there is no equivalent requisite in Europe, even if in the United Kingdom the public interest may play a role when assessing the balance of hardships.

156 *See Bell and Howell Document Mgmt. Prods. Co. v. Altek Sys.*, 132 F.3d 701, 705 n.4 (Fed. Cir. 1997).

157 *Hybritech, Inc. v. Abbott Labs.*, at 1195.

158 *See Titan Titre Corp. v. Case New Holland, Inc.*, 566 F.3d 1372, 1379 (Fed. Cir. 2009).

159 *See Am. Hoist and Derrick Co. v. Sowa and Sons, Inc.*, 725 F.2d 1350, 1360 (Fed. Cir. 1984).

160 *See Roper Corp. v. Litton Sys. Inc.*, 757 F.2d 1266, 1271–72 (Fed. Cir. 1985); *Smith Int'l Inc. v. Hughes Tool Co.*, 718 F.2d 1537, 1575 (Fed. Cir. 1983) (hereinafter *Smith Int'l Inc. v. Hughes Tool Co.*).

161 *See Tucker Anthony Realty Corp. v. Schlesinger*, 888 F.2d 969, 975 (2d Cir. 1989) (citing *Consol. Brands, Inc. v. Mondi*, 638 F. Supp. 152, 155 (EDNY 1986)).

162 *See* Boyce and Hollis (2007), p. 387.

therefore, about the magnitude but the nature of the harm;[163] the injury may not be quantifiable or damages may be impossible to pay. Some examples may be useful. For instance, irreparable harm exists when one party will be put out of business by the injunction or where one party will suffer irrevocable damage to its business reputation.[164]

If the party seeking a preliminary injunction has delayed bringing his request on the matter, the court will be likely to find no irreparable harm and decline to issue the injunction.[165] In the past, when likelihood of success on the merits and irreparable harm were demonstrated, courts tended to interpret the requirement of public interest to be satisfied. This presumed that protecting patent rights amounted to protecting the public interest.[166] Additionally, proving the likelihood of success on the merits, the irreparable harm and the public interest usually implied that the third requirement, the balance of hardships, also favoured the plaintiff.[167] This 'serial assumption' made the four-factor test almost entirely a one-factor test: the likelihood of success on the merit.[168]

In 2006, the Supreme Court rejected the presumption in favour of permanent injunctions upheld by the Federal Circuit.[169] As a consequence, it is 'no longer the law'[170] to presume the requirement of 'irreparable harm' based just on proof of the infringement. Even if interim and permanent injunctions have different prerequisites and serve different purposes,[171] the four-factor test[172] and, in particular, the relevance put by the Supreme Court on the protection of the public interest coincide. Therefore, when analysing the grant of interim injunctions, the elements of balance of hardships and public interest should not be presumed any longer.[173]

After the *eBay* case it has become more difficult for a patent owner obtaining an injunction.[174] Whereas before *eBay* permanent injunctions were granted in 95 per cent of cases, the percentage went down to 72 per cent three years

163 *See*, in Canada, *RJR-Macdonald Inc. v. Canada*, 1994 CanLII 117 (SCC). 164 *Ibid.*

165 *See T.J. Smith and Nephew, Ltd. v. Consol. Med. Equip., Inc.*, 821 F.2d 646, 648 (Fed. Cir. 1987).

166 *See* Section IV.2. 167 *See* Coury (2003), p. 1155. 168 *See* McLeod (2006), par. 27.

169 *See eBay Inc. et al. v. Mercexchange*, L.L.C., 547 U.S. 388 (2006) (hereinafter *eBay*).

170 *See Automated Merchandising Systems, Inc., v. Crane Co.*, 357 Fed. Appx. 297 (Fed. Cir. 2009), p. 6.

171 *See Lermer Germany GmbH v. Lermer Corp.*, 94 F3d, 1575 (1996), p. 1577. For a comment, *see* Tang (2006), p. 239. However, this clear differentiation made in the United States is contrary to the approach of the Court of Justice of the European Union on the issue of the scope of preliminary and permanent injunctions, even though the decisions so far concerned copyright cases. In *L'Oréal and Others* CJEU has mixed the consequences of Article 9, on preliminary injunctions, and Article 11, on permanent injunctions, of the EU Enforcement Directive. *See* CJEU, C-324/09, *L'Oréal and Others v. eBay International AG and Others* [2011], Judgment of the Court (Grand Chamber) of 12 July 2011, ECR I-06011, para. 131.

172 *See* Cotter (2013), p. 102; Dratler (2008), p. 39.

173 It has been suggested that after *eBay* the plaintiff has to prove the balance of hardship and the public interest as well. *See* Cotter (2013), p. 103; and Dratler (2008), pp. 44–45.

174 *See* Manzo (2007). The author has concluded that '[w]hile courts fall on both sides of the question [whether the presumption of irreparable harm survived *eBay*], the better reasoned view appears to be that the presumption has no continued viability', p. 95.

after.[175] However, the implementation of the *eBay* jurisprudence is not uniform.[176] Some district courts have just done what seems obvious and discarded the existence of a presumption of irreparable harm.[177] By contrast, other courts have narrowly interpreted such a presumption and maintained that *eBay* applies only to permanent injunctions.[178] Still, other courts have not decided whether the presumption of irreparable harm also applies to interim injunctions.[179]

IV PRELIMINARY INJUNCTIONS, FUNDAMENTAL RIGHTS AND THE PUBLIC INTEREST

1 *The Right to Be Heard and Preliminary Injunctions*

The right to be heard is a central element of the right to a fair trial and a condition for the guarantee of due process-related entitlements. Indeed, 'the idea that a person ought to be heard before a decision is made or action taken affecting his or her interests is often thought to be the most fundamental element of procedural fairness'.[180] In recognition of this central role, the right to be heard has been recognized as both a fundamental principle[181] and a fundamental right.[182] The procedural guarantees of the right to be heard can be effective instruments in leading to fair

[175] *See* Grumbles, Hughey and Perera (2009), p. 26.

[176] The jurisprudence on preliminary injunctions after the decision in the *eBay* case is mixed. For a list of decisions where preliminary injunctions in patent cases have been granted or denied post-*eBay*, *see* Rabena and Choate (2007), footnote 17, p. 29.

[177] *See Sun Optics, Inc. v. FGX Int'l, Inc.*, No. 07–137, 2007 US Dist. LEXIS 56351 (D. Del. 2 August 2007), where the Court denied a preliminary injunction motion because the patentee had not shown likelihood of success on the merits or irreparable harm and commented that the presumption appears to be inconsistent with the *eBay* case.

[178] *See Christiana Indus., Inc. v. Empire Elecs., Inc.*, No. 06–12568, 2006 US Dist. LEXIS 54210 (E.D. Mich. 4 August 2006), where the court denied the motion of the defendant to reconsider its preliminary injunction order and rejected the argument of the defendant that the *eBay* case eliminated the presumption of irreparable harm for preliminary injunctions.

[179] *See Altana Pharma AG v. Teva Pharms. USA, Inc.*, No. 04–2355, 2007 US Dist. LEXIS 67285 (D.N.J. 6 September 2007), where it has been underscored that '[t]he Court need not consider whether Plaintiffs are entitled to a rebuttable presumption of irreparable harm and whether such presumption, which was previously applied by the Federal Circuit, survived the United States Supreme Court's decision in eBay Inc. v. MercExchange L.L.C., 126 S. Ct. 1837 (2006). Such a presumption, if it is even still valid in light of eBay, would only be applied where a plaintiff makes a clear or strong showing of likelihood of success on the merits. Since, as discussed above, Plaintiffs have not met their burden of showing likelihood of success on the merits, they certainly have not made a clear or strong showing of such success and thus, they would not be entitled to the presumption'.

[180] *See* Galligan (1996), p. 349.

[181] *See* more generally on the concept of hearing principle Galligan (1996).

[182] Such as in several international and regional legal instruments. *See* Article 10 of the Universal Declaration of Human Rights; Article 14(1) ICCPR, and *see* the comment of the UN Human Rights Committee (2007). *See* also Article 6.1 of the ECHR, and for a brief analysis Jacot-Guillarmod (1993), pp. 392–393. *See* Articles 41.2 and 47 of the Charter of Fundamental Rights of the European Union, OJEU C 326 of 26 October 2012, p. 391.

decisions. Courts have noticed that a defect in injunction proceedings, for instance failure to listen to one of the parties, may not be remedied at a later stage. Indeed, 'any prejudice suffered in the meantime may by then have become irreversible and with little realistic opportunity to redress the damage caused'.[183]

The Court of Justice of the European Union has established that the 'observance of the right to a fair hearing is, in all proceedings initiated against a person which are liable to culminate in a measure adversely affecting that person, a fundamental principle of Community law which must be guaranteed even in the absence of any rules governing the proceedings'.[184] The Court of Justice has also emphasized that even if procedural formalities may be simplified to achieve certain goals, such a simplification is not permissible if it undermines the right to a fair hearing.[185] In particular, *inaudita altera parte* provisional measures must guarantee fair trial standards, particularly the right to be heard.[186] The question that must be posed, hence, relates to what is needed to satisfy the hearing principle in intellectual property-related cases and which are the limits of the reduction of formalities governing fast procedures for intellectual property enforcement.

Pursuant to the TRIPS Agreement interim injunctions must be available without hearing the other party where any delay is likely to cause irreparable harm to the right holder. Still, the right to be heard can be identified in Article 50 of the TRIPS Agreement.[187] As drafted, this article is aimed at guaranteeing the defendant's right to receive notice, to be heard and to review the decision. However, there are some particularities in the way these rights are satisfied.

First, Article 50.4 of the TRIPS Agreement provides for procedural safeguards 'after the execution of the measure at the latest'.[188] This means that the defendant will only be informed once the measure is adopted and that the right to be heard will not necessarily be secured *before* the measure is taken.[189] The Court of Justice of the Europe Union has held that observance of the right to a hearing requires persons to be heard before the adoption of decisions affecting them and that this is a 'basic condition governing exercise of a discretionary power by a public authority'.[190]

183 *See* ECtHR, *Micallef v. Malta*, para. 80.

184 *See* ECJ, Case C-7/98, *Krombach v. Bamberski* [2000], Judgment of the Court of 28 March 2000, ECR I-01935, para. 42. *See* also ECJ, Case C-135/92, *Fiskano AB v. Commission of the European Communities* [1994], Judgment of the Court (Fifth Chamber) of 29 June 1994, ECR I-02885, para. 39.

185 *See* ECJ, Case C-49/84, *Leon Emile Gaston Carlos Debaecker and Berthe Plouvier v. Cornelis Gerrit Bouwman* [1985], Judgment of the Court (Fourth Chamber) of 11 June 1985, ECR 1985 01779, para. 10.

186 *See* ECJ, Case-125/79, Case C-125/79, *Bernard Denilauler v. SNC Couchet Frères* [1980], Judgment of the Court of 21 May 1980, ECR 01553, para. 15 *et seq*.

187 Article 9.4 of the EU Enforcement Directive is based on, and to a large extent is identical to, Articles 50.2 and 50.4 of the TRIPS Agreement.

188 *See* also Article 9.4 EU Enforcement Directive.

189 *See* ECJ, Case C-125/79, *Bernard Denilauler v. SNC Couchet Frères* [1980], Judgment of the Court of 21 May 1980, ECR 01553. For a similar view, *see* also UNCTAD/ICTSD (2005), p. 606.

190 *See* ECJ, Case C-315/99, *Ismeri Europa Srl v Court of Auditors of the European Communities* [2001], Judgment of the Court of 10 July 2001, 2001 I-05281, para. 23.

However, if information were always given in anticipation of the measure, preliminary injunctions would be ineffective. In order to ensure the element of 'surprise' and efficiently protect intellectual property rights, a different compromise must be found. A reasonable option is empowering national courts to temporarily suspend the adversarial principle and grant provisional measures without the defendant being heard in a restricted fashion.[191]

Second, where provisional measures have been adopted *inaudita altera parte*, the right to review, including the right to be heard, must take place 'upon request of the defendant'.[192] Naturally, 'a person whose interests are perceptively affected by a decision taken by a public authority must be given the opportunity to make his point of view known'.[193] However, the requirement that the TRIPS Agreement lays down for the defendant to expressly request the review is probably in the limits of the fair trial standards. A different option would have been, for instance, the provision of an automatic hearing without need of formal request. Thus, maximum flexibility should be awarded with respect to any intervention of the defendant. Moreover, any departure from the rule of the TRIPS Agreement that makes the intervention of the defendant more difficult would probably imply a violation of the fair trial criterions.

2 *The Public Interest*

The fourth factor considered when granting an interim injunction in the United States is the protection of the public interest. As the United States Supreme Court held in 1944, 'courts of equity may, and frequently do, go much farther both to give and withhold relief in furtherance of the public interest than they are accustomed to go when only private interests are involved'.[194] Pursuant to this ground, the judge wages the impact of the injunction on the public interest and discards the injunction if such an impact is negative, even if the remaining three criteria are met. The court will assess 'whether there exists some critical public interest that would be injured by the grant of preliminary injunctive relief'.[195] In light of public interest concerns, courts may also require plaintiffs 'an even greater burden of persuasion'[196] to grant the injunction.

[191] *See* ECtHR, *Micallef v. Malta*, no. 17056/06, 15 October 2009, Report of Judgments and Decisions 2009, para. 86 (hereinafter ECtHR, *Micallef v. Malta*).

[192] *See* Article 50.4 TRIPS Agreement.

[193] *See* ECJ, Case C-17/74, *Transocean Marine Paint Association v. Commission of the European Communities* [1974], Judgment of the Court of 23 October 1974, 01063, para. 15.

[194] *See Yakus*, 321 US 441 (1944). *See* Wolf (1984), p. 181; Vaughn (1989), p. 847.

[195] *See Hybritech, Inc. v. Abbott Labs.; Datascope Corp. v. Kontron, Inc.*, 786 F.2d 398, 401, 229 USPQ (Fed. Cir. 1986), p. 43.

[196] Some courts have not directly discarded the injunction invoking the public interest but have claimed that 'where the grant of interim relief may adversely affect the public interest in a manner which cannot be compensated for by an injunction bond, plaintiffs undertake an even greater burden of persuasion'. *See Medical Society of N.Y. v. Toia*, 560 F.2d 535, 538 (2d Cir. 1977).

2.1 The Two Lines of Jurisprudence as to the Meaning of Public Interest

The public interest as a factor considered when granting an injunction may be the most difficult to implement[197] since it evokes nothing less than the 'duty of a court of equity granting injunctive relief to do so upon conditions that will protect all – including the public, whose interests the injunction may affect'.[198] Probably for this reason, this is one of the requisites where the discretion of the court should be given the greatest deference.[199] Indeed, the very notion of 'public interest' is as ubiquitous as blurring. As a proof of that, courts have adopted different views with respect to the meaning of 'public interest'.

The assessment of the impact on the public interest of the grant of an interim injunction is closely related to the public policy pros and cons of the intellectual property protection. This can be seen in the justifications given by courts when deciding on the grant of injunctions in cases relating to patents as well as in cases relating to other categories of intellectual property rights.[200] In this respect, judges have held varying opinions on 'whether the public interest is best served by enjoining further infringement',[201] and similar situations have given place to opposed rulings. It is, in fact, relatively easy to identify periods of time when the courts in the United States were more favourable to implement the 'public interest' criterion. Indeed, the setting up of the Court of Appeals for the Federal Circuit in 1982 marked a turning point. Since then, injunctions became an almost automatic remedy,[202] just the opposite of earlier times, when the public interest was found in 'free competition and the public distrust of monopolies'.[203] The Supreme Court of the United States nevertheless reintroduced in 2006 a note of caution and balance in the *eBay* case.

The two lines of arguments are, however, clear. The traditional trend in the United States jurisprudence holds that the grant of injunctions satisfies the public interest when it permits achieving the purpose of the statute that the

197 *See* Nard (2014), p. 936. 198 *See Inland Steel Co. v. United States* 306 US 153 (1939).

199 *See* Duft (1983), p. 148.

200 *See Continental Paper Bag Co. v. Eastern Paper Bag Co.* 210 US 405 (1908). Also in trademark-related cases it has been held that if public interest is better protected by rejecting an interim injunction, the injunction will not be granted. *See Continental Oil Company v. Crutcher*, 434 F.Supp. 464 (E.D.La. 1977). In the field of trademarks, the public interest 'is most often a synonym for the right of the public not to be deceived or confused'. *See Opticians Ass'n of Am. v. Independent Opticians of Am.*, 920 F.2d 187, 197 (3d Cir. 1990).

201 *See* Manzo (2007), p. 95.

202 *See* the long list of cases in this sense in Creel and Praiss (1990), footnote 98, p. 248.

203 *See* Creel and Praiss (1990), p. 248. Among earlier cases, *see Vitamin Technologists, Inc. v. Wis. Alumni Research Found.*, 146 F.2d 941, 944–45 (9th Cir. 1945) (dictum) – in this cases the (permanent) injunction would have withheld from the general public a cure for rickets in children; *City of Milwaukee v. Activated Sludge, Inc.*, 69 F.2d 577, 593 (7th Cir. 1934) – in this case the permanent injunction would have provoked the shutting-down of sewage treatment plants; *Ballard v. City of Pittsburgh*, 12 F. 783, 786 (C.C.W.D. Pa. 1882); *McCrary v. Pa. Canal Co.*, 5 F. 367, 368 (C.C.E.D. Pa. 1880) (per curiam), p. 1891); *Sanders v. Logan*, 21 F. Cas. 321, 322–23 (No. 12,295) (C.C.W.D. Pa. 1861).

defendant allegedly violates.[204] In this sense, the purpose of patent law is to stimulate innovation by granting and enforcing patents. Pursuant to this rationale, whenever an injunction is instrumental at protecting a patent, the injunction should be granted.[205] As it can be deduced, this generates a situation where injunctions must be automatically granted. However, even under the jurisprudence of the Court of Appeals for the Federal Circuit, compelling public interest grounds have been successfully invoked to impede the award of interim injunctions. Moreover, the *eBay* sentence and the reference made therein to the separation between rights and remedies, as well as the nature of injunctions as a remedy of equity, have resulted in a more inclusive perspective on the role and actual granting of injunctions.

Before the *eBay* case, the prevailing line of thinking associated the public interest with the actual award of injunctions to prevent or impede the continuation of the infringement.[206] Take for instance the *Eli Lilly v. Premo Pharmaceutical Laboratories* case, where the Court held that patent laws are a recognition that temporary monopolies are granted to induce the investment of time and money to research.[207] Consequently, not awarding an injunction would run against that purpose. In *Sanofi-Synthelabo, Inc. v. Apotex, Inc.*, the Court of Appeals also upheld the grant of an interim injunction against the alleged infringer. The Court was not convinced by the allegations of the defendant, who argued that human lives could

204 *See Virginian Railway v. System Federation* No. 40 300 US (1937), p. 552. It has been noted that 'when discussing whether to grant or deny preliminary injunctive relief, courts generally speak of 'the public interest' as synonymous with the broad policy considerations embodied in the substantive law to be applied'. *See* Lewis (1993), p. 855.

205 As stated, 'to the extent a denial of preliminary injunctive relief would be a disincentive to the use of the patented system and research investment, the public will ultimately lose'. *See* Neuner (1980), p. 21.

206 Even after the *eBay* case, courts have held that the public has an interest in maintaining a strong patent system. *See* for instance the cases: o2 *Micro International, Ltd., v. Beyond Innovation Technology Co.*, 2007 WL 869576 (ED Tex. 21 March 2007), p. 3; *Commonwealth Scientific and Industrial Research Organisation v. Buffalo Technology Inc.*, 492 F. Supp. 2d 600 (ED Tex. 2007); *Well Services, Inc. v. Mega Lift Systems, LLC.*, No. H-05–1634, 2007 WL 1231682 (SD Tex. 25 April 2007), p. 15; 800 *Adept, Inc. v. Murex Securities, Ltd.*, 505 F. Supp. 2d 1327 (Dist. Court, MD Florida 12 April 2007), p. 1338; *MPT, Inc. v. Marathon Lahels, Inc.*, No. 1:04-CV-2357, 2007 WL 184747 (ND Ohio 19 January 2007), p. 15. This has happened even in public health related cases, for instance in *Sanofi-Synthelabo v. Apotex, Ine.* 492 F. Supp. 2d 353, 356 (SDNY 2007).

207 It has been held that '[t]his justification for sacrificing short-term price competition in order to foster creativity and improvement of products in long-run is particularly applicable to the pharmaceutical industry'. *See Eli Lilly and Company, v. Premo Pharmaceutical Laboratories, Inc., Federal Pharmacal, Inc., Seymour N. Blackman, Steven Blackman, Johnblackman, Appellants, v. Richard D. Wood, C. Harvey Bradley, Jr., Earl B. Herr, Jr., cornelius W. Pettinga, Eugene L. Step and Arthurr. Whale, Additional Defendants on The counterclaim*, 630 F.2d 120 (3d Cir. 1980). Among the cases with similar reasoning can be quoted *E.I. du Pont de Nemours and Co. v. Polaroid Graphics Imaging, Inc.*, 706 E Supp. 1135, 1146 (D Del. 1989), aft'd, 887 E2d 1095 (Fed. Cir. 1989); *Kemin Foods, L.C. v. Pigmentos Vegetales del Centro S.A. de C.V.*, 240 E Supp. 2d 963, 980–81 (SD Iowa 2003), rev'd on other grounds, 93 F. App'x 225 (Fed. Cir. 2004).

be at stake.[208] On the contrary, the Court justified the injunction claiming that the company had incurred significant costs to develop the product, an investment encouraged by the patent system.[209]

This argument is complemented from different angles. For instance, in *Zenith Labs., Inc. v. Eli Lilly and Co.*[210] an additional point related to litigation costs was added. According to the Court, in case the injunction was not awarded, not only Zenith but also other generic producers would enter the market and 'Lilly would be drawn into further litigation to defend its patent'.[211] The associated costs would also reduce the 'funds available for testing and research and development'.[212] A common element of this line of reasoning is the idea that the public policy at issue in patent cases is the 'protection of rights secured by valid patents'[213] and that 'public policy favours the innovator, not the copier'.[214]

In a large number of cases, however, courts have decided otherwise, and pressing needs or broader social interests have trumped the protection of a specific patent. This line of argumentation has been particularly strong in health-related cases. For instance, in *Hybritech, Inc. v. Abbott Labs.*, a case relating to medical supplies for hepatitis and cancer, the Court of Appeals for the Federal Circuit argued that access to these products outweighed the interests of the right holder.[215] Similarly, in *Scripps v. Genetech* a district court rejected the injunction since the defendant was the sole provider of the drug for haemophilia under litigation.[216] Likewise, in *Ethicon Endo-Surgery v. United States Surgical Corp.*, it was held that the withdrawal from the

208 The generic producer argued that 'if the generic products were removed from the market, consumers would be inclined not to purchase their medication because of the accompanying price increase for the brand name drug, leading to possible deaths'. *See Sanofi-Synthelabo, Inc. v. Apotex, Inc.*, 470 F.3d 1368 (Fed. Cir. 2006).

209 It has been stated that 'we have long acknowledged the importance of the patent system in encouraging innovation'. Indeed, the 'encouragement of investment-based risk is the fundamental purpose of the patent grant, and is based directly on the right to exclude. The district court relied on the testimony of Dr. Hausman in finding that the average cost of developing a block-buster drug is $800 million. Importantly, the patent system provides incentive to the innovator drug companies to continue costly development efforts'. *See Sanofi-Synthelabo, Inc. v. Apotex, Inc.*, 470 F.3d 1368 (Fed. Cir. 2006).

210 *See Zenith Labs., Inc. v. Eli Lilly and Co.*, 460 F. Supp. 812, 826 (DNJ 1978) (hereinafter *Zenith Labs., Inc. v. Eli Lilly and Co.*).

211 *Ibid.* 212 *Ibid.*

213 *Ibid.*, quoting *Smith Int'l Inc. v. Hughes Tool Co.*, 718 F.2d at 1581, 219 USPQ, p. 693.

214 *See Polaroid Corp. v. Eastman Kodak Co.* 228 USPQ 304 (D.Mass. 1985), p 344. In the late 1970, Kodak produced two instant cameras and special film with the objective of competing with the almost legendary Polaroid 'one-step' camera and film. Polaroid brought suit against Kodak for several patent infringements, and Kodak moved for stay of the injunction pending final decision. Among the arguments put forward by Kodak, reference was made to problems for 16 million owners of its instant cameras if the sale of Kodak instant film was enjoined. The public interest, Kodak argued, weighed heavily against an injunction. The Court, however, dismissed outright Kodak's arguments.

215 *See Hybritech, Inc. v. Abbott Labs.*

216 More precisely, the Court denied the injunction holding that 'Genentech makes a strong argument, supported by the declarations of three experts, that hemophiliacs could suffer if there is any delay in bringing recombinant Factor VIII:C to the market ... In addition, recombinant technology may

market of a surgical device 'could have serious disruptive effect on surgical practice', since it was commonly used by many surgeons who had been specifically trained to use it.[217]

Public health protection has not been the sole ground considered when rejecting the grant of an injunction. The provision of goods that are vital for an industrial sector,[218] the possibility of losing jobs and causing problems to third parties – including consumers,[219] the protection of environment,[220] the promotion of competition,[221] cases where 'infringing product is valuable to the public-at-large'[222] or cases where the only advantage to a plaintiff in granting the injunction is to strengthen its position in negotiating a settlement[223] – have also been legitimate reasons to reject issuing injunctions.

2.2 The Public Interest, TRIPS and Differences across Countries

Trying to find a middle ground, some tribunals have held that, if there are no other critical public interests at stake and a conflict is presented between protecting patents and preserving competition, the public interest factor is 'a neutral one'.[224] Similarly, some courts have held that the public has an interest 'both in protecting patent rights and in ensuring that markets are competitive'.[225] In this same line, it has been argued that law is not a single-minded drive toward a policy goal but rather

ultimately provide a more economical and efficient source of Factor VIII:C than human or porcine plasma.' *See Scripps Clinic and Research Foundation, and Revlon, Inc., v. Genetech, Inc and Miles Laboratories, Inc., Defendants*, US District Court for the Northern District of California, 666 F. Supp. 1379 (ND Cal. 20 July 1987).

217 *See Ethicon Endo-Surgery v. United States Surgical Corp.*, 855 F. Supp. 1500, 1517 (1994), p. 1517.

218 For instance the supply of cotton bale wrap to the domestic cotton industry. *See Amoco Corp. v. Exxon Chemical Corp.*, 7 USPQ2d (NDGa 1987), p. 1461.

219 *See Archive Corp. v. Cipher Data Products, Inc.*, 12 USPQ2d (CD Cal. 1988), p. 1469; *Sundance, Inc. v. DeMonte Fabricating Ltd.*, No. 02–73543, 2007 WL 37742 (ED Mich. 4 January 2007), p 2.

220 *See Am. Sterilizer Co. v. Surgikos Inc.*, 17 USPQ2d (ND Tex. 1990), p. 1083.

221 In the case *Illinois Tool Works,* the Federal Circuit Court agreed with the district courts and maintained that 'a public interest in the protection of patent rights' was counterbalanced by the 'continuing right to compete'. *See Illinois Tool Works*, 906 F.2d 679, 59 USLW 2027, 15 U.S.P.Q.2d 1307 (20 June 1990), p. 684. In *Smith & Nephew, Inc. v. Synthes (USA)*, relating to a permanent injunction, the Court held that its award would advance 'consumer access to more competitive, and thus, presumably better, products'. *See Smith & Nephew, Inc. v. Synthes (USA)*, 466 F. Supp. 2d 978, (W.D. Tenn. 2006), p. 985.

222 *See Boehringer Ingelheim Vetmedica, Inc. v. Schering-Plough Corp.*, 106 E Supp. 2d 696, 697, 705 (DNJ 2000).

223 *See Nerney v. New York, N.H & HR. Co.*, 83 F.2d 409, 411 (2d Cir. 1936); similarly, *Foster v. American Machine and Foundry Co.* 492 F.2d 1317 1324 (2d Cir. 1974) (both cases relate to permanent injunctions).

224 *See Tensar Corp. v. Tenax Corp.*, 24 USPQ2d, (DMd 1992), p. 1614.

225 *See Alliance Research Corp. v. Telular Corp.*, 859 F. Supp. 400, 406 (CD Cal. 1994), p. 406. A parallelism can be found in the area of copyright law, where it has been stated that it is in the public interest to encourage authors to publish their works and ensure the widest possible dissemination, something that explains the limitations to protection. *See* Davies (2002), p. 236.

a balance between competing policies;[226] thus any party to a lawsuit can point to a competing policy interest that favours his case.[227]

Even if these arguments may be generally true, they are unhelpful when deciding to award or reject an injunction. The public interest should be a meaningful criterion, and there are tools that enable putting this criterion into practice. In this respect, the times when public interest considerations were considered rarely pivotal[228] or appeared 'difficult for the accused infringer to make use of the public interest prong'[229] are over.

This was certified in the *eBay* case. In its petition, eBay sustained that the Federal Circuit had erroneously replaced traditional principles of equity with a 'virtually irrebuttable presumption that permanent injunctions will issue absent the exceptional circumstance where injunctive relief would pose a harm to the public interest by endangering the public health'.[230] In its sentence, the Supreme Court made clear that there is no public interest presumption in favour of an injunction.[231] On the contrary, a key notion that accompanies that of the public interest is 'flexibility', which ultimately relates to the very same nature of injunctions as equitable remedies. In this sense, the Supreme Court has stated that 'flexibility rather than rigidity has distinguished [equity]. The qualities of mercy and practicality have made equity the instrument for nice adjustment and reconciliation between the public interest and private needs as well as between competing private claims'.[232]

If the 'public interest' occupies a central place, the very notion of 'public interest' also becomes central. There are, however, different views as to what the public interest entails in the context of intellectual property.[233] The public interest can be equated to the economic function that intellectual property rights are meant to play. Accordingly, the public interest would be a broad one, and that being one of enhancing welfare. A different but related perspective holds that the public interest coincides with the stimulus of innovation that patent law is meant to achieve.[234] Certainly, it may also well be that the public interest behind intellectual property is interpreted differently depending on whether innovators or consumers are asked or depending on whether wealthy or developing countries are the ones to respond. The problem with this approach is that the meaning of public interest changes depending on who answers to that question.

226 *See* Lewis (1993), p. 855. 227 *Ibid.*, p. 856. 228 *See* Foster (1986), p. 286.

229 *See* Metcalf (1987), p. 122. Similarly, Hailer (1981), pp. 1403–1404. Also discarding the relevance of the public interest criterion, *see* Armond (2003), p. 137.

230 *See* Petition for Writ of Certiorari, p. I; *eBay* case, p. 2.

231 *See* Iancu and Nichols (2007), p. 403.

232 *See Hecht Co. v. Bowles*, 321 U.S. (1944), pp. 329–330.

233 *See* UNCTAD – Stockholm Network – PIIPA (2007).

234 This has been also nicely captured by courts in the United States. In *Mazer v. Stein* it was held that '[t]he economic philosophy behind the clause empowering Congress to grant patents and copyrights is the conviction that encouragement of individual effort by personal gain is the best way to advance public welfare through the talents of authors and inventors in "Science and useful Arts"'. *See Mazer v. Stein*, 347 US 201 (1954), p. 219.

It is possible, however, to present a broader, more comprehensive view of what the public interest is and how it relates to the intellectual property system and the human being. Within a broader utilitarian approach, Christophe Geiger evokes three philosophical conceptions of the 'common interest'.[235] The first two approaches seem to be almost radically opposed. In the first case, the interest of the State is the common interest, an interest that is identified by the State and reflected into the law. In the second case, by contrast, the individual becomes central and the common interest is defined according to the particular interests of the individual. The third notion equates the common interest with the 'good of mankind'. In this case, the human being occupies the central space, whereas the role of society is 'to define a framework for human development and happiness, according to universal human values'.[236] The question that must to be posed is, naturally, which these universal values are and where their legal translation can be found.

Even if only in a loose sense, international human rights law can be understood as the codification of universal values, a sort of international ethics.[237] Human rights are indeed closely related to the notion of common interest that evokes the 'good of mankind'. Human rights law enshrines norms that synthesize value judgements that go beyond those found in the intellectual property regime[238] and establishes the limits of intellectual property rights protection. Certainly, intellectual property systems reflect 'a balancing of general public interests and private stake holder interests, and in this sense intellectual property rights take into account social welfare considerations as well as those of individual inventors and actors'.[239] However, human rights law goes indeed further since it gives legal expression to the objective of human well-being, and intellectual property protection must serve this objective. In this sense, human rights may inform the shaping and interpretation of the intellectual property system or, put differently, '[i]f we consider the IP system as a tool of public policy, human rights considerations may be helpful in defining the objectives of the policy'.[240]

Human rights are useful not only at identifying policy goals and their legal expression but also when taking judicial decisions in the context of intellectual property cases. In the case of interim injunctions, courts should take into consideration the specific circumstances of the case, the legal interests at stake and the broader prescriptions deriving from human rights law.

In this sense, in the past fifteen years there has been great development at the international level. The relationship between human rights and intellectual

[235] The concept of 'common interest' coincides, for our purposes, with that of the public interest.

[236] *See* Geiger (2015b), p. 8.

[237] *See* Adorno (2002), p. 959; Robinson (2002), pp. 3–4.

[238] Certainly, intellectual property is not exempted from these value judgements. For instance, the Preamble of the TRIPS Agreement recognizes 'the underlying public policy objectives of national systems for the protection of intellectual property, including developmental and technological objectives'.

[239] *See* Abbott (2006).

[240] *See* Wager and Watal (2015), p. 159.

property rights has been treated with great detail and nuance in international bodies, some constitutional courts and also academia.[241] Concepts like the 'core content' of human rights, and the treatment of the interaction of such core content with the protection of intellectual assets, can be of great interest when deciding cases relating to injunctions. There is little doubt, for instance, that adopting a human rights perspective, the public interest element weighs in favour of the defendant 'if it implicates a critical public health or safety interest, such as medical care or the environment'.[242]

In this last respect, the High Court of Delhi has ruled that the public interest in a particular medication must be taken into account when deciding whether to issue a preliminary injunction. The Court stated that 'unlike in cases involving infringement of other products, the Courts have to tread with care [when] pharmaceutical products and more specifically life saving drugs are involved. In such cases, the balancing would have to factor in unknowns such as the likelihood of injury to non-parties and the potentialities of risk of denial of remedies'.[243] As the Protocol 1 to the European Convention on Human Rights recognizes, States have the right to enforce and control the use of property in accordance with the general interest. This central tenet has been emphasized by the European Court of Human Rights, which has stated that 'because of their direct knowledge of their society and its needs, the national authorities are in principle better placed than the international judge to appreciate what is "in the public interest"'.[244]

V CONCLUSIONS

The international regulation of interim injunctions tends to be flexible and allows considerable margin of manoeuvre to States and national judges. Notable differences exist across national legal orders due to a number of factors, including States' different approaches as to the right balance between the protection of intellectual property rights, the public interest and fundamental rights. In practice, national courts still maintain extensive discretion as to whether issuing a preliminary injunction and in setting up the specific conditions for each awarded injunction. Similarly, States can decide whether their legislation sets forth more or less demanding conditions for the award of an interim injunction, for instance a high likelihood of infringement.

Article 50 of the TRIPS Agreement sets forth a flexible regime to determine the award of injunctive relief, which includes the conditions that enable judicial authorities to grant preliminary injunctions and the safeguards for the alleged infringer. Plurilateral and bilateral treaties have broadened the scope of provisional

241 For details and references, *see* Chapter 2. 242 *See* Armond (2003), p. 137.

243 *See F. Hoffmann-LA Roche AG v. Cipla Ltd.*, I.A 642/2008 IN CS (OS) 89/2008 (2008), para. 81.

244 *See* ECtHR, *James and Others v. The United Kingdom*, application no. 8793/79, 21 February 1986, Series A no. 98, para. 46.

measures and have also silenced relevant guarantees in favour of the alleged infringer. Other features observed in different areas of intellectual property enforcement, in particular transplantation of the law, are also evident in the context of interim injunctions.

A number of factors are widely assessed when deciding on the grant of an interim injunction. The likelihood of success on the merits of the case, which subsumes the analysis of the prospects as to the validity of the patent and whether an infringement will be found, is the most commonly recognized factor. Next, the harm that can be avoided or caused if the injunction is granted is also regularly taken into consideration. In this case, it is necessary to find a balance between the continuation of activities that in principle are legal and protection of the right holder from the acts that are potentially infringing. This factor is ultimately related to the balance of convenience, which courts generally perform. Moreover, in the case of the United States, a traditional and recently revitalized factor is that relating to the public interest.

Both the procedure and the consequences of issuing preliminary injunctions are in direct connection with a range of fundamental rights. As for the procedure, the right to be heard is a central element of the right to a fair trial and a condition for the guarantee of due process-related entitlements. The right to be heard is recognized in Article 50 of the TRIPS Agreement and may be particularly threatened in the context of *inaudita altera parte* measures. In the case of patents, the consequences of awarding an interim injunction can be decisive for the provision of vital products, such as medicines, impacting hence on a number of fundamental rights different from the right to be heard, notably on the right to health.

There are similarities between the assessment of the impact on the public interest of the grant of an interim injunction and the public policy pros and cons of the intellectual property system. Before the *eBay* case, the prevailing line of thinking associated the public interest with the actual award of injunctions to prevent or impede the continuation of the infringement. However, in the *eBay* case the Supreme Court of the United States made clear that there is no public interest presumption in favour of an injunction.[245] On the contrary, a key notion that accompanies that of the public interest is 'flexibility'. The public interest is closely connected to human rights entitlements. In a broad sense, international human rights law can be understood as the codification of universal values and the notion of common interest. Human rights are useful not only at identifying policy goals and their legal expression but also when taking judicial decisions in the context of intellectual property cases.

[245] *See* Iancu and Nichols (2007), p. 403.

9

The Award of Damages

I INTRODUCTION

The law on damages in case of intellectual property infringement derives from the general law on damages.[1] The latter has evolved to include consequences arising from both pecuniary and non-pecuniary loss.[2] These consequences will vary depending on the type of intellectual property infringed, the intent or negligence of the infringer and, among other factors, the scale of the infringement. The regulation of damages is still in its infancy in international intellectual property law. However, even if international treaties have only recently started to include articles on damages, the characteristics and consequences of these provisions are of the utmost interest.

In their quest to improve the enforcement of intellectual property rights, states have agreed upon provisions aimed at compensating the right holder and, in some cases, punishing the infringer and discouraging him and others from committing further infringements. The boundaries between compensation, punishment and deterrence are, however, frequently vague. In this respect, the regulation of damages illustrates some of the main difficulties arising from the process of global harmonization of legal standards concerning intellectual property enforcement. The limits of legal harmonization, on the one hand, and the potential clash between some forms of regulation of intellectual property remedies and fundamental rights, on the other hand, become apparent in the area of damages.

Some of the difficulties arise from legal transplantation, one of the techniques used to foster harmonization. States willing to export their own intellectual property standards on damages do so in an uncoordinated and sometimes contradictory

[1] *See* Ross (2005), para. 1.01.

[2] While 'damages' is the term used to allude to the consequences of pecuniary nature arising from intellectual property infringement, other pecuniary consequences also result from the decision on costs.

manner, in particular through trade agreements and technical cooperation. This may put norm-importing states in the situation of creatively interpreting the treaties or deciding which international treaty to infringe, since some treaties contain inconsistent obligations when compared to other treaties. Problems arising from the clash between treaty provisions and constitutional mandates may also create tensions from the point of view of either constitutional law or international law, since states may be forced to disobey basic principles of civil law, in particular when compensation is accompanied by punishment.

The regime on damages exported by the United States in a number of trade agreements requires the adoption of statutory punitive damages for intellectual property infringement, at least in cases of copyright infringement and trademark counterfeiting. For countries of continental law tradition this is a novelty with relevant implications. Although civil procedures have occasionally been used to fulfil objectives that go beyond compensation, the stated objective of such procedures is to compensate the right holder. Constitutional principles related to due process and fair trial may also be compromised in civil law countries importing regimes on punitive damages. Moreover, some countries have adopted both treaties that enshrine punitive damages and other treaties enshrining a compensatory regime on damages. Although the latter does not expressly prohibit punitive damages, it is only through adopting (most likely inconsistent) statutes that both regimes can be implemented simultaneously.

II TAXONOMY OF DAMAGES

Whenever an infringing act, harm and a causal link between both exist, the award of damages may be justified.[3] Different classes of damages have been implemented in response to intellectual property infringement. Although the specific nature and content of each award may vary across jurisdictions, a common terminology can be proposed. The resulting categories or types of damages can be grouped depending on whether they fulfil compensatory or punitive functions. In a number of cases, the same remedy may fulfil both functions and may also pursue deterrent objectives. For this reason, the taxonomy proposed is contentious and some terms may have different uses in different jurisdictions. Nevertheless, this terminology may shed light into an area characterized by heterogeneity across national legal orders and by the existence of sometimes fuzzy lines between compensatory and punitive damages.

[3] In relation to the casual link, damages will be those directly caused or naturally resulting from the tort. However, showing a causal link between the infringement and the loss may be not enough. The intent of the infringer may be decisive, and differences exist depending on the intellectual property category. For copyright cases, *see* Bainbridge (2012), p. 192, quoting the copyright cases *Claydon Architectural Meatlwork Ltd v. DJ Higgins and Sons*, (1997) FSR 475, and *Cambridge Water Co v. Eastern Counties Leather plc.*, (1994) 2 AC 224.

1 *Damages as Compensation*

In order to award compensatory damages all appropriate aspects must be taken into account, in particular the negative economic consequences deriving from the infringement. The latter may include lost profits suffered by the right holder, unfair profits made by the infringer, moral damage inflicted to the right holder and expenses incurred as the result of the dispute and which are different from court costs. In some legal orders courts may set the compensatory damages as a lump sum on the basis of elements such as the amount of the royalties or fees that would have been due if the infringer had requested authorization to use the intellectual property right in question. In general, when estimating damages from a compensatory point of view, lost profits cannot be added to unfair benefits made by the infringer.

1.1 Lost Profits

The objective of the award of damages is to put the right holder in the situation that would have existed if the infringement had not been committed. This has been customarily recognized by statutes[4] and courts,[5] including common law countries, where 'actual' or 'compensatory' damages fulfil this function. In response to this compensatory objective, 'the measure of damages is to be, so far as possible, that sum of money which will put the injured party in the same position as he would have been if he had not sustained the wrong'.[6] This sum of money will include the profits lost by the right holder, which form part of the negative economic consequences integrating the actual prejudice or injury suffered by the right holder.

A condition for the award of lost profits is the existence of intent or negligence on the part of the infringer. Article 45 of the TRIPS Agreement alludes to the intentionality of the infringement and bases the award of compensatory damages on the intent of the infringer. More precisely, it establishes that damages 'adequate to compensate for the injury' must be paid by the infringer who knowingly, or with reasonable grounds to know, engaged in infringing activity. Although exempting innocent infringers from paying for the harm actually inflicted is common practice, this

4 *See* Recital 26 of the Directive 2004/48/EC of the European Parliament and of the Council of 29 April 2004 on the enforcement of intellectual property rights, OJEU L157 of 30 April 2004 (hereinafter EU Enforcement Directive). The Restatement (Second) of Torts, of 1979, § 903. Title 35 USC, § 284 states, '[u]pon finding for the claimant the court shall award the claimant damages adequate to compensate for the infringement . . . '.

5 As the Supreme Court of the United States affirmed in a case concerning patents, the question that has to be posed when setting damages is 'Had the act of infringement not occurred, what would the financial position of the patentee have been?' *See Aro Manufacturing. Co. v. Convertible Top Replacement Co.*, 377 US 476, 507 (1964). In a similar sense, *see Yale Lock Manufacturing Co. v. Sargent*, 117 US 536, 552 (1886).

6 *See Retail Systems Technology Ltd v. McGuire*, [2008] 1 IR 541; in the United States, *see General Tire & Rubber Co. v. Firestone Tyre & Rubber Co Ltd.*, 12 (1975) 1 RPC 203.

may be 'without prejudice to any other remedy'.[7] Hence, while lost profits may not be awarded in case of innocent infringement, unfair profits or compensation plus legal expenses may still be awarded.[8]

Intent and negligence need, however, further elucidation. For instance, in case of infringement, the previous knowledge of the existence of an intellectual property right does not necessarily amount to intent. The case of patents is worth telling. Whereas liability may arise from the manufacturing or importation of a patented invention or use of a patented process, infringing activities such as sale or offer for sale may require additional information. With respect to these infringing activities and in order to award damages, national patent statutes may require notice to the alleged infringer about the existence of the patent, the infringement and a request to cease the infringement.[9] Similarly, in the case of trademarks, damages may only be awarded if the infringer has received sufficient warning from the trademark owner.[10]

1.2 Unfair Profits

Obliging the infringer to pay unfair profits obtained as a result of the infringement instead of actual damages may be more appropriate in several situations. This is, for instance, the case when it is not possible to prove the prevailing party loss or when the benefits of the infringer are higher than the actual damage inflicted to the right holder. In the latter situation and in order to avoid unjust enrichment, it may be fairer to base the award on the account of profits made by the infringer. Similarly, given that lost profits may not be granted in case of innocent infringement, account of unfair profits may be an appropriate method to compensate the right holder.[11]

With regard to intent of the infringer and the award of unfair profits, practice across jurisdictions varies. In some legal orders account of unfair profits obtained by the infringer is limited to cases of wilful or negligent infringement, while in others

7 *See* for instance Article 97.1 of the United Kingdom's Copyright, Designs and Patents Act, of 1988, Chapter 48, and Section 128 (2) of the Irish Copyright and Related Rights Act, of 2000.

8 This is regularly recognized in intellectual property statutes. For instance, in the case of patents, pursuant to Article 68(4) of the Agreement on a Unified Patent Court, 'where the infringer did not knowingly, or with reasonable grounds to know, engage in the infringing activity, the Court may order the recovery of profits or the payment of compensation.' An example in the area of copyright is Article 121(1) of the New Zealand Copyright Act, stating that '[w]here, in proceedings for infringement of copyright, it is proved or admitted that at the time of the infringement the defendant did not know, and had no reason to believe, that copyright existed in the work to which the proceedings relate, the plaintiff is not entitled to damages but, without prejudice to the award of any other remedy, is entitled to an account of profits.'.

9 *See* Article 64.2 Spanish Patent Law, Law N°. 11/1986 of 20 March 1986.

10 *See* Article 42(2) of the Law No. 17/2001 on Trademarks (as amended), 7 December 2001 (hereinafter Spanish Trademark Law, of 2001).

11 *See* Article 97.1 of the United Kingdom's Copyright, Designs and Patents Act, of 1988, Chapter 48: Copyright, Designs and Patents Act, Chapter 48, 15 November 1988 (hereinafter United Kingdom's Copyright, Designs and Patents Act, of 1988), Chapter 48, and Section 128 (2) the Copyright and Related Rights Act, No. 28, 10 July 2000 (hereinafter Irish Copyright and Related Rights Act, of 2000).

this remedy has been tailored to address innocent infringements as well. The TRIPS Agreement recognizes this duality. On the one hand, it identifies lost profits among the appropriate aspects that shall be taken into account when setting the damages in case of negligent or wilful infringement. On the other hand, it also establishes that, in appropriate cases, judicial authorities may order recovery of profits even where the infringer did not knowingly, or with reasonable grounds to know, engage in infringing activity.

The difficulty to lay down a clear divide between compensatory and punitive damages becomes clear in the case of unfair profits. Both continental law and common law regimes allow the expropriation of the benefits obtained by the infringer. Certainly, in this case the measure may exceed the merely compensatory function and be, in fact, supracompensatory. When this happens, it needs to be elucidated whether the payment of unfair profits is not only supracompensatory but also punitive. In the same context, and also to avoid supracompensation and punition, lost profits cannot be added to unfair benefits made by the infringer. Such an addition would go far beyond compensation, amount to unjust enrichment, probably contradict the principle of proportionality and eventually result in punitive damages.[12]

1.3 Moral Damage

The prejudice suffered by the right holder as a result of the infringement may be of economic and non-economic nature. This is why moral damages may be paid to the right holder to compensate 'in full for the "actual prejudice suffered" by him, which also includes any moral prejudice'.[13]

Moral prejudice is closely related to rights connected with the personality of the individual. For instance, a performer shall have the right to respect for his name, his capacity and his performance, which is an inalienable and imprescriptible right attached to his person.[14] Thus, moral prejudice is relatively easy to recognize in case of copyright infringement suffered by individuals. With respect to other categories of intellectual property, such as patents or trademarks, and with respect to damages suffered by legal persons, the situation is different. In the case of trademarks, infringement may certainly produce adverse effects on the reputation of a trademark, provoke loss of goodwill or induce market confusion. These effects are, however, of patrimonial nature and should not be treated as moral damages. In the case of patents, in the rare event it was proven that the infringement damaged the perception of the public

[12] Some courts, however, may take a different stance. Article 68.2 of the Agreement on the Unified Patent Court would seem to favour at least recovering unfair profits that go beyond lost profits. It states that '[t]he infringer shall not benefit from the infringement. However, damages shall not be punitive.'

[13] CJEU, Case C-99/15, *Christian Liffers v Producciones Mandarina, S.L. and Mediaset España Comunicación, S.A*, 17 March 2016.

[14] Article L212-2 of the French Intellectual Property Code.

towards the patented invention, the prejudice could be compensated. However, such a compensation would not be based on the 'moral' damage caused. Instead, the mandate to compensate all relevant aspects, including non-economic consequences, would seem the relevant basis for compensation.

There is no equivalence between moral prejudice and non-economic damage. That is to say, not all damages of non-economic nature are moral damages. Certainly, non-economic damages may also be compensated, but not through the concept of moral prejudice. Additionally, in some occasions not even the infringer will be the responsible of non-pecuniary damages. Take for instance the distress caused by protracted length of proceedings. The European Court of Human Rights has recognized, in the context of copyright litigation, that such a delay must be compensated. However, in this case compensation for lengthy proceedings does not result from the infringement, and both the infringer and the right holder could eventually be entitled to it.[15]

1.4 Aggravated Damages

Aggravated damages compensate the plaintiff for added hurt, distress or insult caused to the right holder by the manner in which the defendant committed the wrong.[16] A broader view holds that they respond to 'an injury to the victim's moral dignity that results from the defendant's denial that the victim is entitled to respect as a moral person'.[17] The focus on the distress caused to the plaintiff is a distinctive feature, intended to compensate the right holder for damages caused by injured feelings.

Although aggravated damages are compensatory,[18] several characteristics may put into question their actual nature. In effect, aggravated damages respond to exceptionally heinous or malicious conduct, which could also have given rise to exemplary damages.[19] Indeed, some have considered aggravated damages a subset of exemplary damages, eventually resulting in significant economic award. Some sustain that aggravated damages are punitive,[20] while leading cases have recognized that the incidental punitive and exemplary effect of aggravated damages may confuse this award with exemplary damages.[21] For some, the nature of aggravated

15 In *Nemec and Others v. Slovakia* the European Court of Human Rights accepted that 'the applicants suffered damage of a non-pecuniary nature, such as distress resulting from the protracted length of the proceedings in their case'. *See* ECtHR, *Nemec v. Slovakia*, no. 48672/99, 15 November 2001, unreported, para. 46.

16 *See* Irish Law Reform Commission (2000), p. 86.

17 *See* Beever (2003), p. 89.

18 In the United Kingdom, *see Rookes v. Barnard*, [1964] 1 All ER 367 (hereinafter *Rookes v. Barnard*). In Ireland, *see Conway v. Irish National Teacher's Organisation*, [1991] 2 IR 305 (hereinafter *Conway v. Irish National Teacher's Organisation*).

19 For exemplary damages, *see* Section 9.2.

20 *See* Ripstein (1999), p. 151; Cane (1997), p. 114; English Law Commission (1997), para. 1.17, p. 17.

21 It has been stated that '[i]t must at present be very difficult for a jury to understand the distinction between aggravated and exemplary damages when there is such a substantial overlap between the

damages 'is something of a compensatory-exemplary hybrid',[22] a view supported by decisions that have linked aggravated damages to 'the cavalier or outrageous conduct of the defendant'.[23] Indeed, 'this direct reliance on the culpability of the defendant as a ground for the assessment of the award is out of character with compensatory awards in general, and therefore suggests a conception of aggravated awards as a compensatory-exemplary hybrid'.[24]

While recognizing the intense relationship and potential overlap between aggravated and exemplary damages, the differentiation is still justified. Aggravated damages are compensatory, since they are assessed with reference to what is necessary to compensate losses suffered by plaintiffs and not 'with reference to what is necessary to punish a defendant for his or her conduct'.[25] Additionally, in many legal orders aggravated damages are allowed, while punitive damages are not. In those legal orders that recognize both aggravated and exemplary damages, maintaining the difference allows responding to infringement in a different but complementary way. In these cases, exemplary damages are awarded only after aggravated damages and take into account the eventual punitive component of the latter.[26]

2 *Punitive Damages and Related Categories*

Some legal orders award damages over and above full compensation for the injury inflicted to the right holder. This is particularly the case of common law countries, where 'exemplary' damages and the related categories of 'additional' and 'punitive and deterrent pre-established damages' are awarded. There is, however, considerable heterogeneity across national legal orders as to the terminology (expressions such as 'vindictive' and 'substantial' damages can be added to the terms already mentioned), the intellectual property categories covered and the content or scope of punitive damages.

Exemplary damages have been traditionally granted in common law jurisdictions in cases of tort and breach of constitutional rights.[27] Non-compensatory categories of damages pursue punishment and deterrence in the context of civil procedures.[28] These have been conceived 'to punish the wrongdoer for his outrageous conduct, to deter him and others from such conduct in the future, and to mark the court's detestation and disapproval of conduct'.[29]

factors which provide the sole justification for both awards'. *See Thompson v. Commissioner of Police*, [1997] 2 All ER 762.

22 *See* Charleton and Kelly (2012), p. 21.

23 *See Conway v. Irish National Teacher's Organisation*, p. 503.

24 *Ibid.*

25 English Law Commission (1997), para. 1.40, p. 26.

26 *See Rookes v Barnard*, para. 2.024.

27 This is the case of Ireland, Canada, Australia, the United Kingdom, New Zealand and United States.

28 *See* Polinsky and Shavell (2000), p. 764. For a historical account, *see* Mesulam (2004), p. 1114; Colby (2003), p. 614.

29 *See Conway v. Irish National Teacher's Organisation*, p. 509.

With regard to punishment, punitive damages are awarded in situations where the conduct of the defendant is particularly malicious or oppressive[30] or 'because of the defendant's evil motive or his reckless indifference to the rights of others'.[31] In these cases, it is understood that awarding only compensation falls short of adequately responding to the infringement and that there is a need to express judicial disapproval or outrage for such a conduct.[32]

Punitive damages also fulfil a deterrent function. They serve both specific and general prevention goals, since they may discourage the infringer from repeating the wrong while also issuing a 'warning to others who are inclined to commit similar wrongs'.[33] In some countries, in fact, deterrence is the sole objective of the award of punitive damages.[34] Words may certainly become tricky and lines blurred, since compensatory damages may also deter potential infringers.

Punitive damages are awarded with respect to different categories of intellectual property rights. In principle, punitive damages are regarded as a remedy of an exceptional nature.[35] As such, they have been awarded, for instance, in patent cases when the defendant 'deliberately, flagrantly and callously' disregarded an interlocutory injunction[36] or in copyright cases where 'the defendant demonstrated an exceptional degree of arrogance'[37] or a 'cynical disregard'[38] of the defendant's rights. Two types of awards – additional damages and statutory damages – share some of the characteristics of exemplary damages while maintaining an independent nature.

2.1 Additional Damages

In some jurisdictions judges may award 'additional' damages in response to violations of specific categories of intellectual property rights.[39] This will happen when the infringement is particularly serious in light of the intentionality of the infringer,

30 *See* Supreme Court of Canada, *Hill v. Church of Scientology*, [1995] 2 SCR 1130 (SCC).

31 Restatement (Second) of Torts, of 1979, § 908(2).

32 *See* Supreme Court of Canada, *Whiten v. Pilot Insurance Co.*, [2002] SCC 18 (hereinafter *Whiten v. Pilot Insurance Co.*).

33 *See* Morris (1931), p. 1174. In a similar sense, punitive damages are awarded 'for the purpose of punishing the defendant, of teaching him no to do again, and of deterring others form following his example'. *See* Prosser (1971), p. 9.

34 A number of statutes establish that deterrence is the sole objective of exemplary damages. In Canada, Article 1621 of the Civil Code of Quebec, SQ 1991, c 64, 18 December 1991 (hereinafter Quebec Civil Code, of 1991), states that '[w]here the awarding of punitive damages is provided for by law, the amount of such damages may not exceed what is sufficient to fulfil their preventive purpose'.

35 The Supreme Court of Canada, in *Whiten v. Pilot Insurance Co.*, has recalled that the main vehicle of punishment is criminal law, while punitive damages should be resorted to only in exceptional cases. Some authors allude to them even as an 'anomaly'. *See* Charleton and Kelly (2012), p. 20.

36 *See* for case law in Canada, *Apotex Inc. v. Merck & Co.*, [2002] 19 CPR (4th) 460 (FCTD).

37 *See* for jurisprudence in Canada, *Pro Arts Inc. v. Campus Crafts Holdings Ltd.*, [1980] 50 CPR (2nd) 230 (Ontario SC).

38 *See* in Canada, *Prism Hospital Software Inc. v. Hospital Medical Records Institute*, [1994] 57 CPR (3rd) 129 (BCSC).

39 In the United Kingdom, in the cases of copyright and related rights, and the United Kingdom's unregistered design right. In Australia, in the cases of copyright and patents.

who has acted deceitfully or scandalously.[40] In some legal orders the criteria that allow the award of additional damages are in fact broader.[41] Although additional damages resemble exemplary damages, they are different and are awarded as a result of a specific statutory provision.[42]

The punitive nature of additional damages has been contested.[43] However, several factors favour studying additional damages in the context of punitive damages. The intentionality of the infringer becomes central, since such damages are awarded in light of circumstances such as the flagrancy of the infringer's conduct both before and after the infringement and the benefit accruing to the defendant by reason of the infringement.[44] For instance, the uncooperative behaviour of the infringer in proceedings has also been used as criterion to award additional damages.[45] Like exemplary damages, additional damages pursue in some cases deterrence.[46] Moreover, they are only granted after a compensatory award has been set.[47]

2.2 Statutory Damages

Damages may be also set by statute. Statutory damages were originally developed in light of the factual and evidentiary difficulties that the calculation of the loss suffered or the discovery of unfair profits may entail.[48] A good example of the potential

40 *See* Bainbridge (2012), p. 193.

41 According to the Australian Copyright Act, No. 63 of 1968, 27 June 1968 (hereinafter Australian Copyright Act, of 1968), Section 115, '[w]here, in an action under this section: (a) an infringement of copyright is established; and (b) the court is satisfied that it is proper to do so, having regard to: (i) the flagrancy of the infringement; and (ia) the need to deter similar infringements of copyright; and (ib) the conduct of the defendant after the act constituting the infringement or, if relevant, after the defendant was informed that the defendant had allegedly infringed the plaintiff's copyright; and (ii) whether the infringement involved the conversion of a work or other subject-matter from hardcopy or analog form into a digital or other electronic machine-readable form; and (iii) any benefit shown to have accrued to the defendant by reason of the infringement; and (iv) all other relevant matters; the court may, in assessing damages for the infringement, award such additional damages as it considers appropriate in the circumstances'.

42 Moreover, 'unlike exemplary damages, a claim for additional damages can be added in after pleadings'. *See* Bainbridge (2002), p. 194.

43 Bainbridge affirms that 'technically they are not punitive, although they may have a punitive element about them'. *See* Bainbridge (2002), p. 193.

44 *See* Article 97.2 of the United Kingdom's Copyright, Designs and Patents Act, of 1988; Article 122 (1) (A) of the Australian Patents Act, of 1990.

45 *See* Federal Circuit Court of Australia, *Tylor v. Sevin*, [2014] FCCA 445. 46 *Ibid.*

47 The court's power to award additional damages is restricted to cases in which it has already assessed damages for the infringement. *See Redrow Homes Limited and Others v. Bett Brothers Plc and Others (Scotland)*, [1997] FSR 828. Affirmed, House of Lords, [1998] FSR 345.

48 The objective of statutory damages is 'to give the owner of a copyright some recompense for injury done him, in a case where the rules of law render difficult or impossible proof of damages or discovery of profits. In this respect the old law was unsatisfactory. In many cases plaintiffs, though proving infringement, were able to recover only nominal damages, in spite of the fact that preparation and

difficulties concerns copyright infringement in the digital domain. In this case, proving the loss may be complex since it is often difficult or just not possible to assess the volume of the infringement, for instance the total number of illicit downloads of copyright protected works. In order to address this situation, statutory damages establish a range within which the amount of the damage can be set.[49] Importantly, when fixing the award, it is not necessary to prove any harm or any benefit arising from the infringement.

The classification of statutory damages among punitive remedies is not devoid of problems. Certainly, statutory damages may pursue compensatory goals, even if the technique chosen does not exactly estimate the actual damage caused. Instead, for the sake of the efficiency of the system, a fix rate is established. A line of thought holds that it is the actual implementation of statutory damages what may give them their punitive nature but not their existence *per se*. In fact, it is up to states to set the rates and eventual caps for pre-established damages. Certainly, in some cases the rate established in the context of statutory damages may seem low.[50]

Some legal orders have straightforwardly linked statutory damages to other goals, most particularly punishment and deterrence. Statutory damages may indeed be awarded with the intention to punish outrageous conduct, to serve as a deterrent that discourages the infringer from behaving in the same way in the future or to act as a general deterrent both for those placed in a similar situation and for the public at large.[51] In these cases, statutory damages will be awarded instead of the compensation for actual loss or recovery of profits, and its amount will at least cover the sum that would have been due if any of the two awards had been chosen.

Compensation, punishment and deterrence may be thus combined in a sole remedy. However, statutory damages are far from being harmonized globally. While in some countries they encompass the three functions, the passage of the time seems to have consolidated punishment as the primary goal at the expense of compensation and

trial of the case imposed substantial expense and inconvenience.' *See Douglas v. Cunningham* 294, US 207 (1935). This may happen with respect to several categories of intellectual property rights. In the United States, statutory damages have been codified for cases of copyright and trademark infringement. *See* Public Law 104-153, 110 Stat. 1386, 2 July 1996 (hereinafter Anticounterfeiting Consumer Protection Act, of 1996); Digital Theft Deterrence and Copyright Damages Improvement Act, of 1999: Public Law 106-160, 113 Stat. 1774, 9 December 1999 (hereinafter Digital Theft Deterrence and Copyright Damages Improvement Act, of 1999); Public Law 105–304, 112 Stat. 2860, 28 October 1998 (hereinafter Digital Millennium Copyright Act, of 1998).

49 In the case of copyright, it implies the imposition of an amount to be determined by the judge in a range between $750 USD and $30.000 USD per infringed work, and up to $150.000 USD if the infringement is wilful. *See* Title 17 USC § 504 (c) (1) Digital Theft Deterrence and Copyright Damages Improvement Act, of 1999. In the digital domain, statutory damages have also been developed for cases of circumvention of copyright protection measures and for acts intended to alter rights management information.

50 Article 43.5 of the Spanish Trademark Law, of 2001, for instance, establishes as compensation for damage 1 per cent of the turnover of the infringing party resulting from the goods or services bearing the trademark unlawfully.

51 *See* Samuelson *et al.* (2013), pp. 546–547.

deterrence in those countries. By contrast, other legal orders specifically state that statutory damages can only pursue compensation.[52] The situation is clearer in those jurisdictions where statutory damages are awarded only in response to innocent infringements. In this case, their intended function is compensation in situations where it would be difficult to estimate either the actual loss experienced by the right holder or the undue profit reaped by the infringer.

Although statutory punitive damages are an ancient institution in the United States,[53] they are still an uncommon remedy in comparative law. Only 24 out of 117 Member States of the World Intellectual Property Organization allow recovery of statutory damages for copyright infringement.[54] This situation may, however, change, particularly in light of the trade agreements promoted by the United States, which are made in the image of the United States legislation as regards damages awards.[55]

3 *Expenses or Legal Costs*

The cost decision shall cover costs incurred in the proceedings. These include costs for simultaneous interpretation, witnesses, court experts, experiments ordered by the court and, among others, letters rogatory. The cost decision shall also include the costs of the successful party, including court fees paid by that party. With respect to fees, a combination of fixed fees and value-based fees may be implemented, whereby a value-based fee may be added to the fixed fee for actions that exceed a certain value.[56]

Practice across jurisdictions is fairly even with regard to the payment of expenses resulting from the dispute, including attorney's fees. While the large majority of countries usually oblige the losing party to pay some or all legal expenses, only in a limited number of nations each party pays its own expenses.[57] In the first group are the Members of the European Union that, by virtue of Article 14 of the Enforcement Directive, must ensure that reasonable and proportionate legal costs and other expenses shall, as a general rule, be borne by the unsuccessful party. In the United States the Supreme Court rejected in 2014 the Federal Circuit's standard for fee-shifting in patent cases under the Patent Act,[58] signalling 'a new era in the granting of

52 Samuelson *et al.* (2013) enumerate the cases of Morocco, Bahrain and Ukraine.

53 The Statute of Monopolies, of 1624, allowed recovery of 'three times so much as the damages' in patent cases.

54 These countries are Azerbaijan, Bahamas, Bahrain, Belarus, Bulgaria, Canada, China, Costa Rica, Dominican Republic, Israel, Kazakhstan, Kyrgyzstan, Liberia, Lithuania, Malaysia, Morocco, Republic of Korea, Republic of Moldova, Russian Federation, Singapore, Sri Lanka, Ukraine, United States and Vietnam. *See* Samuelson *et al.* (2013).

55 *See* Section III.2.1.

56 *See* Preparatory Committee for the Unified Patent Court, Rules on Court fees and recoverable costs, 25 February 2016. Available at www.unified-patent-court.org/news/upc-court-fees-and-recoverable-costs (accessed April 2006)

57 Rowe (1982), p. 651.

58 Octane Fitness, LLC v. ICON Health & Fitness, Inc., 134 S. Ct. 1749 (2014)

attorneys' fees in patent litigation'[59] where district courts have greater discretion in shifting attorneys' fees.

Legal costs cannot be subsumed into damages. Their origin, nature and purpose are different. Even if some international agreements address damages and legal costs in the same article, under the heading of 'damages',[60] legal costs are ancillary remedies of a different nature and are decided independently. In fact, some legal orders have set up a separate procedure for cost decision.[61]

III THE INTERNATIONAL LEGAL FRAMEWORK ON DAMAGES

1 *The Award of Damages in the TRIPS Agreement*

The first norm ever adopted in a multilateral treaty dealing with damages in case of intellectual property infringement was Article 45 of the TRIPS Agreement. This provision enacts the obligation to grant compensatory damages in case of wilful infringement and also enables parties to order the recovery of profits and to set up a system of pre-established damages, even in cases of innocent infringement.

Article 45 of the TRIPS Agreement is divided in two sections. The customary practice of awarding damages adequate to compensate for the injury suffered by the right holder is recognized in the first section. As is usual in the majority of legal orders, injuries must have been caused by an infringer who knew or had reasonable grounds to know that an infringement was committed. The WTO Member States are thus obliged to empower their judicial authorities to award compensatory damages in case of wilful infringement, but they may exempt innocent infringers from payment of compensation.[62]

The second section of Article 45 of the TRIPS Agreement addresses the potential payment of expenses, unfair profits and pre-established damages. With regard to expenses, the TRIPS Agreement obliges parties to allow judicial authorities to order the payment of expenses and specifically states that this may include 'appropriate' attorney's fees.[63] While it is up to the judges to finally decide the award of legal expenses and to decide what 'appropriate' means, States have the obligation to empower judges to do so. On the contrary, the other two elements addressed in this provision – recovery of profits and pre-established damages – are discretional.

[59] Jiam (2015), p. 612. [60] *See* Article 45.2 of the TRIPS Agreement.

[61] In the case of the Unified Patent Court, 'a cost decision may be the subject of separate proceedings following a decision on the merits and, if applicable, a decision for the determination of damages.' *See* Rules 150-157 of the Rules of Procedure of the Unified Paten Court, 18th draft of 19 October 2015.

[62] UNCTAD-ICTSD (2005), p. 593.

[63] The drafters of the TRIPS Agreement had due regard to the diverging practice existing in this area. Attorneys' expenses need not to be recognized, in line with what happens in some jurisdictions. *See* UNCTAD-ICTSD (2005), p. 593. *See* also Section 1.4.

In effect, the second part of Article 45.2 of the TRIPS Agreement is no longer constructed in mandatory terms. It *allows* States to empower judges to order the recovery of profits and/or pre-established damages. This flexibility leaves many options open. Significantly, the TRIPS Agreement does not allude to punitive or deterrent goals of the award of damages. Thus, although not formally excluded, in the TRIPS Agreement damages are not conceived from a punitive standpoint.

Article 45.2 of the Agreement recognizes in fact the diversity existing within this area. Pursuant to this article, recovery of profits and pre-established damages may or may not be awarded, separately or together, and this can happen in the case of both wilful and innocent infringements.[64] Indeed, the TRIPS Agreement only states that the recovery of profits and pre-established damages may be awarded 'even where the infringer did not knowingly, or with reasonable grounds to know, engage in infringing activity', which in fact means that they may be awarded both when the infringer knew and when the infringer was not aware about the infringement.

In light of this openness, other factors become decisive. Local legal traditions by and large favour compensation over punishment, and generally stand against the use of civil remedies to punish intellectual property infringement. Moreover, reflections made in this chapter[65] and in Chapter 2 regarding the principle of proportionality and several components of the right to a fair trial become as well of relevance in regard to punitive damages, and favour the purely compensatory approach. From a different perspective, the chilling effect mentioned in Chapter 3 must also be taken into consideration. Punitive damages may impact on legitimate activities, which may be just abandoned in fear of the consequences. Hence, both local trade and international trade may be ultimately restricted as a result of the potential award of punitive damages.

2 *Preferential Trade Agreements and the Award of Damages*

2.1 Preferential Trade Agreements Negotiated by the United States

Trade agreements negotiated by the United States introduce new obligations and impact upon the nature of the infringement resulting in the award of damages, the consequences of the infringement and the method to estimate the amount of damages. The template is similar in all the agreements and exports the vision of the United States according to which 'civil proceedings may advance punitive as well as remedial goals, and, conversely, that both punitive and remedial goals may be served by criminal penalties'.[66] Like the TRIPS Agreement, United States PTAs recognize the compensatory nature of the award of damages, and all the agreements state that the infringer

64 Importantly, Article 45 of the TRIPS Agreement does not mandate innocent infringers to compensate damages, although Article 37.1 of the agreement obliges *bona fide* acquirer of infringing integrated circuits to compensate the right holder with a sum equivalent to the royalty that would have been paid.

65 *See* Section IV.2.

66 *See Kennedy v. Mendoza-Martinez*, 372 US 144 (1963); *US v. Halper* 109 S Ct. 1892 (1989).

has to pay damages to compensate for the injury caused as a result of the infringement.[67] However, in several respects the similarities with the TRIPS Agreement end here.

All but one trade agreement concluded by the United States oblige its trading partners to take into account the profits of the infringer that were not considered in computing the amount of the compensatory damages.[68] That is, at least in cases of trademark and copyright infringement, right holders are entitled to damages adequate to compensate for the injury as well as profits made by the infringer and not taken into account when computing the actual damages. As abovementioned, the addition of lost profits and unfair benefits is not only supracompensatory but may be punitive as well, hence hardly acceptable in numerous countries.

It is also noticeable that trade agreements subscribed by the United States limit the flexibility concerning the method to determine the amount of damages. In this respect, the TRIPS Agreement just states that damages need to be 'adequate' to compensate for the injury caused. In contrast, United States treaties identify the value of the infringing good or service that must be taken into consideration to determine the final award. In this sense, they establish that in determining the amount of damages, the judicial authorities 'shall consider, *inter alia*, the value of the infringed-on good or service, according to the suggested retail price or other legitimate measure of value submitted by the right holder'.[69] In the case of patents, in line with the United States Patent Act of 1952, one of the PTAs includes a footnote establishing that 'damages adequate to compensate for the infringement shall not be less than a reasonable royalty'.[70]

67 *See* Article 16.11.8 (a) (i) US-Colombia FTA and EIA (2012); Article 16.11.8 (a) (i) US-Peru FTA and EIA (2009); Article 15.9.7 (a) (i) CAFTA-DR-US FTA and EIA (2006); Article 18.10.5 (a) (i) Republic of Korea-US FTA and EIA (2012); Article 17.11.6 (a) (i) US-Australia FTA and EIA (2005); Article 16.10.8 US-Singapore FTA and EIA (2004); Article 17.11.8 (a) (i) US-Chile FTA and EIA (2004); Article 4.24 US-Jordan FTA and EIA (2001); Article 15.11.6 (a) (i) US-Morocco FTA and EIA (2006); Article 15.11.7 (a) (i) US-Panama FTA and EIA (2012); Article 15.10.6 (a) (i) US-Oman FTA and EIA (2009).

68 *See* Article 16.11.7 (a) (ii) US-Colombia FTA and EIA (2012); Article 16.11.7 (a) (ii) US-Peru FTA and EIA (2009); Article 15.9.7 (a) (ii) CAFTA-DR-US FTA and EIA (2006); Article 17.11.6 (a) (ii) US-Australia FTA and EIA (2005); Article16.9.5 (b) and 19.9.8 US-Singapore FTA and EIA (2004); Article 17.11.8 (a) (ii) US-Chile FTA and EIA (2004); Article 4.24 US-Jordan FTA and EIA (2001); Article 15.11.6 (a) (ii) US-Morocco FTA and EIA (2006); Article 15.11.7 (a) (ii) US-Panama FTA and EIA (2012); Article 15.10.6 (a) (ii) US-Oman FTA and EIA (2009). This is not the case of the agreement with Republic of Korea, which establishes the possibility to choose between lost profits or unfair benefits, but not both (it uses 'or' instead of 'and'). *See* Article 18.10.5 (a) (i) and (ii) Republic of Korea-US FTA and EIA (2012);

69 With slight variations, this is what can be found in the following agreements, Article 16.11.8 (b) US-Colombia FTA and EIA (2012); Article 16.11.7(b) US-Peru FTA and EIA (2009); Article 15.9.7 (b) CAFTA-DR-US FTA and EIA (2006); Article 18.10.5(b) Republic of Korea-US FTA and EIA (2012); Article 17.11.6 (b) US-Australia FTA and EIA (2005); Article 16.10.8 US-Singapore FTA and EIA (2004); Article 17.11.8 (b) US-Chile FTA and EIA (2004); Article 4.24 US-Jordan FTA and EIA (2001); Article 15.11.6 (b) US-Morocco FTA and EIA (2006); Article 15.11.7 (b) US-Panama FTA and EIA (2012); Article 15.10.6 (b) US-Oman FTA and EIA (2009).

70 *See* footnote 28 of the Republic of Korea-US FTA and EIA (2012). What a 'reasonable royalty' means is, of course, a matter of contention. The New York District Court identified in *Georgia Pacific v. United States Plywood* up to fifteen different factors to estimate reasonable royalties. *See Georgia Pacific v. United States Plywood*, 318 F. Supp. 1116 (S.D.N.Y. 1970).

The retail price or other measures of value submitted by the right holder are not the most adequate criteria to determine the value of the award. On the one hand, there are other possibilities, which include customary royalties in the relevant market for the infringing product, production costs or the most frequent lost profit.[71] Moreover, courts usually take into account the opinion of experts appointed by the court and measures of value proposed by the infringer to complement the measure of value proposed by the right holder. Thus, referring only to the 'measure of value' proposed by the right holder would contradict that reasonable practice. On the other hand, in the case of patents the key notion is not the price of product but the value or specific contribution of the infringed patent to the invention. If the patent owner can prove that the patented feature causes market demand, then the entire market value of the product may be used to set damages. However, 'sales lost to an infringing product cannot irreparably harm a patentee if consumers buy that product for reasons other than the patented feature'.[72] If the patent forms part of a larger invention and it does not drive the demand for the product, either the market value of the infringing component or a reasonable royalty can be the criteria used to set damages.

The agreements promoted by the United States enact the obligation to set up a regime of pre-established damages that constitute a deterrent to future infringements, at least in cases of trademark counterfeiting and copyright infringement.[73] One of the agreements includes, moreover, the explicit obligation to include punitive damages.[74] Deterrent pre-established damages are regulated in these agreements as an alternative to actual damages, and it is up to the right holder to choose between the two awards. In this context, the position of the right holder is significantly strengthened, since he will be able to choose whether 'deterrence' and/or punishment[75]

[71] Estimated for instance by multiplying the margin of profit of the original product by the proven number of infringing goods, which can vary depending on the substitution rate.

[72] *Apple Inc. v. Samsung Electronics Co., Ltd (Apple I)*, No. 2013-1129 (Fed. Cir. Nov, 2013).

[73] *See* Article 16.11.7 US-Colombia FTA and EIA (2012); Article 16.11.7 US-Peru FTA and EIA (2009); Article 15.9.8 CAFTA-DR-US FTA and EIA (2006); Article 18.10.6 Republic of Korea-US FTA and EIA (2012); Article 17.11.7 US-Australia FTA and EIA (2005); Article 14.10.7 US-Singapore FTA and EIA (2004); Article 17.11.9 US-Chile FTA and EIA (2004); Article 4.25 US-Jordan FTA and EIA (2001); Article 15.11.7 US-Morocco FTA and EIA (2006); Article 15.11.8 US-Panama FTA and EIA (2012); Article 15.10.7 US-Oman FTA and EIA (2009). It could be interpreted that in the US-Jordan FTA and EIA (2001), punitive damages potentially concern all types of infringement, since it is merely stated in Article 4.25 that '[e]ach Party shall ensure that its statutory maximum fines are sufficiently high to deter future acts of infringement with a policy of removing the monetary incentive to the infringer . . . '.

[74] Article 17.11.7 (b) of the US-Australia FTA and EIA (2005) establishes that as an alternative to pre-established damages it is possible to maintain a system of additional damages (hence, punitive), provided that such damages are not regularly awarded in proceedings involving deliberate infringement.

[75] In the case of the US-Australia FTA and EIA (2005).

should be added to compensation,[76] since pre-established damages shall be in an amount sufficient to constitute a deterrent to future infringements and to compensate fully the right holder.

Deterrent damages for intellectual property infringement are controversial mainly in continental law countries, where civil procedure fulfils a compensatory function.[77] As abovementioned, deterrence and punition are closely interconnected. This is probably the reason why some trade agreements try to adjust damages to national approaches and legal traditions. For instance, in the case of the agreement between Chile and the United States, the deterrent function of statutory damages is not mentioned, while the article on damages affirms that these will be set up in light of the national intellectual property system and the objectives set forth in the treaty.[78] In a similar way, some other agreements state that pre-established damages shall not be understood as punitive damages.[79]

With regard to intent, TRIPS only establishes obligations with respect to the infringer who knowingly, or with reasonable grounds to know, engaged in infringing activity. However, the United States PTAs seem to treat all infringers in the same way, since only one out of eleven United States PTAs distinguishes between innocent and wilful infringements,[80] while the rest of the treaties allude just to the 'infringer' or the infringer who 'engaged in infringing activity' without further qualification. There has been a telling evolution in this respect. In 1994, the North American Free Trade Agreement established as a general rule that damages adequate to compensate for an infringement would be awarded 'where the infringer knew or had reasonable grounds to know that it was engaged in an infringing activity'.[81] NAFTA, in fact, was a mild version of what would follow later. In that case, judicial authorities were entitled to award pre-established damages or recovery of profits, or both, only in the case of copyright infringement.[82] Interestingly, it was not mentioned that pre-established damages had to fulfil a deterrent function and, if adopted, these were restricted to cases of wilful infringement.[83] Since then, the language has evolved to require the mandatory imposition, a quantity resulting from the addition of lost profits and unfair benefits and amounts sufficient to compensate and deter future infringement.[84]

76 In the case of CAFTA-DR-US FTA and EIA (2006) as well as in the case of US-Panama FTA and EIA (2012), it is not mentioned that pre-established damages shall be available on the election of the right holder, merely that pre-established damages must be available and are alternative.

77 *See* Sections II.1.1 and 2, and *see also* Section IV.

78 *See* Article 17.11.9 US-Chile FTA and EIA (2004).

79 This is the case of the US-Peru FTA and EIA (2009) and US-Colombia FTA and EIA (2012).

80 Article 4.24 of the US-Jordan FTA and EIA (2001) alludes to damages to be paid with respect to 'knowing infringement of trademark, copyright and related rights'.

81 *See* Article 1715.2 (d) NAFTA FTA and EIA (1994).

82 *See* Article 1715.4 NAFTA FTA and EIA (1994).

83 The scope of Article 1715.4 NAFTA FTA and EIA (1994) is limited to what establishes Article 1715.2 (d).

84 *See* Samuelson *et al.* (2013).

2.2 PTAs Negotiated by the European Union

Recent PTAs of the European Union include a provision on the award of damages in case of intellectual property infringement, as part of the European Union's strengthened attention to intellectual property enforcement norms. A brief description of the European harmonized regime on damages may clarify some of the questions raised by the European PTAs' provision on damages.[85] This is a useful exercise in light of the partial transposition of the European legal framework into some PTAs, an incomplete exportation that may have important consequences for the scope and effects of the corresponding provisions.

Article 13 of the EU Enforcement Directive on damages contains two subsections, which draw a distinction between the infringer who knowingly infringed an intellectual property right or had reasonable grounds to know that an infringement was about to be committed[86] and the infringer who did not know or had no reasonable grounds to know.[87]

In the case of the wilful infringer and the infringer that had reasonable grounds to know, it is stated that damages must be appropriate to the actual prejudice. Two alternatives are offered to satisfy this objective. Under the first option, compensation must take into account all 'appropriate aspects', such as the negative consequences, including loss profits of the right holder, unfair profits realized by the infringer or elements other than economic factors, such as moral prejudice.[88] The second option in cases of wilful infringement is to award damages as a lump sum, on the basis of elements such as the amount of royalties and fees that would have been due if an authorization had been requested.[89] The reference to lump sum damages on the basis of 'at least' the amount of the royalty that should have been paid allows European Union Member States to go beyond the minimum requirement and award double or even triple compensation for lost royalties.[90] However, and contrary to what the European Commission originally proposed, this is just an option left to Member States.[91] Moreover, even in these cases the Enforcement Directive does not include punitive damages. Instead, the objective is 'to provide for full compensation for the prejudice suffered, which is sometimes difficult for the right holder to determine'.[92]

With regard to the infringer who did not know, the Enforcement Directive empowers States to allow judicial authorities to order the recovery of profits and/or the payment of damages, which may be pre-established.[93] Hence, in the harmonized

85 *See* Article 13 EU Enforcement Directive. 86 *See* Article 13.1 EU Enforcement Directive.
87 *See* Article 13.2 EU Enforcement Directive. 88 *See* Article 13.1 (a) EU Enforcement Directive.
89 *See* Article 13.1 (b) EU Enforcement Directive.
90 This was, in fact, foreseen in the European Commission's proposal. *See* Reinbothe (2010), p. 21.
91 Article 17.1 (a) of the proposal of the European Union obliged to give to the right holder the possibility to receive a lump sum payment of twice the licensing fee instead of the proven amount of the actual damage. *See* Reinbothe (2010), pp. 19–20.
92 This was mentioned by the European Commission in an earlier version of the text, which effectively included double damages. *See* European Commission (2003a), p. 23.
93 *See* Article 13.2 EU Enforcement Directive.

European regime, pre-established damages are optional and only mentioned in the case of innocent infringements.

European PTAs either contain the obligation to adopt the European intellectual property legal framework over a number of years[94] or directly enshrine a provision containing most of the aforementioned regime for awarding damages.[95] In the latter case, however, a notable absence must be noted. None of the European PTAs includes the first paragraph of Article 13.1 of the Enforcement Directive. They copy and paste Articles 13.1(a) and (b) of the Enforcement Directive, i.e. the methods and options to award damages, but not the first paragraph of Article 13.1. This paragraph alludes to the intentionality of the infringer and states that in case of wilful infringement, damages must be appropriate to the actual prejudice suffered. Thus, by ignoring this paragraph, intent and the compensatory nature of damages are left out of the text of European trade agreements.

In light of this drafting, where European PTAs provisions are literally transposed or directly applied, lost profits could eventually be awarded even in case of innocent infringements, and the award of damages could also go beyond the reparation of the actual prejudice suffered. That is, a strict liability regime would be set up. Moreover, the award of damages as a lump sum on the basis of elements such as *at least* the amount of royalties and fees, but delinked from the compensatory nature of damages, could entail the grant of punitive damages in cases of both wilful and innocent infringements.

3 *The Award of Damages in Plurilateral Agreements*

3.1 The Anti-Counterfeiting Trade Agreement

In many respects, ACTA codified the minimum common denominator found in the national legal orders of its proponents. While it left it open to Member States to choose the option they would implement – thus, continuing with their national practice was the envisageable outcome – the addition and combination of all possible national options produced peculiar texts. The article on damages is noteworthy in this regard.

ACTA recognizes the compensatory nature of damages, stating that these must be 'adequate to compensate for the injury the right holder has suffered as a result of the infringement'.[96] However, and in line with the PTAs promoted by the Unites States, ACTA establishes that the amount of damages can be set taking into account 'any legitimate measure of value the right holder submits, which may include lost profits, the value of the infringed goods or services measured by the market price, or the

94 *See* Chapter 6, Section IV.5.

95 *See* Article 244 EU-Colombia and Peru FTA and EIA (2013); Article 267 EU-Central America FTA and EIA (2013); Article 10.50 EU-Republic of Korea FTA and EIA (2011); Article 160 EU-CARIFORUM States FTA and EIA (2008).

96 *See* Article 9.1 ACTA.

suggested retail price'.[97] This list is interesting. On the one hand, it improves PTAs subscribed by the United States, since it mentions a reasonable and commonly used measure of value to assess damages, i.e. lost profits.[98] On the other hand, the problems mentioned when addressing damages pursuant to the United States PTAs are also present in the ACTA list of measures of value.[99] These problems include not only an inducement to confusion between market price and compensation but also the fact that it is left to the right holder to submit the adequate measure of value. By contrast, common practice in intellectual property litigation is that both parties submit the measure of value they consider appropriate. In light of these estimates, the final decision is up to the discretion of the judge.

In addition to damages based on the injury inflicted on the right holder, ACTA also enshrines the possibility to award damages based on profits obtained by the infringer 'at least in cases of copyright or related rights infringement and trademark counterfeiting'.[100] As with many other remedies, what in TRIPS is a possibility left to states to transform into domestic legislation, in ACTA becomes an option left to judges.

As it happens with the United States PTAs, taking into account only the measure of value submitted by the infringer is problematic.[101] Moreover, listing the profits lost, the retail price and the market price altogether, as comparable elements, is misguiding. In fact, in order to assess lost profits, the retail price and market price may be aspects taken into consideration. They are not alternative criteria. Instead, retail price and market price can be factored into lost profits. For instance, the retail price and market price may be multiplied by the number of infringing items seized. Certainly, this example illustrates the incorrectness of identifying only these two measures of value. Other criteria, such as production costs or the profits, may be used to determine the amount of damages.[102]

ACTA reinforces and complements Article 45.2 of the TRIPS Agreement by stating that judicial authorities must have the authority to order the losing Party to pay court costs or fees and appropriate attorney's fees or any other expenses as provided for under that Party's law. When compared to the TRIPS Agreement, two new items are mentioned in ACTA, namely, 'court costs or fees' and 'any other expenses as provided for under that Party's law'.[103]

Article 9.3 of ACTA reflects the diverse legal traditions of ACTA members concerning the award of damages and permits choosing among them.[104] It establishes that

97 *Ibid.*

98 As abovementioned, it is frequent to set damages by multiplying the profit lost per original good that has not been sold by a varying number of infringing goods, which depends on the proof of infringement and the substitution rate.

99 *See* Section III.2.1.

100 Article 9.2 ACTA is also in line with the European and US PTAs.

101 *See* Section II.2.2.

102 *Ibid.*

103 *See* Article 9.5 ACTA. *See* Section II.1.3 and related for notes for some examples of legal costs.

104 Indeed, Member States of ACTA claimed that their national legal orders would not be altered. *See* for instance European Commission (2008), p. 2; USTR (2008), p. 4.

at least with respect to infringement of copyright and trademark counterfeiting, each Party shall enable right holders to be awarded damages pursuant pre-established damages, additional damages or presumptions for determining the amount of damages sufficient to compensate the right holder. Pre-established damages and damages based on presumptions may be ordered as an alternative to compensatory damages and damages equivalent to the infringers' profits. In the case of pre-established damages, the United States model of statutory damages seems to have been taken into account, while the option of additional damages reflects some common law countries' approach to damages.[105] The third option clearly crystallizes the continental law approach.[106]

3.2 The Trans-Pacific Partnership Agreement

The TPP Agreement provisions on damages[107] are based upon damages regulation in United States PTAs, although they are not entirely coincidental. While in some instances the TPP Agreement adds some balance, in other respects it strengthens the levels of protection and the value of the award when compared to PTAs.

First, while the TPP Agreement recognizes the compensatory nature of damages, it is the first international agreement to clearly state that 'at least' damages must be compensatory.[108] Thus, if compensation is the floor, as the TPP Agreement establishes, it can be presumed that punishment is an envisaged action.

Second, the regime for the award of damages set forth in the TPP Agreement repeats the problems already described when analysing PTAs and ACTA with respect to the measure of value to compensate for the injury. Pursuant to the TPP, it is up to the right holder to submit a legitimate measure of value, which may include lost profits, the market price or the retail price of goods or services. Certainly, as it happens with ACTA, the TPP text improves the US trade agreements, since it includes lost profits among the possible criteria. However, the identification of other measures of value, in particular market or retail price of infringing goods or services, is problematic.[109] The same happens with respect to the identification of the right holder as the person entitled to submit such a measure of value. While the TPP does not preclude other possibilities,[110] the preference for the right holder's submission of measures of value does not match with current practice in intellectual property litigation, which favours bringing into consideration diverse views and sources in order to estimate the amount due.[111]

105 *See* Section II.2.2.
106 *See* for instance the similarities with Article 13.2 EU Enforcement Directive.
107 *See* Articles 18.74.3 to 18.74.9 of the TPP Agreement.
108 *See* Article 18.74.3 of the TPP Agreement.
109 *See* the aforementioned reasons in Sections III.2.1 and 3.1.
110 Article 18.74.4 of the TPP Agreement alludes to the mentioned measures of value 'among other things'. It adds, moreover, a reference to 'legitimate' measures of value, which allows multiple interpretations.
111 *See* Sections III.2.1 and 3.1.

Fourth, courts must be able to order the payment of unfair profits at least in cases of wilful trademark counterfeiting and copyright and related rights infringement.[112] In a footnote, it is established that parties 'may comply with this paragraph through presuming those profits to be the damages referred to in paragraph 3'. This paragraph establishes the obligation to award, at least, compensatory damages in case of wilful infringement. To correctly interpret this provision, an additional footnote must be taken into consideration. There, it is established that there is no obligation to provide for the parallel award of the diverse remedies set forth in the TPP Agreement.[113] In light of this regime, two options are possible. First, compensation in case of wilful trademark counterfeiting and copyright and related rights infringement is possible by means of awarding either unfair profits or lost benefits. Second, parties are free to combine lost profits and unfair benefits when awarding damages in cases of wilful trademark counterfeiting and copyright and related rights wilful infringement.

Fifth, in case of copyright or related rights protecting works, phonograms or performances, as well as in case of trademark counterfeiting, parties shall provide either pre-established damages, which shall be available on the election of the right holder, or additional damages or both.[114] It is clarified that pre-established damages must be not only compensatory but also deterrent[115] and also that additional damages are punitive damages.[116] The punitive content of damages pursuant to the TPP and the debates that have arisen as a result of the content of PTAs and ACTA invite the further analysis of the award of punitive damages, in particular what it entails for international intellectual property law.

IV THE DEBATE OVER PUNITIVE DAMAGES

Recent international initiatives in the area of enforcement have brought to the forefront the debate on the nature and ultimate function of damages in cases of intellectual property infringement. While bilateral treaties have been used to export or consolidate the regime of one of the Parties to the treaty, in the plurilateral and multilateral arenas the push for opposite visions has so far resulted in a sort of stalemate. This gives rise to tense situations and makes it imperative to engage in a real discussion on whether the compensatory and punitive approaches can be reconciled.

First, as a result of PTAs, a number of countries of civil law tradition have adopted the obligation to impose punitive damages. This compromise impacts on some fundamental principles that instruct their national legal order. Second, in some cases civil law countries that have undertaken to adopt punitive damages in trade agreements have also adopted other treaties that consolidate a regime of damages of

[112] Article 18.74.5 of the TPP Agreement. [113] *See* footnote 110 of the TPP Agreement.

[114] Articles 18.74.6 and 18.74.7 of the TPP Agreement. [115] Article 18.74.8 of the TPP Agreement.

[116] *See* footnotes 112 and 113 of the TPP Agreement.

a merely compensatory nature. Lastly, the regulation of damages in the plurilateral and multilateral contexts shows how difficult – if not impossible – it is to successfully conclude initiatives that aim to harmonize the main intellectual property enforcement remedies.

What follows is an analysis of the difficulties that punitive damages entail in their home countries as well as in civil law countries. Next, the problems from the angle of public international law and in terms of international intellectual property policy-making are also examined.

1 *The Divide between Civil Law and Common Law Traditions*

Civil law legal orders and their highest courts have strongly resisted the incorporation of punitive damages,[117] arguing that these are inconsistent with foundational principles of private law and may encroach on public policy[118] and fundamental rights.[119] The primary reason is clear. In the continental tradition civil law remedies pursue compensatory objectives, while it is the object of criminal law to punish infringers. For this reason, punitive damages in civil law countries still 'stir up memories of very ancient times when legal systems did not make a strict difference between penalty and compensation'.[120]

However, civil law countries increasingly enter into contact with punitive damages. The *exequatur* of foreign sentences from countries where punitive damages are accepted is one of the cases where civil law courts have to deal with the nature and constitutional limitations of the award of damages. Several European courts have rejected the execution of sentences awarding exemplary and punitive

117 Almost all Supreme Courts of continental law countries have, at some stage, manifested their stance against punitive damages. In Spain, *see* STS 7 November 2000, Repertorio de Jurisprudencia Westlaw Aranzadi RJ-9911, or STS 7 December 1995, Repertorio de Jurisprudencia Westlaw Aranzadi RJ-9268; in Germany, *see* BGHZ 118, 312 (343–344) = NJW 1992, 3096 (3104); in Costa Rica, *see* Decision No. 420-F-S1-2012, 28 March 2012, or Decision No. 1153-F-S1-2011, 3 September 2011.

118 Recital 32 of Rome II provides that 'the application of a provision of the law designated by this Regulation which would have the effect of causing non-compensatory exemplary or punitive damages of an excessive nature to be awarded may, depending on the circumstances of the case and the legal order of the Member State of the court seised, be regarded as being contrary to the public policy (ordre public) of the forum'. *See* Regulation (EC) No. 864/2007 of the European Parliament and of the Council of 11 July 2007 on the law applicable to non-contractual obligations (Rome II), OJEU L 199/40 of 31 July 2007. The text is, however, significantly different from Article 24 of Rome II (2003), '[t]he application of a provision of the law designated by this Regulation which has the effect of causing non-compensatory damages, such as exemplary or punitive damages, to be awarded shall be contrary to Community public policy'. *See* European Commission (2003b).

119 As noted, 'the compensatory approach is allowed in civil cases in European law whereas anything beyond that, carrying resonance of criminal penalties, potentially could be argued to move the case into conflict with generally accepted principles of law and with fundamental human rights'. *See* Charleton and Kelly (2012), p. 20.

120 *See* Koziol (2008), p. 741.

damages originating in the United States. When declarations or judgements on enforceability have been sought in Germany, the country's Federal Court of Justice has rejected them on the grounds that they would violate *ordre public*. The Federal Court of Justice has noted that under German law punishment and deterrence are responsibilities of criminal courts.[121] The same has been held in other European jurisdictions, such as Italy, where the Supreme Court of Cassation has recalled that the civil process is suitable for awarding compensation but not for punishing infringers.[122]

Part of the doctrine disagrees with this jurisprudence. The argument made is that there are similarities between the award of damages in common law and civil law traditions,[123] and that the civil process is not necessarily at odds with some sort of punishment. The historical foundations of punitive damages, found in Roman law,[124] could give credit to this argument. In fact, it was only in the eighteenth and nineteenth centuries that the objectives of the civil procedure were limited to compensation, in response to the development of criminal law.[125] Against this backdrop, those arguing in favour of punitive damages in the civil law context examine the present civil legal order to elucidate two aspects in particular: criminal elements of the award of damages and contexts where the objective of the award of damages would be distinct from compensation.[126] Fundamentally, it is argued that in light of the allegedly broad purposes of the award of damages in civil law countries, there should be more flexibility towards punitive damages.

In response to the argument affirming that continental law countries actually award damages that go beyond financial loss and that this implies that objectives other than compensation are sought, it can be responded that the fundamental

121 The leading decision in Germany, the *California – Judgment*, was adopted in 1992. In that case, a German national who had been condemned for sexual abuse in the United States moved to Germany, where he owned some properties. The condemning sentence obliged him to pay punitive and exemplary damages of $400.000 USD, an award that was however rejected by the German Federal Court of Justice because it would violate *ordre public*. *See* BGH, 4 June 1992, 118 Entscheidungen des Bundesgerichtshofes in Zivilsachen [BGHZ] 312 (FRG). *See* also Tolani (2011), p. 186; Koziol (2008), p. 742.

122 The original text of the decision of the Supreme Court of Cassation reads as following: '[n]el vigente ordinamento l'idea della punizione e della sanzione è estranea al risarcimento del danno, così come è indifferente la condotta del danneggiante. Alla responsabilità civile è assegnato il compito precipuo di restaurare la sfera patrimoniale del soggetto che ha subito la lesione, mediante il pagamento di una somma di denaro che tenda ad eliminare le conseguenze del danno arrecato'. *See PJ v. Fimez SPA*, no. 1183, 19 January 2007.

123 Part of the doctrine has emphasized that civil and common law approaches to damages are not totally opposed but share a number of characteristics. *See* Behr (2003), pp. 148–152.

124 In the *Lex Duodecim Tabularum furtum necmanifestum* is awarded *poena dupli*, a punishment that later on was augmented to *poena quadrupli*.

125 *See* Tolani (2011), p. 186.

126 Among others – and drawing the attention on the German legal order – are mentioned 'damages in the context of the protection of personal rights', 'damages for pain and suffering' and 'damages for discrimination under labor law'. *See* Tolani (2011), p. 199.

principles remain the same. Even accepting that the award of damages in continental law countries can imply a deterrent aspect, this is still achieved by fair compensation. In this regard, awards that surpass the actual loss 'are not based on punitive considerations'[127] but pursue full compensation, which must be understood in a broad sense and implies elements of a different nature, particularly satisfaction. The Canadian Supreme Court has recognized that the award of general damages may chase objectives that overpass economic redress,[128] and the German Federal Court of Justice has made clear that satisfaction does not imply a penal component since its objective is not punishment but compensation of intangible aspects such as pain and suffering.[129]

The different approaches of common law and civil law countries towards the nature and functions of the civil and criminal processes determine the acceptability of some of the consequences of punitive damages. For instance, punitive damages may result in improving the plaintiff's position, since the award may exceed the amount of the real damage caused.[130] The plaintiff may end up receiving a large sum of money to which he had no real entitlement,[131] even in cases where the injury has been minimal or non-existent. While this outcome may be acceptable in some common law countries, from the perspective of civil law countries 'no arguments can justify awarding the plaintiff an advantage when he has suffered no corresponding damage and has no unjust enrichment claim against the defendant'.[132]

In light of the traditional compensatory function of the civil process, the pivotal question concerns the situation of civil law countries that adopt treaties enshrining punitive damages.[133] For instance, it has been rightly noted that 'the obligation of statutory damages alters drastically the Chilean general system of compensatory damages upon which IPRs had traditionally relied'.[134] The majority of countries that have negotiated PTAs with the United States face similar situations,[135] and it is doubtful that fulfilling both their constitutional obligations and the treaty provision on damages is feasible.

[127] *See* Jansen and Rademacher (2009), p. 85.

[128] It has stated that punitive damages 'should be awarded only in those circumstances where the combined award of general and aggravated damages would be insufficient to achieve the goal of punishment and deterrence'. *See* Supreme Court of Canada, *Hill v. Church of Scientology*, [1995] 2 SCR 1130 (SCC). *See* also in Canada, *Lubrizol v. Imperial Oil*, [1996] 71 CPR (3d) 26 (FCA).

[129] *See* BGH, NJW 1992, p. 3096 ff. (3103), quoted from Tolani (2011), p. 202.

[130] *See* Salvador Coderch (2000), p. 5. [131] *See* Irish Law Reform Commission (2000), p. 8.

[132] *See* Koziol (2008), p. 752. [133] *See* Section III.2.1 and Section IV.3.

[134] *See* Roffe (2004), p. 44.

[135] Only a small number of countries recognize punitive damages in case of intellectual property infringement. It is not strange, thus, that the jurisprudence of numerous US trade partners has expressed opposition towards punitive damages. The Supreme Court of Costa Rica has for instance re-stated the compensatory function of damages in the civil process and the ban to use this process to enrich the defendant. *See* Decision No. 420-F-S1-2012, 28 March 2012.

2 Punitive Damages and Fundamental Rights

Punitive damages are problematic for a number of reasons in relation to the protection of fundamental rights, particularly of the right to a fair trial. Supreme courts of countries awarding punitive damages have responded to most of the criticism by mandating the fulfilment of criteria that accommodate the award of damages to the requirements of due process. For some, however, this has not been enough and problems persist. It seems, in any case, difficult to replicate this jurisprudence in countries unfamiliar with punitive damages.

An important concern relates to double punishment. Since the very facts at the origin of the civil 'punitive' award may also result in the imposition of a criminal sanction, the *ne bis in idem* principle can be endangered. In common law countries situations where the same facts give rise to both civil and criminal punishment[136] have been addressed in order to comply with the doctrine of double jeopardy[137] and the principle of *autrefois acquit*.[138] Fundamentally, it has been argued that regardless of any punitive content, civil remedies maintain their civil nature, and thus, there is no contradiction with the double jeopardy clause. According to the United States Supreme Court, punishment 'is meted out only in criminal proceedings, and whether proceedings are criminal or civil is a matter of statutory construction'.[139]

This approach does, however, seem overly formalistic. It would be difficult to accept it in civil law traditions, since pursuant to that argument the mere naming of the award and not its substantive consequences appear to determine its nature.[140] Probably in recognition of the shortcomings of this approach, the Supreme Court of the United States has accepted the potential existence of cases where a civil sanction

[136] The Accident Compensation Act, No. 49, 19 September 2001 (hereinafter New Zealand Accident Compensation Act, of 2001), Section 319, on Exemplary damages, establishes that '(2) The court may make an award of exemplary damages for conduct of the kind described in subsection (1) even though – (a) the defendant has been charged with, and acquitted or convicted of, an offence involving the conduct concerned in the claim for exemplary damages; or (b) the defendant has been charged with such an offence, and has been discharged without conviction under section 106 of the Sentencing Act 2002 or convicted and discharged under section 108 of that Act; or (c) the defendant has been charged with such an offence and, at the time at which the court is making its decision on the claim for exemplary damages, the charge has not been dealt with; or (d)the defendant has not, at the time at which the court is making its decision on the claim for exemplary damages, been charged with such an offence; or (e)the limitation period for bringing a charge for such an offence has expired.'

[137] In the United States, the double jeopardy clause protects against a second prosecution for the same offence both after acquittal and after conviction as well as against multiple punishments for the same offence. *See North Carolina v. Pearce*, 395 US 711 (1969).

[138] *See* the cases of England and New Zealand – where before changing the law, courts had expressly forbidden subsequent claims for punitive damages in cases where there had been previously a criminal process – in Irish Law Reform Commission (2000), pp. 57–58.

[139] *See US v. Halper*, 109 S Ct. 1892 (1989).

[140] Something that the Supreme Court of the United States has negated, affirming that 'the determination whether a given civil sanction constitutes punishment in the relevant sense requires a particularized assessment of the penalty imposed and the purposes that the penalty may fairly be said to serve'. *Ibid.*

'in application, may be so divorced from any remedial goal that it constitutes 'punishment' for the purpose of double jeopardy analysis'.[141]

Punitive damages also raise concerns with respect to the legal guarantees of the process resulting in the award.[142] The majority of the safeguards that protect defendants in a criminal trial are absent in the civil process. Relevant absences include the need to satisfy a higher standard of proof in the criminal process and, very importantly, the principle of *nulla poena sine lege*. In effect, punitive damages may violate the principle that punishment must be laid down in the law before the commission of the infringement: a punitive award will be awarded without its content being anticipated in any statute.[143] In fact, in some cases a conduct that is not criminal may even result in a higher and not pre-established penalty than criminal conduct. This would be the case, for instance, when the same conduct results in a standard fine in a criminal process as well as notable punitive damages in a civil proceeding.[144]

The process resulting in the imposition of punitive damages raises additional concerns. For instance, the customary roles of the parties in the process are drastically modified, since the right holder and not the judicial authority will act as prosecutor.[145] In addition to the particular case of punitive statutory damages, a related but distinct problem can be identified. Indeed, in countries where damages must be assessed on the basis of the actual loss inflicted, pre-assessed damages cannot satisfy the minimum requirements of due process and fair trial, since there is no assessment of such a loss.

A third line of preoccupation concerns proportionality and extends to the lack of proportionality between the injury and the award as well as between the compensatory award and the punitive award.[146] Cases concerning exorbitant awards resulting from the imposition of punitive damages have become part of common knowledge, even popular culture.[147] Intellectual property is not an exception, and statutory

[141] *Ibid.* [142] *See* Dobbs (1989), pp. 831–917.

[143] The Law Commission for England and Wales stated in this regard, 'there is a moral duty on legislators to ensure that it is clear what conduct will give rise to sanctions and to the deprivation of liberty'. *See* English Law Commission (1997), p. 99.

[144] In this situation, paradoxically, the defendant would prefer to be sentenced in the criminal process rather than condemned to pay punitive damages.

[145] In defense of punitive damages as private punishment, *see* Sebok (2007), pp. 1004–1005.

[146] The Supreme Court of Canada has stated that punitive damages must be, 'i) Proportionate to the blameworthiness of the defendant's conduct; ii) Proportionate to the degree of vulnerability of the plaintiff; iii) Proportionate to the harm or potential harm directed specifically at the plaintiff; iv) Proportionate to the need for deterrence; v) Proportionate to the advantage wrongfully gained by a defendant from the misconduct; vi) Proportionate considering the overall award, that is, compensatory and punitive damages altogether'. *See Whiten v. Pilot Insurance Co.*

[147] The case of the woman who suffered burns due to the temperature of a McDonald's coffee is widely known by lay people. In that case, the jury awarded punitive damages of $2.700.000 USD and compensatory damages of $200.000 USD. Both awards were later on reduced to $480.000 USD and $160.00 USD, respectively. *See Liebeck v. McDonald's Restaurant, PTS Inc.*, No. D-202 CV-93-02419, 1995 WL 360309 (Bernalillo County, N.M. Dist. Ct.) (1994).

damages have resulted in impressive awards,[148] sometimes rejected by upper courts because of their impact on due process and proportionality considerations.[149] The factors that ultimately result in multi-million awards are diverse and comprise the intention to introduce a very strong deterrent effect,[150] the aggregation of statutory damages for infringement[151] and the recourse to statutory maximums, even when the infringement caused little or no actual harm to the plaintiff and brought the defendant little or no profit.[152]

Exorbitant damages cause problems from the constitutional point of view, particularly in terms of due process[153] and the right to property.[154] The jurisprudence resulting from the leading cases with respect to the general category of punitive damages[155] has been adapted to the area of intellectual property, and statutory

[148] In *Capitol Records Inc. and Others. v. Thomas-Rasset*, the defendant was found to have infringed the plaintiff's copyright in sound recordings using a peer-to-peer file-sharing network. The jury awarded statutory damages of $80.000 USD per song (twenty-four songs), which resulted in a total award of $1.920.000 USD. When reviewing the case, the District Court of Minnesota alluded to the lack of proportionality and stated that '[t]he need for deterrence cannot justify a $1.5 million verdict for stealing and illegally distributing 24 songs for the sole purpose of obtaining free music'. *See Capitol Records Inc. and Others v. Thomas-Rasset* 680 F. Supp. 2D 1045, 1054 (D. Minn. 2010).

[149] *Ibid.* The Court subsequently substituted the award for another of $54.000 USD, which was considered the maximum possible in light of due process considerations.

[150] Something that has been considered to contravene the basic principles of due process, '[i]t is inconsistent with due process principles to make such a large award in order to deter strangers to the litigation'. *See Philip Morris USA v. Williams*, 549 US 346, 353 (2007).

[151] As Judge Wood stated in a case in response to the plaintiff petitions, 'if one multiplies the maximum statutory damage award ($150,000) by approximately 10,000 post-1972 works, Defendants face a potential award of over a billion dollars in statutory damages alone. If Plaintiffs were able to pursue a statutory damage theory predicated on the number of direct infringers per work, Defendants' damages could reach into the trillions. As Defendants note, Plaintiffs are suggesting an award that is "more money than the entire music recording industry has made since Edison's invention of the phonograph in 1877."' *See Arista Records LLC and Others v. Lime Group LLC and Others*, USDC, SDNY (2011), available at: http://amlawdaily.typepad.com/limewiredamagesorder.pdf (last accessed August 2015). However, due process has not been sufficiently considered, *see* Scheuerman (2009), pp. 103–104.

[152] *See* a number of examples in Samuelson and Wheatland (2009), pp. 481–484.

[153] *See BMW v. Gore* 116 S Ct 1589 (1996) (hereinafter *BMW v. Gore*); *Cooper Industries, Inc. v. Leatherman Tool Group, Inc.* 532 US 424 (2001); *State Farm Mutual Auto Insurance Co. v. Campbell* 538 US 408, 429 (2003) (hereinafter *State Farm Mutual Auto Insurance Co. v. Campbell*).

[154] In *State Farm Mutual Auto Insurance Co. v. Campbell*, the Supreme Court of the United States ruled that the punitive award being 'neither reasonable nor proportionate to the wrong committed', 'it was an irrational and arbitrary deprivation of [State Farm's] property', p. 429.

[155] With respect to the general category of punitive damages, the US Supreme Court held that the punitive award granted was excessive and enumerated the factors to consider when deciding the amount of the punitive award: (1) the degree of reprehensibility of the defendant's conduct; (2) the ratio between compensatory damages and punitive damages; (3) the disparity between the punitive damages award and the civil and criminal penalties that could be imposed by state law for comparable misconduct. *See BMW v. Gore*, p. 1599. *See* also the Restatement (Second) of Torts, of 1979, § 908(2), which identifies the following three factors as considerations in measuring punitive damages: (l) the character of the defendant's misconduct; (2) the nature and extent of the plaintiffs

damages for intellectual property infringement in particular.[156] Indeed, some governments have expressly identified disproportionate awards as a crucial problem that new statutes adopting statutory damages should avoid.[157]

Lack of proportionality is not a problem just from the perspective of due process but also because of its impact on other fundamental rights. In this sense and in respect to statutory damages for copyright infringement, it has been noted that excessive awards are 'likely to have other negative spillover effects, such as chilling lawful, even if close to the boundary, uses of copyrighted works, especially those that would promote freedom of speech and freedom of expression'.[158] Although not in the intellectual property context, the European Court of Human Rights has stated that an overly excessive sanction may violate the right to freedom of expression. In *Tolstoy Miloslavsky v. United Kingdom*,[159] English courts had awarded a very substantial compensation in response to the defamation inflicted by the defendant. The European Court accepted that the damages awarded were legally prescribed and thus in line with the European Convention on Human Rights. However, when the Court analysed whether the award imposed was 'necessary in a democratic society', it questioned the proportionality between the illegality committed and the penalty imposed and ultimately found a violation of the right to freedom of expression.

In order to respond to the problems arising from the lack of proportionality, some jurisdictions have laid down a list of factors to be taken into account when fixing the amount of damages[160] as well as some corrective tools to adjust that amount. Among

injuries; (3) the wealth of the defendant. In Canada, the Supreme Court identified the general criteria to set up damages in *Whiten v. Pilot Insurance Co.*

156 The principles enunciated in *BMW v. Gore* have been paraphrased in the context of statutory damages for copyright infringement. In this regard, it has been sustained that '[a]pplying the *Gore* guideposts to copyright statutory damages is relatively straightforward' and that the relative reprehensibility of copyright infringers depends on a number of factors, among others, whether infringers are intentional bad actors, whether it was reasonable to believe that actions were lawful, whether the case involved a novel issue, whether the infringement was part of a pattern of similar misconduct or an isolated event, whether there was recidivism and whether the defendant obstructed efforts to determine liability or damages. *See* Samuelson and Wheatland (2009), p. 472.

157 Canada affirmed that the new *Copyright Modernization Act* 'ensures that Canadians will not face disproportionate penalties for minor infringements of copyright by distinguishing between commercial and non-commercial infringement. Under current law, for commercial and non-commercial infringements, copyright owners can sue for statutory damages ranging from $500 to $20,000 for each work that is infringed. This Bill will dramatically reduce an individual's potential liability in cases of non-commercial infringement. In such cases, statutory damages will be reduced to a one-time payment of between $100 and $5000 for all infringements that took place prior to the lawsuit. For commercial infringement, there will be no change from the current law.' *See The Copyright Modernization Act: Questions and Answers*, available at: http://balancedcopyright.gc.ca/eic/site/crp-prda.nsf/eng/h_rp01153.html#record (last accessed July 2013). The Copyright Modernization Act has been adopted in 2012; *see* Copyright Modernization Act, SC 2012, c 20, 29 June 2012

158 *See* Samuelson and Wheatland (2009), pp. 495–496.

159 *See* ECtHR, *Tolstoy Miloslavsky v. United Kingdom*, no. 18139/91, 13 July 1995, Series A no. 316-B.

160 For a very diverse range of factors that can be taken into account when fixing the award, compare for example Article 56 (b) of the Copyright Act, 19 November 2007, Law Statutes of Israel [2007] Issue 2199, 25 November 2007, p. 34 (hereinafter Copyright Act of Israel, of 2007), and Article 119.5 of

the corrective criteria, mention is made of the possibility to award less than the minimum established as statutory damage if there is more than one work in a single medium and awarding even the minimum amount would result in a total award out of proportion to the infringement.[161] On other occasions, the strategy adopted consists of holding that 'infringements carried out as part of a set of activities shall be deemed as a single infringement'.[162] Finally, in a third response, caps have been placed on the total possible amount of damages.[163]

3 *Conflicting Treaties, Inconsistent Obligations and Conflict of Policies*

The regulation of punitive damages in PTAs gives rise to a confusing legal scenario. Two different situations have to be distinguished, one relating to the inharmonious regulation of this remedy globally, the other concerning the specific situation of countries that adopt multiple treaties where damages are regulated in a different manner.

Several countries have adopted treaties that regulate statutory damages both with the European Union and with the United States,[164] and the number of such countries is likely to rise given the path of adoption of PTAs that regulate enforcement in a meaningful manner. As noted previously, in the European PTAs pre-established damages are optional, target innocent infringements and exclude punitive purposes. In contrast, the agreements promoted by the United States oblige PTA partners to enact statutory damages, which may be applicable both to innocent and wilful infringements and must fulfil a deterrent function.

It may be tempting to address this situation in terms of conflict between treaties and apply Article 30 of the Vienna Convention on the Law of Treaties, which addresses the application of successive treaties relating to the same subject matter.

Singapore Copyright Act, Chapter 63, of 1987: 'Copyright Act, No. 2, Chapter 63, 14 February 1987 (hereinafter Singapore Copyright Act, Chapter 63, of 1987).

161 Article 38.1.3 of the Canadian Copyright Act, RSC, 1985, c C-42, 1985 (hereinafter Canadian Copyright Act, of 1985), establishes that '[i]n awarding statutory damages under paragraph (1)(a) or subsection (2), the court may award, with respect to each work or other subject-matter, a lower amount than $500 or $200, as the case may be, that the court considers just, if (a) either (i) there is more than one work or other subject-matter in a single medium, or (ii) the award relates only to one or more infringements under subsection 27(2.3); and (b) the awarding of even the minimum amount referred to in that paragraph or that subsection would result in a total award that, in the court's opinion, is grossly out of proportion to the infringement'.

162 *See* Article 56 (c) Copyright Act of Israel, of 2007.

163 Article 119(2)(d) of the Singapore Copyright Act, Chapter 63, of 1987 states that 'where the plaintiff has elected for an award of statutory damages in lieu of damages or an account of profits, statutory damages of – (i) not more than $10,000 for each work or subject-matter in respect of which the copyright has been infringed; but (ii) not more than $200,000 in the aggregate, unless the plaintiff proves that his actual loss from such infringement exceeds $200,000'.

164 States that have effectively adopted treaties with the United States and the European Union regulating damages are Panama, Colombia, Peru, Dominican Republic, Costa Rica, Nicaragua, El Salvador, Honduras, Guatemala and Republic of Korea.

In our view, however, such an application is not warranted since, we hold, there is no normative conflict.

The adoption of a strict notion of conflict dismisses the applicability of Article 30 of VCLT. Pursuant to this notion, a conflict only exists when two provisions cannot be applied altogether.[165] This means, for instance, that whenever a conflict occurs between an article drafted in terms of permission and another that lays down an obligation, merely fulfilling the obligation and disregarding the permission will avoid the conflict. In the European PTAs, the provision on statutory damages is drafted as a 'double-may' provision. It establishes that, in case of innocent infringement, 'Parties may provide that the judicial authorities may order the recovery of profits or the payment of damages which may be pre-established'.[166] Hence, Parties are not obliged to provide this possibility at all or may favour the recovery of profits. Applying any of these options will avoid a conflict with the United States PTAs.

However, this notion of conflict is not satisfactory since it is too formalistic and leaves unanswered most of the real conflictive situations in international law. Presently, there is another widely accepted view, according to which a conflict exists when a norm affects the implementation of another norm.[167] This more flexible and pragmatic view does not, however, change our assessment of the relationship between the norms on punitive damages contained in PTAs. In reality, the answer to this situation is that treaties adopted by the European Union and by the United States reflect different approaches to the institution of damages but do not enact obligations that cannot be fulfilled at the same time. Countries may effectively apply both regimes simultaneously by just providing pre-established damages with deterrent effect for both innocent and wilful infringements. European treaties do not say that pre-established damages may not fulfil a punitive function. Although this is not the continental law approach, there is nothing in the European agreements forbidding countries from adopting pre-established damages with punitive content. Hence, countries may respect the European and US agreements by providing statutory punitive damages in case of innocent and wilful infringement.

This possibility is the paradoxical outcome of the competitive exportation of domestic standards to third countries. This is the reason why, in our view, the situation reflects the limits of international regulation of intellectual property via PTAs. Countries that export domestic standards that have not been harmonized due to the existence of fundamental discrepancies with regard to the nature and functions of such norms contribute to the creation of incoherent and conflictive national statutes. The fact that during the ACTA negotiations, the United States and the European Union were not able to reach an agreement concerning the regime on damages reflects the fundamental divide existing in this field. Regardless of this fact

165 *See* Jenks (1953), p. 426. 166 *See* Article 244.2 EU-Colombia and Peru FTA and EIA (2013).
167 *See* International Law Commission (2006a), p. 148.

and being aware of that divide, both the United States and the European Union have continued to export their respective regimes.[168]

V PROPOSALS FOR REFORM

The present international legal framework on damages for intellectual property infringement calls for urgent attention to three distinct areas. First, it is necessary to clarify the functions and nature of the award of damages in each treaty. This will permit stressing the difference between compensatory and punitive damages and also between deterrent and punitive damages. Another area that calls for attention concerns respect for the legal guarantees that the right to a fair trial implies as well as the tense relationship between punitive damages, due process and the principle of proportionality. Finally, it is of foremost importance that the proponents of increased standards of intellectual property protection harmonize their positions or refrain from indiscriminately proposing their own legislation. While this is the most difficult objective, it is the way to avoid the adoption of inconsistent statutes in countries importing intellectual property standards.

1 *Differentiation between Deterrence and Punishment*

International treaties state that the award of damages must compensate the right holder for the infringement suffered. The United States PTAs and the TPP also establish that, in case of trademark counterfeiting and copyright infringement, a system of statutory damages must be set up and shall function so as to constitute a deterrent to infringement. In one isolated PTA and in the TPP, the obligation to include punitive damages is explicitly introduced as an alternative to deterrent pre-established damages.

When observed from the perspective of continental law countries, the latter obligation raises the problem of the alteration of the customary compensatory function of damages. Restitution and compensation seem to be substituted by punishment and deterrence. In order to avoid the problems arising from the award of punitive damages in civil law countries and to clarify and define the function of the award of damages, it is necessary to underline and probably revive the traditional difference between punishment and deterrence.

In the United States and some other jurisdictions, exemplary statutory damages serve strong deterrent and punitive purposes. This needs *not*, however, to be the case of United States trading partners. In our view, to fulfil the agreements with the United States enacting damages with deterrent effect suffices. There is not a single

168 The EU-Republic of Korea FTA and EIA (2011) allows for the coherent application of both the continental law regime and 'punitive damages regime'. The reason may be found, however, not in the desire of facilitating the implementation of the Republic of Korea-US FTA and EIA (2012) but merely in the fact that Republic of Korea already provided for punitive damages.

PTA that mentions punishment as a goal of statutory damages. In reality, the sole objective mentioned besides compensation is deterrence. This is important since the 'original and still meaningful purpose'[169] of pre-established damages was to compensate plaintiffs and reasonably deter infringement. Hence, although punishment may be closely related to deterrence, it is also differentiable.

In light of the above, countries that have undertaken the compromise to incorporate deterrent statutory damages can determine, in the national statutes that implement the required deterrent effect, when the award of damages prevents future infringements. That is, the specific amount or the mechanism to determine that amount depends on the national implementation. Given that this obligation is to be fulfilled in the context of statutory damages, the system to fix statutory damages can be designed so that full compensation is awarded. Full compensation can include satisfaction, as well as compensation, with regard to elements distinct from actual loss. If this is the case, full compensation can play a deterrent effect while not punishing the infringer.

2 *Due Process and Legal Guarantees*

For countries that have traditionally recognized punitive content in the award of damages, as well as for others that started recognizing such content only recently, it is important to bear in mind the limits set forth both in international intellectual property treaties and international human rights treaties. Among the former, multilateral, plurilateral and bilateral treaties state that intellectual property enforcement measures, remedies and procedures must be 'effective, proportionate and dissuasive'. As aforementioned, proportionality is a central element of due process and fair trial as well as a principle of public international law.[170]

The quest for proportionality implies the avoidance of excessive awards. This is something that can be achieved through acting both in the judicial and the normative areas. It is indeed the role of the judge to prevent disproportionate awards and ensure the respect of due process standards when ruling on a specific case. However, there is also a need to act on the normative side in order to set the criteria that may eventually lead to the award of punitive or deterrent damages and ensure the respect of fair trial guarantees.

Guidelines that help set and cap the potential award should discourage disproportionate sentences and guarantee the respect of the right to a fair trial. These guidelines can incorporate important principles and constitute a framework for the adoption of norms of a more specific nature.[171] While some of these principles have been intensely discussed in legal orders that do award punitive damages, they may be further evaluated and, of course, other regimes with less experience may not

169 *See* Samuelson and Wheatland (2009), p. 495.
170 *See* Chapter 2, Section IV.3.1.
171 *See* Samuelson and Wheatland (2009); Koziol (2008), p. 764.

necessarily wish to share foreign jurisprudence. In our view, it is necessary to guarantee the compensatory function of the award of damages, to prohibit the award of punitive damages when the same facts have already resulted in a criminal conviction, to require an increased standard of proof and clearer evidence in case punitive damages are accepted and to limit punitive awards to the most egregious wilful infringements.

3 *Treaty Coherence*

Finally, intellectual property 'exporters' should seek to harmonize their positions with regard to the function and regulation of damages. The United States and the European Union are clearly aware of the differences that they maintain in this area. These differences do not concern just minor aspects. They reflect instead a profound gap that separates the Parties' views on the function and guarantees of the civil process. Unless consensus is found, it is very possible that more and more inconsistent regimes on damages will be adopted.

Fundamentally, the harmonization agenda should guarantee that new treaties codify more clearly how to treat the different categories of damages in case of intellectual property infringement. Unambiguous key elements should be established, devoting particular attention to aspects such as the relationship between the intention of the infringer and the specific award and whether damages – in particular statutory damages – fulfil compensatory, punitive or deterrent objectives.

PART IV

Border Measures

10

The Global Regime on Border Measures

I INTRODUCTION

Customs surveillance of intellectual property infringing goods 'is an efficient way to quickly and effectively provide legal protection to the right-holder',[1] since it makes it possible 'to "nip the infringements in the bud"'.[2] Border control is indeed more efficient than the implementation of other enforcement measures combined since, 'where the release of goods is suspended or goods are detained by customs authorities at the border, only one legal proceeding should be required, whereas several separate proceedings should be required for the same level of enforcement for goods found on the market'.[3]

The World Trade Organization Agreement on Trade-Related Aspects of Intellectual Property Rights introduced the first comprehensive multilateral regulation on border measures relating to goods protected by intellectual property rights. Certainly, both the Berne and the Paris Conventions enacted some articles on border measures, but the provisions established therein were fundamentally constrained to seizures on importation.[4] In fact, the Paris Convention set up a flexible regime where the exceptions outnumbered the obligations:[5] seizure on importation could be substituted by 'prohibition of importation or by seizure inside the country'[6] or, if none of these measures was available, by actions and remedies

[1] *See* Regulation (EU) No. 608/2013 of the European Parliament and of the Council of 12 June 2013 concerning customs enforcement of intellectual property rights and repealing Council Regulation (EC) No 1383/2003, Recital 4, Preamble (hereinafter EU Regulation No. 608/2013).

[2] *See* Bronckers, Verkade and McNelis (2000), p. 20.

[3] *See* Council Regulation (EC) No. 1383/2003 of 22 July 2003 concerning customs action against goods suspected of infringing certain intellectual property rights and the measures to be taken against goods found to have infringed such rights, Recital 4, Preamble (hereinafter Regulation No. 1383/2003).

[4] *See* Articles 13.3 and 16 Berne Convention, and Articles 9 and 10 Paris Convention.

[5] *See* Fukunaga (2008), p. 878. [6] *See* Article 9.5 Paris Convention.

available in such cases to nationals under national law 'until such time as the legislation is modified accordingly'.[7]

In comparison to the Berne and Paris Conventions, the TRIPS Agreement enacted a detailed regime concerning the control on importation of counterfeit and pirated goods. Although the TRIPS Agreement implied a major change, the measures set up therein do not cover all categories of intellectual property rights and border situations. Some countries have considered that the TRIPS Agreement is not comprehensive enough and that 'the "aggressive" enforcement provisions of TRIPS, particularly the border measures, have fallen'.[8] Therefore, it comes as no surprise that border measures are the enforcement-related remedy most frequently regulated in post-TRIPS bilateral and plurilateral treaties.[9]

Legal transplantation is also frequent in the area of border enforcement. Some PTAs' border enforcement sections are heavily influenced by the domestic legislation of the country promoting the intellectual property chapter of the treaty, whereas multilateral and plurilateral treaties have also been modelled upon the customs laws of a reduced number of States. In fact, this was already the case of the TRIPS Agreement,[10] just as it has been in the Anti-Counterfeiting Trade Agreement. Mechanisms distinct from international norm-setting, such as technical cooperation and emulation, also explain the transplantation of some border enforcement statutes into other legal orders.[11]

Plurilateral and bilateral treaties' articles on border enforcement usually focus on the categories of intellectual property rights and border situations that must be controlled. In both cases they generally expand the scope of the TRIPS Agreement. The rest of the subjects commonly addressed in national border measures regulations or in the TRIPS Agreement, such as the procedural provisions, receive heterogeneous and frequently scant attention in plurilateral and bilateral agreements.

The law applied to determine the infringing status of goods subject to customs control, together with the intellectual property categories and border situations under control, are central aspects of new international norms on border enforcement. In particular, in the case of the control of transit, the possibility to apply the law of the country implementing border measures – regardless of whether the products are intended for that country's market and even when the goods are not infringing in the country of destination – is at the centre of the international debate.

The evolution of international norms regulating border enforcement has been particularly controversial given its close connection with international trade, its

7 Articles 9.6 and 10.1 Paris Convention extend the same prescription to false indications.

8 *See* Trainer and Allums (2008), p. 4. *See* for instance European Commission (2005b), pp. 6, 9.

9 *See* Seuba (2013b), p. 12; Grosse Ruse-Khan (2015), pp. 88–99.

10 *See* Blakeney (2001), pp. 40–41; UNCTAD-ICTSD (2005), p. 609; Correa (2007), p. 439.

11 For instance, Chinese Regulations on Customs Protection for Intellectual Property Rights follows the former EU Regulation 1383/2003 on border measures. *See* Hong (2009), p. 298.

implications on a number of fundamental rights and its economic impact. On the one hand, the expansion of the scope of border measures to include the control of products under suspensive procedures or in a free zone or warehouse and the application of the law of the country of the custom procedures under the or 'manufacturing' fiction have the potential to impact basic principles of the international trading regime, the freedom of transit principle in particular. On the other hand, the effect that border measures may have on access to vital products and the connection made between some categories of intellectual property rights and consumer safety also feed the debate on the interrelation between human rights and border enforcement. Moreover, while largely ignored, the economic relevance of new border enforcement undertakings should also be considered. Taxpayers' contributions may end up funding new border measures to control goods not produced or intended for their countries, and the most efficient international transport routes may be circumvented because of the chilling effect of some border enforcement regulations.[12]

II THE REGULATION OF BORDER MEASURES IN THE TRIPS AGREEMENT

1 *Introduction*

The TRIPS Agreement laid down the first multilateral regime for enforcing intellectual property rights at the border, which includes both general principles and detailed rules. Although its scope is narrower than national statutes, Section 4 of Part III of the TRIPS Agreement introduced crucial changes in the international regulation of customs control and created numerous challenges for Member States with no pre-TRIPS border enforcement experience.[13]

Members of the WTO adopted the compromise to impede the importation of counterfeit trademark or pirated copyright goods and agreed that the infringing nature of goods should be determined in accordance with the law of the country of importation. For the purposes of triggering the suspension of release by customs authorities, TRIPS also provided the first globally accepted definitions on 'counterfeit trademark goods' and 'pirated copyright goods'. Other infringements of intellectual property rights and the control of exportation and transit were left at the discretion of the WTO Members.

The WTO Members are obliged to adjust border enforcement procedures for the control of importation to a number of requirements. Putting aside the mandatory control of importation of counterfeit and pirated goods, Members are free to decide which intellectual property categories will be controlled, whether they extend the control to border situations different from importation and the requirements that will apply to the control of exportation and transit. They are also free to identify the

[12] *See* Chapter 3, Sections IV.2.1 and 3.1. [13] *See* Trainer (2008), p. 52.

authority in charge of implementing border measures. Since measures adopted by customs authorities are in principle preliminary,[14] it is left for judicial or administrative authorities to subsequently decide on the existence of an infringement and the ultimate fate of the products.[15]

2 Border Operations That Can Be Controlled

Articles 51 and 52 of the TRIPS Agreement contain the central requirements set up in the section on border measures. Article 51 regulates the suspension of release by customs authorities and Article 52 the content of the application for suspension of release. With respect to customs operations that must be controlled, Members must allow an application to be lodged for the suspension of the release into free circulation of imported counterfeit and pirated products. This *ex parte* action reflects the initial proposal put forward by the European Union in November 1987[16] and the idea that the control of importation is intended to function as a 'safety net in the event that enforcement at the source has not taken place'.[17] This should effectively remedy the lack of control of exportation: countries will block the entrance into their territory of counterfeit and pirated goods that avoided control in countries of manufacture.[18]

Members *may* also set up procedures for the suspension of the release of infringing goods destined for exportation and may foresee that actions will be adopted *ex officio*. Both possibilities are, however, up to the decision of the parties.[19] Moreover, there shall be no obligation to apply such procedures to goods in transit or to parallel imported goods.[20] This freedom has prompted some States to complain about the insufficiency of the TRIPS Agreement and to promote, in the international context, 'a number of actions to tackle the situation, including the extension of the obligation to make available customs measures to goods in transit and for export'.[21] As detailed further in this chapter, these complaints have been transformed into an agenda for

[14] They can, however, become definitive in some legal orders. *See* Chapter 12, Section I.

[15] *See* UNCTAD-ICTSD (2005), p. 609.

[16] During the Uruguay Round negotiations, the European Union stated that the final text should at least include border enforcement provisions that empower customs or other authorities to prevent imports of counterfeit or pirated goods and possibly exports as well. *See* GATT (1987c), pp. 3–4.

[17] *See* Otten and Wager (1996), p. 405; UNCTAD-ICTSD (2005), p. 609.

[18] *See* Micara (2012), p. 74. Some claim that countries controlling exportation invest their resources to protect other countries. According to Dimitrov, 'China has used its Customs resources chiefly to protect *other* countries, by stopping the exportation of counterfeits'. *See* Dimitrov (2009), p. 79.

[19] *See* Section I.2.3.1.

[20] *See* footnote to Article 51. Concerning parallel importation, it is not necessary to suspend the release of goods if products have been put in the commerce by or with the consent of the right holder. Once the right holder has chosen a country to commercialize the product for the first time, he is not entitled to impede its release into free circulation. It has been affirmed that 'the footnote clearly applies to certain cases of infringement of trademark and copyright only, and there is no solid basis to extend it into other fields'. *See* UNCTAD-ICTSD (2005), p. 613.

[21] *See* European Commission (2005b), p. 6.

normative reform, which has materialized through the conclusion of bilateral and plurilateral trade agreements.

In addition to border situations that must be controlled and intellectual property categories that must be supervised, the TRIPS Agreement lays down conditions, rights, limits and procedural requirements for the implementation of border measures. Importantly, the WTO Panel report on *China – Intellectual Property Rights* stated that those requirements refer to importation[22] but not to exportation and transit. In a nutshell, the control of importation of counterfeit and pirated goods, as well as the potential control of importation of goods protected by any other category of intellectual property rights, will be governed by the conditions set forth in Part III Section 4. However, other border operations relating to any right do not need to be adjusted to the same provisions. In reaching this conclusion, the panel relied on the fact that while the extension of border measures to intellectual property infringements – distinct from those mentioned in the TRIPS Agreement – is explicitly conditioned to the satisfaction of the requirements set forth in Part III Section 4,[23] the same condition does not exist with respect to other border situations.[24]

The clarification provided by the WTO Panel has far-reaching legal and economic consequences. In practice, the WTO Panel decision confirms that exports from countries usually targeted as sources of counterfeited and pirated goods are in essence immune to the regime set forth in the TRIPS Agreement,[25] and the same happens with respect to the control of transit.[26] This situation is unsatisfactory for right holders, who see how countries regarded as the main sources of pirated and counterfeit goods are not obliged to control exportation or to apply the conditions in the TRIPS Agreement in case they effectively decide to control exportation.[27] However, it has also been noted that this is not surprising in light of the WTO's origins, which focused on barriers to the *entry* of goods into Members' markets.[28]

With regard to the control of transit, 'at the time TRIPS was negotiated, the practice of seizing goods in transit based on allegations of patent infringement was unknown, so members would not have contemplated such practice as an option when drafting the relevant provision'.[29] While the control of transit is thoroughly analysed in Chapter 11, at this point it can be noted that the title of Article 51 announces that this article deals with the 'Suspension of Release by Customs

[22] *See* WTO Panel Report, *China – measures affecting the protection and enforcement of intellectual property rights*, WT/DS362/R, 26 January 2009 (hereinafter WTO Panel, *China – Intellectual Property Rights*), para. 7.224.

[23] *See* Article 51 TRIPS Agreement, second phrase.

[24] *See* Article 51 TRIPS Agreement, third phrase.

[25] This was clearly the case of China, *see* Grosse Ruse-Khan (2010), pp. 624, 626; Grosse Ruse-Khan (2009a), p. 60.

[26] *See* WTO Panel, *China – Intellectual Property Rights*, para. 7.224.

[27] Compared with the existing obligation in the TRIPS Agreement to deploy border measures against imports, targeting exports is much more important for right holders. *See* Grosse Ruse-Khan (2010), p. 625.

[28] *See* Dinwoodie and Dreyfuss (2009), p. 1218.

[29] *See* Abbott (2009b), p. 47.

Authorities'. Therefore, the TRIPS Agreement does not enshrine border measures concerning goods that do not need to be 'released by customs authorities'. In their daily customs activity, border authorities 'suspend the release' of goods that enter or exit the national jurisdiction. That is, the suspension of release concerns goods that come from or enter into the internal market, i.e. imported, exported and re-exported goods. In contrast, goods in transit are not 'released for free circulation' or 'released for exportation': they are simply meant to transit through the country. Accordingly, customs authorities' action with respect to goods in transit differs from that executed with respect to exported or imported goods.[30]

3 *Categories of Intellectual Property Rights Object of Customs Control*

Border enforcement measures enshrined in the TRIPS Agreement do not refer to all categories of intellectual property rights. Article 51 of the Agreement only establishes the obligation to deploy border measures regarding trademarks and copyrights. Moreover, just counterfeiting and piracy, and not all trademark and copyright infringements, must be controlled, while border measures are optional when applied to other intellectual property rights.

Historically, counterfeiting was the first type of infringement of intellectual property rights controlled at the border. In fact, the Paris Convention already ordered the seizure on importation of goods unlawfully bearing a trademark or trade name, although the regime set forth in the Paris Convention was indeed flexible.[31] The obligation set forth in the TRIPS Agreement to control counterfeits is in line with the Preamble of the Agreement, where parties recognize the need to establish a 'multilateral framework of principles, rules and disciplines dealing with international trade in counterfeit goods'. Pursuant to the TRIPS Agreement, there is no obligation to control trademark violations distinct from counterfeiting, such as 'passing off' or the improper use of a trademark.[32] The same occurs with respect to copyright violations, since the obligation to control pirated goods does not entail the control of other copyright infringements, such as substantial similarity or adaptation without the author's permission.[33]

The TRIPS Agreement lays down the first international definitions of counterfeit and pirated goods, which condition the scope of action at the border.[34] Put into

30 In the European Union customs authorities may either *suspend the release* of the goods or *detain* these goods. These are distinct operations to be applied to goods placed under different procedures. Suspension of release applies to importation ('release for free circulation'), exportation and re-exportation, while detention is the action for goods placed under a suspensive procedure, placed in a free zone or a free warehouse, in the process of being re-exported with notification, introduced into the customs territory or leaving that territory. Thus, two actions (suspension of release and detention) apply to different customs operations. By contrast, the TRIPS Agreement only orders the suspension of release.

31 Article 9 Paris Convention. The Bern Convention also foresaw (an even softer regime for) the control of importation in Article 13.3. *See* Section I.

32 *See* Correa (2007), pp. 439–440; UNCTAD-ICTSD (2005), p. 610.

33 *Ibid.*

34 *See* footnotes 14 and 15.

relation with the prescribed actions, TRIPS definitions reflect the customary practice of focusing primarily on the control of visibly infringing goods, i.e. goods bearing without authorization a trademark identical to that validly registered or that cannot be distinguished and copies made without the consent of the right holder or person duly authorized by the right holder. There are several reasons for focusing the control on visibly infringing goods, the principal being the ease of determining the infringement.[35] Other infringements are more difficult to detect at first sight. This is indeed the case of patent infringement. Determining the existence of a patent violation requires an assessment of the scope of the claims, a much more complex activity than the visual inspection by customs' authorities,[36] and may require analyses that involve laboratory tests and other expert assessment procedures that can hardly be performed by customs authorities.[37] Patents are not, however, the only difficult case. In respect to the more and more frequent obligation to control all types of trademark violations, and not only counterfeits, it has been stated that 'findings of likelihood of confusion based on the degree of similarity of both the signs and the goods require a comprehensive legal analysis which is much less straightforward than determining counterfeit goods'.[38] As this task is usually performed by courts or intellectual property authorities, imposing it on inexpert customs officials may result in wrongful detentions.[39]

Finally, it must be noted that the requirements of the TRIPS Agreement apply to the control of infringements distinct from counterfeiting and piracy. This was made clear in the *China – Intellectual Property Rights* panel report, where it was stated that, in congruence with the second phrase of Article 51,[40] when States decide to avail themselves of the freedom to control infringements distinct from counterfeiting and piracy, the requirements set forth in Part III Section 4, of the TRIPS Agreement apply. The WTO Panel underlined the importance of the phrase 'provided that the requirements of this Section are met' and affirmed that this implies that all the requirements of Section 4 have to be met when controlling the importation of infringing goods, regardless of the intellectual property category concerned.[41] Hence, while countries enjoy an important margin of discretion when regulating the control of the exportation and transit, the same flexibility does not apply to the control of importation.

[35] *See* UNCTAD-ICTSD (2005), p. 610; Correa (2007), p. 440. Elaborating on this aspect, reference has been made to 'the institutional incompetence of the customs authorities to deal with complex matters relating to patent law'. *See* Gupta (2009), p. 265.

[36] *See* Correa (2009), p. 49; Gervais (2006), p. 49; Bronckers, Verkade and McNelis (2000), p. 20.

[37] *See* Kuipers *et al.* (2009), p. 8; Kuipers and Lamme (2013), p. 53.

[38] *See* Grosse Ruse-Khan (2015), p. 91.

[39] *See* Chapter 11.

[40] Which refers to the application of the same section to goods involving other infringements of intellectual property rights, provided that the requirements of this section are met.

[41] Therefore, when the scope of border measures embraces infringements distinct from counterfeiting and piracy, the conditions set forth in Section 4 of Part III of the TRIPS Agreement shall apply to each and every intellectual property covered. *See* WTO Panel, *China – Intellectual Property Rights*, para. 7.223.

4 Action concerning Goods Allegedly Infringing and Infringing Goods

The TRIPS Agreement conceives border measures as a combination of actions potentially taking place at two moments and involving two different authorities. First, customs authorities may suspend the release of the goods, either *ex officio* or because the right holder has lodged an application. Once the right holder has been informed about the suspension of release into free circulation, a reasonable period of time to initiate proceedings leading to a decision on the merits of the case, adopted by the 'competent authorities', is awarded.

The TRIPS Agreement differentiates 'competent authorities' from 'customs authorities'. While it is for 'customs authorities'[42] to suspend the release of goods, if the country does not specifically mandate *ex officio* action, such suspension will normally follow the decision of the 'competent authorities', either judicial or administrative. In some countries, the courts deal with the application for border seizures, a practice that some consider burdensome.[43] In principle, the decision on the infringing nature of the goods will be adopted by the 'competent authorities'.[44] Although it is possible that 'administrative authorities' and 'customs authorities' coincide or pertain to the same administrative branch,[45] at some stage, particularly if the owner of the products opposes the detention, proceedings should move to the judicial domain.

4.1 *Ex officio* Action

The TRIPS Agreement allows parties to prescribe that border measures must be initialled only by the right holder. However, in cases where States control importation *ex officio*, they will adjust their actions to the obligations set forth in Article 58 of the TRIPS Agreement. Accordingly, they must ensure that authorities may seek any useful information from the right holder, they shall notify both the importer and the right holder promptly of the suspension, and they may exempt public authorities from liability if their actions were taken in good faith.[46]

4.2 Remedies: Destruction or Disposal of the Goods

The practice with respect to the destiny of products detained at the border and finally considered to be counterfeit or pirated varies across countries. In terms of

42 These are mentioned in Articles 51, 52 and 53.1 TRIPS Agreement.

43 Against that practice, *see* note to Article 1 of the *Model provisions for national legislation to implement fair and effective border measures consistent with the Agreement on trade related aspects of intellectual property rights*. *See* World Customs Organization (2003), p. 8.

44 In some jurisdictions this is not necessarily the case. For instance, in the European Union, if the alleged infringer does not respond to the seizure of goods within a reduced number of days, goods are considered to be infringing and automatically destroyed.

45 *See* UNCTAD-ICTSD (2005), p. 609; Correa (2007), p. 439.

46 *See* Article 58 TRIPS Agreement.

disposition methods, which encompass both destruction and disposal,[47] a common consequence of infringement in some jurisdictions is the destruction of the goods, while in other countries ethical, economic or opportunity factors may result in a different outcome.

Pursuant to Article 59 of the TRIPS Agreement, competent authorities must be entitled to order the destruction or disposal of infringing goods seized at the border.[48] The decision regarding destruction or disposal will be adopted in accordance with the principles set up in Article 46 of the TRIPS Agreement. This article prescribes that judicial authorities shall have the authority to order that goods they found to be infringing be, without compensation, disposed of outside the channels of commerce in such a manner as to avoid any harm to the right holder or, if this would be contrary to existing constitutional requirements,[49] destroyed. The same possibility applies with respect to materials and implements the predominant use of which has been in the creation of the infringing goods. It also establishes a number of fair trial guarantees, in particular, the possibility of judicial review[50] and the call for proportionality.[51]

Destruction and disposal are not necessarily the only possible options, and more importantly, the application of both of these methods is not automatic and may not be necessary. It must, for instance, be subject to the test of proportionality. Therefore, the obligation set forth in the first sentence of Article 59 is satisfied if competent authorities have the authority to order *either* destruction *or* disposal[52] but does not require them to implement this power 'in a particular way, unless otherwise specified'.[53]

This was addressed in the WTO Panel report *China – Intellectual Property Rights*, where the United States held that the Chinese regulations did not satisfy the requirements of the TRIPS Agreement, particularly those concerning the destiny of products intercepted at the border and found to be infringing patents, trademarks, copyrights or related rights. Chinese Regulations on Customs Protection of Intellectual Property Rights foresaw the possibility of destroying goods found to be infringing and enumerated three disposal options, namely donations to charities, sale of the products to the right holder and auction of the goods after eradicating the infringing features.[54] Destruction was mentioned last in the list of options. According to China, this list was not a 'compulsory sequence of steps',[55] since customs authorities could decide to change the order autonomously. The Chinese

[47] *See* WTO Panel, *China – Intellectual Property Rights*, para. 7.250. [48] *Ibid.*, para. 7.285.

[49] This caveat 'was introduced to reflect a rule in countries such as Brazil where destruction of otherwise useful goods is allegedly unconstitutional'. *See* Gervais (2009b), p. 2354 (footnote 5).

[50] *See* Article 59 TRIPS Agreement.

[51] Pursuant to Article 46 TRIPS Agreement, relevant in the context of border measures by virtue of Article 59 TRIPS Agreement, '[i]n considering such requests, the need for proportionality between the seriousness of the infringement and the remedies ordered as well as the interests of third parties shall be taken into account'.

[52] *Ibid.*, para. 7.246. [53] *Ibid.*, para. 7.238. [54] *Ibid.*, para. 2.3. [55] *Ibid.*, para. 7.197.

viewpoint was upheld by the WTO Panel,[56] which also upheld the validity of donations, sale to the right holder and auction as disposal methods, although it did not agree with the specific procedure for auctioning infringing goods.[57] More importantly, the possibility to choose between donation and destruction was considered enough to satisfy the regime of the TRIPS Agreement.

If the option chosen is the disposal of products, Article 46 establishes that goods shall be placed 'outside the channels of commerce in such a manner as to avoid any harm caused to the right holder'. There is not a single and prescriptive means of disposal. Moreover, the requirement to avoid any harm to the right holder does not entail an absolute guarantee that no harm will be caused. There is an obligation to prevent the occurrence of damages, but given that disposal of infringing goods outside the channels of commerce 'is an alternative to destruction of the goods, it cannot be said that there is an inherent risk of harm simply because the goods have not been completely destroyed. If this was the case, there would be no choice between the methods of disposal.'[58]

5 *Guarantees That Apply*

5.1 Conditions and Protection of Parties Distinct from the Right Holder

The provisions of the TRIPS Agreement on border measures lay down a number of requisites aimed at guaranteeing the protection of parties distinct from the right holder as well as safeguarding activities and objectives distinct from intellectual property protection *per se*. They resemble the qualifications that apply in the case of provisional measures, since they share a very similar nature. Quite often these procedural guarantees and limitations are drafted in mandatory terms, particularly when they relate to the protection of free trade. In a way, they are a reflection of the nature of the TRIPS Agreement as a treaty that lays down both rights and limitations for right holders.[59]

In order to lodge an application for the suspension by the customs authorities of the release of goods, the right holder must show 'valid grounds for suspecting' that importation of counterfeit or pirated goods may take place.[60] This is the first requirement that the right holder must satisfy in order to have the border measure issued. Article 52 prescribes that the right holder shall be required to 'provide adequate evidence to satisfy the competent authorities that, under the laws of the country of importation, there is *prima facie* an infringement'. Hence, the initial suspicion mentioned in Article 51 must be documented with 'adequate evidence', which must be enough to convince competent authorities that an infringement is

56 *Ibid.*, para. 7.348.

57 The panel's disagreement did not focus on auctioning as such but on the fact that the Chinese system did not guarantee that the state of the goods was sufficiently altered to deter further infringement. *See* WTO Panel, *China – Intellectual Property Rights*, para. 7.375.

58 *Ibid.*, para. 7.282.

59 *See* Chapter 4, Sections II.2.2.5 and 2.2.6.

60 *See* Article 51 TRIPS Agreement.

likely to exist. The interpretation of what 'adequate evidence' means is left to the competent authorities.

The TRIPS Agreement establishes an additional condition concerning the provision of information. In order to proceed with the detention of the allegedly infringing goods, the right holder must supply a sufficiently detailed description of the goods to make them readily recognizable by customs authorities.[61] As stated elsewhere, this provision 'only requires information for the customs authorities to identify the allegedly infringing goods, but their inspection to determine whether *prima facie* infringement exist can be made by a different authority'.[62] Contrary to the wording in the TRIPS Agreement, some organizations have held that 'applications should not be rejected and enforcement should not be withheld solely due to the absence of specific details of the shipment or the goods'.[63]

Another threshold set forth in the TRIPS Agreement is the possibility to require the applicant to post a security or equivalent assurance, provided that this requisite does not 'unreasonably' deter recourse to border procedures.[64] Like other articles in the agreement, this provision does not prescribe a specific outcome but the means to arrive to such an outcome, since it merely obliges States to empower authorities to act.[65] The provision of such securities pursues the prevention of abuse as well as compensation to the defendant in case the procedures initiated prove unmerited.[66]

In connection with the obligation to post a security or equivalent assurance, the TRIPS Agreement establishes that judicial authorities shall be able to request that the applicant pay appropriate compensation in favour of the owner, importer and/or consignee of the goods. This may happen in two cases. The first concerns injuries caused through the wrongful detention of goods, while the second relates to injuries caused by the detention of goods if proceedings leading to a decision on the merits of the case are not initiated or the provisional measures prolonging the suspension of the release are not adopted by the competent authority.[67]

When customs authorities suspend the release of the goods on the basis of a decision other than by a judicial or other independent authority, the items protected by industrial designs, patents, layout-designs or undisclosed information *shall* be released ten working days after the applicant has been served notice of the suspension and no provisional relief by the authority has been granted.[68] In order to have the goods released, the owner,

[61] *See* Article 52 TRIPS Agreement. [62] *See* UNCTAD-ICTSD (2005), p. 612; Correa (2007), p. 442.

[63] *See* World Customs Organization (2003), para. 3.03. [64] *See* Article 53.1 TRIPS Agreement.

[65] Competent authorities shall have the authority to provide those guarantees, but this is different from effectively demanding their provision. *See* WTO Panel, *China – Intellectual Property Rights*, para. 7.236. In the section on border enforcement, TRIPS uses this construction as well in the cases of the authority to order the applicant to pay the importer, the consignee and the owner of the goods appropriate compensation and the possibility to order the destruction or disposal of infringing goods.

[66] *See* Article 53.1 TRIPS Agreement.

[67] Article 56 TRIPS Agreement must be put into relation with Article 55 of the same treaty, where the basis of the indemnification is established.

[68] *See* Articles 55 TRIPS Agreement and 53.2 of the TRIPS Agreement.

importer or consignee must satisfy the usual conditions for importing the products and post a security sufficient to protect the right holder.[69] Interestingly, it has been noted that this mandatory provision regulates 'measures that Members are *not* obliged to order under Article 51',[70] since that article establishes the mandatory control of counterfeit trademarks and pirated copyrights but not designs, patents, layout-designs or undisclosed information. This limitation of the right of the right holder to have the products detained operates as a safeguard against undue constraints to importation,[71] and it arguably responds to the underlying idea that 'trade in goods where IP infringements are not easily detectable should receive additional protection against the abuse of border measures and the risk of IP enforcement itself becoming a barrier to legitimate trade'.[72] New regulations establishing the automatic destruction of goods in case the alleged infringer does not respond in due time to the seizure are hardly compatible with this provision and with due process-related guarantees.[73]

Border measures are subjected to tight time limits. Allegedly infringing goods shall be released if, within a period not exceeding ten working days after the applicant has been notified of the suspension, the customs authorities have not been informed that proceedings leading to a decision on the merits of the case have been initiated or the competent authority has taken provisional measures prolonging the suspension of the release. The procedures on the merits of the case alluded to in Article 55 should be commenced by the applicant. In this case, a review, including a right to be heard, shall take place if the defendant so requests. This should enable competent authorities to decide whether these measures shall be modified, revoked or confirmed.

The protection of customs of authorities has also been foreseen in the TRIPS Agreement. Where measures are adopted *ex officio* and in good faith, Members may exempt both public authorities and officials from liability. This is quite a flexible provision as it may protect both judicial and administrative authorities, although it was probably conceived primarily to protect border authorities in the course of their inspection activities. As stated in Article 48.2 of the TRIPS Agreement, 'the burden of proof that actions were not taken or intended in good faith would rest with the party that alleges misconduct; in other words, *bona fide* would be presumed'.[74]

Regular consumers may also be entitled to protection in some specific cases, since Article 60 of the TRIPS Agreement states that small quantities of goods of non-commercial nature contained in travellers' personal luggage or sent in small consignments may be excluded from the application of the section on border measures.

5.2 Guarantees for the Right Holder

In addition to the right to require the suspension of the release into free circulation of goods allegedly infringing intellectual property rights, the TRIPS Agreement also

69 *Ibid.* 70 *See* UNCTAD-ICTSD (2005), p. 614. 71 *See* Dreier (1996), p. 250.
72 *See* Grosse Ruse-Khan (2010), p. 627. 73 See Chapter 12, Section I.
74 *See* UNCTAD-ICTSD (2005), p. 600.

enshrines a number of guarantees in favour of the right holder. These guarantees fundamentally concern procedural rights related to the information that the right holder may receive and the actions that he may undertake.

First, the right holder is entitled to receive information on the measure that is going to be adopted. In this particular regard, judicial or administrative authorities must inform the applicant 'within a reasonable period' on whether they have accepted the application.[75] Additionally, where determined by the competent authorities, the right holder will be informed of the period during which the customs authorities will take action. This period may vary in each country, and in some cases it may take up to a year.[76]

Article 57 of the TRIPS Agreement lays down the right of information in the context of border measures. It establishes that, where a positive determination has been made on the merits of a case, Members may authorize competent authorities to inform the right holder of the names and addresses of the consignor, the importer and the consignee as well as of the quantity of goods. This will allow the right holder 'to act against all those that were possibly involved in the infringement'.[77]

5.3 Guarantees for Both Parties

Both the importer and the applicant must be promptly notified of the suspension of the release of goods.[78] What 'promptly' specifically entails is open to a narrow margin of interpretation. Promptly, indeed, means 'done without delay' or 'immediate',[79] thus implying a very short period of time.

Both the right holder and the importer must have sufficient opportunity to inspect any goods detained by customs authorities, subject to the protection of confidential information.[80] In the case of the right holder, inspection should allow him to substantiate his claims, while in the case of the alleged infringer inspection should permit him to elaborate his defense.

6 *Law That Applies to Border Measures*

The *China – Intellectual Property Rights* report confirmed that WTO Members must apply the same conditions prescribed for the control of importation of counterfeit and pirated goods as those pertaining to the control of importation of goods infringing other categories of intellectual property rights. However, the WTO Panel

75 *See* Article 52 TRIPS Agreement.

76 For instance, in the EU Regulation No. 608/2013, Article 11.1 establishes that '[t]hat period shall begin on the day the decision granting the application takes effect, pursuant to Article 10, and shall not exceed one year from the day following the date of adoption'.

77 *See* UNCTAD-ICTSD (2005), p. 617.

78 *See* Article 54 TRIPS Agreement.

79 *See Oxford Dictionary*, available at: http://oxforddictionaries.com/definition/english/prompt?q=prompt (last accessed June 2015).

80 *See* Article 57 TRIPS Agreement, first phrase.

also stated that in the cases of exportation and transit the requirements set forth in the section on border measures of the TRIPS Agreement do not necessarily apply. The finding of the WTO Panel also applies with respect to the relevant law to determine the infringing status of goods, which will be different in the cases of importation, exportation and transit.

Article 52 of the TRIPS Agreement states that the right holder must provide evidence to satisfy the competent authorities that, 'under the laws of the country of importation, there is *prima facie* an infringement'. Additionally, footnote 14 of the TRIPS Agreement refers to the law of the country of importation to assess the 'counterfeit' and 'pirated' nature of the goods. Therefore, both from the wording of Article 52 and from the references found in footnote 14, it is clear that the relevant law in the case of importation is the law of the country of importation.

Neither the TRIPS Agreement nor the GATT defines 'importation'. This lack of definition may create practical difficulties for the identification of the actual country of importation. To 'import' means 'to bring (goods or services) into a country from abroad'.[81] Hence, from the textual point of view, crossing the border would be enough to consider that an importation has taken place, thus permitting the country of transit to assess the infringing nature of good pursuant to its own law. If such a literal interpretation was correct, each transit operation would imply an act of 'importation' and be impeded by right holders located in the country of transit. This is not, however, the correct reading. The nature and meaning of the operations of transit and importation differ. Article V:1 of GATT distinguishes transit from importation, and several articles of the TRIPS Agreement allude to transit and importation separately.[82]

The case of exportation does not raise special difficulties. If countries decide to empower customs authorities to control exportation, they will associate this possibility to the negative rights granted to the right holder by intellectual property national statutes. This right will be either expressly recognized in the list of negative rights or, as happens in many countries, associated to some other negative entitlements such as, in the case of patents, impeding the sale or offer for sale. Whichever the case, a link will be established between the control of exportation and right holders' rights pursuant to municipal law.[83]

The control of transit is an entirely different matter. In this case, whether the law of the country of importation is relevant to determine the infringing status of goods

81 *See Compact Oxford English Dictionary*, available at: www.askoxford.com/concise_oed/import?view=uk (last accessed June 2015).

82 Not surprisingly, countries regulate differently the control of importation and transit. Several customs procedures imply the entrance of goods into the national territory, even if their status is not that of goods released into free circulation. This is the case of 'external transit', and some may argue that it is also the case of goods placed under supervision in free zones.

83 A discussion touches upon the inclusion of the control of exportation among right holders' rights, something that in light of some fundamental principles of intellectual property law could be not necessarily the case. *See*, in detail, Massaguer (1989), pp. 79–83.

is not related to the prescriptions set forth in Article 52 and footnote 14 of the TRIPS Agreement. The answer to the question of which is the relevant law to assess the infringing status of goods in transit is based upon basic principles of intellectual property law as well as other disciplines of international economic law. The principles of territoriality of intellectual property rights and the freedom of transit are of paramount importance in this context. Moreover, there is no unique answer applicable to all categories of intellectual property rights. The common understanding is that countries cannot block goods that merely transit their customs territory alleging intellectual property infringements pursuant to their local law. However, we argue in Chapter 11 that, if a risk of diversion of counterfeit goods onto the internal market is proven or in cases of clear fraud of the transit procedure, countries may be entitled to stop counterfeits. If countries decide to act in these cases, both the law of the country of importation and the law of the country of customs procedures should be of relevance to assess the counterfeit status of trademark-infringing goods.

III THE REGULATION OF BORDER MEASURES IN PLURILATERAL AGREEMENTS

1 *ACTA Provisions on Border Enforcement*

Intellectual property enforcement at the border was among the most controversial subjects of the negotiations leading to the adoption of the Anti-Counterfeiting Trade Agreement. Chapter II, Section 3, of ACTA codified the norms on the scope of border measures, the initiation of proceedings and the procedure to deal with goods allegedly infringing intellectual property rights caught in the context of the implementation of border measures. The provisions of ACTA are closely related to those of the TRIPS Agreement,[84] and in several respects border measures articles either specify or strengthen TRIPS provisions. Generally speaking, while articles of ACTA on border measures are not as problematic as anticipated in the context of the negotiations, they expand the rights of right holders and make it more difficult for other interested stakeholders to take advantage of the normative space left in the TRIPS Agreement, in the sense that ambiguities and rights of traders and owners of goods are restricted.

1.1 Border Operations Controlled

ACTA obliges its Parties to implement or maintain procedures with respect to the importation and exportation of shipments, both if the initiative to suspend the release of goods is undertaken by customs authorities and when it responds to

[84] *See* Chapter 4, Sections III.1.2 and 1.3.

the right holders' request.[85] However, ACTA does not require the adoption of either *ex officio* or *ex parte* measures to control the transit.

Contrary to the TRIPS Agreement, Parties of ACTA shall control the exportation of allegedly infringing goods and set up *ex officio* procedures.[86] Hence, Parties that so far did not allow customs authorities to act *ex officio* will be obliged to permit it, and States that already foresaw *ex officio* action will be obliged to maintain it.[87] The same applies with regards to exportation: those Members that so far did not allow custom authorities to control exportation will be obliged to enable it, and those that already foresaw the control of exportation will be obliged to maintain it.

ACTA also regulates several aspects concerning the control of transit. It defines 'in-transit goods' as goods under customs transit or transhipment and clarifies that the former means the procedure under which goods are transported under customs control from one customs office to another, while the latter refers to 'the Customs procedure under which goods are transferred under Customs control from the importing means of transport to the exporting means of transport within the area of one Customs office which is the office of both importation and exportation'.[88] Also important for the purposes of the section on border measures is the definition of the notion of 'territory', which means the 'customs territory and all free zones of a Party'.[89]

Importantly, ACTA confirms the right to 'adopt or maintain procedures with respect to suspect in-transit goods or in other situations where the goods are under customs control'.[90] These procedures – suspension of the release and detention – may be adopted on the initiative of customs authorities or at the request of the right holder. Although this is an apparently naïve provision as Parties are free to decide whether to control the transit ('may adopt or maintain'), its effects may be far-reaching. There are two reasons for that.

On the one hand, ACTA allows the adoption of border measures with respect to all categories of intellectual property rights. On the other hand, the existence of infringement will be determined in accordance with the law of the Party providing the procedures. This regime implies that Parties are entitled to control in-transit

85 *See* Article 16.1 ACTA. 86 *See* Section II.2.3.1.

87 *See* Article 16.1(a) and (b) ACTA, and Article 16.2 ACTA.

88 *Ibid.*, Article 5(f) ACTA repeats the definition provided in the Kyoto Convention, on the Simplification and Harmonization of Customs Procedures of 1974, Definition E4/Annex E; and Definition E1/F1.

89 Article V GATT, on 'Freedom of transit', only mentions 'territory' but does not provide a definition, something which has to be understood in the context of an agreement that provides a definition not for 'territory', but for 'customs territory', and defines it as a 'territory with respect to which separate tariffs and other regulations of commerce are maintained'. Whether free zones are included in the definition of 'territory' has been debated. This is probably the reason why footnote 1 to Article 5(m) ACTA states that 'the Parties acknowledge that free zone means a part of the territory of a Party where any goods introduced are generally regarded, insofar as import duties and taxes are concerned, as being outside the customs territory'.

90 'A Party *may* adopt or maintain', Article 16.2 ACTA (emphasis added).

goods and ascertain the infringing nature of the products protected by any category of intellectual property rights in accordance with the local law. If no other conditions are set, the effects of this regime may be noticed not only in the country adopting it but also in third countries.

The potential impact that the treatment of goods in transit could have on free trade and access to intellectual property-protected goods in jurisdictions other than those providing the procedures was a matter of concern in the negotiations leading to the adoption of ACTA. The trade disruption caused by the European Union's customs regulation constantly surfaced the treaty negotiations.[91] Succinctly, it was understood that ACTA could imply the expansion of a regime entailing the indiscriminate control of goods in transit protected by all types of intellectual property categories as well as the application of the law of the country of transit to determine the existence of an infringement. Although the controversy had its origin in the detention of patented goods in transit in the Netherlands, similar arguments were made with regard to the control of trademark products in transit.

1.2 Categories of Intellectual Property Rights Subject to Control

As a matter of principle, ACTA provisions apply to all categories of intellectual property rights that its Parties recognize in their national legal orders. These categories include at least those regulated in the TRIPS Agreement,[92] since being a Member of the WTO is a pre-requisite to becoming Party to ACTA.[93] Therefore, the border measures of ACTA would apply in principle to all categories of intellectual property rights that are the subject of Sections 1 through 7 of Part II of the TRIPS Agreement.[94]

However, two important caveats must be introduced. The first concerns the effects of linking the scope of ACTA to the categories of intellectual property rights that are the *subject* of Sections 1 through 7 of Part II of the TRIPS Agreement, while the second relates to the freedom recognized in ACTA to exclude certain categories of intellectual property from specific areas of enforcement.

Except in those cases where it is explicitly stated otherwise, ACTA applies with respect to 'intellectual property'. While Article 5(h) of ACTA does not provide an exact definition of 'intellectual property', it maintains the reach given to this term by Article 1.2 of the TRIPS Agreement, which specifies that 'intellectual property' refers to the 'categories of intellectual property that are the subject of Sections 1 through 7 of the Part II'. Although the scope of ACTA and the TRIPS Agreement may seem to be identical, in fact it is different, both in general and concerning border measures.

91 *See* in this regard, Grosse Ruse-Khan and Jaeger (2009), pp. 502–503; Seuba (2009); Kumar (2009); Seuba (2010a); Micara (2012).

92 *See infra* analysis on Article 5(h) ACTA.

93 Article 43 ACTA establishes that 'any Member of the WTO may apply to accede to this Agreement'.

94 *See* Chapter 4, Section III.1.1.

First of all, as noted in Chapter 4, it must be recalled that the 'categories' of the TRIPS Agreement do not match with the headings of Sections 1 through 7 of the Agreement but with the categories that are the *subject* of those sections. This is for instance the case of *sui generis* plant variety protection. There are also categories currently protected in various countries that are not the subject of the TRIPS Agreement or ACTA, such as the protection of non-original databases.

In some respects and in comparison to the TRIPS Agreement, ACTA reduces the scope of protection and does not include some forms of protection effectively covered by the TRIPS Agreement and some PTAs.[95] Moreover, the definition of intellectual property contained in Article 5(h) of ACTA must be put into relation with Article 3.2, which states that nothing in the Agreement creates an obligation on a Party 'to apply measures where an intellectual property right is not protected under its laws and regulations'. This means, for instance, that ACTA would not apply in countries such as the United States to the protection of geographical indications.

Early drafts of ACTA stipulated the obligation to provide border measures for in-transit goods suspected of infringing 'intellectual property rights',[96] a compromise watered down later on. The exclusion of patents and confidential information from the scope of border measures in ACTA[97] responded to both legal and social concerns. ACTA was negotiated in the midst of the controversy arising from the effects of the European border measures regulation on public health and free trade. This was, however, the last straw in the context of a more profound tendency reflected in bilateral, plurilateral and even unilateral initiatives to enhance intellectual property enforcement.[98] The heightened reaction to these initiatives as well as the political context that prevailed between 2007 and 2010 – when ACTA was negotiated – partially explain the freedom given to Parties of ACTA to exclude patents and undisclosed information from the scope of the section on border enforcement.

1.3 Action concerning Infringing Goods

While ACTA upholds the TRIPS Agreement and Parties can enable competent authorities to choose between destruction or disposal of infringing goods, ACTA's drafting seems to favour destruction. Indeed, reference to disposal is made after destruction, as if it were a second-best approach, and then only to state that disposal shall be performed in such a manner as to avoid any harm to the right holder.[99] ACTA remains almost totally silent with respect to the guarantees that benefit the contesting Parties in the context of remedies concerning infringing goods. However,

[95] Utility models are covered for instance in the entire enforcement section of the EU-CARIFORUM States FTA and EIA (2008), in Article 148, and a provision on criminal enforcement refers also to utility models in Article 121 Japan-Indonesia FTA and EIA (2008). *See* Chapter 4, Section III.1.3, and Seuba (2015a), pp. 62–64.

[96] *See* Article 2.X:1–2 ACTA Draft of 21 April 2010.

[97] *See* footnote 6 of ACTA.

[98] *See* Correa (2009).

[99] *See* Article 20.1 ACTA.

those guarantees can be found in the TRIPS Agreement by virtue of the referral to the TRIPS Agreement made in Article 1 of ACTA.

Like the TRIPS Agreement, ACTA allows States to exclude parallel imported goods from the application of border measures.[100] Hence, it is required that goods were put in the market by the right holder or with his consent. Therefore, concerns expressed regarding the exclusion from this freedom of goods that have been the object of a compulsory license are relevant in the ACTA context as well.[101] A notable difference, however, is that ACTA border measures apply to all categories of intellectual property rights, with the exception of patents and protection of undisclosed information.[102]

ACTA clarifies that border measures must be implemented in a manner that avoids the creation of barriers to legitimate trade. This is an important condition, which can also be inferred from the Preamble of ACTA as well as the general referral to the objectives and principles of the TRIPS Agreement in Articles 6.1 and 2.3 of ACTA. This provision could be crucial in light of the possibility established in ACTA to control goods that, as will be analysed, are legitimate.[103]

1.4 Guarantees That Apply

1.4.1 PROTECTION OF PARTIES DISTINCT FROM THE RIGHT HOLDER. Several articles of ACTA regulate the provision of information on the part of the right holder. The first article to address the provision of information does so in a general manner and states that the right holder may offer information to assist the competent authorities in taking border measures if requested to do so or may supply information on his own initiative.[104] The reference to the provision of information on the initiative of the right holder is a novelty with respect to the TRIPS Agreement and may imply recognition of private systems of information as valid channels to feed the action of border authorities.

Another article related to the provision of information concerns the application made by the right holder. Article 17 of ACTA orders right holders to provide information on two different aspects. The first part of the relevant provision states that if the right holder presents an application for the suspension of the release of the goods or their detention, he must provide 'adequate evidence to satisfy the competent authorities that, under the law of the Party providing the procedures, there is *prima facie* an infringement of the right holder's intellectual property right'.[105] The second part requires the applicant to supply sufficient information reasonably in his possession to make the suspect goods reasonably recognizable by the

[100] Footnote 5 of ACTA states that there is 'no obligation to apply procedures set forth in this Section to goods put on the market in another country by or with the consent of the right holder'.
[101] *See* Section II.2.2. [102] *See* footnote 6 ACTA. [103] *See* Chapter 11.
[104] *See* Article 15 ACTA. [105] *See* Article 17.1 ACTA.

competent authorities. Certainly, both conditions evoke what it is just usual in the context of interim measures.

In line with a number of trade agreements but presenting a novelty with respect to the TRIPS Agreement, ACTA softens the requirements that the right holder must fulfil in order to ask for information. This is in particular the case of the request of sufficient information to make the suspect goods reasonably recognizable by competent authorities, as already foreseen in the TRIPS Agreement. ACTA, however, adds that such a requirement shall not unreasonably deter recourse to *ex parte* border enforcement procedures.[106] It therefore introduces another criterion to evaluate national border enforcement regulations and facilitate the control of allegedly infringing goods.

ACTA clearly establishes that Parties may disregard – 'deny, suspend, or void' – an application where the applicant has abused border enforcements procedures. Although nothing in the TRIPS Agreement precluded enacting a provision such as this, and it could already be found in local legislation, it is an interesting recognition of the undesired effects of some border enforcement actions. Even more interesting is the compromise stating that the same options – 'deny, suspend, or void' – apply 'where there is due cause'.[107] This vague provision may permit the consideration of a wide range of legal and social grounds to deny, suspend or void an application.

ACTA also allows the defendant to obtain possession of suspect goods provided that three conditions are satisfied. First, a judicial order must be obtained. Second, the alleged infringer must post a bond or other security. Third, this possibility shall only apply in exceptional circumstances.[108] This provision contrasts with the more balanced regime for the release of goods, conditioned to posting a security, found in the TRIPS Agreement, which tries to avoid border measures becoming a barrier to legitimate trade.[109] However, as will be examined later, some PTAs are even more drastic since they categorically forbid the release of allegedly infringing goods.[110] Given the mandatory language of Article 53.2 of the TRIPS Agreement and the general recognition of the preference for the obligations of the TRIPS Agreement found in ACTA[111] and some PTAs,[112] the regime set forth in the TRIPS Agreement – which is more flexible when observed from the point of view of the alleged infringer and the interest in preserving free trade – should prevail whenever conflicts with other treaties or national provisions are detected.

The requirement of a security or equivalent assurance in the case of *ex parte* border procedures 'to protect the defendant and the competent authorities and to prevent abuse' follows *verbatim* the obligation already set forth in the TRIPS Agreement, including the limitation to not 'unreasonably' deter recourse to border

106 *Ibid.* 107 *See* Article 17.4 ACTA. 108 *See* Article 18 ACTA.
109 *See* TRIPS Article 53.2 and Section II.3.1.
110 *See* Article 18.11.20 Republic of Korea-US FTA and EIA (2012).
111 *See* Chapter 4, Section III.1.2. 112 *See* Chapter 4, Section IV.2.1 (last paragraph).

measures protection.[113] The novelty with respect to previously existing obligations is that the security can be provided in the form a bond conditioned to hold the defendant harmless from any loss or damage resulting from the withholding of the goods. This novelty was probably proposed by the United States, since very similar drafting can be found in the majority of trade agreements subscribed to by the United States.[114]

ACTA targets border control of infringements of a commercial nature. Two provisions apply to goods that must or could be seized. First, although ACTA specifically states that even small consignments must be controlled, the section on border measures will only apply to goods of a commercial nature.[115] Additionally, in response to criticism attracted by the initial proposal to search personal luggage,[116] ACTA recognizes the right of Parties to exclude from the application of the Section on border measures 'small quantities of goods of a non-commercial nature contained in travelers' personal luggage'.[117]

1.4.2 GUARANTEES FOR THE RIGHT HOLDER. The provisions on border measures of ACTA expand the rights of the right holder and enable further expansion thanks to the ambiguity arising from the combination of articles dealing with border situations that can be controlled, the categories of intellectual property rights subject to control and the law that will apply to determine the infringing nature of goods. ACTA also lays down a number of additional (*vis-à-vis* the TRIPS Agreement) guarantees and procedural details favouring the right holder. For instance, in line with the TRIPS Agreement, ACTA obliges each Party to inform the applicant within a reasonable period of time whether the application has been accepted.[118] However, transforming into an obligation what in the TRIPS Agreement is left at the discretion of the Members,[119] ACTA establishes that, where competent authorities have accepted the application, they shall also inform the applicant of the period of validity of the application.[120]

Concerning guarantees for the right holder, ACTA not only transforms the options of the TRIPS Agreement into obligations but also creates new obligations. Going a step further towards increased levels of protection compared to the TRIPS Agreement, ACTA addresses different contexts where information must be provided and mentions additional purposes of the provision of information. These include the identification of the goods and the determination of the existence of an infringement

113 Compare Article 53.1 TRIPS Agreement with Article 18 ACTA.

114 *See* Article 15.11.21 CAFTA-DR-US FTA and EIA (2006); Article 17.11.20 US-Australia FTA and EIA (2005); Article 14.9.21 US-Bahrain FTA and EIA (2006); Article 16.11.21 US-Colombia FTA and EIA (2012); Article 15.11.21 US-Morocco FTA and EIA (2006); Article 15.11.21 US-Panama FTA and EIA (2012); Article 15.10.21 US-Oman FTA and EIA (2009).

115 *See* Article 14.1 ACTA.

116 Initial leaks of ACTA texts included a provision stating that 'Parties shall include in the application of this section goods of a commercial nature sent in small consignments'.

117 *See* Article 14.2 ACTA.

118 *See* Article 17.3 ACTA.

119 Article 52 TRIPS Agreement states 'where determined by the competent authorities'.

120 *Ibid.*

as well as information provided once the determination as to infringement has been made or goods have been seized.

With the purpose to assist Parties in the detection of infringing goods, ACTA recognizes a power of the Parties and an additional advantage for the right holder: that of authorizing competent authorities to provide a right holder with information about specific shipments of the goods, including the description and quantity of the goods.[121]

Information may also be provided to determine the existence of infringement. ACTA goes beyond almost all existing agreements in specifying that this information includes the description and quantity of the goods and the identification of the consignor, importer, exporter or consignee as well as the country of origin of the goods and the name and address of the manufacturer of the goods.[122] Part of this information would fall under the scope of Article 57 of the TRIPS Agreement. The difference, however, is that while in the TRIPS Agreement the provision of this information is subjected to the existence of a 'positive determination' on the merits of the case, in the case of ACTA this information will assist in the determination of whether infringement has occurred.

While the two options are left to the discretion of the Parties, ACTA makes compulsory the provision of information in a third scenario once the infringement has been determined. In this case, if the legislation does not already establish the obligation to provide information to determine the existence of the infringement,[123] authorities will provide the right holder with information about the goods, including but not limited to the description and quantity of the goods; the name and address of the consignor, importer, exporter or consignee and, if known, the country of origin of the goods and the name and address of the manufacturer of the goods. This provision expands and converts into an obligation what in Article 57 of the TRIPS Agreement and in many PTAs is a possibility left up to the States to implement.[124]

1.5 Law That Applies to Border Measures

ACTA states that if the right holder presents an application for the suspension of the release or detention of the goods, he must provide 'adequate evidence to satisfy the competent authorities that, under the law of the Party providing the procedures, there is *prima facie* an infringement'.[125] Considered *in abstracto*, the reference to

[121] *See* Article 22(a) ACTA. [122] *See* Article 22(b) ACTA.

[123] Article 22(c) ACTA starts with the caveat 'unless a Party has provided its competent authorities with the authority described in subparagraph (b)', and Article 22(b) of the treaty establishes that, 'a Party may authorize its competent authorities to provide a right holder with information about goods, including, but not limited to, ... to assist in the determination referred to in Article 19'.

[124] However, the obligation to effectively provide this information only applies in the case of imported goods. *See* Article 22(c) ACTA.

[125] *See* Article 17.1 ACTA (emphasis added).

'the law of the Party providing the procedures' is problematic. For instance, in the case of the control of products in transit, if countries do not exclude patents from the scope of border enforcement, it may imply the control of patented products in transit. Such control will be conducted pursuant to the law of country providing the procedures (or the country of transit), which may lead to the kinds of problems that arose in the European context with regard to the seizure of pharmaceutical products in transit. Although the possibility is real, this does not automatically need to be the case.

In effect, the situation described has to be framed in the broader context of other commitments in ACTA and the obligations of ACTA Parties pursuant to their membership to the World Trade Organization. Moreover, it has to be underlined that the possibility to control the transit in accordance to the law of the country applying the procedures does not entail the right to detain the goods and decide on their infringing nature. Something else – a necessary link between the country providing the procedures and the goods – must exist. In Chapter 11 we argue that either there must be either a risk of diversion onto the internal market or it must be clear that there is an abuse of the transit procedure.

2 *Border Measures in the Trans-Pacific Partnership Agreement*

The Trans-Pacific Partnership Agreement article on border measures repeats the pattern already observed in other areas. It fundamentally relies on previous trade agreements concluded by the Unites States to increase standards of protection and improve right holders' rights. In the area of border measures this is done by providing that more intellectual property categories and border situations must be controlled in a way that makes predictable the occurrence of conflicts with fundamental intellectual property and free trade principles.

2.1 Operations and Categories Subject to Control

The TPP foresees the mandatory control of importation of counterfeit, confusingly similar trademark and pirated copyright goods. The control of importation of these goods will take place both *ex parte*[126] and *ex officio*,[127] while the control of exportation is mandatory *ex officio*.[128]

The case of the control of transit exemplifies what happens with respect to other provisions in the Trans-Pacific Partnership Agreement, heavily conditioned by numerous footnotes. In this case, the control of transit of counterfeit, confusingly similar trademark and pirated copyright goods seems in principle an obligation, while in reality it is just a faculty of Member States. In effect, by virtue of a footnote,

126 Article 18.76.1 of the Trans-Pacific Partnership Agreement.
127 Article 18.76.5(a) of the Trans-Pacific Partnership Agreement.
128 Article 18.76.5(b) of the Trans-Pacific Partnership Agreement.

the control of transit becomes discretional and can be substituted by the provision of information to another Party regarding goods that have been examined.[129]

The TPP would be, hence, less demanding than several PTAs both with respect the categories of intellectual property rights object of control and the border operations that must be controlled. Certainly, in respect to TRIPS, the TPP adds the control of confusingly similar trademarks and requires the control of exportation. However, PTAs generally go beyond that and demand the control of exportation and, some PTAs, the control of transit as well.[130] Moreover, the categories of intellectual property rights object of control pursuant to PTAs may also go beyond those mentioned in the TPP.

2.2 Action concerning Infringing Goods

The TPP establishes that competent authorities must be authorized to order the destruction of infringing goods. Even if destruction seems to be the first option, disposal outside the channels of commerce is also possible. These two are, in fact, almost the sole available options, since the TPP foresees that only 'in exceptional circumstances' goods may not be disposed outside the channels of commerce. As it is also common in PTAs, in regard to counterfeit trademark goods, the simple removal of the trademark unlawfully affixed shall not be sufficient, other than in exceptional cases, to permit the release of the goods into the channels of commerce.

2.3 Guarantees That Apply

2.3.1 PROTECTION OF PARTIES DISTINCT FROM THE RIGHT HOLDER. As it happens with provisions relating to provisional measures, the party demanding the suspension of release must provide adequate evidence to convince the competent authorities that there is *prima facie* an infringement and to supply sufficient information to make the suspect goods reasonably recognizable by competent authorities. The TPP, however, repeats the content of ACTA[131] and US PTAs[132] and establishes a limit not foreseen in the TRIPS Agreement. In this regard, it affirms that the requirement to provide information shall not unreasonably deter recourse to these procedures.[133]

The TPP also recognizes the faculty of judicial authorities to require the right holder the provision of reasonable security or equivalent assurance to protect the defendant and the competent authorities and to prevent abuse. As it happens with respect to the provision of information, there is also a limit regarding the provision of a security: it shall not unreasonably deter recourse to these procedures.

[129] *See* footnote 123 of the Trans-Pacific Partnership Agreement. [130] *See* Section IV.2.
[131] *See* ACTA Article 17.1. [132] *See* Section IV.3.3.
[133] *See* Article 18.76.2 of the Trans-Pacific Partnership Agreement.

The TPP focuses on border control of infringements of a commercial nature. In this respect, it specifically states the provision on border measures shall apply to goods of a commercial nature, even if sent in small consignments. However, small quantities of goods of a non-commercial nature contained in travellers' personal luggage and in small consignments may be excluded from the application of the border measures article.[134]

2.3.2 GUARANTEES FOR THE RIGHT HOLDER. In a novelty with respect to TRIPS but in line with ACTA and PTAs,[135] the TPP foresees that the security that can be requested to the applicant may be in the form of a bond conditioned to hold the defendant harmless from any loss or damage resulting from any suspension of the release of goods in the event the competent authorities determine that the article is not an infringing good.

The right of information has been extended to the border measures provision, as it happened in ACTA. In effect, Parties may provide that their competent authorities have the authority to inform the right holder without undue delay of the names and addresses of the consignor, exporter, consignee or importer; a description of the goods; the quantity of the goods and, if known, the country of origin of the goods.[136] This implies providing sensitive information when a decision on the merits of the case has not yet been adopted.[137]

Also in a novelty with respect to TRIPS but in line with United States PTAs, if a Party establishes or assesses an application fee, storage fee or destruction fee, that fee shall not be set at an amount that unreasonably deters recourse to these procedures.[138]

2.4 Law That Applies to Border Measures

The definition of counterfeit trademark goods and pirated copyright goods established in the TPP for the purpose of the nine sub-sections of the article on border measures affirms that the relevant law to assess the infringing status of goods is the law of the country providing the procedures.[139] Hence, whereas in TRIPS mention is made to the country of importation, in the TPP it is the law of the country implementing the border measures the relevant one. As examined with respect to importation and exportation, this is the reasonable option. However, if countries

[134] *See* Article 18.76.9 and footnote 125 of the Trans-Pacific Partnership Agreement.

[135] *See* Article 18.76.3 of the Trans-Pacific Partnership Agreement and compare it with TRIPS Article 53.1, ACTA Article 18, and Article 15.11.21 CAFTA-DR-US FTA and EIA (2006); Article 17.11.20 US-Australia FTA and EIA (2005); Article 14.9.21 US-Bahrain FTA and EIA (2006); Article 16.11.21 US-Colombia FTA and EIA (2012); Article 15.11.21 US-Morocco FTA and EIA (2006); Article 15.11.21 US-Panama FTA and EIA (2012); Article 15.10.21 US-Oman FTA and EIA (2009).

[136] Article 18.76.4 (a) of the Trans-Pacific Partnership Agreement. Article 18.76.4 (a) permits however submitting this information within thirty working days of the seizure or determination that the goods are counterfeit trademark goods or pirated copyright goods.

[137] Weatherall (2015), p. 39. [138] Article 18.76.8 of the Trans-Pacific Partnership Agreement.

[139] *See* footnote 116 (a) and (b), as well as Article 18.76.2 of the Trans-Pacific Partnership Agreement.

decide controlling the transit, the application of the law of the country providing the procedures, without further qualification, is problematic.[140]

IV THE REGULATION OF BORDER MEASURES IN PREFERENTIAL TRADE AGREEMENTS

1 *Introduction*

The protection of intellectual property rights at the border is one of the central topics addressed in PTAs, which have spearheaded future regulation in the multilateral and plurilateral arena. Border measures norms enshrined in some customs unions and free trade agreements either anticipated or coincided with the TRIPS Agreement.[141] In fact, border enforcement has frequently been the sole intellectual property matter addressed in PTAs, sometimes supplemented with articles on general aspects of intellectual property protection. Even today, when comparing the different areas of intellectual property enforcement regulation, border enforcement is, by and large, the one that attracts more attention within PTAs.[142]

PTAs regulating border measures not only anticipated multilateral and plurilateral agreements but tried to remedy the deficiencies that, from the point of view of right holders, can be found in the multilateral context. Probably the most important one,

140 *See* Chapter 11.

141 When examining the regulation of the agreements addressing border measures, it is possible to detect a core regulation that appeared for the first time in NAFTA and was later transplanted into the TRIPS Agreement and to bilateral agreements, the first being those concluded by Mexico as early as 1995. *See* Colombia-Mexico FTA and EIA (1995); Costa Rica – Mexico FTA and EIA (1995).

142 A research conducted in 2013 determined that while 38 PTAs regulate civil enforcement and 36 PTAs regulate criminal enforcement, 52 PTAs regulate border enforcement. *See* EFTA-Albania FTA (2010); Andean Community CU (1988); Australia-Chile FTA and EIA (2009); Chile-Japan FTA and EIA (2007); Chile-Mexico FTA and EIA (1999); China-Costa Rica FTA and EIA (2011); Colombia-Mexico FTA and EIA (1995); Costa Rica-Mexico FTA and EIA (1995); CAFTA-DR-US FTA and EIA (2006); EC Treaty CU and EIA (1958); EFTA-Colombia FTA and EIA (2011); EFTA-Hong Kong, China FTA and EIA (2012); EFTA-Montenegro FTA (2012); EFTA-Peru FTA (2011); EFTA-Serbia FTA (2010); EFTA-Ukraine FTA and EIA (2012); EU-CARIFORUM States FTA and EIA (2008); EU-Colombia FTA and EIA (2013); EU-Republic of Korea FTA and EIA (2011); EU-Peru FTA and EIA (2013); Japan-Indonesia FTA and EIA (2008); Japan-Malaysia FTA and EIA (2006); Japan-Peru FTA and EIA (2012); Japan-Philippines FTA and EIA (2008); Japan-Switzerland FTA and EIA (2009); Japan-Thailand FTA and EIA (2007); Japan-Viet Nam FTA and EIA (2009); Republic of Korea-US FTA and EIA (2012); Mexico-El Salvador FTA and EIA (2001); Mexico-Guatemala FTA and EIA (2001); Mexico-Honduras FTA and EIA (2001); Mexico-Nicaragua FTA and EIA (1998); NAFTA FTA and EIA (1994); Pakistan-China FTA and EIA (2007/2009); Panama-Peru FTA and EIA (2012); Panama-Chinese Taipei FTA and EIA (2004); Peru-Republic of Korea FTA and EIA (2011); Peru-China FTA and EIA (2010); Singapore-Australia FTA and EIA (2003); Thailand-Australia FTA and EIA (2005); US-Australia FTA and EIA (2005); US-Bahrain FTA and EIA (2006); US-Chile FTA and EIA (2004); US-Colombia FTA and EIA (2012); US-Jordan FTA and EIA (2001); US-Morocco FTA and EIA (2006); US-Panama FTA and EIA (2012); US-Oman FTA and EIA (2009); US-Peru FTA and EIA (2009); US-Singapore FTA and EIA (2004). The number of treaties counted could be in fact higher if a more flexible criterion were adopted. *See* Seuba (2013b).

together with that relating to intellectual property categories that fall within the scope of border enforcement, refers to the border situations that will be monitored of control. As previously noted, the TRIPS Agreement does not oblige WTO Members to control the exportation. Moreover, if countries decide to control exportation, they are free to set up conditions distinct to those set forth in the TRIPS Agreement.[143] By contrast, extending border measures to export and transit is among the key targets of last-generation PTAs, particularly those concluded by the European Union and Japan.[144]

Although there are some flagrant cases of vague wording and unclear scope,[145] most frequently PTAs' border measures regimes are specific but incomplete legal frameworks, in the sense that they prescribe clear obligations but only with respect to a limited number of aspects. This feature has significant implications in terms of the relationship between PTAs and other agreements, particularly the TRIPS Agreement, as well as in terms of legal sources of inspiration to complement the regulation resulting from the implementation of PTAs. In addition to the cases of vagueness and incompleteness, it is also worth mentioning that the sections on border measures of PTAs give place to normative conflicts.[146]

2 *Border Operations and Categories of Intellectual Property Rights Controlled*

Articles on border measures contained in PTAs commonly address border situations subject to control and categories of intellectual property rights that must be controlled. However, an important difference regarding the regulation of other aspects exists, particularly with respect to the guarantees that protect right holders and competitors.

2.1 Border Operations Controlled

The control of the importation of goods allegedly infringing intellectual property rights is the most common obligation set forth in sections on border enforcement of PTAs.[147]

143 *See* Section II.2.1. 144 *See* Section IV.2.1.

145 *See* for instance Article 16.11 of the Panama – Chinese Taipei FTA and EIA (2004).

146 This is the case of the conflict between Article 18 ACTA and Article 18.11.20 of the Republic of Korea-US FTA and EIA (2012). While in the first case, in exceptional circumstances, the defendant may obtain possession of suspect goods by posting a bond, in the second case it is totally forbidden to obtain possession of suspect goods.

147 Numerous PTAs explicitly enact this obligation. *See* Andean Community CU (1988); Australia-Chile FTA and EIA (2009); Chile-China FTA and EIA (2006/2010); Chile-Japan FTA and EIA (2007); Chile-Mexico FTA and EIA (1999); China-Costa Rica FTA and EIA (2011); Colombia-Mexico FTA and EIA (1995); Costa Rica-Mexico FTA and EIA (1995; (the current version of the treaty, from 2013 does not regulate border measures); EC Treaty CU and EIA (1958); EFTA-Albania FTA (2010); EFTA-Colombia FTA and EIA (2011); EFTA-Hong Kong, China FTA and EIA (2012); EFTA-Montenegro FTA (2012); EFTA-Peru FTA (2011); EFTA-Serbia FTA (2010); EFTA-Ukraine FTA and EIA (2012); EU-CARIFORUM States FTA and EIA (2008); EU-Colombia and Peru FTA and EIA (2013); EU-Republic of Korea FTA and EIA (2011); EU-Central America FTA and EIA (2013); EU-Peru FTA and EIA (2013); Japan-Indonesia FTA and EIA (2008); Japan-Malaysia FTA and EIA (2006); Japan-Peru FTA and EIA (2012); Japan-Switzerland FTA and EIA (2009); Japan-Thailand

In a number of treaties, border measures have been regulated in a fairly detailed manner, but no specific mention has been made to the control of exportation or importation. In these cases, it is merely stated that authorities may suspend the release of goods into free circulation if the right holder lodges an application and specific procedural conditions are fulfilled.[148] It is highly possible that in most of these PTAs, Parties only had in mind the control of importation, but this may have not always been the case. In fact, a literal interpretation of these agreements permits understanding that the control of both importation and exportation is included. As previously explained, the suspension of release concerns imported, exported and re-exported goods.[149] Hence, PTAs that only allude to the suspension of release without specifically limiting its scope to the control of importation may be read as including the control of exportation as well.

A number of treaties enshrine the obligation to control the exportation of allegedly infringing goods[150] while others foresee this obligation but only in the context of *ex officio* procedures.[151] In other cases, treaties only allude to the suspension of release in general terms without clarifying the border situations included.[152] In the latter case, it can be interpreted that both the importation and exportation are included. Finally, a number of PTAs also allude to the control of exportation but, in line with the TRIPS Agreement, make clear that this is a possibility left up to the Parties to implement.[153]

FTA and EIA (2007); Republic of Korea-US FTA and EIA (2012); Mexico-El Salvador FTA and EIA (2001); Mexico-Guatemala FTA and EIA (2001); Mexico-Honduras FTA and EIA (2001; Mexico-Nicaragua FTA and EIA (1998); Nicaragua-Chinese Taipei FTA and EIA (2008); Peru-Republic of Korea FTA and EIA (2011); NAFTA FTA and EIA (1994); Panama-Peru FTA and EIA (2012).

148 *See* Japan-Philippines FTA and EIA (2008); CAFTA-DR-US FTA and EIA (2006); Pakistan-China FTA and EIA (2007/2009); Peru-China FTA and EIA (2010); Peru-Republic of Korea FTA and EIA (2011); Thailand-Australia FTA and EIA (2005); US-Australia FTA and EIA (2005); US-Bahrain FTA and EIA (2006); US-Chile FTA and EIA (2004); US-Colombia FTA and EIA (2012); US-Morocco FTA and EIA (2006); US-Panama FTA and EIA (2012); US-Oman FTA and EIA (2009); US-Peru FTA and EIA (2009); US-Singapore FTA and EIA (2004).

149 *See* Section I.1.1.

150 *See* Andean Community CU (1988); Chile-China FTA and EIA (2006/2010); Chile-Japan FTA and EIA (2007); China-Costa Rica FTA and EIA (2011); EC Treaty CU and EIA (1958); EFTA-Albania FTA (2010); EFTA-Montenegro FTA (2012); EFTA-Serbia FTA (2010); EFTA-Ukraine FTA and EIA (2012); EU-CARIFORUM States FTA and EIA (2008); EU Colombia FTA and EIA (2013); EU-Republic of Korea FTA and EIA (2011); EU-Central America FTA and EIA (2013); EU-Peru FTA and EIA (2013); Japan-Indonesia FTA and EIA (2008); Japan-Malaysia FTA and EIA (2006); Japan-Peru FTA and EIA (2012); Japan-Switzerland FTA and EIA (2009); Japan-Thailand FTA and EIA (2007); Nicaragua-Chinese Taipei FTA and EIA (2008); Panama-Peru FTA and EIA (2012); Singapore-Australia FTA and EIA (2003); Thailand-Australia FTA and EIA (2005).

151 *See* CAFTA-DR-US FTA and EIA (2006); Republic of Korea-US FTA and EIA (2012); US-Bahrain FTA and EIA (2006); US-Chile FTA and EIA (2004); US-Colombia FTA and EIA (2012); US-Morocco FTA and EIA (2006); US-Panama FTA and EIA (2012); US-Oman FTA and EIA (2009); US-Peru FTA and EIA (2009); US-Singapore FTA and EIA (2004).

152 *See* Japan-Philippines FTA and EIA (2008).

153 *See* Chile-Mexico FTA and EIA (1999); Colombia-Mexico FTA and EIA (1995); Costa Rica-Mexico FTA and EIA (1995); EFTA-Hong Kong, China FTA and EIA (2012); Mexico-El Salvador FTA and EIA (2001); Mexico-Guatemala FTA and EIA (2001); Mexico-Honduras FTA and EIA (2001); Mexico-Nicaragua FTA and EIA (1998); NAFTA FTA and EIA (1994).

A reduced number of treaties also allude to products in transit or under other suspensive procedures.[154] The European Union is particularly persistent in proposing the inclusion of this obligation, as the European Union itself anticipated in 2005.[155] However, the categories of intellectual property rights that should be controlled while products are in transit vary from treaty to treaty. In the case of the United States PTAs, the control of products in transit is specifically mandated when actions of customs authorities are adopted *ex officio*.[156] Other PTAs expressly re-affirm what was already established in the TRIPS Agreement, i.e. the control of transit is optional,[157] while in the majority of PTAs there is no mention of the obligation to control products in transit.

2.2 Categories of Intellectual Property Rights Covered

In the context of border measures and together with the obligation to control exportation and, incidentally, transit, the most important novelty set forth in PTAs is the extension of the intellectual property rights categories under control. In quantitative terms, this expansion is the most frequent TRIPS-*plus* provision in the context of border measures, since a large number of PTAs expand the mandate of the TRIPS Agreement to control counterfeit and pirated goods and require the control of not only trademarks and copyrights in general but also other categories of intellectual property rights.

In effect, a large number of PTAs reaffirm the obligation to apply border measures to counterfeit trademark goods and pirated copyright goods.[158] Importantly, other

154 *See* EC Treaty CU and EIA (1958); EU-CARIFORUM States FTA and EIA (2008); EU Colombia FTA and EIA (2013); EU-Republic of Korea FTA and EIA (2011); EU-Central America FTA and EIA (2013); EU-Peru FTA and EIA (2013); Nicaragua-Chinese Taipei FTA and EIA (2008); Panama-Peru FTA and EIA (2012).

155 *See* European Commission (2005b), pp. 13–14.

156 *See* CAFTA-DR-US FTA and EIA (2006); Japan-Switzerland FTA and EIA (2009); Republic of Korea-US FTA and EIA (2012); US-Bahrain FTA and EIA (2006); US-Chile FTA and EIA (2004); US-Colombia FTA and EIA (2012); US-Morocco FTA and EIA (2006); US-Panama FTA and EIA (2012); US-Oman FTA and EIA (2009); US-Peru FTA and EIA (2009); US-Singapore FTA and EIA (2004).

157 *See* Chile-Mexico FTA and EIA (1999); Colombia-Mexico FTA and EIA (1995); Costa Rica-Mexico FTA and EIA (1995); EFTA-Hong Kong, China FTA and EIA (2012).

158 *See* Australia-Chile FTA and EIA (2009); Chile-China FTA and EIA (2006/2010); Chile-Mexico FTA and EIA (1999); China-Costa Rica FTA and EIA (2011); CAFTA-DR-US FTA and EIA (2006); EFTA-Hong Kong, China FTA and EIA (2012); EU-CARIFORUM States FTA and EIA (2008); EU-Republic of Korea FTA and EIA (2011); Japan-Indonesia FTA and EIA (2008); Japan-Peru FTA and EIA (2012); Mexico-El Salvador FTA and EIA (2001); Mexico-Guatemala FTA and EIA (2001); Mexico-Honduras FTA and EIA (2001); Mexico-Nicaragua FTA and EIA (1998); Nicaragua-Chinese Taipei FTA and EIA (2008); NAFTA FTA and EIA (1994); Pakistan-China FTA and EIA (2007/2009); Panama-Peru FTA and EIA (2012); Peru-China FTA and EIA (2010); Peru-Republic of Korea FTA and EIA (2011); US-Australia FTA and EIA (2005); US-Bahrain FTA and EIA (2006); US-Chile FTA and EIA (2004); US-Colombia FTA and EIA (2012); US-Jordan FTA and EIA (2001); US-Morocco FTA and EIA (2006); US-Panama FTA and EIA (2012); US-Oman FTA and EIA (2009); US-Peru FTA and EIA (2009); US-Singapore FTA and EIA (2004).

agreements refer not only to counterfeit and pirated goods but to all types of trademark[159] and copyright[160] infringements, thus enlarging the scope of goods that will be controlled.[161] A more reduced number of PTAs include the obligation to control categories of intellectual property rights distinct from trademarks and copyright. This is the case of treaties that order the control of patents,[162] designs,[163] geographical indications,[164] utility models[165] and plant varieties.[166]

Some agreements do not identify a particular category of rights to be controlled at the border. By contrast, an obligation to deploy border measures that will apply to, generically, 'intellectual property rights' is enacted.[167] A large number of PTAs mention the control of all categories of intellectual property rights but frame it in terms of a possibility and not necessarily as an obligation.[168] Finally, in some isolated cases, parties undertake the obligation to apply border measures to a number of intellectual property rights categories and commit to increasing that number or consider the application of border measures to other categories of intellectual property rights.[169]

159 *See* Andean Community CU (1988); EU (28) Enlargement CU and EIA (2013); Chile-Japan FTA and EIA (2007); EFTA-Colombia FTA and EIA (2011); EFTA-Peru FTA (2011); EU Colombia FTA and EIA (2013); EU-Central America FTA and EIA (2013); EU-Peru FTA and EIA (2013); Japan-Malaysia FTA and EIA (2006); Japan-Philippines FTA and EIA (2008); Japan-Switzerland FTA and EIA (2009); Japan-Thailand FTA and EIA (2007); Singapore-Australia FTA and EIA (2003); Thailand-Australia FTA and EIA (2005).

160 *See* Chile-Japan FTA and EIA (2007); EFTA-Colombia FTA and EIA (2011); EFTA-Peru FTA (2011); EU (28) Enlargement CU and EIA (2013); EU Colombia FTA and EIA (2013); EU-Central America FTA and EIA (2013); EU-Peru FTA and EIA (2013); Japan-Malaysia FTA and EIA (2006); Japan-Philippines FTA and EIA (2008); Japan-Switzerland FTA and EIA (2009); Japan-Thailand FTA and EIA (2007); Republic of Korea-US FTA and EIA (2012); Singapore-Australia FTA and EIA (2003); Thailand-Australia FTA and EIA (2005).

161 *See* this question in Section II.2.2.

162 *See* Chile-Japan FTA and EIA (2007); EC Treaty CU and EIA (1958); EU-Republic of Korea FTA and EIA (2011); Japan-Philippines FTA and EIA (2008); Japan-Switzerland FTA and EIA (2009); Nicaragua-Chinese Taipei FTA and EIA (2008).

163 *See* EC Treaty CU and EIA (1958); EU-CARIFORUM States FTA and EIA (2008); EU-Republic of Korea FTA and EIA (2011); Japan-Philippines FTA and EIA (2008); Japan-Switzerland FTA and EIA (2009).

164 *See* EC Treaty CU and EIA (1958); EU-CARIFORUM States FTA and EIA (2008); EU-Republic of Korea FTA and EIA (2011); Nicaragua-Chinese Taipei FTA and EIA (2008).

165 *See* Japan-Philippines FTA and EIA (2008); EC Treaty CU and EIA (1958).

166 *See* Chile-Japan FTA and EIA (2007); EC Treaty CU and EIA (1958); EU-Republic of Korea FTA and EIA (2011); Nicaragua-Chinese Taipei FTA and EIA (2008).

167 *See* CAFTA-DR-US FTA and EIA (2006); EFTA-Albania FTA (2010); EFTA-Montenegro FTA (2012); EFTA-Serbia FTA (2010); EFTA-Ukraine FTA and EIA (2012); Japan-Switzerland FTA and EIA (2009); Nicaragua-Chinese Taipei FTA and EIA (2008).

168 *See* Chile-Mexico FTA and EIA (1999); Colombia-Mexico FTA and EIA (1995); Costa Rica-Mexico FTA and EIA (1995); EFTA-Colombia FTA and EIA (2011); EFTA-Peru FTA (2011); Japan-Malaysia FTA and EIA (2006); Mexico-El Salvador FTA and EIA (2001); Mexico-Guatemala FTA and EIA (2001); Mexico-Honduras FTA and EIA (2001); Mexico-Nicaragua FTA and EIA (1998); NAFTA FTA and EIA (1994).

169 *See* Chile-Mexico FTA and EIA (1999); Colombia-Mexico FTA and EIA (1995); Costa Rica-Mexico FTA and EIA (1995); EFTA-Colombia FTA and EIA (2011); EFTA-Peru FTA (2011); EU-CARIFORUM States FTA and EIA (2008).

3 *Specific Regulation of Border Measures in PTAs*

The extension and content of articles on border measures in PTAs vary significantly, which makes it difficult to offer a homogeneous picture of their regulation in these agreements. As noted, the majority of PTAs focus primarily on the categories of intellectual property rights and the border situations that must be controlled, in both cases generally expanded *vis-à-vis* the TRIPS Agreement. The other areas commonly addressed in national legal orders or in the TRIPS Agreement command relatively limited attention. Against this scenario, we now look into those areas where PTAs go beyond the TRIPS Agreement: action with respect to infringing goods, remedies and guarantees for the Parties.

It is rare to find a comprehensive TRIPS-*plus* border enforcement regulation in a PTA. Indeed, the majority of PTAs enshrine TRIPS-*plus* norms in the context of border measures but avoid addressing each and every aspect regulated in the TRIPS Agreement. Notwithstanding the fact that parties to a PTA are already obliged to comply with the TRIPS Agreement, reiteration of the content of border measures in the TRIPS Agreement is very frequent.[170] Interestingly, in addition to repeating the border enforcement articles of the TRIPS Agreement, some PTAs also allude to this Agreement to state that the rights and obligations set forth therein apply to new situations regulated in the PTA. Similarly, some PTAs allude to the TRIPS Agreement taking it as baseline to add new rights and obligations[171] or to extend to other stakeholders (the exporter and the holder of the goods) specific rights that, pursuant to the TRIPS Agreement, would only benefit the importer.[172] Of course, there are also provisions that enshrine new (TRIPS-*extra*) obligations.[173]

Although references to the TRIPS Agreement are frequent, this is not always the case. Sometimes parties take for granted the existence and full implementation of the TRIPS Agreement and merely regulate aspects not regulated before without ever repeating – or alluding to – the TRIPS Agreement or obligations set forth therein.[174]

[170] Not only this. In fact, some PTAs include an express reference *in totum* to the legislation of border measures found in the TRIPS Agreement. *See* Article 93 Japan-Viet Nam FTA and EIA (2009); some EFTA agreements that incorporate by reference all the Enforcement Section of the TRIPS Agreement. *See* Article 6.13 EFTA-Colombia FTA (2008).

[171] *See* Articles 16–13 to 16–17 EFTA-Peru FTA (2011); Article 4 Singapore-Australia FTA and EIA (2003) (with reference only to exportation).

[172] *See* Article 163.2 EU-CARIFORUM States FTA and EIA (2008); Article 273.3 EU-Central America FTA and EIA (2013); Article 10.67.3 EU-Republic of Korea FTA and EIA (2011).

[173] For instance, complementing the obligation to suspend the release into free circulation, it is established that '[e]ach Party shall provide that the application to suspend the release of goods shall apply to all points of entry to its territory and remain applicable for a period of not less than one year from the date of application, or the period that the good is protected by copyright or that the relevant trademark registration is valid, whichever is shorter'. *See* Article 18.10.19 Republic of Korea-US FTA and EIA (2012); Article 17.11.19 US-Australia FTA and EIA (2005); Article 14.9.20 US-Bahrain FTA and EIA (2006); Article 15.11.20 US-Morocco FTA and EIA (2006); Article 15.10.20 US-Oman FTA and EIA (2009). A different example is found in Article 18.10.24 Republic of Korea-US FTA and EIA (2012).

[174] This is for instance the case of the Thailand-Australia FTA and EIA (2005), which only alludes to exportation.

3.1 Action

PTAs that regulate border measures order the suspension of the release of allegedly infringing goods and foresee that this may take place *ex parte* or, in a number of agreements, *ex officio*. Some agreements also regulate the procedure that must be followed to detain and inspect the goods and may also regulate the *ex parte* initiation of proceedings leading to a decision on the merits of the case.

Those PTAs that allude to *ex officio* action either maintain the freedom codified in the TRIPS Agreement to adopt border measures *ex officio*[175] or lay down the obligation to effectively empower customs authorities to act *ex officio*.[176] Hence, an important difference between the TRIPS Agreement and a substantial number of PTAs is the obligation to allow customs authorities to adopt border measures on their own initiative, thus anticipating some of the contents of ACTA.

3.2 Remedies

The ultimate fate of infringing products detained at the border has also been regulated in a number of PTAs. The TRIPS Agreement states that competent authorities must be entitled to order the destruction or disposal of infringing goods.[177] It also establishes a number of conditions to be fulfilled in case goods are going to be destroyed, including the possibility to seek a review by a judicial authority and the conformity of such disposal or destruction with other constitutional requirements.[178] While some agreements replicate this regulation,[179] other PTAs show a preference – sometimes an obligation – for the destruction of the goods.

The regulation of the destruction of the goods has some variations in the concerned agreements. In some cases, it is simply established that authorities must have the power to order the destruction of infringing goods.[180] In other cases, such a possibility becomes an obligation to be implemented in accordance with local laws, which may order that simplified procedures be set up for the destruction of the

175 Thus, it is unnecessary to recall this freedom. *See* for instance the cases of Chile-Mexico FTA and EIA (1999); Costa Rica-Mexico FTA and EIA (1995); Mexico-El Salvador FTA and EIA (2001); Mexico-Guatemala FTA and EIA (2001); Mexico-Honduras FTA and EIA (2001); Mexico-Nicaragua FTA and EIA (1998); NAFTA FTA and EIA (1994).

176 *See* Australia-Chile FTA and EIA (2009); Chile-China FTA and EIA (2006/2010); China-Costa Rica FTA and EIA (2011); CAFTA-DR-US FTA and EIA (2006); EFTA-Hong Kong, China FTA and EIA (2012); EFTA-Montenegro FTA (2012); EU Colombia FTA and EIA (2013); EU-Republic of Korea FTA and EIA (2011); EU-Peru FTA and EIA (2013); Japan-Thailand FTA and EIA (2007); Republic of Korea-US FTA and EIA (2012); Pakistan-China FTA and EIA (2007/2009); Panama-Peru FTA and EIA (2012); Peru-China FTA and EIA (2010); Peru-Republic of Korea FTA and EIA (2011); US-Australia FTA and EIA (2005); US-Bahrain FTA and EIA (2006); US-Chile FTA and EIA (2004); US-Jordan FTA and EIA (2001); US-Morocco FTA and EIA (2006); US-Panama FTA and EIA (2012); US-Oman FTA and EIA (2009); US-Peru FTA and EIA (2009); US-Singapore FTA and EIA (2004).

177 *See* Section II.2.3.2. 178 *Ibid.*

179 In some cases they also include the guarantees mentioned. *See* Chile-Mexico FTA and EIA (1999); Mexico-El Salvador FTA and EIA (2001); Mexico-Guatemala FTA and EIA (2001); Mexico-Honduras FTA and EIA (2001); NAFTA FTA and EIA (1994).

180 *See* EFTA-Montenegro FTA (2012); Costa Rica-Mexico FTA and EIA (1995).

goods.[181] Some treaties prescribe, as a general rule, the destruction of infringing goods but accept that, in exceptional cases, destruction may not be the preferred option.[182] Ethical considerations have been taken into account and are mentioned in a limited number of treaties that enact the obligation to destroy the goods. In these cases, it is established that a judicial decision is necessary before destroying the goods and, in the case of counterfeit trademark goods, that goods may also be donated to charity for use outside the channels of commerce.[183]

3.3 Guarantees

The requisites that the TRIPS Agreement establishes to guarantee the protection of parties other than the right holder, and preserve other activities and objectives such as free trade, are very frequently absent in articles on border enforcement of PTAs.

The attention paid to this aspect in each agreement varies enormously. While some agreements devote only one article to border measures regulation, or just a single paragraph within a longer article, other treaties include several articles in this respect. Naturally, differences arise not only because of the extension of the provisions. In this regard, there are also notable differences between PTAs that enshrine more extensive regulation: while in some cases they merely copy and paste the TRIPS Agreement,[184] other extensive and detailed PTAs go beyond TRIPS.[185]

While the existing diversity in terms of extension and content makes it difficult to generalize, the main purpose of PTAs' border enforcement regulation is the expansion of the categories of intellectual property rights and border situations subject to control. It seems that they assume that already existing national and international norms will provide the necessary checks and balances that are absent in the texts. Therefore, the relevance of the missing guarantees should be addressed taking into account existing international commitments, which may have already enshrined those guarantees. Although this does not preclude a general image of imbalance and a number of consequences may arise from such absences, the guarantees have not been proscribed, and they may apply by virtue of the membership of PTAs' Parties to the TRIPS Agreement.[186]

It is however debatable whether resorting to the TRIPS Agreement is always a good solution. As noted, the TRIPS Agreement lays down guarantees and procedural

[181] *See* Article 123.8 Japan-Switzerland FTA and EIA (2009).

[182] *See* Australia-Chile FTA and EIA (2009); CAFTA-DR-US FTA and EIA (2006); US-Australia FTA and EIA (2005); US-Bahrain FTA and EIA (2006); US-Morocco FTA and EIA (2006); US-Chile FTA and EIA (2004); US-Singapore FTA and EIA (2004); US-Oman FTA and EIA (2009).

[183] This will only be possible when the removal of the trademark eliminates the infringing characteristic of the good and the good is no longer identifiable with the removed trademark. *See* US-Colombia FTA and EIA (2012); US-Panama FTA and EIA (2012); US-Peru FTA and EIA (2009).

[184] A good example in this sense would be the Mexico-Central America FTA and EIA (2012).

[185] This being notably the case of the PTAs of the United States.

[186] *See* Chapter 6, Sections V.5 and VI.

requirements that apply to the control of imports. Border operations such as the control of exportation and transit are not covered, and their legal regime will be different.[187] This is important, since PTAs expand the border situations under control. In the context of this expansion they add new rights for right holders, while tending to neglect guarantees for alleged infringers. Invoking the TRIPS Agreement may not be an option, simply because the guarantees of the TRIPS Agreement were conceived to apply in the context of importation but not necessarily, and not mandatorily, in other border situations.

Among the requirements that the right holder must satisfy when requesting the suspension of the release of allegedly infringing goods into free circulation, the most common ones are the provision of evidence of *prima facie* infringement of the right holder's intellectual property right,[188] the supply of a sufficiently detailed description of the goods to make them readily recognizable by the customs authorities[189] and the provision of a security or equivalent assurance.[190]

While the large majority of agreements do not enshrine the conditions set forth in the TRIPS Agreement, some treaties explicitly reaffirm the conditions mentioned

187 *See* Section II.1.1.1.

188 *See* Australia-Chile FTA and EIA (2009); Chile-China FTA and EIA (2006/2010); Chile-Mexico FTA and EIA (1999); China-Costa Rica FTA and EIA (2011); Costa Rica-Mexico FTA and EIA (1995); CAFTA-DR-US FTA and EIA (2006); Republic of Korea-US FTA and EIA (2012); Mexico-El Salvador FTA and EIA (2001); Mexico-Guatemala FTA and EIA (2001); Mexico-Honduras FTA and EIA (2001); Mexico-Nicaragua FTA and EIA (1998); NAFTA FTA and EIA (1994); Pakistan-China FTA and EIA (2007/2009); Peru-China FTA and EIA (2010); Peru-Republic of Korea FTA and EIA (2011); US-Australia FTA and EIA (2005); US-Bahrain FTA and EIA (2006); US-Chile FTA and EIA (2004); US-Colombia FTA and EIA (2012); US-Morocco FTA and EIA (2006); US-Panama FTA and EIA (2012); US-Oman FTA and EIA (2009); US-Peru FTA and EIA (2009); US-Singapore FTA and EIA (2004).

189 *See* Australia-Chile FTA and EIA (2009); Chile-China FTA and EIA (2006/2010); Chile-Mexico FTA and EIA (1999); China-Costa Rica FTA and EIA (2011); Costa Rica-Mexico FTA and EIA (1995); CAFTA-DR-US FTA and EIA (2006); Republic of Korea-US FTA and EIA (2012); Mexico-El Salvador FTA and EIA (2001); Mexico-Guatemala FTA and EIA (2001); Mexico-Honduras FTA and EIA (2001); Mexico-Nicaragua FTA and EIA (1998); NAFTA FTA and EIA (1994); Pakistan-China FTA and EIA (2007/2009); Peru-China FTA and EIA (2010); Peru-Republic of Korea FTA and EIA (2011); US-Australia FTA and EIA (2005); US-Bahrain FTA and EIA (2006); US-Chile FTA and EIA (2004); US-Colombia FTA and EIA (2012); US-Morocco FTA and EIA (2006); US-Panama FTA and EIA (2012); US-Oman FTA and EIA (2009); US-Peru FTA and EIA (2009); US-Singapore FTA and EIA (2004).

190 In some cases, agreements repeat the formulation of the TRIPS Agreement and establish that this is a possibility, such as in Australia-Chile FTA and EIA (2009); Chile-China FTA and EIA (2006/2010); Chile-Mexico FTA and EIA (1999); China-Costa Rica FTA and EIA (2011); EFTA-Albania FTA (2010); EFTA-Colombia FTA and EIA (2011); EFTA-Peru FTA (2011); EFTA-Serbia FTA (2010); EFTA-Ukraine FTA and EIA (2012). At the same time, in other cases it is established that this is an obligation, such as in Costa Rica-Mexico FTA and EIA (1995); CAFTA-DR-US FTA and EIA (2006); Republic of Korea-US FTA and EIA (2012); Mexico-El Salvador FTA and EIA (2001); Mexico-Guatemala FTA and EIA (2001); Mexico-Honduras FTA and EIA (2001); Mexico-Nicaragua FTA and EIA (1998); NAFTA FTA and EIA (1994); Pakistan-China FTA and EIA (2007/2009); Panama-Peru FTA and EIA (2012); Peru-China FTA and EIA (2010); Peru-Republic of Korea FTA and EIA (2011); US-Australia FTA and EIA (2005); US-Bahrain FTA and EIA (2006); US-Chile FTA and EIA (2004); US-Morocco FTA and EIA (2006); US-Panama FTA and EIA (2012); US-Oman FTA and EIA (2009); US-Peru FTA and EIA (2009); US-Singapore FTA and EIA (2004).

therein and propose more specific regulation. This is the case of PTAs promoted by highly developed countries. For instance, United States PTAs usually specify the characteristics of the security that may be required on the part of the right holder[191] and the period of validity of the request of suspension of release.[192] They also relax some requirements of the TRIPS Agreement, such as the provision of information on the part of the right holder, which in some PTAs 'shall not unreasonably deter recourse to these procedures'.[193] In the case of the European agreements, new PTAs enact demanding and expansive border measures, although in some instances they also pay attention to the protection of the interests of parties other than the right holder. In this regard, and bearing in mind the inclusion of exportation and transit in the European agreements, the explicit extension of the importer' rights to the exporter and the holder of the goods is a positive feature.[194]

4 *Law That Applies to Border Measures*

The law to be applied to determine the legality of the products allegedly infringing intellectual property rights is – together with the extension of intellectual property rights categories and border situations under control – the most controversial aspect of new international norms on border enforcement. The possibility to apply the law of the country of customs procedures, regardless of fact that products may not be intended for its national market, is at the centre of international debate. So far, the legality of such power seems to depend on the specific category of intellectual property rights covered and the potential of diversion of the goods into the internal market.[195] However, plurilaterals and PTAs have been used to expand or consolidate that possibility.

While PTAs may specifically allude to the law of the country of importation, they may also remain silent in this regard or identify a different law. These possibilities have to be put into relation with border situations subject to control in the specific PTA. Half of the agreements that regulate border measures state that the relevant law regulating the suspension of the release of the goods is the law of the country of importation.[196] It is not clear whether this is the law that will apply to products in

[191] A bond conditioned to hold the defendant harmless from any loss or damage resulting from the withholding of the goods, *see* Article 15.11.21 CAFTA-DR-US FTA and EIA (2006); Article 17.11.20 US-Australia FTA and EIA (2005); Article 14.9.21 US-Bahrain FTA and EIA (2006); Article 16.11.21 US-Colombia FTA and EIA (2012); Article 15.11.21 US-Morocco FTA and EIA (2006); Article 15.11.21 US-Panama FTA and EIA (2012); Article 15.10.21 US-Oman FTA and EIA (2009).

[192] Such a provision reads as following, 'the application to suspend the release of goods shall remain in force for a period of not less than one year from the date of application, or the period that the good is protected by copyright or the relevant trademark registration, whichever is shorter'.

[193] *See* Article 17.11.17 US-Chile FTA and EIA (2004); Article 17.11.19 US-Australia FTA and EIA (2005).

[194] *See* Article 163.2 EU-CARIFORUM States FTA and EIA (2008).

[195] *See* Chapter 11.

[196] *See* Australia-Chile FTA and EIA (2009); Chile-China FTA and EIA (2006/2010); Chile-Mexico FTA and EIA (1999); China-Costa Rica FTA and EIA (2011); Colombia-Mexico FTA and EIA (1995); Costa Rica-Mexico FTA and EIA (1995); CAFTA-DR-US FTA and EIA (2006); Republic of Korea-US FTA and EIA (2012); Mexico-El Salvador FTA and EIA (2001); Mexico-Guatemala FTA and EIA

transit as mention is also made of the control of transit. In addition, there are problems akin to those arising from the TRIPS Agreement.[197]

The options found in treaties that do not identify the law of the country of importation as the relevant law to decide on the infringement are varied. In some cases, treaties do not mention any law at all. This may be so for a number of reasons: the PTA may only enshrine a general obligation to provide for procedures concerning the suspension of the release of infringing goods,[198] the agreement may address only a very specific topic in the domain of border measures,[199] the PTA may have transplanted the articles of the TRIPS Agreement on border measures but not the footnotes of the Agreement – including those on the counterfeit and pirated status of goods[200] – or the treaty may be fairly complete but remain silent on this question.

Indeed, a number of PTAs identify a different law than that of the country of importation. Such cases are not numerous, and their exact meaning is not always entirely clear. Some treaties declare that the relevant law is the law of the country of customs procedures or, similarly, the law of the party implementing the measures.[201] Other agreements do not identify any specific law but declare that, in order to apply for the suspension of release of the trademark infringing goods, it is required to have the trademark registered (arguably in the country of customs procedures) and, in the case of pirated goods, to consider whether the goods are infringing in the country of production.[202] Finally, there are treaties that do not directly identify the applicable law but establish the liberty of the parties in this regard. This means that it is in principle up to that country's legal order to decide whether the law is that of the country of importation or some other law.[203] Each and every one of these cases creates tensions with fundamental principles of intellectual property law and international trade law, as the analysis in Chapter 11 will attest.

(2001); Mexico-Honduras FTA and EIA (2001); Mexico-Nicaragua FTA and EIA (1998); Pakistan-China FTA and EIA (2007/2009); Panama-Peru FTA and EIA (2012); Peru-Republic of Korea FTA and EIA (2011); US-Australia FTA and EIA (2005); US-Bahrain FTA and EIA (2006); US-Chile FTA and EIA (2004); US-Colombia FTA and EIA (2012); US-Morocco FTA and EIA (2006); US-Panama FTA and EIA (2012); US-Oman FTA and EIA (2009); US-Peru FTA and EIA (2009); US-Singapore FTA and EIA (2004).

197 *See* this same chapter and Chapter 11.

198 *See* Article 164 Chile-Japan FTA and EIA (2007); Article 16.5 EFTA-Colombia FTA and EIA (2011); Article 119.2 Japan-Indonesia FTA and EIA (2008).

199 The obligation to provide *ex officio* action, Article 4.26 US-Jordan FTA and EIA (2001).

200 *See* Mexico-Nicaragua FTA and EIA (1998); Mexico-El Salvador FTA and EIA (2001); Mexico-Guatemala FTA and EIA (2001); Mexico-Honduras FTA and EIA (2001).

201 *See* EU-Republic of Korea FTA and EIA (2011); Peru-China FTA and EIA (2010). In the case of EU-CARIFORUM States FTA and EIA (2008), it is declared that the law of the country of customs will apply for designs and geographical indications.

202 *See* EU Colombia FTA and EIA (2013); EU-Peru FTA and EIA (2013).

203 For instance, in the relevant norm of the Andean Community, this matter is left at the discretion of the national law of the country that applies the measures. *See* Article 250 of Decision No. 486 on Common Intellectual Property Regime of 14 September 2000, Andean Community CU (1988).

11

Border Measures and Free Trade

I INTRODUCTION

Plurilateral, regional and bilateral agreements have significantly expanded the scope of border measures against goods that allegedly infringe intellectual property rights. The possibility of controlling products under any suspensive procedure, the increase in the number of intellectual property types subject to border control and the application of the law of the country of customs procedures even when no direct link exists between the goods and such a country may result in a regime difficult to reconcile with basic principles of both intellectual property law and international trade law.

The relevance of customs regulation expands beyond the country applying border measures, particularly concerning exportation and transit. Regarding exportation, border measures impede shipments of locally manufactured products that infringe intellectual property rights to third countries. In the case of transit, the goal is to impede the arrival of products to foreign jurisdictions, even if these products are not infringing in the countries of origin and destination. In this case, when the link between allegedly infringing products and the country of transit is weak or inexistent, the possibility of creating an illicit trade barrier becomes clear.

The tension between border measures and free trade is widely recognized in international and regional intellectual property law. Indeed, the objective of balancing the protection of intellectual property and the protection of free trade was at the forefront in the negotiations of the TRIPS Agreement.[1] The Agreement expressly states that all enforcement procedures 'shall be applied in such a manner as to avoid the creation of barriers to legitimate trade'.[2] In the plurilateral context, the

[1] Ensuring the compatibility between free trade rules and intellectual property norms was a chief objective of the Uruguay Round negotiations, announced as early as September 1986 by the Ministers of the GATT. *See* GATT (1986), paras. 7–8. *See* also GATT (1988a), para. 2; Bronckers, Verkade and McNelis (2000), pp. 29–30.

[2] *See* Article 41.1 TRIPS Agreement.

Anti-Counterfeiting Trade Agreement also states that Parties must ensure that enforcement procedures are applied avoiding the creation of barriers to legitimate trade.[3] Similarly, EU Regulation No. 608/2013 states that measures adopted to keep illicit products off the European market should be adopted 'without impeding legitimate trade'.[4]

Some norms presently in force, as well as certain other interpretations of border enforcement rules, may put into question whether the command to ensure the free flow of legitimate trade is respected and, ultimately, whether fundamental principles of trade law and intellectual property law are obeyed. Answers may vary depending on the intellectual property rights category at issue, but the principles are essentially the same. This is why it is of interest to look into the jurisprudence of the Court of Justice of the European Union on the control of goods subject to suspensive procedures as well as recent normative developments in the European context. In this regard, it is also pertinent to recall the relevance of a very basic tenet of intellectual property, i.e. the territoriality principle, and examine the substantive rights of right holders in order to ascertain whether the control of transit is included among these rights. Finally, an analysis from the point of view of international trade rules is also merited, since these norms capture the ongoing tension between international trade and intellectual property.

II THE TERRITORIALITY PRINCIPLE AND THE RIGHTS CONFERRED BY A PATENT

The expansion of intellectual property rights types subject to border control, the increasing number of customs situations where such controls can be undertaken and the possibility of invoking the law of the country of customs procedures to assess the infringing status of goods make it necessary to review these developments against fundamental principles of intellectual property law and the rights conferred by each category of intellectual property rights.

1 *The Territorial Nature and Independence of Patents*

A patent confers the rights enumerated in the corresponding statute, for a limited duration of time and within a specific territory. When considering the spatial scope of a patent it is usual to refer to the principle of territoriality. This principle implies

3 *See* Article 6.1 of the Anti-Counterfeiting Trade Agreement.

4 *See* Recital 2 of the Introduction EU Regulation No. 608/2013. Its antecessor, Regulation No. 1383/2003, affirmed that whereas 'the marketing of ... goods infringing intellectual property rights does considerable damage' and that 'such goods should, in so far as is possible, be kept off the market' this should be done 'without impeding the freedom of legitimate trade'. Recital 2 Council Regulation (EC) No. 1383/2003 of 22 July 2003 concerning customs action against goods suspected of infringing certain intellectual property rights and the measures to be taken against goods found to have infringed such rights, OJEU L 196/7 of 2 August 2003 (hereinafter Regulation No. 1383/2003).

that the protection conferred by a patent only covers the sovereign territory of the granting state. That is, the spatial efficacy of the laws governing a patent right is delimited by the territoriality principle, i.e. it covers the national territory.[5] Therefore, patent validity, the definition of infringement and the claims resulting from infringements are to be judged according to the *lex loci*.[6]

Both national and international intellectual property law recognize the territoriality principle. There are numerous examples of national statutes explicitly stating that intellectual property is protected within the national territory in accordance with the national law.[7] Internationally, the Paris Convention enshrines the principle of independence, according to which an invention may be protected differently in each national legal system, and the protection granted in one jurisdiction does not affect the protection offered elsewhere.[8] This can be observed in many different areas, ranging from patentability criteria to a patent's validity, scope and duration.[9] In a related fashion, the TRIPS Agreement codifies minimum standards and allows the WTO Members to adopt higher levels of protection. This implies that intellectual property law should have no extra-territorial effects and that each state is responsible for the level of protection it grants. Likewise, in a separate decision, the WTO Members have explicitly recognized 'the territorial nature of the patent rights'.[10]

The principles of territoriality and independence do, however, not imply a total disregard of what occurs abroad. That is to say, national patent law may take into account activities taking place in other countries if such activities ultimately impact

5 The Restatement (Third) of the Foreign Relations Law of the United States is clear: 'patents are considered territorial, having legal effect only in the territory of the issuing state'. *See* Restatement (Third) of the Foreign Relations Law of the United States, § 415 cmt. i. For Europe, *see* Article 22.4 Council Regulation (EC) No. 44/2001 of 22 December 2000 on jurisdiction and the recognition and enforcement of judgements in civil and commercial matters, OJ L 012 of 16 January 2001, which establishes that 'The following courts shall have exclusive jurisdiction, regardless of domicile: 4. in proceedings concerned with the registration or validity of patents . . . the courts of the member state in which the deposit or registration has been applied for, has taken place . . . '

6 *See* Jaeger, Grosse Ruse-Khan, Drexl and Hilty (2010).

7 The United States Patent Act states that a person may be liable for patent infringement if he/she 'makes, uses, offers to sell or sells any patented invention, *within* the United States' (emphasis added). *See* United States Patent Act 35 USC § 271(a). More broadly, Article 10.4 of the Spanish Civil Code establishes that 'intellectual property and industrial property rights will be protected within the Spanish territory in accordance with the Spanish law'. *See* Civil Code (approved by Royal Decree of 24 July 1889).

8 *See* Article 4*bis*(1) of the Paris Convention; WIPO (2004), pp. 245–246.

9 Courts have had the chance to reflect on the grounds and importance of this principle. For instance, in 1972 a US District Court noted that 'Courts in the foreign countries whose patents are involved here would disagree with this court's determinations on the validity of the patents. Those Courts would at any rate be faced with the hard choice of accepting the inexpert determination of a foreign court or creating an unseemly conflict with the judgment of the court of another country.' *See Packard Instrument Co. v. Beckman Instruments Inc.*, 346 F. Supp. 408, 175 USPQ (BNA) 282 (N.D.Ill. 1972).

10 Paragraph 6(i) of the WTO General Council Decision of 30 August 2003 establishes that 'it is understood that this will not prejudice the territorial nature of the patent rights in question'. *See* WTO General Council (2003).

on the national jurisdiction. This is exemplified by the possibility of impeding the importation of products made using a patented process,[11] the prohibition of exportation of components of patented products so as to introduce the combination of such components abroad in a manner that would infringe the patent if such combination occurred within the importing state[12] or, similarly, the exportation of components that are meant for use only in a patented device.[13]

In a similar vein, but observed from a different perspective, patent law also takes into consideration the interest of preserving free trade while ensuring the territorial enforceability of patent rights. In this sense, a notable exception to the patent owner's rights, relating to the use of articles on foreign vessels, aircraft and land vehicles, was developed to guarantee the free flow of trade. In *Brown v. Duchesne*, the United States Supreme Court constrained the literal territorial scope of a United States patent. A French vessel in US territory used a gaff on board covered by a patent. While this amounted to an unauthorized use in the national territory, the Supreme Court did not consider it an infringement.[14] This case, which was preceded by a similar case that resulted in an amendment to the English patent law,[15] gave place in 1925 to the present Article 5*ter* of the Paris Convention, which foresees an exception to the rights of the patent owner regarding devices forming part of vessels, aircraft or land vehicles.

2 Rights Conferred by a Patent

The territoriality principle implies that the title holder will be able to claim his rights if the jurisdiction where the right is protected and the place of infringement coincide,[16] in accordance with the legal norms in force therein. However, only by analysing the rights conferred by each category of intellectual property rights will it be possible to determine the specific rights of the right holder and whether these rights include potential claims with respect to specific border situations, such as transit.

In light of the current trends in international and regional intellectual property law, the study of patents is particularly relevant. Article 28 of the TRIPS Agreement states that where the subject matter of a patent is a product, the owner has the right to prevent third parties from making, using, offering for sale, selling or importing that

[11] See Article 5*quarter* Paris Convention and Article 28.1.b TRIPS Agreement.

[12] The United States introduced this provision in response to a case where separated components of a patented invention were exported and later assembled and sold abroad. *See Deepsouth Packing Co. V. Laitram Corp.*, 406 US 518 (1972).

[13] *See* for both prohibitions 35 USC § 271(f), Sections 1 and 2 respectively.

[14] *See* Chisum (1996–1997), p. 605.

[15] In 1852, and in reaction to the ruling *Caldwell v. Vanvlissengen*, the English Parliament amended the patent law to exclude from liability ships coming from third countries and that, either in English waters or ports, could be regarded as infringing patent rights.

[16] *See* von Mühlendahl and Stauder (2009), p. 654.

product. Next, where the subject matter is a process, the owner can prevent third parties from using the process or using, offering for sale, selling or importing for these purposes at least the product obtained directly by that process. Therefore, the main characteristic of patents is the granting of a negative right, a *ius prohibendi* regarding specific acts undertaken in the granting state.

The control of transit is certainly not included in the list of activities that the right holder can impede. However, arguing that the right holder can just not control the transit may be an overly formalistic explanation. There are other reasons that render it undesirable to impede transit. These reasons have to do with the territorial nature of intellectual property rights, particularly strong in the case of patents. An intellectual property right confers a national entitlement, a power over protected products in the domestic market. This is why activities such as transit, which in principle bear no relationship to the domestic market, cannot be included in the list of negative rights granted by a patent.

In some jurisdictions title holders' dissatisfaction with this state of things has led them to resort to legal fictions that enable the control of patented products in transit. Dutch courts have applied a legal fiction called the 'local manufacturing fiction', according to which 'goods in transit should be regarded by way of fiction as goods which have been produced in The Netherlands'.[17] A similar proposal was put forward by Philips and the Belgian government in the context of the CJEU process regarding the joined *Philips* and *Nokia* cases.[18] The fiction that the products were manufactured in the country administering the customs procedures would trigger the competence of the local courts, even if in reality the products only transit the national territory.

Although 'it is hard to imagine a greater departure from the principle of independence of patents than the "manufacture fiction"',[19] the use of legal fictions in intellectual property law is common. For instance, in some jurisdictions patent law does not mention the control of exportation among the activities that patent owners can impede. However, this has not impeded courts from inferring the existence of a link between the control of exportation and the sale (or 'introduction into commerce') of the patented product.[20] However, with regard to the control of transit, if any legal fiction had to be accepted at all, it would not be that of local

[17] This permits that '[g]oods which in their country of origin and destination do not infringe IP rights can still be detained by customs and found to infringe an IP right in the Netherlands'. *See* Kuipers *et al.* (2009), p. 12; van den Brink (2008).

[18] Philips and the Belgian government defended a fiction pursuant to which goods declared for warehousing or for transit and covered by an application for action 'are deemed to have been manufactured in the Member State where that application is made, even though it is not in dispute that they were manufactured in a non-member State'. *See* CJEU, joined cases C-446/09 and C-495/09, *Koninklijke Philips Electronics NV (C-446/09) v. Lucheng Meijing Industrial Company Ltd and Others and Nokia Corporation (C-495/09) v. Her Majesty's Commissioners of Revenue and Customs* [2011], Judgment of the Court (First Chamber) of 1 December 2011, ECR I-12435, para. 53 (hereinafter *Philips v. Nokia*).

[19] *See* Abbott (2009b), p. 49.

[20] *See* Massaguer (1989), p. 131.

manufacture but be that of the assimilation of transit to either sale or importation. Even in these cases, the assimilation is unacceptable.

The differences between importation and transit are clear. When imported, goods are introduced in the national territory to exploit them there. In contrast, the introduction of goods in transit into the national territory is just a circumstantial event. In fact, the contact with the national soil is merely instrumental, since the goal is reaching a final destination in a different country where the product will be effectively exploited.[21]

The differences between sale and transit are also notable. In the case of sale, there is a wish to change the power over the goods, something that does not occur in transit. In the operation of transit the carrier merely puts the sender in contact with the addressee, but he is not entitled to introduce the products into the market of the transited country.[22] Of course, transit may also imply changing the carrier or the means of transport in the transited country. In cases that imply a change of the power over the goods, such as transhipment, the right holder could try to assimilate transit to other prohibited actions – such as sale – and therefore impede the transit. Nevertheless, numerous national courts have affirmed that transhipment and similar operations do not imply the introduction of protected goods into the national market.[23] In such cases, contact with the national market is merely circumstantial, while changing the power over the goods does not imply a change of their final destination.

3 *Border Measures in the European Union: Lessons for the Global Regime*

3.1 The Rapid Expansion of the European Border Enforcement Regulation

The European Union's border measures regime combines the application of the law of the country of customs procedures to products under any customs situation together with a large number of intellectual property types and border situations subject to customs control. The seizures of products in transit in the European customs territory and the jurisprudence of the CJEU on this matter exemplify the tension existing between free trade and the control of goods allegedly infringing intellectual property in the jurisdiction of transit.

EU Regulation No. 608/2013 currently in force confirms and expands the central aspects of the controversial – and repealed – Regulation No. 1383/2003. It consolidates the expansion of controls at the border, in terms of both the intellectual property rights categories controlled by customs authorities and border situations that enable authorities to take action. The sophisticated European legal framework resulting from a relatively fast succession of regulations is in fact aimed

21 *Ibid.*, pp. 142–144. 22 *Ibid.*, p. 134.

23 In 1915, the German Federal Court of Justice stated in *Taeschner-Pertussin* that the transferal of the power of disposition of goods to the carrier did not imply the introduction of the products into the national market in a way that could be considered as infringing the national patent. *See* Massaguer (1989), pp. 144–145.

at curbing intellectual property infringements occurring not only on European soil but also in third countries.

The first step in the process of the European Union's expansion of its border measures regime was carried out in 1986 when Regulation No. 3842/86 ordered border measures to be taken with respect to the importation of counterfeit goods.[24] Eight years later, Regulation No. 3295/94 mandated the detention of not only counterfeit but also pirated merchandise. Controls had to be implemented in cases of importation, exportation, re-exportation and entry for a suspensive procedure.[25] Notably, patent infringements were not covered until the late 1990s, when Regulation No. 241/1999[26] included patent and supplementary protection certificates. By that time, only a limited number of intellectual property rights categories remained out of the scope of the European Regulation.

That gap was almost totally closed by Regulation No. 1383/2003, which prescribed the control of goods protected by plant variety rights, geographical indications and designations of origin. Ten years later, EU Regulation No. 608/2013 also included trade names in so far as they were protected as exclusive property rights under national law. Regulation No. 608/2013 also covered topographies of semiconductor products and utility models and devices primarily designed, produced or adapted for the purpose of enabling or facilitating the circumvention of technological measures.[27]

Following the European Commission's proposals, EU Regulations No. 1383/2003 and 608/2013 strengthened the position of right holders in several respects. The intellectual property rights categories covered were broadened, right holders were accorded cost-free access to the system, the destruction of allegedly infringing goods was facilitated, an European Union application was created, and the scope for *ex officio* action by customs authorities was expanded.

Article 1.1 of Regulation No. 1383/2003 distinguished two sets of situations. On the one hand, it allowed customs authorities to take action against goods suspected of infringing intellectual property rights entered for release for free circulation, export or re-export.[28] On the other hand, it also covered goods suspected of infringing intellectual property rights and found during checks when entering or leaving the customs territory, when placed under a suspensive procedure or in the process of

24 *See* Council Regulation (EEC) No. 3842/86 of 1 December 1986 laying down measures to prohibit the release for free circulation of counterfeit goods, OJ L 357/1 of 18 December 1986 (hereinafter Regulation No. 3842/86).

25 *See* Council Regulation (EC) No. 3295/94 of 22 December 1994 laying down measures to prohibit the release for free circulation, export, re-export or entry for a suspensive procedure of counterfeit and pirated goods, OJ L 341/18 of 30 December 1994 (hereinafter Regulation No. 3295/94).

26 *See* Council Regulation (EC) No. 241/1999 amending Regulation (EC) No. 3295/94 laying down measures to prohibit the release for free circulation, export, re-export or entry for a suspensive procedure of counterfeit and pirated goods, OJ L 27 of 2 February 1999 (hereinafter Regulation No. 241/1999). This regulation amended Regulation No. 3295/94 in response to the recommendation put forward by the Commission. *See* European Commission (1998).

27 *See* Article 2.1 letters (j) (k) (l) Regulation No. 608/2013.

28 *See* Article 1.1 subsection (a) Regulation No. 1383/2003.

being re-exported subject to notification or, finally, when placed in a free zone or warehouse.[29] In fact, Regulation No. 1383/2003 allowed taking action in all kinds of customs situations regarding goods not subject to intra-community trade. Notably, as the third recital of the regulation established, the transhipment of goods was also included.

EU Regulation No. 608/2013 substantially covers the same situations but does so in clearer language. It covers goods subject to customs supervision or control within the customs territory of the European Union in accordance with the European Customs Code.[30] Pursuant to EU Regulation No. 608/2013, authorities must supervise goods particularly in the following situations: when declared for release for free circulation,[31] in the cases of exportation[32] or re-exportation,[33] when entering or leaving the customs territory of the European Union[34] and when placed under a suspensive procedure or in a free zone or free warehouse.

Controversies have mainly revolved around goods placed under a suspensive procedure or in a free zone or free warehouse. These goods are not intended for the European Union market, and their relation with Europe is limited to transiting the European territory. Suspensive or 'special procedures' – in the terminology used in the 2008 Modernised Customs Code – include several possibilities: transit (external and internal); storage (temporary storage, customs warehousing and free zones); specific use (temporary admission and end-use) and processing (inward and outward processing).[35]

In terms of litigation and trade disputes, the most controversial situations have been those arising from the detention of products under external transit, warehousing and transhipment. The external transit regime allows non-Community goods to move from one point to another within the European Union customs area without subjecting such goods to import duties or other charges.[36] This status is indicated for products arriving in or leaving from different states integrating the European customs area, generally due to better transport connections or lower costs.

[29] *See* Article 1.1 subsection (b) Regulation No. 1383/2003.

[30] Article 1 EU Regulation No. 608/2013. According to Article 4 of the European Customs Code, customs procedures include (a) release for free circulation, (b) transit, (c) customs warehousing, (d) inward processing, (e) processing under customs control, (f) temporary admission, (g) outward processing, (h) exportation.

[31] The procedure allowing third-country goods to circulate freely throughout the Community in the same way as goods made in the Community is called release for free circulation.

[32] Exportation consists of sending European goods outside the European customs area.

[33] Re-exportation refers to the departure from the European Union of non-Community goods introduced into the European territory without having been released for free circulation at any time.

[34] As Article 91 of the European Customs Code establishes, 'goods brought into the customs territory of the Community shall, from the time of their entry, be subject to customs supervision'. Until a customs-approved treatment or use is assigned to goods, they remain under customs supervision.

[35] *See* Article 135 Regulation (EC) No. 450/2008 of the European Parliament and of the Council of 23 April 2008 laying down the Community Customs Code, OJ 145 of 4 June 2008 (hereinafter Modernised Customs Code).

[36] *See* CJEU, Case C-383/98, *The Polo/Lauren Company LP v. Pt Dwidua Langgeng Pratama International Freight Forwarders* [2000], Judgment of the Court (First Chamber) of 6 April 2000, ECR I-2519, para. 26 (hereinafter *Polo v. Lauren*).

Concerning transhipment, EU Regulation No. 608/2013 permits customs authorities to take action when goods are found during checks on products entering or leaving the customs territory of the European Union.[37]

Pursuant to EU Regulation No. 608/2013, goods are suspected of infringing an intellectual property right if there are indications that where such goods are found in a Member State, they are the subject of an act infringing an intellectual property right.[38] In addition, each category of intellectual property rights covered is defined in accordance with the European Union or Member State's regulation, reaffirming that the relevant law is the law of the customs procedures. If applied without limitation or further qualification to goods in transit, this regime may conflict with the principles of territoriality and freedom of transit, and in the case of some of intellectual property categories, it does not match with the substantive rights conferred by the title.

As discussed later, the CJEU has required additional connections with the country where the procedures are initiated in order to determine the infringing status of products in transit. Indeed, in response to the heated debates arising from the detention of medicines in transit, EU Regulation No. 608/2013 also states that 'customs authorities should, when assessing a risk of infringement of intellectual property rights, take account of any substantial likelihood of diversion of such medicines onto the market of the Union'.[39] However, the particular reference to pharmaceutical products in transit hardly represents the definitive and global solution to the necessary 'compromise between the imperatives of international trade, free movement of goods, and protection against intellectual property rights infringements'[40] that border measures must achieve.

3.2 The Jurisprudence of the Court of Justice of the European Union

On various occasions the CJEU has dealt with the interaction between the principle of territoriality, the rights conferred by different categories of intellectual property

37 Article 1(b). *See* Vrins and Schneider (2006a), p. 95. The new regulation does not mention Articles 91 and 177 of the Modernised Customs Code. These articles correspond to Articles 37 and 183 of the repealed European Customs Code, which were expressly mentioned in Regulation No. 1383/2003.

38 *See* Article 2.7.a EU Regulation No. 608/2013. It follows, therefore, Regulation No. 1383/2003, which stated that the law of the Member State within which the goods are placed in any of the customs situations shall apply when deciding whether an intellectual property right has been infringed. In fact, Article 10 Regulation No. 3295/1994 already stated that '[t]he law in force in the Member State within the territory of which the goods are placed in one of the situations referred to in Article 1(1)(a) shall apply as regards: (a) referral to the authority competent to take a substantive decision and immediate notification of the customs service or office referred to in paragraph 1 of that referral; (b) reaching the decision to be taken by that authority. In the absence of Community rules in this regard, the criteria to be used in reaching that decision shall be the same as those used to determine whether goods produced in the Member State concerned infringe the rights of the holder.'

39 *See* Recital 11 and Article 1.5 EU Regulation No. 608/2013.

40 *See* Vrins and Schneider (2006a), p. 66.

rights and the push for enforcing local intellectual property rights that may have extra-territorial effects. While in most of the cases the Court has dealt with controversies arising from trademark litigation, fundamental aspects of its jurisprudence are transferable to other categories of intellectual property rights.

In 2000, in the context of *The Polo/Lauren Company LP v. Pt Dwidua Langgeng Pratama* case, the CJEU linked the validity of border measures regulation to the European Union's common commercial policy. The Court affirmed that provisions on intellectual property affecting cross-border trade constitute an essential element of international trade legislation and that the external transit of non-Community goods does have an effect on the internal market. Alleging the possible diversion of those goods onto the European market, the Court upheld the legality of the regulation.[41] The risk that counterfeit goods in external transit may be fraudulently brought on to the European market had, in fact, already been underlined by the General Advocate as a factor to take into consideration when examining the regulation.[42]

In *Montex Holdings Ltd. v. Diesel SpA*, a cargo from a non-European Union country was in transit through Germany, heading towards Ireland, a country where the goods were not trademark protected. In response to several preliminary questions, the Court affirmed that 'external transit does not constitute use of the mark liable to infringe the right of the mark's proprietor to control the putting of the goods in question on the Community market, because it does not imply any marketing of those goods'.[43] This led the Court to conclude that the proprietor of a trademark can prohibit the transit of goods bearing the trademark and placed under the external transit procedure 'only if those goods are subject to the act of a third party while they are placed under the external transit procedure which necessarily entails their being put on the market in that Member State of transit'.[44] The CJEU also made it clear that the risk of diversion was not merely theoretical. It held that the right holder must demonstrate either 'the existence of a release for free circulation' or 'another act necessarily entailing their being put on the market' in the transit State.[45] In a previous case, the Court stated that 'placing non-Community products under a suspensive customs procedure does not make it possible for them to be put on the market in the Community in the absence of release for free circulation'.[46]

Advocate General Jacobs was even clearer in *Unilever NV and Others*. This case concerned genuine trademarked goods that the applicant was trying to introduce

41 'There is a risk that counterfeit goods placed under the external transit procedure may be fraudulently brought on to the Community market.' *See Polo v. Lauren*, paras. 33–34.

42 *See* Opinion of Advocate General Jacobs, Case C-405/03, 26 May 2005, para. 34.

43 *See* ECJ, Case C-281/05, *Montex Holdings Ltd. v. Diesel SpA* [2006], Judgment of the Court (Second Chamber) of 9 November 2006, ECR I-10881, para. 25 (hereinafter *Montex Holdings*).

44 *Ibid.*, para. 27.

45 *Ibid.* para. 25.

46 *See* ECJ, Case C-405/03, *Class International BV v. Colgate-Palmolive Company and Others* [2005], Judgment of the Court (Grand Chamber) of 18 October 2005, ECR I-8735, para. 47 (hereinafter *Class International*).

into the European Economic Area. The defendants blocked the products at the Dutch border invoking legislation prohibiting the entry of counterfeit products, but it soon became clear that this was not the case. Among the questions answered by the Advocate General was whether a trademark owner may oppose the entry of legally trademarked goods from third countries into the territory of a Member State. It was recalled that trademark owner exclusive rights are granted in order to enable the proprietor to protect his specific interests as proprietor. In this context, Advocate General Jacobs affirmed that he could 'not see how the essential function of a trademark can be compromised solely by the fact that goods genuinely bearing that mark are subject to the external transit procedure and hence by definition are not in free circulation within the Community'.[47] Advocate General Jacobs also recalled the *Rioglass and Transremar* case,[48] where the CJEU affirmed that the mere passing in transit did not involve any marketing of the goods and therefore could not infringe any rights.[49]

The jurisprudence of the CJEU on Article 30 of the Treaty Establishing the European Community[50] may also be helpful in establishing the limits of border enforcement of intellectual property rights. Article 30 of the EC Treaty authorizes prohibiting or restricting importation, exportation and transit of goods invoking the protection of industrial and commercial property. Intellectual property rights enforcement would be therefore a legitimate basis to move away from free trade principles. Even so, the CJEU made it clear that these actions could be taken only 'to protect the specific subject-matter of the right of industrial and commercial property'.[51] In the area of patents and in the context of the jurisprudence related to the exhaustion of rights doctrine, the CJEU has stated that the specific subject matter of a patent is to use an invention for placing the goods resulting from said invention onto the market for the first time.[52] It is hardly tenable that the mere transit of a product could affect this specific subject matter, since the invention would not

47 *See* Opinion of Advocate General Jacobs, Case C-405/03, 26 May 2005, para. 29.

48 In *Rioglass and Transremar* the Court affirmed that 'Article 28 EU is to be interpreted as precluding the implementation pursuant to a legislative measure of a Member State concerning intellectual property, of procedures for detention by the customs authorities of goods lawfully manufactured in another Member State and intended, following their transit through the territory of the first Member State, to be placed in the market in a non-member country'. *See* ECJ, Case C-115/02, *Administration des douanes v. Rioglass* S.A. [2003], Judgment of the Court (Sixth Chamber) of 23 October 2003, ECR I-12705, para. 30 (hereinafter *Rioglass and Transremar*).

49 Jacobs stated (referring to the *Rioglass* jurisprudence) that 'if the Court took that view with regard to goods in free circulation in the Community it would apply a fortiori to non-Community goods in respect of which import formalities have not been completed'. *See* Opinion of Advocate General Jacobs, Case C-405/03, 26 May 2005, para. 32.

50 *See Treaty on European Union and the Treaty on the Functioning of the European Union.*

51 *See* ECJ, Case C-23/99, *Commission of the European Communities v. French Republic* [2000], Judgment of the Court of 26 September 2000, ECR I-7653, para. 38 (hereinafter *Commission v. France*).

52 *See*, for instance, Case C-15/74, *Centrafarm BV and Adriaan de Peijper v. Sterling Drug Inc.* [1974], Judgment of the Court of 31 October 1974, ECR 01147, para. 9.

be used nor the product placed onto the national market where the right holder's rights are recognized.

So, under a very similar legal regime to the present one, the CJEU linked the detention and the suspension of release of protected goods in transit to the potential diversion of those goods onto the transited market. In itself, the transit of goods through a country where they are protected does not imply an infringement. The background argument is that only by placing the goods onto the internal market can the subject matter of a specific intellectual property right or the rights of the title holder be infringed. Consequently, the detention of goods in transit would only be warranted if those goods threatened the right holder's competitive position in the country of transit.

Some countries have introduced alternative regimes allowing action to be taken with respect to goods in transit. An option consists of anticipating the moment and location of the protection of an intellectual property right. This is the case of Switzerland, where the patent owner can impede the transit of patent-infringing goods if he can also prohibit the import into the country of destination.[53] Hence, Swiss law permits anticipating the moment of the protection that the same title holder could demand in the country of destiny. Although it relates to patents, Swiss authorities justify such anticipation 'in view of the increasing international dimension of counterfeiting and piracy'[54] and in order to 'prevent Switzerland from becoming a transit country for pirated goods'.[55]

The Swiss option is far from unproblematic when assessed against both the prohibition of extraterritoriality of intellectual property rights and the rights conferred to the right holder. This is the case for two reasons. First, local authorities might find themselves in the difficult situation of examining the validity of the intellectual property right in the country of importation. Second, the right holder may prevent the transit even if his rights in the transit country have not been affected at all. In this last regard, the CJEU adopted in 2011 a significant judicial decision on the temporary detention and eventual destruction of goods placed under a suspensive procedure.[56] In its reply to the joined *Philips* and *Nokia* cases,[57] the CJEU restated its previous jurisprudence, holding that the mere placement of goods under a suspensive procedure does not entitle right holders to request the detention of goods and that no infringement of intellectual property rights can be found if there is no evidence of the potential diversion of goods.

The preliminary ruling responded to two questions – one on copyright and design law and the other on trademark law – that originated from Belgian, English and Welsh courts. The CJEU was asked whether goods coming from a non-Member

[53] *See* Article 8.3 of the Patents Act; Swiss Federal Institute of Intellectual Property, *Interpretation of the Patents Act*, available at: www.ige.ch/fileadmin/user_upload/Juristische_Infos/e/j10030e.pdf (last accessed June 2015).

[54] *Ibid.* [55] *Ibid.* [56] Customs warehousing and external transit, in this case.

[57] *See Philips v. Nokia*.

State that are imitations of goods protected in the European Union by a trademark right or copies of goods protected by copyright, a related right or a design can be classified as 'counterfeit' or 'pirated' goods on the basis that they are brought into the European customs territory, even if not released for free circulation.[58] The Court was also requested to rule on whether products placed under suspensive procedures could be detained and a decision on their infringing status adopted. Right holders and some states argued that this could be possible if the 'local production fiction' were applied.[59] To back their case, they invoked a number of consumer safety concerns.

The Court's decision consolidates previous jurisprudence and elaborates it further. The decision introduces arguments relating to the international trade regime and the convenience of maintaining equilibrium between the protection of intellectual property and free trade. It also addresses concerns over consumer safety and excludes border enforcement of intellectual property rights as the adequate means to address those concerns.[60] The decision of the CJEU analyses separately the temporary detention of goods placed under a suspensive procedure and the substantive decision following the temporary detention of goods placed under a suspensive customs procedure.

With regard to temporary detention, the Court restates that mere transit and customs warehousing cannot be regarded as implying a sale in the European Union. Therefore, goods placed under a suspensive procedure cannot infringe rights in the European Union simply because they are placed in such circumstances. However, if these goods are the subject of a commercial act directed to European consumers, intellectual property rights may be infringed. Direct commercial acts will allow detaining the goods placed under a suspensive procedure. The risk of fraudulent diversion to European consumers may also arise in other circumstances, even when goods have not yet been directed towards European consumers. Customs authorities can, in effect, detain the goods or suspend their release when there are indications that commercial activities may take place in the near future or are being disguised.[61] Suspicion, based on a number of facts of the case, will suffice for that purpose.[62]

58 *Ibid.*, para. 49. *See* question in paras. 40 and 47.

59 *Ibid.*, para. 53. *See* Section II.2.

60 *See* Chapter 12.

61 According to the CJEU, a customs authority can act when there are indications before it that one or more of the operators involved in the manufacture, consignment or distribution of the goods in warehousing or transit, while not having yet begun to direct the goods towards European Union consumers, are about to do so or are disguising their commercial intentions. *See Philips v. Nokia*, para. 60.

62 Including the following: the destination of the goods is not declared, the lack of precise or reliable information as to the identity or address of the manufacturer or consignor of the goods, a lack of cooperation with the customs authorities or the discovery of documents suggesting that there is a likelihood of a diversion of those goods to European Union consumers. *See Philips v. Nokia*, para. 61.

If goods have already been detained, judicial authorities will have to ascertain whether they infringe an intellectual property right. This decision cannot be taken on just suspicion, but it must be based on an examination of whether there is proof of an infringement. Goods cannot be classified as 'goods infringing an intellectual property right' if it is not proven that they are intended to be put on sale in the European Union.[63] Evidence that goods may infringe an intellectual property right in Europe may include the existence of a sale of goods to a customer in the European Union, of an offer for sale or advertising addressed to European consumers or of documents or correspondence concerning the goods in question showing that diversion of those goods to European Union consumers is envisaged.[64]

3.3 Trademark Reform and Border Enforcement

The CJEU jurisprudence in the *Nokia* and *Philips* joined cases was criticized by right holders and some European institutions. Indeed, even respected judges have criticized the current state of affairs and, while abiding by the jurisprudence of the CJEU, have underlined the need for change.[65] All of them probably share the basic understanding that, 'in cases where the infringement as well as the intention to infringe, copy or counterfeit are clear and beyond doubt, manufacturers or traders should not be able to rely on the benefits of the transit procedure to carry on manifestly illicit activities'.[66]

The European Commission, the Council and the Parliament tried to respond to the perceived need for change by embarking on a delicate reform of the trademark regulation and directive, and in December 2015 the new legislation in the field was adopted.[67] Reconciling free trade and trademark enforcement without unduly restricting access to legitimate products in third countries and respecting basic intellectual property principles is indeed a delicate endeavour, as reflected in the different proposals put forward by European institutions.

63 *Ibid.*, para. 70. 64 *Ibid.*, para. 71.

65 Judge Kitchin noted, in the context of the Nokia case, that 'I recognise that this result is not satisfactory. I can only hope it provokes a review of the adequacy of the measures available to combat the international trade in fake goods by preventing their transhipment through Member States'. *See* *Nokia v. HMRC*, [2009] EWHC 1903 (Ch), Case No: HC 09CO1457, para. 80.

66 *See* Jaeger, Grosse Ruse-Khan, Drexl and Hilty (2010), p. 17.

67 *See* Regulation (EU) 2015/2424 of the European Parliament and of the Council of 16 December 2015 amending Council Regulation (EC) No 207/2009 on the Community trade mark and Commission Regulation (EC) No 2868/95 implementing Council Regulation (EC) No 40/94 on the Community trade mark and repealing Commission Regulation (EC) No 2869/95 on the fees payable to the Office for Harmonization in the Internal Market (Trade Marks and Designs), OJEU L 341/21 of 24 December 2015, entering into force on 23 March 2016. *See* also the Directive (EU) 2015/2436 of the European Parliament and of the Council of 16 December 2015 to approximate the laws of the Member States relating to trade marks, OJEU L 336/1 of 23 December 2015 (hereinafter EU Directive 2015/2436).

In its initial proposal, the European Commission recalled the criticism made by stakeholders with regard to the implications of the *Nokia* and *Philips* judgement. In their view, the sentence placed an inappropriately high burden of proof on right holders and hindered the fight against counterfeiting. For this reason, the European Commission held that there was 'an urgent need to have in place a European legal framework enabling a more effective fight against the counterfeiting of goods as a fast-growing activity'[68] and proposed an amendment to the trademark regulation. The amendment entitled European trademark owners to prevent all third parties from bringing goods into the customs territory of the European Union without being released for free circulation there, where such goods come from third countries and bear without authorization a trademark that is essentially identical to the trademark registered in respect of those goods or that cannot be distinguished in its essential aspects from that trademark, regardless of their release for free circulation.[69]

If the proposal of the European Commission had gone through without any further qualification, it would have implied a substantive change in the European normative framework and a reversal of the CJEU jurisprudence. In fact, it would have implied granting European right holders greater powers than those enjoyed by trademark owners in comparable economies. In effect, although some countries do allow the control of trademark protected goods in transit,[70] in the United States goods can only be detained if they have entered the stream of interstate commerce.[71]

The European Council added some wording to the European Commission's proposal with the intention of achieving a more nuanced text. Pursuant to the final text of the EU's Directive 2015/2436, the right of the trademark proprietor to detain products in transit shall lapse if during the proceedings 'evidence is provided by the declarant or the holder of the goods that the proprietor of the registered trade mark is not entitled to prohibit the placing of the goods on the market in the country of final destination'.[72] This wording puts the onus of proving the right holder's power on the owner of the goods. In our view, it would have been more reasonable and easier to require the right holder to prove that his mark is also validly registered in the country of destination.[73]

[68] *See* EU Commission (2013b), p. 9.

[69] *See* the proposed Article 9.5 of the Proposal for a Regulation of the European Parliament and of the Council amending Council Regulation (EC) No. 207/2009 on the Community trade mark, 2013/0088 (COD).

[70] *See* Vanrell (2013), p. 55; AIM (2014), pp. 2–6.

[71] It is not sufficient, hence, 'that the infringing goods have been packed into a freight car in Canada and are passing through the United States to a customer in Mexico'. *See* Scungio (2013), p. 54.

[72] *See* Article 10.4 and Recital 23 of the EU Directive 2015/2436.

[73] This has been proposed by Rapporteur Cecilia Wikström. *See* Committee on Legal Affairs (2014), Amendment 6 Proposal for a Directive Recital 22.

III FREEDOM OF TRANSIT PURSUANT TO ARTICLES V AND XX(D) OF GATT

1 *The Cumulative Nature of the WTO Obligations*

The impact of border measures on free trade must be studied in light of the obligations arising from the WTO General Agreement on Tariffs and Trade. Article V of GATT establishes a capital principle of the multilateral trade system, i.e. the principle of freedom of transit. In the same Agreement, Article XX lays down several general exceptions to these provisions.

The WTO panels and the Appellate Body have stated on numerous occasions that since the WTO Agreement is a 'single undertaking' it follows that 'WTO obligations are cumulative and Members must comply with all of them at all times'.[74] Therefore, both the relevant articles of GATT and the TRIPS Agreement must be taken into account when analysing disputes arising from the implementation of border measures with regard to intellectual property protected goods. In fact, the interaction between the TRIPS Agreement and other WTO agreements has already been addressed by the WTO adjudicative organs, which have underlined that there is no hierarchy between the TRIPS Agreement and GATT 1994 and that both may be applicable in the same dispute.[75]

The GATT and the TRIPS Agreement share the goal of avoiding the use of intellectual property rights to create barriers to legitimate trade. This common objective may help to attribute sense to general principles of GATT not yet implemented in the TRIPS Agreement. For instance, the notion of GATT on 'disguised restriction to international trade' may be analysed in light of restrictions arising from certain levels of intellectual property enforcement. The interaction can also work the other way around and consider the TRIPS Agreement as an agreement containing 'new rules and disciplines concerning the applicability of the basic principles of GATT 1994'.[76] In this regard, the provisions of the TRIPS Agreement on border measures could be considered as specifying the provisions of GATT on the same subject. It must be noted, however, that the interpretative interaction does not preclude independent examination of the same facts pursuant to both the GATT and the TRIPS Agreement.

2 *The Freedom of Transit Principle*

Article V of GATT sets the legal framework for the principle of freedom of transit. Article V:1, which is based on the 1921 Barcelona Convention and Statute on Freedom of Transit,[77] states that goods and means of transport shall be deemed to

[74] *See* WTO Panel Report, *Turkey – Restrictions on imports of textile and clothing products*, WT/DS34/R, 31 May 1999, para. 9.92.

[75] *See* WTO Panel Report, *European Communities – Protection of trademarks and geographical indications for agricultural products and foodstuffs*, WT/DS290/R, 15 March 2005, para. 7.87.

[76] As the Preamble of the TRIPS Agreement affirms.

[77] *See* WTO (1995), p. 214.

be in transit when the passage across the territory of a contracting party 'with or without trans-shipment, warehousing, breaking bulk, or change in the mode of transport, is only a portion of a complete journey beginning and terminating beyond the frontier of the contracting party'. Having established the definition of 'traffic in transit,' Article V:2 lays down the fundamental principle of freedom of transit.

This principle was interpreted for the first time by a WTO Panel in April 2009 in the *Colombia – Indicative prices and restrictions of ports of entry* dispute.[78] With regard to Article V:2, the WTO Panel agreed with the parties that sub-section 1 – i.e. the definition of transit – informed the scope of obligations under Article V:2. The WTO Panel also specified the meaning of the first and second sentences of Article V:2.[79] Pursuant to the first sentence of that article, freedom of transit requires extending unrestricted access via the most convenient routes for the passage of goods in international transit whether the goods have been trans-shipped, warehoused or break-bulked or have changed modes of transport. Accordingly, goods in international transit from any WTO Member State must be allowed entry whenever they are destined for the territory of a third country.[80] As far as the second sentence of Article V:2 is concerned, the panel considered that 'the obligation in Article V:2, second sentence is clear on its face: Members shall not make distinctions between goods which are "traffic in transit" based on the flag of vessels; the place of origin, departure, entry, exit or destination of the vessel; or on any circumstances relating to the ownership of goods, of vessels or of other means of transport'.[81]

3 Conditions Imposed to Delays and Restrictions on Products in Transit

Article V:2 of GATT requires extending unrestricted access to products in transit. Thus, it would seem that restrictions on products protected by intellectual property rights would not be acceptable. However, since Article V contains other sub-sections, it must be contextualized in the broader framework of the entire GATT as well as the multilateral trading system. In this regard, Articles V:3, V:4 and XX(d) of GATT are fundamental.

[78] The WTO Panel set up to issue the report recognized that the task was 'arduous since it will be necessary to interpret article V of the GATT without any meaningful guidance'. *See* WTO Panel Report, *Colombia – Indicative prices and restrictions on ports of entry*, WT/DS366/R, 27 April 2009, para. 7.388 (hereinafter WTO Panel, *Colombia – Indicative prices and restrictions on ports of entry*).

[79] In its first sentence, Article V:2 prescribes that '[t]here shall be freedom of transit through the territory of each contracting party, via the routes most convenient for international transit, for traffic in transit to or from the territory of other contracting parties'. In its second sentence, Article V:2 establishes that '[n]o distinction shall be made which is based on the flag of vessels, the place of origin, departure, entry, exit or destination, or on any circumstances relating to the ownership of goods, of vessels or of other means of transport'.

[80] 'Reasonably, in the Panel's view, a Member is not required to guarantee transport on necessarily any or all routes in its territory, but only on the ones "most convenient" for transport through its territory.' *See* WTO Panel, *Colombia – Indicative prices and restrictions on ports of entry*, para. 7.401.

[81] *Ibid.*, para. 4.402.

To begin with, Article V:3 modulates freedom of transit by stating that contracting parties may require that goods in transit be entered at the proper custom house. In case such traffic in transit complies with applicable customs laws and regulations, Article V:3 establishes that goods shall not be subject to any unnecessary delays or restrictions and shall be exempt from customs duties and from all transit duties. Two points may be raised with respect to this sub-section.

First, by virtue of Article V:3 of GATT, the WTO members' customs authorities are entitled to detain products protected by intellectual property rights in the application of their 'custom laws and regulations'. However, Article V:3 of GATT also forbids *unnecessary delays* or *restrictions*. This terminology is no stranger to the WTO jurisprudence where the so-called 'necessity test' is well known. According to this test, if the party had other less trade-restrictive and equally effective alternatives to achieve a certain public policy goal, it should have chosen those alternative measures.

Accepting that goods can be temporally detained, attention must focus on measures integrating the inspection regime. In this particular case, if the national border enforcement regulation is in line with Article 55 of the TRIPS Agreement, which relates to the duration of the suspension and prescribes a relatively short period for the right holder to inspect the goods, it is difficult to challenge the border enforcement regulation *as such* for resulting in 'unnecessary delays'. This, however, does not preclude a different conclusion regarding specific cases where time frames may be significantly longer. That is to say, even if local law fulfils the requirements prescribed by the GATT, it would still be possible to challenge the local regulation *as applied*.

Together with the potential infringement of Article V:3 of GATT caused by unnecessary delays, in case of detentions of products in transit it is equally important to evaluate the scope of *unnecessary restrictions*. If it is established that the TRIPS Agreement has been infringed by the unlawful detention of products or the application of the law of the country of transit without any further link to the national market (because there is no risk of diversion onto the national market or abuse of the transit procedure aimed at engaging in a manifestly illicit activity), it can also be sustained that interruptions of the flow of protected products in transit amount to unnecessary restrictions in the sense of Article V:3 of GATT. The risk of diversion onto the national market and the possibility of determining the counterfeit status of goods in the country of destination would be decisive factors in determining the existence of unnecessary restrictions.

4 *The Reasonableness of Border Measures Regulations*

Article V:4 of GATT lays down a fundamental rule regarding the principle of freedom of transit. It establishes that '[a]ll charges and regulations imposed by contracting parties on traffic in transit to or from the territories of other contracting parties shall be reasonable, having regard to the conditions of the traffic'. Hence,

Article V:4 imposes an open standard (*reasonableness*) against which specific regulations shall be assessed. In this context, if an infringement of Article V:4 of GATT resulting from the local border enforcement regulation was found, it would be necessary to amend the corresponding provisions.

The WTO adjudicative organs have shown their preference for a literal interpretation,[82] which implies relying on the ordinary or of the words.[83] The dictionary meaning of 'reasonable' alludes to 'as much as is appropriate or fair; moderate',[84] 'not extreme or excessive'.[85] It is clear, therefore, that deciding on whether something is reasonable requires an evaluation of all the relevant circumstances, implying a case-by-case analysis. This case-oriented analysis has, in fact, been performed by the WTO adjudicative organs when the term *reasonable* has appeared in disputes.

The WTO Panel in the *Mexico – Measures affecting telecommunications services* case dealt with the meaning of 'reasonable terms, conditions and rates' in the context of GATS.[86] The WTO Panel stated that 'reasonable can be defined as something of such an amount, size, number, etc., as is judged to be appropriate or suitable to the circumstances or purpose'.[87] From that sense of 'reasonable' the WTO Panel inferred that, regarding 'rates', reasonable meant that they must 'represent the costs incurred in providing the service'.[88] Similarly, in *US – Hot-Rolled Steel* case, the Appellate Body insisted on the need to adopt a case-by-case approach when deciding on the meaning of 'reasonable'. It stated that 'the word "reasonable" implies a degree of flexibility that involves consideration of all of the circumstances of a particular case.'[89]

82 The Appellate Body – quoting Sir Ian Sinclair – has manifested that only 'where the meaning imparted by the text itself is equivocal or inconclusive, or where confirmation of the correctness of the reading of the text itself is desired, light from the object and purpose of the treaty as a whole may usefully be sought'. *See* WTO Appellate Body Report, *United States – Import prohibition of certain shrimp and shrimp products*, WT/DS58/AB/R, 8 October 1998, para. 114.

83 The Appellate Body has recalled that dictionaries are a 'useful starting point'. *See* WTO Appellate Body Report, *European Communities-Customs classification of frozen boneless chicken cuts*, WT/DS269/AB/R, WT/DS286/AB/R, 12 September 2005, para. 175. *See* also Yu (2011f), p. 733; Gervais (2009a), p. 552.

84 *See The Concise Oxford Dictionary* (tenth ed.), revised, 2001, p. 1193.

85 *See Merriam Webster Online Dictionary*, available at: www.webster.com/cgi-bin/dictionary.

86 The United States challenged Mexico's compliance with the GATS and the specific undertakings of Mexico in relation to the GATS. The Reference Paper contained in the Mexico's *GATS Schedule of Specific Commitments* establishes in its Article 2.2(b) that interconnection provided by a major supplier must be ensured on *terms, conditions* and *rates* that are *reasonable*. On the other hand, *GATS Annex on telecommunications* 5(a) establishes that '[e]ach Member shall ensure that any service supplier of any other Member is accorded access to and use of public telecommunications transport networks and services *on reasonable* and non-discriminatory *terms and conditions*, for the supply of a service included in its Schedule'.

87 *See* WTO Panel Report, *Mexico – Measures affecting telecommunications services*, WT/DS204/R, 2 April 2004, para. 7.182.

88 *Ibid.*

89 *See* WTO Appellate Body Report, *United States – Anti-Dumping measures on certain hot-rolled steel products from Japan*, WT/DS184/AB/R, 24 July 2001, paras. 84–85.

The meaning of 'reasonable' is therefore contextual. Article V:4 of GATT reinforces this point when, after having stated that regulations must be reasonable, it adds 'having regard to the conditions of the traffic'. The reasonability, thus, will be assessed in a different manner depending on which are the 'conditions of the traffic'. Again, it is necessary to establish the meaning of 'conditions of the traffic'.

On the one hand, 'conditions' refer to 'the state of something or someone, with regard to appearance, fitness, or working order'.[90] On the other hand, in accordance with Article V:1 GATT, 'traffic' is the term used to refer to in-transit goods and merchandise. Thus, the 'conditions of the traffic' are the characteristics of the merchandise. Accordingly, regulations regarding transit must be reasonable and take into account the characteristics of the goods.

Hence, the analysis of intellectual property border enforcement regulations in the context of Article V:4 of GATT must take into consideration that goods under control may have different levels of protection (or no protection at all) in different countries, namely the country of origin, the country of transit and the country of destination. The question that needs to be answered is whether it is 'reasonable' to control goods that are in transit and could be protected in the country of transit. In our view, the territoriality and independence principles, as well as the 'strong link to global trade and the traditional WTO/General Agreement on Tariffs and Trade (GATT) approach toward further trade liberalization',[91] favour a qualified response. Control would be possible (i.e. *reasonable*) if a link between the goods and the market of transit can be effectively established or if the infringement pursuant the law of the country of destination of goods is also apparent on its face and abuse of the transit procedure for conduct of a manifestly illicit activity can be effectively determined.

An additional answer to the question of whether such a control is 'reasonable' can be inferred from potential trade-restrictive effects of the control of goods in transit. Interestingly enough, the literal interpretation of the term 'reasonable' in Article V:4 of GATT obliges taking into account the context in which the term is applied. However, Article 31.1 of the Vienna Convention on the Law of Treaties commands something different when it mandates taking into account the context. That article makes it necessary to assess the location of the interpreted provision in a specific treaty as well as the relevance of that treaty in a specific legal regime. In order to ascertain the meaning of the 'reasonability' prescribed by Article V:4 of GATT to regulations, it is pertinent to consider the fact that this prescription is contained in a section of an article that establishes freedom of transit as a general rule.[92] It is also

90 *See The Concise Oxford Dictionary* (tenth ed.), revised, 2001, p. 279.

91 *See* Grosse Ruse-Khan (2010), p. 628.

92 Article V:4 GATT enshrines an exception to that general rule, in the sense that Members may adopt regulations and impose reasonable charges to the traffic. As the freedom of transit is the general rule, exceptions must be interpreted narrowly. This is why the 'reasonableness' criteria must be defined in the context of what the article prescribes, namely freedom of transit.

important to note that this treaty is part of a complex system of treaties and institutions that have the promotion of free trade as their mainspring.

Article V:4 is part of GATT of 1947, which was adopted with a view to reducing tariffs and other barriers to trade and eliminating discriminatory treatment in international commerce. Indeed, trade liberalization aimed at the improvement of human well-being was the underlying goal of GATT 1947. Moreover, when states decided to create the WTO and signed the Marrakech Agreement, they laid down the institutional machinery necessary to promote free trade. The promotion of free trade is, in fact, the cross-cutting goal of all WTO agreements, including the TRIPS Agreement. Having in mind the trade-liberalization objectives of the GATT, the WTO Agreement and the WTO itself, it can be affirmed that regulations regarding traffic in transit are not reasonable if they restrict the trade of legitimate products.

5 *The Potential Invocation of Article XX(d) of GATT*

Article V of GATT must be read in conjunction with Article XX(b) of the same Agreement. Indeed, should the existence of the inconsistencies of Article V of GATT be proven, the Party in breach could still find its border measures justified pursuant to Article XX(d) of GATT. Both customs enforcement and the protection of intellectual property are recognized in Article XX(d) as grounds that permit measures derogating from the obligations of GATT, provided that the measures adopted respect the obligations set up in the *chapeau* clause of Article XX, including the prohibition of arbitrary or unjustifiable discrimination between countries and the prohibition of disguised restrictions on international trade.[93]

The measure at issue must not only come under one or another of the exceptions listed under Article XX. It must also satisfy the requirements imposed by the opening clauses of Article XX.[94] The first condition, in any case, is to identify a provisional justification under exception (d), which requires demonstrating two elements: 'First, the measure must be one designed to "secure compliance" with laws or regulations that are not themselves inconsistent with some provision of the GATT 1994. Second, the measure must be 'necessary' to secure such compliance. A Member who invokes

[93] The chapeau of Article XX and the text of Article XX(d) GATT provide that '[s]ubject to the requirement that such measures are not applied in a manner which would constitute a means of arbitrary or unjustifiable discrimination between countries where the same conditions prevail, or a disguised restriction on international trade, nothing in this Agreement shall be construed to prevent the adoption or enforcement by any contracting party of measures: (d) necessary to secure compliance with laws or regulations which are not inconsistent with the provisions of this Agreement, including those relating to customs enforcement, the enforcement of monopolies operated under paragraph 4 of Article II and Article XVII, the protection of patents, trade marks and copyrights, and the prevention of deceptive practices'.

[94] *See* WTO Appellate Body Report, *United States – Standards for reformulated and conventional gasoline*, WT/DS2/AB/R, 20 May 1996, p. 22.

Article XX(d) as a justification has the burden of demonstrating that these two requirements are met.'[95]

In determining whether a measure is designed to secure compliance with laws and regulations as provided in Article XX, a WTO Member raising a defense should identify the laws or regulations for which it seeks to secure compliance, establish that they are not themselves WTO-inconsistent and demonstrate that the measure at issue is designed to secure compliance with the relevant laws or regulations.[96] Any national rules that are necessary for the implementation of the TRIPS Agreement would be regarded as laws or regulations that are not inconsistent within the meaning of Article XX(d) of GATT.[97] Nevertheless, if it is established that intellectual property border regulation and measures are inconsistent with the TRIPS Agreement, the justification under Article XX(d) could hardly be sustained.

The Party defending its national border measures regulation would probably maintain not only the consistency but also the necessity of the measures.[98] In the context of the WTO law, the Appellate Body has accepted that a measure that is not absolutely indispensable may still be deemed necessary if it overcomes a weighing and balancing process.[99] In *Brazil – Tyres*, the Appellate Body placed great emphasis on this weighing and balancing process. Although the Appellate Body recognized that 'to be characterized as necessary, a measure does not have to be indispensable', it also emphasized that the contribution of that measure to the fulfilment of the objective 'must be material, not merely marginal' and, importantly, that contribution must be 'weighed against its trade restrictiveness'.[100]

According to the Appellate Body, the weighing and balancing process 'is comprehended in the determination of whether a WTO-consistent alternative measure that the Member concerned could "reasonably be expected to employ" is available, or whether a less WTO-inconsistent measure is "reasonably available"'.[101] The fact that

95 *See* WTO Appellate Body Report, *Korea – Measures affecting imports of fresh, chilled and frozen beef*, DS161/AB/R, WT/DS169/AB/R, 11 December 2000, para. 157 (hereinafter WTO Appellate Body Report, *Korea – Various Measures on Beef*).

96 *See* WTO Panel Report, *United States – Import prohibition of certain shrimp and shrimp products*, WT/DS58/R, 15 May 1998, para. 7.174. *See* also WTO Panel Report, *United States – Customs bond directive for merchandise subject to Anti-Dumping / countervailing duties*, WT/DS345/R, 29 February 2008, para. 7.295.

97 *See* McGovern (1995), p. 21.12–1.

98 In this regard, the increasing importance attached to the fight against counterfeiting, piracy and other intellectual property infringements could be a sound basis to sustain the necessity of some border measures.

99 Overcoming thus the interpretation that held that a 'necessary' measure is 'located significantly closer to the pole of "indispensable" than to the opposite pole of simply "making a contribution to"'. *See* WTO Appellate Body Report, *Korea – Various Measures on Beef*, para. 161.

100 *See* WTO Appellate Body Report, *Brazil – Measures affecting the import of retreated tyres*, WT/DS332/AB/R, 3 December 2007, para. 210.

101 *See* WTO Appellate Body Report, *Korea – Various Measures on Beef*, para. 166. The Appellate Body also followed this approach to the word 'necessary' as used in paragraph (b) of Article XX in WTO Appellate Body Report, *European Communities – Measures affecting asbestos and asbestos-containing products*, WT/DS135/AB/R, 12 March 2001, paras. 171–172.

very different legal frameworks exist among WTO Members to address the same problems arising from intellectual property infringement and customs control would be an important factor when assessing either the availability of WTO-consistent alternative measures or the availability of less WTO-inconsistent measures. In this regard, in the joined *Nokia* and *Philips* cases, the CJEU identified a number of measures that the European Union border authorities could adopt to tackle the problems that the border measures at stake intended to address. According to the CJEU, both the efficacy of the border measures regulation and the consumer safety concerns invoked to justify the disputed border measures could be addressed by resorting to other provisions found in general European customs law, unrelated to intellectual property.[102] In our view, this should imply limiting the control of transit merely to the case of diversion onto the national market. In the case of true counterfeits, it is advisable to empower customs authorities to act on the grounds of an abuse of the transit procedure for the conduct of a manifestly illicit activity.

According to the WTO Dispute Settlement Body, 'the burden of proof rests upon the party, whether complaining or defending, who asserts the affirmative of a particular claim or defense. If that party adduces evidence sufficient to rise a presumption that what is claimed is true, the burden then shifts to the other party, who will fail unless it adduces sufficient evidence to rebut the presumption.'[103] However, even if the country applying the border regulation can demonstrate that it respects this highly demanding test, measures and norms would still be assessed against the requirements set forth in the chapeau of Article XX, i.e. they could not be applied in a manner that would constitute a means of arbitrary or unjustifiable discrimination or a disguised restriction of international trade. As mentioned above, restrictions that find their origin either in highly demanding levels of intellectual property enforcement or levels that contradict basic intellectual property principles may be seen as disguised restrictions to international trade.

6 *The Prohibition to Impede Legitimate Trade*

Intellectual property enforcement norms found in international agreements usually enshrine a limitation to the reach of such measures through the prohibition to restrict legitimate trade.[104] Potential impediments to legitimate trade have also been at the centre of the argumentation of the CJEU when limiting the detention of products subject to suspensive procedures. The Court has noted that imitations and copies transiting the European Union customs area may comply with the intellectual property provisions in the state of origin and destination. In light of the objective

[102] *See Philips v. Nokia*, paras. 75, 76, and 77.

[103] *See* WTO Appellate Body Report, *United States – Measures affecting imports of woven shirts and blouses*, WT/DS33/AB/R, 23 March 1997, p. 14.

[104] Article 41 TRIPS Agreement has been replicated in Article 6.1 ACTA, and similar provisions can be found in many PTAs.

of the 'development of world trade through the progressive abolition of restrictions on trade between States, it is essential that those goods be able to pass in transit' via the European Union 'without that operation being hindered, even by a temporary detention'.[105] According to the Court, detaining goods without proof of their potential diversion to European Union consumers would create that type of hindrance.

This question was raised in the context of a controversy between India, Brazil and the European Union resulting from the European seizures of patented products in transit. India, Brazil and other developing countries, both in the WTO consultation phase of the dispute[106] and later in meetings of the TRIPS Council,[107] argued that the European Union's customs regulation and the implementing measures were disrupting legitimate trade.[108]

A central aspect of the discussion was the 'legitimacy' of the trade that was being disrupted. The fact that the products in question were legal in both the exporting and importing countries, the widespread use of generic medicines to achieve better and more affordable health care and the human rights component of the objective to enable access to medicines created a scenario that made it difficult for the European Union to defend the seizures and the regulation backing them.[109] In this context, it is useful to recall that the WTO Panel report *Canada – Generics* gave a definition of 'legitimate'. According to the WTO Panel, the term 'must be defined in the way that it is often used in legal discourse – as a normative claim calling for protection of interests that are "justifiable" in the sense that they are supported by relevant public policies or other social norms'.[110]

This reasoning has resulted in useful findings, according to which 'any trade for which a justifiable public policy or interest exists or which is supported by other social norms is legitimate'.[111] For instance, international trade in pharmaceutical products permits facilitating access to health, which is not only a public policy goal but also a human right.[112] In order to identify 'what and whose public policy or social norms are relevant', the objectives and principles of the TRIPS Agreement may be

105 *See Philips v. Nokia*, para. 63. 106 *See* WTO (2010a).

107 *See* WTO Council for Trade-Related Aspects of Intellectual Property Rights (2010), para. 253.

108 The controversy was settled with the compromise by the European Union to amend its customs regulations and to adopt interim guidelines for its customs officials. The goal was to harmonize customs actions with the more orthodox jurisprudence of the European Court of Justice with regard to transit, risk of diversion and patented products. Press Information Bureau, Government of India, Ministry of Commerce and Industry, *Indian EU Reach an Understanding on Issue of Seizure of Indian Generic Drugs in Transit*, 28 July 2011, available at: http://pib.nic.in/newsite/erelease.aspx?relid=73554 (last accessed June 2015). It remains unclear whether the amended framework will suffice to keep to that compromise, since seizures of legal patented goods in transit are still possible. *See* Baker (2012).

109 With regard to these elements and the legitimacy of the trade that was being disrupted, *see* Seuba (2010a), p. 10; Grosse Ruse-Khan (2011), pp. 696–697.

110 *See* WTO Panel Report, *Canada – Patent protection of pharmaceutical products*, WT/DS/114/R, 17 March 2000 (adopted 7 April 2000), para. 7.69.

111 *See* Grosse Ruse-Khan (2015). 112 *See* Seuba (2009); Kumar (2009); Seuba (2010a), p. 10.

useful,[113] since they permit adopting a flexible approach to the needs of the public interest and are valid for all the WTO Members.

IV CONCLUSIONS

The increased sophistication of intellectual property border enforcement regulation may turn into a difficult relationship with fundamental principles of international trade law. The dilution of the connection between the allegedly infringing goods and the jurisdiction of customs control has resulted in the detention of goods merely transiting a country, something particularly problematic in the case of products protected by patents. The legal framework enabling this type of detentions is exported via plurilateral and bilateral agreements. While the jurisprudence of some regional courts, notably the CJEU, has moderated maximalist implementations, the interpretation delivered by the CJEU may not be adopted by other courts and may also change in light of regional normative developments.

In spite of the fact that goods placed under a suspensive customs procedure cannot, merely by the fact of being so placed, infringe intellectual property rights applicable in local jurisdiction,[114] part of the doctrine and some institutions favour the control of products in transit even if they bear no direct relationship to the local market.[115] The European experience has proved that even when the law of customs procedures is identified as the relevant law to determine the existence of an infringement, it is still necessary to establish an additional connection between the products and the *lex loci* in order to allow the application of the latter. In the case of products in transit, it is necessary to prove the eventual diversion of products into the national market. Hence, countries that have subscribed to treaties ordering the application of the law of customs procedures, including cases of products in transit, can encounter trade-disruptive effects by requiring a direct connection between the goods and their jurisdiction. Basic intellectual property principles, such as the territoriality principle and trade principles, in particular the freedom of transit, require this adjustment. Other avenues for controlling goods in transit, such as anticipating the moment of control on the part of the right holder that could ultimately impede the importation into the country of final destination, remain controversial.

The control of transit should be an exception in the context of a regime inspired by free trade and territoriality principles. In response to the growing volume of trade in counterfeit goods and concomitant consumer-related concerns, the control of transit should be exceptionally acceptable in the case of trademark counterfeited goods provided some conditions were fulfilled. In effect, if a risk of diversion of

[113] *See* Grosse Ruse-Khan (2011).

[114] *See inter alia*, as regards rights concerning designs, *Commission v. France*, paras. 42–43, and, as regards rights conferred by trademarks, *Rioglass and Transremar*, para. 27, *Class International.* para. 47, and *Montex Holdings*, para. 21.

[115] *See* Vrins (2010), p. 362.

counterfeit goods onto the internal market can be proven or in cases of clear fraud of the transit procedure, countries may be entitled to stop counterfeits.

If countries decide to act in cases of risk of diversion or fraud, both the law of the country of importation and the law of the country of customs procedures should be of relevance. In case of risk of diversion, the local jurisdiction and law may be triggered and therefore the *lex loci* used to assess the infringing status of goods. In the case of fraudulent use of the transit procedure to traffic counterfeits, a double check should be performed. First, an assessment of the counterfeit nature of goods in the country of destination must be conducted. Second, if the answer to that question is positive, a decision as to whether the goods are also counterfeits pursuant to the law of the country of transit must be sought.

12

Border Measures and Human Rights

I THE INTERFACE BETWEEN HUMAN RIGHTS AND BORDER ENFORCEMENT

Positive, conflictive and ambiguous relations between border enforcement and human rights can be identified through analysing customs norms and practices worldwide. From the perspective of the right holder, norms on border enforcement fulfil an important function as they permit materializing the protection of intellectual property rights. Therefore, to the extent that intellectual property protection may be instrumental to the fulfilment of some fundamental rights,[1] border enforcement plays a relevant and positive function for the protection and promotion of human rights.

Rules on customs procedures and judicial mechanisms that deal with allegedly infringing goods in different customs situations implement the right to a remedy and the right to a fair trial. Border enforcement norms concretize due process standards in the specific context of customs control and, together with them, the possibility to respect rights related to the administration of justice. This is one of the reasons that explain why enforcement norms are of interest not to just right holders but also to alleged infringers. Indeed, right holders and alleged infringers share a human rights' concern with regard to norms on border enforcement and, more specifically, its balanced design and implementation. Still, incrementalist pressure on international enforcement regulation may have negative effects on the balance of rights and guarantees that national enforcement regulation tries to achieve.

For consumers and users, norms on customs enforcement may be equivocal. On the one hand, these norms may negatively impact on the entry of products into the national market. Consequently, access to goods that permit satisfying rights such as the right to health, the right to food or the right to culture may be impinged upon.

[1] This is for instance the case of the right to property and the right to enjoy the material and moral benefits arising from inventions and creations. *See* Chapter 2, Section I.3.

On the other hand, this impact may occur with respect to products of different quality, ranging from goods of bad quality to goods of standard quality. This introduces an additional layer of complexity that makes it necessary to adopt a nuanced approach. Since border controls may be instrumental in protecting consumer safety and impeding access to unsafe products, it is reasonable to assume that they may also contribute to protecting several human rights. Hence, while border measures may restrict access to life-saving products, they may also be instrumental in forestalling the consumption of poisonous products.

Taking into consideration the multifaceted set of interactions described above and the fact that customs procedures may sometimes have contradictory effects when observed from the human rights perspective, this chapter addresses three different cases of interaction. The first relates to the impact of the implementation of border measures on access to vital products, particularly those that apply to products in transit. The second concerns arguments made in favour of border measures as an instrument to ensure consumer safety and whether these measures are acceptable, or even necessary, to implement a number of human rights. The third case of interaction touches upon ambiguous relations and pays particular attention to border measures regulation of 'bad' normative quality.

II THE IMPACT OF BORDER MEASURES ON ACCESS TO GOODS

1 *Customs Enforcement and the Broader Intellectual Property Trade-Off*

The relationship between intellectual property enforcement and human rights tends to concentrate in the area of civil rights. This is why several chapters of this book touch upon the relationship between intellectual property enforcement and due process or privacy, among other civil rights. Nevertheless, as noted elsewhere, economic and social rights may also be impacted by enforcement norms.[2] The case of border enforcement is particularly telling and invites an expanded analysis of the interactions between human rights and intellectual property enforcement. The impact of border enforcement norms on access to goods is one of the key elements of this analysis.

The positive relationship between economic welfare and intellectual property protection is frequently invoked to support the granting of exclusive rights.[3] In this sense, intellectual property rights are generally perceived as incentives for the development of products that a purely competitive market would not provide.[4]

[2] *See* Seuba (2015c), pp. 181–182. *See* Chapter 2, Section I.2.

[3] In the health context, the broad public policy goal of intellectual property protection is 'to promote innovation, through garnering and directing resources towards beneficial research and development'. *See* WIPO (2007a), p. 3.

[4] This general statement does not apply with respect to all types of intellectual property, such as trademarks or database protection.

Hence, intellectual property protection is instrumental in ultimately satisfying human demands. This objective runs in parallel to other socioeconomic outputs, such as the contribution of intellectual property rights to tax revenue, employment and scientific and cultural advancement.[5] In this context, border measures are usually presented as cogs of the wheel necessary for the fulfilment of these goals and the reaping of benefits resulting from intellectual property protection.[6]

The acceptance of other, non-desirable, effects of intellectual property protection on access to goods is part of the instrumentalist approach. Actually, the fundamental trade-off of intellectual property protection, as well as the social benefits described previously, build upon the assumption that society is willing to pay the cost of restricting access to products for a period of time in exchange for new products and creations. During the period of exclusivity, right holders and licensees can exclude others from undertaking activities that relate to protected products. The entire intellectual property system, including border enforcement, reflects this very basic rationale.

Intellectual property protection at the border impacts on a number of activities that determine access to products in a given market, such as production, exportation, importation and sale. Changes in the legal regime on border measures influence exportation and importation, both in the national jurisdiction and in third jurisdictions, and therefore impinge on the supply of domestic and foreign markets. In the case of import controls, the effects are limited to the country applying the measures and impact on activities such as national production, consumption and public and private expenditure. The cases of exportation and transit are different since the national regime impacts on the provision of goods elsewhere, even if the goods are not infringing in the countries of origin and/or destination. The resulting impact on the availability of products and their prices is translated into consumption and access. Whether such impact is acceptable depends on several factors, some of which are external to the intellectual property system. The latter includes the impact of restrictions on products closely related to the satisfaction of a number of fundamental rights, such as the right to culture, the right to food and the right to health.

2 *The Impact of Border Measures on the Right to Health in Third Countries*

2.1 Systemic Integration in Practice

The possibility of controlling patented goods in transit has raised numerous questions in light of the WTO law.[7] The relevance of norms in both GATT and the TRIPS Agreement when ruling on the legality of the detention of pharmaceutical products in transit was discussed in 2009 in the context of the WTO Dispute Settlement System.

[5] *See* Chapter 3, Section I. [6] *See* Vrins and Schneider (2006a), pp. 4–19.

[7] *See* Chapter 11, Sections III and IV.

It was in that context that the possibility of taking into account international human rights law to interpret disputed WTO norms was raised.[8]

In its request for consultations to the European Union, India argued that the European measures and regulation enabling the detention of products in transit had had 'a serious adverse impact'[9] on public health and the provision on medicines. Accordingly, India argued, the relevant TRIPS Agreement provisions relating to border measures had to be 'interpreted and implemented in light of the objectives and principles set forth in Articles 7 and 8 of the TRIPS Agreement, the Doha Ministerial Declaration on the TRIPS Agreement and Public Health adopted on 14 November 2001 and in the light of Article 12(1) of the International Covenant on Economic, Social and Cultural Rights, which recognizes the right of all persons to the enjoyment of the highest attainable standard of physical and mental health'.[10]

The other complainant State was Brazil. Even if Brazil did not raise the same arguments as India in the context of the WTO Dispute Settlement System,[11] it did so in the WTO General Council and in the TRIPS Council. With regard to the 'Dutch seizures case' the Brazilian Ambassador affirmed in the WTO General Council that 'the protection of intellectual property cannot supersede the protection of more fundamental values, such as the protection of life and the right to promote public health'.[12] At a meeting of the TRIPS Council, he also pointed out in several instances the implications that the measures had on access to health.[13]

Given that the controversy involved WTO norms subject to diverging interpretations and the fact that the measures provoked a scarcity of products affecting vital needs in third countries, it was argued that WTO norms should be clarified in accordance with Members' obligations pursuant to international human rights law. That assumption reflected a very concrete view in the context of the debate on the openness of the WTO Dispute Settlement System towards other public international law norms. As noted in Chapter 2, public international law can be seen as a coherent legal order enacting rules that permit addressing the relationships of norms integrating different sub-regimes.[14] Norms on treaty conflicts and interpretation are instrumental in substantiating such a view. The principle of systemic integration has acquired central importance in this context since it holds that in interpreting international norms, obligations binding on the parties and distinct from the interpreted norm also need to be taken into account.[15]

If human rights are of relevance when adjudicating WTO intellectual property disputes, it can be inferred that States may have the obligation to act differently.

[8] The potential of border measures to become a barrier for international trade has been clear in cases concerning the detention of products in transit. *See* Grosse Ruse-Khan and Jaeger (2009), pp. 502–503; Abbot (2009b); Abbot (2009c); Seuba (2009); Kumar (2009); Seuba (2010a); Micara (2012).

[9] *See* WTO (2010a), p. 3. [10] *Ibid.* [11] *See* WTO (2010b).

[12] *See* WTO General Council (2008), para. 11; ICTSD (2009).

[13] *See* Knowledge Ecology International (2009). [14] *See* Chapter 2, Section IV.3.

[15] See Chapter 2, Section IV.3.1.

The question that needs to be posed, however, is that relating to what extent States bear any responsibility for the human rights situation in third countries.

2.2 States' Responsibility for Health Protection in Third Countries

The control of goods in transit and its impact on access to goods in third countries have attracted numerous comments revolving around the relationship between border measures and human rights. The end-users of goods in transit reside in third countries. Therefore, availability-related problems resulting from border enforcement regulation take place in countries distinct from those implementing the controversial customs procedures. That is, the effects of the detention of goods in transit are manifest in third countries where supply is interrupted or hindered as a result of border measures taken in the State of transit. In the distribution chain, cuts occur even in the absence of infringement in both the country of origin and the destination.

Whether this situation relates to the protection of human rights was raised in 2009. In the context of the European seizures of pharmaceutical products in transit and given the nature of the seized goods – medicines – and their relevance to the protection of health, commentators held that the Dutch seizures had an impact on the right to health in third countries.[16] Implicitly, that argument assumed that the Netherlands and other States taking similar measures have a responsibility as to the protection of the right to health in third countries. Indeed, if the detention of goods in transit were a human rights issue, only the State taking the measure could be considered responsible.

Those invoking human rights entitlements in the context of controversies deriving from border measures assume that States have obligations pursuant to human rights treaties towards other States or individuals residing in third States. In the case of economic and social rights, the basis of such a claim can be found in the International Covenant on Economic, Social and Cultural Rights. With regard to international obligations, Article 2.1 of the ICESCR provides that States parties to the Covenant undertake 'to take steps, individually and through international assistance and cooperation, especially economic and technical, to the maximum of its available resources, with a view to achieving progressively the full realization of the rights recognized in the present Covenant by all appropriate means'. The Committee on Economic, Social and Cultural Rights, the body in charge of supervising the ICESCR, has held that this general undertaking includes the adoption of internal legislative, economic or administrative measures.[17]

The ESCR Committee and other United Nations human rights bodies have also underlined the existence of obligations *vis-à-vis* other States.[18] This holding has been

16 *See* Seuba (2009), p. 19; Grosse Ruse-Khan and Jaeger (2009), pp. 502–538; Kumar (2010), pp. 155–169; Micara (2012), pp. 73–101; UN Human Rights Council (2009), para. 92; Seuba (2010a).

17 *See* UN Committee on Economic, Social and Cultural Rights (1990), paras. 13–14.

18 *See* UN High Commissioner for Human Rights (2002); UN High Commissioner for Human Rights (2001).

expressed both in the context of the general comments concerning specific human rights prepared by the ESCR Committee and in the comments that it delivers in response to the periodic reports submitted by State Members to the ICESCR. The ESCR Committee has underlined the importance of international cooperation to achieve full respect to human rights. It has also affirmed that States must respect the enjoyment of the right to health in other countries and has urged them to take into account international human rights commitments when signing economic agreements or participating in international economic organizations.[19] As part of the core obligations under the right to health, the ESCR Committee has also emphasized the responsibility of States and other actors to deliver assistance and cooperation, especially economic and technical assistance, to enable other countries to fulfil their core obligations.[20]

The ESCR Committee has in fact gone further. It has elaborated – taking as a basis the classic trilogy of obligations to respect, protect and fulfil human rights – the international obligations of States with respect to a number of human rights. In the case of the right to health, pursuant to the obligation to respect, States should under no circumstance hinder access to health in third countries. Pursuant to the obligation to protect, States should impede actions adopted by private companies that may impact access to health in third countries; and, finally, by virtue of the obligation to fulfil, States must provide assistance to other countries in order to enable them to fully respect the right to health.[21]

In the context of restrictions to access caused by border enforcement regulation, the ESCR Committee has stated that States must 'refrain at all times from imposing embargoes or similar measures restricting the supply of another State with adequate medicines and medical equipment'.[22] Although the ESCR Committee had in mind situations of urgency when delivering this statement – rather than constraints resulting from certain intellectual property statutes – it seems reasonable to infer the existence of a duty to keep internal regulations from becoming an obstacle to access to vital products. This duty would exist regardless of the intellectual property status of products when access is part of a human right, in particular if access to specific products forms part of the core obligations resulting from a number of social rights.[23] This is the case, for instance, of essential medicines. The duty to impede internal regulations from becoming an obstacle to access to vital products, framed under the more general principle of international cooperation, would allow invoking human rights arguments if they were

[19] *See* UN Committee on Economic, Social and Cultural Rights (2000), para. 38; UN Economic and Social Council (1995), paras. 7, 42, and 47.

[20] *See* UN Committee on Economic, Social and Cultural Rights (2000), para. 38; UN Economic and Social Council (1995), para. 45.

[21] *Ibid.*, paras. 38–41. [22] *Ibid.*, para. 41.

[23] *See* UN Committee on Economic, Social and Cultural Rights (2006), para. 35.

necessary for interpretation in the context of disputes with other States, particularly in WTO adjudicative bodies when interpreting the provisions of GATT and the TRIPS Agreement.[24]

III BORDER MEASURES, QUALITY OF PRODUCTS AND THE RIGHT TO HEALTH

1 *The Link between Intellectual Property Infringement, Consumer Safety and the Control of Transit*

Depending on the category of intellectual property rights concerned and the product involved, infringement of intellectual property rights can be associated with consumer safety threats. This is the case of counterfeit goods, in particular pharmaceuticals, automotive parts, electrical components, toys and household goods, which may involve products of substandard quality endangering health and safety.

While the link between counterfeiting and consumer safety does not always exist, and caution must therefore be paid when using the terms 'counterfeit' and 'pirated' to refer to intellectual property and consumer safety threats altogether, generally[25] it is true that 'certain types of counterfeit goods can have harmful effects on consumer health and safety, causing serious illness or death'.[26] A clear case in point is that of counterfeit medicines, which 'can be ineffective in treating ailments or may lead to adverse reactions, drug resistance, or even death'.[27]

The threat to consumer safety posed by products that infringe certain types of intellectual property rights has been invoked to justify border measures regulation permitting the control of goods in transit. The European Union, for instance, has defended that, in addition to intellectual property protection, European border measures against goods in transit pursue public health objectives, namely health protection in third countries. This claim has been made both in the context of international controversies involving the European regulations as well as in regional legislative reforms.

In the international context, in relation to the dispute concerning the detention of medicines in transit, the European Union submitted to the TRIPS Council that 'it is important to allow the customs authorities to control goods in transit suspected to infringe IP rights so that they can stop the traffic of potentially dangerous products,

24 *See* Seuba (2010a), p. 23.

25 *See* among the first references on this particular subject, Outterson (2006), pp. 526–543; Outterson (2009).

26 *See* US Government Accountability Office (2010), p. 10. *See* also European Alliance for Access to Safe Medicines (2008); Forzley (2003).

27 *See* US Government Accountability Office (2010), p. 11. Similarly, *see* Commission of the European Communities (2006), p. 2; Wall and Large (2010), p. 1094; Satchwell (2004); Forzley (2003).

such as fake medicines'.[28] European representatives contextualized this activity in the broader framework of the European Union's responsibility with respect to the protection of health in third countries. In this regard, both the European Commissioner for Trade and the European Commissioner for Taxation and Customs Union noted that, '[e]specially in the case of counterfeit medicines, which is a problem that mainly concerns developing countries, the EU considers it a duty to also prevent – to the extent possible – any adverse effects trade in such products could have in vulnerable populations in their countries'.[29]

The European Union adopted in 2015 a new trademark directive and regulation.[30] In particular, the reform intends to adjust border enforcement regulation of goods protected by trademarks. The new legislation keeps the wording of the initial proposal submitted by the European Commission, awarding ample powers to right holders, who are entitled to prevent third parties from bringing goods into the customs territory of Member States even if they are not released for free circulation. This applies to goods that come from third countries and bear without authorization a trademark that is essentially identical to the trademark registered in respect of such goods.[31] Succinctly, this basically implies the recognition of the power to impede the transit. Nevertheless, the new EU Directive 2015/2436 brings some balance and provides that the entitlement of the trademark owner 'shall lapse if, during the proceedings to determine whether the registered trade mark has been infringed, … evidence is provided by the declarant or the holder of the goods that the proprietor of the registered trade mark is not entitled to prohibit the placing of the goods on the market in the country of final destination'.[32]

It is noteworthy however that the report tabled by Rapporteur Cecilia Wikström on the European Commission's proposal contained important amendments. The first of those proposed that border controls should apply to counterfeit goods and not merely trademark-infringing products.[33] Importantly, the second amendment established that 'in order not to hamper legitimate flows of goods, this rule

28 In the same context, it also stated that 'a significant and worrying level of trade in illegal medicines indicating a potentially serious public health and safety issue, which fully justify the control of medicines in transit suspected to infringe IP rights'. *See* Ip-health (2009).

29 *See* Ashton and Kovács (2009).

30 *See* Regulation (EU) 2015/2424 of the European Parliament and of the Council of 16 December 2015 amending Council Regulation (EC) No 207/2009 on the Community trade mark and Commission Regulation (EC) No 2868/95 implementing Council Regulation (EC) No 40/94 on the Community trade mark, and repealing Commission Regulation (EC) No 2869/95 on the fees payable to the Office for Harmonization in the Internal Market (Trade Marks and Designs), OJEU L 341/21 of 24 December 2015, entering into force on 23 March 2016. *See* also the Directive (EU) 2015/2436 of the European Parliament and of the Council of 16 December 2015 to approximate the laws of the Member States relating to trade marks, OJEU L 336/1 of 23 December 2015 (hereinafter EU Directive 2015/2436). *See* Chapter 11, Section II.3.3.

31 *See* Article 10.4 of the EU Directive 2015/2436. *See* also Recitals 21 to 23.

32 *See* Article 10.4 of the EU Directive 2015/2436.

33 The reference to their counterfeit nature cannot be found however in the relevant Article 10.4, only in Recital 21.

should only apply if the proprietor of a trade mark is able to show that the trade mark is validly registered also in the country of destination'.[34] As we detail next, Wikström's proposal, even if it was not retained by the European legislator, was in line with a regulation that could satisfy not only intellectual property goals but also free trade and human rights purposes.

2 *Is There a Human Rights Justification for the Control of In-transit Goods Invoking Health Protection in Third Countries?*

The analysis made in Section II in relation to the international obligations of States arising from human rights commitments concluded that States may also bear responsibility for the protection of health in third countries. It also raised the question of whether customs authorities have the obligation to control goods that, although not intended to be commercialized in their country, may have harmful effects on foreign consumers. If the answer is positive, another question will also need clarification, i.e. is the control of intellectual property infringements the best approach to achieve the goal of protecting the health of citizens in third countries and, if so, which categories of intellectual property rights should be targeted?

The legal grounds of the link established above between access to vital products and States' obligations towards third countries – by virtue of which they should not impede the transit of patented products – would also apply to the control of the quality of products that could endanger human health. As will be developed further, ensuring the quality of products is one of the interrelated elements of the right to health. Therefore, States in a position to influence the quality of products consumed in foreign markets are bound to exercise that influence, in the same way that they are bound not to obstruct access to medicines in third countries. Whether this implies any action related to intellectual property protection, such as the control of counterfeit goods in transit, is a matter for discussion.

A brief reference to the interrelated and essential elements of the right to health, as well as to some of the obligations arising from the right to health, is useful for discussing the obligation of states to exercise some control over counterfeits. The ESCR Committee has stated that the right to health contains a number of interrelated and minimum elements, these being the *availability*, *accessibility*, *acceptability* and *quality* of health goods, services and programs.[35] From this point of view, the quality of products is of vital interest to the 'quality' dimension of the right to health.

A number of human rights obligations lie behind the positive and negative actions that States must undertake pursuant their ICESCR membership. The ESCR Committee has spelled out some of the implications of the obligations to *respect*, *protect* and *fulfil* the right to health. For the purpose of addressing the existence of an

34 *See* Committee on Legal Affairs (2014), Amendment 6 Proposal for a Directive Recital 22; *see* also Article 10.4 of the EU Directive 2015/2436.

35 *See* UN Committee on Economic, Social and Cultural Rights (2000), para. 12.

eventual obligation of States to control counterfeit products, the obligation to *protect* is particularly relevant. By virtue of this obligation, States must prevent and react against infringements of a right committed by third parties. States have a positive duty to intervene and impede what in principle are private acts. With regard to pharmaceutical products, the implementation of this obligation takes concrete form in activities that relate to quality control of the products, such as pharmaceutical registration, inspection and pharmacovigilance.[36]

The obligation to protect may have an important international dimension. The ESCR Committee has mentioned some important examples, such as preventing 'third parties from violating the right in other countries, if they are able to influence these third parties by way of legal or political means'.[37] This would mean, for instance, that if intellectual property border enforcement legislation permitted it, States could control the conduct of the owners and consignees of goods, which could potentially imperil public health in third countries. Although this would not be the only available mechanism, targeting counterfeit goods could be a reasonable objective.

It has, however, been held that border control of counterfeit products in transit may also cause problems for the protection of public health. NGOs have stated that 'even if enforcement is limited to counterfeit trademark infringement, the risk of confusing similarly named, coloured or shaped medicines with counterfeits is high. Especially because ill-equipped customs agents will be asked to evaluate complex trademark violation issues.'[38] Therefore, if all trademark infringements were the object of control, legal products could be detained *ex officio* by customs authorities while in transit, and trademark holders could activate *ex parte* procedures to control the flow of goods to countries where their trademark would not prevail. In order to avoid this, 'the generic producer would need to ensure that its brands remain at sufficient distance also from all protected trademarks in all transit countries in order to ensure that the medicines are not seized in transit'.[39] Arguably, this would increase transaction costs and prevent traders from using the most efficient transit routes, thus adding further barriers to the global trade in generics.[40]

While acknowledging the merit of these claims, a powerful public health rationale for detaining truly counterfeit products in transit exists. NGOs' and academia's resistance to the use of intellectual property protection to achieve public health objectives responds to the abuse made of the term 'counterfeit' by interested parties. It must therefore be made clear that counterfeiting is a specific infringement, not to be confused with other intellectual property infringements. In particular, patent infringement bears no relationship whatsoever to quality concerns, and thus there is no possible link between the control of patented goods in transit and health protection in third countries.[41] However, this is not the case of counterfeit products.

36 *See* Seuba (2006).
37 *See* UN Committee on Economic, Social and Cultural Rights (2000), para. 39.
38 *See* Médecins Sans Frontières (2014). 39 *See* Grosse Ruse-Khan (2015). 40 *Ibid.*
41 *See* Seuba (2010a), p. 31.

The defining criterion that identifies a counterfeit product is its deliberate mislabelling with respect to identity or source. Counterfeit products may indeed be of substandard quality, and some of the problems associated with substandard medicines are related to trademark law. In this sense, one of the mechanisms to commercialize substandard products is through deception about the identity of the product's source.

The control of the transit of counterfeit products by invoking the infringement of intellectual property rights is not the only available means to protect consumers. There are in fact many other mechanisms to foster international cooperation in the context of the quality of medicines.[42] When asked about the specific relationship between the control of products in transit and quality concerns, the Court of Justice of the European Union noted that customs authorities have several tools at their disposal unrelated to intellectual property protection. According to the CJEU, consumer safety concerns can be addressed by resorting to provisions found in general European customs law, unrelated to intellectual property. For the Court, 'precautionary considerations may militate in favour of an immediate seizure of goods identified as posing such risks, irrespective of the customs procedure under which they are placed. In such a context, the question whether the operators responsible for the manufacture and distribution of those goods direct them to consumers in the European Union or in nonmember States is irrelevant'.[43] The Court also noted that goods posing health risks can be treated on the basis of Articles 56, 58 and 75 of the European Customs Code.[44] These articles fundamentally entitle the destruction of the goods or the imposition of restrictions or prohibitions on them or any other necessary measures invoking a broad array of reasons, some of which relate directly to the protection of health.

This does not, however, exclude taking trademark aspects into account. In our view, a plausible option to ensure that only products that pose a real public health risk are detained consists of adopting a double check system. In the first instance, the detection of counterfeit goods at the border could be used as a proxy to determine the possible existence of products of dubious quality. The determination of the counterfeit nature of these goods would take into consideration whether the right holder in the country of transit is also the right holder in the country of destination. Additionally, the consignee and the owner of the goods should be allowed to respond to the seizure by proving that the products have been authorized by health

[42] Such as these measures, '[i]nstead, the EU should invest its efforts into improving the quality of medicines exported from the European Union to third countries, by increasing support for drug regulatory authorities in third countries and by strengthening the WHO pre-qualification program'. *See* Médecins Sans Frontières (2014).

[43] *See* CJEU, joined cases C-446/09 and C-495/09, *Koninklijke Philips Electronics NV (C-446/09) v. Lucheng Meijing Industrial Company Ltd and Others and Nokia Corporation (C-495/09) v. Her Majesty's Commissioners of Revenue and Customs* [2011], Judgment of the Court (First Chamber) of 1 December 2011, ECR I-12435, para. 76.

[44] *See* Council Regulation (EEC) No. 2913/92 of 12 October 1992 establishing the Community Customs Code, OJ L 302 of 19 October 1992, p. 1.

authorities in the country of destination. If that is the case, and the right holder cannot prove that he has grounds to impede the commerce of such a product in the country of destination, even if he is the trademark owner therein, the product should be allowed to continue its journey and the dispute be solved in the country of destination.

IV HUMAN RIGHTS AND THE QUALITY OF THE BORDER ENFORCEMENT LAWS

It has already been noted that a regime lacking balance is hardly compatible with basic due process principles, such as equality of arms. Chapter 2 analysed the 'quality of the law' and the compatibility of intellectual property enforcement statutes 'with the rule of law', while other chapters have devoted particular attention to specific civil enforcement remedies. The present section claims that the 'bad quality' of the law can be observed in the context of border enforcement regulation, both as a result of statutes that do not erect the necessary checks and balances and other statutes that have been poorly drafted.

Take for instance the comparison between the TRIPS Agreement and the European regulation concerning action with respect to allegedly infringing goods. The TRIPS Agreement mandates the release of goods in case proceedings leading to a decision on the merits of the case have not been initialled or provisional measures have not been adopted within a period of ten working days after the applicant has been served notice of the suspension.[45] However, the European Union has inverted the logic behind that rule and has established that the destruction of the goods will follow, without any further procedure on the merits of the case, if the alleged infringer does not respond in due time to the seizure.[46] Hence, practical considerations and right holders' interests have prevailed over considerations relating to a fair hearing and the need to prove an infringement, or at least to show the will to prove the existence of an infringement by starting procedures on the merits of the case.

The (good) drafting of the laws is also a key aspect of the 'quality' requirement. Border measures, and the control of importation in particular, may have an impact on human rights not only in third countries but also within national boundaries. Restrictions to access based in border enforcement grounds may also be based on flawed legal grounds, which make such restrictions particularly condemnable from the human rights point of view. In 2012, the High Court of Kenya delivered

45 Article 55 of the TRIPS Agreement.

46 Regulation (EC) No 1383/2003 allowed a procedure for destroying certain goods without there being any obligation to initiate proceedings to establish whether an intellectual property right has been infringed. Regulation (EC) No 608/2013 has made the procedure compulsory with regard to all infringements of intellectual property rights and orders to apply it where the declarant or the holder of the goods does not explicitly oppose destruction.

a sentence[47] on the national Anti-Counterfeit Act,[48] a statute related to – among other aspects – the importation of generic pharmaceutical products. The petitioners were HIV/AIDS carriers who argued that the Kenyan Act violated their rights to health, life and dignity given the constraints it created for the availability of medicines.[49] The definition of 'counterfeit good' was crafted in a way that created confusion between counterfeit and generic drugs, echoing similar problems at the international level.[50] The plaintiffs alleged that the confusion would ultimately result in the prohibition of the importation and manufacture of generic medicines in Kenya.

The problematic definition established that with regard to medicine, counterfeit meant 'the deliberate and fraudulent mislabelling of medicine with respect to identity or source, whether or not such products have correct ingredients, wrong ingredients, have sufficient active ingredients or have fake packaging'[51] without the authority of the owner of an intellectual property right in force in Kenya or elsewhere with respect to protected goods. While the authorities claimed that this definition coincided with that of the WHO,[52] the judge relied on the arguments of the petitioners and the United Nations Special Rapporteur on the Right to Health, who joined the case as an interested party.

According to the Special Rapporteur, the definition of counterfeit adopted in the Kenyan Anti-Counterfeit Act would be highly problematic from the point of view of the right to health. More precisely, it was claimed that such a definition would lead to situations where 'medicines that are approved by regulatory authorities as being safe and effective are seized on the grounds that they are "counterfeit"; generic medicines destined for importation to Kenya being seized due to the uncertainty surrounding possible infringement of the Act upon delivery; significant delays of shipments of imported generic drugs at ports of entry to Kenya for inspection or legal clarification purposes; seizure of medicines at Kenyan ports by customs officials and police officers who are not specially trained to recognize the difference between counterfeit and generic products and an increase in the price of ARVs within Kenya which would make them expensive and financially inaccessible to those who need them'.[53]

The sentence of the Court held that 'the definition of 'counterfeit' in section 2 of the Act was likely to be read as including generic medication'.[54] For the Court, the

[47] *See* High Court of Kenya, *Patricia Asero Ochieng, Maurine Atieno, Joseph Munyi, and AIDS Law Project v. Attorney General*, Petition No. 409 of 2009, 20 April 2012 (hereinafter *AIDS Law Project v. the Republic*).

[48] *See* The Anti-Counterfeit Act, Act No. 13 of 2008, Legal Notice No. 115, 7 July 2009 (hereinafter Anti-Counterfeit Act).

[49] The petitioners held that 'the Act may deny them the right to enjoy the highest attainable standard of health as the cost of the HIV medication may substantially increase if they are denied an opportunity to purchase generic drugs'. *See AIDS Law Project v. the Republic*, para. 11.

[50] *See* Chapter 13, Section II.1.2.

[51] *See* Section 2 (d) Anti-Counterfeit Act.

[52] *See AIDS Law Project v. the Republic*, para. 74.

[53] *Ibid.*, para. 36.

[54] *Ibid.*, para. 78.

problem was the ambiguity of the provision. From the point of view of the Court '[i]t would be in violation of the state's obligations to the petitioners with respect to their right to life and health to have included in legislation ambiguous provisions subject to the interpretation of intellectual property holders and customs officials when such provisions relate to access to medicines essential for the petitioners' survival'.[55]

V CONCLUSIONS

Positive, conflictive and ambiguous relations between border enforcement and human rights can be identified through analysing customs norms and practices worldwide. Norms on border enforcement fulfil an important function as they permit materializing the protection of intellectual property rights. To the extent that fundamental rights relate to intellectual property, border enforcement plays a relevant and positive function for the protection of right holders' human rights. For consumers and users, norms on customs enforcement may be equivocal. On the one hand, they may negatively impact on the entry of products into the national market. As a result, access to goods may be impinged upon. On the other hand, border controls may be instrumental to protecting consumer safety and impeding access to unsafe products.

Border measures are usually presented as necessary to reap the benefits resulting from intellectual property protection. Likewise, intellectual property protection at the border impacts on a number of activities that determine access to products in a given market. The consideration of human rights entitlements in the context of controversies deriving from border measures assumes that States have obligations pursuant to human rights treaties, towards other States or individuals residing in third States. We hold that while a duty to impede internal regulations from becoming an obstacle to access to vital products exists, States in a position to influence the quality of products consumed in foreign markets are bound to exercise that influence. The crux of the matter is to what extent this implies any action related to intellectual property protection.

The obligation to protect human rights has an important international dimension. In the case of border enforcement, States can control the conduct of the owners and consignees of goods, which can imperil public health in third countries. Although targeting counterfeit goods is not the only available mechanism, it can still be a reasonable objective. In our view, a plausible option to ensure that only products that pose a real public health risk are detained consists of adopting a double check system. In the first instance, the detection of counterfeit goods at the border could be used as a proxy to determine the possible existence of products of dubious quality. The determination of the counterfeit nature of these goods would take into consideration whether the right holder in the country of transit is also the right holder in the country of destination. The right holder should be the responsible for proving that

55 *Ibid.*, para. 94.

extreme. Additionally, the consignee and the owner of the goods should be allowed to respond to the seizure by proving that the products have been authorized by health authorities in the country of destination. If that is the case, and the right holder cannot prove that he has public health grounds to impede the commerce of such a product in the country of destination, even if he is the trademark owner therein, the product should be allowed to continue its journey and the dispute be solved in the country of destination.

Finally, statutes that do not erect the necessary checks and balances for right holders and alleged infringers, as well as statutes that have been poorly drafted and include misguiding pseudo-legal terms, are examples of the 'bad quality' of the law. In this sense, the blurring Kenyan definition of counterfeit products and the European system of automatic destruction of allegedly infringing products are presented as examples of problematic border enforcement statutes when observed from the point of view of human rights protection.

PART V

Criminal Enforcement

13

The Global Regime on Criminal Enforcement

I CRIMINALIZATION OF INTELLECTUAL PROPERTY INFRINGEMENT

In addition to civil and border enforcement, criminal penalties have also been identified as a possible means of enforcing intellectual property rights.[1] While common legislation in the area of criminal enforcement can be found, national legal orders diverge widely with regard to 'the extent to which enforcement of intellectual property rights should be subject to criminal law'[2] and with regard to which intellectual property infringements deserve criminal sanctions.[3] This disagreement prevails even between countries that share the same legal tradition and have harmonized their intellectual property systems to a great extent.[4]

National and regional differences on criminal enforcement have so far resulted in a global regime made up of norms limited both in number and in scope. In fact, despite the recent promotion of new international norms on criminal enforcement,

[1] Recital 28 to the EU Enforcement Directive 2004/48/EC of 29 April 2004 states that, 'in addition to the civil and administrative measures, procedures and remedies provided for under this Directive, criminal sanctions also constitute, in appropriate cases, a means of ensuring the enforcement of intellectual property rights'. *See* Directive 2004/48/EC of the European Parliament and of the Council of 29 April 2004 on the enforcement of intellectual property rights (OJEU L157 of 30 April 2004), OJEU L195 of 2 June 2004 (hereinafter EU Enforcement Directive)

[2] *See* Geiger (2012b), p. 167.

[3] Some developing countries extensively use criminal sanctions for intellectual property infringement; '[i]n the year 2004, for example, the United States prosecuted only 1.33% of criminal intellectual property cases, while Japan has 23.06% of criminal prosecutions. On the other hand, most developing countries apply very high ratio of criminal prosecutions; Taiwan has 60.61% of criminal prosecution while Vietnam prosecution is 77.42%. The exceptional high ratio of criminal prosecution is Thailand which went up to 96.19%. Only 3% left for all civil litigation related to intellectual property matters'. *See* Pinyosinwat (2007), pp. 4–5.

[4] The efforts and failure to adopt a European directive on criminal enforcement are a proof of this. *See* Amended Proposal for a Directive of the European Parliament and of the Council on criminal measures aimed at ensuring the enforcement of intellectual property rights of 26 April 2006, COM (2006) 168 final (hereinafter Proposal for Directive on criminal measures). *See* also European Union Subcommittee of the International Trademark Association (2010).

this area of law is the least harmonized when compared with civil and border enforcement. Certainly, this is changing due to the adoption of bilateral and plurilateral agreements that contain new obligations on criminal enforcement. Nevertheless, despite the proliferation of these treaties, norms on criminal enforcement advance at a slower pace than those on civil or border enforcement. In this regard, it is noticeable that even in cases where countries already punish intellectual property infringements by means of criminal sanctions, they resist the adoption of international obligations that would repeat what is already found in their national legal orders.[5]

There are a number of reasons for being cautious about the expansion of the international normative framework on criminal enforcement. On the one hand, criminal law is closely related to sovereignty;[6] hence, 'the question of which conduct is punishable is essentially a political question to be answered by the legislature'.[7] States have been traditionally wary of adopting international commitments to typify new crimes.[8] In this respect, while international criminal law has significantly expanded, codification has chiefly focused on the most serious forms of criminality.[9] On the other hand, the *ultima ratio* nature of criminal law is related to the gravity of the punishment, which partially explains the close link between criminal law and the social and moral stance towards criminality. Or, as Christophe Geiger puts it, the fact that criminal provisions are closely linked to moral and cultural conceptions within society.[10]

The expansion of criminal enforcement is frequently justified by the gravity of the consequences of certain intellectual property infringements. Counterfeit medicines and the health-related problems they may cause provide a good example. Although this is not automatically the case, counterfeit medicines tend to be of substandard quality,[11] hence endangering both individual and public health.[12] Moreover, their

5 For instance, although the opposition to the criminalization of patent infringement in the EU-Colombia and Peru FTA and EIA (2013) was ultimately successful, criminal enforcement provisions in the draft proposal were already part of the national legislations. *See* Seuba (2009), p. 47.

6 The WTO Panel 'acknowledge[d] the sensitive nature of criminal matters and attendant concerns regarding sovereignty'. *See* WTO Panel Report, *China – measures affecting the protection and enforcement of intellectual property rights*, WT/DS362/R, 26 January 2009, para. 7.501 (hereinafter WTO Panel, *China – Intellectual Property Rights*).

7 *See* Wechsler (2012), p. 148.

8 In this sense, one author stated that '[c]riminal law – together with the disposition of the police monopoly on the use of force – has traditionally been thought of as an area belonging to the core of national sovereignty and competence'. *See* Mylly (2012), p. 215.

9 This is for instance the case of those falling within the notion of *delicta iuris gentium*, or reflecting new preoccupations, such as drug trafficking or money laundering.

10 *See* Geiger (2015c).

11 A study of the World Health Organization determined that 15.6 per cent of 'counterfeit' drugs (pursuant to the WHO definition) contain correct quantities of active ingredients but fake packaging. *See* WHO (2014). *See* also Harms (2007), p. 17.

12 *See* WHO (2006), pp. 105–106.

commercialization is based on deceiving consumers[13] and causes economic harm.[14] Similar arguments can be raised with respect to fake foods, toys or spare parts.[15] Other cases of criminalization of intellectual property infringements, such as copyright piracy on a commercial scale, may be linked to organized crime. However, this relationship is frequently overstated in order to justify the expansion of criminal enforcement.[16]

Synergies and areas of confluence between intellectual property protection, consumer safety and other specially protected legal interests do indeed exist. In response to that relationship, criminal punishment of intellectual property infringement would provide an additional way of protecting legitimate interests, such as health and safety.[17] However, it has been rightly noted that consumer protection may be merely the friendly flag of uncontrolled strengthening of intellectual property rights,[18] an expansion that finds its most severe expression in criminal law. The need and convenience of using intellectual property rights, and not consumer law, to protect those interests are disputable, since this strategy can easily contribute to confusion between the private interests of right holders and the larger interest of the public.

Although punishing counterfeiting and piracy at the domestic level is not new,[19] recent years have evidenced a strong pressure to anticipate the moment of intervention of criminal law in order to lower the bar of criminalization. In response, it has been suggested that a careful sector-by-sector analysis of the consequences of intellectual property infringement in terms of economic and social harm is necessary.[20] The objectives of this nuanced approach are clear: targeting those intellectual property rights infringements that endanger important legal interests, distinguishing individual infringers from members of large-scale organized crime networks, differentiating between intellectual property rights categories and avoiding the generalization of a type of punishment that may have detrimental effects with regard to fundamental rights.

The grounds and moment of intervention of criminal law concerning certain categories of intellectual property rights are controversial. Patent infringement

13 For instance, 'the appellant was the prime mover in a *fraud* on the public to produce and sell convincingly packaged and labelled household name perfumes and clothing as genuine'. *See R v. Priestly (Ronald William)* (1996) 2 Cr App Rep (S) 144 (emphasis added).

14 In the context of the World Trade Organization, the European Union, Japan, Switzerland and the United States have affirmed that counterfeiting – in general – 'has harmful effects on society as a whole: it puts public health and safety at risk, threatens legitimate commerce, and entails loss of jobs and government tax revenues. This activity is also often linked to organized crime and other types of crimes'. *See* WTO Council for Trade-Related Aspects of Intellectual Property Rights (2006), para. 2.

15 *See* Hilty (2012), p. 9.

16 A good example of exaggeration, among many, is Treverton *et al.* (2009).

17 This was for instance the justification argued for the adoption of the Proposal for Directive on criminal measures.

18 *See* Ohly (2012), p. 37.

19 Laws criminalizing counterfeiting can be traced back to the nineteenth century. *See* Harms (2007), p. 5.

20 *See* Geiger (2012a), p. 3.

provides a case in point. Not only is patent infringement unrelated to consumer safety threats or deception,[21] but society benefits from competitors taking the risk of inventing around the patented innovation, since this enables the introduction of new products in the market, thereby fostering competition. The criminalization of patent infringement has been criticized[22] since it may hinder such benefits: not only competitors but researchers themselves may want to avoid the risk of committing a criminal infringement when inventing around patents.[23] Moreover, 'the probabilistic nature of patents makes criminal law sanctions for most breaches of patents problematic: both the validity and exact scope of patents are highly uncertain before tested in courts'.[24]

It is against this backdrop of ambiguous and frequently tense relationships that the forthcoming sections present the norms that make up the international regime on criminal enforcement of intellectual property. However, a note of caution is advised. The analysis of Preferential Trade Agreements may give the impression that criminal enforcement has evolved dramatically and that a sophisticated international regime has emerged. In reality, however, this only applies to a reduced number of countries that have adopted demanding commitments in the context of trade agreements.[25] Most other countries, however, consider Article 61 of the TRIPS Agreement as the primary – and in many cases the only – legally binding standard regulating infringements of international intellectual property rights.

In addition, the use of criminal law seems to denote a stricter stance towards intellectual property enforcement that favours strong protection. Similarly, conventional views have promoted the understanding that developing countries are, in general, less likely to protect intellectual property than developed countries. However, if both statements were true, it may come as a surprise that some developing countries are intense users of criminal law to fight intellectual property infringements,[26] while developed countries are far more prudent.[27]

II CRIMINAL ENFORCEMENT IN THE TRIPS AGREEMENT

The World Trade Organization's Agreement on Trade-Related Aspects of Intellectual Property Rights was the first international treaty to require the adoption of criminal sanctions against some intellectual property infringements.[28] Prior to the adoption of

[21] *See* Ohly (2012), p. 40. [22] *See* Anderson (2005); Lowe (2006), p. 3.

[23] As the European Parliament put it, '[g]iven that most research projects are highly complex, inventors are constantly exposed, when carrying out their work, to the risk of infringing patent rights. Treating patent infringements as criminal offences could deter inventors and academics from developing innovations'. *See* European Parliament (2007a), p. 9.

[24] *See* Mylly (2012), p. 243. [25] No more than fifteen. *See* Section III.

[26] *See* Vechayanon (1998), p. 33; UNCTAD-ICTSD (2005), p. 621.

[27] In Europe, about 90 per cent of the enforcement of intellectual property rights is channelled through civil remedies, while only 10 per cent is achieved through criminal proceedings. *See* Broncкers, Verkade and McNelis (2000), p. 17.

[28] *See* Watal (2010), p. 613.

the TRIPS Agreement, the major international treaties on intellectual property contained obligations that Parties could choose to implement through the adoption of criminal sanctions.[29]

While it has been held that the obligation to criminalize intellectual property rights infringements derives from the Paris and Berne Conventions,[30] in these treaties the criminalization of intellectual property infringement was just one option among others.[31] This is also the approach chosen by the Nairobi Treaty on the Protection of the Olympic Symbol, as well as the Convention for the Protection of Producers of Phonograms against Unauthorized Duplication of their Phonograms, both of which can be satisfactorily implemented with or without laying down criminal sanctions.[32] In light of the pre-existing normative framework, perceived as weak by developed countries and industry representatives, these very same groups demanded the adoption of new standards for criminal enforcement of intellectual property rights.[33]

The provisions on criminal enforcement in the TRIPS Agreement set a common standard of criminal measures, particularly low when compared to the demands made during the negotiations of the treaty and the content of some intellectual property chapters set forth in trade agreements. Nevertheless, the TRIPS Agreement still implied a very important change. On the one hand, criminal enforcement of intellectual property rights was new to many countries that 'were now required to establish a new set of crimes and needed law enforcement to become familiar with the various forms of IPR and how to identify a possible IPR crime'.[34] On the other hand, the provisions on criminal enforcement of the TRIPS Agreement are still a key element of the enforcement part of the treaty and have been the object of the most relevant claim of the main ruling in the WTO Dispute Settlement System dealing with enforcement,[35] the *China – Intellectual Property Rights* case. The adoption of criminal measures fulfils the objective of providing a deterrent,[36] identified in Articles 41 and 61 of the TRIPS Agreement.[37] Indeed, no other enforcement remedy has a deterrent effect comparable to that of criminal sanctions, since individuals themselves must pay for the infringement of intellectual property rights, even with imprisonment.[38]

[29] For instance, Article 6ter of the Paris Convention establishes that parties must '*prohibit by appropriate measures* the use, without authorization by the competent authorities, either as trademarks or as elements of trademarks, of armorial bearings, flags, and other State emblems, of the countries of the Union, official signs and hallmarks indicating control and warranty adopted by them . . . ' (emphasis added).

[30] *See* Harms (2007), p. 5. [31] *See* Grosse Ruse-Khan (2012), p. 171. [32] *Ibid.*

[33] *See* Yu (2012), pp. 288–289. [34] *See* Trainer (2008), p. 59.

[35] *See* Harris (2008), pp. 118–119; Pauwelyn (2010), p. 414 (pointing out that the criminal threshold claim 'was no doubt its most important claim in this dispute').

[36] *See* Grosse Ruse-Khan (2012), p. 174.

[37] According to Article 41.1 of the TRIPS Agreement, the WTO Member States must provide 'remedies which constitute a deterrent to further infringements', while Article 61 of the TRIPS Agreement affirms that 'remedies available shall include imprisonment and/or monetary fines sufficient to provide a deterrent'.

[38] *See* Chow (2002), p. 217.

1 *The Scope of Criminal Measures*

Article 61 of the TRIPS Agreement obliges WTO Member States to provide for criminal procedures and penalties to be applied at least in cases of wilful trademark counterfeiting or copyright piracy on a commercial scale.[39] The criminalization of other intellectual property infringements is left to WTO Member States. Article 61 establishes four conditions or limitations on that obligation: (i) the application of criminal sanctions is limited to trademarks and copyrights, as opposed to all forms of intellectual property rights covered by the TRIPS Agreement;[40] (ii) violations must consist in counterfeiting and piracy, not merely trademark or copyright infringement;[41] (iii) there must exist willfulness;[42] and (iv) infringements must be committed 'on a commercial scale'.[43]

A number of these requirements were considered ambiguous by commentators, who held that Article 61 'created confusion for Member States that have little or no experience in IPR enforcement'.[44] Some of these pre-requisites, such as the definition of 'commercial scale', were interpreted by the WTO Panel in the *China – Intellectual Property Rights* case, as detailed later, and have become in fact the key concepts and object of discussion in bilateral and plurilateral treaties.

1.1 Trademarks and Copyrights

Pursuant to the TRIPS Agreement, WTO Member States must criminalize certain types of trademark and copyright infringements. While trademark and copyright are the only categories of intellectual property rights where criminal sanctions are mandatory, the TRIPS Agreement leaves the adoption of criminal measures in reaction to the infringement of other intellectual property categories at the discretion of the Parties.

1.2 Counterfeiting and Piracy

The TRIPS Agreement mandates WTO Members to provide for criminal procedures and penalties at least in cases of wilful trademark counterfeiting or copyright piracy on a commercial scale. This means that only those trademark and copyright infringements that amount to counterfeiting and piracy must be prosecuted. According to the TRIPS Agreement, 'counterfeit trademark goods' mean any goods

> including packaging, bearing without authorization a trademark which is *identical* to the trademark validly registered in respect of such goods, or which *cannot be*

[39] Article 61 TRIPS Agreement states that, '[m]embers shall provide for criminal procedures and penalties to be applied at least in cases of wilful trademark counterfeiting or copyright piracy on a commercial scale'.

[40] *See* WTO Panel, *China – Intellectual Property Rights*, para. 7.518. [41] *Ibid.*, paras. 7.519–7.522.

[42] *Ibid.*, para. 7.523. [43] *Ibid.*, para. 7.524. [44] *See* Trainer (2008), p. 55.

> *distinguished in its essential aspects* from such a trademark, and which thereby infringes the rights of the owner of the trademark in question under the law of the country of importation.[45]

The TRIPS Agreement also defines 'pirated goods' as

> any goods which are copies made without the consent of the right holder or person duly authorized by the right holder in the country of production and which are made directly or indirectly from an article where the making of that copy would have constituted an infringement of a copyright or a related right under the law of the country of importation.[46]

These definitions of pirated and counterfeit goods are unique in a multilateral treaty. They are helpful not only in defining the criminal conduct that WTO Member States must prosecute pursuant to Article 61 of the TRIPS Agreement[47] but also in clarifying the meaning and use of these terms. The WTO Panel in the *China – Intellectual Property Rights* case made clear that there was a difference between defining 'counterfeiting' and 'piracy' or defining 'counterfeit' and 'pirate'.[48] However, subject to the necessary precisions, the WTO Panel considered that the definitions in footnote 14 were relevant to understanding the terms used in Article 61 of the TRIPS Agreement.[49] This clarification is especially timely, since 'counterfeiting' and 'piracy' are terms frequently used in international fora and debates with varied meanings and purposes. The use of the term 'counterfeiting' has attracted the most disagreement and confusion, particularly (but not only) because of its relationship with public health.[50]

There is a partial overlap between the meanings of 'counterfeit' in the area of public health and intellectual property, which explains why some products are considered 'counterfeits' in both contexts. In intellectual property law, the use of a trademark identical or not distinguishable from the original without the permission of the right holder amounts to counterfeiting,[51] while in the public health context the defining criterion for identifying a counterfeit product is its deliberate mislabelling with respect to identity or source.[52] Certainly, this deliberate mislabelling may include or imply the use of a trademark without the permission of the right holder, hence the overlap between intellectual property and public health approaches.

45 *See* footnote 14(a) to Article 51 TRIPS Agreement (emphasis added).

46 *See* footnote 14(b) to Article 51 TRIPS Agreement.

47 As affirmed by the WTO Panel, footnote 14 to Article 51 of the TRIPS Agreement is relevant to define the scope of Article 61 of the Agreement. *See* WTO Panel, *China – Intellectual Property Rights*, para. 7.522.

48 In the words of the WTO Panel, '[t]he terms used in the first sentence of Article 61 denote classes of acts or activity whilst the terms used in footnote 14 denote classes of goods only. This reflects the fact that Article 61 provides for criminal enforcement against infringing acts whilst Section 4 of Part III (in which the terms defined in footnote 14 are used) provides for enforcement at the border against infringing goods.' *See* WTO Panel, *China – Intellectual Property Rights*, para. 7.521.

49 *Ibid.* 50 *See* Chapter 12, Section IV. 51 *See* footnote 14 TRIPS Agreement.

52 *See* WHO (1992).

'Counterfeit' is a term used in the context of both public health and intellectual property, a connection that has accentuated the pejorative connotation of 'counterfeit' and has been instrumental in raising the importance of intellectual property enforcement. As a result, 'counterfeits' would not only be of economic and legal concern to right holders, they would also present a public health problem. The use of the term 'counterfeit' has introduced intellectual property debates in public health fora, something that has been criticized[53] for unduly mixing 'the legitimate interests in protecting the public against the circulation of sub-standard or unsafe products (particularly medicines) with those related to the protection of IPRs'.[54] In a related fashion, the terms 'pirate', 'counterfeit', 'substandard' or 'spurious' are often used to allude to products that infringe a range of intellectual property rights,[55] which reflects confusion with regard to patent, trademark, and drug safety issues,[56] deriving from an obvious lack of rigor.[57]

1.3 Wilfulness and Commercial Scale

Two other conditions are required for the application of criminal measures to intellectual property rights infringements pursuant to the TRIPS Agreement. First, the acts of counterfeiting and piracy must be committed on a commercial scale, and second, they must be committed wilfully.

The meaning of 'commercial scale' has proved to be particularly controversial.[58] The vagueness of the term has prompted interpretations that equate 'commercial scale' to commercial advantage or mere economic gain. Vagueness has also fed the fear of those who argue that any infringement by a company is a 'commercial scale infringement' given that a company is a commercial legal person and pursues commercial objectives.[59]

The WTO Panel in the *China – Intellectual Property Rights* case clarified the meaning of 'commercial scale' in the context of the TRIPS Agreement. The WTO Panel had to deal with the complaint of the United States against China, where the United States held that China violated Article 61 of the TRIPS Agreement since it failed to provide criminal sanctions and criminal procedures against acts of piracy committed at a commercial scale. China stated that its quantitative approach to 'commercial scale', focusing on the magnitude of the infringement, satisfied the

53 *See* South Centre/Center for International Environmental Law (CIEL) (2008), p. 1.

54 *See* Correa (2012), p. 67. 55 *See* Outterson and Smith (2006), pp. 526–542.

56 *See* Outterson (2009).

57 While lack of rigor may have obvious commercial intentionality, it may also be gratuitous. Even in the academic domain some areas of knowledge seem to have validated the use of the terms 'piracy' and 'theft' as synonymous of patent infringement. This is particularly the case among some economists. *See* for instance Buchanan and Wilson (2012); Engel and Kleine (2013).

58 *See* Creemers (2009); Xue (2009a); Xue (2009b); Gervais (2009a); Grosse Ruse-Khan (2012); Yu (2012); Adam (2011).

59 *See* EGA (2006).

TRIPS Agreement. By contrast, the Unites States held that 'commercial scale' referred to activities that reported a financial return or even to activities that have no commercial purpose but are of a significant magnitude.[60]

The WTO Panel noted that the terms integrating the expression 'commercial scale' need to be read altogether. For that reason, both the qualitative ('commercial') and quantitative ('scale') components of the expression must be taken into account.[61] Accordingly, the WTO Panel held that 'commercial scale' is 'the magnitude or extent of typical or usual commercial activity. Therefore, counterfeiting or piracy on a "commercial scale" refers to counterfeiting or piracy carried on at the magnitude or extent typical or usual commercial activity with respect to a given product in a given market'.[62] In other words, according to the 'cautious understanding of the notion of "commercial scale"'[63] adopted by the WTO Panel, acts of commercial scale require a specific magnitude that is contextual to a given product in a given market.[64]

Some have been critical of the contextual nature of the specific meaning of 'commercial scale'. The underlying criticism underscores the difficulty complainants may have in proving that context and argues that this 'puts a rather heavy evidentiary burden on complainants especially when dealing with opaque markets such as the Chinese market where obtaining reliable information, or even convincing people to submit it (without fear of some form of governmental retaliation) may be difficult'.[65] As analysed below, some bilateral and plurilateral agreements have introduced definitions of 'commercial scale' which in fact make the meaning of this concept even more controversial. In reality, these agreements broaden the definition given to 'commercial scale' in the *China – Intellectual Property Rights* panel report. While this trend has naturally very important consequences for those subscribing the treaties, the definition set forth in bilateral and plurilateral treaties should not affect the understanding of 'commercial scale' at the multilateral level.[66]

The other qualification found in Article 61 of the TRIPS Agreement requires 'willfulness of conduct'. This means that the infringement must be intentional, i.e. the act is deliberate. This condition has been treated in a straightforward way. As the WTO Panel in the *China – Intellectual Property Rights* case held, 'willful' alludes to the infringer's intent and reflects the criminal nature of the enforcement procedures at issue.[67] In our opinion, however, this definition is insufficient since it does not clarify whether the intentionality refers to the act that infringes the right or the offender's intention to infringe the right.

60 *See* WTO Panel, *China – Intellectual Property Rights*, para. 7.480. 61 *Ibid.*, para. 7.538.
62 *Ibid.*, paras. 7.577–7.578. 63 *See* Geiger (2016), p. 651.
64 *See* WTO Panel, *China – Intellectual Property Rights*, para. 7.577.
65 *See* Pauwelyn (2010), p. 415.
66 In this respect, the WTO Panel in the *China – Intellectual Property Rights* case made clear that these definitions are not to be used for determining the term 'commercial scale' in the context of the TRIPS Agreement. *See* WTO Panel, *China – Intellectual Property Rights*, para. 7.581.
67 *See* WTO Panel, *China – Intellectual Property Rights*, para. 7.523.

2 Remedies Established in Article 61

In addition to identifying the infringements that will result in criminal sanctions, and the conditions that must be fulfilled to criminalize those infringements, the TRIPS Agreement also lays down guidance on the type of remedies that must be available. The sanctions can be divided into primary and accessory remedies; the former include imprisonment and monetary fines, and the latter the seizure, forfeiture and destruction of the infringing goods.

With regard to primary remedies, the TRIPS Agreement requires that criminal sanctions shall include imprisonment 'and/or' monetary fines. The alternative conjunction 'or' in between 'imprisonment' and 'monetary fines' implies that Member States will satisfy their obligations if they provide 'monetary fines' but not a prison sentence. There is, however, a minimum level of exigency that either imprisonment or monetary fines must fulfil. In this regard, Article 61 of the TRIPS Agreement provides a somewhat vague standard, since it states that remedies must be 'sufficient to provide a deterrent, consistently with the level of penalties applied for crimes of a corresponding gravity'. While this mandate does not indicate what offences are to be considered of similar gravity, which could pose a problem in terms of legal certainty, this openness is considered appropriate 'given the social factors informing the interpretation of criminal behavior and the necessary observance of national sovereignty in determining these kinds of social rules'.[68]

In addition to the primary obligation, the TRIPS Agreement sets forth that the available remedies 'shall also include the seizure, forfeiture and destruction of the infringing goods and of any materials and implements the predominant use of which has been in the commission of the offence'.[69] Importantly though, the TRIPS Agreement states that 'seizure, forfeiture and destruction' will apply 'in appropriate cases', thus leaving a considerable margin of discretion to decide what the appropriate cases are.[70] As will be seen in the next section, this flexibility has been profoundly amended in new plurilateral and bilateral treaties.

III CRIMINAL ENFORCEMENT IN PLURILATERAL AGREEMENTS

1 The Anti-Counterfeiting Trade Agreement

With regard to other areas of intellectual property enforcement, the Anti-Counterfeiting Trade Agreement integrates the existing multilateral legal framework on criminal enforcement[71] while at the same time taking it one step further. When comparing ACTA with the TRIPS Agreement, the former identifies new

[68] *See* Gibson (2012), p. 246. [69] *See* Article 61 TRIPS Agreement.

[70] *See* Grosse Ruse-Khan (2012), p. 175.

[71] In the Preamble, ACTA declares that it intends to 'provide effective and appropriate means, complementing the TRIPS Agreement'. On the relationship between the TRIPS Agreement and ACTA, *see* Seuba (2015a).

criminal offences and potential infringers,[72] and details previously agreed-upon criminal offences in a more stringent fashion. In addition, some of the terms left open in the TRIPS Agreement are defined in ACTA, thus limiting the flexibility that the TRIPS Agreement availed to WTO Member States. Not all articles in the agreement are, however, clearly delimited. In fact, some provisions on criminal measures have attracted severe criticism given the uncertainty they create with regard to which specific acts shall be punished.

1.1 Scope of Criminal Enforcement: Categories and Offences

With respect to the intellectual property rights categories that must be subject to criminal sanctions, the first two criminal offences mentioned in ACTA had already been enacted in the TRIPS Agreement, i.e. trademark counterfeiting and the piracy of copyright and related rights. Similarly to the TRIPS Agreement, ACTA requires that such infringements must be committed wilfully and on a commercial scale. There are, however, two major differences in this respect between ACTA and the TRIPS Agreement.

The first of these concerns the reference that ACTA makes to 'related rights piracy', not just 'copyright piracy', thus extending the scope of application of criminal sanctions.[73] The second difference concerns the specific delimitation of the meaning of 'commercial scale'. According to ACTA, 'commercial scale' includes at least those activities that are 'carried out as commercial activities for direct or indirect economic or commercial advantage'.[74] Although the definition is not conclusive and has an uncertain reach, it lowers the bar to 'mere willfulness independently of the commercial nature of the activity'.[75] Moreover, as it happens in the Trans-Pacific Partnership and a number of PTAs, the quantitative component or magnitude required in the context of the TRIPS Agreement disappears from ACTA. In this way, ACTA 'broadens considerably' the notion of commercial scale, which becomes 'far less flexible than the market or product-based interpretation of the WTO Panel'.[76]

ACTA identifies several new criminal offences that Parties must prosecute. In some cases these offences are presented as a clarification or extension of the basic obligation set up in the TRIPS Agreement to criminalize wilful counterfeiting and piracy on a commercial scale, while on other occasions the new illicit act is presented as such.

Among the criminal offences that ACTA presents as an extension of those found in the TRIPS Agreement is the criminalization of the importation or exportation of counterfeit trademark goods or pirated copyright goods on a commercial scale. Indeed, the TRIPS Agreement only mentions counterfeiting and piracy but not

[72] In Article 23.5, ACTA sets up the obligation to establish the liability, which may be criminal, of legal persons. ACTA also obliges to punish those aiding at committing the infringement, according to Article 23.4 of the treaty.

[73] For instance in the case of performers' rights.

[74] *See* Article 23.1 ACTA.

[75] *See* Gervais (2012), p. 270.

[76] See Geiger (2016), p. 652.

exportation and importation.[77] In any case, as it will be explained, this is not an utterly new obligation at the international level, since several PTAs also envisaged it before ACTA was concluded.[78]

On other occasions ACTA establishes an entirely new obligation with respect to the TRIPS Agreement. This applies to the adoption of criminal procedures and penalties in cases of wilful importation and use, in the course of trade and on a commercial scale, of labels or packaging to which a mark[79] has been applied without authorization.[80] Again, this obligation is anticipated in a number of PTAs,[81] and it may have an important significance. It can for instance be invoked 'by holders of trademarks against 'parallel importers' or, more generally, against generic pharmaceutical producers who refer to their products as generic versions of trademarked products'.[82] To illustrate the potential relevance of this possibility, Frederick Abbott describes the common practice of parallel traders within the European Union. They, in effect, normally repackage and re-label medicines to include additional languages and information, and 'they use the trademark of the original manufacturer "without authorization". Understood literally, ACTA could attach criminal liability to this conduct'.[83]

ACTA also replicates in other respects the content of PTAs promoted by the United States. It establishes criminal responsibility for acts that contribute to the commission of the infringement. It states that, with regard to the criminal offences identified in the Agreement, Parties shall ensure that criminal liability for aiding and abetting is available under their law.[84] Even if the specific scope and practical consequences of the criminalization of aiding and abetting will depend on the normative implementation and judicial interpretation at the national level, it signifies a relevant expansion of criminal liability of potentially important impact. In any case, the criminalization of these actions seems to anticipate the inclusion in future agreements of new criminal offences, such as the incitement or attempt to commit criminalized acts.[85]

77 *See* footnote 9 to Article 23.1 ACTA.

78 *See* Article 15.11.26(a) CAFTA-DR-US FTA and EIA (2006); footnote 34 to Article 18.10.26 Republic of Korea-US FTA and EIA (2012); Article 17.11.26(b) US-Australia FTA and EIA (2005); Article 16.11.26 US-Colombia FTA and EIA (2012); Article 16.11.26 US-Peru FTA and EIA (2009); Article 125.2 Japan-Switzerland FTA and EIA (2009).

79 It must be identical to, or not distinguishable from, a trademark registered in the territory and which is 'intended to be used in the course of trade on goods or in relation to services which are identical to goods or services for which such trade mark is registered'. *See* Article 23.2 ACTA.

80 *See* Article 23.2(a) and (b) ACTA.

81 *See* Article 17.11.28 US-Australia FTA and EIA (2005); Article 18.10.28 Republic of Korea-US FTA and EIA (2012); Article 17.11.28 US-Australia FTA and EIA (2005); Article 14.10.28 US-Bahrain FTA and EIA (2006); Article 16.11.28 US-Colombia FTA and EIA (2012); Article 16.11.28 US-Peru FTA and EIA (2009); Article 15.11.27 US-Morocco FTA and EIA (2006).

82 *See* Abbott (2015), p. 40. 83 *Ibid.* 84 *See* Article 23.4 ACTA.

85 In the European context, and with regard to the Proposal for Directive on criminal measures, it has been explained that '[t]he European Parliament made further amendments to exclude 'attempts' from the scope of the offence and also to try to clarify incitement. The European Economic and

In some respects, however, ACTA can be considered softer than PTAs. This is, for instance, the case of the criminalization of pirated copies of movies made in cinema halls.[86] In effect, in contrast to a number of agreements concluded by the United States,[87] ACTA establishes that parties *may* criminalize the 'unauthorized copying of cinematographic works from a performance in a motion picture exhibition facility open to the public'. This drafting leaves open the possibility not to do so, a flexibility excluded both in the TPP and some bilateral trade agreements.

1.2 Penalties

ACTA repeats and clarifies the content of the TRIPS Agreement with regard to sanctions that may be imposed. It states that Parties must enact sanctions that include imprisonment as well as fines that are sufficient to provide a deterrent and are consistent with crimes of corresponding gravity.[88] ACTA also clarifies that there is no obligation in either the TRIPS Agreement or in ACTA 'for a Party to provide for the possibility of imprisonment and monetary fines to be imposed in parallel'.[89]

ACTA complements and expands the references found in the TRIPS Agreement with respect to the seizure, forfeiture and destruction of the infringing goods, materials and implements used in the commission of the offence. First, ACTA eliminates the reference found in the TRIPS Agreement to the provision of these measures 'in appropriate cases', which means that States are free to determine in their legislation which are these cases. Instead, this flexibility is substituted by an obligation to entitle competent authorities to decide on the applicability of seizure, forfeiture or destruction of goods. Second, while PTAs order to entitle judicial authorities to decide, ACTA orders to entitle 'competent authorities' to implement the named measures, entitling therefore administrative authorities as well.

ACTA also lays down a detailed regime with regard to seizure. It clarifies what objects can be seized, including suspected counterfeit trademark goods or pirated copyright goods and materials, as well as implements used in the commission of the alleged offence – already identified in Article 61 of the TRIPS Agreement as sizable goods.[90] In addition, ACTA includes an obligation to allow judicial authorities to order the seizure of 'documentary evidence relevant to the alleged offence, and the assets derived from, or obtained directly or indirectly through, the alleged infringing activity'.[91] In an effort to facilitate seizure, ACTA states that where the identification of items subject to seizure is required by national law, the 'Party shall not require the items to be described in greater detail than is necessary to identify them'.[92]

Social Committee similarly expressed concern about the 'intent' element of incitement, believing that intent is not enough as there must also be some material act.' *See* Gibson (2012), p. 255.

86 *See* Article 23.3 ACTA.

87 *See* for instance Article 18.10.29 of the Republic of Korea-US FTA and EIA (2012).

88 *See* Article 24 ACTA.

89 *See* footnote 12 to Article 24 ACTA and above with respect to the TRIPS Agreement.

90 *See* Article 25.1 ACTA. 91 *Ibid.* 92 *See* Article 25.2 ACTA.

In the case of forfeiture or destruction of goods, ACTA repeats the provisions of the TRIPS Agreement, and announces a number of new obligations. First, it upholds the right of competent authorities to order the forfeiture or destruction of all counterfeit trademark goods or pirated copyright goods. It adds, however, that '[i]n cases where counterfeit trademark goods and pirated copyright goods are not destroyed, the competent authorities shall ensure that, except in extraordinary circumstances, such goods shall be disposed of outside the channels of commerce in such a manner as to avoid causing any harm to the right holder'.[93] Moreover, paralleling an obligation found in some PTAs, ACTA establishes that Parties shall ensure that the forfeiture or destruction of infringing goods shall occur without compensation to the infringer.[94]

Finally, ACTA also lays down a new obligation concerning the value of the forfeited or seized assets. It establishes that judicial authorities must have the authority to order the seizure or the forfeiture of 'assets the value of which corresponds to that of the assets derived from, or obtained directly or indirectly through the allegedly infringing activity'.[95]

2 *The Trans-Pacific Trade Agreement*

The Trans-Pacific Trade Agreement enshrines the most complete and demanding international text relating to criminal enforcement of intellectual property rights. In several important respects, it sets an unprecedented low bar regarding the criminalization of intellectual property infringement.

2.1 Scope of Criminal Enforcement

The TPP continues the trend initiated in bilateral trade agreements and followed in ACTA, essentially broadening the scope of criminal enforcement in cases of intellectual property infringement. Pursuant to the TPP, new activities and intellectual property infringements must be criminalized, while blurring definitions determine such criminalization. In particular, as it happened in ACTA, the definition of 'commercial scale' significantly broadens the scope of criminal liability. Moreover, according to the TPP, offences previously unknown to international intellectual property law must be object of criminal penalties.

The TPP identifies five offences that require criminal sanctions. These are the wilful trademark counterfeiting or copyright or related rights piracy on a commercial scale, the wilful importation or exportation of counterfeit or pirated goods on a commercial scale, the wilful importation and domestic use, in the course of trade and on a commercial scale, of a label or packaging that violates trademark rights, the unauthorized copying of a cinematographic work from a performance in a movie

[93] *See* Article 25.3 ACTA. [94] *Ibid.* [95] *Ibid.*

theatre that causes significant harm to a right holder in the market for that work, and, finally, aiding and abetting with respect to the previously mentioned offences.

Three out of the five offences mentioned allude to the 'commercial scale' of infringing activities. A *de minimis* definition is provided, according to which 'commercial scale' includes at least 'acts carried out for commercial advantage or financial gain'[96] as well as 'significant acts, not carried out for commercial advantage or financial gain, that have a substantial prejudicial impact on the interests of the copyright or related rights holder in relation to the marketplace'.[97] It is further clarified that the volume and value of infringing goods may be taken into consideration in determining such a prejudicial impact.[98] The TPP text not only goes beyond the TRIPS Agreement but modifies the interpretation that the WTO Panel in the *China – Intellectual Property Rights* case gave to 'commercial scale'.

The change can be particularly noticed when examining the terms integrating the definition of 'commercial scale' pursuant to the TPP. In particular, the meaning of 'financial gain' is vague and makes room for a broad scope of potential offences. In principle, as noted in Chapter 14, if 'financial gain' was literally interpreted, all activities generating economic savings would fall within that term. This would include, thus, private activities. However, the TPP clarifies that for the purposes of criminal enforcement and regarding the definition of 'commercial scale', 'financial gain' can be understood as 'commercial purpose'.[99] This means that, pursuant to the TPP, 'commercial scale' entails acts carried out for commercial advantage or commercial purpose.

Requiring a 'commercial purpose' may be more limited than 'financial gain' but, still, is vague and involves a broad range of options for criminal offences. On the one hand, 'commercial purpose' is certainly narrower than 'financial gain'. In this sense, even if the expression 'commercial purpose' is ambiguous and allows different interpretations, it also permits excluding a large number of acts where there is 'financial gain' but there is no 'commercial purpose'. This is the case, in particular, of private acts such as private copies of protected materials. On the other hand, however, it is also clear that the combination of the qualitative and quantitative criteria identified in the *China – Intellectual Property Rights* panel report – according to which both the nature of the act and its magnitude where relevant – in the TPP is substituted by a new standard of just qualitative nature. This standard, also present in a number of bilateral trade agreements, takes into consideration the commercial advantage and the commercial purpose, but not necessarily the magnitude of the infringement.

The TPP also requires the criminalization of the wilful importation or domestic use, in the course of trade and on a commercial scale, of labels or packaging infringing a trademark. In the analysis of ACTA it was already mentioned the

96 *See* Article 18.77.1(a) TPP 97 *See* Article 18.77.1(b) TPP.
98 *See* footnote 127 to Article 18.77.1(b) TPP. 99 *See* footnote 89 TPP.

potential impact that this offence could have on parallel importation.[100] Such a criminalization would target the separate importation of goods and labels with a view to later combination. As noted by Kimberlee Weatherall, this would not be particularly problematic because it requires willingness and is limited to situations of identical trademarks or trademarks that cannot be distinguished.[101] The problems could manifest, however, due to 'the combination of a broad definition of "counterfeiting" with a broader set of signs which may these days be registered as trademarks'.[102]

Two relatively new criminal offences end the list enshrined in the TPP. Like in some PTA,[103] the TPP requires punishing the unauthorized copying of cinematographic works from performances in movie theatres if this causes 'significant harm to a right holder in the market for that work'.[104] Besides, in line with ACTA, aiding and abetting is also the object of criminal liability. This must be read in conjunction with the rest of the offences, since it is with respect to the offences for which the TPP requires criminal punishment that Parties must ensure that criminal liability for aiding and abetting is available under their law.[105] The comments made with respect to ACTA and the criminalization of aiding and abetting are fully applicable in the case of TPP, since provisions in both treaties are almost identical.

2.2 Penalties

The TPP requires the imposition of penalties that include sentences of imprisonment as well as monetary fines. Providing for either one or the other penalty is, thus, no longer an option like in the TRIPS Agreement. Moreover, the reading of the text gives the impression that these penalties are cumulative and that they can be implemented altogether. However, in line with ACTA, a footnote to the very same article clarifies that there is no obligation to provide for 'imprisonment and monetary fines to be imposed in parallel'.[106] In any case, the most important guidance in the very same sub-section indicating the type of penalties requested by the TPP is the mandate to set penalties that are consistent with crimes of a corresponding gravity.[107]

Chapter 14 of this book introduces the objectives of criminal sanctions in the area of intellectual property enforcement. Essentially, it holds that the main criterion to determine whether criminal sanctions should be imposed is whether infringing acts have particularly damaging social consequences. This, naturally, does not exclude the right holder, but the central object of criminal punishment in the area of intellectual property should focus on broader legal interests.[108] By contrast, the

[100] *See* Section III.1.1. [101] Weatherall (2015), p. 51. [102] *Ibid.*, p. 52.
[103] *See* Article 18.10.29 Republic of Korea-US FTA and EIA (2012). [104] *See* Article 18.77.4 TPP.
[105] *See* Article 18.77.5 TPP. [106] *See* Article 18.77.6(a) and footnote 132 TPP.
[107] *See* Article 18.77.6(a) TPP.
[108] Public interest-related aspects in criminalization of intellectual property rights infringement were underlined, for example, by the representatives of India and Hong Kong at the negotiations of the TRIPS Agreement. *See* Adam (2011), p. 346.

TPP puts the emphasis on a blurring and broad definition of commercial scale – i.e. the impact on the right holder' interests – while alluding to circumstances such as threats to health or security to be taken into account to determine the penalties.[109]

The sub-sections relating to the seizure of evidence, suspected goods and related materials, as well as the forfeiture of assets deriving from the infringing activity, and the destruction or forfeiture of infringing goods, materials and implements, and any other label or packaging,[110] are essentially identical to ACTA, which has been already analysed. Broadly speaking, they certainly go beyond the TRIPS Agreement and, for instance, explicitly allow seizing documentary evidence, assets, labels or packaging. Like it happens in many PTAs, the TPP also explicitly identifies the destruction of infringing goods in the context of criminal sanctions.

IV CRIMINAL PROCEDURES AND PENALTIES IN PREFERENTIAL TRADE AGREEMENTS

Preferential Trade Agreements that specifically regulate criminal measures[111] usually replicate the minimum standards set forth in the TRIPS Agreement. Sometimes they merely copy and paste what was previously agreed in TRIPS,[112] but in a number of recent treaties Parties have decided to go further than what is required in that Agreement.

The expansion generally concerns both the covered categories of intellectual property rights and the acts that must be punished. However, the expansion is also exemplified in a specific mention of the obligation to entitle authorities to initiate criminal procedures *ex officio*, either for counterfeit and pirated goods[113] or for goods

[109] *See* Article 18.77.6(b) TPP. [110] *See* Article 18.77.6(c), (d) and (e) TPP.

[111] *See* Australia-Chile FTA and EIA (2009); Chile-Japan FTA and EIA (2007); Chile-Mexico FTA and EIA (1999); Colombia-Mexico FTA and EIA (1995); Costa Rica-Mexico FTA and EIA (1995); CAFTA-DR-US FTA and EIA (2006); EFTA-Mexico FTA and EIA (2001); EFTA-Montenegro FTA (2012); EU-CARIFORUM States FTA and EIA (2008); EU-Colombia and Peru FTA and EIA (2013); EU-Republic of Korea FTA and EIA (2011); EU-Peru FTA and EIA (2013); Japan-Indonesia FTA and EIA (2008); Japan-Malaysia FTA and EIA (2006); Japan-Peru FTA and EIA (2012); Japan-Philippines FTA and EIA (2008); Japan-Switzerland FTA and EIA (2009); Japan-Thailand FTA and EIA (2007); Japan-Viet Nam FTA and EIA (2009); Republic of Korea-US FTA and EIA (2012); Mexico-El Salvador FTA and EIA (2001); Mexico-Guatemala FTA and EIA (2001); Mexico-Honduras FTA and EIA (2001); Mexico-Nicaragua FTA and EIA (1998); NAFTA FTA and EIA (1994); US-Australia FTA and EIA (2005); US-Bahrain FTA and EIA (2006); US-Chile FTA and EIA (2004); US-Colombia FTA and EIA (2012); US-Jordan FTA and EIA (2001); US-Morocco FTA and EIA (2006); US-Panama FTA and EIA (2012); US-Oman FTA and EIA (2009); US-Peru FTA and EIA (2009); US-Singapore FTA and EIA (2004).

[112] *See* Article 15–46 Chile-Mexico FTA and EIA (1999); Article 164.3 Chile-Japan FTA and EIA (2007); Article 184 Japan-Peru FTA and EIA (2012).

[113] *See* Article 17.38(d) Australia-Chile FTA and EIA (2009); Article 15.11.26(b)(iv) CAFTA-DR-US FTA and EIA (2006); Article 18.10.27(f) Republic of Korea-US FTA and EIA (2012); Article 17.11.27(d) US-Australia FTA and EIA (2005); Article 14.10.27(d) US-Bahrain FTA and EIA (2006); Article 17.11.22(e) US-Chile FTA and EIA (2004); Article 4.26 US-Jordan FTA and EIA (2001); Article 15.11.26 (b)(iv)

infringing other intellectual property rights categories[114] as well as the liability of legal persons.[115] Some PTAs also reflect the relevance of the digital environment and require the criminalization of activities taking place on the Internet.[116]

1 *The Scope*

1.1 Categories of Intellectual Property Rights

All agreements that lay down an obligation to implement criminal sanctions do refer at the minimum to trademark counterfeiting and copyright piracy on a commercial scale. Some PTAs expand this obligation to encompass either intellectual property in general (provided that the infringement is committed on a commercial scale)[117] or some specific intellectual property rights categories distinct from trademarks and copyrights. Among the latter are treaties that enshrine a commitment to 'consider' the adoption of criminal sanctions for other intellectual property rights infringements.[118] Some agreements go further and contain a detailed list of rights the infringement of which may result in criminal sanctions. These include patents, utility models, industrial designs, trademarks or layout-designs of integrated circuits, copyrights or related rights, plant breeder's rights,[119] geographical indications and undisclosed information.[120]

1.2 Offences

A relatively small number of PTAs incorporate new situations and acts that provide for the application of criminal law. While most of these treaties have been promoted by the United States, Japan has also shown a keen interest in the enforcement of

US-Morocco FTA and EIA (2006); Article 15.11.26(b)(iv) US-Panama FTA and EIA (2012); Article 16.9.21(a)(iv) US-Singapore FTA and EIA (2004).

114 In Article 125.4 of the Japan-Switzerland FTA and EIA (2009), the obligation to act *ex officio* is also foreseen for the cases of infringement committed wilfully and on a commercial scale of rights to patents, utility models, industrial designs, trademarks or new varieties of plants, or the acts of unfair competition (there is no mention of copyright though).

115 Certainly, the obligation to establish the liability of legal persons is only found in one agreement, which sets forth moreover that, 'such liability shall be without prejudice to the criminal liability of the natural persons who have committed the criminal offences'. *See* Article 10.56 EU-Republic of Korea FTA and EIA (2011).

116 *See* Article 17.11.23 US-Chile FTA and EIA (2004); Article 18.10.30 Republic of Korea-US FTA and EIA (2012).

117 *See* Article 127 Japan-Malaysia FTA and EIA (2006).

118 In Article 10.55 of the EU-Republic of Korea FTA and EIA (2011) this compromise specifically targets geographical indications and designs.

119 *See* Article 121 Japan-Indonesia FTA and EIA (2008); Article 129.3 Japan-Philippines FTA and EIA (2008); Article 125.1(a) and (b) Japan-Switzerland FTA and EIA (2009); Article 140 Japan-Thailand FTA and EIA (2007).

120 *See* Article 125.1(c) and (d) Japan-Switzerland FTA and EIA (2009). With respect to industrial secrets, *see* also Article 18–21-4 Colombia-Venezuela-Mexico FTA and EIA (1995).

intellectual property rights through criminal sanctions. The European Union has generally refrained from codifying criminal enforcement in PTAs. However, this has not always been the case, and the agreement with the Republic of Korea not only mandates the provision of criminal sanctions at least in cases of wilful trademark counterfeiting and copyright and related rights piracy but also creates new obligations with respect to particular acts, such as the criminalization of aiding and abetting.[121] As it has been noted, this exceeds the European Union *acquis* on the matter.[122]

PTAs concluded by the United States require Parties to punish the wilful importation or exportation of counterfeit or pirated goods. These treaties provide for criminal penalties in cases of exportation and importation to the same extent as the trafficking or distribution of such goods in domestic commerce.[123] The agreement between Japan and Switzerland expands this criminalization to transit and makes it applicable to patents, utility models, industrial designs, rights relating to new varieties of plants, geographical indications and acts of unfair competition.[124]

Some PTAs also call for the adoption of criminal procedures and penalties for knowingly transporting, transferring or otherwise disposing of counterfeit labels for a number of products (including phonograms, copies of computer programs or documentation, packaging for a computer program, or a copy of a motion picture or other audiovisual work),[125] and counterfeit documentation or packaging for a computer program.[126]

A notable feature of many PTAs – mostly promoted by the United States – is the frequent reference to the provision of criminal penalties against the circumvention of effective technological measures that are used by authors, performers and producers of phonograms to protect their copyrighted works. PTAs that cover this specific area diverge widely. Some mention that Parties will provide criminal penalties 'when appropriate'[127] or 'in appropriate circumstances',[128] while others mandate the adoption of criminal sanctions.[129]

121 *See* Article 10.57 EU-Republic of Korea FTA and EIA (2011).

122 See Geiger (2016), p. 654.

123 *See* Article 15.11.26(a) CAFTA-DR-US FTA and EIA (2006); Article 18.10.26 Republic of Korea-US FTA and EIA (2012); Article 17.11.26(b) US-Australia FTA and EIA (2005); Article 16.11.26 US-Colombia FTA and EIA (2012); Article 16.11.26 US-Peru FTA and EIA (2009); Article 15.11.26(a) US-Morocco FTA and EIA (2006); Article 15.11.26(a) US-Panama FTA and EIA (2012).

124 *See* Article 125.2 Japan-Switzerland FTA and EIA (2009).

125 *See* Article 17.11.28(a) US-Australia FTA and EIA (2005); Article 14.10.28(a) US-Bahrain FTA and EIA (2006); Article 16.11.28(a) US-Colombia FTA and EIA (2012); Article 16.11.28(a) US-Peru FTA and EIA (2009); Article 15.11.27(a) US-Morocco FTA and EIA (2006).

126 *See* Article 17.11.28(b) US-Australia FTA and EIA (2005); Article 14.10.28(a) US-Bahrain FTA and EIA (2006); Article 16.11.28(b) US-Colombia FTA and EIA (2012); Article 16.11.28(b) US-Peru FTA and EIA (2009); Article 15.11.27 (b) US-Morocco FTA and EIA (2006).

127 *See* Article 17.28 Australia-Chile FTA and EIA (2009).

128 *See* Article 17.7.5(a) US-Chile FTA and EIA (2004).

129 *See* Article 15.5.7(a) CAFTA-DR-US FTA and EIA (2006); Article 18.4.7(a) Republic of Korea-US FTA and EIA (2012); Article 17.4.7(a) US-Australia FTA and EIA (2005); Article 14.4.7(a) US-Bahrain FTA and EIA (2006); Article 17.7.6(a) US-Chile FTA and EIA (2004); Article 16.7.4(a) US-Colombia FTA and EIA (2012); Article 16.7.4(a) US-Peru FTA and EIA (2009); Article 4.13 US-Jordan FTA and

Acts against rights management information committed wilfully and for the purposes of commercial advantage or private financial gain will also be subject to criminal sanctions under a number of PTAs mostly promoted by the United States.[130] In some cases, treaties establish that prohibited acts may be exempted from criminal liability if they are performed by a non-profit library, archive, educational institution or broadcasting entity established without a profit-making.[131]

Some treaties also specify that whoever manufactures, assembles, modifies, imports, exports, sells, leases or otherwise distributes 'a tangible or intangible device or system, knowing [or having reason to know] that the device or system is of assistance in decoding an encrypted program-carrying satellite signal without the authorization of the lawful distributor of such signal' may be liable to criminal sanctions.[132] Such sanctions may apply to those who wilfully 'receive and make use of, or further distribute, a program-carrying signal that originated as an encrypted program-carrying satellite signal knowing that it had been decoded without the authorization of the lawful distributor of the signal'.[133]

There are two other significant cases of criminalization. While the first has been enacted in just one treaty, it is significant because it anticipated the content of ACTA and TPP and is likely to reappear in future agreements. This case concerns the use of, or attempt to use, audiovisual recording devices to transmit or make a copy of a motion picture or other audiovisual work from their performance in a public motion picture exhibition facility.[134] The second case is interesting because it is the only one where the right holder is the potential offender. In effect, a small number of PTAs establish an obligation to provide for 'administrative, civil, or criminal sanctions if the inventor or the patent applicant willfully makes a wrongful or misleading declaration of the origin or source'.[135] Clearly, criminal sanctions are not mandatory in this case, but it illustrates the imbalance characterizing PTAs: that in only two treaties – and in a manner that permits the non-application of any criminal sanctions at all – is the right holder mentioned as the potential offender.

EIA (2001); Article 15.5.8(a) US-Morocco FTA and EIA (2006); Article 15.5.7(a) US-Panama FTA and EIA (2012); Article 16.4.7(a) US-Singapore FTA and EIA (2004).

130 *See* Article 17.29(b) Australia-Chile FTA and EIA (2009); Article 18.4.8(a) Republic of Korea-US FTA and EIA (2012); Article 17.4.8(a) US-Australia FTA and EIA (2005); Article 14.4.8(a) US-Bahrain FTA and EIA (2006); Article 16.7.5(a) US-Colombia FTA and EIA (2012); Article 16.7.5(a) US-Peru FTA and EIA (2009); Article 15.5.9(a) US-Morocco FTA and EIA (2006); Article 15.5.8(a) US-Panama FTA and EIA (2012); Article 16.4.8(a) US-Singapore FTA and EIA (2004).

131 *See* Article 16.7.5(a) US-Colombia FTA and EIA (2012); Article 16.7.5(a) US-Peru FTA and EIA (2009); Article 17.29(b) Australia-Chile FTA and EIA (2009).

132 *See* Article 17.33.1(a) Australia-Chile FTA and EIA (2009); Article 18.7.1 Republic of Korea-US FTA and EIA (2012); Article 17.7.1 US-Australia FTA and EIA (2005); Article 14.7.1(a) US-Bahrain FTA and EIA (2006); Article 17.8.1 US-Chile FTA and EIA (2004); Article 16.8.1 US-Colombia FTA and EIA (2012); Article 16.8.1 US-Peru FTA and EIA (2009); Article 15.8.1 US-Morocco FTA and EIA (2006); Article 15.8.1 US-Panama FTA and EIA (2012); Article 16.6.1 US-Singapore FTA and EIA (2004).[133] *See* Article 17.33.1(b) Australia-Chile FTA and EIA (2009).

134 *See* Article 18.10.29 Republic of Korea-US FTA and EIA (2012).

135 *See* Article 6.5.6 EFTA-Colombia FTA and EIA (2011); Article 6.5.6 EFTA-Peru FTA (2011).

1.3 Wilfulness and Commercial Scale

No PTA defines the term 'willful', and the only indirect reference to the meaning of this notion can be found in the agreement between the United States and Chile, where it is declared that 'evidence of reproduction or distribution of a copyrighted work, by itself, shall not be sufficient to establish willful infringement'.[136] Given that all Parties to PTAs are also Parties to the WTO, the notion of wilfulness seems readily exportable into the PTAs context. As noted when analysing the TRIPS Agreement, according to the WTO Panel in the *China – Intellectual Property Rights* case 'willful' alludes to the infringer's intent and reflects the criminal nature of the enforcement procedures at issue.[137]

One of the characteristics of PTAs is that they often provide the specific meaning of terms and parameters that were left open in the TRIPS Agreement. This is particularly the case of the 'commercial scale' requisite. While the TRIPS Agreement leaves open the definition of commercial scale, some PTAs lay down a specific definition of this criterion or identify situations where commercial scale can be ascertained.

Treaties that provide a definition of commercial scale are largely coincidental as all of them have been subscribed by the United States or by countries that have concluded a prior agreement with the United States. The first aspect to be noticed is that all these treaties constrain the definition of 'commercial scale' to the case of copyright and related rights infringement. What 'commercial scale' implies with respect to other intellectual property infringements is still open to interpretation.

When the definition of 'commercial scale' is included in the text, it is done by way of examples of infringements that amount to it. The first case is that of 'significant infringements of copyright that are not committed for the purpose of commercial advantage or financial gain' if these are committed wilfully. The second case concerns 'willful infringements that have no direct or indirect motivation of financial gain, provided that there is more than a *de minimis* financial harm'.[138] These broad and ambiguous standards do not clearly indicate which infringements will be punishable. However, they seem to be in the direction set up in the agreement between the United States and the Republic of Korea, where it is established that 'financial gain' includes the 'receipt or expectation of anything of value'.[139] Certainly, this is an extremely broad standard in the context of criminal procedures.

136 *See* note 33 to Article 17.11.22(a)(i) US-Chile FTA and EIA (2004).

137 *See* WTO Panel, *China – Intellectual Property Rights*, para. 7.523.

138 *See* Article 17.38 Australia-Chile FTA and EIA (2009); Article 17.11.26(a)(i)(ii) US-Australia FTA and EIA (2005); Article 14.10.26 US-Bahrain FTA and EIA (2006); Article 17.11.22(a) US-Chile FTA and EIA (2004); Article 16.11.26(a)(b) US-Colombia FTA and EIA (2012); Article 16.11.26(a)(b) US-Peru FTA and EIA (2009); Article 15.11.26(a) CAFTA-DR-US FTA and EIA (2006); Article 15.11.26(a) US-Morocco FTA and EIA (2006); Article 15.11.26(a) US-Panama FTA and EIA (2012); Article 16.9.21 US-Singapore FTA and EIA (2004).

139 *See* note 33 to Article 18.10.26 Republic of Korea-US FTA and EIA (2012).

2 *Sanctions*

Many PTAs replicate the obligation, set forth in the TRIPS Agreement, to provide for penalties for the offences enacted, including 'imprisonment and/or monetary fines that are sufficient to provide a deterrent to infringement', and are 'consistent with the level of penalties applied for crimes of an analogous gravity'.[140] The reference to the second condition – similar to crimes of corresponding gravity – tends to be neglected in the agreements of the United States.[141]

The majority of PTAs do not provide details with respect to the severity of the sanctions. In fact, only one agreement indicates that penalties must be 'effective, proportionate and dissuasive'.[142] Several PTAs insist on the deterrent nature of the penalties,[143] and some mention that 'policies or guidelines that encourage penalties to be imposed by judicial authorities at levels sufficient to provide a deterrent to future infringements' shall be adopted.[144]

PTAs also go further than the TRIPS Agreement with respect to the seizure, forfeiture and destruction of infringing goods and related materials. In a number of cases, PTAs eliminate the reference found in the TRIPS Agreement to the seizure, forfeiture and destruction of goods 'in appropriate cases' and instead include an obligation to enable judicial authorities to adopt the necessary actions. In fact, in some cases the drafting seems to make seizure, forfeiture and destruction almost compulsory.[145]

Many PTAs also describe the objects that can be seized, forfeited or destroyed. Regarding seizure, mention is made of the seizure of suspected counterfeit or pirated goods as well as related materials and implements that have been used in the commission of the offence. In addition to this obligation, set forth in the TRIPS Agreement, a number of PTAs also require the seizure of assets that are 'legally traceable to the

140 Sometimes this can be inferred from the general reference made to enforcement provisions of the TRIPS Agreement (this is the case of the PTAs subscribed by EFTA and Article 95 Japan-Viet Nam FTA and EIA (2009)). On other occasions, the reference is explicit, such as in Article 17.38(a) Australia-Chile FTA and EIA (2009); Article 18–31 Colombia-Venezuela-Mexico FTA and EIA (1995); Article 14–30 Costa Rica-Mexico FTA and EIA (1995) (superseded by a new treaty, Mexico-Central America FTA and EIA (2012), which however does not include enforcement provisions on intellectual property rights); Article 15 EFTA-Montenegro FTA (2012); Article 271 EU-Central America FTA and EIA (2013); Article 16–59 Mexico-Northern Triangle FTA and EIA (2001); Article 17–29 Mexico-Nicaragua FTA and EIA (1998); Article 1717 NAFTA FTA and EIA (1994).

141 *See* for instance the case of Article 15.11.26(a) CAFTA-DR-US FTA and EIA (2006), with the exception of Article 17.11.22(b) US-Chile FTA and EIA (2004).

142 *See* Article 10.59 EU-Republic of Korea FTA and EIA (2011).

143 *See* Article 18.10.27(a) Republic of Korea-US FTA and EIA (2012); Article 17.11.27(a) US-Australia FTA and EIA (2005); Article 14.10.27(a) US-Bahrain FTA and EIA (2006); Article 16.11.27(a) US-Colombia FTA and EIA (2012); Article 16.11.27(a) US-Peru FTA and EIA (2009); Article 15.11.26(b)(i) US-Morocco FTA and EIA (2006); Article 15.11.26(b)(i) US-Panama FTA and EIA (2012).

144 *See* Article 15.11.26(b)(i) CAFTA-DR-US FTA and EIA (2006); Article 14.10.27(a) US-Bahrain FTA and EIA (2006); Article 15.11.26(b)(i) US-Morocco FTA and EIA (2006); Article 16.9.21(a)(i) US-Singapore FTA and EIA (2004).

145 *See* Article 18–31 Colombia-Venezuela-Mexico FTA and EIA (1995).

infringing activity and documentary evidence relevant to the offence'.[146] In some cases it is stated that there is no need to individually identify the items that are subject to seizure as long as they fall within the general categories specified in the legal order.[147]

Something similar occurs with regard to the forfeiture and destruction of the goods. While the TRIPS Agreement merely mentions that 'in appropriate cases' remedies shall include forfeiture and destruction of the goods, many PTAs mandate that judicial authorities shall have the authority to order the forfeiture of assets legally traceable to the infringing activity and the forfeiture and destruction of all goods found to be counterfeit or pirated. With the sole exception of the PTA between the European Union and the Republic of Korea, which also alludes to counterfeit goods,[148] PTAs constrain the forfeiture and destruction of materials and implements[149] that have been used in the making of the infringing goods to the case of copyright piracy. In addition, PTAs that regulate forfeiture and destruction frequently specify that these actions shall take place without compensation to the defendant.[150]

146 *See* Article 17.38(b) Australia-Chile FTA and EIA (2009); Article 10.58 EU-Republic of Korea FTA and EIA (2011); Article 15.11.26(b)(ii) CAFTA-DR-US FTA and EIA (2006); Article 18.10.27(b) Republic of Korea-US FTA and EIA (2012); Article 17.11.27(b) US-Australia FTA and EIA (2005); Article 14.10.27(b) US-Bahrain FTA and EIA (2006); Article 17.11.22(c) US-Chile FTA and EIA (2004); Article 16.11.27(b) US-Colombia FTA and EIA (2012); Article 16.11.27(b) US-Peru FTA and EIA (2009); Article 15.11.26(b)(ii) US-Morocco FTA and EIA (2006); Article 15.11.26(b)(ii) US-Panama FTA and EIA (2012); Article 16.9.21(a)(ii) US-Singapore FTA and EIA (2004). In Article 125.5 of the Japan-Switzerland FTA and EIA (2009) reference is made to confiscation of 'crime proceeds and properties derived from such crime proceeds' in the cases of infringement of rights to patents or trademarks or copyrights or related rights. With respect to documentary evidence, *see* Article 140.3 of the Japan-Thailand FTA and EIA (2007).

147 *See* footnote 17–23 to Article 17.38 Australia-Chile FTA and EIA (2009); Article 15.11.26(b)(ii) CAFTA-DR-US FTA and EIA (2006); Article 18.10.27(b) Republic of Korea-US FTA and EIA (2012); footnote 17–29 to Article 17.11.27(b) US-Australia FTA and EIA (2005); Article 14.10.27(b) US-Bahrain FTA and EIA (2006); Article 17.11.22(c) US-Chile FTA and EIA (2004); Article 16.11.27(b) US-Colombia FTA and EIA (2012); Article 16.11.27(b) US-Peru FTA and EIA (2009); Article 15.11.26 (b)(ii) US-Morocco FTA and EIA (2006); Article 16.9.21(a)(ii) US-Singapore FTA and EIA (2004).

148 *See* Article 10.60.2 of the EU-Republic of Korea FTA and EIA (2011) with respect to both to trademark counterfeiting and copyright piracy.

149 At least with respect to wilful copyright and related rights piracy, *see* Article 17.38(c) Australia-Chile FTA and EIA (2009); Article 17.11.27(c) US-Australia FTA and EIA (2005); Article 14.10.27(c) US-Bahrain FTA and EIA (2006); Article 17.11.22(d) US-Chile FTA and EIA (2004); Article 16.11.27(c) US-Colombia FTA and EIA (2012); Article 16.11.27(c) US-Peru FTA and EIA (2009); Article 15.11.26 (b)(iii) US-Morocco FTA and EIA (2006); Article 15.11.26(b)(iii) US-Panama FTA and EIA (2012); Article 16.9.21(a)(iii) US-Singapore FTA and EIA (2004); Article 15.11.26(b)(iii) CAFTA-DR-US FTA and EIA (2006); Article 18.10.27(d) Republic of Korea-US FTA and EIA (2012).

150 *See* Article 17.38(c) Australia-Chile FTA and EIA (2009); Article 17.11.27(c) US-Australia FTA and EIA (2005); Article 14.10.27(c) US-Bahrain FTA and EIA (2006); Article 17.11.22(d) US-Chile FTA and EIA (2004); Article 16.11.27(c) US-Colombia FTA and EIA (2012); Article 16.11.27(c) US-Peru FTA and EIA (2009).

14

Criminal Enforcement and Human Rights

I INTRODUCTION

Criminal enforcement of intellectual property pursues a double objective. On the one hand, it aims at deterring and responding to the most serious violations of intellectual property rights. On the other hand, it is also instrumental in the protection of social goods, such as public health, property and consumer safety. In the context of criminal enforcement, the interests of the right holder are taken into consideration in the broader framework of social interests. This is in contrast to the norms on civil enforcement, which respond to the private nature of intellectual property rights and put private parties at the centre.

Chapter 13 detailed how new international treaties broaden the scope of criminal measures in response to intellectual property infringement. Such an expansion may alter the objective of criminal enforcement and, in some instances, may also impact on fundamental rights. The definition of key concepts in the context of criminal enforcement may alter the focus traditionally put on the social effect that certain activities must have in order to be considered criminal offences and, instead, take as reference the damage suffered by the right holder. This is the case of the definitions relating to terms such as 'commercial scale', 'financial gain' and 'economic advantage'. In parallel, expanding the scope of criminal measures in response to intellectual property infringement may impinge on fundamental rights such as the right to a fair trial, the right to privacy and the right to freedom of expression. In this respect, a key question relates to the compatibility of the normative expansion of criminal measures with basic principles of justice, in particular legal certainty, proportionality and due process.[1]

An in-depth analysis of the impact of criminal measures targeting intellectual property rights on each and every fundamental right goes beyond the remit of this chapter. Instead, this chapter addresses the major aspects of the intersection between

[1] *See* Gracz (2013), p. 21.

criminal enforcement and human rights and identifies the most relevant cases of tension. Particular emphasis is placed upon a fundamental principle of criminal law, namely the principle of legal certainty, which is critical in the context of criminal enforcement but seems to be frequently overlooked in international normative processes.

II PROTECTION OF FUNDAMENTAL RIGHTS

1 *Freedom of Expression*

The relationship between criminal enforcement of intellectual property and freedom of expression is vast and materializes in very different contexts. Think, for instance, about enforcement in the digital domain. Penalties such as the termination of Internet connection or the blocking of access to webpages in response to intellectual property infringement bear a direct connection to freedom of expression. The tension between enforcing intellectual property rights through criminal law and the right to freedom of expression has been addressed in different fora, including courts and international bodies.

The debates revolving around the interface between the two legal areas have generally focused on three main topics and have echoed the broader debate arising from the intersection of fundamental rights and criminal enforcement of intellectual property rights. One area of concern has been the expansion in the scope and severity of criminal liability for private users' activities.[2] A different area relates to the vague content of some provisions laying down criminal sanctions for intellectual property infringement.[3] The third, and probably broader, area of discussion is the one relating to the principle of proportionality and whether new criminal enforcement measures are adequate in light of this principle.

In respect to the latter, the principle of proportionality occupies centre-stage in the relationship between criminal enforcement and fundamental rights[4] and recognizes courts' considerable discretion in its application and implementation. The case of the right to freedom of expression is a telling one, since the principle of proportionality is instrumental in curbing the abuse of criminal procedures for the enforcement of intellectual property rights[5] that have a detrimental effect on this fundamental right. International treaties that recognize the right to freedom of expression also allow it to be legitimately restricted. This is the case of the

[2] *See* in this sense, for instance, UN Human Rights Council (2011), paras. 33–37.

[3] *See* more generally on this, Geiger (2015c).

[4] *See* Geiger (2016); Gunn (2005); Sweet and Mathews (2008); Kaminski (2014).

[5] The issue of misuse has been brought forward for example by the European Parliament in its legislative resolution on the directive proposal on criminal enforcement. *See* European Parliament (2007a), Article 7. *See* also Hilty, Kur and Peukert (2006), p. 975.

International Covenant on Civil and Political Rights, which invokes a 'strict'[6] test of proportionality for such a limitation.[7] At the regional level, the European Court of Human Rights has also developed a proportionality test[8] in order to guarantee against interference with the right to freedom of expression. While the Court has held that exceptions to freedom of expression 'must be narrowly interpreted and the necessity for any restrictions must be convincingly established',[9] the principle of proportionality requires taking into account the nature and severity of the penalties that would be imposed.[10] Consequently, the principle of proportionality can assist applying cautious criminal sanctions that are compatible with restrictions that might occur to the right to freedom of expression.

Criminalization of intellectual property activities taking place in the digital environment raises specific human rights concerns. As a matter of principle, the UN Human Rights Council has emphasized that 'the same rights that people have offline must also be protected online'.[11] This is relevant because some of the new criminal sanctions applied in response to intellectual property infringement are based upon a strict liability system, which could have a potential 'chilling effect' that might affect the securing of the right to freedom of expression.[12] Freedom of expression protects both individual rights and the public interest. This is clear in cases where attempts are made to adopt intellectual property legislation that could allow the blocking of content or monitoring and identification of critics on the

6 The UN Human Rights Committee has stated that Article 19.3 of the Covenant 'lays down specific conditions and it is only subject to these conditions that restrictions may be imposed: the restrictions must be "provided by law"; they may only be imposed for one of the grounds set out in subparagraphs (a) and (b) of paragraph 3; and they must conform to the *strict* tests of necessity and proportionality' (emphasis added). *See* UN Human Rights Committee (2011), para. 22.

7 *See* Human Rights Committee, *Vladimir Velichkin v. Belarus*, Communication no. 1022/2001, 20 October 2005, UN Doc CCPR/C/85/D/1022/2001 (2005), para. 7.3. For a description of the criteria that satisfy the test of proportionality, *see* Gunn (2005), p. 467 *et seq*.

8 For one of the first analyses on the evolution of the principle of proportionality and its application in the jurisprudence of the European Court of Human Rights, *see* Eissen (1993). The author concludes by stating that '[o]ver the years proportionality has put down solid and lasting roots in the case-law of the European Court of Human Rights, and these roots will in all likelihood go even deeper, continuing to broaden the scope of the principle . . . Indeed the extent to which this has already occurred suggests that it has even now acquired the status of a general principle in the Convention system, a status which it already has in numerous municipal legal systems and in community law,' p. 146.

9 *See* ECtHR, *Thorgeirson v. Iceland*, no. 13778/88, 25 June 1992, Series A no. 239, para. 63.

10 *See*, for instance, ECtHR, *Neij and Sunde Kolmisoppi v. Sweden*, no. 40397/12, 19 February 2013. In this judgement, the European Court of Human Rights found that the criminal penalties imposed on the applicants interfered with their right to freedom of expression protected by Article 10 of the European Convention on Human Rights. However, the Court applied the balancing test of proportionality and decided 'that the nature and severity of the penalties imposed are factors to be taken into account when assessing the proportionality of interference with the freedom of expression guaranteed by Article 10 . . . In the present case, the Court considers that the prison sentence and award of damages cannot be regarded as disproportionate,' pp. 11–12.

11 *See* UN Human Rights Council (2012), p. 2. *See*, for an analysis on this perspective, Land (2013).

12 *See* in this respect UN Human Rights Council (2011), para. 28; Manta (2011), p. 516.

Internet.[13] These regulations may present particularly difficult problems from different angles. The first of these concerns cases where criminal sanctions against intellectual property infringement are perceived by the public[14] as restricting the freedom of expression[15] in a way that could have a 'chilling effect on expressive activities'.[16] The second concern has to do with the tangible menace of criminal liability and the real threat it poses for online intermediaries.[17]

In addition, vague and ambiguous definitions of key criteria[18] that determine the threshold for the application of criminal sanctions to acts of infringement could lead to unacceptable restrictions to the right to receive and impart information.[19] Vague definitions of crucial notions may result as well in criminalization of low-level infringement and *de minimis* behaviour, thus impacting on the principles of proportionality and legality. The new provisions on criminal enforcement might bring with them a broad scope of criminal penalties and severe consequences of their application.[20] Therefore, criminalized actions and the corresponding sanctions should require a sound justification,[21] and imprisonment sentences should also be closely scrutinized.[22]

2 *Fair Trial*

The right to a fair trial[23] becomes fully relevant when applying criminal law in cases of intellectual property infringement. The content, judicial interpretation and development of the overarching right to a fair trial, as well as the fairness, proportionality and reasonableness that prescribe due process requirements, condition the regime for the criminal enforcement of intellectual property rights. In particular, the

13 *See* Kaminski (2014); Land (2013); UN Human Rights Council (2011).

14 As one author explained, '[w]hether the society respects a given law and obeys particular legal norms depends not only on the normative reality, but also on the way in which the society *perceives* the particular branch of law. What the general public thinks the law says and how it apprehends respective legal acts is equally important for the internalisation of the legal norms as what the law actually says'. (emphasis in original). *See* Gracz (2013), p. 26 *et seq.*

15 *See* Hardy (2002), p. 306. 16 *See* Manta (2011), p. 516.

17 *See* for a detailed analysis on this aspect Kaminski (2014), pp. 615–616. 18 *See* Section 3.1.

19 *See* UN Human Rights Council (2014), para. 51. As it has been stated, 'criminalizing low-level infringement impinges on an Internet user's right to receive information'. *See* Kaminski (2014), p. 614. *See* also for a comment in this sense Strowel (2009), p. 82.

20 *See* also Weatherall (2016).

21 *See* ECtHR, *Dudgeon v. the United Kingdom*, no. 7525/76, 22 October 1981, Series A no. 59. *See* also Griffiths (2012).

22 *See* ECtHR, *Incal v. Turkey*, no. 22678/93, 9 June 1998, Reports 1998-IV. *See* also on this Geiger (2016).

23 *See* Article 14 ICCPR; Article 6 ECHR; Article 47 EU Charter of Fundamental Rights; Article 8 American Convention on Human Rights. Due process rights are recognized in international human rights instruments such as in Articles 7 and 10 UDHR; Articles 13 and 14 ICCPR. The UN Human Rights Committee explained that, '[t]he procedural guarantees of article 13 of the Covenant incorporate notions of due process also reflected in article 14'. *See* UN Human Rights Committee (2007), para. 62.

right to a fair trial provides a rich legal framework, integrating procedural rules that need to be considered for efficient and fair enforcement legislation.[24]

The right to a fair trial includes the right to effective access to a court[25] and the right to effectively participate in proceedings,[26] which are covered by the requirement of a 'fair hearing'.[27] The principle of equality of arms is also 'one feature of the wider concept of fair trial',[28] and it is inherent to the fairness of criminal proceedings.[29] The requirement of 'fairness' implies looking beyond the procedures in an oral hearing and approaching criminal proceedings as a whole. This, together with the non-derogable nature of the fundamental principles of the right to a fair trial,[30] ascertains that these principles must be upheld in cases of intellectual property infringement when assessing and enforcing the procedural rules on 'any criminal charge'[31] of the defendant.[32]

In such proceedings, the independence and impartiality of the tribunal established by law are indispensable and inalienable safeguards.[33] Equally, the request to

24 *See* Chapter 3, Section III.2.

25 *See* ECtHR, *Golder v United Kingdom*, no. 4451/70, 21 February 1970, Series A no. 18.

26 *See* ECtHR, *Stanford v United Kingdom*, no. 16757/90, 23 February 1994, Series A no. 282-A, para. 26.

27 The European Court of Human Rights established the condition of 'fair hearing' under Article 6 of the European Convention on Human Rights. This requirement is also found in Article 14.1 of the International Covenant on Civil and Political Rights, which provides that '[a]ll persons shall be equal before the courts and tribunals. In the determination of any criminal charge against him, or of his rights and obligations in a suit at law, everyone shall be entitled to a fair and public hearing . . . ' *See* the comment of the UN Human Rights Committee (2007).

28 *See* ECtHR, *Monnell and Morris v. the United Kingdom*, no.(s) 9562/81, 9818/82, 2 March 1987, Series A no. 115, para. 62.

29 For a detailed analysis of the principle of 'equality of arms' in the context of intellectual property enforcement, *see* Seuba (2015c).

30 The UN Human Rights Committee stated, '[a]rticle 4, paragraph 2, of the Covenant explicitly prescribes that no derogation from the following articles may be made: . . . article 15 (the principle of legality in the field of criminal law, i.e. the requirement of both criminal liability and punishment being limited to clear and precise provisions in the law . . . ' *See* UN Human Rights Committee (2001), para. 7. *See* also para. 11.

31 The UN Human Rights Committee defined 'criminal charges' as they 'relate in principle to acts declared to be punishable under domestic criminal law. The notion may also extend to acts that are criminal in nature with sanctions that, regardless of their qualification in domestic law, must be regarded as penal because of their purpose, character or severity'. *See* UN Human Rights Committee (2007), para. 15.

32 *See also* on this issue Griffiths (2012), pp. 199–200.

33 *See* Article 14.1 ICCPR; Article 10 UDHR; Article 6.1 ECHR; Article 47 EU Charter of Fundamental Rights; Articles 7.1 and 26 of the African Charter on Human and Peoples' Rights; Articles 8.1 and 27.2 of the American Convention on Human Rights. The general principle of 'an independent and impartial tribunal established by law' is one of customary international law, meaning that it is binding on all states at all times, thus an absolute right. *See* UN Human Rights Committee (2007), para. 19; UN Human Rights Committee (2001), para. 16. *See* also HRC, *Gonzales del Rio v. Peru*, no. 263/1987, CCPR/C/46/D/263/1987, 2 November 1992, para. 5.1. The ECtHR also settled criteria about the meaning of 'an independent and impartial tribunal established by law'. *See* ECtHR, *De Wilde, Ooms and Versyp ('Vagrancy') v. Belgium*, no. 2832/66, 2835/66; 2899/66, 18 June 1971, Series A no. 12, para. 78; *Ringeisen v. Austria*, no. 2614/65, 16 July 1971, Series A no. 15; *Neumeister v. Austria*, no. 1936/63, 27 June 1968, Series A no. 17.

set up 'adequate and effective safeguards against arbitrary interference and abuse'[34] as well as the demand to ensure that any interference with the rights covered by human rights instruments shall be 'in accordance with the law' are relevant principles in the context of criminal enforcement of intellectual property rights. In this respect, individuals must be protected against arbitrary interference[35] by the competent authorities, and the scope of rules of law should be clear and detailed in order to avoid such interference.[36]

3 *Privacy*

The right to privacy,[37] which protects personal information,[38] is of relevance in the context of criminal proceedings for the enforcement of intellectual property.[39] Criminal enforcement connects to the disclosure of personal data and monitoring of communications, especially in cases relating to copyright infringement. Criminal proceedings relate, therefore, with the broad interpretation of the scope of 'private life' and 'correspondence' as set forth in the jurisprudence of the European Court of Human Rights.[40] These terms include email correspondence and the use of the Internet.[41]

34 The ECtHR has prohibited 'arbitrary interference and abuse' in the specific context of intellectual property litigation. The Court has stated that '[a]n Anton Piller order is granted without the defendant's being notified or heard and is capable of producing damaging and irreversible consequences for him ... For these reasons it is essential that this measure should be accompanied by adequate and effective safeguards against arbitrary interference and abuse'. ECtHR, *Chappell v. the United Kingdom*, no. 10461/83, 30 March 1989, Series A no. 152-Apara. 57.

35 *See Malone v. the United Kingdom*, no. 8691/79, 2 August 1984, Series A no. 82, para. 68.

36 *See* ECtHR, *Kopp v. Switzerland*, no. 23224/94, 25 March 1998, para. 72. *See* also Kaminski (2014) on the possible problem of criminalization of intellectual property law and arbitrary enforcement in relation to freedom of expression, pp. 617–618.

37 *See* Article 17 ICCPR; Article 8 ECHR; Article 7 EU Charter of Fundamental Rights; Article 11 American Convention on Human Rights.

38 In addition to personal information, the right to privacy has been invoked to protect a wide range of other areas, from personal identity, *see*, e.g., ECtHR, *Burghartz v. Switzerland*, no. 16213/90, 22 February 1994, Series A no. 280-B, to the right to establish and to develop relationships with others, *see*, e.g., ECtHR, *X v. Iceland*, no. 6825/74, 18 May 1976.

39 However, it can be noted that the exact meaning of the right to privacy is still open to discussions. As an author stated, '[t]hinking about punishment and the right to privacy is difficult in the first place because of the lack of firm establishment of any well-defined right to privacy'. *See* Hudson (2006), p. 138. For more debates on defining the right to privacy more generally, *see*, for example, the volume of Claes *et al.* (2006); and for earlier attempts in this sense, *see*, for instance, Parker (1974) or Wacks (1980).

40 *See* for example ECtHR, *Halford v. United Kingdom*, no. 20605/92, 25 June 1997, Reports 1997-III, 'within the scope of 'private life' and 'correspondence' in Article 8 para. 1 (art. 8–1), ... the Court in its case-law had adopted a broad construction of these expressions', para. 42.

41 *See* for example ECtHR, *Liberty and others v. the United Kingdom*, no. 58243/00, 1 July 2008, '[t]elephone, facsimile and email communications are covered by the notions of 'private life' and 'correspondence' within the meaning of Article 8', para. 56.

While the right to privacy protects the individual against arbitrary interference by public authorities, thus essentially entailing a negative obligation on States to abstain from such interference,[42] it also entails positive obligations[43] and goes beyond relations between individuals and authorities. In this respect, States have the obligation to adopt measures to secure respect for private life, both in the context of relations between the individual and public authorities and in the context of interpersonal relations.[44] The European Court of Human Rights has alluded to a positive obligation on States to ensure an 'effective deterrence against grave acts'[45] concerning personal information, a positive obligation the extends to many different areas, including relations between Internet users and the Internet service providers.

Along similar lines, the UN Human Rights Committee has underlined that the right to privacy concerns 'protection against both unlawful and arbitrary interference. That means that it is precisely in State legislation above all that provision must be made for the protection of the right set forth in that article.'[46] Therefore, international standards governing criminal proceedings and their implementation make clear that any interference with human rights can only take place on the basis of law, which requires all parties to 'comply with the provisions, aims and objectives'[47] of the International Covenant on Civil and Political Rights. More broadly, human rights instruments and related jurisprudence identify minimum procedural guarantees or relevance in the context of criminal enforcement of intellectual property rights and are part of the 'enabling environment for effective intellectual property protection'.[48]

III THE RELEVANCE OF THE PRINCIPLE OF LEGAL CERTAINTY

Chapter 13 underlined that adopting new international norms on criminal enforcement is difficult given the particularly close relationship between criminal enforcement, national sovereignty and domestic values. International criminal law has progressed in areas where a globally shared conviction on the need to protect a relevant legal interest by means of criminal sanctions exists. This has been, for instance, the case of grave violations of humanitarian law, which compromise core legal interests such as life and physical or mental human integrity. However, international norms dealing with criminal enforcement are scarce and eventually problematic if there is no shared perception or common understanding with respect to their need or function. This is often the case of, precisely, criminal sanctions against intellectual property infringements.

42 *See* ECtHR, *Marckx v. Belgium*, no. 6833/74, 13 June 1979, Series A no. 31, para. 31.
43 *See* for instance, ECtHR, *K.U. v. Finland*, no. 2872/02, 2 December 2008, Reports of Judgments and Decisions 2008 (hereinafter ECtHR, *K.U. v. Finland*), para. 42.
44 *See* ECtHR, *M.C. v. Bulgaria*, no. 39272/98, 4 December 2003, Reports of Judgments and Decisions 2003-XII (extracts), para. 150.
45 *See* ECtHR, *K.U. v. Finland*, para. 43.
46 *See* UN Human Rights Committee (1988), para. 2.
47 *Ibid.*, para. 3.
48 *See* Yu (2011f), p. 1114. *See* also Gracz (2013).

In the case of criminal enforcement, the 'constructive ambiguity' that characterizes the negotiation of new international treaties[49] may result in controversial norms. In this regard, while in certain areas of intellectual property ambiguous drafting has facilitated the conclusion of agreements acceptable to all Parties – and may also facilitate national implementation given the intrinsic flexibility it implies – in the area of criminal enforcement the situation is different for a number of reasons.

First, some countries transplant internationally agreed-upon texts word for word into their domestic legal orders without further refinement. This implies that all the virtues but also all the potential problems in the specific context of criminal enforcement – i.e. ambiguity – of the international text are replicated internally.[50] Second, although norms on enforcement contained in plurilateral and bilateral agreements have in principle not been conceived to be directly applicable, this possibility depends on the national stance towards direct applicability of international law.[51] The eventual direct application of criminal enforcement provisions enshrined in international agreements and the demanding criteria set up by the principle of legality make it of the utmost importance that a thorough assessment is conducted on whether the new norms on criminal enforcement fulfil the minimum requirements that any criminal law statute should meet.

The principle of legality prescribes not only the non-retroactivity of criminal laws and penalties but also the need for clarity, concision and predictability.[52] *Lex scripta, lex certa, lex previa* and *lex stricta* are the four pillars of this principle,[53] as codified in the main multilateral human rights covenants.[54] Legal certainty 'expresses the fundamental premise that those subject to the law must know what the law is so as to be able to plan their actions accordingly'.[55] The individual must 'know from the wording of the relevant provision and, if need be, with the assistance of the courts' interpretation of it, what acts and omissions will make him liable'[56] as well as the

[49] *See* Watal (1999). [50] *See* Chapter 6, Section VI.

[51] It depends in fact on the content of the obligations enacted in the treaty and the permeability of the national legal order towards international law, whether or not they establish subjective rights and in a sufficiently clear and detailed manner. Obligations such as '[m]embers shall ensure', '[p]arties shall make available' and '[m]embers shall guarantee' may create subjective rights. Certainly, this will depend on a range of factors, but this terminology, in principle, may entitle private right holders invoking treaty provisions in the context of national litigation.

[52] 'In its broadest sense, the principle of legality encompasses the following in respect of criminal provisions: (1) the principle of non-retroactivity (nullum crimen, nulla poena sine lege praevia); (2) the prohibition against analogy (nullum crimen, nulla poena sine lege stricta); (3) the principle of certainty (nullum crimen, nulla poena sine lege certa); and (4) the prohibition against uncodified, ie unwritten, or judge-made criminal provisions (nullum crimen, nulla poena sine lege scripta).' *See* Kress (2010), paras. 29–31.

[53] *See* Haveman (2003), pp. 39–40; Lamb (2002), pp. 773–774; Robinson (1988), pp. 396–397.

[54] *See* Article 15 ICCPR; Article 7 ECHR; Article 49 EU Charter of Fundamental Rights.

[55] *See* Tridimas (1999), p. 163.

[56] *See* ECtHR, *Kokkinakis v. Greece*, no. 14307/88, 25 May 1993, Series A no. 260-A, para. 52.

corresponding penalties.[57] That is, norms must clearly define the offences and the penalties associated to those offences.[58] The UN Human Rights Committee has for instance affirmed that the 'broad definition' of a crime may negatively impact fundamental rights, including rights of non-derogable nature.[59] According to the Committee, the vagueness of the definitions directly contradicts the principle of legality.[60] This is particularly so in the case of 'ambiguous wording of the provisions and the use of several evidentiary presumptions to the detriment of the defendant'.[61]

In contrast to these demands, some criminal enforcement provisions in bilateral and plurilateral agreements contradict the principle of legal security in its dimension of *lex certa*. These provisions fail to meet the 'duty on legislators to ensure that it is clear what conduct will give rise to sanctions and to the deprivation of liberty'.[62] The analysis of the global regime on criminal measures for the enforcement of intellectual property rights shows at least four cases where, given the impact on legal certainty, the lack of precision could be particularly detrimental for the right to a fair trial.

1 *Commercial Scale*

According to many international agreements, the commercial scale of the infringement is decisive for the provision of criminal measures. Scholars have underlined both the relevance[63] and the additional requirement[64] that the proof of 'commercial scale' implies, since goods must not be only infringing but also traded on a commercial scale. Although some definitions of 'commercial scale' have been put forward in the regional context,[65] the TRIPS Agreement is silent in that regard.

57 In the European Union, for example, the Court of Justice established the principles of 'legal certainty' and 'legality of criminal offences and penalties', which are 'satisfied where the individual can know from the wording of the relevant provision and, if need be, with the assistance of the courts' interpretation of it, what acts and omissions will make him criminally liable'. *See* ECJ, Case C-308/06, *International Association of Independent Tanker Owners (Intertanko) and Others* v. *Secretary of State for Transport*, [2008] ECR I-04057, para. 71.

58 *See* Mylly (2012), p. 242.

59 *See* HRC, Estonia, ICCPR, A/58/40, vol. I, 2003, 41, para. 79(8).

60 For instance, 'extremist activity' has been considered too vague to satisfy the principle of legality. *See* HRC, Russian Federation, ICCPR, A/59/40, vol. I, 2003, 20, para. 64(20). *See* similarly, HRC, Morocco, ICCPR, A/60/40, vol. I, 2004, 35, para. 84(20).

61 *See* HRC, Israel, ICCPR, A/58/40, vol. I, 2003, 64, para. 85(14).

62 *See* Irish Law Reform Commission (1997), p. 99.

63 *See* Hilty (2012), p. 18.

64 *See* Grosse Ruse-Khan (2012), p. 176.

65 This is the case of the Directive 2004/48/EC of the European Parliament and of the Council of 29 April 2004 on the enforcement of intellectual property rights, OJEU L157 of 30 April 2004 (hereinafter EU Enforcement Directive), which provides a definition of 'commercial scale' although for application in the civil context. According to the Recital 14 of the EU Enforcement Directive, '[a]cts carried out on a commercial scale are those carried out for direct or indirect economic or commercial advantage; this would normally exclude acts carried out by end consumers acting in good faith'.

As noted in Chapter 13, the definition of 'commercial scale' was a central topic in the *China – Intellectual Property Rights* panel report.[66]

In that case, the WTO Panel rejected arguments in support of an expansive meaning of 'commercial scale' and favoured a cautious and flexible approach.[67] In doing so, it rejected claims made by the United States, which held that 'commercial scale' was tantamount to merely 'commercial' and that Article 61 of the TRIPS Agreement only excludes *de minimis* activities.[68] In fact, for the United States, in the case of expensive products such as professional software, a single sale of an infringing product could qualify as commercial scale.[69]

The WTO Panel observed that the notion of 'commercial scale' was contextual and varied across markets and products within the same market. In this sense, the WTO Panel held that the notion of 'commercial scale' referred to 'counterfeiting or piracy carried on at the magnitude or extent of typical or usual commercial activity with respect to a given product in a given market'.[70] The WTO Panel further clarified that 'what constitutes a commercial scale for counterfeiting or piracy of a particular product in a particular market will depend on the magnitude or extent that is typical or usual with respect to such a product in such a market, which may be small or large'.[71]

Although not entirely coincidental, the WTO Panel's position was similar to the Chinese stance, which held that commercial scale implied 'a significant magnitude of infringement activity', thus providing a broad standard '[that is] subject to national discretion and local conditions'.[72] It seems that the WTO Panel's verdict 'permits assessment of the obligations under the Agreement in terms of penalties to the specific circumstances and needs of the country in question, thus adopting a differentiated approach'.[73] It has been held that 'this means that the demonstration of what constitutes "commercial scale" depends on quantitative analyses and assessment that inevitably introduce subjective considerations'.[74] More generally, the WTO Panel decision has been perceived as allowing considerable flexibility for interpretation, entailing 'significant policy space for WTO Members'.[75]

In contrast to the flexibility of the TRIPS Agreement, plurilateral and bilateral agreements provide for a definition of 'commercial scale' that may give rise to a range of problems. In the case of plurilateral agreements, according to ACTA, 'acts carried out on a commercial scale include at least those carried out as commercial activities for direct or indirect economic or commercial advantage',[76]

66 *See* WTO Panel Report, *China – measures affecting the protection and enforcement of intellectual property rights*, WT/DS362/R, 26 January 2009 (hereinafter WTO Panel, *China – Intellectual Property Rights*). *See*, for a comment, Creemers (2009); Xue (2009a); Xue, (2009b); Gervais (2009); Grosse Ruse-Khan (2012); Yu (2012); Yu (2010c); Watal (2010).

67 *See* Geiger (2015b), p. 114. 68 *See* WTO Panel, *China – Intellectual Property Rights*, para. 7.481.

69 *Ibid.*, Annex A-5, para. 2. 70 *Ibid.*, para. 7.577. 71 *Ibid.* 72 *Ibid.*, para. 7.481.

73 *See* Geiger (2015b), p. 119. 74 *See* Correa (2012), p. 72.

75 *See* Grosse Ruse-Khan (2012), p. 181. 76 *See* Article 23.1 ACTA.

and the TPP alludes to 'financial gain' when defining 'commercial scale' but clarifies that the term can be understood as 'commercial purposes'.[77]

Some PTAs also establish at least two possibilities of what, in the case of copyright, implies 'commercial scale'. First, it includes 'significant willful infringements for purposes of commercial advantage or private financial gain', thereby adding 'significant' to the text already found in ACTA and alluding to 'financial gain'. The second possibility identified in PTAs is new and concerns those 'willful infringements that have no direct or indirect motivation of financial gain, provided that there is more than a *de minimis* financial harm'.[78] Some treaties delete the condition requiring at least '*de minimis* financial harm' and merely require 'significant wilful copyright or related rights infringements that have no direct or indirect motivation of financial gain'.[79]

The lack of clarity of the ACTA definition of the 'commercial scale' benchmark of criminal sanctions was understood by many to violate fundamental human rights. For instance, it was stated that the relevant provision had 'a very uncertain scope' and was 'highly problematic with regard the principle of legal certainty and legality of criminal offenses'.[80] This criticism fuelled the debate on the impact that ACTA had on fundamental rights, in particular the discussion focusing on criminal sanctions. This debate and preoccupation were, in combination with the lack of transparency of the ACTA negotiations, at the centre of the overwhelming rejection of the ratification of the treaty by the European Union Parliament.[81]

Chapter 13 featured the important changes introduced by TPP regarding the definition of 'commercial scale'. The reference made in TPP to 'commercial advantage', as potentially synonymous to 'financial gain', and therefore synonymous to 'commercial scale', is too broad and too unspecific for justifying criminal sanctions. Certainly, it allows excluding from criminal liability infringing activities that generate positive economic personal consequences. However, it is not by any means clear the precise scope of the resulting double criterion. In effect, if commercial advantage and commercial purpose are put at the centre of the definition of commercial scale and the quantitative requirement is removed, the scope of criminal sanctions becomes much broader and uncertain.

Similar problems occur with respect to several PTAs that oblige to provide for criminal sanctions in cases of, as abovementioned, 'significant willful infringements for purposes of commercial advantage or private financial gain', as well as 'willful infringements that have no direct or indirect motivation of financial gain, provided that there is more than a *de minimis* financial harm'.[82] The interpretation of these provisions is far from clear. On this case, unlike TPP, there is not even a footnote

77 *See* footnote 88 TPP. 78 *See* Article 15.11.26(a) CAFTA-DR-US FTA and EIA (2006).

79 *See* Article 18.10.26 Republic of Korea-US FTA and EIA (2012). 80 *See* Geiger (2015b), p. 105.

81 ACTA was rejected on 4 July 2012 with 478 votes against, 39 in favour and 165 abstentions. *See* European Parliament (2012a). *See* also Matthews and Zikovska (2013).

82 *See* Article 15.11.26(a) CAFTA-DR-US FTA and EIA (2006).

stating the 'financial gain' may be understood as 'commercial advantage'. On the contrary, it is stated that 'commercial scale' includes 'financial gain', the latter including the 'receipt or expectation of anything of value'.[83] On the other hand, numerous questions would require an answer. For instance, which infringements are 'significant'? At which stage does an infringement start to be 'significant' for the purposes of criminal sanctions? The meaning of '*de minimis* financial harm' is not provided; thus, which is the '*de minimis*' standard? What are the exact criteria that apply to 'indirect motivation of financial gain'? Do they include innocent infringements, or could traditional copyright limitations still be applicable?[84]

The cases identified above reflect the same problem, i.e. the difficulty of ascertaining when an individual becomes an offender. The problem, however, goes beyond ambiguity. On many occasions – including with respect to the concept of 'commercial scale' – ambiguity has been praised as indicating flexibility,[85] thereby opening the door to an interpretation that better suits national circumstances. The problem in this case is double. First, the principle of legality and certainty requires clearer wording. Second, while the wording is unclear, it is sufficiently clear at the same time as to enlarge the scope of potential criminal offenders.

Given the ambiguity of some treaties, the reference to 'commercial advantage' could cover 'any commercial activity, which was intended to make money, save money, or improve a commercial entity's market position (or undermine a competitor's)',[86] while the reference to 'private financial gain' would include many other infringements of uncertain nature. In that situation, not only legal certainty but also the principle of proportionality would ultimately be at stake,[87] since both the seller of a limited amount infringing goods and the member of an organized band devoted to selling pirated goods would be responsible.[88] Probably anticipating this situation, the trade agreement between Chile and the United States established that nothing in the treaty 'prevents prosecutors from exercising any discretion that they may have to decline to pursue cases'.[89]

2 *The Wilfulness Requirement*

International norms on criminal enforcement require the infringement to be committed wilfully.[90] Direct intention or *means rea* must therefore be proved, while acts

83 *See* note 33 to Article 18.10.26 Republic of Korea-US FTA and EIA (2012).

84 *See* also Geiger (2015c).

85 For many, the lack of definition of 'commercial scale' in the context of the TRIPS Agreement is for instance an important flexibility and allows Member States an important margin of discretion. *See* in this sense, Correa (2009), p. 41; Xue (2009a), p. 295.

86 *See* Gibson (2012), p. 255.

87 Particularly in those cases where there is no reference to the exclusion of *de minimis* infringements.

88 Against this view, *see* Guo (2007), p. 53.

89 *See* footnote 34 to Article 17.11.22 US-Chile FTA and EIA (2004).

90 This is commonly observed, from Article 61 of the TRIPS Agreement to Article 18.77.1 of the TPP.

committed out of recklessness or negligence would in principle not amount to criminal responsibility. However, requiring direct intention does not necessarily coincide with the practice found in various countries, which have adopted less demanding standards and also consider a criminal offence those acts committed out of gross negligence or recklessness.[91]

Even when direct intention is required, doubts may persist as to the specific significance of wilfulness. These doubts relate to aspects such as the criteria to appreciate the intention, and are also extended to the specific act that has to be committed wilfully. With respect to the latter, in the context of the European Union directive proposal on criminal enforcement,[92] there was a lack of clarity on what act exactly would be considered as intentional, whether the act that infringes (general intent) or the willingness of the person to infringe the right (specific intent).[93] The same question may be posed with respect to criminal provisions for intellectual property infringement in plurilateral and bilateral agreements. According to the European Parliament, specific intent should be required, i.e. the criminalization should only proceed if the person committed his or her action knowing that an intellectual property right would be infringed.[94] This is not, however, a unanimous view. As a proof of this, the European Commission had not endorsed the opinion of the European Parliament, and it withdrew the directive proposal.[95]

It has also been noted that the standards to appreciate an intention can 'diverge significantly'.[96] Even though domestic legislations establish the legal basis for the element of 'wilfulness' in intellectual property rights infringement cases, it has been observed that in the United States,[97] for example, primarily the courts are entrusted with the assessment of wilful intent, and they have interpreted this requirement differently.[98] In contrast, in European countries the national laws are more specific in defining the standard of the 'intention' condition.[99] The proposals that left the

91 In Austria 'recklessness' is sufficient *means rea* for both trademark counterfeiting and copyright piracy. *See* the Trademarks Protection Act of 1970 (as last amended up to 2011) and Federal Law on Copyrights on Literary and Artistic Works and Related Rights of 1936 (as last amended in 2010). In Denmark the criminal intent required is actual intent or 'gross negligence', also in relation to both trademark counterfeiting and copyright piracy. *See* the Consolidate Trademark Act No. 109 of 2012 and Consolidated Act on Copyright No. 1144 of 2014.

92 *See* Amended Proposal for a Directive of the European Parliament and of the Council on criminal measures aimed at ensuring the enforcement of intellectual property rights of 26 April 2006, COM (2006) 168 final.

93 *See* Chartered Institute of Patent Agents (2005).

94 *See* European Parliament (2007a), Article 2.

95 *See* OJEU C 252 of 18 September 2010, p. 9.

96 *See* Geiger (2015c), p. 121.

97 *See* the provisions covered by the Copyright Act of 1976, Pub. L. No. 94–553, 90 Stat. 2541, Titles 17 and 18 USC § 506 and Trademark Counterfeiting Act of 1984, Pub. L. No. 98–473, 98 Stat. 2178, Title II § 1502(a).

98 *See* Gervais (2012), p. 269. However, the Supreme Court of the United States acknowledged that 'willful . . . is a word of many meanings, its construction often being influenced by its context'. *See* *Spies v. United States*, 317 US 492, 497 (1943).

99 In Italy, for instance, most of the trademark-related offences require 'general intent', meaning that the perpetrator acted 'consciously and willfully', and other trademark offences require 'specific intent', which means that the perpetrator acted 'consciously and willfully' *and* with a specific intent of gaining

terms 'intention' or 'willful' undefined have been heavily criticized for unduly expanding the offences and the offenders.[100]

3 *The Use of the Term 'Counterfeit'*

As noted in previous chapters, in particular in Chapter 12, 'counterfeit' has become a sort of popular term used to designate any intellectual property-infringing good as well as products raising quality-related concerns. This is problematic since it entails making use of a term that in the legal language refers to goods infringing trademark law – usually attracting severe consequences – to unrelated quality aspects and to intellectual property infringements that bear no relationship with trademarks. One of the problems arising from such confusion is the potential attraction of criminal liability. Indeed, 'the conceptualization of any infringement of IPRs as "counterfeiting" may have significant consequences, notably the criminalization of infringements that in most countries – particularly developed countries – are only subject to civil sanctions. Thus, any copyright violation (even if not "piracy") or patent infringement may be subject to a fine or imprisonment'.[101]

The majority of PTAs enshrine a definition of 'counterfeit' and 'pirated' goods that parallels the one found in the TRIPS Agreement. In principle, therefore, the definition of 'counterfeit' should not be particularly problematic. Nevertheless, not only some professional fora but also some national legal orders have adopted confusing definitions of 'counterfeit'. In response, when national courts have dealt with such definitions, they have pointed out the problems that they pose in terms of legal certainty. The case of Kenya is worth telling.

In 2008, Kenya adopted the national Anti-Counterfeit Act, which ordered the criminalization and seizure of counterfeit goods.[102] The problem with the Anti-Counterfeit Act was that the definition of counterfeit goods could be read as

a profit arising from his criminal action. *See* Article 474 and Article 648 respectively, of the Penal Code (approved by Royal Degree No. 1398 of 1930). In the Netherlands, in copyright cases, to establish criminal intent the law requires an intentional copyright infringement, which means that the person had the intention to infringe a copyright or that the person should have known that its actions infringe a copyright (see Articles 31, 31A and 31B of the Dutch Copyright Act of 23 September 1912). Article 32 of the same act, on the other hand, requires a culpable infringement, which means that there are reasonable grounds for the infringer to know that its actions infringe a copyright.

100 *See* Lowe (2006), p. 3.

101 *See* Correa (2012), p. 72.

102 *See* Anti-Counterfeit Act, Act no. 13 of 2008, Legal Notice no. 115 of July 2009 (hereinafter Anti-Counterfeiting Act 2008), Section 32 established that '[i]t shall be an offence for any person to – (a) have in his possession or control in the course of trade, any counterfeit goods; (b) manufacture, produce or make in the course of trade, any counterfeit goods; (c) sell, hire out, barter or exchange, or offer or expose for sale, hiring out, barter or exchange any counterfeit goods; (d) expose or exhibit for the purposes of trade any counterfeit goods; (e) distribute counterfeit goods for purposes of trade or any other purpose; (f) import into, transit through, tranship within or export from Kenya, except for private and domestic use of the importer or exporter as the case may be, any counterfeit goods; (g) in any other manner, dispose of any counterfeit goods in the course of trade'.

including legal generic medicines.[103] A complaint was presented to the High Court of Kenya, arguing that the potential confusion could impinge upon the trade of generic medicines, thereby affecting access to medicines and the right to health. The decision of the High Court of Kenya gave reason to the complainants,[104] declared that the enforcement of the contentious bill would violate the right to life, human dignity and health,[105] and underlined the need of clarity and concision in this domain. An additional problem from the human rights perspective is '[t]he possible application of sanctions in cases where there is no willful violation of a trademark or copyright, or where production or commercialization is not made on a commercial scale',[106] based on the drafting of a law that is hardly compatible with the principle of legality.

This case permits raising the broader problem resulting from the interchangeable use of the terms 'counterfeit' and 'substandard', in the case of 'counterfeit' with different meanings depending on the source and the context. These terms are, moreover, often put into relation with patent infringement or other intellectual property infringements, to the extent that it is not uncommon to find official documents that allude to patent infringement – or any other intellectual property rights infringement – as 'counterfeiting'.[107] This expansion entails that, 'for instance, the infringement of one or more claims of a patent is comparable to the fraudulent use of a trademark'.[108]

For the World Health Organization, the defining criterion for identifying a counterfeit product is the deliberate mislabelling with regard to identity or source. If such mislabelling does not occur, there is no counterfeit. Importantly, the mislabelling can affect aspects distinct from the trademark. As the WHO states, 'counterfeiting can apply to both branded and generic products and counterfeit products may include products with the correct ingredients or with the wrong ingredients,

[103] The Anti-Counterfeit Act 2008 states in Article 2 that '"counterfeiting" means taking the following actions without the authority of the owner of any intellectual property right subsisting in Kenya or elsewhere in respect of protected goods – (a) the manufacture, production, packaging, re-packaging, labelling or making, whether in Kenya or elsewhere, of any goods whereby those protected goods are imitated in such manner and to such a degree that those other goods are identical or substantially similar copies of the protected goods; (b) the manufacture, production or making, whether in Kenya or elsewhere, the subject matter of that intellectual property, or a colourable imitation thereof so that the other goods are calculated to be confused with or to be taken as being the protected goods of the said owner or any goods manufactured, produced or made under his licence; (c) the manufacturing, producing or making of copies, in Kenya or elsewhere, in violation of an author's rights or related rights'. *See* Chapter 12, Section IV.

[104] *See* High Court of Kenya, *Patricia Asero Ochieng, Maurine Atieno, Joseph Munyi, and AIDS Law Project v. Attorney General*, Petition No. 409/2009, 20 April 2012 (hereinafter *Patricia Asero Ochieng et al. v. Attorney General*).

[105] *See Patricia Asero Ochieng et al. v. Attorney General*, para. 72.

[106] *See* Correa (2012), p. 67.

[107] The OECD for instance uses the expressions 'counterfeiting' and 'piracy' to refer to all kind of intellectual property infringements. The OECD stated that its study 'focused on the infringement, through counterfeiting and piracy, of trademarks, copyrights, patents and design rights ... ' *See* OECD (2009), p. 1.

[108] *See* Correa (2012), p. 60.

without active ingredients, with insufficient active ingredients or with fake packaging'.[109] From the public health perspective, a counterfeit drug is a medicine whose identification does not match with reality. This may occur with respect to products protected by different categories of intellectual property rights or with respect to products not protected by intellectual property rights at all. In this context, counterfeiting may be related but is in principle independent from intellectual property infringement and includes drugs with misleading information with respect to the origin, composition and/or manufacturer of the product.

Counterfeit products with incorrect ingredients are part of the broader phenomenon of substandard pharmaceuticals, i.e. products whose composition and ingredients do not conform to the pharmaceutical standards set for them[110] and that may be either ineffective or dangerous.[111] From the perspective of public health, substandard medicines represent the most important public health problem,[112] although the phenomenon of counterfeiting attracts most of the attention.[113]

There is an important ongoing international debate on how to tackle the problems derived from the lack of quality of certain pharmaceutical products. In fact, some of the problems and practices associated with substandard medicines are related to trademark law and are the object of criminal sanctions. In this sense, one of the mechanisms for commercializing substandard products is through deception about the identity of the product's source. However, there are no arguments to link patent infringement and product quality, and in any case, definitions of counterfeit in the intellectual property context should not introduce terminology that may ultimate create confusion *vis-à-vis* generic products.

4 *Technological Protection Measures and Rights Management Information*

The aspects identified in relation to the core concepts of the international legal framework on criminal enforcement of intellectual property rights – such as 'commercial scale', the 'wilfulness' requirement or the definition of 'counterfeiting' – show the practical implications of the principle of legal certainty that underpins the rule of law. Arguments similar to those raised with respect to the definitions of those terms are also relevant with regard to the criminalization of the circumvention of technological measures and the violation of rights management information.

Several bilateral agreements concluded by the United States lay down criminal measures in response to circumvention activities of effective technological measures. These measures will 'be applied when any person, other than a nonprofit library, archive, educational institution, or public non-commercial broadcasting entity, is found to have engaged willfully and for purposes of commercial advantage

[109] *See* IMPACT (2011). [110] *See* Behrens *et al.* (2002), pp. 1–2. [111] *See* WHO (2004), p. 133.
[112] *See* Caudron *et al.* (2008), p. 1068. [113] *Ibid.*

or private financial gain in any of the foregoing activities'.[114] The reference to 'private financial gain' as a benchmark to apply criminal measures is also found in the context of the provisions on rights management information.[115]

Again, as it happens with other key terms in the context of criminal enforcement, the interpretation of these provisions is unclear and suggests the existence of too ample a scope. On the one hand, it was already noted that relying on 'commercial advantage' shifts the focus from the social interest to the right holder's interests. On the other hand, in these agreements express mention is made to 'private financial gain', which opens a potentially tremendous broad field. The threshold established therein seems really low, since non-commercial activities may become the object of criminal prosecution.

IV CONCLUSIONS

Recent initiatives in international intellectual property law-making have significantly expanded the scope of criminal measures in response to intellectual property infringement.[116] There are, however, several aspects that need to be carefully analysed.

Important doubts exist with respect to the concrete meaning and scope of some provisions on criminal enforcement enshrined in several international agreements of plurilateral and bilateral nature. This was the case of articles set forth in ACTA, and it is also currently the case of the TPP. Both of them were preceded, and followed, by bilateral trade agreements that enact articles giving rise to similar concerns with respect to the principle of legal certainty. In particular, the lack of precision relates to the concept of 'commercial scale' and, more broadly, the bar that needs to be satisfied to give place to criminal sanctions. The standard applied to demonstrate 'wilfulness' is also far from clear, and the misuse of the term 'counterfeit' brings up similar concerns.

Further, criminal enforcement of intellectual property rights is justified when a compelling public interest exists.[117] In this respect, the threat of criminal penalties may have an impact not only on legal activities entirely but also on the public interest and fundamental rights. A key tool in that context is the proportionality test, recognized as an important instrument for balancing interests in the sphere of intellectual property. As noted in this chapter with respect to freedom of expression and more broadly in Chapter 2, the principle of proportionality may have a decisive

114 *See* Article 18.4.7(a) (ii) Republic of Korea-US FTA and EIA (2012); Article 15.5.7(a) 2 (ii) CAFTA-DR-US FTA and EIA (2006); Article 17.4.7 US-Australia FTA and EIA (2005) (emphasis added).

115 *See* Article 18.4.8(a) Republic of Korea-US FTA and EIA (2012).

116 There are also opinions that suggest that ACTA for example is endorsed as an improvement to the TRIPS Agreement; 'the ACTA is not meant to add to substantive rights but only to ensure the more effective enforcement of those rights already provided for in the TRIPS Agreement'. *See* Mercurio (2012), p. 369.

117 *See* Wechsler (2012), p. 150.

impact in cases where criminal measures for intellectual property rights infringement might interfere with respect to fundamental rights.

Even more important than clarifying the drafting of criminal enforcement articles and its actual implementation *vis-à-vis* the principle of proportionality is deciding to what extent criminal law is the appropriate mechanism to respond to specific intellectual property infringements. There are both practical and substantive objections to this practice.

From the practical point of view, the mere presence of criminal sanctions for intellectual property infringement within the national legal order does not suffice to convince judges to apply them. This may be caused by concerns arising from the impact of sanctions as well as the social perception that this type of sanctions may be excessive. Moreover, among the practical reasons that explain the reduced use of criminal procedures in cases of intellectual property infringement are the time-consuming proceedings of criminal law, the stricter proof requirements in criminal cases and the costs involved in imposing criminal penalties.[118]

On the substance, there is still little empirical data on the intersection between norms of intellectual property rights and criminal law enforcement.[119] A comprehensive assessment on the feasibility of criminal sanctions for intellectual property rights infringement is still missing, and many questions remain unanswered, such as those related to the implementation, compliance and effectiveness of these laws. As examined in Chapter 3, criminal enforcement of intellectual property rights requires significant investment and relevant costs associated with its implementation. Given the availability of other tools to prevent and react against infringement and the severe impact of criminal measures, alternative solutions may be cheaper, faster and fairer.[120] The search for effective protection of intellectual property rights is more and more based on growing evidence of the problems caused by counterfeiting and piracy, as testified by an impressive volume of published data.[121] However, when proposing a framework for criminal enforcement of intellectual property rights, the cost of combating acts of intellectual property rights infringement through the adoption and implementation of criminal sanctions is not properly weighted.

From a substantive point of view, approaching infringement of intellectual property rights through the lenses of criminal law has profound consequences.

118 *See* Geiger (2015c). At the same time, it has been observed that 'criminal enforcement is not the preferred method of enforcing IPRs in developed countries. In contrast, criminal enforcement is now the main tool of enforcement in developing countries'. *See* Harms (2007), para. 28.

119 In recent years, however, a few studies have been conducted on the particular issues of copyright infringement through peer-to-peer file sharing, and they provide interesting data on the appropriateness of criminal sanctions on these acts. *See*, for example, Hargreaves (2011); Huygen *et al.* (2009); Karaganis (2011); Karaganis and Renkema (2013).

120 For instance increasing public awareness of intellectual property rights and designing strategies to properly inform consumers of the danger of counterfeiting and piracy. *See* also Bitton (2013).

121 *See* Chapter 3.

In this sense, it has been noted that criminal law should take into account but not mainly focus on the economic consequences of intellectual property infringement. The need for a differentiated approach where infringements would only be punished in the case of actual social harm or particularly risky consequences for consumers has been underlined.[122] Against this proposal, new norms reinterpreting standards such as 'commercial scale' seem to depart even more from the public interest objectives that pursue criminal law. As a result, it is doubtful whether these are the right criteria for deciding which acts of intellectual property infringement should be criminalized.[123]

The need for reform in the field criminal enforcement of intellectual property rights appears evident,[124] and human rights norms provide a good tool for that purpose. Recent international normative initiatives, however, persist in approaches to criminal enforcement that create tensions between intellectual property law and other legal systems, such those governing human rights.[125] Instead, criminalization of intellectual property law implicates principles of justice that make it necessary to consider a balanced set of rules, requiring compliance with obligations of procedural justice and respect for fundamental rights. The latter, thus, should guide lawmakers in their work as to ensure a functional statutory intellectual property regime and reinforce in this way the acceptability of the intellectual property regime in the eyes of society.

[122] *See* Geiger (2010). *See* also Hilty (2012); Lefranc (2012); Hilty, Kur and Peukert (2006); Moohr (2002); Manta (2011); Geiger (2016); McManis and Pelletier (2012), p. 210.

[123] *See* Geiger (2014b), p. 131; Hilty, Kur and Peukert (2006), p. 976.

[124] *See* also on this Geiger (2015c), p. 140.

[125] *See* also Ellis (2011), p. 64; DeLaurell (2012), p. 175.

Epilogue

Norms creating rights and obligations, and norms on the enforcement of those rights and obligations, integrate the intellectual property legal regime, which also includes norms relating to the granting and maintenance of intellectual property rights. The intellectual property regime forms part of the broader legal order, and its norms interact with general principles of law and with norms belonging to other legal systems, including those touching upon competition, human rights, trade and development.

The relationship between primary and secondary norms, in particular between those establishing substantive rights and those on adjudication, is multifaceted. While norms on enforcement may just seem instrumental for the fulfilment of primary norms, the picture is more complex. In reality, norms on enforcement also shape the extent of substantive rights and obligations. On one hand, substantive rights are explicitly subject to the provisions found in enforcement-related sections of national statutes or international treaties. Norms on enforcement, hence, determine the method and scope of substantive protection. On the other, aspects such as the conditions for awarding an interim injunction or the methods for estimating damage awards drastically shape substantive rights. In this sense, the power to exclude and the economic value of an intellectual property right are directly determined by enforcement norms, which may also transform the right to exclude into a right to compensation.

Optimum enforcement does not refer to a pre-established set of things or predetermined situation. In reality, norms of different nature and of different legal regimes interact to protect diverse legal interests. In light of the numerous intersections and the existing sophisticated nets of legal interests, intellectual property enforcement is better understood as a process, a weighing and balancing process. Enforcement describes an action, not a pre-established outcome. In this regard, intellectual property law intends to fulfil a much more complex objective than safeguarding the right to exclude. While the latter is the most visible aspect of intellectual property entitlements, it is just a mechanism for the fulfilment of broader policy goals. Other rights, remedies, processes and institutions are of relevance to fulfil those goals and are also taken into account in the weighing and balancing process to enforce intellectual property rights.

The correlation between rights and remedies exists, thus, in the context of a broader legal framework. The weighing and balancing process to enforce intellectual property rights goes hand in hand with legal concepts such as judicial discretion and flexibility. The former is a traditional legal principle, while the latter is a loose term that has gained momentum in international intellectual property discussions. In that context, flexibility alludes to the in-built space of intellectual property norms and how states and other relevant stakeholders can make use of it. Far from leading to arbitrary outcomes or to a weakened protection of intellectual property rights, judicial discretion and flexibility are key tools to reaching and enforcing fair and equitable decisions in light of what is prescribed by the law and the circumstances of the case.

In the majority of cases, norms integrating the global regime for the enforcement of intellectual property rights leave national authorities ample space for adjustment. Even if the drafting of international rules is frequently vague and may lack balance, competent authorities have sufficient margin to shape intellectual property enforcement norms. The chapters of this book include numerous examples of the existing possibilities. Thus, regardless of the global picture arising from enforcement norms found in many bilateral and plurilateral agreements, there are various options to improve them and to guarantee a fair and balanced enforcement of intellectual property rights. The combination of comparative law and fundamental rights is probably the most productive strategy for improving international texts, but broader policy goals and general principles of law may be instrumental as well.

In light of this contextualized approach to intellectual property enforcement, it comes as no surprise that debates in the area of enforcement connect closely to debates revolving around substantive or material intellectual property norms. The correct balance between the interests of right holders and the broader interests of society is the chief concern of legislators, judges and authorities charged with enforcing intellectual property rights. Access to information and to vital products, for instance, are among the topics that both substantive and enforcement norms alike influence. In fact, on many occasions the latter is just the means to materialize the former. This is not, however, always the case, and specificities also exist. That is to say, there are cases where enforcement norms bear an independent relation to fundamental rights. For instance, many chapters of this book have emphasized the relevance of the right to a fair trial in the context of intellectual property enforcement norms and activities.

Recent international normative advances in the area of enforcement have been partially accomplished by means of the intense transplantation of intellectual property norms. New norms and new treaties promote in effect harmonization by means of legal transplantation. There is nothing inherently negative in using experience gained in other nations when developing new intellectual property norms. Likewise, there is nothing negative in proposing to other nations the adoption of norms that have worked well at the national level. What is puzzling yet is the pattern observed in many international treaties, consisting of the proposal of norms that only reflect the interests of right holders. Actually, biased proposals do not reflect the statutes of nations making those proposals, which are more balanced.

In actual practice, biased norms militate against the interests of right holders they intend to protect. At least two reasons can be mentioned. Right holders may one day become intellectual property infringers. In fact, this is a daily occurrence in numerous areas of business. In this scenario, right holders themselves will expect a reasonable and fair legal framework to protect them when they become alleged infringers. On the other hand, biased international norms face rejection by the public and deeper legitimacy challenges, which sometimes cause the failure of the treaties enacting those norms. Recent plurilateral initiatives are telling examples. Biased normative proposals do not seem, therefore, a mature and efficient tool to promote new norms or to promote the enforcement of intellectual property rights.

How will norms on intellectual property enforcement be in, say, fifteen years' time?

A first attempt to respond to this question may be found in economic analysis of intellectual property. The scale and impact of intellectual property infringement are among the central topics of interest of policy-makers, both at the global and national levels. It could not be otherwise, given the economic, scientific and cultural relevance of intellectual property in contemporary societies. Economic analysis is helpful to both designing and implementing enforcement norms. In the first case, quantification of all relevant factors, positive and negative, gives a sense and a guide for normative action. In the second case, the economic impact of remedies is closely related to fundamental legal principles. In this regard, notions such as proportionality or unjust enrichment bear a close connection with key remedies and their actual implementation. Economic analysis of intellectual property enforcement may, therefore, play a relevant role in the design of future intellectual property norms, particularly those relating to damages, injunctions and criminal enforcement.

The present situation at the international level makes it tempting to predict a stalemate of multilateralism and the advancement of bilateralism and plurilateralism. While such an outcome is possible, it would be based on a flawed approach to enforcement. Economies at different level of development and diverse legal traditions share much more concerning enforcement than one would expect when observing international debates. In reality, fundamental principles of balance and fairness are universal, as universal as numerous human rights of chief relevance in the area of enforcement. It is perfectly possible to propose an agenda for multilateral normative action in the area of enforcement – and even the content of many of its norms – if the foundations of such an agenda are rightly identified: a common understanding of the systemic role of enforcement in the broader legal system, the fundamental principles of balance and fairness, and the guidance and limits resulting from human rights entitlements.

Bibliography

Abbott FM (2004a) The Doha Declaration on the TRIPS Agreement and Public Health and the contradictory trend in bilateral and regional free trade agreements. Quaker United Nations Office, Occasional Paper no. 14

(2004b) WTO Dispute Settlement practice relating to the Agreement on Trade-Related Intellectual Property Rights. In: Ortino F and Petersmann E-U (eds.) *The WTO Dispute Settlement System: 1995–2003*. Kluwer Law International, The Hague, pp 421–453

(2006) TRIPS and human rights: Preliminary reflections. In: Abbott FM, Kaufmann C and Cottier T (eds.) *International Trade and Human Rights: Foundations and Conceptual Issues*. University of Michigan Press, Ann Arbor, pp 145–170

(2009a) *Innovation and technology transfer to address climate change: Lessons from the global debate on intellectual property and public health*. ICTSD Issue Paper no. 24, Geneva. http://ictsd.org/downloads/2009/07/innovation-and-technology-transfer-to-address-climate-change.pdf (last accessed May 2015)

(2009b) Seizure of generic pharmaceuticals in transit based on allegations of patent infringement: A threat to international trade, development and public welfare. *WIPO Journal* 1: 43–50

(2009c) Worst fears realised: The Dutch confiscation of medicines bound from India to Brazil. *Bridges Monthly* 1: February–March

(2015) An overview of the Agreement: Contents and features. In: Roffe P and Seuba X (eds.) *The ACTA and the Plurilateral Enforcement Agenda: Genesis and Aftermath*. Cambridge University Press, Cambridge, pp 31–45

Abbott FM and Correa C (2007) *World Trade Organization Accession Agreements: Intellectual Property Issues*. Quaker United Nations Office, Geneva

Abbott FM and Cottier T (2003) Dispute prevention and dispute settlement in the field of intellectual property rights and electronic commerce: US – Section 211 Omnibus Appropriations Act 1998 ('Havana Club'). In: Petersmann E-U and Pollack MA (eds.) *Transatlantic Economic Disputes: The EU, the US, and the WTO*. Oxford University Press, Oxford, pp 429–449

Abbott FM, Cottier T and Gurry F (2007) *International Intellectual Property in an Integrated World Economy*. Wolters Kluwer Law and Business, Aspen Publishers, New York

Abdel Latif A (2015) Developing countries and the contestation of ACTA at the TRIPS Council. In: Roffe P and Seuba X (eds.) *The ACTA and the Plurilateral Enforcement Agenda: Genesis and Aftermath*. Cambridge University Press, Cambridge, pp 357–375

Abi-Saab G (1999) Fragmentation or unification: Some concluding remarks. *New York University Journal of International Law and Politics* 31: 919–933

Adam A (2011) What is 'commercial scale'? A critical analysis of the WTO decision in WT/DS362/R. *EIPR* 33: 342–348
Addanki S (1998) Economics of patent damages: A practical guide. *Practicing Law Institute/Pat.*: 845–851
Andenas M and Zleptnig S (2006) Proportionality and Balancing in WTO Law: A Comparative Perspective. *EAIEL Policy Paper* No. 2
Adorno R (2002) Biomedicine and international human rights law: In search of global consensus. *Bulletin of the World Health Organization* 80: 959–963
Akester P (2006) The political dimension of the digital challenge: Copyright and free speech restrictions in the digital age. *Intellectual Property Quarterly* 1: 16
Allison JR and Lemley M (1998) Empirical evidence on the validity of litigated patents. *American Intellectual Property Law Association Quarterly Journal* 26: 185–275
Anderson D (1998) Negotiation and dispute settlement. In: Evans M (ed.) *Remedies in International Law: The Institutional Dilemma*. Hart Publishing, Oxford, pp 111–121
Anderson R (2005) The second IPR Enforcement Directive – A threat to competition and to liberty. Foundation for Information Policy Research. www.fipr.org/copyright/ipred2.html (last accessed September 2015)
Andrews N (2012) Fundamental principles of civil procedure: Order out of chaos. In: Kramer XE and van Rhee CH (eds.) *Civil Litigation in a Globalising World*. Asser Press, The Hague, pp 19–38
Angelopoulos CJ (2008) Freedom of expression and copyright: The double balancing act. *Intellectual Property Quarterly* 3: 328–353
Armond M (2003) Introducing the defense of independent invention to motions for preliminary injunctions in patent infringement lawsuits. *California Law Review* 91: 117–162
Arrow KJ (1962) Economic welfare and the allocation of resources for invention. In: Nelson R (ed.) *The Rate and Direction of Inventive Activity*. Princeton University Press, Princeton, pp 609–625
Ashton C and Kovács L (2009) Letter addressed by Catherine Ashton-European Commissioner for Trade-and László Kovács-Commissioner for Taxation and Customs Union-to Médecins Sans Frontières. CAB24/CA/PH/caD(09)256A(09)324 (on file with the author)
Aufricht H (1952) Supersession of treaties in international law. *Cornell Law Quarterly* 37: 655–700
Aust A (2nd ed.) (2007) *Modern Treaty Law and Practice*. Cambridge University Press, Cambridge
Austin J (1832) *The Province of Jurisprudence Determined*. John Murray, London
Bainbridge D (9th ed.) (2012) *Intellectual Property*. Pearson, Essex
Baker BK (2012) Settlement of India/EU WTO dispute re seizures of in-transit medicines: Why the proposed EU border regulation isn't good enough. School of Law Faculty Publications, Paper No. 37
Band J and Gerafi J (2014) Infringement-risk in copyright-intensive industries. Policybandwidth. http://infojustice.org/wp-content/uploads/2014/01/band-gerafi01062014.pdf (last accessed April 2015)
Bastian E-M and Knaak R (1995) Trade mark infringement proceedings in the countries of the European Union. *IIC* 26: 149–174
Beever A (2003) The structure of aggravated and exemplary damages. *Oxford Journal of Legal Studies* 23: 87–110
Behr V (2003) Punitive damages in America and German law – Tendencies towards approximation of apparently irreconcilable concepts. *Chicago-Kent Law Review* 78: 105–161

Behrens RH, Awad AI and Taylor RB (2002) Substandard and counterfeit drugs in developing countries. *Tropical Doctor* 32: 1–2

Bello H (1995) International decisions. *American Journal of International Law* 89: 772

Bently L and Sherman B (3rd ed.) (2008) *Intellectual Property Law*. Oxford University Press, Oxford

Bercovitch DJ and Rubin JZ (1992) *Mediation in International Relations*. St. Martin's Press, London

Berryman J (2007) Thirty years after: Anton Piller orders and the Supreme and federal Courts of Canada. *Journal of International Commercial Law and Technology* 2: 128–140

(2009–2010) Challenging shibboleths: Evidence based policy making, the Supreme Court of Canada and Anton Piller orders. *Advocates Quarterly* 36: 509–534

Bindschedler R (1992) Conciliation and mediation. In: Bernhardt R and Macalister-Smith P (eds.) *Encyclopedia of Public International Law*. North Holland, Amsterdam/New York, pp 721–725

Bitton M (2013) Rethinking the Anti-Counterfeiting Trade Agreement's criminal copyright enforcement measures. *Journal of Criminal Law and Criminology* 102: 67–118

Blair RD and Cotter TF (1998) An economic analysis of damages rules in intellectual property law. *William and Mary Law Review* 39: 1585–1694

(2005) *Intellectual Property: Economic and Legal Dimensions of Rights and Remedies*. Cambridge University Press, Cambridge

Blakeney M (2001) *Border Control of Intellectual Property Rights under TRIPS*. Sweet and Maxwell, London

(2004a) Enforcement of intellectual property rights: Challenges, remedies and public awareness. In: WIPO National Seminar on Intellectual Property for Faculty Member and students of Ajman University, organized by the World Intellectual Property Organization (WIPO), in cooperation with Ajman University of Science and Technology (AUST), the Association of Arab Universities and the Association of Arab Private Institutions for Higher Education Ajman, May 5 and 6, 2004, WIPO/IP/UNI/DUB/04/7

(2004b) International intellectual property jurisprudence after TRIPS. In: Vaver D and Bentley L (eds.) *Intellectual Property in the New Millennium*. Cambridge University Press, Cambridge, pp 3–19

(2005) Guidebook on Enforcement of Intellectual Property Rights. http://trade.ec.europa.eu/doclib/docs/2005/april/tradoc_122641.pdf (last accessed August 2015)

(2012) *Intellectual Property Enforcement. A Commentary on the Anti-Counterfeiting Trade Agreement (ACTA)*. Edward Elgar, Cheltenham, UK and Northampton, MA

Blakeney M and Mengistie G (2011) Intellectual property policy formulation in LDCs in Sub-Saharan Africa. *African Journal of International and Comparative Law* 19: 66–98

Boyce JR and Hollis A (2007) Preliminary injunctions and damages rules in patent law. *Journal of Economics and Management Strategy* 16: 385–405

Brandreth B (2005) Remedies, costs and enforcement. In: Fysh M (ed.) *The Modern Law of Patents*. Lexis Nexis Butterworths, London, pp 455–500

Brewster R (2009) Shadow unilateralism: Enforcing international trade law at the WTO. *University of Pennsylvania Journal of International Law* 30: 1133–1146

(2011) The surprising benefits to developing countries of linking international trade and intellectual property. *Chicago Journal of International Law* 12: 1–54

Bridy A (2012) Graduate response American style: 'Six strikes' measured against five norms. *Fordham Intellectual Property, Media and Entertainment Law Journal* 23: 1–66

Bronckers MCEJ, Verkade DWF and McNelis NM (2000) *TRIPS Agreement: Enforcement of Intellectual Property Rights*. Office for Official Communications of the European Communities, Luxembourg

Brown A, Guadamuz A and Hatcher J (2010) The impact of free trade agreements on information technology based business. *Geopolitics, History, and International Relations* 2: 62–123

Buchanan JA and Wilson BJ (2012) *An experiment on protecting intellectual property*. http://ideas.repec.org/p/chu/wpaper/12–09.html (last accessed September 2015)

Burk D and Cohen J (2001) Fair use infrastructure for rights management systems. *Harvard Journal of Law and Technology* 15: 41–83

Burrell R and Colleman A (2005) *Copyright Exceptions: The Digital Impact*. Cambridge University Press, Cambridge

Burrell R and Weatherall K (2008) Exporting controversy? Reactions to the copyright provisions of the US-Australia free trade agreement: Lessons for U.S. trade policy. *University of Illinois Journal of Law, Technology and Policy* 2: 259–319

Busaniche B (2012) Intellectual property rights and free trade agreements: A never ending story. In: Bollier D and Helfrich S (eds.) *The Wealth of the Commons*. http://wealthofthecommons.org/contents (last accessed April 2015)

Calabresi G and Melamed AD (1972) Property Rules, Liability Rules, and Inalienability: One View of the Cathedral. *Harvard Law Review* 85: 1089–1121

Cane P (1997) *The Anatomy of Tort Law*. Oxford University Press, Oxford

Cannizzaro E (2000) *Il principio della proporzionalità nell'ordinamento internazionale*. Università di Macerata, Milano

Carter EL (2009) Harmonization of copyright law in response to technological change: Lessons from Europe about fair use and free expression. *University of La Verne Law Review* 30: 312–345

Casalonga C and Langlais F-X (2010) Bilan de trois ans de mesures provisoires en droit des brevets. *Cahiers de Droit de L'Entreprise* 6: 33–40

Casanovas y La Rosa O (2001) *Unity and Pluralism in Public International Law*. Martinus Nijhoff, The Hague

Casey B (2012) The impact of intellectual property theft on the economy. Prepared by the Chairman's Staff of the US Congress Joint Economic Committee (on file with author)

Castel-Fodor K-J (2013) Providing a release valve: The US-China experience with the WTO Dispute Settlement System. *Case Western Law Review* 64: 201–238

Caudron J-M *et al.* (2008) Substandard medicines in resource-poor settings: A problem that can no longer be ignored. *Tropical Medicine and International Health* 13: 1062–1072

Charleton P and Kelly S (2012) *Copyright as one of several competing rights in European Law*. Fordham Intellectual Property Conference

Chisum DS (1996–1997) Normative and empirical territoriality in intellectual property: Lessons from patent law. *Virginia Journal of International Law* 37: 603–618

Chow D (2002) *A Primer on Foreign Investment Enterprises and Protection of Intellectual Property in China*. Kluwer Law International, The Hague

(2011) Counterfeiting as an externality imposed by multinational companies on developing countries. *Virginia Journal of International Law* 51: 785–823

Claes E, Duff A and Gutwirth S (eds.) (2006) *Privacy and the Criminal Law*. Intersentia, Antwerpen, Oxford

Colby TB (2003) Beyond the multiple punishment problem: Punitive damages as punishment for individual, private wrongs. *Minnesota Law Review* 87: 583–678

Conley ND (1987) An economic approach to patent damages. *American Intellectual Property Law Quarterly Journal* 15: 354–390

Conner K and Rumelt RP (1991) Software piracy: An analysis of protection strategies. *Management Science* 37: 125–139

Cordray ML (1994) GATT v. WIPO. *Journal of the Patent and Trademark Office Society* 76: 121–143

Cornish W and Llewelyn D (2005) The enforcement of patent rights in the United Kingdom. In: Health C and Petit L (eds.) *Patent Enforcement Worldwide: A Survey of 15 Countries, Writings in Honour of Dieter Stauder*. Hart Publishing, Oxford and Portland, OR, pp 87–108

Cornish WR, Drexl J, Hilty R and Kur A (2003) Procedures and remedies for enforcing IPRs: The European Commission's proposed directive. *European Intellectual Property Review* 25: 447–449

Correa C (2007) *Trade Related Aspects of Intellectual Property Rights: A Commentary on the TRIPS Agreement*. Oxford University Press, Oxford

(2009) The push for stronger enforcement rules: Implications for developing countries. In: *The Global Debate on the Enforcement of Intellectual Property Rights and Developing Countries. International Centre for Trade and Sustainable Development*, Issue Paper no. 22, Geneva, pp 27–80

(2012) Anti-counterfeiting: A Trojan horse for expanding intellectual property protection in developing countries? In: Geiger C (ed.) *Criminal Enforcement of Intellectual Property: A Handbook of Contemporary Research*. Edward Elgar, Cheltenham, UK and Northampton, MA, pp 59–74

Correa C, Velasquez G and Seuba X (2012) *IPR, R&D, Human Rights and Access to Medicines: An Annotated Bibliography*. South Centre, Geneva

Cot J-P (1972) *International Conciliation*. Europa Publications Ltd

Cotter TF (2013) *Comparative Patent Remedies, A Legal and Economic Analysis*. Oxford University Press, Oxford

Cottier T and Foltea M (2012) Global governance in intellectual property protection: Does the decision-making forum matter? *The WIPO Journal* 3: 139–165

Coury L (2003) C'est what? Saisie! A comparison of patent infringement remedies among the G7 economic nations. *Fordham Intellectual Property Media and Entertainment Law Journal* 13: 1101–1159

Cowan TA (1971) Law without force. *California Law Review* 59: 683–694

Creel TL and Praiss DM (1990) The revolution in preliminary injunctions against patent infringement. *John Marshall Law Review* 24: 225–262

Creemers R (2009) The effects of World Trade Organization case DS362 on audiovisual media piracy in China. *EIPR* 31: 568–576

Cullet P (2004) Intellectual property rights and food security in the South. *The Journal of World Intellectual Property* 7: 261–286

D'Erme R, Geiger C, Grosse-Ruse Kahn H, Heinze C, Jaeger T, Matulionyte R and Metzger A (2013) The impact of the Anti-Counterfeiting Trade Agreement on the legal framework for IP enforcement in the European Union. In: Geiger C (ed.) *Constructing European Intellectual Property: Achievements and New Perspectives*. Edward Elgar, Cheltenham, UK and Northampton, MA, pp 394–408

Damrosch LF (1997) Enforcing international law through non-forcible measures. *Recuil des Cours* 9: 19–24

Dasgupta P (2011) Modern Economics and the Idea of Citizenship. In: Pontifical Council for Justice and Peace (ed.) *Social and Ethical Aspects of Economics*. Pontifical Council for Justice and Peace, Vatican City, pp 47–58

Davey WJ (2000) WTO dispute settlement: Segregating the useful political aspects and avoiding 'over-legalization'. In: Bronckers M and Quick R (eds.) *New Directions in International Economic Law: Essays in Honour of John H. Jackson*. Kluwer Law International, The Hague, pp 291–309

(2005) The WTO Dispute Settlement System: The first ten years. *Journal of International Economic Law* 8: 17–50

Davies G (2nd ed.) (2002) *Copyright and the Public Interest*. Sweet and Maxwell, London

De Werra J (2001) The legal system of technological protection measures under the WIPO Treaties, the DMCA, the European Union Directives and other national laws (Japan, Australia). *RIDA* 189: 66–213

DeLaurell R (2012) The Anti-Counterfeiting Trade Agreement of 2010: Two problems and one unanswered question. *Global Business Law Review* 2: 175–192

Dimitrov MK (2009) *Piracy and the State: The Politics of Intellectual Property Rights in China*. Cambridge University Press, Cambridge

Dinwoodie G (2006a) Some remarks on the limits of harmonization. *John Marshall Review of Intellectual Property Law* 5: 596–604

(2006b) The international intellectual property law system: New actors, new institutions, new sources. *Marquette Intellectual Property Law Review* 10: 205–214

Dinwoodie G and Dreyfuss RC (2009) Designing a global intellectual property system responsive to change: The WTO, WIPO, and beyond. *Houston Law Review* 46: 1187–1234

Dinwoodie G, Hennessey WO and Perlmutter S (2001) *International Intellectual Property Law and Policy*. Lexis Nexis, Newark/San Francisco/Charlottesville

Diver CS (1983) The Optimal Precision of Administrative Rules. *The Yale Law Journal* 93: 65–109

Doane M (1994) TRIPs and international intellectual property protection in an age of advancing technology. *American University International Law Review* 9: 465–497

Dobbs DB (1989) Ending punishment in 'punitive' damages: Deterrence–measured remedies. *Alabama Law Review* 40: 831–917

Drahos P (1999) The universality of intellectual property rights: Origins and development. In: *WIPO, Intellectual Property Rights and Human Rights*. WIPO, Geneva, pp 13–41

(2001) *A Philosophy of Intellectual Property*. Aldershot, Ashgate

(2007) Weaving webs of influence: The United States, Free Trade Agreements and dispute resolution. *Journal of World Trade* 41: 191–210

Dratler J (2008) eBay's practical effect: Two differing visions. *Akon Intellectual Property Journal* 2: 35–55

Dreier T (1996) TRIPS and the enforcement of intellectual property rights. In: Beier FK and Schriker G (eds.) *From GATT to TRIPS: The Agreement on Trade-Related Aspects of Intellectual Property Rights.* Max Planck Institute for Foreign and International Patent, Copyright and Competition Law, Munich, pp 248–277

Dreyfuss RC (2004) TRIPS-Round II: Should users strike back? *University of Chicago Law Review* 71: 21–35

Dreyfuss RC and Lowenfeld AF (1997) Two achievements of the Uruguay Round: Putting TRIPS and dispute settlement together. *Virginia Journal of International Law* 37: 275–335

Dubuisson F (2012) Les implications juridiques et économiques du téléchargement d'œuvres sur Internet: Les clés du débat. In: Doutrelepont C, Dubuisson F and Strowel A (eds.)

Le Téléchargement D'œuvres sur Internet: Perspectives en Droits Belge, Français, Européen et International. Larcier, Bruxelles, pp 19–45

Duchêne A and Serfes K (2012) Patent settlements as a barrier to entry. *Journal of Economics and Management Strategy* 21: 399–429

Duft BJ (1983) Patent preliminary injunctions and the United States Court of Appeals for the Federal Circuit. *Journal of the Patent Office Society* 65: 131

Dupuy PM (1999) The danger of fragmentation or unification of the international law system and the International Court of Justice. *New York University Journal of International Law and Politics* 31: 791–807

Dusollier S (2003) Fair use by design in the European copyright directive of 2001. *Communications of the ACM* 46: 51–55

Eissen MA (1993) The principle of proportionality in the case-law of the European Court of Human Rights. In: Macdonald RStJ, Matscher F and Petzold H (eds.) *The European System for the Protection of Human Rights*. Martinus Nijhoff Publishers, Dordrecht/Boston/London, pp 125–146

Ellis R (2011) Conflicts at the intersection of ACTA and human rights: How the Anti-Counterfeiting Trade Agreement violates the right to take part in cultural life. *American University Intellectual Property Brief* 2: 64–71

Elsig M and Pollack MA (2012) Agents, trustees, and international courts: The politics of judicial appointment at the World Trade Organization. *European Journal of International Relations* 0: 1–25

Emmert F (1990) Intellectual property in the Uruguay Round-negotiating strategies of the Western industrialized countries. *Michigan Journal of International Law* 11: 1317–1399

Engel C and Kleine M (2013) Who is afraid of pirates? An experiment on the deterrence of innovation by imitation, *Research Policy* 44(1) DOI: 10.2139/ssrn.2269635

Felgueroso J (2002) TRIPS and the Dispute Settlement Understanding: The first six years. *AIPLA Quarterly Journal* 30: 165–231

Ficsor M (2002) The Law of Copyright and the Internet, *The 1996 WIPO Treaties, Their Interpretation and Implementation*. Oxford University Press, Oxford

(2005) Copyright in the Digital Environment: The WIPO Copyright Treaty (WCT) and the WIPO Performance and Phonograms Treaty (WPPT). WIPO/CR/KRT/05/7

(2010) Protection of 'DRM' under the 'WIPO Internet Treaties': Interpretation, implementation and application. In: Stamadoudi I (ed.) *Copyright Enforcement and the Internet*. Kluwer Law International, The Netherlands, pp 257–302

Finger JM and Schuler P (1999) Implementation of the Uruguay Round Commitments: The development challenge. *World Bank Development Research Group, Policy Research*, Working Paper no. 2215

Fink C (2009a) Enforcing intellectual property rights: An economic perspective. In: *The Global Debate on the Enforcement of Intellectual Property Rights and Developing Countries. International Centre for Trade and Sustainable Development*, Issue Paper no. 22, Geneva, pp 1–26

(2009b) Enforcing Intellectual Property Rights: An Economic Prospective. WIPO Enforcement Committee, WIPO/ACE/5/6

(2011) Intellectual property rights. In: Chauffour J-P and Maur J-C (eds.) *Preferential Trade Agreement Policies for Development: A Handbook*. World Bank, Washington, DC, pp 387–405

Firth A (2008) 'Holding the line': The relationship between the public interest and remedies granted or refused, be it for breach of confidence or copyright. In: Torremans P (ed.)

Intellectual Property and Human Rights: Enhanced Edition of Copyright and Human Rights. Kluwer Law International, The Netherlands, pp 421–446

Footer ME (2010) The (re)turn to soft law in reconciliating the antinomies in WTO law. *Melbourne Journal of International Law* 11: 241–276

Forzley M (2003) *Counterfeit Goods and the Public's Health and Safety*. International Intellectual Property Institute, Washington, DC

Foster JJ (1986) The preliminary injunction – a 'new' and potent weapon in patent litigation. *Journal of the Patent and Trademark Office Society* 68: 281

Franck TM (1988) Legitimacy in the international system. *American Journal of International Law* 82: 705–759

Fukunaga Y (2008) Enforcing TRIPS: Challenges arising from adjudicating minimum standards agreements. *Berkeley Technology Law Journal* 23: 867–931

Galligan DG (1996) *The hearing principle*. In: Galligan DG (author) *Due Process and Fair Procedures, A Study of Administrative Procedures*. Oxford University Press, Oxford, pp 348–391

Gao C (2000) A Comparison between Pre-Trial Remedies for Trade Mark Infringements in Canada and China (unpublished thesis). www.collectionscanada.gc.ca/obj/s4/f2/dsk3/ftp04/MQ57541.pdf (last accessed August 2015)

Garner BA (7th ed.) (1999) *Black's Law Dictionary*. West Publishing Co., Saint Paul

Geiger C (2007) The role of the three-step test in the adaptation of copyright law to the information society. *e-Copyright Bulletin*, UNESCO, January–March

(2010) Of ACTA, 'pirates' and organized criminality – How 'criminal' should the enforcement of intellectual property be? *IIC* 41: 629–631

(2012a) Introduction. In: Geiger C (ed.) *Criminal Enforcement of Intellectual Property: A Handbook of Contemporary Research*. Edward Elgar, Cheltenham, UK and Northampton, MA, pp 1–8

(2012b) The Anti-Counterfeiting Trade Agreement and criminal enforcement of intellectual property: What consequences for the European Union? In: Rosen J (ed.) *IP Rights at the Crossroads of Trade*. Edward Elgar, Cheltenham UK and Northampton, MA, pp 167–181

(2014a) Challenges for the enforcement of copyright in the online world: Time for a new approach. In: Torremans P (ed.) *Research Handbook on the Cross-Border Enforcement of Intellectual Property*. Edward Elgar, Cheltenham, UK and Northampton, MA, pp 704–730

(2014b) The rise of criminal enforcement of intellectual property rights . . . and its failure in the context of copyright infringements on the Internet. In: Frankel S and Gervais D (eds.) *The Evolution and Equilibrium of Copyright in the Digital Age*. Cambridge University Press, Cambridge, pp 113–142

(2015a) Assessing the implications of ACTA for the European Union: Legitimate aim but wrong means. In: Roffe P and Seuba X (eds.) *The ACTA and the Plurilateral Enforcement Agenda: Genesis and Aftermath*. Cambridge University Press, Cambridge, pp 313–328

(2015b) Copyright as an access right, securing cultural participation through the protection of creators' interests. *Max Planck Institute for Innovation and Competition Research Paper No. 15–07*

(2015c) The Anti-Counterfeiting Trade Agreement (ACTA) and beyond: Towards a differentiated approach to criminal enforcement of intellectual property rights at global level. In: Roffe P and Seuba X (eds.) *The ACTA and the Plurilateral Enforcement Agenda: Genesis and Aftermath*. Cambridge University Press, Cambridge, pp 100–114

(2016) Towards a Balanced International Legal Framework for Criminal Enforcement of Intellectual Property Rights. In: Ullrich H *et al.* (eds.) *TRIPS plus 20. From Trade Rules to Market Principles*. Springer, Berlin, pp 645–679

Geiger C and Izyumenko E (2017a) Intellectual property in front of the European Court of Human Rights. In: Geiger C, Nard C and Seuba X (eds.) *Intellectual Property and the Judiciary*. Edward Elgar, Cheltenham, UK and Northampton, MA (forthcoming)

(2017b) Human Rights and Intellectual Property in European Judicial Practice. Edward Elgar, Cheltenham, UK and Northampton, MA (forthcoming)

Geist M (2003) Why we must stand on guard over copyright. www.michaelgeist.ca/2003/10/why-we-must-stand-on-guard-over-copyright/ (last accessed May 2015)

(2010a) The case for flexibility in implementing the WIPO Internet treaties: An examination of the anti-circumvention requirements: In: Geist M (ed.) *From 'Radical Extremism' to 'Balanced Copyright': Canadian Copyright and the Digital Agenda*. Irwin Law, Toronto, pp 204–246

(2012) The trouble with ACTA: An analysis of the Anti-Counterfeiting Trade Agreement. In: EU DG for External Policies (ed.) Workshop: The Anti-Counterfeiting Trade Agreement (ACTA). EXPO/B/INTA/FWC/2009–01/Lot7/25, pp 25–45

(2015) Slaying the ACTA myths. In: Roffe P and Seuba X (eds.) *The ACTA and the Plurilateral Enforcement Agenda: Genesis and Aftermath*. Cambridge University Press, Cambridge, pp 345–356

Genovesi LM (2013) La aplicación industrial y la utilidad como requisitos de patentabilidad: diferencias y semejanzas. Consecuencias de su aplicación. In: Seuba X (ed.) *Propiedad Intelectual, Competencia y Aspectos Regulatorios del Medicamento*. PUJ-ICTSD, Bogotá, pp 331–382

Genovesi M and Kors J (2005) Medidas cautelares. In: Kors J (ed.) *Patentes de Invención: Diez Años de Jurisprudencia*. La Ley, Buenos Aires, pp 153–181

Georgiev D and Van der Borght K (2006) *Reform and Development of the WTO Dispute Settlement System*. Cameron May, London

Gergen MP *et al.* (2012) The Supreme Court's accidental revolution? The test for permanent injunctions. *Columbia Law Review* 112: 203–249

Gerhardsen TIS (2006) WTO TRIPS Council stumbles over inclusion of enforcement. www.ip-watch.org/2006/10/27/wto-trips-council-stumbles-over-inclusion-of-enforcement/ (last accessed May 2015)

Gervais D (2006) The international legal framework of border measures in the fight against counterfeiting and piracy. In: Vrins O and Schneider M (eds.) *Enforcement of Intellectual Property Rights Through Border Measures*. Oxford University Press, Oxford, pp 37–63

(2009a) China – Measures affecting the protection and enforcement of intellectual property rights. *American Journal of International Law* 103: 549–554

(2009b) Of clusters and assumptions: Innovation as part of a full TRIPS implementation. *Fordham Law Review* 77: 2353–2377

(2012) Criminal enforcement in the US and Canada. In: Geiger C (ed.) *Criminal Enforcement of Intellectual Property: A Handbook of Contemporary Research*. Edward Elgar, Cheltenham, UK and Northampton, MA, pp 269–285

(2nd ed.) (2003) *The TRIPS Agreement: Drafting History and Analysis*. Sweet and Maxwell, London

(3rd ed.) (2008) *The TRIPS Agreement: Drafting History and Analysis*. Sweet and Maxwell, London

Giblin R (2014) Evaluating graduated response. *Columbia Journal of Law and the Arts* 37: 147–209

Gibson J (2012) The Directive proposal on criminal sanctions. In: Geiger C (ed.) *Criminal Enforcement of Intellectual Property: A Handbook of Contemporary Research*. Edward Elgar, Cheltenham, UK and Northampton, MA, pp 245–266

Gielen C (2002) Netherlands: Procedural matters – Preliminary ruling of ECJ re duration of provisional injunctive measures in TRIPS Member States. EIPR 24: N5 (case comment)

Global Options (2003) *An Analysis of Terrorist Threats to the American Medicine Supply*. Signature Book Printing, Gaithersburg

Godin PD (1996) Anton Piller orders in an age of scepticism: Charter application and other safeguards for judicially-ordered searches. *University of Toronto Faculty of Law Review* 54: 107–148

Govaere I (2011) With eyes wide shut: The EC strategy to enforce intellectual property rights abroad. In: Dashwood A and Maresceau M (eds.) *Law and Practice of EU External Relations, Salient Features of a Changing Landscape*. Cambridge University Press, Cambridge, pp. 401–428

Gracz K (2013) On the role of copyright protection in the information society, Anti – ACTA protests in Poland as a lesson in participatory democracy. *Journal of Intellectual Property, Information Technology, and E-Commerce Law* 4: 21–35

Greenleaf G *et al.* (2007) Not a fair trade: Australia's TPM protection and AUSFTA-inspired reforms. University of New South Wales Faculty of Law Research Series, Paper no. 19, University of New South Wales. http://law.bepress.com/cgi/viewcontent.cgi?article=1021&context=unswwps-flrps (last accessed May 2015)

Griem JM and Brook A (2008) eBay and preliminary injunctions. *The National Law Journal*. https://www.milbank.com/images/content/9/9/993/051208-NLJ-Jack-Griem.pdf (last accessed April 2017)

Griffiths J (2012) Criminal liability for intellectual property infringement in Europe: The role of fundamental rights. In: Geiger C (ed.) *Criminal Enforcement of Intellectual Property: A Handbook of Contemporary Research*. Edward Elgar, Cheltenham, UK and Northampton, MA, pp 191–212

(2015) Enforcement of intellectual property rights and the rights to a fair trail. In: Geiger C (ed.) *Research Handbook on Human Rights and Intellectual Property*. Edward Elgar, Cheltenham, UK / Northampton, MA, pp 438–454

Grosse Ruse-Khan H (2008a) A comparative analysis of policy space in WTO law. Max Planck Institute for Intellectual Property, Competition and Tax Law Research Paper Series No. 02–02 (reproduced in: Kur A (ed.) (2011) *Intellectual Property Rights in a Fair World Trade System: Proposals for Reform of TRIPS*. Edward Elgar, Cheltenham, UK and Northampton, MA, pp 167–207)

(2008b) A pirate of the Caribbean? The attractions of suspending TRIPS obligations. *Journal of International Economic Law* 11: 313–364

(2009) Re-delineation of the role of stakeholders: IP enforcement beyond exclusive rights. In: Xuan L and Correa C (eds.) *Intellectual Property Enforcement: International Perspectives*. Edward Elgar, Cheltenham, UK and Northampton, MA, pp 43–61

(2010) China – Intellectual property rights: Implications for the TRIPS-plus border measures. *The Journal of World Intellectual Property* 13: 620–638

(2011) A trade agreement creating barriers to international trade?: ACTA border measures and goods in transit. *American University International Law Review* 26: 645–726

(2012) Criminal enforcement and international IP law. In: Geiger C (ed.) *Criminal Enforcement of Intellectual Property: A Handbook of Contemporary Research*. Edward Elgar, Cheltenham, UK and Northampton, MA, pp 171–190

(2015) Legal framework for enforcement: Border measures. In: Roffe P and Seuba X (eds.) *The ACTA and the Plurilateral Enforcement Agenda: Genesis and Aftermath*. Cambridge University Press, Cambridge, pp 88–99

Grosse Ruse-Khan H and Jaeger T (2009) Policing patents worldwide? EC border measures against transiting generic drugs under EC and WTO intellectual property regimes. *International Review of Intellectual Property and Competition Law* 40: 502–538

Grumbles E, Hughey R and Perera S (2009) The Three Year Anniversary of eBay v. MercExchange: A Statistical Analysis of Permanent Injunctions. *Intellectual Property Today*, November: 25–29

Gunn TJ (2005) Deconstructing proportionality in limitations analysis. *Emory International Law Review* 19: 465–498

Guo J (2007) Protection and enforcement of intellectual property rights: A WTO case against China. *Italian Intellectual Property Yearbook* 2007: 33–68

Gupta A (2009) Border enforcement of intellectual property rights in India: Recent developments. *Trade, Law and Development* 1: 192–221

Gursey J (1995) *Copyright Theft*. Aslib/Gower Publishing, London

Gutowski RJ (1999) The marriage of intellectual property and international trade in the TRIPS Agreement: Strange bedfellow or a match made in Heaven? *Buffalo Law Review* 47: 713–762

Hailer DB (1981) Granting preliminary injunctions against dealership terminations in anti-trust action. *Virginia Law Review* 67: 1395–1422

Hardy T (2002) Criminal copyright infringement. *William and Mary Bill of Rights Journal* 11: 305–341

Hargreaves I (2011) Digital Opportunity: A Review of Intellectual Property and Growth: An Independent Report. www.ipo.gov.uk/ipreview-finalreport.pdf (last accessed April 2015)

Harms L (2007) The enforcement of intellectual property rights by means of criminal sanctions: An assessment. *WIPO Advisory Committee on Enforcement*. WIPO/ACE/4/3

Harris DP (2008) The honeymoon is over: The U.S.-China WTO intellectual property complaint. *Fordham International Law Journal* 32: 96–187

Hart HLA (2nd ed.) (1997) *The Concept of Law*. Oxford University Press, Oxford

Hathaway O and Shapiro SJ (2011) Outcasting: Enforcement in domestic and international law. *The Yale Law Journal* 121: 252–349

Haveman R (2003) The principle of legality. In: Haveman R, Kavran O and Nicholls JN (eds.) *Supranational Criminal Law: A System Sui Generis*. Intersentia, Antwerp, Oxford, New York, pp 39–78

Heath C (2005) Comparative overview and the TRIPS enforcement provisions. In: Heath C and Petit L (2nd ed.) (eds.) *Patent Enforcement Worldwide: A Survey of 15 Countries, Writings in Honour of Dieter Stauder*. Hart Publishing, Oxford and Portland, OR, pp 5–67

Heath C and Cotter TF (2015) Comparative overview and the TRIPS enforcement provisions. In: Heath C (ed.) *Patent Enforcement Worldwide, Writings in Honour of Dieter Stauder*. Hart Publishing, Oxford and Portland, OR, pp 3–53

Helfer L (2003) Human rights and intellectual property: Conflict or coexistence. *Minnesota Intellectual Property Review* 5: 47–61

(2004) Intellectual property rights in plant varieties: International legal regimes and policy options for national governments. *Food and Agriculture Organization of the United Nations*, FAO Legislative Study no. 85

Henckels C (2008) Overcoming jurisdictional isolationism at the WTO-FTA nexus: A potential approach for the WTO. *European Journal of International Law* 19: 571–599

Hestermeyer H (2007) *Human Rights and the WTO: The Case of Patents and Access to Medicines*. Oxford University Press, Oxford

Hilty R (2012) Economic, legal and social impacts of counterfeiting. In: Geiger C (ed.) *Criminal Enforcement of Intellectual Property: A Handbook of Contemporary Research*. Edward Elgar, Cheltenham, UK and Northampton, MA, pp 9–23

Hilty RM, Kur A and Peukert P (2006) Statement of the Max-Planck Institute for Intellectual Property, Competition and Tax Law on the Proposal for a Directive of the European Parliament and the Council on Criminal measures aimed at ensuring the enforcement of intellectual property rights. *IIC* 37: 970–977

Hinze G (2016) Brave new world, ten years later: Reviewing the impact of policy choices in the implementation of the WIPO Internet treaties' technological protection measure provisions. *Case Western Reserve Law Review* 57: 779–821

Holcombe RG (1997) A theory of public goods. *Review of Austrian Economics* 10: 1–22

Hong X (2009) An anatomical study of the United States versus China at the World Trade Organization on intellectual property enforcement. *European Intellectual Property Review* 31: 292–299

Hoorens S *et al.* (2012) Measuring IPR infringements in the internal market, development of a new approach to estimating the impact of infringements on sales. *Prepared for the European Commission, Internal Market and Services Directorate-General*. RAND Corporation, Brussels

Hudec R (1970) The GATT legal system: A diplomat's jurisprudence. *Journal of World Trade Law* 4: 615–665

Hudec R (1993) *Enforcing International Trade Law: The Evolution of the Modern GATT Legal System*. Butterworth Legal Publishers

(1998) The role of the GATT Secretariat in the evolution of the WTO Dispute Settlement procedure. In: Bhagwati J and Hirsch M (eds.) *The Uruguay Round and Beyond: Essays in Honour of Arthur Dunkel*. Springer, Berlin, pp 101–121

(1999) The new dispute settlement procedure: An overview of the first three years. *Minnesota Journal of Global Trade* 8: 1–53

Hudson B (2006) Secrets of the self: Punishment and the right to privacy. In: Claes E, Duff A and Gutwirth S (eds.) *Privacy and the Criminal Law*. Intersentia, Antwerpen, Oxford, pp 137–161

Hui KL and Png I (2013) Piracy and the legitimate demand for recorded music. *Contributions to Economic Analysis and Policy* 2: 1–25

Husovec M and Peguera M (2015) Much ado about little: Privately litigated Internet disconnection injunctions. *IIC* 46: 10–37

Huygen A *et al.* (2009) *Ups and downs: Economic and cultural effects of file sharing on music, film and games*. Ministers of Education, Culture and Science, Economic Affairs and Justice, The Netherlands

Iancu A and Nichols WJ (2007) Balancing the four factors in permanent injunction decisions: A review of post-eBay case law. *Journal of the Patent and Trademark Office Society* 89: 395

ICTSD (2009) Brazil Slams EU for Seizure of Generic Drugs. *Bridges* 13. www.ictsd.org/bridges-news/bridges/news/brazil-slams-eu-for-seizure-of-generic-drugs (last accessed June 2015)

Jackson JH (1996) Appraising the launch and functioning of the WTO. *German Yearbook of International Law* 39: 20–41

(1998a) *Designing and implementing effective dispute settlement procedures: WTO Dispute Settlement*, appraisal and prospects. In: Krueger AO (ed.) *The WTO as an International Organization*. The University of Chicago Press, Chicago and London, pp 161–180

(1998b) *The World Trade Organization: Constitution and Jurisprudence*. Royal Institute of International Affairs, London

Jacot-Guillarmod O (1993) Rights related to good administration of justice (Article 6). In: Macdonald RSTJ, Matscher F and Petzold H (eds.) *The European System for the Protection of Human Rights*. Martinus Nijhoff Publishers, Dordrecht/Boston/London, pp 381–404

Jaeger T, Grosse Ruse-Khan H, Drexl J and Hilty R (2010) Statement of the Max Planck Institute for Intellectual Property, Competition and Tax Law on the review of the EU legislation on customs enforcement of intellectual property rights. Max Planck Institute for Intellectual Property, Competition and Tax Law Research Paper No. 10–08

Jansen N and Rademacher J (2009) Punitive damages in Germany. In: Koziol H and Wilcox V (eds.) *Punitive Damages: Common Law and Civil Law Perspectives*. Springer, Wien, New York, pp 75–86

Jenks CW (1953) Conflict of law-making treaties. *British Yearbook of International Law* 30: 401–453

Jennings R and Watts A (9th ed.) (eds.) (1992) *Oppenheim's International Law*. Longman, London

Jiam H (2015) Fee-shifting and octane: An empirical approach toward understanding 'exceptional'. *Berkeley Technology Law Journal* 30: 612–644

Jimenez H, Martin B and Palao I (2013) Observatorio de Piratería y Hábitos de Consumo de Contenidos Digitales. Gfk. www.cedro.org/docs/default-source/textos-de-interés/observatorio-pirateria2013.pdf?sfvrsn=6 (last accessed April 2015)

Jonsén J and Söllner S (2007) The 'breakthrough' of the right to food: The meaning of General Comment no. 12 and the Voluntary Guidelines for the interpretation of the human right to food. *Max Planck Yearbook of United Nations Law* 11: 391–415

Judge E and Al-Sharieh S (2012) Join the club: The implications of the Anti-Counterfeiting Trade Agreement's enforcement measures for Canadian copyright law. *Alberta Law Review* 49: 677–744

Kahn-Freund O (1974) On uses and misuses of comparative law. *The Modern Law Review* 37: 1–27

Kalbfus B and Wehlau A (2012) The conflict between ex parte injunctions and the right to be heard: Protective letters at European level as a possible solution. *European Intellectual Property Review* 34: 410–415

Kaminski M (2011) An overview and the evolution of the Anti-Counterfeiting Trade Agreement. *Albany Law Journal of Science and Technology* 21: 385–444

(2014) Copyright crime and punishment: The First Amendment's proportionality problem. *Maryland Law Review* 73: 587–634

Kamperman Sanders A (2015) Provisions on civil enforcement – Section 2 of ACTA. In: Roffe P and Seuba X (eds.) *The ACTA and the Plurilateral Enforcement Agenda: Genesis and Aftermath*. Cambridge University Press, Cambridge, pp 80–87

Karaganis J (ed.) (2011) *Media Piracy in Emerging Economies*. Social Science Research Council, New York

Karaganis J and Renkema L (2013) Copy culture in the US and Germany. *The American Assembly*, Columbia University, New York

Kelsen H (1967) *Pure Theory of Law*. University of California Press, Berkeley

Keplinger JM (2007) Enforcement of IP rights in the digital environment: The role of the World Intellectual Property Organization. *Gewerblicher Rechtsschutz und Urheberrecht, Internationaler Teil* 56: 648–649

Kleinfeld J (2011) Enforcement and the concept of law. *The Yale Law Journal Online* 121: 293

Koh H (1997) Why do nations obey international law? *The Yale Law Journal* 106: 2599–2656

Korff D and Brown I (2011) Opinion on the compatibility of the Anti-Counterfeiting Trade Agreement (ACTA) with the European Convention on Human Rights and the EU Charter of Fundamental Rights. www.greens-efa.eu/fileadmin/dam/Documents/Studies/ACTA_fundamental_rights_assessment.pdf (last accessed November 2016)

Koziol H (2008) Punitive damages – A European perspective. *Louisiana Law Review* 68: 741–764

Kress C (2010) Nulla poena nullum crime sine lege. In: *Max Plank Encyclopedia of Public International Law*. www.uni-koeln.de/jur-fak/kress/NullumCrimen24082010.pdf (last accessed September 2015)

Kühnen T (author) and Peterreins F (tr.) (7th ed.) (2015) *Patent Litigation Proceedings in Germany: A Handbook for Practitioners*. Carl Heymanns Verlag, Cologne, pp. 564–605

Kuipers G and Lamme O (2013) How do I stop goods in transit? *The Netherlands. Managing Intellectual Property* March: 53

Kuipers G *et al.* (2009) Netherlands, Report Q208, border measures and other means of customs intervention against infringers. www.aippi.nl/uploads/Q208%20NL%201.PDF (last accessed June 2015)

Kumar S (2009) Freedom of transit and trade in generic pharmaceuticals: An analysis of the EU border enforcement law and the international intellectual property regime. *EIPR* 31

(2010) International trade, public health, and intellectual property maximalism: The case of European border enforcement and trade in generic pharmaceuticals. *Global Trade and Customs Journal* 5: 155–169

Kur A (2004) The enforcement directive – Rough start, happy landing? *IIC* 35: 821–830

Kur A and Grosse Ruse-Khan H (2008) Enough is enough: The notion of binding ceilings in international intellectual property protection. Max Planck Institute for Intellectual Property, Competition and Tax Law Research Paper Series no. 09–01

Kur A and Grosse Ruse-Khan H (2011) Enough is enough: The notion of binding ceilings in international intellectual property protection. In: Kur A (ed.) *Intellectual Property Rights in a Fair World Trade System*. Edward Elgar, Cheltenham, UK and Northampton, MA, pp 359–407

Kur A and Harhoff D (2014) Great data, nice tale, but what's the message? The OHIM/EPO Study on the economic relevance of IP-intensive industries in the EU. *IIC* 45: 617–620

Kwak K and Marceau G (2002) Overlaps and Conflicts of Jurisdiction between the WTO and RTAs. Conference on Regional Trade Agreements World Trade Organization. www.wto.org/english/tratop_e/region_e/sem_april02_e/marceau.pdf (last accessed May 2015)

Lamb S (2002) Nullum crimen, nulla poena sine lege in international criminal law. In: Cassese A, Gaeta P and Jones JRWD (eds.) *The Rome Statute of the International Criminal Court: A Commentary*. Oxford University Press, Oxford, pp 733–766

Lamond G (2001) Coercion and the nature of the law. *Legal Theory* 7: 35–57

Land M (2013) Toward an international law of the Internet. *Harvard International Law Journal* 54: 393–458

Landes WM and Posner RA (1979) Adjudication as a private good. *The Journal of Legal Studies* 8: 235–284

Lang A and Scott J (2009) The hidden world of WTO governance. *European Journal of International Law* 20: 575–614

Lanjouw JO and Lerner J (1996) Preliminary injunctive relief: Theory and evidence from patent litigation. *NBER Working Paper Series* 5689

(1997) The enforcement of intellectual property rights: A survey of the empirical literature. *NBER Working Paper Series* 6296

Lanjouw JO and Schankerman M (2001) Enforcing intellectual property rights. *NBER Working Paper Series* 8656

(2004) Protecting intellectual property rights: Are small firms handicapped? *The Journal of Law and Economics* 47: 45–74

Laycock D (2008) How remedies become a field: A history. *The Review of Litigation* 27: 161–267

Leathley C (2007) An institutional hierarchy to combat the fragmentation of international law: Has the ILC missed an opportunity? *New York University Journal of International Law and Politics* 40: 259–306

Lee E (2011) Measuring TRIPS compliance and defiance: The WTO compliance scorecard. *Journal of Intellectual Property Law* 18: 401–445

Lefranc D (2012) Historical perspective on criminal enforcement. In: Geiger C (ed.) *Criminal Enforcement of Intellectual Property: A Handbook of Contemporary Research*. Edward Elgar, Cheltenham, UK and Northampton, MA, pp 101–127

Legrand P (1997) The impossibility of 'legal transplants'. *Maastricht Journal of European and Comparative Law* 4: 111

Leichkis Y (2007) On fire ants and claim construction: An empirical study of the Eastern District Court of Texas as a preeminent forum for patent litigation. *Yale Journal of Law and Technology* 9: 195–233

Lemley M and Volokh E (1998) Freedom of speech and injunctions in intellectual property cases. *Duke Law Journal* 48: 147–242

Lerner J (1995) Patenting in the shadow of competitors. *The Journal of Law and Economics* 38: 463–496

Lewis OH (1993) The wild card that is the public interest: Putting a new face on the fourth preliminary injunction factor. *Texas Law Review* 72: 849

Lorcher T (2003) WTO dispute settlement and arbitration. *International Arbitration Law Review* 6: 203

Loughlan P (2007) 'You wouldn't steal a car': IP and the language of theft. *European Intellectual Property Review* 29: 401–405

Lowe V (1996) *Res judicata* and the rule of law in international arbitration. *African Journal of International and Comparative Law* 8: 38–50

(1999) Overlapping jurisdiction in international tribunals. *Australian Yearbook of International Law* 20: 191–204

(2006) The law of unintended consequences: A perspective on the draft directive on criminal measures to enforce intellectual property rights. *The Criminal Lawyer* 163: 3

Lowenfeld AF (1994) Remedies along with rights: Institutional reform in the new GATT. *American Journal of International Law* 88: 477–488

Malbon J, Lawson C and Davison M (2014) *The WTO Agreement on Trade-Related Aspects of Intellectual Property Rights: A Commentary*. Edward Elgar, Cheltenham, UK and Northampton, MA

Manta ID (2011) The puzzle of criminal sanctions for intellectual property infringement. *Harvard Journal of Law and Technology* 24: 469–518

Manzo ED (2007) Injunctions in patent cases after eBay. *The John Marshall Review in Intellectual Property Law* 7: 44–96

Marceau G (2001) Conflicts of norms and conflicts of jurisdictions: The relationship between the WTO Agreement and MEA's and other treaties. *Journal of World Trade* 35: 1081–1131

Marshall H (2005) The enforcement of patent rights in Germany. In: Health C and Petit L (eds.) *Patent Enforcement Worldwide: A Survey of 15 Countries, Writings in Honour of Dieter Stauder*. Hart Publishing, Oxford and Portland, OR, pp 109–138

Massaguer J (1989) *Los efectos de la patente en el comercio internacional*. Librería Bosch, Barcelona

Matsushita M, Schoenbaum TJ and Mavroidis P (2nd ed.) (2006) *The World Trade Organization: Law, Practice and Policy*. Oxford University Press, Oxford

Mattei H (2003) A theory of imperial law: A study on U.S. hegemony and the Latin resistance. *Indiana Journal of Global Legal Studies* 10: 383–448

Matthews D (2008) The fight against counterfeiting and piracy in the bilateral trade agreements of the EU. Briefing Paper, European Parliament, EXPO/B/INTA/2008/28

Matthews D and Zikovska P (2013) The rise and fall of the Anti-Counterfeiting Trade Agreement (ACTA): Lessons for the European Union. *IIC* 44: 626–655

Matulionyte R (2011) ACTA' s digital chapter: Remaining concerns and what can be done. *Queen Mary Journal of Intellectual Property* 1: 248–271

(2015) ACTA's digital chapter: Remaining concerns and what can be done. In: Roffe P and Seuba X (eds.) *The ACTA and the Plurilateral Enforcement Agenda: Genesis and Aftermath*. Cambridge University Press, Cambridge, pp 115–142

Max Planck Institute for Innovation and Competition (2013) Principles for Intellectual Property Provisions in Bilateral and Regional Agreements. www.ip.mpg.de/fileadmin/ipmpg/content/forschung_aktuell/06_principles_for_intellectua/principles_for_ip_provisions_in_bilateral_and_regional_agreements_final1.pdf (last accessed May 2015) (reproduced in: *IIC* 44: 878–873)

May C (2007) *The World Intellectual Property Organization: Resurgence and the Development Agenda*. Routledge, London

Mazzeschi R (2002) Book Review of Enzo Cannizzaro. *Il principio della proporzionalità nell'ordinamento internazionale*. *European Journal of International Law* 13: 1031–1036

McGovern E (3rd ed.) (1995) *International Trade Regulation*. Globefield Press, Exeter

McInnes MP (1987–1988) The right to silence in the presence of Anton Piller: A question of self incrimination. *Alberta Law Review* XXVI: 332–344

McLachlan C (2005) The principle of systemic integration and Article 31(3)(c) of Vienna Convention. *International and Comparative Law Quarterly* 54: 279–320

McLeod R (2006) Injunction junction: Remembering the proper function and form of equitable relief in trademark law. *Duke Law and Technology Review* 13: 1–22

McManis C (2009) Human rights as a constraint on intellectual property rights: The case of patent and plant variety protection rights, genetic resources and traditional knowledge. In: Grosheide W (ed.) *Intellectual Property and Human Rights: A Paradox*. Edward Elgar, Cheltenham, UK and Northampton, MA, pp 272–299

McManis CR and Pelletier JS (2012) Two tales of a treaty revisited: The proposed Anti-Counterfeiting Trade Agreement (ACTA). In: Rosén J (ed.) *Intellectual Property at the Crossroads of Trade*. Edward Elgar, Cheltenham, UK and Northampton, MA, pp 182–236

McNelis N (2003) What obligations are created by World Trade Organization Dispute Settlement Reports? *Journal of World Trade* 37: 647–672

Mercurio B (2012) Beyond the text: The significance of the Anti-Counterfeiting Trade Agreement. *Journal of International Economic Law* 15: 361–390

(2015) ACTA: Anatomy of a failed agreement. In: Roffe P and Seuba X (eds.) *The ACTA and the Plurilateral Enforcement Agenda: Genesis and Aftermath*. Cambridge University Press, Cambridge, pp 329–337

Merrills JG (2006) The means of dispute settlement. In: Evans M (2nd ed.) (ed.) *International Law*. Oxford University Press, Oxford, pp 533–560

(4th ed.) (2005) *International Dispute Settlement*. Cambridge University Press, Cambridge

Messen J and Meurer M (2012) The direct costs from NPE disputes. Boston University School of Law, Law and Economics Research Paper no. 12–34

Mesulam S (2004) Collective rewards and limited punishment: Solving the punitive damages dilemma with class. *Columbia Law Review* 104: 1114–1149

Metcalf LC (1987) Preliminary injunctions and their availability: How to defend against the early injunction. *AIPLA Quarterly Journal* 15: 104

Metzger A (2010) A primer on ACTA: What Europeans should fear about the Anti-Counterfeiting Trade Agreement. *Journal of Intellectual Property, Information Technology and E-Commerce Law* 1: 109–116

Meurer MJ (1989) The settlement of patent litigation. *The Rand Journal of Economics* 20: 77–91

Meyer CM (1983) Dataphase Systems, Inc. v. C.L. Systems, Inc.: Preliminary injunctions. Civil Procedure 830–849

Micara AG (2012) TRIPS-plus border measures and access to medicines. *Journal of World Intellectual Property* 15: 73–101

Montesquieu CdS (2001) *The Spirit of Laws*. Batoche Books, Kitchener, 2001

Moohr GS (2002) The problematic role of criminal law in regulating use of information: the case of the Economic Espionage Act. *North Carolina Law Review* 80: 853–921

Morin J-F and Gold ER (2014) An integrated model of legal transplantation: The diffusion of intellectual property law in developing countries. *International Studies Quarterly* 58: 781–792

Morris C (1931) Punitive damages in tort cases. *Harvard Law Review* 44: 1173–1194

Mota SA (2000) TRIPS-five years of disputes at the WTO. *Arizona Journal of International and Comparative Law* 17: 533–554

Muntañá Mora M (1993) A GATT with teeth: Law wins over politics in the resolution of international trade disputes. *Columbia Journal of Transnational Law* 31: 103–180

Murphy SD (1991) The ELSI case: An investment dispute at the International Court of Justice. *Yale Journal of International Law* 16: 391–452

Mursak Hermann R (2012) WHO negotiations to address medical R&D global gaps head deep into night. Intellectual Property Watch. www.ip-watch.org/2012/11/29/who-negotiations-to-address-medical-rd-global-gaps-head-deep-into-night/ (last accessed April 2015)

Mylly T (2012) Criminal enforcement and European Union law. In: Geiger C (ed.) *Criminal Enforcement of Intellectual Property: A Handbook of Contemporary Research*. Edward Elgar, Cheltenham, UK and Northampton, MA, pp 213–244

Nard C (3rd ed.) (2014) *The Law of Patents*. Wolters Kluwer, New York

Netanel NW (1996–1997) The next round: The impact of the WIPO Copyright Treaty on TRIPS Dispute Settlement. *Virginia Journal of International Law* 37: 441–498

Neuner R (1980) Injunctive relief available to the owners of patents and trademarks. *APLA Quarterly Journal* 8: 14

New W (2005) TRIPS Council issues still alive for WTO Ministerial. www.ip-watch.org/2005/10/28/trips-council-issues-still-alive-for-wto-ministerial/ (last accessed May 2015)

Nimmer D (1995) The end of copyright. *Vanderbilt Law Review* 48: 1385–1420

Nurton J (2013) EPO/OHIM study puts a value on European IP. *Managing Intellectual Property*. 30 September, available at www.managingip.com/Article/3260914/EPOOHIM-study-puts-a-value-on-European-IP.html (last accessed April 2017)

Ohly A (2012) Counterfeiting and consumer protection. In: Geiger C (ed.) *Criminal Enforcement of Intellectual Property: A Handbook of Contemporary Research*. Edward Elgar, Cheltenham, UK and Northampton, MA, pp 24–41

Okediji RL (2000) Toward an international fair use doctrine. *Columbia Journal of Transnational Law* 39: 75–176

(2002) TRIPS Dispute Settlement and the sources of (international) copyright law. *Journal of the Copyright Society of the USA* 49: 584–633

(2004) Development in the Information Age: Issues in the Regulation of Intellectual Property Rights, Computer Software and Electronic Commerce. ICTSD and UNCTAD, Issue Paper no. 9, Geneva

Opinion of European Academics on Anti-Counterfeiting Trade Agreement (2011). *Journal of Intellectual Property, Information Technology and E-Commerce Law* 2: 65–72

Oppenheim L (1905) *International Law*. Logmans, London

Orakhelashvili A (2007) The acts of the Security Council: Meaning and standards of review. *Max Planck Yearbook of United Nations Law* 11: 143–195

Otten A (1997) El Acuerdo sobre los ADPIC: Visión general. In: Iglesias Prada JL (ed.) *Los Derechos de la Propiedad Intelectual en la Organización Mundial del Comercio. El Acuerdo sobre los Aspectos de los Derechos de la Propiedad Intelectual Relacionados con el Comercio*. IDEI, Tomo I, Madrid, pp 21–44

(1998) Implementation of the TRIPS Agreement and prospects for its future development. *Journal of International Economic Law* 1: 523–536

Otten A and Wager H (1996) Compliance with TRIPS: The emerging world view. *Vanderbilt Journal of Transnational Law* 29: 391–414

Outterson K (2006) Counterfeit drugs: The good, the bad and the ugly. *Albany Law Journal of Science and Technology* 16: 526–543

(2009) Import safety rules should not hinder legitimate generic drug markets. *Boston University School of Law Working Paper no. 09–25*

Outterson K and Smith R (2006) Counterfeit drugs: The good, the bad and the ugly. *Albany Law Journal of Science and Technology* 16: 525–543

Parker RB (1974) A definition of privacy. In: Barendt E (ed.) (2001) *Privacy*. Ashgate, Darmouth

Pauwelyn J (2003) *Conflict of Norms in Public International Law. How WTO Law Relates to Other Rules of International Law*. Cambridge University Press, Cambridge

(2004a) Bridging fragmentation and unity: International law as a universe of interconnected islands. *Michigan Journal of International Law* 25: 903–927

(2004b) Going global, regional or both? Dispute settlement in the Southern African development Community (SADC) and overlaps with the WTO and other jurisdictions. *Minnesota Journal of Global Trade* 13: 231–304

(2005) The transformation of world trade. *Michigan Law Review* 104: 1–66

(2010) The dog that barked but didn't bite: 15 years of intellectual property disputes at the WTO. *Journal of International Dispute Settlement* 1: 389–429

Perkins D and Mills G (1996) Patent infringement and forum shopping in the European Union. *Fordham International Law Journal* 20: 549–601

Petersmann E-U (1997) Constitutionalism and international organizations. *Northwestern Journal of International Law and Business* 17: 398–469

(2006) Justice as conflict resolution: Proliferation, fragmentation, and decentralization of dispute settlement in international trade. *University of Pennsylvania Journal of International Economic Law* 27: 273–366

Petit L (2005) The enforcement of patent rights in France. In: Health C and Petit L (eds.) *Patent Enforcement Worldwide: A Survey of 15 Countries, Writings in Honour of Dieter Stauder*. Hart Publishing, Oxford and Portland, OR, pp 139–170

Pham N (2010) The Impact of Innovation and the Role of Intellectual Property Rights on US Productivity, Competitiveness, Jobs, Wages, and Exports. NDP Consulting. www.amchamchile.cl/sites/default/files/NDP_IP_Jobs_Study_Hi_Res.pdf (last accessed April 2015)

Piller C (2006) How piracy opens doors for Windows. *Los Angeles Times*. http://articles.latimes.com/print/2006/apr/09/business/fi-micropiracy9 (last accessed April 2015)

Pinyosinwat J (2007) A model of intellectual property rights enforcement for developing countries. *IIP Bulletin*. www.iip.or.jp/e/e_summary/pdf/detail2006/e18_19.pdf (last accessed April 2015)

Pires de Carvalho N (2002) *The TRIPS Regime of Patent Rights*. Kluwer Law International, The Hague

(2nd ed.) (2005) *The TRIPS Regime of Patent Rights*. Kluwer Law International, The Hague

Polinsky AM and Shavell S (2000) Punitive damages. In: Bouckaert B and De Geest G (eds.) *Encyclopedia of Law and Economics*, Vol. II. Edward Elgar, Cheltenham, UK and Northampton, MA, pp 764–781

Priest G (1986) What economists can tell lawyers about intellectual property: Comments on Cheung. In: Palmer JP and Zerbe RO (eds.) *Research in Law and Economics: The Economics of Patents and Copyrights* 8: 19–24

Prosser W (4th ed.) (1971) *Handbook of the Law of Torts*. West Publishing, St. Paul

Psychogiopoulou E (2012) Copyright enforcement, human rights protection and the responsibilities of internet service providers after Scarlet. *European Intellectual Property Review* 8: 552–555

Rabena JF and Choate KE (2007) Injunctive relief in the ITC post eBay. *Akon Intellectual Property Journal* 1: 27–41

RAE (22nd ed.) (2001) *Diccionario de la Lengua Española (DRAE)* Madrid

Rayna T and Barbier L (2010) Fighting consumer piracy with graduated response: An evaluation of the French and British implementations. *International Journal of Foresight and Innovations Policy* 6: 294–314

Raz J (1975) *Practical Reason and Norms*. Hutchinson & Co. (Publishers) Ltd., London

Reichman JH (1995) Universal minimum standards of intellectual property protection under the TRIPS component of the WTO. *The International Lawyer* 29: 345–388

(1997) Enforcing the enforcement procedures of the TRIPS Agreement. *Virginia Journal of International Law* 37: 335–356

(2003) The TRIPs Agreement comes of age: Conflict or cooperation in the post-transitional phase? In: Cottier T and Mavroidis PC (eds.) *Intellectual Property: Trade, Competition, and Sustainable Development*. University of Michigan Press, Ann Arbor, pp 115–140

Reichman JH and Lange D (1998) Bargaining around the TRIPS Agreement: The case for ongoing public-private initiatives to facilitate worldwide intellectual property transactions. *Duke Journal of Comparative and International Law* 9: 11–68

Reinbothe J (2010) The EU Enforcement Directive 2004/48/EC as a tool for copyright enforcement. In: Stamatoudi IA (ed.) *Copyright Enforcement and the Internet*. Kluwer Law International, The Hague, pp 3–28

Reinbothe J and Howard A (1991) The state of play in the negotiations on TRIPS (GATT/ Uruguay Round). *European Intellectual Property Review* 5: 157–164

Reinbothe J and von Lewinski S (2002) *The WIPO Treaties 1996: The WIPO Copyright Treaty and The WIPO Performances and Phonograms Treaty, Commentary and Legal Analysis*. Butterworths Lexis Nexis, London

(2nd ed.) (2015) *The WIPO Treaties on Copyright, A Commentary on the WCT, the WPPT, and the BTAP*. Oxford University Press, Oxford

Ricketson S (2015) Proposed international treaty on droit de suite/resale royalty right for visual artists. Resale Right, http://resale-right.org/wp-content/uploads/2016/03/SG15-0565_Ricketson_Study-Definitive_2015-07-06_EN-3.pdf, last accessed April 2016

Ricketson S and Ginsburg JC (2nd ed.) (2006) *International Copyright and Neighbouring Rights, The Berne Convention and Beyond*. Oxford University Press, Oxford

Ripstein A (1999) *Equality, Responsibility and the Law*. Cambridge University Press, Cambridge

Rob R and Waldfogel J (2006) Piracy on the high C's: Music downloading, sales displacement, and social welfare in a sample of college students. *The Journal of Law and Economics* 49: 29–62

Robinson M (2002) Ethics, human rights and globalization. Second Global Ethic Lecture, The Global Ethic Foundation University of Tübingen, Germany. www.weltethos.org/1-pdf/20-aktivitaeten/eng/we-reden-eng/speech_Robinson_eng.pdf (last accessed November 2015)

Robinson PH (1988) Legality and discretion in the distribution of criminal sanctions. *Harvard Journal on Legislation* 25: 393–460

Rock A (1984–1985) The Anton Piller order: An examination of its nature, development and present position in Canada. *Advocates Quarterly* 5: 191–213

Roffe P (2004) Bilateral agreements and a TRIPS plus world: The Chile-USA Free Trade Agreement. TRIPS Issues Papers no. 4, Quaker International Affairs Programme, Ottawa

Roffe P and Genovesi LM (2009) Propuesta de estrategia y plan de acción: implementación del Acuerdo de Promoción Comercial con los EEUU en el área de propiedad intelectual. Banco Interamericano de Desarrollo, Vicepresidencia de Sectores y Conocimiento, Sector de Integración y Comercio, Washington, DC. http://idbdocs.iadb.org/wsdocs/getdocument.aspx?docnum=2054292 (last accessed May 2015)

Roffe P and Seuba X (2015) Introduction: ACTA and the international debate on intellectual property enforcement. In: Roffe P and Seuba X (eds.) *The ACTA and the Plurilateral Enforcement Agenda: Genesis and Aftermath*. Cambridge University Press, Cambridge, pp 1–28

Rogers T and Szamosszegi A (2010) *Fair Use in the US Economy*. Computer and Communications Industry Association, Washington, DC

Romano CPR (2007) The shift from the consensual to the compulsory paradigm in international adjudication: Elements for a theory of consent. *New York University Journal of International Law and Politics* 39: 791–872

Romet I and Veron P (2011) On the way to fair balance, the French approach to patent litigation. *Who's Who Legal*. http://whoswholegal.com/news/features/article/28961/on-fair-balance-french-approach-patent-litigation (last accessed July 2015)

Ross JC and Wasserman JA (1993) Trade-related aspects of intellectual property rights. In: Stewart TP (ed.) *The GATT Uruguay Round: A Negotiating History (1986–1992)*, Volume II. Kluwer Law International, The Hague, pp 2264–2315

Ross TP (2005) *Intellectual Property Law: Damages and Remedies*. Law Journal Press, New York

Roucounas E (1987-VI) Engagements parallèles et contradictoires. *Recueil des Cours* 206: 197

Roudaut MR (2012) From sweatshops to organized crime: The new face of counterfeiting. In: Geiger C (ed.) *Criminal Enforcement of Intellectual Property: A Handbook of Contemporary Research*. Edward Elgar, Cheltenham, UK and Northampton, MA, pp 75–100

Rowe TD (1982) The legal theory of attorney fee shifting: A critical overview. *Duke Law Review* 1982: 651–680

Salvador Coderch P (2000) Punitive damages. *InDret* 1: 1–17

Samuelson P (2003) Digital Rights Management {and, or, vs.} the law. *Communications of the ACM* 46: 41–45

Samuelson P and Wheatland T (2009) Copyright statutory damages: A remedy in need of reform. *William and Mary Law Review* 51: 439–511

Samuelson P, Hill P and Wheatland T (2013) Statutory damages: A rarity in copyright laws internationally, but for how long? *Journal of the Copyright Society of the USA* 60: 529

Samuelson PA (1954) The pure theory of public expenditure. *Review of Economics and Statistics* 36: 387–389

Sandler T (2013) Public goods and regional cooperation for development: A new look. *Integration and Trade* 17: 13–24

Saperstein L (1997) Copyrights, criminal sanctions and economic rent: Applying the rent seeking model to the criminal law formulation process. *The Journal of Criminal Law and Criminology* 87: 1470–1510

Sarnoff JD (2009) Flexible application of injunctive relief in intellectual property enforcement (with reference to lessons from the emerging US jurisprudence). In: Correa C and Li X (eds.) *Intellectual Property Enforcement, International Perspectives*. Edward Elgar, Cheltenham, UK and Northampton, MA, pp 98–132

Satchwell G (2004) *A Sick Business: Counterfeit Medicines and Organized Crime*. Stockholm Network, London

Savin A (2006) Book comment. Intellectual property: Economic and legal dimensions of rights and remedies. *The Economic Journal* 116: F159–F161

Scheinin M (2007) Access to justice before international human rights bodies: Reflections on the practice of the UN Human Rights Committee and the European Court of Human Rights. In: Francioni F (ed.) *Access to Justice as a Human Right*. Oxford University Press, Oxford, pp 135–152

Scheuerman SB (2009) Due process forgotten: The problem of statutory damages and class actions. *Missouri Law Review* 74: 103–152

Schlicher JW (2000) Measuring patent damages by the market value of inventions – The Grain Processing, Rite-Hite, and Aro Rule. *Journal of the Patent and Trademark Office Society* 82: 503–535

(2nd ed.) (2003) *Patent Law: Legal and Economic Principles*. Thomson West

Schwartz DL and Kesan JP (2014) Analyzing the role of non-practicing entities in the patent system. *Cornell Law Review* 99: 425–456

Scotchmer S (2004) *Innovation and Incentives*. MIT Press, Cambridge, MA, London

Scungio MA (2013) How do I stop goods in transit? The United States. *Managing Intellectual Property* March: 54

Sebok AJ (2007) Punitive damages: From myth to theory. *Iowa Law Review* 92: 957–1036

Seuba X (2006) A human rights approach to the WHO Model List of Essential Medicines. *Bulletin of the World Health Organization* 84: 405–411

(2008) Intellectual property rights and human rights. In: Correa C and Yusuf A (eds.) *Intellectual Property And International Trade: TRIPS Agreement*. Kluwer International Law, The Netherlands, pp 387–419

(2009) *Border measures concerning goods allegedly infringing intellectual property rights: The seizures of generic medicines in transit*. ICTSD Programme on IPRs and Sustainable Development, Working Paper

(2010a) Free trade of pharmaceutical products: The limits of intellectual property enforcement at the border. *ICTSD Programme on IPRs and Sustainable Development,* Issue Paper no. 27

(2010b) *La Protección De La Salud Ante la Regulación Internacional De Los Productos Farmacéuticos*. Marcial Pons, Madrid

(2010c) Mainstreaming the TRIPS and human rights interactions. In: Correa C (ed.) *Research Handbook on the Protection of Intellectual Property under WTO Rules: Intellectual Property in the WTO*, Volume 1. Edward Elgar, Cheltenham, UK and Northampton, MA, pp 192–215

(2013a) Checks and balances in the intellectual property enforcement field: Reconstructing EU trade agreements. In: Geiger C (ed.) *Constructing European Intellectual Property: Achievements and New Perspectives*. Edward Elgar, Cheltenham, UK and Northampton, MA, pp 409–433

(2013b) Intellectual property in Preferential Trade Agreements: What treaties, What content? *The Journal of World Intellectual Property* 16: 240–261

(2013c) The relevance of the principles for intellectual property provisions in bilateral and regional agreements vis-à-vis European Preferential Trade Agreements. *IIC* 44: 943–947

(2014a) Implementation issues arising from intellectual property chapters contained in trade agreements between the European Union and developing countries. In: Dexl J, Grosse Ruse-Khan H and Nadde-Phlix S (eds.) *EU Bilateral Trade Agreements and Intellectual Property: For Better or Worse?* Springer, Berlin, pp 293–303

(2015a) ACTA initial provisions and general definitions. In: Roffe P and Seuba X (eds.) *The ACTA and The Plurilateral Enforcement Agenda: Genesis and Aftermath*. Cambridge University Press, Cambridge, pp 46–65

(2015b) General obligations with respect to enforcement. In: Roffe P and Seuba X (eds.) *The ACTA and the Plurilateral Enforcement Agenda: Genesis and Aftermath*. Cambridge University Press, Cambridge, pp 66–79

(2015c) Human rights and intellectual property law at bilateral and multilateral levels: Substantive and operational aspects. In: Geiger C (ed.) *Research Handbook on Human Rights and Intellectual Property*. Edward Elgar, Cheltenham, UK and Northampton, MA, pp 173–200

Shapiro SJ (2011) *Legality*. Harvard University Press, Cambridge, MA

Shavell S (2002) Law versus morality as regulators of conduct. *American Law and Economics Law Review* 4: 227–257

Shelton D (2006) International law and 'relative normativity'. In: Evans MD (2nd ed.) (ed.) *International Law*. Oxford University Press, Oxford

Sherkow JS (2014) Preliminary injunctions post-Mayo and Myriad. *Stanford Law Review Online* 67: 1–8

Sherlock A (1989) European Court of Human Rights – execution of an 'Anton Piller order' and Article 8. *European Law Review* 14: 476

Siegel DE (2002) Legal aspects of the IMF/WTO relationship: The fund's articles of Agreement and the WTO agreements. *American Journal of International Law* 96: 561–599

Sloss D (2009) *The Role of Domestic Courts in Treaty Enforcement: A Comparative Study*. Cambridge University Press, Cambridge

Smith BL (1996) Enforcing TRIPS Part III in WTO Dispute Settlement. In: Hansen H (ed.) *International Intellectual Property Law and Policy. Volume* 6, Juris Publishing, Huntingdon, p 46

Smith RC (2013) Discovery and compulsion: How regulatory and litigation issues relating to intellectual property rights are challenging the fundamental right to the protection of personal data. *Queen Mary Journal of Intellectual Property* 3: 2–21

Sobrino Heredia JM (2009) Procedimientos de aplicación de las normas internacionales (II): la solución pacífica de las controversias internacionales (los medios de arreglo diplomático y el arbitraje. In: Diez de Velasco M (17th ed.) (ed.) *Instituciones de Derecho Internacional Público*. Tecnos, Madrid, pp 926–943

Soentgen J (2012) Disposing of counterfeit goods: Unseen challenges. WIPO Magazine 6. www.wipo.int/wipo_magazine/en/2012/06/article_0007.html (last accessed April 2015)

South Centre/Center for International Environmental Law (CIEL) (2008) *The International Medical Products Anti-Counterfeiting Taskforce (IMPACT): Is the WHO on the Right Track?* Intellectual Property Quarterly Update, Third Quarter

Spenneman C (2015) ACTA, East African enforcement legislation and generic medicines: A comparison. In: Roffe P and Seuba X (eds.) *The ACTA and the Plurilateral Enforcement Agenda: Genesis and Aftermath*. Cambridge University Press, Cambridge, pp 244–258

Stauder D (2005a) Enforcing industrial property rights: Patent protection from a comparative viewpoint. In: Heath C and Sanders K (eds.) *New Frontiers of Intellectual Property Law: IP and Cultural Heritage, Geographical Indications, Enforcement and Overprotection*. Hart Publishing, Oxford and Portland, OR, pp 291–302

(2005b) Introduction. In: Heath C and Petit L (2nd ed.) (eds.) *Patent Enforcement Worldwide: A Survey of 15 Countries, Writings in Honour of Dieter Stauder*. Hart Publishing, Oxford and Portland, OR, pp. 1–4

Stauder D and Llewelyn D (2004) Oskar Hartwieg's thoughts on the English legal system. In: Vaver D and Bentley L (eds.) *Intellectual Property in the New Millennium: Essays in Honour of William R. Cornish*. Cambridge University Press, Cambridge, pp 47–57

Stewart TP (1993) *The GATT Uruguay Round: A Negotiating History*. Kluwer Law International, The Hague

Straus J (2000) Reversal of the burden of proof, the principle of 'fair and equitable procedures' and preliminary injunctions under the TRIPS Agreement. *Journal of World Intellectual Property* 3: 807–823

Strowel A (2009) Internet piracy as a wake-up call for copyright law makers–Is the 'graduated response' a good reply? *WIPOJ* 1: 75–86

Strowel A and Tulken F (2005) Freedom of expression and copyright under civil law: Of balance, adaptation and access. In: Griffiths J and Suthersanen U (eds.) *Copyright and Free Speech: Comparative and International Analyses*. Oxford University Press, Oxford, pp 287–313

Su E (2000) The winners and the losers: The Agreement on Trade-Related Aspects of Intellectual Property Rights and its effects on developing countries. *Houston Journal of International Law* 23: 169–218

Suthersanen U (2005) Towards an international public interest rule? Human rights and international copyright law. In: Griffiths J and Suthersanen U (eds.) *Copyright and Free Speech: Comparative and International Analyses*. Oxford University Press, Oxford, pp 97–125

Sweet AS and Mathews J (2008) Proportionality balancing and global constitutionalism. *Columbia Journal of Transnational Law* 47: 72–164

Szott Moohr G (2005) Defining overcriminalization through cost-benefit analysis: The example of criminal enforcement laws. *American University Law Review* 54: 783–806

Takeyama LN (1994) The welfare implications of unauthorized reproduction of intellectual property in the presence of demand network externalities. *The Journal of Industrial Economics* 42: 155–166

Tang YH (2006) The future of patent enforcement after eBay v. MercExchange. *Harvard Journal of Law and Technology* 20: 235–252

Taniguchi Y (2009) The WTO Dispute Settlement as seen by a proceduralist. *Cornell International Law Journal* 42: 1–21

Taubman A (2012) *A Practical Guide to Working with TRIPS*. Oxford University Press, Oxford

Tekeste E and Muñoz V (2008) *The Changing Structure and Governance of Intellectual Property Enforcement*. South Centre, Geneva

Teubner G (1998) Legal irritants: Good faith in British law or how unifying law ends up in new divergences. *The Modern Law Review Limited* 61: 11–32

The Law Dictionary, *Featuring Black's Law Dictionary Free Online Legal Dictionary* (2nd ed.). http://thelawdictionary.org/enforce/ (last accessed April 2015)

Therein J (2001) Exorcising the specter of a pay-per-use society: Toward preserving fair use and the public domain in the digital age. *Berkeley Technology Law Journal* 16: 979–1043

Thompson WC (2004) *Bootleg Billions: The Impact of the Counterfeit Goods Trade on New York City*. City of New York Office of the Comptroller (on file with author)

Thorley S and Fysh M (2015) Interim injunctions – The UK approach. Centre for International Intellectual Property Studies, Training Program for Technically Qualified Judges of the Unified Patent Court

Tolani M (2011) US punitive damages before German courts: A comparative analysis with respect to the ordre public. *Annual Survey of International and Comparative Law* XVII: 185–207

Tomuschat C (3rd ed.) (2014) *Human Rights, Between Idealism and Realism*. Oxford University Press, Oxford

Trachtman J (1998) Trade and . . . Problems, cost-benefit analysis and subsidiarity. *European Journal of International Law* 9: 32–85

(1999) The domain of WTO Dispute Resolution. *Harvard International Law Journal* 40: 333–377

Trainer TP (2008) Intellectual property enforcement: A reality gap (insufficient assistance, ineffective implementation). *John Marshall Review of Intellectual Property Law* 8: 47–79

Trainer TP and Allums VE (2008) *Protecting Intellectual Property Rights across Borders*. Thomson West, St. Paul

Treverton GF *et al.* (2009) Film Piracy, Organized Crime and Terrorism. RAND Corporation. www.rand.org/content/dam/rand/pubs/monographs/2009/RAND_MG742.pdf (last accessed April 2015)

Tridimas T (1999) *The General Principles of EC Law*. Oxford University Press, Oxford

Tullock G (1971) Decisions as public goods. *Journal of Political Economy* 79: 913–918

Urbas G (2005) Criminal enforcement of intellectual property rights: Interaction between public authorities and private interests. In: Heath C and Sanders K (eds.) *New Frontiers of Intellectual Property Law: IP and Cultural Heritage, Geographical Indications, Enforcement and Overprotection*. Hart Publishing, Oxford and Portland, OR, pp 303–322

van den Brink J (2008) *Comeback for the legal fiction of the Anti Piracy Regulation?* Kennedy van der Laan Newsletter (on file with author)

van Overwalle G (2009) Patents in agricultural biotechnology and the right to food. *Paper Commissioned by the UN Human Right Council Special Rapporteur*, Olivier De Schutter, for the Scientific Report on Intellectual Property Rights and Right to Food

Vander S (2009) Provisional measures. In: Stoll P-T, Busche J and Arend K (eds.) *WTO: Trade-Related Aspects of Intellectual Property Rights*, Martinus Nijhof, Brill, The Netherlands, pp 738–750

Vandoren P (1999) The implementation of the TRIPS Agreement. *Journal of World Intellectual Property* 2: 25–34

Vanrell JE (2013) How do I stop goods in transit? Uruguay. *Managing Intellectual Property* March: 55

Vasak K (1977) A 30-year struggle: The sustained efforts to give force of law to the Universal Declaration of Human Rights. *The UNESCO Courier* 29

Vaughn LB (1989) A need for clarity: Toward a new standard for preliminary injunctions. *Oregon Law Review* 68: 839

Vechayanon W (1998) Intellectual property rights enforcement and the role of Intellectual Property Court in Thailand. In: *The Intellectual Property and International Trade Law Forum: Special Issue*. The Central Intellectual Property and International Trade Court, Bangkok, pp 30–44

Veron P and Mandel O (2005) 20 ans d'interdiction provisoire de contrafaçon de brevet d'invention a travers l'analyse de 200 decisions. *Properiete Industrielle: Edute* 3

Vidal-Quadras M (2013) La recepción de la cláusula Bolar en Europa. In: Seuba X (ed.) *Propiedad Intelectual, Competencia y Aspectos Regulatorios del Medicamento*. PUJ-ICTSD, Bogotá, pp 295–330

Villiger ME (2011) The rules of interpretation: Misgivings, misunderstandings, miscarriage? The 'crucible' intended by the International Law Commission. In: Cannizzaro E (ed.) *The Law of Treaties Beyond the Vienna Convention*. Oxford University Press, Oxford, pp 105–122

Vitkauskas D and Dikov G (2012) *Protecting the Right to a Fair Trial under the European Convention on Human Rights*. Council of Europe, Strasbourg

von Mühlendahl A and Stauder D (2009) Territorial intellectual property rights in a global economy – Transit and other 'free zones'. In: Prinz zu Waldek und Pyrmont W, Brauneis R, Adelman MJ, Drexl J and Nack R (eds.) *Patents and Technological Progress in a Globalized World. Liber Amicorum Joseph Strauss*. Springer, Berlin, pp 653–673

Vrins O (2010) The real story of a fiction: Transit after Montex under Regulation EC 1383/2003. *Journal of Intellectual Property Law and Practice* 5: 358–371

Vrins O and Schneider M (2006a) Regulation (EC) 1383/2003. In: Schneider M and Vrins O (eds.) *Enforcement of Intellectual Property Rights through Border Measures*. Oxford University Press, Oxford, pp 65–173

(eds.) (2006b) *Enforcement of Intellectual Property Rights through Border Measures*. Oxford University Press, Oxford

Wacks R (1980) *The Protection of Privacy*. Sweet and Maxwell, London

Wager H and Watal J (2015) Human rights and international intellectual property law. In Geiger C (ed.) *Research Handbook on Human Rights and Intellectual Property*. Edward Elgar, Cheltenham, UK and Northampton, MA, pp. 149–172

Wall DS and Large J (2010) Jailhouse frocks: Locating the public interest in policing counterfeit luxury fashion goods. *British Journal of Criminology* 50: 1094–1116

Watal J (1999) Intellectual property rights and agriculture: Interests of developing countries. Paper presented at The Conference on Agriculture and the New Trade Agenda in the

WTO 2000 Negotiations. http://siteresources.worldbank.org/INTARD/864477-1112355387702/20424604/watal.pdf (last accessed November 2016)

(2001) *Intellectual Property Rights in the WTO and Developing Countries*. Kluwer Law International, The Hague

(2010) US–China intellectual property dispute: A comment on the interpretation of the TRIPS enforcement provisions. *The Journal of World Intellectual Property* 13: 605–619

Watson A (1978) Comparative law and legal change. *The Cambridge Law Journal* 37: 313–336

(2nd ed.) (1993) *Legal Transplants: An Approach to Comparative Law*. University of Georgia Press, Athens

Weatherall K (2010) ACTA – Australian Section by section analysis (April public draft). http://works.bepress.com/kimweatherall/21 (last accessed November 2016)

(2015) Section by Section Commentary on the TPP Final IP Chapter Published 5 November 2015 – Part 3 – Enforcement. http://works.bepress.com/kimweatherall/33 (last accessed November 2016)

(2016) Safeguards for defendant rights and interests in international intellectual property enforcement treaties. *Sydney Law School Research Paper No. 16/52*

Wechsler A (2012) Criminal enforcement of intellectual property law: An economic approach. In: Geiger C (ed.) *Criminal Enforcement of Intellectual Property: A Handbook of Contemporary Research*. Edward Elgar, Cheltenham, UK and Northampton, MA, pp 128–150

Weil P (1983) Towards relative normativity in international law? *American Journal of International Law* 77: 413–442

Wellman C (2000) Solidarity, the individual and human rights. *Human Rights Quarterly* 22: 639–657

Werden GJ *et al.* (1999) Economic analysis of lost profits from patent infringement with and without noninfringing substitutes. *American Intellectual Property Law Quarterly Journal* 27: 305–333

Wolf AD (1984) Preliminary injunctions: The varying standards. *Western New England Law Review* 7: 173–237

Wu YT (2014) How will eBay v. Mercexchange affect preliminary injunctions? *NTUT Journal of Intellectual Property Law and Management* 3: 34–55

Xuan L (2009) Ten general misconceptions about the enforcement of intellectual property rights. In: Xuan L and Correa C (eds.) *Intellectual Property Enforcement: International Perspectives*. Edward Elgar, Cheltenham, UK and Northampton, MA, pp 14–42

Xue H (2009a) An anatomical study of the United States versus China at the World Trade Organization on intellectual property enforcement. *EIPR* 31: 292–298

(2009b) Enforcement for development: Why not an agenda for the developing world? In: Li X and Correa CM (eds.), *Intellectual Property Enforcement: International Perspectives*. Edward Elgar, Cheltenham, UK and Northampton, MA, pp 133–156

Yang T (2006) International treaty enforcement as a public good: Institutional deterrent sanctions in international environmental agreements. *Michigan Journal of International Law* 27: 1132–1184

Yankwich LR (1957) The art of being a judge. *University of Pennsylvania Law Review* 105: 374–389

Yu PK (2004) Currents and crosscurrents in the international intellectual property regime. *Loyola of Los Angeles Law Review* 38: 323–444

(2006) TRIPs and its discontents. *Marquette Intellectual Property Law Review* 10: 369–410

(2007a) International enclosure, the regime complex, and intellectual property schizophrenia. *Michigan State Law Review* 2007: 1–33
(2007b) The international enclosure movement. *Indiana Law Journal*: 82: 827–907
(2009a) A tale of two development agendas. *Ohio Northern University Law Review* 35: 465–573
(2009b) The objectives and principles of the TRIPS Agreement. *Houston Law Review* 46: 979–1046
(2010a) Enforcement, economics and estimates. *WIPO Journal* 2: 1–19
(2010b) The graduated response. *Florida Law Review* 62: 1373–1430
(2010c) The US – China dispute over TRIPS enforcement. Drake University Law School, Occasional Papers in Intellectual Property Law 5
(2011a) Are developing countries playing a better TRIPS game? *UCLA Journal of International Law and Foreign Affairs* 16: 311–342
(2011b) Intellectual property and human rights in the nonmultilateral era. *Florida Law Review* 64: 1045–1100
(2011c) Six secret (and now open) fears of ACTA. *SMU Law Review* 64: 975–1094
(2011d) The TRIPS enforcement dispute. *Nebraska Law Review* 89: 1046–1131
(2011e) TRIPS and its Achilles' heel. *Journal of Intellectual Property Law* 18: 479–531
(2011f) TRIPS enforcement and developing countries. *American University International Law Review* 26: 727–782
(2012) Shaping Chinese criminal enforcement norms through the TRIPS Agreement. In: Geiger C (ed.) *Criminal Enforcement of Intellectual Property: A Handbook of Contemporary Research*. Edward Elgar, Cheltenham, UK and Northampton, MA, pp 286–309
(2013) The ACTA/TPP country clubs. In: Beldiman D (ed.) *Access to Information and Knowledge: 21st Century Challenges in Intellectual Property and Knowledge Governance*. Edward Elgar, Cheltenham, UK and Northampton, MA, pp 258–283
(2015) The ACTA Committee. In: Roffe P and Seuba X (eds.) *The ACTA and the Plurilateral Enforcement Agenda: Genesis and Aftermath*. Cambridge University Press, Cambridge, pp 143–154
(2016) The Transplant and Transformation of Intellectual Property Laws in China. In: Lee N, Bruun N and Li M *Governance of Intellectual Property Rights in China and Europe*. Edward Elgar, Cheltenham, UK and Northampton, MA, pp 20–42
Zapatero MP (2003) *Derecho del Comercio Global*. Thomson – Civitas, Madrid
Zekos GI (2007) The case for giving to private parties access to the WTO dispute settlement system. *Journal of World Investment and Trade* 8: 441–451
Zuckerman A (2007) Editor's note. The privilege against self-incrimination may not confer a right to refuse disclosure of incriminating documents that came into existence independently of the disclosure order. *Civil Justice Quarterly* 26: 395–403

DOCUMENTS INTERNATIONAL ORGANIZATIONS

GATT (1986) *Ministerial Declaration on the Uruguay Round*. MIN.DEC
GATT (1987a) Guidelines Proposed by the European Community for the Negotiation on Trade-Related Aspects of Intellectual Property Rights. MTN.GNG/NG11/W/16
(1987b) Statement by the United States at Meeting of 25 March 1987. MTN.GNG/NG11/W/2
(1987c) Submissions from Participants on Trade Problems Encountered in Connection with Intellectual Property rights, European Communities, Japan, United States. MTN. GNG/NG11/W/7

(1988a) Statement by Thailand at the Meeting of 12–14 September 1988. MTN.GNG/NG11/W/27

(1989) Enforcement of Trade-Related Intellectual Property Rights – Communication from India. MTN.GNG/NG11/W/40

International Law Commission (2001a) Draft articles on Responsibility of States for Internationally Wrongful Acts, with commentaries

(2001b) Draft Articles on Responsibility of States for Internationally Wrongful Acts. Supplement no. 10 (A/56/10), chp.IV.E.1

(2006a) *Conclusions of the Work of the Study Group on the Fragmentation of International Law: Difficulties Arising from the Diversification and Expansion of International Law.* United Nations

(2006b) Fragmentation of International Law: Difficulties Arising from the Diversification and Expansion of International Law, Report of the Study Group of the International Law Commission, Finalized by Martti Koskenniemi. A/CN.4/L.682

OECD (2008) *The Economic Impact of Counterfeiting and Piracy*. OECD, Paris

(2009) *Magnitude of Counterfeiting and Piracy of Tangible Products: An Update*. OECD, Paris

UN Committee on Economic, Social and Cultural Rights (1990) General Comment no. 3, The Nature of States Parties' Obligations (Art. 2, Para. 1, of the Covenant). E/1991/23

(1998) General Comment no. 9, Substantive Issues Arising in the Implementation of the International Covenant on Economic, Social and Cultural Rights. E/C.12/1998/24

(2000) General Comment no. 14, The Right to the Highest Attainable Standard of Health. E/C.12/2000/4

(2001) Human Rights and Intellectual Property, Statement by the Committee on Economic, Social and Cultural Rights. E/C.12/2001/15

(2006) General Comment no. 17 (2005), The right of Everyone to Benefit from the Protection of the Moral and Material Interests Resulting from any Scientific, Literary or Artistic Production of Which He or She is the Author (Article 15, Paragraph 1 (c), of the Covenant). E/C.12/GC/17

(2010a) E/C.12/2010/SR.3, 4 and 5

(2010b) E/C.12/COL/CO/5

UN Economic and Social Council (1995) The Interpretation and Practical Application of the Obligations Incumbent upon States Parties to the International Covenant on Economic Social and Cultural Rights. E/C.12/1995/SR.22

UN ECOSOC Sub-Commission on the Promotion and Protection of Human Rights (2001) The Impact of the Agreement on Trade-Related Aspects of Intellectual Property Rights on Human Rights: Report of the High Commissioner. E/CN.4/Sub.2/2001/13

UN General Assembly (1982) Manila Declaration on the Peaceful Settlement of International Disputes. A/RES/37/10

UN High Commissioner for Human Rights (2001) Access to Medication in the Context of Pandemics such as HIV/AIDS. E/CN.4/RES/2001/33

(2002) Access to Medication in the Context of Pandemics such as HIV/AIDS. E/CN.4/RES/2002/32

UN Human Rights Committee (1988) General comment no. 16, Article 17 (Right to Privacy) The Right to Respect of Privacy, Family, Home and Correspondence, and Protection of Honour and Reputation. HRI/GEN/1/Rev.9, Vol. I

(2001) General comment no. 29, States of Emergency (Article 4). CCPR/C/21/Rev.1/Add.11

(2004) General Comment no. 31, The Nature of the General Legal Obligation Imposed on States Parties to the Covenant. CCPR/C/21/Rev.1/Add.13

(2007) General comment no. 32, Article 14, Right to Equality before Courts and Tribunals and to Fair Trial. CCPR/C/GC/32

(2011) General comment no. 34, Article 19, Freedom of Opinion and Expression. CCPR/C/GC/34

UN Human Rights Council (2007) Implementation of General Assembly Resolution 60/251 of 15 March 2006 Entitled 'Human Rights Council', Human Rights and International Solidarity. A/HRC/4/8

(2009) Report of the Special Rapporteur on the Right of Everyone to the Enjoyment of the Highest Attainable Standard of Physical and Mental Health, Anand Grover. A/HRC/11/12

(2011) Report of the Special Rapporteur on the Promotion and Protection of the Right to Freedom of Opinion and Expression, Frank La Rue. A/HRC/17/27

(2012) The Promotion, Protection and Enjoyment of Human Rights on the Internet. A/HRC/RES/20/8

(2013) Access to Medicines in the Context of the Right of Everyone to the Enjoyment of the Highest Attainable Standard of Physical and Mental Health. A/HRC/RES/23/14

(2014) Report of the Special Rapporteur in the Field of Cultural Rights, Farida Shaheed, Copyright Policy and the Right to Science and Culture. A/HRC/28/57

UN Sub-Commission on the Promotion and Protection of Human Rights (2000) Intellectual Property Rights and Human Rights. E/CN.4/SUB.2/RES/2000/7

(2001) Intellectual Property and Human Rights. E/CN/4/SUB.2/RES/2001/21

UNCTAD – Stockholm Network – PIIPA (2007) Defining the Public Interest in Intellectual Property. http://unctad.org/sections/dite_totip/docs/dite_pcbb_iaso051_en.pdf (last accessed December 2015)

UNCTAD-ICTSD (2005) *Resource Book on TRIPS and Development*. Cambridge University Press, Cambridge

UNSG High-Level Panel on Access to Medicines (2015) Terms of Reference. https://static1.squarespace.com/static/562094dee4b0d00c1a3ef761/t/568d535a1c12106651299f6e/1452102490740/TOR+on+new+template+5Jan16+FINAL.pdf (last accessed May 2016)

WHO (1992) Counterfeit Drugs: Report of a Joint WHO/IFPMA Workshop. WHO/DMP/CFD/92

(2004) Combating counterfeit medicines. *WHO Drug Information* 18: 133–137

(2006) Public Health, Innovation and Intellectual Property Rights, Report of the Commission on Intellectual Property Rights, Innovation and Public Health. www.who.int/intellectualproperty/documents/thereport/ENPublicHealthReport.pdf (last accessed November 2016)

(2014) General Information on Counterfeit Medicines. www.who.int/medicines/services/counterfeit/overview/en/ (last accessed September 2015)

WIPO (1987) Comité de Expertos sobre la armonización de ciertas disposiciones de leyes para la protección de las invenciones, Exclusiones de la protección por patente. Memorándum de la Oficina Internacional de la OMPI. HL/CE/IV/INF/1

(1997) Proposed Treaty on the Settlement of Disputes between States in the Field of Intellectual Property. WO/GA/XXI/2

(2003) *Guide to the Copyright and Related Rights Treaties Administered by WIPO and Glossary of Copyright and Related Rights Terms*. World Intellectual Property Organization (WIPO), Geneva

(2nd ed.) (2004) *WIPO Intellectual Property Handbook: Policy, Law and Use*. World Intellectual Property Organization (WIPO), Geneva

(2007a) Development Agenda. WIPO Doc. A/43/16, Annex A, 12 November 2007

(2007b) Human health and the IP system: Innovation, access and public welfare. WIPO Symposium on Current Issues in Intellectual Property and Public Health. www.wipo.int/export/sites/www/policy/en/global_health/pdf/public_health_ip.pdf (last accessed June 2015)

(2007c) Study on the Economic, Social and Cultural Impact of Intellectual Property in the Creative Industries

(2012) *Guide on Surveying the Economic Contribution of the Copyright-Based Industries*. World Intellectual Property Organization (WIPO), Geneva

(2013) WIPO Draft Guidelines on Assessing the Economic, Social and Cultural Impact of Copyright on the Creative Economy

World Bank (2001) *Global Economic Prospects and the Developing Countries 2002*. World Bank, Washington, DC

World Customs Organization (2003) Model Provisions for National Legislation to Implement Fair and Effective Border Measures Consistent with the TRIPS Agreement. www.tafa-r.org.tw/forum/20110816/20110816WCOModelLawfinal.pdfwww.tafa-r.org.tw/forum/20110816/20110816WCOModelLawfinal.pdf (last accessed June 2015)

World Health Organization (2001) Globalization, TRIPS and Access to Pharmaceuticals. WHO Policy Perspectives on Medicines no. 003

WTO (1995) Analytical index of the GATT. WTO, Geneva. www.wto.org/english/res_e/booksp_e/gatt_ai_e/art5_e.pdf

(2001) Article 5 of the Dispute Settlement Understanding, Communication from the Director-General. WT/DSB/25

(2010a) European Union and a Member State – Seizure of Generic Drugs in Transit, Request for consultations by Brazil. WT/DS409/4

(2010b) European Union and a Member State – Seizure of Generic Drugs in Transit, Request for consultations by India. WT/DS408/1, G/L/921, IP/D/28

(2010c) European Union and a Member State – Seizure of Generic Drugs in Transit, Request for consultations by Brazil. WT/DS409/1, IP/D/29, G/L/922

(2013) Annual Report (2013) of the Council for TRIPS. IP/C/67

WTO Council for Trade-Related Aspects of Intellectual Property Rights (1995a) Procedures for Notification of, and Possible Establishment of a Common Register of National Laws and Regulations under Article 63.2. IP/C/2

(1995b) Format for Listing of 'Other Laws and Regulations' to be Notified under Article 63.2. IP/C/W/8/Rev.1

(1995c) Checklist of Issues on Enforcement. IP/C/5

(1997) Notifications of Laws and Regulations Relating to Articles 3, 4 and 5 of the TRIPS Agreement: Format for One Option. IP/C/9

(2006) Enforcement of Intellectual Property Rights. Joint Communication from the European Communities, Japan, Switzerland and the United States. IP/C/W/485

(2010) Minutes of Meeting Held in the Centre William Rappard on 8–9 June 2010. IP/C/M/63

WTO General Council (2002a) Decision on the Implementation of Paragraph 6 of the Doha Declaration. IP/C/W/405

(2002b) Request for Mediation by the Philippines, Thailand, and The European Communities, Communication from the Director-General. WT/GC/66

(2003) Implementation of paragraph 6 of the Doha Declaration on the TRIPS Agreement and Public Health, Decision 30 August 2003. WT/L/540

(2005) Amendment of the TRIPS Agreement, Decision of 6 December 2005. WT/L/641

(2008) Intervention by Brazil, TRIPS Council Agenda Item M (Other Business), Public Health Dimension of the TRIPS Agreement. www.ip-watch.org/files/RemediosIntervencao-do-Brasil-Conselho%20Geral-03%2002%202008.doc (last accessed June 2015)

DOCUMENTS EUROPEAN UNION AND EUROPE

Commission of the European Communities (2005a) Communication from the Commission to the Council, the European Parliament and the Economic and Social Committee on a Customs Response to Latest Trends in Counterfeiting and Piracy. COM(2005) 479

(2005b) Proposal for a European Parliament and Council Directive on Criminal Measures Aimed at Ensuring the Enforcement of Intellectual Property Rights, {SEC(2005)848} / COM/2005/0276 final, COD 2005/0127

(2006) Explanatory Memorandum of the Amended Proposal for a Directive of the European Parliament and of the Council on Criminal Measures Aimed at Ensuring the Enforcement of Intellectual Property Rights of 26 April 2006, COM (2006) 168 final

Committee on Legal Affairs (2014) Report on the proposal for a directive of the European Parliament and of the Council to approximate the laws of the Member States relating to trade marks (recast). COM(2013)0162 – C7-0088/2013 – 2013/0089(COD)

Directorate General Internal Market and Services (2013) Synthesis of the responses 'Civil enforcement of intellectual property rights: public consultation on the efficiency of proceedings and accessibility of measures'. http://ec.europa.eu/internal_market/consultations/docs/2012/intellectual-property-rights/summary-of-responses_en.pdf (last accessed April 2015)

Directorate General Taxation and Customs Union (TAXUD) (2014) A serious problem for everyone. http://ec.europa.eu/taxation_customs/customs/customs_controls/counterfeit_piracy/combating/index_en.htm (last accessed April 2015)

European Commission (1998) Report from the Commission on the implementation of Council Regulation (EC) No 3295/94 of 22 December 1994 as regards border controls on trade in goods which may be counterfeit or pirated, and Proposal for a Council Regulation (EC) amending Regulation (EC) No 3295/94 laying down measures to prohibit the release for free circulation, export, re-export or entry for a suspensive procedure of counterfeit and pirated goods. COM(1998) 25 final, OJ C 108/63

(2003a) Proposal for a Directive of the European Parliament and of the Council on Measures and Procedures to Ensure the Enforcement of Intellectual Property Rights. COM(2003) 46 final

(2003b) Proposal for a Regulation of the European Parliament and the Council on the Law Applicable to Non-Contractual Obligations (Rome II). COM(2003) 427 final

(2005a) Communication from the Commission to the Council, the European Parliament and the Economic and Social Committee on a Customs Response to Latest Trends in Counterfeiting and Piracy. COM(2005) 479

(2005b) Strategy for the Enforcement of Intellectual Property Rights in Third Countries. OJEU C 129/3

(2008) The Anti-Counterfeiting Trade Agreement: Fact Sheet. http://trade.ec.europa.eu/doclib/docs/2008/october/tradoc_140836.11.08.pdf (last accessed August 2015)

(2009a) Commission Staff Working Document, IPR Enforcement Report 2009. SEC(2009) 1360. http://trade.ec.europa.eu/doclib/docs/2009/october/tradoc_145204.pdf (last accessed May 2015)

(2009b) The Anti-Counterfeiting Trade Agreement (ACTA): Fact sheet. http://trade.ec.europa.eu/doclib/docs/2009/january/tradoc_142039.pdf (last accessed June 2015)
(2010a) Commission Staff Working Document, Analysis of the application of Directive 2004/48/EC of the European Parliament and the Council of 29 April 2004 on the enforcement of intellectual property rights in the Member States Accompanying document to the Report from the Commission to the Council, the European Parliament and the European Social Committee on the application of Directive 2004/48/EC of the European Parliament and the Council of 29 April 2004 on the enforcement of intellectual property rights. SEC(2010) 1589 final
(2010b) Report from the Commission to the European Parliament, the Council, the European Economic and Social Committee and the Committee of the Regions, Application of Directive 2004/48/EC of the European Parliament and the Council of 29 April 2004 on the Enforcement of Intellectual Property Rights. COM(2010) 779 final
(2012) Commission Staff Working Document, Online services, Including e-commerce, in the Single Market. SEC(2011) 1641 final
(2013a) Commission Staff Working Document, Report on the Protection and Enforcement of Intellectual Property Rights in Third Countries. SWD(2013) 30 final. http://trade.ec.europa.eu/doclib/docs/2013/march/tradoc_150789.pdf (last accessed May 2015)
(2013b) Proposal for a Regulation of the European Parliament and of the Council amending Council Regulation (EC) No. 207/2009 on the Community trade mark. COM(2013) 161 final, 2013/0088 (COD)
(2014) Communication from the Commission to the European Parliament, the Council and the European Economic and Social Committee, Trade, Growth and Intellectual Property – Strategy for the Protection and Enforcement of Intellectual Property Rights in Third Countries. COM(2014) 389 final
European Parliament (2007a) Legislative resolution of 25 April 2007 on the amended proposal for a directive of the European Parliament and of the Council on criminal measures aimed at ensuring the enforcement of intellectual property rights (COM(2006)0168 – C6-0233/2005 – 2005/0127(COD)). P6_TA(2007)0145
(2007b) Report on the amended proposal for a directive of the European Parliament and of the Council on criminal measures aimed at ensuring the enforcement of intellectual property rights (COM(2006)0168 – C6-0233/2005 – 2005/0127(COD)). A6–0073/2007
(2012a) ACTA before the European Parliament, press release of 4 July 2012. www.europarl.europa.eu/news/en/news-room/20120703IPR48247/European-Parliament-rejects-ACTA (last accessed May 2015)
(2012b) Legislative resolution of 4 July 2012 on the draft Council decision on the conclusion of the Anti-Counterfeiting Trade Agreement between the European Union and its Member States, Australia, Canada, Japan, the Republic of Korea, the United Mexican States, the Kingdom of Morocco, New Zealand, the Republic of Singapore, the Swiss Confederation and the United States of America (12195/2011 – C7-0027/2012 – 2011/0167 (NLE)). P7_TA-PROV(2012)0287
European Union Agency for Fundamental Rights and Council of Europe (2016) *Handbook on European Law Relating to Access to Justice*. Publications Office of the European Union, Luxembourg
European Union Subcommittee of the International Trademark Association (2010) Task Force on Criminal Sanctions of the Anti-Counterfeiting and Enforcement Committee (ACEC) Criminal prosecution of counterfeiting and piracy in Member States of the European Union. www.inta.org/Advocacy/Documents/INTAEUCriminalSanctions20082009.pdf (last accessed September 2015)

DOCUMENTS UNITED STATES

American Association of Law Libraries *et al.* (2010) Concerns with April 2010 ACTA text. www.librarycopyrightalliance.org/storage/documents/consolidatedtextcomments423.pdf (last accessed April 2015)

Committee on Armed Services United States Senate (2012) Inquiry into the Counterfeit Electronic Parts in the Department of Defense Supply Chain. Report 112–167. www.armed-services.senate.gov/imo/media/doc/Counterfeit-Electronic-Parts.pdf (last accessed April 2015)

Economics and Statistics Administration and United States Patent and Trademark Office (2012) Intellectual Property and the US Economy: Industries in Focus. www.uspto.gov/news/publications/IP_Report_March_2012.pdf (last accessed April 2015)

Industry Functional Advisory Committee on Intellectual Property Rights for Trade Policy Matters (2004) The US-Central American Free Trade Agreement (FTA), The Intellectual Property Provisions, Report of the Industry Functional Advisory Committee on Intellectual Property Rights for Trade Policy Matters (IFAC-3). www.ustr.gov/archive/assets/Trade_Agreements/Regional/CAFTA/CAFTA_Reports/asset_upload_file571_5945.pdf (last accessed May 2015)

Intellectual Property Enforcement Coordinator (2012) 2011 US Intellectual Property Enforcement Coordinator Annual Report on Intellectual Property Enforcement. www.whitehouse.gov/sites/default/files/omb/IPEC/ipec_annual_2011_report.pdf (last accessed May 2015)

(2013) 2013 Joint Strategic Plan on Intellectual Property Enforcement. www.whitehouse.gov/sites/default/files/omb/IPEC/2013-us-ipec-joint-strategic-plan.pdf (accessed May 2015)

Office of the United States Trade Representative (USTR) (2008) Trade Facts: The Anti-Counterfeiting Trade Agreement. https://ustr.gov/archive/assets/Document_Library/Fact_Sheets/2008/asset_upload_file760_15084.pdf (last accessed August 2015)

United States Copyright Office (1998) The Digital Millennium Copyright Act of 1998. www.copyright.gov/legislation/dmca.pdf (last accessed June 2016)

United States Trade Representative (2014) 2014 Special 301 Report. www.ustr.gov/sites/default/files/USTR%202014%20Special%20301%20Report%20to%20Congress%20FINAL.pdf (last accessed May 2015)

US Customs and Border Protection Office of International Trade (2012) Intellectual Property Rights – Fiscal Year 2011 Seizure Statistics, Prepared by CBP Office of International Trade. Washington DC US Customs and Border Protection and US Immigration and Customs Enforcement. www.ice.gov/doclib/iprcenter/pdf/ipr-fy-2011-seizure-report.pdf (last accessed April 2015)

US Government Accountability Office (GAO) (2010) Intellectual Property: Observations on Efforts to Quantify the Economic Effects of Counterfeit and Pirated Goods. GAO Report 10–423. www.gao.gov/new.items/d10423.pdf (last accessed April 2015)

DOCUMENTS, OTHER COUNTRIES

Allen Consulting Group (2003) Counterfeiting of Toys, Business Software and Computer and Video Games. Report to the Australian Toy Association, the Business Software Association of Australia and the Interactive Entertainment Association of Australia, Sydney

English Law Commission (1997) Aggravated, Exemplary and Restitutionary Damages

Irish Law Reform Commission (1997) Aggravated, Exemplary and Restitutionary Damages

(2000) Report on Aggravated, Exemplary and Restitutionary Damages. LRC 60–2000

DOCUMENTS, JOINT STUDIES

European Patent Office (EPO) and the Office for Harmonization in the Internal Market (Trade Marks and Designs) (OHIM) (2013) Intellectual Property Rights Intensive Industries: Contribution to Economic Performance and Employment in the European Union. Industry-Level Analysis Report

OECD and EUIPO (2016) Trade in Counterfeit and Pirated Goods. Mapping the economic impact. OECD and EUIPO, Paris

DOCUMENTS, OTHER

AIM (2014) Comments on transit controls of goods suspected of infringing IPRs. Brussels

Alliance against IP Theft (2005) Comments on the European Commission's proposal for a Directive on criminal measures (on file with author)

Centre for Economics and Business Research (2000) The economic impact of counterfeiting in selected industries of the EU economy. CEBR, London (on file with author)

Chartered Institute of Patent Agents (2005) Preliminary Comments on the proposed Directive on criminal measures aimed at ensuring the enforcement of intellectual property rights and the Council Framework Decision on measures to strengthen the criminal law framework to combat intellectual property offences

Commission on Intellectual Property Rights (2002) Integrating Intellectual Property Rights and Development Policy. London

The Economist (2005) BSA or Just BS. Software Theft Is Bad; So Is Misstating the Evidence. www.economist.com/node/3993427 (last accessed April 2015)

European Generic and Biosimilar Medicines Association (EGA) (2006) Amended Proposal for a European Parliament and Council Directive on Criminal Measures Aimed at Ensuring the Enforcement of Intellectual Property Rights (on file with author)

Europe Economics (2008) Jobs, Tax and Contribution to the UK Economy: The Impacts of Reducing Illicit Peer-to-Peer File-Sharing. www.europe-economics.com/publications/fileshare08.pdf (last accessed April 2015)

European Alliance for Access to Safe Medicines (2008) The Counterfeiting Superhighway

Frontier Economics (2011) Estimating the Global Economic and Social Impacts of Counterfeiting and Piracy. Report Commissioned by Business Action to Stop Counterfeiting and Piracy. www.iccwbo.org/Advocacy-Codes-and-Rules/BASCAP/BASCAP-Research/Economic-impact/Global-Impacts-Study/ (last accessed April 2015)

Gallup Organization (2007) Global Consumer Awareness, Attitudes, and Opinions on Counterfeiting and Piracy. Third Global Congress Combating Counterfeiting and Piracy, Geneva. www.ccapcongress.net/archives/Geneva/Files/Stewart.pdf (last accessed April 2015)

IFPI (2011) Music at the Touch of a Button. Digital Music Report

International Anti-Counterfeiting Coalition (2005) The Negative Consequences of International Intellectual Property Theft: Economic Harm, Threats to the Public Health and Safety, and Links to Organized Crime and Terrorist Organizations. White Paper (on file with authors)

International Medical Products Anti-Counterfeiting Taskforce (IMPACT) (2011) Facts, activities, documents developed by the Assembly and the Working Groups 2006–2010. http://apps.who.int/medicinedocs/documents/s20967en/s20967en.pdf (last accessed September 2015)

International Trademark Association (1998) The Economic Impact of Trademark Counterfeiting and Infringement. Estimation of the Impact of Trademark Counterfeiting and Infringement on Worldwide Sales of Apparel and Footwear. www.inta.org/Advocacy/Documents/INTACounterfeitingEconomicImpact1998.pdf (last accessed April 2015)

INTERPOL (2011) Global Operation Strikes at Online Supply of Illegal and Counterfeit Medicines Worldwide. www.interpol.int/News-and-media/News-media-releases/2011/PR081 (last accessed April 2015)

Ip-health (2009) Intervention by European Communities at the TRIPS Council (Dutch seizures) (on file with author)

Knowledge Ecology International (2009) Statement by Brazil at TRIPS Council: Public health dimension of TRIPS Agreement. http://keionline.org/blogs/2009/03/04/brazilian-intervention-at-trips-council (last accessed June 2015)

(2012) Welcome Trust tells WHO it opposes R&D Treaty and the de-linkage of R&D costs from drug prices. http://keionline.org/node/1608 (last accessed April 2015)

Le Monde (2012) Le budget de la Hadopi passe à 8 millions d'euros

Managing Intellectual Property (1997) Interim relief: A worldwide survey, Germany

Médecins Sans Frontières (2014) Civil Society letter regarding proposed rules for EU trademark legislation. www.msfaccess.org/content/civil-society-letter-regarding-proposed-rules-eu-trademark-legislation (last accessed June 2015)

Motion Picture Association of America (2006) Worldwide Study of Losses to the Film Industry and International Economies Due to Piracy. Industry Report. www.iccwbo.org/WorkArea/DownloadAsset.aspx?id=2147491008 (last accessed April 2015)

Netcoalition-CCIA (eds.) (2010) Response of Netcoalition and the Computer & Communications Industry Association to the Intellectual Property Enforcement Coordinator's Request for Comments on the Joint Strategic Plan (on file with author)

TERA Consultants (2010) *Building a Digital Economy: The Importance of Saving Jobs in the EU's Creative Industries*. www.iccwbo.org/Advocacy-Codes-and-Rules/BASCAP/BASCAP-Research/Economic-impact/Building-a-Digital-Economy-TERA-study (last accessed April 2015)

Trade – Human Rights – Equitable Economy (3D) (2009) Seeds of hunger: Intellectual property rights on seeds and the human rights response

Index

For EU product safety concerns, contact us at Calle de José Abascal, 56–1°, 28003 Madrid, Spain or eugpsr@cambridge.org.

www.ingramcontent.com/pod-product-compliance
Lightning Source LLC
LaVergne TN
LVHW052214200926
848481LV00001B/108

* 9 7 8 1 1 0 8 4 0 0 8 9 3 *